S0-ESD-478

an introduction to **teaching**
in the elementary school

an introduction to **teaching**
in the elementary school

OSCAR T. JARVIS
University of Texas at El Paso

MARION J. RICE
University of Georgia

WM. C. BROWN COMPANY PUBLISHERS
Dubuque, Iowa

Copyright ©1972 by Wm. C. Brown Company Publishers

Library of Congress Catalog Card Number: 72-78492

ISBN 0—697—06238—4

All rights reserved. No part of this publication may be reproduced, stored in a retrieval system, or transmitted, in any form or by any means, electronic, mechanical, photocopying, recording, or otherwise, without the prior written permission of the copyright owner.

Printed in the United States of America

contents

Preface vii
Prologue ix

Part I
An Introduction to Teaching

1. The Changing Functions of the Elementary Teacher 3
2. Understanding the Elementary Child in Culture 12

Part II
Planning for Curriculum Development

3. Setting Curriculum Objectives 43
4. Understanding Curriculum Patterns 55
5. The Pre-Primary Curriculum 74
6. The Primary School Program 95
7. The Intermediate School Program 117
8. Instruction for Exceptional Children 131
9. The School's Media Center 145

Part III
Teaching the Skills Subjects

10. Reading: Key to Man's Cultural Heritage 161
11. Language and Communication 188
12. Teaching Mathematics 234

Part IV
Teaching the Unit Study Subjects

13. Teaching Science 251
14. Social Studies, Democracy, and Citizenship 264
15. Health and Safety in the School 288

Part V
Teaching the Fine Arts and Recreation

16. Teaching Music Through Singing and Listening 319
17. Teaching Art Through Self-Expression 343
18. Physical Development Through Movement and Exercise 361

Part VI
Organizing for Instruction

19. Vertical and Horizontal Organizational Patterns 383
20. Evaluating and Reporting Pupil Growth 399
21. Classroom Management and Teaching 422

Part VII
The Teacher Confronts Major Issues

22. Integration: The Challenge of Democracy in Race Relations....461
23. The Culturally Disadvantaged: Challenge to Performance Teaching 484
24. Collective Negotiations and Activism 510

Epilogue: Change and the Elementary School 521
Index 535

preface

An Introduction to Teaching in the Elementary School was written with one central purpose in mind—to provide a requisite and introductory overview of what teaching in the elementary school is for the student who is beginning his initial professional preparation. As an orientation, the content of this text precedes other segments of the professional preparation program such as human growth and development, children's literature, methods, and student teaching.

This volume begins with a review of the elementary school in historical perspective as set forth in the *prologue*. It ends with a resume of current changes that are taking place within the elementary school as described in the *epilogue*. Seven major aspects about teaching in the elementary school are treated between the prologue and epilogue sections of this text. *Part I* explicates a general introduction to teaching including the elementary teacher's changing role and the salient information one needs to know about schooling children in the context of the American culture. What the future professional should understand about planning for curriculum development in the elementary school is the focal point of *Part II*. This section addresses itself to curriculum objectives and patterns; the program of the preprimary, primary, and intermediate schools; exceptional children; and the media center program.

Teaching the skills, content, and creative and recreative courses in the elementary school is the theme of Parts III, IV, and V of this text. *Part III* treats the skills areas of reading, language, and mathematics. *Part IV* describes instruction in elementary school science, social studies, and health and safety, while *Part V* covers the teaching of music, art, and physical education.

The concepts, practices, and procedures of organizing for instruction about which the undergraduate student of elementary education should be knowledgeable are made explicit in *Part VI*. In this section, the prospective student is provided with an orientation to vertical and horizontal patterns in school organization, evaluating and reporting pupil progress, and strategies of classroom management.

The section of this volume immediately preceding the concluding *epilogue, Part VII*, treats the major issues which confront the professional who enters teaching in the

1970s. These issues include race relations, education for culturally disadvantaged children, and the matter of collective negotiations in education.

A unique feature of *An Introduction to Teaching in the Elementary School* is the "appraisal" section at the end of each chapter. More often than not, textbooks in education are written in a sterile fashion in which the authors examine all aspects of the designated topics included in their monographs but fail to proffer an assessment or point of view concerning the topics. In this volume, we have set forth in the "appraisal" segment of each chapter a definite assessment of that chapter's content. While we make no claim that our appraisals brook no questioning or even that they will be acceptable to a majority of our colleagues in education, we have set them forth intrepidly in the confidence that the students of these pages will appreciate a candid assessment of their content.

Teaching in the modern elementary school is a complex task. It requires total professional commitment if it is done properly. This text will have served its purpose if it makes clear to the prospective teacher the nature of the task that is required in the 1970s and if it contributes to his commitment to a profession whose major underpinnings are humanitarian in nature.

Oscar T. Jarvis
Marion J. Rice

prologue

The elementary teacher of the 1970s joins an undertaking vastly different from that of a hundred years ago. At that time the public school system was still in its infancy, notwithstanding antecedents two centuries old. While most children then received some common schooling, the average pupil received less than four years, terms lasted a few months, and most teachers themselves had merely an elementary education, with professional training restricted to a few days in an institute.

Today, practically every educable child of elementary school age is in school for six to eight years (depending on the organizational pattern), the terms normally run nine months, and the standard teaching certificate is normally contingent upon the teacher's having a baccalaureate degree. Moreover, even rural children enjoy the benefits of an enriched curriculum, whereas at one time their elementary schooling was restricted largely to the three R's. Thus, the present commitment to elementary education is not only different in size, encompassing a horde of children and an army of teachers, but it is improved in quality. Notwithstanding the nostalgic inclination to find in our educational past some golden age of virtue, comparative testing as early as 1906 and 1919 indicated that the increased commitment to a professionally directed public school system was bearing a richer fruit. Under a more humane and efficient pedagogy, coupled with longer schooling, children acquired more knowledge than did their peers a half century earlier.[1]

Any educational system is the heir of its past and the culture which gives it birth. Over the years developments within American education have been gradual and continuous. Avant garde movements, notwithstanding their appeal to the intelligentsia, have seldom wrought a revolution. The schools have been transformed, not only in their plant but in their spirit, but the change has been evolutionary rather than revolutionary. Our educational past, as conservator of the conventional wisdom, is thus prologue to the present and guardian of the future.

1. Tests administered in 1846 in Springfield and in 1845 in Boston were readministered in 1906 and 1919. See: Rudolph R. Reeder, *The Springfield Tests, 1846-1906* (Springfield, Mass.: Holden Patent Book Co., 1908); O. W. Caldwell and S. A. Courtis, *Then and Now in Education; 1845-1923* (Yonkers: World Book Co., 1924).

A prospective teacher will find in the history of education more than antiquarian dust. First, there is the record of institution building, and institutions are the work of a culture. Education, like the realm of politics, has its heroes, but these heroes attain this stature when they work with and not against the stream of culture. Second, the history of education reveals a constant leitmotif in which the efficient organization of the schools for mass instruction, formalism, is periodically challenged by natural or child-centered methods. Today, practically every elementary teacher is in some way a disciple of Rousseau and pilgrim to Yverdon, where Pestalozzi established the first child-centered school.

This *prologue* is divided into three parts. The first demonstrates the relationship of education and culture; the second presents eight themes of our educational present reaching into the past; and the third, dry with statistics, indicates the present dimensions of our educational effort.

Education is a Part of the Culture

Education is not synonymous with a culture, but the forces which affect the culture also affect education. The interrelation of culture and education are evident from the period of early settlement to the civil rights controversies of the 1960s. To know something of the culture is to know something of education.

The English heritage not only included language, morals, and manners, but educational practices which placed responsibility on the parent and institutional responsibility on church and charity. Although there was an English system of education which led to the university, and which was duly imported to the colonies, the system was one of neglect for the masses. But in the colonies, religious differences led to the establishment of two different educational traditions which exert their influence even today.

In the South, Anglicans supported charity or private schools; in the middle colonies, parochialism flourished; but in New England the Dissenters laid the basis for future public schools. In the homogeneous theocracy of New England, where the state was first the servant of the church, the common law principle of parental responsibility was modified by a Massachusetts legislative act of 1647 which imposed the responsibility for the support of education on the inhabitants of a political entity, the town.

While the educational excellence of New England may have been overestimated and the educational retardation of the South overemphasized—the Civil War destroyed a flourishing educational structure characterized by public support of private and church schools—the fact remains that the New England devotion to public as opposed to pauper education was transferred wherever settlers from New England went. The educational primacy of New England in the colonial period was maintained into the nineteenth century, and Massachusetts was long noted for its educational firsts—whether college, primary school, high school, or normal school. Thus different conceptions of the value of schooling led to considerable differences in the education of children, which in time became a part of differences in regional resources.[2]

2. Ellwood P. Cubberley, *Public Education in the United States* (Boston: Houghton Mifflin Company, 1934), pp. 12-40; William M. French, *America's Educational Tradition* (Boston: D. C. Heath and Company, 1964), pp. 1-33; Edgar W. Knight, *Education in the United States,* 2d ed. (Boston: Ginn and Company, 1941), pp. 50-67; Adolph E. Meyer, *An Educational History of the American People,* 2d ed. (New York: McGraw-Hill Book Company, 1967), pp. 3-117.

An example of the relationship of culture and education in the Progressive Education Movement is the interaction of two different intellectual currents—expressionism in art and Freudianism. The emphasis on creativity and the tendency to view any exercise of teacher authority as repression have their inspiration, if not their genesis, in the popularization of Freudian psychology and aesthetic expressionism in the first two decades of the century. There is a world of difference in art as expression and art as a subject to be learned.[3]

The most recent cultural force, which is continuing to have a profound impact on the development of American education, is the social rights revolution and education for minority groups. The extent to which educational practice follows the general culture is well demonstrated by segregation, *de facto* and *de jure,* and was not challenged by educators in North or South, notwithstanding the fine talk of the equality of educational opportunity. The *Brown* decision of 1954 is a monument to the inability of schools to operate differently from the general context of the culture. Implementation of the decision depended upon the coercive influence of national power, and it was the 1970 school term, more than a school generation after *Brown,* before there was massive integration.

Not only has the civil rights movement contributed to new patterns of school attendance, but it has contributed to a new ethnic parochialism. While the rage for Black Studies may wane during the 1970s as black educators find that educational performance does not automatically follow a change in reading content, it will undoubtedly leave in the textbooks a more sympathetic treatment of minorities as well as multi-ethnic illustrations. It is still too early to know if it will also leave a legacy of inverse racism.

The cultural approach to education does not imply a simple determinism. Ideas are the product of human intelligence, and it is impossible to look at the development of American education without looking at its philosophers and doers. Ideas from abroad, coming from men like Rousseau, Pestalozzi, Froebel, and Herbart, have deposited not merely a strata of practice, but remain as sources of educational inspiration. And we have a pantheon of domestic heroes, whether their contributions have been in the form of texts, as with a Webster and McGuffey; in the form of school management and organization, as with William T. Harris; in teacher education, as with Francis T. Parker and William H. Kilpatrick; in the public school movement, as with Horace Mann and Henry Barnard.

But all educational innovations are not readily accepted. Jefferson's dream of universal education in Virginia, first sketched in 1779, was not achieved for a hundred years. There was no experience and no sentiment for public education to which he could appeal.[4] Joseph Neef, a teacher under Pestalozzi, came to the United States in 1806 and wrote treatises on Pestalozzian methods in 1808 and 1813. But he wrote in a period of educational decline, and his works went unheeded.[5] Pestalozzian influence became ascendant, however, with the establishment of public education and professional schools after the mid-century.

In the history of education, therefore, there exist two forces which affect educa-

3. Lawrence A. Cremin, *The Transformation of the School: Progressivism in American Education, 1876-1957* (New York: Alfred A. Knopf, 1961), pp. 202-15.
4. Cubberley, *Public Education,* p. 89.
5. Meyer, *Educational History,* pp. 234-35.

tion—those which exist in the general culture and those which are more peculiar to education as an institutionalized subculture.

Out of the Past

The usual treatment of American educational history is chronological. It begins with a discussion of English antecedents, early colonial practices, changes toward secularization in the late eighteenth century, the common school revival and establishment of free schools, and eventually brings the account up to the present day. Space does not permit even a truncated chronological treatment in this introduction. Instead, the device of showing historical continuity around selected topics will be utilized. The purpose is not to provide a comprehensive précis of American educational history, but to indicate how the interaction of culture and leaders helped to shape the school system, and how, in the course of time, substantial changes were made of which we today are the legatees. In turn, current theory and practice affect the future.

State and Local Control of Education. A distinctive characteristic of American education is its organization into fifty separate state systems. Legally, there is no national system, and common elements in philosophy, curriculum, and organization depend on a common cultural base and educational diffusion, not on a national structure.

At the time the second national constitution was ratified in 1789, education in the United States, true to its English tradition, was still primarily a parental and charitable matter. A number of the new states nevertheless had included declarations about the support of education in the constitutions which replaced colonial charters. These declarations were more important for asserting the principle of state primacy rather than initiating a practice, for it was another half century and more before state systems of education were established. In Europe, the only country which had established a national system of state schools was the Kingdom of Prussia.

It is therefore not surprising that the Constitution of 1787 was silent on the subject of schools. The Massachusetts compulsory school attendance and town school tax law of 1647, emulated only in Connecticut, had developed from the tradition of piety and salvation and not from republican equality. The public school movement had to wait for the egalitarian spirit which came with Jacksonian democracy. In view of the lack of public commitment to education, the extensive national largesse in the form of land grants (see Federal Aid) showed a national interest in education which, for its time, exceeded the means of implementation.

Coupled with state primacy was the concept of local control. In Massachusetts, the General Court as early as 1647 had established the pattern by requiring towns to maintain schools. School attendance was easy in the early town, because, by law, all inhabitants had to reside within one-half mile of the town meeting house. With the expansion of population, new settlements arose within the towns, many miles away from the original settlement. Eventually, the town was divided into various school districts, and each district was eventually given the right to elect trustees, levy taxes, and select teachers, as in Connecticut in 1786 and in Massachusetts in 1789. From New England, the small district school system spread throughout the United States, and was at one time applied even on a ward basis in cities.

The result of the district system was to create a highly fragmented system of education, with all the virtues and vices which small administrative units entail. Districts with a rich tax base and commitment to education provided schools of unusual excellence, but for each school of this nature there were hundreds so impoverished that the wretched schooling offered made a mockery of equal education. During the last forty years the number of district schools has decreased from over one hundred twenty-five thousand to one-fifth the number. The area of the country having the smallest number of school districts is the Southeast. This results from the fact that the public school systems in the South were financially dependent upon the states, when created after the Civil War, and lacked the strong local attachment of those in New England and Middle West states.

In most states, the primary source of local support for schools is the property tax. With the increase in schools costs, 1969 saw one of the highest rates of rejections for school bond indebtedness in years. Many school finance specialists have for a number of years held that the property tax, tied to the local district, is an inadequate base for educational support, and argue that the only equitable means is through state and national minimum foundation programs.

Federal Aid to Education. National support of education is older than the state systems of public education. While the national constitution made no provision for education, Congressional enactments in 1785 and 1787 had laid the basis for national support by reserving every sixteenth section of township lands in the Northwest Territory for the support of education. On admission of Ohio, the first state to be admitted from the old Northwest, it was agreed that the sixteenth section would be ceded to the state, in exchange for no state taxation of national lands. This practice was extended to all new states except Texas, which as a former republic owned its own domain, and Maine and West Virginia, which were formed from older states. Eventually, over 145 million acres of public lands were ceded to the states in support of education, a not inconsiderable endowment since the traditional price of $1.25 per acre once represented a purchasing power many times that of today.

During the nineteenth and early twentieth century, a variety of bills were enacted which extended Federal support to education. But these measures were primarily in the support of agricultural, technical, and vocational education. While the office of U.S. Commissioner of Education had been established in 1867, this office remained primarily a statistical and information gathering office for a hundred years. The Blair Bill of 1881 and repeated bills for national aid to education after World War I were not enacted. The National Defense Education Act of 1958 was primarily directed toward the secondary and college levels. It was 1965 before passage of the Elementary and Secondary Education Act provided assistance for specified objectives at the elementary level. This legislation was more a product of concern with the social rights revolution and the problem of minorities than it was with general educational assistance to the states.

While there have been proponents of a national foundation program for the support of education for over a hundred years, the early enactment of such a statute is unlikely. Notwithstanding the fact that there is growing recognition that the illiterate of Appalachia, for example, come to people the ghettoes of Chicago, the sentiment for a national minimum standard of educational effort has yet to emerge. Hence, the inequalities in the distribution of national wealth and income are perpetuated in the great variations in educational opportunity provided from state to state.

Pluralism in Education. The dominance of public education in America often obscures the fact that while the state has a responsibility to educate its future citizenry, it does not enjoy an educational monopoly.

Basic to this pluralism in education is the English common law principle imposing on a parent the responsibility to provide an education for his children suitable to his station in life. For the affluent, this implied a tutor or grammar school; for the middle class, a reading and writing school; and for the innumerable poor, a life of ignorance or some charity education.

It is against this background that the much extolled laws of Massachusetts are remarkable: the one of 1642 required compulsory schooling; the one of 1647, public support of education. Together they reversed the common law principle by requiring an education of the sons of drayers as well as divines, although over two centuries would elapse before the public high school emerged to begin the eradication of class differences in access to higher education and before the schools were made completely free.

The idea of public responsibility for education did not in the colonial period pass to the other colonies. In the middle colonies, the diversity of sects promoted parochialism, and in the South, the dominance of Anglicans established a charity approach to education. On examination, however, the New England example was unique. A religious intolerance furthered the working of a theocracy, in which sacred wish and secular execution were identical. The need for education for salvation, a view held by other Protestants, thus provided for Dissenters in Massachusetts the basis of a sacred education under secular auspices. When the sacred influence waned toward the end of the eighteenth century, the New England school, in structure and in spirit, was easily converted to a public school, in contrast to the pauper idea which replaced the charity school in the South. The Massachusetts model hence served as a model for the country in the attempt to develop public education.

Public support of education, however, in the earliest years did not necessarily imply public control of education. In the South, only North Carolina had established a public school system, free of the taint of pauperism, prior to the Civil War. However, extensive public support was given to academies, of which there were 2,640 in the southern states in 1850.[6] Many of these were church related, but this served as no bar to public support, whether in Massachusetts or Georgia.

The real break in the tradition of state aid to private and church schools, which continues in England to this day, came with the increase in the Catholic population and the demands of Catholics for access to public support. The tacit acceptance of state support to different denominations lasted only so long as they were Protestant. The result of the petition of Catholics in New

---

6. Cubberley, *Public Education,* p. 247.

York City for a share of the school funds in 1840 was followed by other sects likewise petitioning and others opposed. Finally, the New York legislature created for the city a board of education, and stopped the debate over sectarian support by prohibiting the allocation of public school funds to any school which taught or practiced religious doctrine. Eventually, older states amended their constitutions with a similar prohibition, and the constitutions of newer states included such restrictions when admitted.

The restriction of public funds to nonsectarian schools does not imply the corollary right to restrict education to public schools. While it may coerce a parent to educate his child, it may not compel the parent to send the child to a public school. In a 1922 Oregon case, the Supreme Court held invalid a statute requiring attendance at a public school.[7]

In recent years, however, the issue of state support for sectarian schools has again been raised, particularly in states with a large Roman Catholic enrollment. In a number of states, aid in the form of public textbooks and transportation has been sanctioned under the child-benefit theory.[8] And at the national level, Congress in the Elementary and Secondary Education Act of 1965 made it a matter of public policy to provide support within a school district to eligible children attending parochial or private schools.

While the nonpublic school population of the country is only about ten percent, the distribution varies greatly by state. In Illinois, about twenty-five percent of the elementary public school population is nonpublic, compared to less than three percent in Georgia. Nonpublic schooling is primarily parochial education. In 1961-62, less than three percent of nonpublic elementary students were in schools not related to a church. Of those in church related schools, some 4.5 million, about ninety-three percent, were in Roman Catholic schools.

As a result of this pupil and sectarian distribution, considerations of public support to sectarian education frequently assume the stance of religious controversy, with Catholics supporting and Protestants opposing state aid. The public assumption of the parochial educational load would require a considerable expansion of public effort, particularly in some states.

The recognition of sectarian support has nevertheless been accompanied by an increased secularization of the schools. Not only must they be nondenominational, they must be unreligious.

Piety, Morals, and Values. Educational thinkers since the beginning of educational consciousness have been concerned not merely about the skills and knowledge of the young, but the relationship of education to character development. Variations of this theme have accompanied the development of education in the United States. If the schools are today concerned about values, it is not because there is a new concern, but because it is a concern as old as education. Education, religion, morality, and good government have long been equated.

One of the dominant concerns in the colonies was with religion, and the Massachusetts law of 1647, often referred to as

7. Pierce v. Society of Jesus and Mary, 268 U.S. 510 (1925).
8. Cochran v. Louisiana State Board of Education, 281 U.S. 370 (1930); Everson v. Board of Education, 330 U.S. 1 (1947).

the "Old Deluder Act" because of its reference in those words to Satan, attempted to provide knowledge of scripture to battle the wiles of the devil. To a people whose God was a personal and persuasive presence, it was natural to fight the antigod of darkness with Biblical piety. Thus the early texts were religious tracts, and the child was expected to proceed in his reading from Hornbook to Catechism, Psalter, and Bible. In the eighteenth century *The New England Primer,* combining Cotton Mather's *Spiritual Milk for American Babes* and the *Westminster Catechism,* leaped into popularity, and well into the nineteenth century constituted the chief beginning text for use of Dissenters and Lutherans.

By the end of the eighteenth century, the religious sentiment had waned and books more secular in tone became popular. But whether the reader was Webster's *Third Part,* Bingham's *Orator,* or some other compilation, they had one thing in common: the emphasis on selections, or pieces, to emphasize patriotism and the virtues of work and charity. The most famous readers of the nineteenth century were the McGuffey series, of which over 120 million had been sold by 1920.

Following the early lead of Webster, McGuffey substituted a secular for a religious morality. Homilies and selections emphasized the American virtues of courage, honesty, temperance, truth, obedience, kindness, frankness, and reliability. Even within the first lesson in the first reader, diligence in study and care of property were emphasized. In a period when reading material was scarce, the text was read and reread. Just as the Bible served as a unifying cultural-moral force in an earlier age, the McGuffey readers served a similar secular purpose in the schools for some three generations.[9]

The simple overlap of school, religion, and morality which continued throughout the nineteenth century has come under increasing attack in recent years. The flag salute, long a symbol of patriotic commitment, may no longer be a required school observance.[10] Schools may release children for religious instruction during the school day off school grounds,[11] but nondenominational religious instruction may not be given in school.[12] While the Bible may not be read or prayers offered for a religious purpose, the Bible may be read and religion studied for its historical and literary effect.[13]

But the purpose of moral instruction is to form the ideas of the young, not to study comparative history. The usual solution of the Bible prayer and reading question is to ignore the Supreme Court mandate where the practice is supported by local opinion, whether it is Indiana or Utah.[14] The fact that religious and patriotic practices in the schools do not lead to tolerance is witnessed by the anti-Catholic riots of the 1840s, and persecution of Jehovah's Witnesses a cen-

9. William Marshall French, *America's Educational Tradition: An Interpretative History* (Boston: D. C. Heath and Company, 1964), pp. 72-75.

10. West Virginia State Board of Education v. Barnette, 319 U.S. 624 (1943).

11. Zorach v. Clauson, 343 U.S. 306 (1952).

12. McCollum v. Board of Education, 33 U.S. 203 (1948).

13. Engel v. Vitale, 370 U.S. 421 (1962); School District of Abington Township, Pennsylvania v. Edward Lewis Schempp, 374 U.S. 203 (1963).

14. Clarence J. Karier, *Man, Society, and Education: A History of Educational Ideas* (Glenview, Illinois: Scott, Foresman and Company, 1967), p. 305.

tury later. Nor does it lead to a reduction in racial prejudice.

The question of indoctrination does not arise in homogeneous societies, simply because there is no difference in the way of the culture and the way of the school.[15] Thus in American Samoa a standard explanation for school practices is simply *fa Samoa*, it is the Samoan custom. But where there are different religions, different ethnic groups, and various minorities, it is inevitable that values should be perceived in different ways. Consequently, the question of values not only intrudes prominently in social studies, but is a matter of importance in all curriculum development. While there is no longer agreement on American values—in fact, much value clarification is a subtle attack on American folk values—the concern with this aspect of the curriculum is a continuation of the old problem of how to use education to further man's moral nature.

The Purposes of Education: Social and Individual. Among the conflicting values in American education in recent years has been the differing emphases in the purpose of education. The individualist emphasis, expressly associated with the aesthetic-expressive and child-centered movement of the 1920s, has its spiritual roots in the romanticism of Rousseau and its methodological inspiration in the Pestalozzian pedagogy of love, buttressed by the popularization of Freudian psychoanalysis which tended to view any exercise of teacher authority as repression.[16]

The fact that the Progressive Education Association died in 1955 without lamentation of mourners perhaps reflects the fact that the public emphasis in American education has tended to be social rather than individual, whether expressed in the language of salvation, patriotism, national development, or reform. The personal salvation envisioned by the Puritan had a communal objective and thus required a communal responsibility, and was not a matter of merely individual concern. After the establishment of the Republic, the schools were unabashedly enlisted in the development of a national spirit, and history as well as readers were used to inculcate the desired image of democratic rectitude and royal degeneracy, an emphasis further strengthened by the heady winds of the French Revolution. The eclipse of Federalism and rise of Jacksonian democracy was subsequently followed by the triumph of the free school movement. And the justification of the need for public education was social rather than individual: a democracy required an educated citizenry and a developing industry demanded literate manpower. A secular folk morality, embodied in the school readers, complemented this interpretation.

The 1890s were a period of social reform, with populism leading to muckraking. It was against this background that Dewey developed his instrumental form of pragmatism, one in which the individual stood in transactional relationship to his environment and one in which the social environment enhanced the development of human traits.[17] But Dewey, unlike his later colleague Counts, did not see the schools as a vehicle for reconstructing the social or-

---

15. Joseph S. Junell, "Do Teachers Have the Right to Indoctrinate?" *Phi Delta Kappan* 51, no. 4 (December 1969): 182-85.

16. Cremin, *Transformation of the School*, pp. 202-15.

17. Ibid., p. 63. Karier, *Man, Society, and Education*, pp. 144-48; Cremin, *op. cit.*, p. 63.

der,[18] a view which made the concept of progressive education even more suspect during the 1930s.

Viewed against the social purposes of the school, the individualistic emphases of reformers such as Kilpatrick[19] and Rugg[20] appeared self-centered and egocentric. The experimental schools which epitomized the spirit of individual progressivism in education were all too frequently schools for the upper middle class which ignored the educational problems of the poor and the challenge of Americanization.[21] The creation of schools to reflect a conception of development within a child's world was the antithesis of older types of pedagogy which attempted to make schools more effective socially by making them more efficient psychologically. The former is inward looking, whereas the latter meets the educational needs of the child within the context of social requirements.

The advent of Sputnik in 1957 served, among other things, to once more direct attention to the social purposes of education. While some educators lamented the fact that the first large scale post-war national assistance to education came in the form of the National Defense Education Act of 1958, the title of the act, as well as its provisions, reflect a preoccupation with a particular social objective, the capitalization of scientific manpower. The National school aid bill of 1965 likewise indicated, in the allocation of funds, a preoccupation with the social purposes of education.

Public schooling is part of the political process, as is any other institution dependent upon taxation. Irrespective of how much public schools may speak the language of the individual, the individual in any culture, even in a democracy, is not an atom, but a member of the society. In a democracy, furthermore, he is not a subject, but a citizen, a term which implies a nexus of responsibility to other citizens as well as the corporate body in which he resides. The extreme child-centered wing of progressive education fell into disrepute not merely because it followed an impressionistic curriculum, but because such a curriculum was socially irresponsible. A democratic culture can encourage a tremendous individuality in the arts, in material goods, and in manners to emphasize personal tastes and preferences. Any social order, however, implies concurrence with respect to social purposes, and it is this need for stability which tends to make public education orthodox rather than heterodox. Thus, after periods of individual emphasis, public education may be expected to reemphasize the broader social purposes of education. The revival of interest in subject matter in the 1960s was not merely a triumph of the essentialist position, long reflected by William T. Bagley,[22] but was also a return to a concern for the social consequences of education.

18. George S. Counts, *Dare the Schools Build a New Social Order?* (New York: John Day Company, 1932).

19. William Heard Kilpatrick, *Foundations of Method* (New York: Macmillan Company, 1925).

20. Harold Rugg and Ann Shumaker, *The Child-Centered School* (Chicago: World Book Company, 1928). With the depression years, Rugg shifted his position, and attempted to make one of the first revisions in social studies to present his interpretation of the educational needs of the new industrial order.

21. Cremin, *Transformation of the School,* p. 212.

22. Ibid., p. 191; Meyer, *Educational History,* pp. 324, 468.

Individualization, Monitorial, and Graded Schools. Repeated calls for the practicing and prospective teacher "to individualize" instruction abound in the literature. While these calls are more exhortatory than practical, the new teacher is frequently amazed to find that individual teaching, at least recitation hearing, once dominated the schools and that the achievement of a graded system, permitting instruction of children in groups, was once regarded as a great advance in educational efficiency.

The district school organization, which once dominated the American scene, inevitably made the rural school a one room school. In the one room school, there was a wide age span and an even greater performance span, since some pupils attended regularly, others infrequently, and times for entry were not restricted to a particular time of the year and birthday. The composition of the student body required individualization—assignments, help, and recitation were usually made individually or to a handful of children.[23] Even in cities where larger attendance made possible a division of labor among teachers, the early practice was for a class to consist of pupils in all sequences, so that each class, in effect, was a separate school.[24] This early form of school is an extreme example of what is now popularly called multigrading (see chapter 19). Another development in this trend was the erection in the city of school buildings in which a large number of students, as many as two hundred, were assigned to a teacher with several assistants. Off the large room, in which double desks were fastened in neat rows, there were small recitation rooms, in which the assistant teachers worked with pupils in small groups. Except for the fixed desks, stern discipline, and paucity of study materials, the arrangement has a modern flavor.

But while the ungraded school was to continue for many a year, by the middle of the nineteenth century progressive cities had begun to adopt the graded school plan, modeled after Prussia and extensively described by Mann in his 1844 *Seventh Annual Report.* From the use of teachers and assistant teachers, called ushers, with a large group of students divided into recitation groups, it was but a step to provide a separate room with a teacher for recitation groups.

The shift from individual to group instruction was facilitated by two major developments. The first was the Lancastrian system, which in the first decades of the nineteenth century was the rage in the cities, when charitable societies still carried the burden of teaching the poor. The essential features of the system were the collection of a large number of pupils in one room under one master, who taught a carefully structured lesson to older and brighter boys, the monitors, who in turn taught the lesson to the youngsters in their charge. In a day when the costs of private instruction were some $12.00 a year, the Lancastrian costs of less than $2.00 a year appealed to charities where costs were a pressing concern. At the same time, the attention to organization, sanitation, methods, group instruction, and the grading of materials suitable to different performance levels created a more optimistic base for public education and showed the importance of teacher training

23. Cubberley, *Public Education,* p. 327.
24. Ibid., p. 305.

xx   prologue

and class instruction.[25] The monitorial system included one aspect of instruction which is now becoming increasingly popular—the use of older students, or even students on the same grade level, as teaching helpers.[26]

A second contribution which facilitated the emergence of the graded school was the development of graded texts; *The McGuffey Eclectic Readers* (first and second readers of which appeared in 1836) were the most notable example. Arithmetic, long a difficult subject which had been taught mainly at the college level, was finally organized for elementary instruction with the publication of Warren Colburn's *First Lessons in Arithmetic on the Plan of Pestalozzi* in 1821. About 1834 or 1835, Joseph Ray issued his graded series in arithmetic—*The Child's Arithmetic, Mental Arithmetic,* and *Practical Arithmetic*. These enjoyed for many years a great popularity west of the Alleghenies because of their clarity of organization and clear statement of fundamental principles.[27]

Throughout the later history of American education, attempts have been made to improve the efficiency of instruction for individuals. Some of the most notable examples are the older Winnetka and Dalton plans, the individual pupil project, and, more recently, teaching machines, tutor texts, and computerized instruction. In contrast with the earlier individual assign, study and recite methods, supervised by the teacher, these methods facilitate independent learning and the completion of learning tasks according to student performance.

While some school people have concentrated on the improvement of individual instruction, others have been concerned primarily with group instruction. Some of these have included the Batavia plan, which involved the use of assistant teachers to tutor retarded students, and was an effort to maintain semi-annual promotion for all students without the need for retention. The plan, in essence, was a continuation of the older assistant teacher plan previously utilized, and was revived in Quincy, Massachusetts in the late 1870s by Colonel Parker. It owes its name to the school system in New York where it was fully described in 1914. A modern variation of the Batavia plan is the extensive use of teaching assistants, which came into vogue with federal assistance in the 1960s. It is unfortunate that there is no adequate research to indicate the optimum way of utilizing teaching assistants for pupil growth.

Other variations, emphasizing help to the more able student, was the frequent reclassification of pupils, once every ten weeks, to permit more able pupils to advance more rapidly. William T. Harris, Superintendent in St. Louis and later Commissioner of Education, was a leader in this approach as early as 1880.

Differentiated courses of study, based on pupil abilities, were tried before the advent of psychological test construction. A two course plan, lasting eight years for slower and six years for brighter students, was known as the Cambridge Plan where it was inaugurated prior to 1910. As early as 1898, a three-track plan, divided into slow,

25. Ibid., pp. 128-37; Meyer, *Educational History*, pp. 146-47; French, *America's Educational Tradition*, pp. 50-51.
26. The buddy system is used perhaps more extensively in reading. A series: Reading Helper Books has been developed for this purpose by Book-Lab, Inc., of Brooklyn, N.Y.
27. Cubberley, *Public Education*, pp. 292-95; Meyer, *Educational History*, pp. 200-201; French, *America's Educational Tradition*, pp. 71-75.

average, and superior groups, had been tried out in Baltimore which gave its name to that effort. Children progressed by age from grade to grade, but the amount of work expectancy differed by group to which assigned. By the beginning of the first World War, there was common knowledge, if not practice, of such ideas as flexible grading, different courses of study, and special classes to meet the varying needs of pupil growth.[28]

In view of the long history of trying to meet different pupil needs from changes in organization, curriculum, and managemnt, the prospective teacher may pointedly ask "How?" any time the issue of individualization is raised.

Hornbooks, Texts, and Multi-Media. One of the most significant factors in shaping instruction and the quality of the schools is the kind of learning material available to the pupil. While it has long been popular in schools of education to criticize textbook teaching, the size of the school text publishing industry and the persistence of texts in school are concrete evidence of the utility of the invention.

Even the poorest schools in the United States have riches of material beyond the imagination of a colonial teacher. The almost complete absence of teaching equipment, books, and supplies, combined with the individual method of recitation and other inefficient teaching methods, was so wasteful of time that children might go to school on and off for years and merely get a start in reading and writing.[29] Books were scarce, and the double seat, when it replaced log benches, not only conserved on aisle space but made it possible for two students to share a text. Although paper making from rags began in Germantown as early as 1690, for another hundred and fifty years paper remained scarce and expensive. It was not until the latter 1860s that economical paper from wood pulp was developed. The first U.S. pencil manufacturing establishment did not open until 1827, and it was in the 1830s before the steel nib made the quill pen obsolete for writing. Thus one of the early requirements of a schoolmaster was the ability to make and repair quill pens. There were no blackboards, maps, or other visual aids. Slates did not come into use until the 1820s. Printed copy books for writing appeared in 1795, but it was another half century before they came in common use. A writing master originally spent much time in setting copy.

The writing and publication of textbooks, which became common in the early nineteenth century, represented both a technological and methodological revolution. The impact of textbooks far exceeded the subsequent introduction of such innovations as the magic lantern, stereopticon, radio, standard 16-mm films for classroom use in the 1930s, and educational television in the 1950s. Among the early texts in reading which made a lasting imprint on the character of education were Noah Webster's *Blue-backed Speller,* Part I of his three part *Grammatical Institute of the English Language,* Caleb Bingham's *American Preceptor,* Lindley Murray's *The English Reader,* and the *McGuffey Readers.* Lindley Murray's *English Grammar* was so extensively revised and circulated that Murray did for syntax what Webster did for spelling and word usage. In arithmetic, texts by

28. Cubberley, *Public Education,* pp. 513-35.
29. Ibid., p. 57; Knight, *Education in the U.S.,* pp. 123-25.

xxii   prologue

Nicholas Pike, Colburn, and Day had a lasting influence.

Publication of texts encouraged the expansion of the curriculum from the two R's, reading and 'riting, to include the third "R" of the elementary school—'rithmetic. It also encouraged the early teaching of geography and history. Jedidah Morse's *American Universal Geography* appeared in 1784; Nathanial Dwight's *A Short but Comprehensive System of the Geography of the World* in 1795; and William C. Woodbridge's *Rudiments of Geography* in 1821. Eventually, the study of geography became a popular subject in the elementary schools. In the 1820s Samuel Goodrich, a prolific producer of elementary texts under the name of Peter Parley, published *A History of the United States*. Late in the 1830s Noah Webster also published a United States history. Both contained the Constitution of the United States, and thus initiated the study of civics in elementary schools.

As early as 1830, the form of the elementary program had taken shape, largely brought about as a result of the newer teaching made available by texts. In the primary grades, reading and writing had been expanded to include simple numbers and elementary language. In the intermediate grades arithmetic, geography, and history were added, the art of penmanship replaced simple writing, and grammar was added to elementary language usage. In the latter part of the nineteenth century the major changes came in the elementary curriculum with the addition of elementary science, art, music, and simple manual training for the boys, and physical training.[30] Figure P. 1, taken from Cubberley, shows the progressive growth of the elementary curriculum from 1775 to 1900. By the end of the century, the main outlines of the curriculum had become established. Subsequent changes have largely been concerned with grouping in broad curriculum

30. Cubberley, *Public Education,* pp. 300, 473.

1775	1825	1850	1875	1900
READING Spelling Writing Catechism Bible Arithmetic	READING 　Declamation SPELLING* Writing 　Good Behavior 　Manners and Morals ARITHMETIC*	READING DECLAMATION SPELLING WRITING 　Manners 　Conduct MENTAL ARITH.* CIPHERING	READING 　Literary 　　Selections SPELLING PENMANSHIP* Conduct PRIMARY ARITH. ADVANCED ARITH.	READING LITERATURE* Spelling Writing* . . . . ARITHMETIC
	Bookkeeping GRAMMAR Geography	Bookkeeping Elem. Lang. GRAMMAR Geography History U.S.	. . . . Oral Lang.* GRAMMAR Home Geog. TEXT GEOG. U.S. HISTORY Constitution	. . . . ORAL LANG.* Grammar Home Geog. TEXT GEOG.* History 　Stories* TEXT HIS.*
		Object Lessons	Obj. Lessons* Elem. Science* Drawing* Music* Phy. Exercises	Nature 　Study* Elem. Sci.* Drawing* Music* Play Phy. Train.* Sewing Cooking Manual 　Training
	Sewing and Knitting	. . . .	. . . . . .	

CAPITALS = Most important subjects.
　Roman = Least important subjects.
　　　　* = New methods of teaching now employed.
Underlined = Subjects of medium importance.

Fig. P.1. The Development of the Elementary School Curriculum. From: Ellwood P. Cubberley, **Public Education in the United States** (Boston: Houghton Mifflin Company, 1934), p. 473.

strands, i.e., language arts, science, and social studies. In contrast to curriculum innovation resulting from American textbook development, these latter curriculum developments came primarily as a result of changes in teacher education, such as the formal Pestalozzian object lesson introduced by Sheldon at Oswego, and new ideas of education, such as the Froebelian conception of education through play.

The modern elementary teacher not only has a more attractive environment in which to teach, but a veritable cafeteria of learning materials. A teacher may choose between such varied approaches as simulation and programmed learning, films and television, teaching tapes, and, in limited instances, computer-assisted instruction.

But the improved learning revolution, which multi-media technology was supposed to bring about, has not yet occurred.[31] This results from the fact that most of the new media are not alternate *communication* systems, but alternate *delivery* systems. A message is the same message whether received aurally or decoded from written sound equivalents. Furthermore, at a given instructional moment, it is difficult to combine but two sense impressions concurrently, as in the combination of pictures and sound, or pictures and reading. The effective concurrent use of pictures, reading, and sound are limited to types of chained associative learning, as in label learning. With food in a cafeteria, one may choose today apple pie and tomorrow coconut custard, but the chemistry of the body, impervious to tastes, converts the food into the requirements of human energy. Likewise the chemistry of the mind reduces a communication to its message components, irrespective of the delivery system by which transmitted.

While it is common among media advocates to assume the media are the messages, messages are only transmitted and received through language. While both still and moving pictures facilitate associative learning, they are not a substitute for explanation. Even such an advocate of multi-media resources as Dale recognizes that the textbook is the most efficient way of presenting the content of any systematic body of subject matter. Textbooks will persist because no adequate substitute has been found.[32]

Formalism and Naturalism: Competing Philosophies and Methods. Formalism may be defined as an emphasis on the transmission of subject matter and efficient teaching methodologies controlled by the teacher. Naturalism may be defined as an emphasis on the growth of the child and learning methods emphasizing child activity. Much of the history of American education in the nineteenth and twentieth centuries may be interpreted as an effort at these two types of reform—one to provide a more efficient way for students to acquire knowledge, the other to create a freer environment for individual learning. Formalism assumes that rationality is based in knowledge; naturalism places more emphasis on emotions and sentiments, an individual expression.

The lack of wealth and the paucity of education first encouraged formalism in American education, not merely because of the age of this tradition, but because

31. James D. Finn, *"Take-off to Revolution,"* in Alfred de Grazia and David A. Sohn, eds., *Revolution in Teaching: New Theory, Technology, and Curriculum* (New York: Bantam Books, 1964), pp. 23-31.

32. Edgar Dale, "Instructional Resources," in *The Changing American School,* Sixty-fifth Yearbook of the National Society for the Study of Education, Part II, ed. John I. Goodlad (Chicago: University of Chicago Press, 1966), pp. 84-109.

it could produce results. Developing countries inevitably emphasize formal methods, and thus the United States in the early nineteenth century embraced the Lancastrian structured system in preference to Pestalozzian methods. The time was not yet ripe.

In addition to the traditional English heritage, formalism in the American elementary school has been furthered by such diverse movements as the Lancastrian method, formal Pestalozzianism of the Oswego School, Herbartian methodology, and the curriculum reform movement of the 1960s. Nineteenth and twentieth century naturalism have their philosophic roots in Rousseau and pedagogic roots in Pestalozzi. It is hard to find any significant movement of either nineteenth century American reform which is not traceable back to Pestalozzi and Rousseau. Various Pestalozzian influences were expressed in the writing of instructional materials throughout the nineteenth century, but it was the Froebelian influence of the kindergarten movement which made the biggest impact. Pestalozzian influences are clearly evident in the Parker schools at Quincy and Chicago, and his eclecticism—stealing, as he admitted—had wide influence throughout the country. The Parker school and the Dewey school, both in Chicago, represented the apogee of the nineteenth century movement toward naturalism.

It is important to understand that formalism does not necessarily imply either poor methodology or an inadequate curriculum, although the two may unhappily concur. The Jesuits were the teachers par excellence of the Counter Reformation, and perhaps the most notable exponents of modern formalism. While their very excellence perpetuated a classical curriculum, so good were the Jesuit teachers that Sir Francis Bacon gave them a compliment which might be literally translated: "They are so good I wish they were on our side."[33]

Formalism facilitates the establishment of an educational structure and the diffusion of methods which teachers may copy and adapt. Hence, the appeal of the earliest Lancastrian methods previously described —they were clear and direct. Formal Pestalozzianism was introduced in the middle of the nineteenth century by Sheldon at Oswego, New York. Unlike the early methods which Joseph Neef had attempted to popularize in the first decade, the Pestalozzian version popularized by Sheldon was worked out by the Mayos for use in England. Though these formal object lessons were so verbal that they made a travesty of Pestalozzi's sense pedagogy, there were some fortunate by-products: object study did shift more emphasis to real objects, real objects to nature study, and nature study to the development of elementary science. The use of inquiry to interpret sense data did not have to await *Science: A Process Approach* materials. The use of real objects also required oral language, and helped in the shift in emphasis from grammar to usage. The utilization of real objects instead of mere ciphers had already been adopted by Colburn for the teaching of arithmetic, and the principle of observation applied in the teaching of geography by Arnold Guyot.

The concept of behavioral objectives also had its antecedents in the Pestalozzian concept of learning elements. It was carried to an extreme form by the German pedagogue Grube, but nevertheless enjoyed a great vogue in this country in the latter

---

33. Sir Francis Bacon, *Advancement of Learning* (London: J. M. Dent and Co., 1965), p. 17.

nineteenth century. It was Pestalozzianism gone to seed, like some of the current emphasis on minute behavioral objectives. The development of object lessons, like the later five formal steps of Herbartianism, nevertheless contributed to the professional competences of teachers.[34]

Superficially, Herbartianism is an associational psychology, but a transcendent type of associationalism more akin to Thorndikian connectionism than to Lockian sensationalism. This results from Herbart's ideas of knowledge, which presage the structure of the discipline movement of the 1960s. Knowledge is not a mere compendium of facts, as in Morse's geography or Davenport's history. It consists of an ordered arrangement, logically related. Nor is learning the mere memorization of isolated facts, but the organization of new material into a previous mental repertory. Learning is hence not passive, but is an active mental process of discrimination and incorporation. The task of the teacher is to facilitate learning by arranging and presenting material consistent with the student's previous state of knowledge.

Following this conceptualization, five systematic steps were developed, and exercised considerable influence, especially at the secondary level, for many years. The importance of Herbartianism in American pedagogy is indicated by the organization of the National Herbart Society in 1892, predecessor of The National Society for the Study of Education. Psychological theories of subject matter learning in the classroom continue to show an affinity for Herbartian thought, such as those of Asubel and his receptive learning model, because Herbart was essentially concerned with teaching and transmitting knowledge. The concern with the assessment of preinstructional behavior as an entering point, as well as the more naive concept of readiness, are both anticipated in the Herbartian concept of the apperceptive mass.

In the curriculum reform of the 1960s, formalism was concerned with two different outcomes—process as well as knowledge (products). While most of the projects emphasize active pupil involvement, and thus are superficially more akin to progressive than to traditional education, the substantive outcomes of the curriculum reform movement are depicted in terms of a product which is controlled by the curriculum. Whether the object is process or knowledge, the approach is formal, because the outcome is not left to pupil planning.[35] In part, the shift in emphasis in the 1960s resulted from the growing criticism of the child-centered schools crescendoing with the life-adjustment movement of the 1950s. Much of the curriculum students will study in the elementary schools in the 1970s will reflect the formal attempt to control the outcome of pupil learning through a structured curriculum.

Naturalism in American education first had to await the development of an educational system; there must be an educational structure before there can be a revolt. Throughout the nineteenth century the strongest inspiration of naturalism came from Europe, and the ideas of Rousseau, Pestalozzi, and Froebel—a blend of romanticism, the pedagogy of love, and mysticism

---

34. Cubberley, *Public Education*, pp. 396-97; Knight, *Education in the U.S.*, p. 516.
35. See Robert Glaser, "The Design of Instruction," in *The Changing American School*, Sixty-fifth Yearbook of the National Society for the Study of Education, Part II, ed. John I. Goodlad (Chicago: University of Chicago Press, 1966), pp. 215-42.

—encouraged a century of educators. The improvement of pedagogy was continually inspired by the work of Pestalozzi, and this child-centered emphasis was given additional encouragement by the introduction of kindergartens in the middle of the nineteenth century. The central idea of the kindergarten movement was the natural, self-directed activity of the child, focused toward moral and social ends. The kindergartens were developed primarily as private ventures separate from the public schools, unlike the earlier infant school movement in Boston, modeled after the Owenite schools of New Lanark, which led to the development of the primary division of the grammar school.[36]

At the end of the nineteenth century, Colonel Francis Parker, who had studied Pestalozzian and Froebelian methods in Europe, was the leading exponent of child-centered methods and precursor of twentieth century progressivism. An avowed eclectic, first at Quincy, and then at the Cook County Training School in Chicago, he was the leading exponent of naturalist methods, and his school became a veritable mecca for educational reformers.

By the end of the century, the child study movement under G. Stanley Hall was in full swing. Eventually, the heritage of Rousseau mingled with the strains of educational science, expressionism, and Freudian psychology to justify an even greater emphasis on the child as the center of education. Soon the radicalism of Froebel was to appear the essence of conservatism, as reformers gave even greater emphasis to child purposes and planning. Fertilized by the primitivism of G. Stanley Hall and the child study movement, the twentieth-century movement fused neo-Rousseauism, Freudianism, and expressionism into a radical bohemianism which was not merely a pedagogic revolt of naturalism versus formalism, but a revolt against traditional values.[37] The social utilitarianism, implicit in the Owenite schools, was forgotten.[38] Among some of the most notable of the schools of the first three decades of the twentieth century were Fairhope, the Children's School, and the Play School, progressive schools associated with the charisma of such teachers as Marietta Johnson, Margaret Naumburg, and Caroline Platt. Characterized by studied informality and emphasizing art and expression, these schools were the antithesis of rational purposes in education, and eventually confused educational bohemianism with the naturalistic revolt against formalism.[39]

To give direction to the reform movement in education, the Progressive Education Association was organized in 1919. The key ideas of this wide and diverse movement are indicated in the original platform: freedom to develop naturally, self-governing pupil conduct, interest the motive of all work, correlation between different subjects, the teacher as guide, and school-parent cooperation. Some of its most exciting work came in the field of creative expression through art, literature, music and dramatics, and students interested in these aspects of education may profitably consult the *Progressive Education* issues of 1926, 1927, 1928, and 1931.[40] The decade of the 1930s brought depression and the issue of social reform, and exciting work in the

---

36. Cubberley, *Public Education,* pp. 455-59; Knight, *Education in the U.S.,* pp. 519-20; French, *America's Educational Tradition,* pp. 133-34; Meyer, *Educational History,* pp. 241-44.
37. Cremin, *Transformation of the School,* p. 338.
38. Karier, *Man, Society, and Education,* pp. 157-58; 226-30.
39. Cremin, *Transformation of the School,* p. 207.
40. Ibid., p. 247.

field of social studies was developed by Rugg at the Lincoln School, but these ideas were never accepted as were the ideas in the arts.

Long before the Progressive Education Association died in 1955, the steam had gone out of the movement. But not before many substantial changes had been made in the schools. The project method of Kilpatrick and the integrated day had been widely accepted, and even the most conservative schools were more akin to progressive ideas than they were to the traditional schools of the nineteenth century. The environment, curriculum, methods, and discipline had all been transformed; what had been the avant garde, the experimental, had now become the educational mainstream.[41]

The naturalistic revolt against formalism was not the only factor in bringing about educational change. Many of these changes were implicit in the culture, as it shifted from a rural to an urban society and from an agrarian to an industrial economy. The contribution of the experimental schools was not to change American education, but to give individuals, endowed with messianic fervor, an opportunity to find a clientele which would support their enthusiasms and help translate ideas into practice. With the process of time, many of these were accepted and incorporated into the mainstream of American education.

Much of the controversy over formal, or subject-centered, and natural, or child-centered, methods in education result from different philosophical conceptions of the purposes and methods of education. The challenge of elementary schools of the future is somehow to unite both formal training, which supports the rational transmission of culture, and natural methods, designed to further the spontaneity of the individual. It is for this reason that teachers of the 1970s may once again turn to the study of the philosophical and methodological writings of John Dewey. While progressives regarded Dewey as the philosopher of the movement, Dewey always emphasized the social purposes in education and was a constant critic of the excesses of child-centered education. Dewey was thus criticized by both conservatives and progressives. While the ambiguity of Dewey inevitably contributed to variations in interpretation, Dewey was always committed to rationality as the basis of moral and social life.[42]

As early as 1926 he characterized the studied lack of adult guidance in the child-centered school as stupid because it misconstrued conditions of independent thinking. He warned against the impressionistic, child-centered curriculum as an invitation to intellectual failure, and held that the organization of systematic subject matter was not hostile to individuality, but a means through which individuality was achieved.[43] Learning for Dewey was not merely doing, but always required insight and cognitive connections, as in the formation of habits.[44] The inquiry approach, the

41. Ibid., pp. 306-8; Cubberley, *Public Education,* p. 516; Meyer, *Educational History,* p. 329.

42. John Dewey, *Philosophy and Civilization* (New York: Capricorn Books, 1963), p. 34.

43. John Dewey, "How Much Freedom in the New School?" *The New Republic,* 9 July 1930, pp. 204-6; "Progressive Education and the Science of Education," *Progressive Education* 5 (1928): 197-204; Cremin, *Transformation of the School,* pp. 234-35; Karier, *Man, Society, and Education,* p. 147.

44. John Dewey, *Democracy and Education* (New York: Macmillan Company, paperback, 1961) (originally published in 1916), pp. 139-40; Ernest E. Bayles and Bruce L. Hood, *Growth of American Educational Thought and Practice* (New York: Harper and Row, Publishers, 1968, p. 261.

most popular of the methodologies of the 1960s, is a revival of Dewey's problem solving and reflective teaching methods sketched a half-century previously.[45]

The instrumentalism of Dewey is part of the wider movement of pragmatism, with which Charles S. Pierce and William James are associated. Pragmatism is an indigenous American philosophical development. In the years ahead, the schools may find, within the context of American culture and theory, practices which unite the best of formal and natural traditions, utilizing them as complementary rather than competing modes of instruction and learning.

The Elementary Education Establishment

Teachers as well as administrators need to know something of the dimensions of the education establishment. Its size and economic impact are often unappreciated by the classroom teacher preoccupied with the particular problems of teaching Johnny. As teacher, he is not alone, and there are millions of Johnnies.[46]

Enrollment, Teachers, and Holding Power. In the fall of 1970, there were 36,800,000 children enrolled in grades K-8, accounting for over 99 percent of children of school age. Of this number, 32,430,000 were enrolled in regular public schools and accounted for 88 percent of the school population. There were 4,170,000 enrolled in regular nonpublic schools. The remainder were enrolled in special purpose public and private schools, such as schools for American Indians and military dependents and schools for exceptional children.

In the fall of 1969 there were 1,251,000 elementary teachers in 73,216 public and 15,340 nonpublic elementary schools. The retention rate in fall 1961 in the eighth-grade was 978 per 1,000 pupils entering the fifth-grade compared to 741 in fall 1924. Higher retention in the elementary school was reflected in higher retention in the secondary school. The number of students graduating from high school in 1969 was 759 per 1,000 fifth-grade enrollees, over twice that of the 1932 figures of 302.[47]

School Years Completed. As a result of the increase in the number of persons attending elementary school and the increase in school holding power, the percentage of persons 25 years of age and older with less than five years schooling decreased from 23.8 percent in 1910 to 5.9 percent in 1968. There were nevertheless significant ethnic differences. While less than 5 percent of the white population might be deemed functionally illiterate on the basis of number of school years completed, over 17 percent of the nonwhite population, mainly Negro, had less than five years of schooling.

Whereas the median number of years of schooling completed was 8.1 in 1910, in 1968 it was 12.1. Again, there are substantial racial and regional differences. While the white population had a median level of 12.1, it was 9.5 for the nonwhite population. Differences between white and nonwhite educational attainment measured by number of school years completed is most pronounced in the Southern states where separate segregated schools were a legal part of the social structure. Thus in

45. John Dewey, *How We Think* (Boston: D. C. Heath and Co., 1933).
46. Unless otherwise indicated, all statistics in this section are taken from *Digest of Educational Statistics 1969* (Washington, D.C.: U.S. Government Printing Office, 1969).
47. *Digest of Educational Statistics,* 1970, p. 2.

South Carolina and California, median years of school completed in 1960 for whites was 10.3 and 12.1, and for nonwhites, 5.9 and 10.5. Thus nonwhites in California had a higher school attainment mean than whites in South Carolina.

Education and Earning Power. Educational attainment is directly related to jobs, income, and other opportunities. In 1968, persons with less than eight years of elementary school constituted only 9.3 percent of all occupational groups, but over three-fourths of these were in low paying operative, service, and manual labor jobs. Annual income of men 25 years and older in 1966 with less than eight years of schooling was $3,520 compared to $7,494 for a high school graduate. Success in gaining school competency in the elementary school, however, is a prerequisite to high school retention. Students who do not learn to read, write, and cipher effectively in the elementary grades are most likely to drop out of school at the legal school leaving age.

Expenditures. The expenditures for public elementary and secondary education in 1969-70 were estimated to amount to about 38 billion dollars, a figure still less than half of the national defense budget. Major support for local schools continued to be provided by the local school district, with support as follows: local, 53.9 percent; state, 33.7 percent; and national, 8.1 percent. State and local support of education, including higher education, is generally the largest item of state and local expenditure, accounting for 40 cents of every tax dollar.

There is nevertheless a wide variation in local and state financing of education. In 1968-69, local support ranged from a high of 85.5 percent in New Hampshire to a low of 4.3 percent in Hawaii. Generally, states which followed the Massachusetts model of local school initiative—New England and North Central—have high local support levels. In states where the public school system was first created at the state level, as in the South, there is a high level of state support. In the West the tradition is mixed. Consequently, the per capita property tax is highest in states which support education primarily from local sources.[48]

Education is one of the many components which enter into the computation of the Gross National Product (GNP). In 1968, seven percent of the GNP went for education, twice the 1930 percentage. Since GNP and educational expenditures reflect inflationary pressures, comparison of educational effort on the basis of percentage of GNP is one means of ascertaining if there is an increasing financial, or hold-the-line, commitment to education.

Compulsory School Age. The compulsory ages of schooling in most states is from seven to sixteen, with the permissive range generally from six to twenty-one. The average public school year in the United States is almost 180 days. Average daily attendance is usually high, over 91 percent of enrollment. Pupils attend an average of 164 school days per year.

School Systems. In the fall of 1967, there were 20,173 school systems. There were 172 school systems which enrolled 25,000 students or more. They accounted for less than 1 percent of the systems, but for 17 percent of elementary schools, enrolled 30 percent of the elementary students,

---

48. National Education Association—Research Division, *Rankings of the States, 1970* (Washington, D.C.: NEA, 1970), Tables 73, 84.

and employed 27 percent of the elementary teachers.

In contrast, there were 8,355 school systems with pupil enrollments of less than 300. They accounted for 40 percent of the systems, but enrolled only 2 percent of elementary pupils and employed less than 3 percent of the teachers. Six states accounted for most of these very small school districts, with over 7,000 systems. Whereas Hawaii operated as one school system—its late territorial heritage—some states with small populations, such as Nebraska and South Dakota, had over 1,000 each.

There was very little difference in pupil expenditure (figures cited include secondary expenditures) for the largest and smallest systems—$538 to $549 in 1961-62. The average per pupil expenditure in that year was $513, compared to $717 in 1969-70.[49]

Large school systems have school buildings with large enrollments; small systems, small buildings with concomitant enrollments. The average number of elementary pupils enrolled in a school in the largest systems was 816, over twice the size of the school district enrollment of the smallest systems. Here the average school enrollment was 69 pupils. The teacher ratio is also higher in the largest systems, 28 compared to 19. The average elementary school, however, is large: 500 pupils and 19 teachers with a teacher-pupil ratio of 1:27.

Transportation. With the increase in size of school systems and size of schools, as well as construction of all-weather surfaced roads, the percentage of children transported to school has drastically increased. In 1929-30, less than 8 percent of the pupils were transported at an average cost of $28.81 per pupil. In 1967-68, over 40 percent of the pupils were transported, at an average cost per pupil of $55.00.

Teachers. In the fall of 1969, there were 1,087,000 public elementary teachers; 150,000 were employed in regular non-public schools; and another 4,000 were employed by the Bureau of Indian Affairs, other federal agencies, and college training schools. To be a public school teacher in the United States is to be a public employee; the opportunities for private or parochial employment are limited.

The standard teaching degree was a baccalaureate, held by some 72 percent of elementary teachers in 1965-66. Elementary education was largely a woman's world, with about 90 percent of the teachers female.

In addition to there being few men teachers, there are also striking differences in age and experience: women teachers tend to be older and more experienced. While there are more young women teachers than young men teachers—12.8 compared to 3.4 percent—men increasingly tend to withdraw from teaching. Thus women elementary teachers have a mean age of 40.5 compared to a mean age of 35 for men. In 1965-66, 85 percent of women elementary teachers had 20 or more years of teaching experience while only 15 percent of the elementary men teachers had this experience. Most elementary teachers are married and have children, as is shown in figure P.2.

Salaries. Based on unadjusted dollars, the salary of elementary school teachers doubled during the period 1955 to 1968, increasing from a mean of $3,852 to $7,676. While inflation has reduced purchasing power, average teacher salaries are nevertheless over two-and-a-half times what they were

49. Ibid., table 114.

Teacher Characteristics	DIS.
Highest Degree Held	
No 4-Year Degree	12.9
Bachelor's Degree	71.4
Master's Degree	14.9
Sixth Year Degree	.8
Doctor's Degree	....
Average years of teaching experience	13.4
Average number of hours per week to teaching	46.5
Average salary	$6,119
Average age in years	41.1
Marital Status	
Married	67.5
Widowed, separated, divorced	12.3
Single	20.2

Fig. P.2. Selected Characteristics of Elementary School Teachers 1965-1966. From National Education Association— Research Division, **American Public School Teacher, 1965-1966** (Washington, D.C.: NEA, 1967), pp. 37-38.

in terms of 1929-30 purchasing power, based on the Consumer Price Index of the U.S. Department of Labor.

There are still wide variations in salaries of elementary teachers, as shown in the following comparisons for a bachelor's degree with no experience for the Southeast and the Far West—the lowest and highest paying regions.

	Southeast	Far West
Lowest Salary	$4,400	$5,650
Highest Salary	7,133	8,400
Mean Salary	5,817	6,720
Difference Between H-L	2,733	2,750
Percent Diff of Lowest	62	49

Salary extremes are thus relatively greater in the Southeast.[50]

On the whole, however, there are increasing inducements for career preparation and teaching of elementary teachers. In 1969-70, mean minimum-maximum scheduled salaries for all reporting systems were $7,673 and $12,002. What a teacher receives depends on the system in which he teaches.

School Housing. Growing school systems are constantly building new rooms to house public school children. During the decade 1958-68, over 700,000 instructional rooms were built, almost one-half of the instructional rooms in use in 1964-65. Construction of teaching stations has added to the increasing needs for capital expenditure, placing an additional stress on the requirments for public financial support in addition to growing expenditures for current operations. At the same time, from eighteen to twenty thousand school rooms are abandoned each year due to obsolescence, consolidation, destruction, urban renewal, and other causes. School construction has generally kept up with enrollment growth, so that in the fall of 1968 only about one-half of one percent of elementary children were attending school on curtailed session, primarily in six states—California, New York, Rhode Island, Montana, Florida, and Louisiana. In 1968, there was an instructional room for every twenty-six pupils, compared to one for every twenty-eight pupils in 1958. To provide the recommended ratio of one room for every twenty-five elementary and every twenty secondary pupils in 1964-65, an additional 285,000 rooms would have been required. Thus, even a slight reduction in the number of pupils per room requires a substantial additional capital investment in school housing.

Finances. It was estimated in the fall of 1968 that the United States received some 37 billion dollars for public elementary and secondary education. Notwithstanding this impressive figure, public school

50. National Education Association—Research Division, *Salary Schedules for Teachers, 1969* (Washington, D.C.: NEA, 1969), pp. 9-10.

revenue receipts, as percent of personal income, amounted to only five percent.

While there has been increasing emphasis on federal aid to education, there has been a significant shift also from local to state support, as indicated below:

PERCENT DISTRIBUTION

Year	Local	State	National
1919-20	83.2	16.5	0.3
1967-68	53.0	39.1	7.9

Over the years, expenditures objects have changed less than have sources of revenue. Percentage allocations for current expenditures, capital outlay, and administration were almost the same in 1965-66 as in 1919-20. The biggest changes were a decline in instructional costs and an increase in fixed charges and other services. The "fixed charges" category reflects benefits to teachers in the form of teacher retirement and social security costs; the "other services" category primarily reflects the increasing expenditures on public school transportation.

Public school revenue receipts in 1969-70 per pupil in ADA were $907, with a low of $524 per pupil in Alabama and a high of $1,430 for New York. This difference reflects differences in per capita income, which in 1968 was $2,337 in Alabama and $4,151 in New York. Differences in economic wealth by state are reflected in differences in level of educational support. Some of the poorer states actually exert more effort for educational support than wealthier states. Thus Mississippi, which ranked 50th in per capital personal income in 1968, ranked 24th in allocation of percentage of personal income to support public education.[51]

Need For Elementary Teachers. The regular elementary teacher has seldom been the beneficiary of special stipends and institutes, notwithstanding the fact that he is the backbone of the elementary program. In recent years, the supply of regular elementary teachers has begun to balance the demand, so that few school systems now report extreme difficulty in filling vacancies.

There is nevertheless a difference in the supply of available teachers, and the supply of qualified teachers. Based on quality criteria, which include such factors as increased enrollment, teacher turnover, replacement of teachers with substandard classifications, reduction of overcrowded classes, and special instructional services, supply (in 1969) was estimated to be 35 percent of demand. Not only are there special needs for such elementary personnel as librarians and as teachers of exceptional children, but limited comparisons also indicate that the supply of beginning teachers is not as large as needed in subject-area assignments in elementary schools and in junior-high school subjects.[52]

There is nevertheless a substantial difference between supply and demand, based on theoretical standards, and supply and demand based on actual standards and the job market. In recent years there has been a substantial increase in the training of elementary teachers, and it is now estimated that the supply of baccalaureate level elementary teachers will exceed demand for the next ten years. Estimates for 1972 indicate a supply of 104,000 elementary teachers for 37,000 positions. While the scope of elementary certification, frequently from

---

51. NEA, *Rankings of the States, 1970,* pp. 31, 44-45.

52. National Education Association, Research Division, *Teacher Supply and Demand in Public Schools, 1969* (Washington, D.C.: NEA 1970), p. 50.

grades 1 through 8, facilitates job placement, regular elementary teachers may anticipate a competitive job market.[53] While employment conditions may adversely affect individuals, the possibility of greater selectivity among elementary teachers may contribute to raising the quality of elementary instruction.

Summary

The elementary teacher who joins the profession in the 1970s will join a vast undertaking significant in a number of ways. From the standpoint of finances, elementary education is a significant part of the Gross National Product; from the standpoint of numbers, it marshals an army of children and teachers; from the standpoint of output, it represents a heavy investment in the capitalization of manpower.

But elementary education is more than finances, numbers, and manpower. The elementary school represents a place where the ideals of American culture, reflected in its system of knowledge and its morals, are transmitted to the young. Adults who join this enterprise undertake no mean task, even when they win no laurels; they are joined together in the continued development of the national character, and need apologize to no man for their calling.

Public education has been criticized in the past, and will continue to be criticized in the future. Its very nature as a public activity, with many diverse clients having different perceptions, invites criticism, as do other public institutions. Perhaps educational ingenuity will permit greater diversity in meeting these different needs. But the prospective teacher can enter his profession with the confidence that public education of the young is a noble calling and an exciting undertaking. The volume of criticism is one measure of its importance and its continuing vitality.

SELECTED REFERENCES

BAYLES, ERNEST E., and HOOD, BRUCE L. *Growth of American Educational Thought and Practice.* New York: Harper and Row, Publishers, 1967.

CREMIN, LAWRENCE A. *The Transformation of the School: Progressivism in American Education, 1876-1957.* New York: Alfred A. Knopf, 1961.

CUBBERLEY, ELLWOOD, P. *Public Education in the United States.* Boston: Houghton Mifflin Company, 1934.

Educational Statistics 1969, Digest of. Washington, D.C.: U.S. Government Printing Office, 1969.

FRENCH, WILLIAM MARSHALL. *America's Educational Tradition: An Interpretive History.* Boston: D. C. Heath and Company, 1964.

GOODLAD, JOHN I., ed. *The Changing American School. Sixty-fifth Yearbook of the National Society for the Study of Education, Part II,* Chicago: University of Chicago Press, 1966.

KARIER, CLARENCE J. *Man, Society, and Education: A History of American Educational Ideas.* Glenview, Ill.: Scott, Foresman and Company, 1967.

KNIGHT, EDGAR W. *Education in the United States.* 2d ed., Boston: Ginn and Company, 1941.

MEYER, ADOLPH E. *An Educational History of the American People.* New York: McGraw-Hill Book Company, 1967.

National Education Association—Research Division. *The Amercian Public School Teacher, 1965-66.* Washington, D.C.: National Education Association, 1967.

———. *Rankings of the States, 1970.* Washington, D.C.: National Education Association, 1970.

53. "Teacher Job Shortage Ahead," *NEA Research Bulletin* 49, no. 3 (October 1971): 69-74.

To the Teachers of America's Children

There is not a coin small enough, ever stamped by the hand of man, to pay the salary of a poor teacher;

there is not gold enough in the mines of the world to measure the value of a teacher who lifts the souls of children to the true dignity of life and living.

—Francis W. Parker
Talks on Pedagogics

PART ONE

an introduction to teaching

Photo: Courtesy of El Paso (Texas) Independent School District.
Photography: Seth J. Edwards, Jr.

the changing functions of the elementary teacher

1

Throughout the history of elementary education in the United States, the function or role that the teacher has been expected to fulfill has changed periodically. In large measure, this is true because the elementary school simply mirrors the culture in which it is set. Presently, the elementary teacher's role is changing again. Before investigating the nature of that changing role, let us briefly review some of the major roles which elementary teachers have been expected to perform in the past.

Initial Role of the Elementary Teacher

The earliest of elementary teachers in America were expected to offer religious instruction in some Christian belief in addition to instructing children in reading, writing and, later, arithmetic.[1] In fact, church and school instruction were further related in that frequently the teacher was also a minister of the gospel. An early role of teaching in colonial America's schools then was one of offering religious instruction in addition to instruction in the three R's.[2]

Our New England forefathers subscribed to the notion that everyone ought to be taught to read. The first law passed to insure that children would be taught to read was enacted by the colonial legislature of Massachusetts in 1642. This law was superseded by the law of 1647 which decreed that every Massachusetts town which had fifty or more householders must acquire a teacher to provide instruction in reading and writing and that the constituents of each town must pay a suitable wage to such a teacher.[3]

These New Englanders had narrow sectarian purposes in mind in mandating that every child should be taught to read; that he should receive religious instruction and understand the capital laws of the country.[4] Ironically, this mandate to achieve literacy broadened the role and scope of the colonial

1. Ellwood P. Cubberley, *Public Education in the United States* (Boston: Houghton Mifflin Company, 1934) p. 473.
2. For a thorough discussion of the teacher's changing role, see: Gordon C. Lee, "The Changing Role of the Teacher," in *The Changing American School, Sixty-fifth Yearbook of the National Society for the Study of Education, Part II,* ed. John I. Goodlad (Chicago: University of Chicago Press, 1966), pp. 9-31.
3. Cubberley, *Public Education,* p. 18.
4. Ibid., p. 17.

3

teacher's responsibilities as schools were established and teachers were employed who were less closely tied to a given religious sect. This introduced secularized teaching in American public education—a principle which was to become a basic characteristic of our nation's schools.[5]

Historically, the teacher has always been expected to prepare children for effective participation in public affairs. Likewise, he has been expected to teach children for vocational competence. For example, arithmetic was added to the curriculum of the colonial schools by 1775 when it became evident that children needed to master the fundamental operations of mathematics if they were to become competent in such adult pursuits as navigation, surveying, and merchant accounting. One can similarly trace the impact of the emergence of various courses in the school's curriculum on the role which the teacher has fulfilled for any given time period in our nation's history.

One of the major functions of the early teacher was the teaching of morality. After the adoption of the nation's constitution, the relationship between school and church was weakened as the impact of the constitutional provisions for separation of church and state began to manifest itself in the states. As a result, teachers concerned themselves more with teaching moral virtues and less with teaching a given religious creed. However, teachers were expected to uphold the moral code implicit in the Old and New Testaments. In fact, a prime consideration in employing a teacher was whether or not he subscribed to the moral code held by the community in which the school was located. Furthermore, the citizens of the community insisted upon some control of the teacher's life to insure the fact that he would set an appropriate moral example for their children[6]—a stricture which appears to be of less importance in our contemporary schools because there is a great variety of acceptable behavior.

Inherent in the role of the early teacher in the nation's schools was that he teach his charges patriotism and love of country. This became a universally expected function of all elementary teachers as the country expanded and public education developed.

Of course, teachers have long been charged with the responsibility of developing in their students acceptable social behavior congruent with democratic principles. This has demanded that the role of the teacher be modified to include teaching children certain affective learnings and interpersonal skills which promote acceptable social attitudes and behavior.

By the beginning of this century, the curriculum of the elementary school had been expanded to include approximately eighteen subjects, an expansion which further altered the role of the teacher.[7] That is, there was evidence of great concern for the general education of children in this nation, as witness the offering of such subjects as reading, literature, spelling, arithmetic, grammar, geography, history, science, music, manual training, and drawing. The teacher now had to concern himself with the total educational development of his pupils; their learnings in cognitive, affective and psychomotor areas.

The teaching role of the elementary teacher in the nation's schools has been modified many times. Each modification has broadened the teacher's role or respon-

5. Lee, "Changing Role," p. 11.
6. Ibid., pp. 12-13.
7. For a graphic portrayal of the evolutionary process of the elementary curriculum, 1775-1900, see figure P-1 of this text.

sibility. Up to the turn of this century, he had been expected to assume at one time or another the responsibility for: teaching religion; improving the literacy level of his charges; preparing children for effective participation in public affairs; developing his students' vocational competencies; providing by instruction and example learnings in morality; teaching patriotism and love of country; developing acceptable attitudes and social behavior among his students; and, eventually, being concerned with the total educational betterment of his pupils.[8]

This basic role of the teacher has continued to change in the twentieth century. Now, let us investigate some of those changes.

Changing Role of the Elementary Teacher

There have been two great movements in the twentieth century which have greatly altered the role of the elementary school teacher. These events which have exerted an effect on teaching and consequently the teacher's role include the progressive education movement,[9] particularly in the second and third decades of this century, and the reform movement toward discipline-centered curricula in the 1960s.[10]

Progressive Education Movement. From the genesis of the graded elementary school to the progressive education era in America's schools, teachers largely fulfilled their role in a formal manner. Through employing the assign-study-recite-test technique, they administered standardized lessons to the group and, more often than not, attempted to exact uniform achievement from their students. Teaching them reading, morality, general knowledge, patriotism, and acceptable social behavior was largely teacher centered and students learned by rote. The educational literature is replete with criticisms of this type of teaching and learning in the elementary school.[11]

In retrospect, one can view the years from 1900 to America's entrance into World War II in 1941 as transitional years during which the teacher's role in the elementary school was changing from that of a stern disciplinarian and an exactor of uniform standards to that of a diagnostician and guider of learning. In fulfilling this new role, the teacher's methods were expected to change from teacher centeredness (assign-study-recite-test) to pupil centeredness (learning-by-doing in experience or activity units). This movement was spawned by such leaders of the progressive education movement as John Dewey and William Heard Kilpatrick.[12]

As the impact of systematic psychology on education began to be evidenced in this

---

8. Lee, "Changing Role," pp. 10-15.

9. For a discussion of the progressive education movement, see John T. Wahlquist, *The Philosophy of American Education* (New York: Ronald Press Company, 1942), chap. 6.

10. For a comprehensive discussion of the reform movement in elementary curriculum following 1951, see John I. Goodlad, "The Curriculum," in *The Changing American School, Sixty-fifth Yearbook of The National Society for the Study of Education, part II,* ed. John I. Goodlad (Chicago: University of Chicago Press, 1966), pp. 32-58.

11. See, for example: Hughes Mearns, "Salvation by Information," *North American Review,* 229 (January 1930): 65-72; William J. Shearer, *The Grading of Schools,* 3d ed. (New York: H. P. Smith Publishing Company, 1899) pp. 21-23. John T. Wahlquist, *Philosophy of American Education,* pp. 84-138.

12. See John Dewey, *School and Society* (Chicago: University of Chicago Press, 1915); William Heard Kilpatrick, *Remaking the Curriculum* (New York: Newson & Company, 1936); John Dewey, *Experience and Education* (New York: Macmillan Company, 1938): John Dewey, *Democracy and Education* (New York: Macmillan Company, 1916).

period, progressive educationists began to enunciate increasing concern for the individual learner, for differentiated instruction, and for less formal learning experiences in which children would become less passive and more active in the teaching and learning process.

As one might suspect, all teachers and all schools did not make this transition overnight. In fact, one can still find vestiges of Procrustean methods still being employed by some of the nation's teachers in the 1970s. What was established in the preponderance of America's schools in the 1900s prior to World War II, however, was gradual change in the teacher's role from an authoritarian figure in a formalized learning setting to that of a democratic teacher in an informal learning atmosphere where an attempt was being made to meet the individual interests and needs of the children. The teacher's role remained basically the same; that is, he still strove to teach for literacy, vocational competency, patriotism and the like.

The Reform Movement. After the war years, World War II and the Korean War, the teacher's role expectancy began to change drastically. This was occasioned largely by the launching of Sputnik I in October of 1957. Our nation was shocked in assessing the fact that our schools were failing to teach adequately in the sciences and humanities. Under the general welfare clause of the constitution, the federal government entered education to stay. Huge sums of money were pumped into education with the passage of the 1958 National Defense Education Act and later with the passage of the 1965 Elementary and Secondary Education Act.

With the passage of the 1958 legislation, the reform movement in elementary education in this nation began to gain momentum.[13] Teachers once again began to stress the mastery of content in the new discipline-centered curricula which were developed in the nation, e.g., School Mathematics Study Group materials.

Learning by induction or discovery gained prominence in the late 1950s and early 1960s. As a result of such teaching, coupled with such major situations as the moral awakening of the public conscience to the civil rights issue; the war in Viet Nam; the new curricula in science, mathematics, social studies and English; and an increased, improved technology—the products of our schools, the children, have become different from those of any previous era in the nation's history.

Thus, we witness the changing of the teacher's role in the American culture. Prior to World War II, the teacher was expected to educate children narrowly according to more or less puritanical principles to which this nation had been dedicated since its inception. It appears evident that since the onrush of the Space Age, the teacher's role has changed to one of educating children broadly, through inquiry methods and highly structured curricula, to become autonomous individuals capable of living effectively in a highly technological culture. This does not mean that teaching for literacy, morality, vocational competence, patriotism or acceptable social behavior, for example, is of any less consequence. It does mean that the teacher's role in teaching for these outcomes has become more sensitive and congruent with the increased sophistication and complexity of the times in which we live.

13. Goodlad, "The Curriculum," pp. 41-45.

Educational Criticism

As the American teacher changed the methods with which he performed his role expectation in the first half of the twentieth century from those of a teacher of subject-centered orientation to child-centered or experience-oriented procedures, he, along with the school, became the recipient of criticism from certain educators known as "essentialists." Essentialists such as Bagley, Finney, Morrison and Breed contended that the new progressive teachers, known as "Progressives," were guilty of overemphasizing pupil interests—individualism and freedom—when it seemed clear that the children should master essential knowledge and accept truths of the society by imposing whatever discipline and authority was necessary.[14] The essentialists stated that low standards in the schools and a lack of ordered procedure was a result of the progressives' concern for democratic teaching procedures which were based upon pupil interest and needs in an activity or experience curriculum.[15]

The criticism of the progressives took many forms in the 1940s, 50s and 60s. Barzun complained that just about everyone was dissatisfied with education in the mid-1940s except those who were in charge of it.[16] Keats charged that the progressives were responsible for a leveling influence in the public schools. Furthermore, they, the progressives, would not admit that an intellectually elite group of students required a greater scientific and abstract curriculum. This neglect resulted in scaling down the curriculum to a level of work geared to students of only average ability. He also asserted that the progressives were concerned with the happiness of their charges to such an extent that hard work and academic achievement among pupils were sacrificed.[17] Trace stated in 1961 that over the past thirty years educators had come to believe that it was not too important for students to have a thorough knowledge of such basic subjects as literature, the basic sciences and history. He further contended that students were expected to become familiar with the intricacies of family living and how to adjust to the environment as they find it; hence, in his opinion, children actually learned very little about the basic subjects in the nontraditional or progressive schools.[18]

Of course, the accusations of the essentialists have not gone unchallenged by educators with more progressive leanings. One can find able rebuttals to such charges.[19] In essence, these arguments and facts are only important in their historical perspective since we have actually entered the era of the reform movement in curriculum which is a mid-point between progressivism and essentialism.

The reform movement in curriculum reached its zenith in the 1960s when new

---

14. R. Freeman Butts and Lawrence A. Cremin, *A History of Education in American Culture* (New York: Henry Holt and Company, 1953), p. 494.

15. William E. Drake, *The American School in Transformation* (New York: Prentice-Hall, Inc., 1955), p. 465.

16. Jacques Barzun, *Teacher in America* (New York: Doubleday & Company, Inc., 1944), p. 11.

17. John Keats, *Schools Without Scholars* (Boston: Houghton Mifflin Company, 1958), p. 108.

18. Arthur S. Trace, Jr., *What Ivan Knows That Johnny Doesn't* (New York: Random House, Inc., 1961), p. 182.

19. See, for example, Douglas Rugh, "The Scapegoat Value of American Public Education," *School and Society* 82 (14 July 1955): 20-22; Joseph Justman, "Wanted: A Philosophy of American Education," *School and Society* 83 (12 May 1956): 159-61.

curricula were developed in arithmetic, science, social studies and English.[20] The new curricula associated with this movement placed renewed emphasis upon the mastery of subject matter content and the perfection of certain cognitive processes and psychomotor skills. In a sense, the reform movement was an eclectic or compromise position between the traditionalists or essentialists and the nontraditionalists or progressives in that learnings in the content areas were more structured for students but they were planned to incorporate more of the students' known interests and needs. Stated another way, the new curricula, which will be discussed in detail in Parts III and IV of this volume, were restructured more like the parent disciplines from which they were derived, e.g., mathematics, history and geography, and greater insistence was made by teachers that children master the content workways and processes of these curricula. This pleased many essentialists. Also, the new curricula were planned and developed more scientifically to appeal to students in substantive or processes units of work. This pleased many progressivists. The teacher's role in the curriculum reform movement is subsequently discussed.

Role of the New Elementary Teacher

There are several movements which presently are taking place that will shape the role of the elementary teacher in the 1970s. These movements include education to: (1) suit national purposes, (2) stress the mastery of cognitive processes and subject matter, (3) develop autonomous individuals, and (4) provide specialized training.[21] Let us examine these movements as they relate to a changed role for the new elementary teacher.

Education to Suit National Purposes. With the emergence of the curriculum reform movement in education, the emphasis has shifted from a predominant child-centered orientation to one in which national needs and goals are stressed. For example, the schools at most levels responded to the national concern, expressed by statute in the 1958 NDEA legislation, by "beefing-up" instruction in science, math and foreign language in order to close the science and technology gaps existing between the Soviet Union and the United States. One can assess the results of that effort as we enter the 1970s. America now has the rocketry, the technology and the scientists necessary to maintain its lead in the conquest of space for the next several years. The teacher of the 1970s, therefore, will be called upon to teach for a basic literacy in terms of the significant political and social problems which this nation faces.[22]

Education to Stress Mastery of Cognitive Processes and Subject Matter. As part and parcel of the reform movement in curriculum, the new elementary teacher will be expected to have a basic academic orientation in teaching children. That is, he will teach the new curricula which emphasize—even demand—cognitive processes and subject matter mastery by students.[23] If we

20. See, John U. Michaelis et al., *New Designs for the Elementary School Curriculum* (New York: McGraw-Hill Book Company, 1967.)

21. For a more comprehensive discussion of these points, see: Lee, "Changing Role," pp. 20-31.

22. Ibid., pp. 20-21.

23. For a review of these new curricula, see Glenys G. Unruh, ed., *New Curriculum Developments* (Washington, D.C.: Association for Supervision and Curriculum Development, 1965), 106 pp.

educate to meet national problems having political and social significance in the 1970s, then teachers must help each child master as much as he can of the basic processes and products of the academic disciplines, e.g., English, mathematics, history and geography.

Education to Develop Autonomous Individuals. The new elementary teacher will be expected to view education as a continuing process; hence, he will dedicate his efforts toward developing self-regulating students who will be able to continue educating themselves once their formal learning experiences have come to an end. In the decade ahead, teachers will seek to develop the intellectual powers (cognitive processes) of their charges as a base for continued learning.

Education to Provide Specialized Training. Teachers of the reform movement era will not be as concerned with the concept of teaching the "whole child" as were their counterparts who were identified with the progressive education era. Instead, the new teacher will devote his major efforts towards becoming a specialist in one or more of the disciplines in order that he can effectually teach cognitive facts and skills as well as develop the intellectual processes of his students in a specialized area. This orientation automatically means that other agencies, e.g., home, church, YMCA, YWCA, Boy Scouts and Girl Scouts, must increasingly attend to the teaching of many of the affective learnings which teachers in previous times strove mightily to attain. Stated another way, this suggests that the school and its teachers in the reform movement era will address themselves more to meeting the intellectual and academic needs of children.

Not only is teaching the so-called average or normal child becoming more specialized in the elementary school—the teaching of exceptional children is also becoming more specialized. Presently, a great movement is being waged to have specialists teach disadvantaged learners as well. Whether the specialists are accustomed to teaching normal, exceptional or disadvantaged learners, the prevailing view is that the new elementary teachers perceive each child individually *as student* and attend to the intellectual and academic needs of each rather than trying to meet the *all-embracing* needs of the "whole child"— as espoused in the progressive era.[24]

In sum, the new elementary teacher's role has changed to be congruent with and fulfill national goals, to stress subject matter mastery, to develop autonomous students who will be capable of continuing to teach themselves in the years ahead and to attend to the intellectual and academic needs of children through specialized teaching. A new view of the child *as student* has emerged replacing the notion of the progressives that the "whole child" had to be attended to by the school.

The New Teacher and Classroom Management

Chapter 21 will treat classroom management in detail. However, it should be pointed out here that the horizontal organization of the elementary school will change rapidly in the 1970s to accommodate the new emphasis on specialized instruction. As the teacher's role changes from a pluralistic and diversified one to a singular and specialized one, the self-contained classroom likely will fall into increasing disuse. Re-

24. Lee, "Changing Role," pp. 22-23.

placing the self-contained classroom horizontally will be team teaching and departmentalization, two alternative horizontal plans which yield themselves better to specialized teaching than does the self-contained classroom plan. Actually, the sixties marked the beginning of this movement.[25]

Under the team teaching and departmentalized organizational arrangements, which are discussed at greater length in chapter 19, the new elementary teacher, in performing his role, will act more as a resource person and organizer of materials and technology as children are engaged in learning subject matter and perfecting their cognitive skills.[26] In so acting, his methods will be markedly different from those advocated by the essentialists—stern disciplinarian and dispenser of facts following the assign-study-recite-test teaching strategy—or those espoused by the progressives—diagnostician and guider of learning in largely experience or activity units.

Becoming an Effective Elementary Teacher

One can find a plethora of research and summaries of research that treat the abilities and traits of successful teachers.[27] Generally, the correlations between certain traits or abilities and teaching success are positive but not high. The reason for this seems to reside in the fact that measures of teaching success are usually derived from supervisor's ratings. These ratings often are lacking in reliability and validity. It seems more appropriate here therefore to raise certain questions about teaching which appear to have relevance for teaching in the elementary school during the 1970s—a period which will be the era of the reform movement and it will be characterized by more substantively oriented curricula and specialized instruction. Some of the relevant questions which can be raised about who is suited to teach in this era follow.

As a teacher, do I:

1. believe that developing autonomous students who are capable of continuing to learn or educate themselves in order that they can become effectual citizens is the primary raison d'etre for teaching?
2. want to continually develop expertise in a given curricular area in order that I can effectively teach my charges the subject matter and cognitive skills they need in order that they will become literate and vocationally competent individuals?
3. embrace the emergent view of the individual child *as student* in the modern elementary school rather than to attempt to attend to the *whole child*?
4. want to prepare students for participation in public affairs who are sensitive to and capable of coping with the social, political and economic problems of the times?

25. For discussions of the increasing incidence of team teaching and departmental teaching in the nation's elementary schools, see: "Team Teaching," *NEA Research Bulletin* 45, no. 4 (December 1967), pp. 114-15; "Departmentalization in Elementary Schools," *NEA Research Bulletin* 44, no. 1 (February 1966), pp. 27-28.

26. For a discussion of the new elementary teacher's role in specialization, see Alexander Frazier, "The New Elementary School Teacher," *The New Elementary School* (Washington, D.C.: Association for Supervision and Curriculum Development, NEA, and Department of Elementary School Principals, NEA, 1968), pp. 96-112.

27. See: David G. Ryans, *Characteristics of Teachers: A Research Study* (Washington, D.C.: American Council on Education, 1960); Marie A. Mehl et al., *Teaching in Elementary School*, 3d ed. (New York: Ronald Press Company, 1965), pp. 479-97; William B. Ragan, *Teaching America's Children* (New York: Holt, Rinehart and Winston, 1961), pp. 25-43.

5. want to differentiate instruction in attending to the intellectual and academic needs of my charges?
6. believe that the general welfare of the society is contingent upon an intelligent and well-informed citizenry?
7. recognize the importance and significance of teaching in meeting the goals of the society collectively while at the same time contributing to the self-fulfillment of each person individually?
8. enjoy working with people?
9. attempt to develop and maintain a well-balanced emotional life?
10. keep myself physically fit?
11. believe that appropriate teaching must be directed to all types of students—the exceptional as well as the so-called average or normal students?
12. have and maintain a sense of humor?

In sum, the effective elementary teacher of the curriculum reform era quite likely will fit the following description of a teacher advanced by Farrell.[28]

> ... Does the teacher see each student as unique from him, though possessing that which embraces us all—our common humanity; or does he assume that the class exists as audience for the extension of his, and only his personality? Aware, as he must be, of the dependency of his charges upon him, does he exploit that dependency by creating disciples en masse or a coterie that perpetually yearns to hear the latest word from the master; or does he envision and plan for a time of his own obsolescence when each student can function autonomously without him? ...
>
> To the degree that one can infer intent clearly, to that degree can he distinguish the great teacher as separate from the great personality; for the great teacher, regardless of intensity of personality, will consciously or unconsciously seek students to be ultimately free from, not bound to, himself...
>
> In short, if a teacher commands the respect of his students, if he envisions his central task as that of imparting knowledge to advance human freedom, if he is willing to sacrifice himself for the principles he teaches, then he is a great teacher, whether he teaches in a rural one-room elementary school, in an august university, or in a slum school in Harlem. He may go unheralded in literature, uncodified in textbooks, unobserved by outsiders, but by the strength of a democracy he shall be known.

Appraisal of the Changing Functions of the Elementary Teacher

Twentieth century America is so different from Colonial America in science and technology that the inhabitants of today appear to belong to another planet, not merely to a different era. The jets and rockets of today shriek of the changing world in which we live, a world so remote from the agricultural idyll that Jefferson envisioned from the heights of Monticello that we are alternately bereaved and frightened by the consequences of our inventiveness and daring.

Although patterns of behavior do not always change as rapidly as do the artifacts of a culture, it is still a truism that social institutions change as technology and science change. It was therefore inevitable that the role of the elementary teacher would change as the country moved in an accelerating tempo from an agrarian to an industrial society and as the knowledge base generated by the new sciences geometrically expanded. Since education is both a child and a progenitor of culture, it is not surprising to find that in a religious age the elementary pedagogue was also a sectarian teacher or that in a scientific age he became a mentor for scientific learning. The

---

28. Edmund J. Farrell, "Toward the Definition of a Great Teacher," *Phi Delta Kappan* 45, no. 9 (June 1964): 454.

changing role of the elementary teacher is a reflection of the changes in our culture.

But under the facade of change there is also a reality of continuity, a reality which is engendered and transmitted by two forces—the nature of culture and the nature of the learner. Rarely are there sharp breaks in a culture, merely cumulative impacts in time. From the vantage point of time we single out certain events or trends and contrast them with another point in time to dramatize and emphasize the differences. And so it is with teaching. The dichotomies in education reflected by such labels as essentialist, progressive, and curriculum reform are points on a continuum, reflecting different emphases and values rather than different systems of education.

In addition to the stability of culture in the midst of change, there is also the permanence of human learning rooted in an animal organism. Elementary education begins at the beginning of formal instruction, and there is and will continue to be less variability in elementary than in secondary and higher education. Literacy in a literate society begins with reading, writing, and numbers, keys to the realms of vicarious and abstract transmission of culture. Methods and approaches may change, but these fundamental tasks impart a uniformity to elementary instruction across the millenia of history.

The history of education reveals the attempts of reformers and critics to make the process of education more meaningful to young learners, but an examination of reform movements under any label indicates that the old most often persists in the substance of the new. The rhetoric of change is often more dramatic than the change itself. And when changes take place in education, they often mirror the changes generated in society, not in education as a causal agent. The rise of the progressive movement coincided not only with new conceptions in child development, but with shifts in child rearing practices in much of the country; the curriculum reform era coincided with national concerns about scientific manpower development.

The changes in educational philosophy represented in different approaches to curriculum and teaching are just as much a part of our history as war and industrialization. These changes in educational philosophy are not mere reflections of narrow pedagogical views; they are attempts to reconcile the system of education with moral and scientific views of the nature of man and of society.

As a teacher, you will wish to become more familiar with these ideas in other courses, not merely to be able to answer questions on tests but to develop your own educational philosophy and view of teaching and learning. A teacher does not bring solely a bag of teaching tricks and a store of knowledge to the classroom. He brings to his pupils his own personality and own conception of the nature of teaching and learning. The great teachers of the past, whether a Plato, a Rousseau, a Pestalozzi, or a Montessori, brought to the act of teaching profound conceptions of the nature of man and of society. Their formulations of curriculum and of teaching reflected these fundamental views. You will enrich your own life if you place the idea of your own role as a teacher into the perspective of our changing culture and the nature of man and project them into the future. The children you teach will not live in the world of your generation, but that of one yet to emerge.

Selected References

Frazier, Alexander. "The New Elementary School Teacher," *The New Elementary School*. Washington, D.C.: Association for Supervision and Curriculum Development, NEA, and Department of Elementary School Principals, NEA, 1968, pp. 96-112.

Goodlad, John I., et al. *The Changing School Curriculum*. New York: The Fund for the Advancement of Education, 1966.

Lee, Gordon C. "The Changing Role of the Teacher," *The Changing American School, Sixty-fifth Yearbook of the National Society for the Study of Education, part II*. ed. John I. Goodlad. Chicago: The University of Chicago Press, 1966, pp. 9-31.

Perrodin, Alex F., ed. *The Student Teacher's Reader*. Chicago: Rand McNally & Company, 1966.

Unruh, Glenys G., ed. *New Curriculum Developments*. Washington, D.C.: Association for Supervision and Curriculum Development, 1965.

Williams, Lois, et al. *Six Areas of Teacher Competence*. Burlingame, California: California Teachers Association, 1964.

2

understanding the elementary child in culture

The effective teaching of children in the school is generally held to require competency in four major areas: knowledge of subject matter; skill in teaching; appreciation of the school as a social institution; and an understanding of the child as an individual as well as a learner. It is to this fourth competency—understanding of the child—that this chapter is addressed.

The subject matter for acquiring an understanding of the child in his many facets has its theoretical foundations in the field of child growth and development, one of the oldest and most extensive disciplines in pedagogy. The field of child growth and development draws on the behavioral sciences, but in its formative period was most closely identified with biology and genetic psychology. For that reason, much of child growth and development is tinged with maturational determinism.[1] Only recently has it begun to give serious attention to the contributions of anthropology and sociology, especially in connection with the important concept of culture as a system of learned behavior and the relationship of social class to socialization and school learning.

A prospective elementary teacher generally takes at least one course in child growth and development, in which norms are given with respect to such diverse dimentions as physical growth and moral behavior. A chapter in a general text, such as this, most frequently gives a summary of some of the high spots in child growth and development. This chapter departs from conventional overviews in several ways. The authors are more concerned with indicating perceptions of children and behavioral considerations which interfere with learning than with the delineation of age or grade norms. The emphasis is on developing a view of the child as a product of his culture, and the view emphasized is more anthropological than psychological. This emphasis is deliberate. For too long approaches to understanding children have focused on descriptions of children's behavior, without consideration being given the cultural context in which it occurs. The child was regarded as a biological animal, but not as a social animal.

This book espouses the viewpoint that the teacher is one of the most important

---

1. For a lucid discussion of this, see Gladys G. Jenkins, et al., *These Are Your Children,* 3d ed. (Chicago: Scott, Foresman and Company, 1966).

instruments of enculturation. Culture and group processes are the means by which the child acquires his culture and becomes a socialized individual. The culture of the school is inextricably interwoven with the child's enculturation. This chapter begins with a section on biology and culture, and considers such topics as socialization, values, emotional growth, prejudice, intelligence, physical appearance, motor development, and interests. In every section, the positive role of the school and the teacher is emphasized. It is hoped that this treatment, which focuses on the understanding of the elementary child in the context of cultural development, will assist the prospective teacher approach teaching with confidence and inspire new zeal in experienced teachers.

This chapter largely ignores the emphasis given to physical growth in the preschool years and the rapid growth of the pubescent and adolescent years with the attendant emotional problems. While early maturing children in the intermediate school (see chapter 7) experience these psychosocial crises, this emphasis would call undue attention to the adolescent stage and detract from the principle of emphasis on enculturation.

Biology and Culture

Two major forces interact on the development of man—biology and culture. The species *Homo sapiens* has certain characteristics which set man apart from all other animals. These characteristics permit certain behaviors and prohibit others. Thus man can learn to swim underwater, but he cannot learn to breathe under water. He lacks the gills of an aquatic animal for absorbing dissolved oxygen from water. On the other hand, his culture may provide him with an artificial environment with which to invade the fishy domain—an aqualung, diver's suit, or submarine. Biology and culture are thus equally important in the development of the child.

Man and Biology. As such, man is the result of millions of years of organic development. In this long process, a special species emerged called *Homo sapiens*. This species has certain distinctive physical characteristics which set him apart from other animals: bipedal, erect locomotion; hands with opposable thumbs; stereoscopic vision; a highly developed central nervous system; and a complex oral communication system.

Walking is a landmark in the physical development of the child, and follows a sequence of pushing, rolling, hitching, crawling, and creeping. The tremendous significance of walking is species specific: the head is held erect and the hands and arms are freed for the complex interaction of eye, mouth, and hand which has such tremendous importance for early brain cell formation. The opposable thumb not only makes possible the grasping of objects, but the manipulation of objects, and is the organic basis of technology. But what a man does with his hands depends on his culture and the opportunity for learning. A hand can guide a plow, set a lathe, drive a nail, move a pencil, throw a spear, pull a bow, or strum a guitar. But there is nothing in the biology of the hand that requires any one of these activities.

Another distinctive characteristic of man is his large brain. At birth the head of an infant is disproportionate to the size of his body. About 21 percent of his total length is in the head, compared to about 8 percent in an adult. But this monstrous disproportion is the basis of learning and culture, a biological fact which sets man apart from all others. Compare the brain volume of a man and a whale, the largest mammal. In man the brain volume is about 1,500 cc. and the whale 3,000 cc. The weight of a man's brain is about 2 percent of his body. The weight of a whale's brain in proportion to his total weight is infinitesimal.

But more important than the size of the brain is the ratio of the weight of the brain to the weight of the spinal cord. In frogs and fishes the ratio is less than one; the brain weighs less than the spinal cord. In lower mammals, it is between two and four; in apes fifteen. But in man the brain weighs fifty-five times as much as the spinal cord. In man most of the brain is made up of the cerebrum, the part that controls learned behavior. The capacity of man to learn has a basis in his physical nature that developed over aeons of walking erect, using tools, and talking. The billions of nerve connections in the cerebrum provide the biological basis of intelligence. If the cerebrum fails to develop, either as a result of lethal chromosomes or injury, there is no physical basis for the acquisition of intelligent behavior, notwithstanding the opportunities for learning provided by the culture.

Man is born helpless, and acquires his humanity through learning. This fundamental aspect of humanness is emphasized when the capacity of learning in other animals is compared with that of man. Animal behavior ranges from tropisms, in which behavior is automatic without prior learning, as in wasps and ants, to learned behavior, as in the rat killing capacity of cats.[2] Certainly, the capacity to learn is a function of the physiological system, so that the more elaborate the nervous system in higher vertebrates, the higher the learning capacity. Hence, monkeys and apes learn better than elephants, dogs, and horses. But no other animal challenges man in his capacity to learn.

Man and Culture. At some time in the evolution of man, a new phenomenon appeared. In place of the simple responses to chemical stimuli, as with plants and lower organisms, a new type of behavior appeared, a behavior based on learning. The first material evidence of this behavior are the remains of stone tools, so that the emergence of nonorganic behavior is first associated with man's capacity to make tools. Tool-making and other aspects of culture are beyond the organic, and are manifestations of behavior based on intelligence and learning. The nineteenth century sociologist Spencer applied the label *supraorganic* to cultural behavior. The term supraorganic expresses a sequence of development—as well as study—inorganic is the domain of the physical sciences; organic, the biological sciences; and the supraorganic, the social sciences, of which education is an applied field. But the term now used in preference to the more descriptive concept of the supraorganic is the term culture.

There are many definitions of culture. A simple and comprehensive definition of culture is the totality of *things* and *behaviors* man uses to adjust to his environment. Culture has a content consisting of artifacts, the things man makes; the behaviors of man using his body and the artifacts he creates; and the meanings man ascribes to these behaviors. A child is born into a culture,

2. Z. Y. Kuo, "Genesis of Cat's Responses to Rats," *Journal of Comparative Psychology* 11 (October 1930): 1-35.

and he acquires the traits of the culture as a result of enculturation—by example, imitation, play, practice, and direct teaching. Both culture and enculturation therefore may be thought of in terms of learning—culture as the repertory of knowledge and behaviors to be learned, and enculturation as the process by which a culture is transmitted and acquired by the young.

Cross-cultural comparison, that is, the studies of people living in different cultures, have revealed two significant aspects for understanding human behavior. There are practices common to every culture, from age grading to weather control. Children in every culture are treated somewhat different according to age, but whether these result in adult age sets, as among the Masai, or a vague recollection of common schooling together, as in the United States, depends upon the pattern of cultural expectancies. Whether a people attempt to provide scientific information about the weather, or to control the weather through magic, depends upon the cultural inventory. But what a child learns depends on his culture. Studies of differences of artistic expression among children of different cultures indicate that the perception of the environment is related to the structure of the culture. Thus while men of all races share a common biological mechanism for learning, what they learn is often vastly different, because of the tendency of races and cultures to become geographically isolated.

Because the human infant requires years of nurture before he reaches maturity, the primary agency of enculturation is the family. Hence, the child first acquires the cultural patterns of the parents, not because of biology, but because of the *opportunity* to learn. There is nothing in the genetic composition of any stock which precludes the learning of another culture. After the traits of one culture are learned, however, acquisition of second culture traits are more difficult because previous enculturation has established a repertory of behaviors and psychological adjustments which make acculturation—the acquisition of the behaviors of another culture—more difficult. The concept of enculturation therefore emphasizes the importance of early learning and the importance of the preschool (see chapter 5) in providing learning opportunities for children who would otherwise be denied learning by lack of experience.

One of the most important facets of culture, if not the most important, is language. Language provides the means by which meaning is attributed to behaviors in a culture. A teacher only has to be present on some occasion in which the language used is different from his to understand that without a knowledge of the language, it is almost impossible to perceive behavior with any understanding. It is for this reason that in the study of other cultures, first importance is placed on a knowledge of the language. A language is not merely a means to talk, to communicate. It is the vehicle by which a culture is understood. Children who are deficient in language use consequently are handicapped in their ability to understand the culture.

Language is also the means by which one generation transmits knowledge to another. Language is the basis of cultural accumulation because prior knowledge can be preserved in the descriptive symbols and retrieved. Skill in language in a literate society predisposes children to success in reading and writing, since reading and writing are means of decoding and encoding language into signs that stand for speech. Enculturation that emphasizes communication skills in the early years thus contributes to school success, because schooling itself emphasizes cultural transmission through language use.

Culture not only affects what is learned, but the capacity to retain what is learned through practice. The experience of Captain Fitz-Roy with the reversion of his Fuegian proteges to savagery[3] is merely one example of the extinction of learned behaviors acquired in one culture because the traits of the original culture do not require their use. Where there is a fit between the culture of the school and the culture of the home, there is a greater opportunity to retain and extend school learning. Incongruence between the culture of the school and the out-of-school culture may explain why, with increased age and the development of a pattern of non-verbal interests, the performance of children from subcultures, especially lower class, deviate increasingly from the norm.

Hence one of the great tasks of the teacher is to help lower class students substitute vicarious cultural expectancies for presently expected performance. Since a culture is also a system of organized values, schooling may be regarded as a way of assuring, in a system of universal education, that all children, irrespective of their cultural background, are exposed to a common interpretation of the value system which transcends subcultural and class lines. One of the great problems of American education today is the fact that it appears to espouse values which are only pertinent to some groups in the culture, rather than being universally applicable.

In recent years it has become fashionable to question the relevancy of school enculturation to the needs of certain groups, especially minority groups and learners who come from lower social classes. While school success is no guarantee of social mobility, the relationship of amount of schooling to income and the acquisition of material traits suggests that school enculturation facilitates improvement of the material culture. Since the material culture is one of the most tangible motives for cultural change, much school motivation is related to the expectancy of delayed rather than immediate material rewards. While the concept of material reward is unappealing to educators who think in terms of developing the intellectual potentialities of children, it is consistent with an observation which appears to be consistent across cultures: material traits in a culture are accepted or changed more quickly than are traits associated with home, family, and religion acquired in the earliest years of intimate personal enculturation. Much of the criticism of American education today by minority and lower class groups is stated in the language of relevance. Teachers would be able to interpret these criticisms more intelligently for their own work with students if they understood that the criticism is not directed so much at *education* per se, but at the failure of education to make students sufficiently competent to achieve the material rewards attained by other groups.

Sex is biologically determined by the uniting of an X (female) or Y (male) bearing sperm with an ovum, always X. Sex classification, which results from the

3. Editors of Life, *The Wonders of Life on Earth* (New York: Time Incorporated, 1960), pp. 136-37.

chance pairing of chromosomes, is the most important single basis for determining the participation of an individual in a culture.[4] This primary biological difference serves as a differentiating basis for activities between boys and girls in all cultures, but the kind of sex typing varies from culture to culture. Notwithstanding the fact that in most cultures there is usually a sharp division of labor based on sex, there is nothing in biology which ascribes the role of weaver to a male Yoruba or to a female Navajo.

Vocational sex typing is equally characteristic of literate and preliterate cultures. The practice of medicine by women is rare in the United States, but common in Russia. The employment of women in heavy construction work is common in Russia, but rare in the United States. Normally, sex typing is accepted and boys and girls learn the social expectancies ascribed to boy and girl roles which are embedded in the *mores* of the culture. School practices merely extend the enculturation which accompanies sex typing. While the sexes normally are not segregated for education in American public schools, teachers enforce the conventional expectancies of girl and boy behaviors. Since girls are not expected, normally, to enter professions requiring scientific and mathematical expertise, they are given little social encouragement in these areas at home or in school. The learning performance and vocational choices of children are thereby affected by their culture (see "Interests").[5]

Healthy adjustment in any culture requires appropriate identification with ascribed sex roles. Teachers should be aware of the fact that some boys and girls do have difficulty in making these adjustments often because of the behavior they have learned at home. In such cases, the teacher may create situations which encourage success in the performance of the appropriate role. The rigid assignment of activities by sex, however, may have unfortunate reactions on developing a wide range of interests.

Race and Culture. A biological development which has had far reaching consequences, because of cultural interpretations, is the division of the one species *Homo sapiens* into different races or stocks. The variation in man, resulting in differences in pigmentation, hirsuteness, hair color, eye color, body shape, and face shape, is biologically explained as a result of genetic drift, mutations, isolated breeding populations, and hybridization.

Before the great historical migrations, which took populations to different parts of the world, races were merely local populations, separated from other populations and the common gene pool by geographic isolation. Since many of these populations were so isolated that they were unable to share in the inventions of other groups—human inventiveness is rare—they also differed in the nature of their cultures.

In the eighteenth century, when scientific interest in all fields began to quicken, early students of man erroneously made the conclusion that culture was determined by race, a conclusion which reflected the ethnocentrism of the white European scientists of the period. The justification of the enslavement of pre-literate peoples, such as American Indians and Africans, also led to the de-

---

4. Ralph Linton, *The Cultural Background of Personality* (New York: Appleton-Century-Crofts, Inc., 1945), p. 64.
5. Roland R. Renne, "Woman Power and the American Economy," *Journal of Home Economics* 49, no. 2 (February 1957): 83-86.

velopment of an elaborate apology which, in brief, held that they ought to be slaves because they were innately inferior. This type of explanation easily overlooked the fact that American Indians and some Africans had achieved cultures by the tenth century A.D. which were equal and sometimes superior to those of northern Europe.

The confounding of race and culture persists even today. Many educated individuals, including teachers, frequently accept the easy folkways of the culture which attribute differences in personality, character, intelligence, and achievement to an individual's skin color. But discriminatory treatment on the basis of pigmentation can result in patterns of behavior which appear to be a function of race, when, as Dobshansky points out, rearing in a culture without race prejudice would result in a different set of social expectancies and a different organization of behavior.[6] The different racial and ethnic stocks to which American boys and girls belong are unequally distributed in the population. Indians are found largely in the Southwest, Negroes in the Southeast and in the large urban centers, and children of mixed, Spanish-speaking stocks in the Southwest and some urban areas. But whether or not a teacher's assignment involves the teaching of minority children, care must be exercised in the teaching of all children to develop an objective attitude toward race and a value acceptance of all Americans.

In this section it has been emphasized that while biology provides the physical foundation of behavior, behavior is not determined by biology but results from the interaction of biology and culture. While the central nervous system provides the neurological structure for learning, the opportunity to learn is provided by the culture. Every group of people possesses a distinctive culture, and the process of learning—enculturation—takes place within the framework of the culture. But it is always a determinate group of people who carry and transmit a culture. In the next section we look at learning from another perspective—that of the group into which a child is reared. The process of acquiring the approved behaviors of a group is called socialization. It is but another way in which we look at the process by which children become human.

Socialization, Values, and Emotional Growth

The term *socialization* has many similarities to the previously discussed concept of *enculturation,* but it is useful to emphasize the processes by which a child becomes a member of a group. Briefly, socialization is the process by which an individual acquires and internalizes the values of his group. While social control through sanctions is exercised by every society, the social order is primarily maintained as a result of children learning and behaving in accordance with the norms of the group. This is the meaning of socialization as frequently used in sociology.[7]

The concept of socialization has important implications for schooling. In the first place, the school is one of the most important agencies of socialization. Next to the family, it occupies the largest block of time in the life of normal children. Through the content of teaching and the patterns

6. T. Dobshansky, "What is Heredity," *Science* 100, no. 2601 (3 November 1944): 406.
7. Talcott Parsons and Robert F. Bales, *Family, Socialization and Interaction Process* (Glencoe, Ill.: Free Press, 1955).

of behavior—of teacher-pupil and pupil-pupil—the school sets certain norms and encourages children to internalize these norms. From the standpoint of norm identity, a child who is able to internalize the desired norms and incorporate them into his behavior is showing increasing evidences of socialization. School evidences of socialization are such routine but important behaviors as acceptance of taking turns, not interrupting another speaker, continuing to work when the teacher is not in the room, and waiting until the end of the period to go to the water fountain. Antisocial groups, such as gangs of delinquent boys, also enforce patterns of socialization,[8] but such groups are regarded as social deviants from the prevailing group norms. Socialization inevitably requires some loss of freedom, but without agreement on some minimum rules of behavior no group could exist.

Socialization may also be viewed from the standpoint of the development of personality and the integration of personal behavior, a point of view emphasized in psychology. Erikson, from a psychoanalytic point, has conceptualized eight stages of social learnings according to different ages.[9] Three of these are preschool learnings: learning trust versus mistrust, autonomy versus shame, and initiative versus guilt. The socialization task especially appropriate to the elementary years is the learning of industry versus inferiority. This is the stage of beginning to master more formal skills of life. In play, the individual child progresses from free to organized play; in peer relations, conforming to norm behaviors; in knowledge, by mastering school subjects; and in discipline, increasing willingness to work independently and to accept responsibility. In the adolescent period, the question of identity learning becomes all important. Mastery of the previous socialization tasks facilitates subsequent socialization.

In the socialization of the child, early affection in interpersonal relations appears very significant in the development of an integrated personality and subsequent relations with others. From the well-known experiments of maternal deprivation in monkeys[10] and studies of maternal deprivation in infant rearing,[11] it appears that love is a prerequisite to the development of a socialized individual who can adjust to himself and to others. This thesis does not imply that the individual must be smothered in love: it does imply that the individual first needs to learn to be dependent on others. In doing so, he learns that other people are important. As the child progressively becomes less dependent with age, he can generalize these sentiments in his relations with other people.[12]

Notwithstanding the fact that the basic personality of the child has already been shaped prior to the time the child begins school, teachers in school can do much to reduce negative traits and emphasize positive characteristics. For many children, the

8. Albert K. Cohen, *Delinquent Boys: The Culture of the Gang* (Glencoe, Ill.: Free Press, 1955).
9. E. H. Erikson, "The Problem of Ego Identity," *Journal of the American Psychoanalytic Association* 4, no. 1 (January 1956): 56-121.
10. Harry F. Harlow, "The Nature of Love," *The American Psychologist* 13 (December 1958): 673-85.
11. W. Goldfarb, "Effects of Psychological Deprivation in Infancy and Subsequent Stimulation," *American Journal of Psychiatry*, no. 102 (July 1945): 18-33.
12. Boyd R. McCandless, *Children: Behavior and Development,* 2d ed. (New York: Holt, Rinehart and Winston, Inc., 1967), p. 432.

teacher provides the only sympathetic understanding of themselves as a person. In providing the child with emotional support, the teacher should never be under the illusion that she can be a surrogate mother. This kind of identification is not necessarily helpful to the child and is often emotionally disconcerting for the teacher.

But a teacher can do many things to assist the child in his adjustment to himself by helping him make a better adjustment to the school. The teacher can demonstrate that he likes his work and accepts children;[13] he can display a warm and positive manner to children and their interest;[14] he can help the child adjust to the group and enhance his social acceptance.[15] Since teachers have a tendency to favor children from higher income over low income homes, it is imperative that teachers be fair in their dealings with lower social class children.[16] Much school rejection by children from lower income groups reflects their perception of teacher rejection.[17] The school therefore reinforces the low esteem in which low income children hold themselves, and contributes by its own negative socialization to the lack of school adjustment (see chapter 23).

McCandless gives one of the harshest indictments of the aversive school socialization of lower class children in a biting chapter entitled "The Middle-Class Teacher and the Every-Class Child."[18] More important than the failure of acceptance, as important as it is, is the failure of teachers to teach for *proficiency*. In McCandless's view, much of the attempt to improve the self-concept of the lower class child is doomed to failure because it does not address itself to the essential fact that the lower class child needs, above all, to acquire the basic skills for schooling. Reading is the preeminent school skill. Lack of success in school tasks is not only disastrous for success in school, but in terms of satisfactory social development. The failure of school socialization is a matter of enormous proportions. About 18 percent of the entire public school population is economically deprived in terms of federal definition, i.e., the family unit of five earns less than $3,000 annually. Schooling as a social institution in any culture primarily draws its personnel from persons of or aspiring to middle-class status. This results in part from the reward system which provides relatively low rewards for teaching. In the judgment of the authors of this book, the failure of the middle class teacher to teach effectively children from disadvantaged backgrounds does not arise so much from a lack of interest or of motivation, but comes from a lack of knowledge and experience. A major fault lies in the teacher training institutions, which train their teachers as if

---

13. H. E. Whitley, "Mental Health Problems in the Classroom," *Understanding the Child* 23, no. 4 (October 1954): 93-103.

14. C. M. Christensen, "Relationship between Pupil Achievement, Pupil Affect-Need, Teacher Warmth, and Teacher Permissiveness," *Journal of Educational Psychology* 51 (June 1960): 169-74.

15. L. K. Frank and M. H. Frank, "Teachers' Attitudes Affect Children's Relationships," *Education* 75 (September 1954): 6-12.

16. Hilde T. Himmelweit, "Socioeconomic Background and Personality," *International Social Science Bulletin* 7, no. 1 (1955): 29-35.

17. J. E. Dittes and H. H. Kelley, "Effects of Different Conditions of Acceptance upon Conformity to Group Norms" *Journal of Abnormal and Social Psychology* 53, no. 1 (July 1956): 100-07.

18. McCandless, *Children: Behavior and Development,* pp. 575-611.

they were to teach in middle-class schools. Many beginning teachers have had no previous intellectual, much less practical, experience in working with children from low income families. The changing patterns of integration in this country make realistic training even more imperative.

Prejudice

Perhaps one of the great school challenges of the next decade is the reduction of racial prejudice. The elimination of prejudice is a school goal because it affects both teacher and pupils. Prejudice is the root of one of the great American contradictions—the promise of democracy and discrimination against minority groups (see chapter 22). A consideration of prejudice, often neglected as part of the developmental process, appropriately belongs to this chapter because prejudice is acquired as are all behaviors and attitudes—it is learned. If prejudice is learned, then the logical corrollary follows: the schools can assist children to reduce, if not eliminate, prejudice by exposure to those learning experiences which counteract prejudice.

Prejudice may be defined as a negative attitude toward groups and individuals resulting from false generalizations and fixed overgeneralizations.[19] Prejudice is thus not some mysterious, untreatable force, but primarily reflects the lack of correct knowledge acquisition in the early stages of socialization. A child is born without prejudice, and acquires prejudice as a result of cultural influences.

The learning of prejudice begins in early childhood. The first prejudices a child learns are learned from his parents. These are his first teachers. Most prejudices acquired by children are unconsciously learned and unconsciously taught. While some parents verbalize their feelings, the most common method of learning prejudice is by example. Eventually, the child learns that certain groups and certain neighborhoods are to be avoided or treated different from family friends and home neighborhood. Many of you who read these lines can recall some experience in which you first were the object of prejudice or were involved in some act of discrimination which somehow left you disillusioned, even frustrated, and perhaps fearful.

But children have a number of traits which help them to adjust. They are helpless, they are plastic, and they are pragmatic. While very young children are not race or class conscious, by the time they begin school they are aware of differences in the way people look and behave. Now not merely their family and acquaintances shape their prejudices, but all the institutions of the culture which touch the child: his school, his church, his organized activities and his pattern of housing. Whether at play or at worship, at school or at home, the experiences of most American children teach prejudice. What they see, what they hear, what they read, reinforce the behavioral patterns of prejudice. But rarely are they verbally taught to hate. They accept the mores of the culture as right and proper. Later they hear the Sermon on the Mount or the Declaration of Independence without feeling any contradiction of living in a segregated suburb, attending a segregated school, or working in

---

19. This discussion is based upon "Prejudice and Ethnocentrism," in Milton Kleg, Marion J. Rice, and Wilfrid C. Bailey, *Race, Caste, and Prejudice:* (Athens, Ga.: Anthropology Curriculum Project, University of Georgia, 1970).

a segregated office. Prejudiced? Most children attain adulthood without any consciousness of the relationship between cultural conditioning and prejudice.

Because of the discrimination against minorities which has resulted from prejudice, there has been little research in the reduction of prejudice until the last decade. As a sensitive area, the interrelationships of race and prejudice have even been studiously avoided by schools in the process of integration.

From what we know about human behavior, however, two lines of attack on prejudice are open to the schools. The first is to provide integrated schools. While contact does not lead to mutual trust and understanding between different ethnic groups, integration provides an operational context in which children can grow up and learn together. The second thing schools can do is to make realistic information available to children at an early age about race and prejudice. The recent study of Kleg indicates some favorable change in attitudes and reduction in prejudice following objective instruction about race and prejudice.[20] As a result of the need for a frontal attack on prejudice, especially racial prejudice, some school systems are beginning to introduce social studies lessons which expose children to the nature of prejudice.[21]

Most teachers today are products of a racially segregated society. Even outside the South, patterns of de facto living have contributed to sentiments which support prejudice. Consequently, teachers in every section need to know more about race and prejudice, and strive to avoid behaviors and expressions of attitudes which help shape prejudice.

Intelligence and Culture

People vary in ability. At a very early age, children acquire the labels "dumb," "smart," "bright," and "sharp" to characterize their own performance and that of their schoolmates. The preoccupation of schools and teachers with grading further emphasizes the importance of intellectuality. For some, it becomes a stimulus to further effort; for many, a dread day of reckoning to be escaped as soon as possible. The child in school is constantly faced with the spectre of intelligence, because schools and teachers are concerned with it. He is classified and labeled on the basis of his intelligence; opportunities are opened or doors closed on the basis of this quality. However, once he ends schooling the matter of intelligence looms of less importance. Adult behavior is approved or disapproved on the basis of conformity to job or social expectancies, although the common labels of childhood may still be used in informal appraisal.

One of the most important aspects of human growth is the growth in intelligence. One of the major tasks of the school is to facilitate this growth. Notwithstanding the ambiguities surrounding the concept, teachers are concerned in the fostering of intelligence. This section is designed to indicate how the teacher is a mediator between culture and the child in the acquisition of the behaviors related to intelligent behavior.

20. Milton Kleg, "Race, Caste, and Prejudice: The Relationship of Change in Knowledge to Change in Attitude" (unpublished doctoral dissertation, The University of Georgia, Athens, 1970).

21. Frank Jennings, *Cultural Diversity in our Community—A Social Studies Unit for Grades 1-3;* (San Diego, Calif.: San Diego City Schools, 1970) idem, *The People of Our Community . . . for Grades Four, Five, and Six* (San Diego, Calif.: San Diego City Schools, 1970).

Definitions of Intelligence. There are many definitions of intelligence. These range in emphasis from unitary to factorial definitions. On the one hand there is the definition of Terman which defines intelligence as the ability to carry on abstract thinking.[22] At the other extreme is Guilford's conceptual model of a multi-factored intellect consisting of the interaction of operations, products, and contents which theoretically provide for 120 cells representing specific abilities.[23] In between this dichotomy there are a number of other well-known approaches to the definition of intelligence. One of these is that of Spearman, who regards intelligence as consisting of a general factor, *g*, which underlies all tasks, and a specific factor, *s*, related to the performance of a given task.[24] The ability of a child to learn mathematics, according to Spearman's approach, would depend on the interaction of *g* and *s* factors. A person inferior in *g* would not likely excel at a specific task, however, because this factor is a prerequisite to all tasks.

One of the approaches best known to elementary teachers is that of Thurstone,[25] who converted his theoretical factorial approach to intelligence into a measuring device, the *Chicago Primary Abilities Test.* Thurstone rejected the general factor approach of Spearman and regarded intelligence as a composite of eight primary mental abilities. Consequently, Thurstone placed more emphasis on the capacity of an individual to excel in specific tasks because of specific abilities than did Spearman.

Defining Intelligence by Measurement. These various approaches in defining intelligence reflect the implicit premise that intelligence is a quality inherent in the individual. From what has been said about enculturation and socialization, however, it should be apparent that behavior depends upon learning, and learning depends upon the opportunities to learn. From a cultural standpoint, intelligence might be defined simply as behavior suitable to the performance of a task, whether the task is making an historical inference or milking a cow. Intelligence associated with achievement on Madison avenue might have little value for survival on an Indian reservation in New Mexico.

In the context of the school, however, certain conventions have been established with respect to the measurement of intelligence. The school, it must be remembered, is primarily concerned with learning expressed in language. In 1900, elementary school teachers did not ask a child to shoe a horse, sum an account, or steer a ship to measure intelligence. Neither do we ask a child in the 1970s to repair a radio, roof a house, or run a computer to measure intelligence. Over the centuries the constant of schooling has been the manipulation of symbols and the use of language.

The first successful test of intelligence was constructed by Alfred Binet. It succeeded in distinguishing between dull and bright children in school because it was not based upon some abstract idea of intelligence, but actually reflected teachers' expectancies of

22. Lewis M. Terman, *Measurement of Intelligence* (Boston: Houghton Mifflin Co., 1916), p. 42.
23. J. P. Guilford, "Intelligence: 1965 Model," *American Psychologist* 21, no. 1 (January 1966): 20-26.
24. Carl E. Spearman, *The Abilities of Man: Their Nature and Measurement* (New York: Macmillan Company, 1927).
25. L. L. Thurstone and Thelma G. Thurstone, *Factorial Studies of Intelligence,* Psychometric Monographs no. 2 (Chicago: University of Chicago Press, 1941).

students' school behavior as defined by the culture. By a process of trial and error, Binet found that there were certain school behaviors which were highly correlated. Children who were best on tests of judgment were also best on tests designed to measure such things as vocabulary, memory, and attention.[26]

In the United States, Terman adopted the ideas of Binet and applied them to the performance of normal and superior children. In 1916 he published the Stanford Revision of the Binet Tests, which immediately became the standard intelligence measuring instrument in this country. It was subsequently revised in 1937 and again in 1960. Another widely used test with children is the *WISC*, the *Wechsler Intelligence Scale for Children*. Both the *Stanford* and the *WISC* are individual tests, and require administration by a trained professional. The importance of the Stanford test for teachers is the fact that group tests of intelligence, commonly used in the school, incorporate many elements of individual testing.

Some of the better known group tests of intelligence for children are the *California Test of Mental Maturity, Otis-Lennon Quick-Scoring Mental Ability Tests,* and the *Kuhlmann-Anderson Intelligence Tests*. These tests are usually administered by teachers in the class setting, and generally have high predictive value for success in school. These tests predict success in school because they purportedly measure school behaviors. Take the elementary form of the *California Test of Mental Maturity* as an example. It provides a five-category profile—memory, spatial relationship, logical reasoning, numerical reasoning, and verbal concepts. An analysis of the sub-categories and actual test items of the CAT indicate that it tests the kinds of learning children reputedly acquire in school. Intelligence is viewed in terms of intelligence tests scores, which therefore primarily define school behavior. For this reason, some school critics advocate the elimination of intelligence testing, especially because the symbolic verbal and mathematical behavior emphasized on intelligence tests are allegedly biased against children from minority and lower income families.

These criticisms, however, are somewhat invalid when it is recognized that, by definition, these tests of intelligence are largely restricted to behavior in school occasioned by the use of language. Language efficiency is a highly desired trait in every culture, and is often a prerequisite to prestigious positions, such as lawyer, politician, preacher, professor, or other professions emphasizing language use. The measure of a good plumber, however, is not his ability to talk about fitting pipes, but his ability to actually fit pipes. The intelligence of a plumber lies in his hand and his eye, not so much in his words. But if he aspires to own or manage a plumbing business and not lay pipes, there is an advantage in language efficiency.

But whether intelligence is exhibited in language or a trade or a skill, it never results automatically as an innate capacity. It is acquired through culture and is exhibited only in performance. The school is a specialized instrument of the culture, just as the apprentice system is for training tradesmen. Contrary to what many scholars believe to be true, an intelligence test does not measure a capacity for learning, it

---

26. Lee J. Cronbach, *Essentials of Psychological Testing,* 2d ed. (New York: Harper and Brothers, 1960), pp. 160-70.

merely measures a particular performance. Only further opportunity for learning and performance testing will indicate whether the individual can increase his performance as measured by some testing device.

There is a practical advantage in the use of intelligence tests—it permits teachers to identify pupils who require different experiences. One of the common assumptions teachers make is that they can always identify their brightest and slowest children. However, this is not always the case. In a well controlled study, teachers with a median of twelve years of teaching experience were asked to judge both the highest and lowest achievers. They were more unsuccessful than successful.[27]

Expansion of School Learning. Intelligence is a measure of performance. The performance opportunities of children in elementary school are primarily limited to symbolic performance through language. Two conclusions are important for elementary teaching. The first is that the improvement of children's language performance is a matter of highest priority.

There is a second corollary. The performance opportunities of elementary children should be expanded (see "Interests"). Notwithstanding what we know of children's abilities, interests, psychological motivation, social class structure and learning, and emotional growth and personality development, the curriculum of the elementary school provides children with an opportunity to display a limited repertory of behavior. It is likely that as long as this type of curriculum exists, the school will continue to fail a large number of children, notwithstanding improvement in the technology of teaching. The solution is not to limit children's performance by limiting their learning opportunities, but to expand contacts with the culture. At the present time, children have few opportunities for learning except play and bookish schooling. Certainly, some opportunities to revive the kind of learnings available to children when they learned to work at home and on the farm seem to be required.

This does not mean a deemphasis on formal learning and knowledge. In fact, higher proficiency is required for all children. Neither does it assume an early "vocational" curriculum for some children. But it does assume that children who get more satisfaction from the use of their hands and bodies should have an opportunity to do so. Since language is also associated with the artifacts of a culture, more experience with the artifacts of a culture might be one of the most useful ways of increasing language competency. Consequently, an expansion of the curriculum might thus contribute to the general objective of schooling.

Readiness and Learning

One of the favorite terms in child development and in early childhood education is "readiness." The usual explanation of why a child hasn't learned, or can't learn, is that he is "not ready." Child psychologists frequently define readiness for physical learning in terms of maturation, and for intellectual learning in terms of mental maturity as defined by standardized IQ tests. In addition, they generally add every other aspect of human development, so that the concept of readiness expands to be

27. A. M. Alexander, "Teacher Judgment of Pupil Intelligence and Achievement is not Enough," *Elementary School Journal* 53 (March 1953): 396-401.

almost equivalent to the developmental process from birth to maturity.[28] As a result, "readiness" is a nonoperational teaching concept.

Another disadvantage of the concept of readiness is the tendency to apply the term restrictively to children's learning. If readiness is a function of maturation rather than learning, the obvious conclusion, then, is to delay teaching. Hunt pointed out that this unfortunate conclusion not only applied to learning in the schools, but also long dominated child rearing practices. Child specialists even went so far as to advise parents not to play with young children too much because they might be overstimulated.[29]

Notwithstanding the fact that many new preschool programs are predicated on the assumption of providing young children with many rich encounters with the environment prior to schooling, readiness as a concept is frequently preferred to learning. One reason is that its very ambiguity is more compatible to the informal processes of learning which are espoused by many child specialists. The school teacher, on the other hand, is acutely conscious of his role as a formal and deliberate instrument of learning.

In the section on culture it was emphasized that the acquisition of culture—enculturation—is the acquisition of behavior through learning. The humanity of man largely consists in the capacity to learn—his behavior is not limited to a few tropistic, innate patterns but dependent on his opportunity to learn. What a child needs to learn at a given age depends upon the social expectancies set by the culture.

This premise can be illustrated by the cultural task of learning to read. One of the school learning expectancies set in our culture for six-year-olds is the initiation of reading. Some previous learnings which facilitate learning to read are phoneme-grapheme discrimination and knowledge of letter names (see chapter 10). If a child has not previously learned these skills at home—and many disadvantaged learners have not (see chapter 23), waiting for a child to get "ready" merely deprives him of the opportunity to learn. He therefore becomes less ready with the passage of time, and the gap between actual and expected school performance is increased rather than narrowed.[30] It is also questionable if many of the recommended reading readiness activities are actually functional, when compared to time taught in the specific activity.[31] Furthermore, many of the readiness activities are actually the beginning steps in reading.[32]

The authors of this book propose an operational definition of readiness in terms of performance. *Readiness is the ability to perform a task as a result of previous learning.* If a child is "ready," he can perform the task and go on to the next one. If he is not able to perform the task, it is

28. See, for example, Arden N. Frandsen,, *Educational Psychology* (New York: McGraw-Hill Book Company, Inc., 1961), pp. 61-106.
29. J. McV. Hunt, *Intelligence and Experience* (New York: Ronald Press Company, 1961), p. 5.
30. *Hancock County School Improvement Project: Third Annual Report* (Sparta, Ga.: Hancock County School District, 1969).
31. For a typical emphasis on reading readiness, see Arthur W. Hulman, *Teaching Reading* (Columbus, Ohio: Charles E. Merrill Books, Inc., 1961), pp. 22-70.
32. For example, the directions in the following book concern the initial teaching of reading: readiness is a tautology. Bank Street College of Education, *Teacher's Guide to Readiness Experiences* and *In The City* and *People Read* (New York: Macmillan Company, 1967).

the responsibility of the teacher to teach the child, not to delay teaching in the hope that some maturational process will eventually permit him to perform successfully. Because of differences in background and previous experiences, the time required to learn a given performance will vary from individual to individual.

This definition of readiness, stated in performance terms, automatically eliminates standardized IQ and reading readiness tests as readiness measures: they are not sufficiently performance specific. Furthermore, performance after teaching is frequently substantially higher than predicted from readiness measures. This approach to readiness eliminates the ambiguity surrounding the concept of readiness, and suggests that the hierarchy of simpler skills leading to more complex performances should be operationally stated as part of the learning sequence (see chapter 3). As a result, the teacher can adjust his teaching to the actual performance of the child rather than depend on the transfer of some assumed "readiness" activities to specific learning tasks.

Physical Appearance

Childern are concerned about the way they look. They early learn that the first impression, if not the most lasting that one person makes on another, depends on the general looks of his body and the way he handles it (see "Motor Development"). Teachers, as well as other adults, oftentimes dismiss the concern of children with their overall physical appearance as a matter of vanity and of no significant, long-range concern. However, teachers in particular need only to recall the extent to which they prejudge and type people by their physical appearance to realize that the question of looks is a very real and important one, even for young children.

In the first place, the way a child looks depends upon a very real human organism —his own body. And body build is related to certain physical skills that are considered important. Even though most men long ago ceased to be hunters the physique for successful hunting is also advantageous for sports and skills of athletic prowess. The excessively fat or the excessively skinny boy or girl are at a real, not nominal, disadvantage in games and sports. The well-knit, strongly muscled, not too-tall, not too-short, well-proportioned youngster is more than a cultural stereotype; his physical advantage is a real asset for participation in games and sports[33] and it reacts favorably on his self-concept.[34] Consequently, the child's perception of his own self interacts with his perception of acceptance by others—parents, siblings, friends, teachers—and aids or hinders emotional development and self-adjustment. It is for this reason that Havighurst identified as one of the important developmental tasks of the middle childhood years the need for the child to accept himself as a growing organism.[35]

33. Bruch takes the position that excessive deviation from the average in body build is a handicap in the performance of motor skills because the nature of the body build discourages the child from the necessary practice to acquire the skill, not in the body skill per se. However, if the lack of initial success is a deterrent to further practice, it would seem that physical configuration per se is a positive disadvantage. See H. Bruch, "Developmental Obesity and Schizophrenia," *Psychiatry* 21, no. 1 (February 1958): 65-70.

34. Laverne C. Johnson, "Body Cathexis as a Factor in Somatic Complaints," *Journal of Consulting Psychology* 20, no. 2 (August 1956): 145-49.

35. R. J. Havighurst, *Human Development and Education* (New York: Longman's, 1953).

In this section emphasis is placed on two aspects of physical development—physical appearance, early maturation, and the relationship to self-concept.

Body Build, Ideal Type, and Temperament. Western man has long been fascinated with the relationship of body build to temperament. Over 2,500 years ago Hippocrates divided men into two classes —the long thins and the short thicks. This classification has basically persisted despite changes in nomenclature in many articles written on the subject. Students who recall little else from Shakespeare are likely to remember the classical stereotype of the fat, jolly man in these words of Caesar:

> Let me have men about me that are fat:
> Sleek-headed men and such as sleep o'nights:
> Yond Cassius has a lean and hungry look;
> He thinks too much: such men are dangerous.

The work of Sheldon in the area of body build and temperament has had tremendous influence. Working with college men, students in late adolescence, he developed a three-fold classification: the *endomorph,* short, big-bellied, and fat; the *mesomorph,* broadshouldered, muscular, slim-hipped, and of medium height; and the *ectomorph,* tall and skinny.[36] While few researchers accept the extreme position taken by Sheldon and his coworkers,[37] studies of children, especially boys, indicate that perceptions related to physique indicate the early formation of typologies.

Walker studied preschool children of ages two, three, and four and found that certain traits, based upon the observations of nursery teachers, were already in evidence. The endomorphs were assertive and revengeful; the mesomorphs were easily angered, quarrelsome, ambitious, self-assertive, leaders in play, noisy, easily angered, revengeful, and self-confident; the ectomorphs were the introverts, almost the opposite of the stereotype of the mesomorphs. As early as the preschool years, it appears that the perception of male behavior of endormorphs is negative, that of mesomorphs assertive but boyish and socially acceptable, and that of the ectomorphs as nice but withdrawn. While the mesomorphic build of boys was related to a higher degree of gross, physical activity, a mesormorphic build in girls appeared to be more highly related to approved social behavior.[38]

The Staffieri study pertained to boys ages four through ten. His criterion groups were long lean and short thick boys, based on a ratio of height in inches to weight in pounds. These boys were given 15-inch silhouettes of adult and child representations of endo-, meso-, and ectomorphs. Irrespective of age, the children reflected the stereotyping of physique: endomorphs were described as socially offensive; ectomorphs as retiring, nervous, and shy; and the mesomorphs as manly, outgoing, active, and with other ideal attributes. The subjects were also asked to choose the silhouette of the preferred type, and it was in-

---

36. Morphology has to do with structure of arrangement. The prefixes *endo* and *ecto* are taken from biological descriptions of the embryo in the double layered stage of the gastrula. The outer *ectoderm* gives rise to the skin and nervous system; the inner *endoderm* gives rise to the digestive tract and related inner organs. Hence the very nomenclature, when understood, is related to unfavorable perceptions.

37. W. H. Sheldon, E. M. Hartl, and E. McDermott, *Varieties of Delinquent Youth* (New York: Harper and Brothers, 1942).

38. R. N. Walker, *Body Build and Behavior in Young Children; I. Body and Nursery School Teachers' Ratings,* Monograph for Social Research and Child Development 27, serial no. 84, 1962.

variably of the ideal stereotype—the mesomorph. They also identified the silhouette which looked like them with considerable accuracy. Popularity and leadership were also highly related to physique perception.[39] Studies of high school students indicate similar stereotyping.[40]

Studies of physique have generally involved white subjects, so that generalizations about physique and self-concept normally are limited to white students. A study by Brodsky, however, involved both Negro and white college students, and indicated no difference in the way the two groups responded in their answers to a questionnaire related to five male types. As with the previously cited studies involving younger students, the same negative image of the endomorph, positive image of the mesomorph, and half-negative image of the ectomorph emerged.[41] It thus appears that perceptions of desirable physical appearance is primarily cultural rather than racial.

Social Advantage of Early Physical Growth. Advanced physical growth is frequently related to the mesomorphic type, leading to both a physical and a social advantage. There is a wide range in rates of physical growth, so that averages tend to be meaningless. Some boys and girls of the same age, however, are much more developed physically than other boys and girls of the same age. The advantages of early maturing are most positively seen in the middle school years, with the emphasis on organized athletics, and in the high school years, where early maturing boys have an advantage in mate selection. By the time boys and girls reach the sixth grade, however, early pubescence begins to set them apart in attitude and interest, exaggerating the range of behavior as well as physical size. If there has not been a prior adjustment of self-concept to physique, prepubescence more frequently exaggerates the emotional and personality problems associated with differences in physical self-perception.

Studies of early and late maturing boys have been made using adult ratings and subject perceptions. Invariably, adults perceived more desirable physical and social qualities in early maturers as compared with late maturers, and emphasized these differences even more than did the boys.[42] In a study of late maturing as compared with early maturing boys using the Thematic Apperception Test, late maturers perceived themselves in more derogatory terms than early maturers who tended to see themselves in a more heroic image.[43] On the other hand, it appears that early maturing girls are at a handicap in our society, because of the differences in social expectancies for girls. A stocky build for girls is a handicap, and the difference between sexually mature girls and immature boys

39. J. R. Staffieri, "A Study of Social Stereotype of Body Image in Children," *Journal of Personality and Social Psychology* 7, no. 1, (September 1967): 101-3.

40. W. C. Washburn, "The Effects of Physique and Intrafamily Tension on Self-Concept in Adolescent Males," *Journal of Consulting Psychology* 26, no. 5 (November 1962): 460-66; J. B. Cortes and Florence M. Gatti, "Physique and Self-Description of Temperament," *Journal of Consulting Psychology* 29, no. 5 (November 1965): 432-39.

41. C. M. Brodsky, *A Study of Norms for Body Form-Behavior Relationships,* (Washington, D.C.: Catholic University of America Press, 1954).

42. Mary C. Jones and Nancy Bayley, "Physical Maturing Among Boys as Related to Behavior," *Journal of Educational Psychology* 41 (March 1950): 129-48.

43. P. H. Mussen and Mary C. Jones, "Self-Conceptions, Motivations, and Interpersonal Attitudes of Late- and Early-maturing Boys," *Child Development* 28 (June 1957): 242-56.

is striking, both physically and socially.[44] In contrast with boys, however, the advantage of late maturing for girls seems to disappear in the late teens.[45] The evidence for girls seems to be more equivocal than for boys, a fact that may reflect more variability and less stereotyping in perceptions of female behavior.

Personality, Physique, and the Teacher. There is no convincing evidence that personality is a function of bodily build. Nevertheless, it is very clear that in American culture the muscular body of the mesomorph is regarded much more favorably than that of the thin ectomorph, and the ectomorph is preferable to the fat endomorph. If cultural stereotypes have any influence on social adjustment, it is clear that the mesomorphs have a greater possibility of developing a healthy personality and making a better total adjustment to the context of the school.

Teachers are just as subject to social stereotyping as other population groups. Since they come in contact with large numbers of children in group situations, where differences in physical appearance are accentuated, the teacher must be careful that his perceptions of children do not automatically mirror the cultural bias. In his evaluation of children, especially the more deviant types, he must be careful to check their real performance rather than reflect the stereotype. If he does not, his own treatment may fulfill the prophecy of the thin child as a shy introvert and the fat boy as a hostile extrovert.

Since children tend to treat each other in terms of cultural stereotypes, it appears desirable to provide children at an early age with more realistic information about their physical growth (see chapter 15, "Health and Safety"). Even when girls and boys are quite handsome and attractive, they can perceive themselves as ugly and physically undesirable. Often the mere provision of factually accurate written material, suitable to the age of the learner, is sufficient to allay their fears.

The high school curriculum, with its emphasis on athletics, unwittingly reinforces the social stereotype which gives every advantage to muscularly built boys. Notwithstanding the fact that few boys actually participate in competitive sports, the universal hero is the successful athlete, an image which is a part of the total cultural pattern. Notwithstanding the fact that athletic programs for the younger years are supposed to deemphasize competitive contact sports (see chapter 18), most of the institutions, especially for boys, put a premium on athletic prowess. This attitude is nowhere more prevalent than in the Little Leagues, which imitate the professionals not only in costume but in the urge to win. In such competitions, every advantage is on the side of the larger, muscular competitors—the mesomorph.

Perhaps one of the most useful things schools could do for children is to get them to compete on the basis of physical maturity, such as height and weight, in place of age-grade competition. As noted previously, there may be a considerable variation in the size of the children in any grade in elementary school. The less adept chil-

---

44. H. E. Jones, "Adolescence in Our Society," in *The Family in a Democratic Society,* Anniversary Papers of the Community Service Society of New York (New York: Columbia University Press, 1949), pp. 70-82.

45. Mary C. Jones and P. H. Mussen, "Self-Conceptions, Motivations, and Interpersonal Attitudes of Early- and Late-Maturing Girls," *Child Development* 29 (December 1958): 491-501.

dren, especially the over-fat and over-thin, frequently adjust to competitive play by withdrawal, with consequent negative reactions on self-concept and personality. The school emphasis on the age as the norm often means that older boys and girls refuse to play on teams with younger children, to which they are most suited, because acceptance of such a situation is public advertisement of their assumed inferiority. It is probable that the schools themselves, and other institutions which follow the school pattern of age-grade placement, are the agencies which transmit and fix in children the cultural stereotypes associated with physique.

Differences in physical development are one reason for differences in children's interest. While all muscular boys do not pursue athletics and some thin boys strive inordinately for athletic success, interests are mainly learned. One of the greatest justifications for a rich elementary curriculum is to provide an opportunity for children to find some area in which they can succeed and find a lasting interest.

Motor Development

An extensive examination of motor development more appropriately belongs to the chapters in this book dealing with health and with recreation. However, motor development is not related merely to athletic skill, but applies to such skills as playing the piano and to writing (see chapter 11, "Language Arts"). Furthermore, a whole series of social expectancies are built around motor skills, from dancing to driving a car. In addition to contributing to physical health, effective motor development and coordination are related to a vast expenditure of human effort in work and play.

The wise development of motor skills consequently is significant for individual pleasure and happiness as well as for laying the foundation for economic and industrial production.

The child who comes to school already has acquired certain foundation skills, such as self-feeding, dressing, walking and running. A beginning elementary teacher can only appreciate the extent of this accomplishment if he has had children of his own or taught nursery school, where much adult effort is consumed in child care. During the elementary years, the child develops skill in finer coordination of the smaller muscle groups used in athletics, such as grasping and throwing balls, in writing, and in using tools.

Practice, Guidance, and Motivation in Skill Development. The old adage "Practice makes perfect" applies to motor skills as well as to other areas of development. Nevertheless, the *quality* of the practice is often far more important than the *quantity* of the practice, a maxim that teachers might well remember in assigning class or homework. Because young children seem less aversive to repetitive tasks than older children, the years of middle childhood are perhaps ideal for mastering the skills expected in a particular culture. They are also less self-conscious and less likely to be overwhelmed by adult standards, than are junior high and high school students.

While many skills, such as play and home chores, are learned by imitation with little direction, the quality of this learning is often deficient and gives the child little satisfaction. It is for this reason that more complex skills, such as playing a musical instrument or writing, are normally learned as a result of teaching rather than mere imitation. Imitation and practice alone are not sufficient; the quality of the practice is extremely important. What is required is practice with understanding; this involves teaching. Hence, a wider range of teacher competencies are required in the elementary schools if children are to have an opportunity to develop skills in areas of their interest.

A third prerequisite in the development of skills is motivation. Psychologists and teachers agree on the importance of motivation for all human learning, but both are often at a loss as to the practical means of motivating the uninterested or negative child.

In general, motivation is either internal or external. Internal motivation comes from the satisfaction obtained from an activity, whereas external motivation comes from the prestige or approval of significant others in the life of the child. One child may play a musical instrument because of the personal satisfaction he derives from musical mastery whereas another child may play an instrument because of the peer association being member of a school orchestra or band may bring. Many activities are engaged in by children as a result of feelings of inadequacy. This well-known compensatory mechanism not only is a means of facilitating personal adjustment, but is also responsible for the development of a great variety of skills in a culture. The development of multiple interests, therefore, should be encouraged rather than discouraged by teachers.

Skill development is usually somewhat easy in the first stages, whether it is catching a ball or drawing a figure. Improvement normally requires much additional practice, even when the learning tasks are programmed in small, sequential sequences. It is here that the approval of teachers and adults for effort expended rather than the quality of the performance becomes all important. The verbal encouragement that comes from such words as "Fine!", "That's a good try!", "Gee, that's great!" often makes the difference between continued effort or abandonment.

The importance of good teaching is itself one of the most important factors in motivation. Over forty years ago the German psychologist, Ferdinand Hoppe, a student of Kurt Lewin, postulated that actual achievement is less important to the experience of success and failure than were the aspirations of the learner at the time of action.[46] Children who are chronic failures in school set their aspirations with little regard for their achievements, whereas those who experience success are realistic in their aspirations.[47] In synthesizing the result of the work of Hoppe and Sears, Barker concluded that the social pressure of the school to succeed unbalances the mechanism of setting aspirations in accordance with one's abilities. The result is exaggerated failure for some children, and the unrealistic setting of expectations.

An indispensable element of good teaching, therefore, requires helping students to set goals for themselves in which they experience success. Success in accomplishing the task, in turn, becomes a motivating element for continued application and additional success. This principle of motivation-

---

46. Roger G. Barker, "Success and Failure in the Classroom," *Progressive Education* 19 (April 1942): 221-24.

47. P. S. Sears, "Levels of Aspiration in Academically Successful and Unsuccessful Children," *Journal of Abnormal and Social Psychology* 35 (October 1940): 498-536.

through-success is not only applicable to the improvement of motor skills, but applies to all areas of teaching. The setting of micro-learning objectives (see chapter 3) finds a rationale not only in the structuring of learning, but also in the psychology of motivation and success feedback.

Sex differences in motor development become noticeable about the beginning of kindergarten and the first grade. These become more marked the older the child, since certain skills are considered by a culture more appropriate for one sex than another. Most of these differences result from sex typing rather than physical differences. Girls develop more fine muscle skills, because they are encouraged to color with crayons, cut with scissors, sew, and play dolls whereas boys are encouraged to engage in motor skills which require speed and strength. The deprivation of girls from certain learning experiences in a culture is one means by which the culture develops appropriate identification with masculine and feminine roles, a developmental task especially important in heterosexual relations. The role of female deprivation in learning is characteristic of preliterate as well as literate cultures. Mead attributed the deficit in female Manuan fishing skills to the denial of this opportunity in childhood.[48]

Two aspects of motor development should be mentioned—handedness and awkwardness. Handedness refers to the fact that most people prefer to use their dominant hand, either right or left. Ambidextrous individuals are rare. Right handedness is dominant in most cultures and, in consequence, the artifact and manipulative content of the world is made for right handed people. Educators have long debated the desirability of changing dominant left-handedness to right-handedness. When it was thought that handedness was hereditary, there was less inclination to attempt to change it. It is now thought that handedness is culturally induced, and that in the long run there are definite cultural advantages which accrue from a switch from left-handedness to right-handedness.[49] These include facility in writing.[50] The most desirable time to change handedness is in the early years, preferably before six, and where there are indications that the child uses both hands interchangeably. However, if left-hand habits have not been strongly established, primary teachers may undertake a shift to right-handedness if the child appears willing to change and aversive reactions do not occur.[51]

The awkward child is at a disadvantage in the evaluation of his peers as well as adults. Awkwardness may result from delayed physical development, lack of opportunity to develop muscle control, poor physical condition, emotional tension, or the mere fact of laziness through overindulgence. Of particular concern today is the negativism that many older children display toward anything that smacks of productive work and manual labor, an attitude that is fostered by sedentary activ-

48. Margaret Mead, *Coming of Age in Samoa* (New York: William Morrow and Company, 1928), pp. 20-38.
49. L. T. Dayhaw, "Guiding Handedness in the Development of the Child," *Education* 74 (November 1953): 196-99.
50. G. F. Reed and A. C. Smith, "A Further Experimental Investigation of the Relative Speeds of Left and Right-Handed Writers," *Journal of Genetic Psychology* 100 (June 1962): 275-88.
51. G. Hildreth, "The Development and Training of Hand Dominance," *Journal of Genetic Psychology* 75 (December 1949): 197-275; idem, *Journal of Genetic Psychology* 76 (March 1950): 39-144.

ities and spectator sports.[52] Since motor development can be improved through practice, one of the objectives of elementary physical education should be the reduction of awkwardness through providing children with the needed opportunity for practice when they first come to school. The tendency to neglect the primary grades and emphasize motor development in the latter grades often extracts a heavy premium: even when children eventually overcome their early awkwardness, they too often carry with them perceptions of inadequacy which handicap their adjustment to themselves and to the school.

Interests

An interest may be defined as a learned motive in which a person persists when he is free to make a choice as to his activity.[53] The three key words in this definition are learning, persistence, and choice.

Interests are learned, whether the learning results from the general process of socialization or from formal schooling. All too often, children's interests are referred to as if they were innate rather than acquired. In fact, reference to children's interests is simply another way of delineating the socially approved expectancies in a particular culture by age group. Nowhere is this more clearly seen than in reading, an interest usually associated with schooling. The affirmed reading interest of children at any age reflects the kind of books adults select, approve, and encourage children to read.[54] Interest in sports likewise reflects the repertory of culturally approved sports. Such cultural preferences of English for rugby and cricket and Americans for football and baseball are well-known. Where children do not have an opportunity to acquire an interest, or the trait is socially disapproved, there is little possibility for an interest to show itself.

Persistence is important in the development of an interest. Young and old both manifest momentary likes, which fail to become an interest because of their temporary nature. Many a parent has longed for his child to become proficient in music, art, or ballet; contracted for private lessons; given all possible encouragement; and then seen the interest abandoned because the child derived little satisfaction from the effort. Such transient interests are properly classified as whims, and are displayed in school as well as in the home.

Parental and teacher encouragement are often needed to fix an interest, but it should not be expected that every like will become an interest, even with prodding. After all, children cannot know what gives them satisfaction until they have had an opportunity to explore alternatives. At the same time, the acquisition of skill through practice is often prerequisite to the development of the interest. Thus, a teacher needs to exercise discrimination in encouraging a child to persist or in helping him to explore another area which might become an interest. Many long and profitable interests occur as a byproduct of schooling. The so-called extracurricular interest clubs often provide some of the most effective channels for maintaining an identity with the school

---

52. L. E. Tyler. "The Development of Vocational Interests: The Organization of Likes and Dislikes in Ten-Year-Old Children," *Journal of Genetic Psychology* 86 (March 1955): 33-44.

53. H. G. Shane, "Children's Interests," *NEA Journal* 46 (April 1957): 237-39.

54. P. Witty, Ann Comer, and Dilla McBean, "Children's Choices of Favorite Books: A Study Conducted in Ten Elementary Schools," *Journal of Educational Psychology* 37 (May 1946): 266-78.

as well as foreshadowing vocational interests. Unfortunately, these outlets are infrequently found in the lower grades.

A third element in an interest is that of choice. So important is this element that the child-centered curriculum theoretically emphasized children's interests and needs, even though these interests were always manipulated by adults to achieve adult learning goals. There is an element of contradiction in the ascription of choice to interest, when the first aspect of interest emphasized the opportunity to learn. The contradiction is more apparent than real, because it is assumed that the choice will be restricted to the opportunities to learn within the context of American culture. An American child could learn to play a biwa if provided an opportunity, but it is doubtful if either he or his listeners would derive much satisfaction because of differences in the tonal qualities of the Japanese pentatonic from the western diatonic scale.

Irrespective of the culture, adults are expected to stimulate children's interests by providing them with an opportunity to explore the cultural inventory. Choice, however, involves the right of children to make initial selections as to possible interests, even though they turn out to be whims. With proper teaching, an interest may be developed. An activity which is forced upon a child and which fails to stimulate or challenge him eventually becomes boring, even if not met with outright hostility. The principle of providing a variety of interest centers in the elementary classroom to stimulate diverse interests has long been espoused, but most often fails because, except for subject matter, such centers all too frequently have a bookish orientation. What is needed is a type of curriculum which will permit children to explore a diversity of active interests, everything from plumbing and electricity to creative dramatics and gardening. Suggestions for the development of such a wide variety of children's interests have long been espoused, and were a facet of Progressive Education but have generally been neglected because of the design and organization of American schools. Even more important may be the incongruity between this type of education, best exemplified in the British infant schools, and the personality of the American child resulting from different child rearing practices and social expectancies. Nevertheless, a revival of interest may be expected in this model, not merely for the development of children's interests but for all of schooling.[55]

However desirable that instruction capitalize upon children's interests, the point of view taken in this book is that schooling as a social institution does not begin in children's interests, but in the needs of a society for a trained citizenry. Because of the social expectancies of a literate society, most children become interested in school. For those who do not become interested in school learning tasks, the challenge is to find more efficient ways of teaching them, rather than attempting to define school learning and proceed with instruction in terms of their interests. After all, there will be some adult definition of interest. However, the curriculum of the elementary school requires broadening to develop a range of interests and skills, without abandoning the concern for competency in the basic skills and knowledge of a literate society.

55. See, for example, Charles E. Silberman, *Crisis in the Classroom* (New York: Random House, 1970).

Teachers also need to keep in mind that interests change with age and are sex typed. In the area of play, for example, the shift in interest from simple and isolated play to organized play and team sports reflects an increase in muscular power and coordination. Many interests change as a result of successful experiences in school. Boys typically show a greater interest in mathematics with age than girls, an interest that reflects the emphasis on mathematics for boys as a basic subject for success in the scientific professions and in business.

Art is an interest which shows shift toward feminine dominance in the preteen years as a result of sex typing (see chapter 17). English boys show a greater preference for drawing than American boys because drawing in England is considered more sex-appropriate for males.[56]

As an instrument of socialization, schools and teachers influence interests through sex typing. Teachers should always bear in mind that some studies of creativity indicate that many creative males score high on femininity indices of such scales as the Minnesota Multiphasic Personality Inventory (MMPI) and the California Psychological Inventory (CPI).[57] These scales naturally reflect the definition of masculinity-femininity as defined in terms of American culture. The implication for schooling is that boys and girls should be encouraged to pursue a wide variety of interests, and that the rigid conformity of sex typing enforced through denigrative identification should be discouraged.

Appraisal of Understanding Elementary Children

The elementary teacher is invariably admonished to improve his teaching by increasing his technical, subject matter competencies and by increasing his understanding of children. He is encouraged to collect data on children not merely to report to parents but to have objective information about pupil behavior to help solve learning problems (see chapter 20). Certainly, teachers need to be sensitive to the whole range of factors which confront humans in any social situation.

Teachers can use such knowledge successfully in many cases. In fact, because the teacher is in contact with the child under many different conditions over a longer period of time, he has many opportunities to observe the child. The teacher has a chance to see the child display a range of emotions and behaviors: aggression, withdrawal, anxiety, happiness, optimism, cheating, lying, confidence, rudeness, politeness, and so on. In most cases, exercise of his role as a teacher, sympathetic or firm as the case may be, is often sufficient to help the child with his difficulties and successes.

In other cases, more study is needed by the teacher. Here are three examples in Miss Smith's class. She is an elementary science teacher, and firmly committed to teaching her students *science*. But she also knows that no matter how well she prepares or teaches there will be difficulties arising from conditions which concern her students which have nothing to do with science.

Now there was Harry, always shy and apparently lost in daydreams; Richard, alter-

---

56. Jerome Siller, "Socioeconomic Status and Conceptual Thinking," *Journal of Abnormal and Social Psychology* 55, no. 3 (November 1957): 365-71.

57. Donald W. Mackinnon, "The Nature and Nurture of Creative Talent," *American Psychologist* 17 (July 1962): 484-94.

nately brilliant and disruptive; and Jane, who always found some excuse to not work on a committee with Nancy. Harry was thin as a fence pole, lacked coordination, and was the last to be chosen in games. Miss Smith provided him with a book on different physical types, and the very fact that he now knew that he was not a physical freak helped him considerably. Richard, it turned out, was an unusually brilliant boy who had been held back a grade because of a long illness. After consultation with the principal, fourth grade teacher, parents, and Richard, it was decided to place him in the fourth grade class. Since he found some competition in the class, he had to study more and had no time to interrupt the class.

Nancy was a Negro; Jane had never lived in a community where there were Negroes. Yet she had anxieties about being near Nancy that almost made her unable to function. Miss Smith first changed the committee assignments and later introduced the concepts of race and prejudice in her science teaching. She then began to deliberately structure opportunities for multi-ethnic work. Eventually, Jane appeared to be relieved of many of her anxieties, and no longer requested committee changes, changed places in line, or sat at a different table in order to avoid associating with Nancy.

Many problems of growth and development do not, of course, have such happy endings. The solution of these problems, however, are normally beyond the skills of a classroom teacher, who is not trained to be a clinical psychologist or a psychiatrist. The best way for the classroom teacher to use his understanding of his children is to assist them within the context of teaching. If that is not successful he should use his knowledge of them to refer them to trained personnel for diagnosis and treatment, just as he does in cases requiring dental, medical, or similar care.

The point of view taken here is that the classroom teacher is, above all, a teacher. He should try to expand his knowledge of children's growth and development to facilitate his teaching. He should also be alert to the various characteristics that interfere with learning. But the teacher is not trained, and should not be expected to function, as a clinician.

SELECTED REFERENCES

BALDWIN, ALFRED L. *Theories of Child Development.* New York: John Wiley and Sons, Inc., 1967.

BANDURA, ALBERT, and WALTERS, RICHARD H. *Social Learning and Personality Development.* New York: Holt, Rinehart and Winston, Inc., 1963.

CROW, LESTER D., and CROW, ALICE. *Child Development and Adjustment.* New York: Macmillan Company, 1962.

GESELL, ARNOLD. *Studies in Child Development.* New York: Harper and Row, Publishers, 1948.

———. *Youth: The Years from Ten to Sixteen.* New York: Harper and Brothers, 1956.

HUNT, J. McV. *Intelligence and Experience.* New York: Ronald Press Company, 1961.

HURLOCK, ELIZABETH B. *Child Development.* 4th ed. New York: McGraw-Hill Book Company, 1964.

KLAUSMEIER, HERBERT J., and GOODWIN, WILLIAM. *Learning and Human Abilities.* 2d ed. New York: Harper & Row Publishers, 1966.

KLEG, MILTON; RICE, MARION J.; and BAILEY, WILFRID C. *Race, Caste, and Prejudice.* Athens, Ga.: Anthropology Curriculum Project, University of Georgia, 1970.

LINTON, RALPH. *The Cultural Background of Personality.* New York: Appleton-Century-Crofts, Inc., 1945.

MCCANDLESS, BOYD R. *Children: Behavior and Development.* 2d ed. New York: Holt, Rinehart and Winston, Inc., 1967.

MONTAGU, ASHLEY. *The Direction of Human Development.* Rev. ed. New York: Hawthorn Books, Inc., 1970.

MURPHY, LOIS BARCLAY. *The Widening World of Childhood.* New York: Basic Books Inc., 1962.

PRESCOTT, DANIEL E. *The Child in the Educative Process.* New York: McGraw-Hill Book Company, 1957.

SMART, MOLLIE S., and SMART, RUSSELL C. *Children: Development and Relationships.* New York: Macmillan Company, 1967.

PART TWO

planning for curriculum development

Photo: Courtesy of El Paso (Texas) Independent School District.
Photography: Seth J. Edwards, Jr.

setting curriculum objectives

3

An elementary school should have clearly defined curriculum objectives. If the school is to achieve its objectives, they must be lucidly understood by teachers, children, and parents alike. In fact, one might rightly hypothesize: the more clearly the objectives are stated and understood by all those concerned with the school and its functions, the more likely the school's objectives will be achieved.

The nation has always had some objectives for the school and education to accomplish although the objectives have changed somewhat and become more numerous with time. For example, the earliest objectives of education when free public education was established were primarily two in number. First, education was to provide each child with the opportunity of self-fulfillment in terms of his own ability and the contribution he could make to a democratic society. And, second, education was intended to insure the nation that it would have a literate citizenry.[1]

Importance of Objectives

Curriculum objectives in the elementary school are important to teachers, children, and parents for a number of reasons. Some of the more important ones are discussed in the following paragraphs.[2]

1. OBJECTIVES SERVE AS GUIDELINES FOR PROGRAM DEVELOPMENT. The stated curriculum objectives provide the framework or guidelines which govern teaching and learning situations in the elementary school. Stated another way, curriculum objectives constitute what the professional staff and the citizenry believe are important and should be taught in school. Viewed from this perspective, each course of study in the elementary school curriculum will have specific objectives in the cognitive, affective and psychomotor domains which contribute towards the accomplishment of the school's general or global curriculum objectives.[3]

1. Ralph W. Tyler, "Purposes for Our Schools," *California Elementary Administrator* 32, no. 3 (March 1969): 9.
2. For a thorough discussion of the purposes which curriculum objectives serve, see William B. Ragan, *Modern Elementary Curriculum* (New York: Holt, Rinehart and Winston, Inc. 1966), pp. 113-17.
3. For a discussion of cognitive and affective objectives, see: Benjamin S. Bloom et al., *Taxonomy of Educational Objectives—Handbook I: Cognitive Domain* (New York: David McKay Company, Inc., 1956); David R. Krathwohl et al., *Taxonomy of Educational Objectives—Handbook II: Affective Domain* (New York: David McKay Company, Inc., 1964).

2. OBJECTIVES ARE FORMULATED TO PROMOTE A GIVEN PHILOSOPHY OF EDUCATION. The global curriculum objectives which are stated for the elementary school are usually of such nature that they reflect a given philosophy about the type of education which should be provided for children. One would expect to find in an essentialist oriented school, for example, stated curriculum objectives which clearly serve societal needs. Conversely, the curriculum objectives of a progressive oriented school most likely would be stated more in terms of a child-centered point of view placing major emphasis upon meeting the immediate interests of children.

When the classroom teachers collectively and individually subscribe to the basic philosophy underlying the school's statement of curriculum objectives, they are more likely to be well-adjusted in their teaching role and effecient in teaching performance. When teachers are not in agreement with the philosophical basis of the curriculum objectives, role conflict may exist between the goals the institution desires to achieve and the idiographic or personal goals teachers wish to achieve.[4] One can see, therefore, how important it is that teachers participate in formulating the curriculum objectives and the philosophical basis of the elementary school.

3. OBJECTIVES SERVE TO INSURE THAT SOCIETAL NEEDS ARE MET. Even in the progressivists' child-centered school, there frequently appear some societal oriented curriculum objectives. One can find global curriculum objectives in the preponderance of America's elementary schools since 1958, for example, dealing with improved learnings in mathematics, science, and foreign language to meet national purposes even though many of the schools pride themselves on being child-centered.

The principle that if the child is not educated, the State will suffer is as old as education itself in this nation.[5] One can anticipate that in the future, therefore, curriculum objectives, at least in part, will be shaped in terms of important societal needs such as that imposed upon the schools by the federal congress with the passage of the National Defense Education Act in 1958.

4. OBJECTIVES GIVE DIRECTION TO THE SELECTING OF CHILDREN'S LEARNING EXPERIENCES. Unless the school has clearly delineated curriculum objectives, which hopefully its staff helped to formulate and accept, teachers may allow the prescribed textbook content to become the governing medium for determining what is learned by their charges. With clear notions of the purposes for which they educate, however, teachers can select content from textbooks and other materials which help them achieve the desired curriculum objectives. In short, the stated curriculum objectives become the desired end for which children are educated and teachers select materials and plan learning experiences which facilitate the accomplishment of the final objectives.

5. OBJECTIVES PROVIDE A SET OF DESIRED LEARNING OUTCOMES WHICH CAN BE EVALUATED TO DETERMINE HOW EFFECTUAL THE INSTRUCTIONAL PROGRAM IS. The school's stated objectives provide a set of learning outcomes for children such as

---

4. For a theoretical discussion of the role expectations of the institution as it relates to the personal need dispositions of the staff, see J. W. Getzels and E. G. Guba, "Social Behavior and the Administrative Process," *The School Review* 65 (Winter 1957): 423-41.

5. Ellwood P. Cubberley, *Public Education in the United States* (Boston: Houghton Mifflin Company, 1934), p. 19.

factual information, attitudes and appreciations, and skills that can be used as a basis for measurement and evaluation to determine the degree to which the staff has been effectual in achieving specified curriculum goals. There can be no meaningful evaluation in the elementary school in the absence of clearly defined curriculum objectives—the ends for which teachers teach and children learn. The curriculum objectives, therefore, represent what teachers attempt to accomplish with children in the teaching and learning situations.

Once one understands the importance of stated curriculum objectives in the elementary school, he has the requisite understanding to study objectives of education in a democracy. Let us examine curriculum objectives which are consonant with education in a democracy.

Objectives of Education in a Democracy

Before we examine a listing of curriculum objectives that has gained universal acceptance in the nation, let us investigate values in a democracy as pre-determiners of objectives. As we shall see, the emergent values in the society largely shape any statement of curriculum objectives.

Values as Predeterminers of Objectives. Curriculum objectives in large measure depend upon those values which are regarded as highly important in promoting and directing human development.[6] What the professional staff and the citizenry believe should be taught about material, social, truth, moral, aesthetic, and spiritual values, for example, weighs mightily upon the global curriculum objectives for the elementary school. As an illustration, if moral values are to be emphasized, curriculum objectives dealing with such concepts as justice, fair play, and honesty will be delineated and stressed in teaching.

One of the major problems in setting curriculum objectives is to first resolve the matter of values. One can reflect on recent history and see changes in values which have affected curriculum objectives in the elementary school. The progressivists in the 1920s and 1930s, for example, created a climate at school heavily laden with social values in which children were supplied with love, understanding, and emotional support based upon the theory that pupil behavioral outcomes would be improved if these conditions obtained. Or, as recently as the decade of the 1960s, one can see the impact of the discipline-centered curricula with a set of curriculum objectives which maximized the truth value where intellectuality was brought to the fore and learning by discovery came into vogue.

The issue in setting curriculum objectives for the elementary school, therefore, becomes a matter of establishing priorities and balances among values. Among that subset of values mentioned earlier—social, truth, moral, aesthetic, and spiritual values, which should be maximized? Or, should there be balance among these values as reflected in the global curriculum objectives for the school? How much should fadism, changing societal conditions, and philosophy, for example, as evidenced in the values of the society at any given time, impinge upon the continuing curriculum objectives of the elementary school? These are hard questions that must be answered before one attempts to establish and periodi-

---

6. For a discussion of values as they relate to goal setting in education, see Philip H. Phenix, *Philosophy of Education* (New York: Henry Holt and Company, 1958), pp. 549-51.

cally revise curriculum objectives for the school.

A Listing of Curriculum Objectives. One of the best listings of global curriculum objectives for the elementary school is that devised by the Educational Policies Commission of the National Education Association in 1938.[7] Their statement of objectives follows.

The Objectives of Self-Realization

The Inquiring Mind: The educated person has an appetite for learning.
Speech: The educated person can speak the mother tongue clearly.
Reading: The educated person reads the mother tongue efficiently.
Writing: The educated person writes the mother tongue effectively.
Number: The educated person solves his problems of counting and calculating.
Sight and Hearing: The educated person is skilled in listening and observing.
Health Knowledge: The educated person understands the basic facts concerning health and disease.
Health Habits: The educated person protects his own health and that of his dependents.
Public Health: The educated person works to improve the health of the community.
Recreation: The educated person is participant and spectator in many sports and other pastimes.
Intellectual Interests: The educated person has mental resources for the use of leisure.
Aesthetic Interest: The educated person appreciates beauty.
Character: The educated person gives responsible direction to his own life. He also develops moral and spiritual values.

The Objectives of Human Relationship

Respect for Humanity: The educated person puts human relationships first.
Friendships: The educated person enjoys a rich, sincere, and varied social life.
Cooperation: The educated person can work and play with others.
Appreciation of the Home: The educated person appreciates the family as a social institution.
Conservation of the Home: The educated person conserves family ideals.
Homemaking: The educated person is skilled in homemaking.
Democracy in the Home: The educated person maintains democratic family relationships.

The Objectives of Economic Efficiency

Work: The educated producer knows the satisfaction of good workmanship.
Occupational Information: The educated producer understands the requirements and opportunities for various jobs.
Occupational Choice: The educated producer has selected his occupation.
Occupational Efficiency: The educated producer succeeds in his chosen vocation.
Occupational Adjustment: The educated producer maintains and improves his efficiency.
Occupational Appreciation: The educated producer appreciates the social value of his work.
Personal Economics: The educated consumer plans the economics of his own life.
Consumer Judgment: The educated consumer develops standards for guiding his expenditures.
Efficiency in Buying: The educated consumer is an informed and skillful buyer.
Consumer Protection: The educated consumer takes appropriate measures to safeguard his interests.

The Objectives of Civic Responsibility

Social Justice: The educated citizen is sensitive to the disparities of human circumstance.
Social Activity: The educated citizen acts to correct unsatisfactory conditions.
Social Understanding: The educated citizen seeks to understand social structures and social processes.
Critical Judgment: The educated citizen has defenses against propaganda.
Tolerance: The educated person respects one's differences of opinion.
Conservation: The educated citizen has a regard for the nation's resources.

---

7. Educational Policies Commission, *The Purposes of Education in American Democracy* (Washington, D.C.: National Education Association, 1938), pp. 51-123.

Social Applications of Science: The educated citizen measures scientific advance by its contribution to the general welfare.

World Citizenship: The educated citizen is a cooperating member of the world community.

Law Observance: The educated citizen respects the law.

Economic Literacy: The educated citizen is economically literate.

Political Citizenship: The educated citizen accepts his civic duties.

Devotion to Democracy: The educated citizen acts upon an unswerving loyalty to democratic ideals.

In attempting to accomplish each of these curriculum objectives, teachers stress them at every grade or instructional level and student mastery is expected as children progress through the elementary school. The values implied in this listing of global objectives for the elementary school are well-balanced. Although other statements of objectives for the elementary school have appeared more recently, this work of the 1938 Educational Policies Commission contines to be a useful guideline for formulating curriculum objectives.[8]

Objectives for Tomorrow's School

The curriculum objectives embodied in the listing of the 1938 Educational Policies Commission are just as relevant for children of the 1970s as they were for children in former years. Of course, there will always be selected objectives which may receive more attention at certain times because of emergent societal conditions. It seems clear, therefore, that the major curriculum objectives for tomorrow's elementary school can be reduced to about five in number: (1) realizing self-fulfillment, (2) becoming an intelligent citizen, (3) achieving social mobility, (4) preparing for the work world, and (5) learning how to continue to learn.[9] These objectives are discussed in the following paragraphs of this chapter.

Realizing Self-Fulfillment. One of the maladies of our present technological culture is that it fosters a generation of young people who are individually in danger of becoming anonymous nonentities. That is, as a result of technology and automation, in some schools children frequently have little to identify with which provides personal satisfaction or self-realization. In schools of this nature, children may be frequently found to be narrowly educated to fit into a particular niche in life with limited chances for full and complete self-realization; in short, they are being miseducated when this condition prevails.[10]

Fortunately, many schools are not like the ones alluded to above. In any event, a check on the dehumanizing effect of educating too narrowly is for the teachers to make, individually and collectively—periodic assessments to determine if, as a result of education, each child has a wider range of realistic choices that he can make personal-

8. Other well-known curriculum objectives for the elementary school can be found in: Nolan C. Kearney, *Elementary School Objectives* (New York: Russell Sage Foundation, 1953); *A Report to the President,* The Committee for The White House Conference on Education (Washington, D.C.: Government Printing Office, 1956), pp. 91-92.

9. See Tyler, "Purposes for Our Schools," pp. 9-14.

10. Ibid., p. 10; also see: Harold G. Shane, "Elementary Education: Objectives," *NEA Journal* 51, no. 6 (September 1962): 41-43; Francis H. Horn, "The Ends for Which We Educate," *The Educational Forum* 28, no. 2 (January 1964): 133-43; L. Thomas Hopkins, "Education for Becomingness," *Childhood Education* 40, no 9 (May 1964): 470-4; Arthur W. Combs, "Fostering Self-Direction," *Educational Leadership* 23, no. 5 (February 1966): 373-76.

ly in life. If the answer to this question is affirmative, the child is being educated for self-realization. Each year of schooling, therefore, should open new avenues of opportunity to each child and the teacher's instructional efforts should be bent towards giving him the requisite skills, knowledges, and attitudes which will enable him to select from a broad array of alternative opportunities that lead to self-realization and fulfillment.

Becoming an Intelligent Citizen. Living in contemporary America is an extremely complex process. There are so many perplexing problems with which children, as well as adults, are confronted. Some of the major problems confronting the citizenry, for example, include: (1) racial integration of schools and housing, (2) fair and equal employment opportunities for all Americans, (3) monetary inflation, (4) drug abuse, (5) pollution of the environment, (6) crime in the street, (7) the in-migration of the rural poor into the inner city, (8) the out-migration of the affluent from the cities to suburbia, (9) the plight of economically deprived families, (10) technology's unwillingness or inability to control itself, and (11) the increasing anonymity of the individual in the mass society.[11] It is imperative that a literate citizenry be educated in order that these problems can be successfully resolved. Teachers, then, must intensify their efforts to attend to the maximum development of each child's intellectual processes and functioning as a major curriculum goal now and in the future.

It should also be added that simply to increase the literacy level of the populace in an attempt to deal with these problems is not enough. Teachers must also teach for changed attitudes, appreciations, and values as curriculum objectives if the school is to educate children who want to resolve the present, vexing problems that are prevalent and persistent in the society. The reason for this is simple; how one feels about a problem is at least as important as what he knows about it. In short, one's feelings control his behavior irrespective of what he knows.[12]

Achieving Social Mobility. Education in America has long been viewed as a means whereby one could improve himself through formalized training at school so that he could get a better job and enjoy or become a participant in the benefits which American life has to offer. Stated another way, the school in the American society has been and still remains a major medium for social mobility—the method whereby the American dream becomes a reality for those who succeed at school.[13]

For many disadvantaged children, the school has not been too effectual in preparing them for full participation in the American life. The reasons for this seem elementary: (1) they do not possess the elaborated language codes which are essential for achieving in the middle class

---

11. As related background reading see: Jacques Ellul, *The Technological Society* (New York: Vintage Books, 1967); Jose Ortega Y Gasset, *The Revolt of the Masses* (New York: W. W. Norton & Company, Inc., 1932); Daniel J. Boorstin, *The Image: A Guide to Pseudo-Events in America* (New York: Harper Colophon Books, 1961); William Murdoch and Joseph Connell, "All About Ecology," *Center Magazine* 3, no. 1 (January 1970): 56-63; Benjamin Solomon, "A Perspective For Educators on the Racial Issue in Education," *Phi Delta Kappan* 47, no. 9 (May 1966): 518-23; Robert J. Havighurst, "Who Are the Disadvantaged," *Education* 85, no. 8 (April 1965): 455-7.

12. Earl C. Kelley, "The Place of Affective Learning," *Educational Leadership* 22, no. 7 (April 1965): 455-7.

13. Tyler, "Purposes for Our Schools" pp. 10-11.

oriented school, (2) they have had little association with formally educated people, (3) they suffer from nutritional and health problems, (4) they are lacking in positive self-concepts including confidence in their ability to learn.[14] Of course, many other reasons could be given as to why the school, with its middle-class orientation, has not helped disadvantaged learners become full participants in the mainstream of American life.

Fortunately, educators are making new attempts to achieve the social mobility curriculum objective for disadvantaged children as they have been achieving so successfully for advantaged learners in former years. Some of these new attempts include: (1) pre-school training for children of disadvantaged background,[15] (2) compensatory training for pupils who are already enrolled in school,[16] improved nutrition and health care including breakfast and lunch at school, dental care, and the like. It suffices to say that the school and its teachers can become effective in helping all children achieve social mobility if they provide educational programs suited to the unique strengths and weaknesses of the pupils served.

Preparing for the Work World. A vital curriculum objective of the elementary school is to initiate instruction which helps children understand the world of work and stimulates their interest in thinking about tentative vocational choices. In the elementary years, teachers can help children develop responsibility, punctuality, thoroughness in work, and intellectual and social skills which are requisite for attaining vocational success in adult life. In intermediate years, teachers can offer instruction central to the theme of career exploration.[17] Such instruction frequently is provided in a unit of work dubbed "The World of Work." In teaching this unit, teachers should cover data which show that the era of unskilled labor and farm labor is virtually over and that the vocational opportunities for the future lie in such fields as engineering, science, social services and the skilled and service trades.

Teaching about the world of work in the elementary school, therefore, should be of the survey nature with respect to the objective of acquainting children about vcoational opportunities. Teaching which develops such habits as responsibility and punctuality, while relevant to other curriculum objectives, also contributes toward preparing children for the work world.

Learning How to Continue to Learn. In light of the rapidity with which we gain new knowledge and of the incidence of changing conditions in our society, it is no longer possible to teach an unchanging set of facts to children in the elementary school which will be relevant to their needs throughout their lives. Rather, a major objective of education today is to equip children with those skills and attitudes which will better enable them to become autonomous individuals capable of learning on their own while they are in school and in post-school years. This is not to imply, how-

---

14. Ibid., J. W. Getzels, "Pre-School Education," *Teacher's College Record* 68, no. 3 (December 1966): 219-28.
15. Educational Policies Commission, *Universal Opportunity for Early Childhood Education,* (Washington, D.C.: National Education Association and American Association of School Administrators, 1966), pp. 3-12; Lendon K. Smith, "The Doctor Looks at the Nursery School," *Education* 87, no. 8 (April 1967): 474-7.
16. George W. Jones, "Compensatory Education for the Disadvantaged," *NEA Journal* 56, no. 4 (April 1967): 21-23.
17. Tyler, "Purposes for Our Schools," pp. 11-12.

ever, that there is not a constant subset of facts, such as the multiplication table, which will continue to be both useful and necessary.

Of course, teaching children how to learn on their own has long been an established curriculum objective but the truth is that, more often than not, teachers pose the problems and questions for the students instead of the pupils finding them as they study. Or, the teacher and the textbooks become readily available answer sources that tend to eliminate the necessary teaching and learning situations so structured that the children are required to find answers to their problems and questions from other dependable sources. To master the objective then of "learning how to continue to learn," traditional teaching and learning procedures in the elementary school will have to be changed so that school experiences become exercises in and examples of continued learning.[18] Teaching children how to learn independently is surely one of the most important, if not the most important, curriculum objective of the modern elementary school.

Criteria to Guide Objectives Formulation

Clear and definitive criteria are needed by those who are concerned with formulating objectives for the elementary school. Ragan has suggested the following criteria to guide the formulation of curriculum objectives.[19]

1. The objectives of the school are formulated cooperatively by pupils, teachers, parents, and administrators.
2. The objectives of the school are written and placed in the hands of teachers, administrators, and parents.
3. The objectives of the school are stated in terms of desirable growth in behavior.
4. Physical, mental, social, and emotional growth are emphasized.
5. Individual differences in interests, needs, and abilities of pupils are recognized in the statement of objectives.
6. The objectives of the school reflect a belief in democratic living.
7. There is continuous effort to develop an understanding of the objectives of the school by administrators, teachers, and parents.
8. The objectives of the school are subject to continuous study and periodic revision.

An Appraisal of Curriculum Objectives

The preceding discussion of global objectives was designed to introduce to you the orthodox view of objectives which you will encounter in much of the professional literature. In this section, an alternative view of objectives is presented. This view is presented not to make you cynical about objectives, but to suggest how you as a teacher might utilize objectives more effectively for school planning.

One of the favorite pastimes of educational specialists is the listing of curriculum objectives. The statement of objectives is always a part of a school self-study or self-evaluation, and seldom is there a school which cannot produce on request an elaborate list of idealized objectives. One of these lists, previously outlined in this chapter, dates from an NEA Educational Policies Commission report of 1938. During the past thirty years it has been imitated in many forms, and will undoubtedly be reflected in the objectives of the elementary school in which you teach.

18. Ibid., p. 13.
19. William B. Ragan, *Teaching America's Children* (New York: Holt, Rinehart and Winston, Inc., 1961), p. 101.

An examination of this list will immediately indicate that the objectives are stated as general goals, equated with democratic society itself. As such, it is a statement of general philosophy and is not functional in the more limited context of schooling. While the objectives purport to be related to the elementary school, frequently they are stated in terms of paragons of adult virtue. They apply to adult life, not to elementary children. Furthermore, many of the objectives are somewhat contradictory. One under *Human Relationship* has to do with "Friendships: The educated person enjoys a rich, sincere, and varied social life." Another under *Civic Responsibility* suggests "Social Activity: The educated citizen acts to correct unsatisfactory conditions." As adults we know that we have to exercise certain options for the use of our time, and that outside of our job hours there is little time to do many of the things considered important. An educated person might display some of these characteristics; seldom would he display all. In fact, many of them have nothing to do with education as related to schooling, but with a general sense of values growing out of socialization. The illiterate is just as capable of enjoying social relationships as an educated person, and is frequently capable of working with community agencies to correct unsatisfactory societal conditions. The 1938 statement of objectives is an interesting example of the confusion between socialization and formal education and school performance and adult performance.

A general characteristic of educational objectives is the overstatement of what education, as related to the institution of schooling, may accomplish. One of the objectives under *Civic Responsibility* has to do with "Conservation: The educated citizen has a regard for the nation's resources." In view of the concern with environmental abuse in the 1970s, one might rightfully conclude that the elementary school has been sadly ineffective. But schools will always be ineffective in meeting their objectives as long as professional educators state the aims of education as broad as public policy or life itself. A review of the actual teaching content in elementary curricula in the last decades indicates that the objective of conservation was not educationally programmed. But even if it had been, the environmental pollution of today would not mean that the schools had failed on this objective. It would simply emphasize the fact that conflicting values and institutions in the adult world are not amenable to exorcism by elementary schooling.

Failure to distinguish between the specialized and general functions of the school as a social institution is one cause of ambiguity in curriculum objectives. The clients—public and pupils—are frequently not nearly as confused about these distinctions as are professional school personnel.

To the general public, the school represents a particular institution with a particular function. This particular function has to do with knowledge and skills that a youngster does not normally acquire in the process of rearing—of socialization. Some of these skills are the traditional ones of reading, writing, and arithmetic. These are required in the elementary school, and on the degree of competency in these areas are built most of the fabric of our symbolic education.

But the school as an institution is more than a place of schooling. Wherever people are brought together, subsidiary social functions corollary to the main function emerge. If the main function of the school is schooling—and many educators would question this—a school nevertheless becomes involved in the health, welfare, and safety of its charges far beyond the original purpose.

In his contacts with his pupils, a teacher attempts to model and require good manners and courtesy, respect and consideration, application and perseverance, tolerance and fair play, and other behavior characteristics which are deemed desirable for group life. In this role, however, the teacher is not acting so much as a teacher as he is fulfilling the expectancies we have of adults in their relationships with children. We expect more from teachers simply because they are in contact with pupils more than other adults are, even their parents. There is, therefore, never any conflict between the teacher in the role of subject teacher and the teacher as model adult in the general process of socialization. If the public emphasizes the first more than the latter it is because it takes the latter for granted as implicit part of the contract of any adult who trains youth.

The conflict which comes between school and community frequently arises from the avowed role of the school as a change agent in community mores. Many social reformers see the school as a focal point where parents, the community, and government agencies can unite in cooperative efforts for social amelioration. This vision is as old as the Utopias.

It was said that the objectives of ancient Persian educators were three—to teach a boy to ride a horse, shoot a bow, and tell the truth. These objectives were stated not as philospic ends, but as performance tasks. As such, they presage the more recent movement among curriculum evaluators to state objectives operationally or behaviorally rather than globally. As such, they have two immediate values: they indicate the type of measure to be used in determining the task performance level, and they indicate the teaching content necessary to achieve the task.

Teachers, as managers of the education of children, implicitly organize their work in terms of operational objectives. They know that the achievement of a specific objective, such as the ability to read, is achieved through a sequence of small performance tasks. Within the confines of their classrooms, teachers do not deal in global objectives very much, but in the more specific detailed objectives. Frequently these are not made explicit, but may be inferred from the teaching cycle. If they cannot be inferred from the overt behavior of teacher and pupils in the classroom, it is likely that the teacher does not have a clear teaching objective in mind (see Epilogue). Consequently, his efforts, and that of the pupils, are inefficient and often ineffectual.

Schools and teachers taking positions not acceptable to their adult patrons frequently find themselves in positions of conflict. Some of this arises from the curriculum content, such as teaching about "evolution" in science or the "United Nations" in social studies. In such cases, however, the professional staff of the schools will more generally have the support of the community than not; this is related to teaching.

However, where the schools become action agencies for social reform, the community support is frequently lacking, unless the community in effect has captured the school and is seeking to use it for ends beyond the conventional objectives of schooling. Teachers are frequently inactive in community and policy matters beyond the purview of the schools. This is particularly true in urban areas. It is possible that the proper channels for teachers to express their interests or desires concerning political activity are through community agencies and affiliations other than the schools. A person does not become a second-class citizen because he becomes a teacher. Most communities are reluctant, however, for teachers to use the schools as a substitute for the political arena. In working with general school objectives, teachers who are more community action oriented need to consider their specialized role as a teacher and the generalized role they may play as a citizen. In the delimitation of school objectives, too little attention has been given to those which are within the domain of the school and those which lie within the realm of general social policy and social reform.

Since the area of teaching and pupil performance objectives overlap with other chapters, this chapter is restricted to a discussion of global objectives. As a teacher, you will probably be called upon at some time in your career to serve on some kind of curriculum or school objectives committee. You will find that many of your colleagues will list the kind of global objectives previously described in this chapter. You may talk aesthetic values when you may not have music and art teachers and little or no sequential program to develop aesthetic knowledge and appreciation. You may outline objectives of democratic participation, notwithstanding the fact that some of your children come from a community in which there are rigid patterns of segregation.

If your school and community are really committed to using objectives to test the adequacy of a school program, the listing and reality testing of school objectives is not a fruitless exercise, but may lay the foundation for a new look at school programming. In this context, global objectives can serve the useful purpose of stating an ideal, comparing it with the existing conditions, and stating what needs to be done to bring that ideal into the realm of reality. Frequently this will require an organization of priorities—seldom does a school or community have the financial resources to bring about all of the desired changes.

You may find that your service on a school objectives committee is a perfunctory one. You and your associate teachers may be expected to develop some type of philosophic statement which has to be updated to conform to accreditation or evaluation procedures. If this is the case, do not let service on such a committee interfere with your professional commitment to teaching children. Just as you accept, as part of your teaching role, the chore of helping children with coats and boots in bad weather, accept service on such a committee with the same degree of aplomb. Simply remember the ideas about objectives in this chapter, and draw upon them and similar sources to make an acceptable if operationally useless statement. You as a teacher will continue to teach the things that you consider important. It is therefore essential that you be clear about your own teaching objectives.

SELECTED REFERENCES

BLOOM, BENJAMIN S. et al. *Taxonomy of Educational Objectives, Handbook I: Cognitive Domain.* New York: David McKay Company, Inc., 1956.

COMBS, ARTHUR W. "Fostering Self-Direction," *Educational Leadership* 23, no. 5 (1966): 373-76.

CROSBY, MURIEL. "Who Changes the Curriculum and How?" *Phi Delta Kappan* 51, no. 7 (1970): 385-89.

Educational Policies Commission. *The Purposes of Education in American Democracy.* Washington, D.C.: National Education Association, 1938.

GOODLAD, JOHN I., ed. *The Changing American School—Sixty-fifth Yearbook of the National Society for the Study of Education: Part II.* Chicago: University of Chicago Press, 1966.

HOPKINS, L. THOMAS. "Education for Becomingness," *Childhood Education* 40, no. 9 (May, 1964): 470-74.

HORN, FRANCIS H. "The Ends for Which We Educate," *The Educational Forum* 28, no. 2 (1964): 133-43.

HOWE, HAROLD, II. *Picking Up The Options.* Washington, D.C.: National Department of Elementary School Principals, NEA, 1968.

KEARNEY, NOLAN C. *Elementary School Objectives.* New York: Russell Sage Foundation, 1953.

KRATHWOHL, DAVID R., et al. *Taxonomy of Educational Objectives—Handbook II: Affective Domain.* New York: David McKay Company, Inc., 1964.

MAGER, ROBERT F. *Developing Attitude Toward Learning.* Palo Alto, California: Fearon Publishers, 1968.

MAGER, ROBERT F. *Preparing Instructional Objectives.* Palo Alto, California: Fearon Publishers, 1962.

SHANE, HAROLD G. "Elementary Education: Objectives," *NEA Journal* 51, no. 6 (1962): 41-43.

SHANE, HAROLD G. "A Curriculum Continuum: Possible Trends in the 70's," *Phi Delta Kappan* 51, no. 7 (1970): 389-92.

understanding curriculum patterns

4

There are several factors which should be taken into consideration before one undertakes a study of variant curriculum patterns that may be used in the elementary school. These factors include: (1) orientation of the curriculum, (2) planning for curriculum development, and (3) organizing for teaching and learning. These factors will be discussed before we treat the different curriculum patterns here. The concluding section of this chapter investigates selected principles of curriculum organization.

A Definition of Curriculum

The curriculum of the elementary school has been defined differently. In former years, many educators conceived of it as a collection of courses in the different subjects which children must study and master. These educators frequently viewed several school activities and child experiences such as school lunch and recess as being extracurricular in nature.[1] In recent years, however, *curriculum* has come to be referred to as every experience in which children engage that the school sponsors, e.g., academic studies, playground experiences, plays, debates and the like.[2]

Presently, a course of study is commonly thought of as a listing of cognitive, affective and skill learnings to be achieved in the various course offerings of the curriculum. In addition to the suggested learnings appearing in each course of study, selected activities, resource materials bibliographies and evaluation instruments are normally included.

As a general rule, the courses of study, commonly referred to as curriculum guides, are developed for the school system as a whole. The intrabuilding faculties then determine in some manner what will be taught in each elementary school.

Orientation of the Curriculum

There are three basic orientations to the curriculum of the elementary school.

1. See Williard S. Elsbree, Harold J. McNally, and Richard Wynn, *Elementary School Administration and Supervision,* 3d ed. (New York: American Book Company, 1967), p. 81.
2. Oscar T. Jarvis and Haskin R. Pounds, *Organizing, Supervising and Administering the Elementary School* (West Nyack, N.Y.: Parker Publishing Company, 1969), p. 41.

They include: (1) the society-centered, (2) the child-centered and (3) the discipline-centered orientations.[3] Let us investigate the basic differences in these curricular orientations.

Society-Oriented Curriculum. A society-oriented curriculum is one in which the objectives of education are considered to be primarily social.[4] That is, the faculty selects and teaches to elementary children those learnings which are known to be necessary for effectual adult living. Stated another way, the school is an agent of society and as such transmits to children certain knowledges and skills that each child should possess in order that he might become a responsible and productive citizen.[5] When a school faculty has this orientation to curriculum, it basically believes that the school primarily serves as society's enculturation agent by seeing that children master that body of knowledge (factual information) and that set of skills (cognitive and psychomotor) which are essential for adult living, thereby meeting the pupils' deferred needs. Little emphasis is attached to the affective learnings, i.e., values, attitudes appreciation and interests, in the society-oriented curriculum although much importance traditionally is attached to teaching patriotism, capitalism, rugged individualism and the like.[6]

There are therefore many identifying characteristics of a society-oriented curriculum. For example, pupils are subjected to rigorous discipline and are required to master prescribed subject matter.[7] Of course, there are other identifying characteristics such as textbook centeredness but these suffice to illustrate the society-oriented curriculum. In its true form, the society-oriented curriculum is congruent with the views of the essentialists which were discussed in chapter 1.

Opponents of the society-oriented curriculum, largely the progressivists, have raised some serious objections to it. Some of their more frequent objections include the following.

First, the society-oriented curriculum attaches little importance to the interests and needs which children evidence. Hence, children frequently are not motivated to do their best work since the prescribed learnings may not be relevant and central to their interests and needs.

A second objection is that in a textbook-centered, society-oriented curriculum student learnings are geared to happenings and facts of the past. As a result contemporary problems involved in everyday living with which children must learn to cope receive little attention. More progressive-minded educators believe that greater emphasis should be placed upon teaching children how to deal intelligently and constructively with problems in our present and ever-changing society.[8]

Third, the uniformity of teaching normally associated with the society-oriented curriculum makes meeting individual, instruc-

---

3. John I. Goodlad, "The Curriculum," in *The Changing American School: The Sixty-fifth Yearbook of the National Society for the Study of Education, Part II*, ed. John I. Goodlad (Chicago: University of Chicago Press, 1966), pp. 40-41.

4. Henry J. Otto and David C. Sanders, *Elementary School Organization and Administration*, 4th ed. (New York: Appleton-Century-Crofts, 1964), p. 42.

5. Jarvis and Pounds, *Organizing, Supervising and Administering*, p. 42.

6. John T. Wahlquist. *The Philosophy of American Education* (New York: Ronald Press Company, 1942), p. 86.

7. Otto and Sanders, *Elementary School Organization*, p. 42.

8. Ibid., p. 41.

tional needs a difficult task. More than that, the society-oriented curriculum tends to breed conformity in student outcomes— a situation which the progressivists believe to be alien to a democratic society.[9]

Fourth, each subject offering in the society-oriented curriculum is normally considered to be an entity of itself. It may be difficult, therefore, for the students to relate the learnings acquired in the different courses.

These and other objections to the society-oriented curriculum on the part of child-centered protagonists led, at the turn of the twentieth century, to a new curricular orientation which came to be known as the child-centered curriculum. Now, let us examine this orientation.

Child-Centered Curriculum Orientation. A child-centered curriculum is one in which learning experiences for children are primarily determined by the developmental needs, interests and aptitudes of the learners. This approach stands at the opposite end of the curriculum orientation continuum from that of the society-oriented curriculum which is predicated on meeting societal needs.

In the child-centered approach, learning experiences are jointly planned by teachers and children in broad units of work which characteristically include many activities and projects which are highly interesting to pupils. These activities or projects are planned and conducted largely on children's expressed *immediate interests,* e.g., music, crafts, reading, science, and writing;[10] and immediate *needs,* e.g., physical and safety, affection and belonging, achievement, approval, and aesthetic.[11]

Whereas the society-oriented curriculum attaches only minor importance to affective learnings, the child-centered curriculum places considerable emphasis on the learnings which involve the values, attitudes, appreciations, interests and emotional sets of children. Characteristically, much concern is shown for children's individual freedom, motivation, self-activity, self-expression and social adjustment when the curriculum is one of child-centered orientation. Furthermore, the child-centered protagonists contend that subject matter is what the individual student needs to know in order to do what he is interested in doing within the activity curriculum.[12] This point of view is in sharp contrast to the society-centered orientation which considers subject matter as a body of factual information to be imparted to students, parceled out over twelve grades and dug out by pupils until they master it; or, failing to do so, withdraw from school.[13]

There are many identifying characteristics of the child-centered school. Some of those most frequently mentioned follow.

First, the daily schedule of activities or learning experiences is quite flexible and tentative. Through pupil-teacher planning in the broad units of work, the children and the teacher will plan what is to be studied in terms of expressed student interests and

9. Wahlquist, *Philosophy of American Education,* p. 87.

10. See Karl C. Garrison, *Psychology of Adolescence,* 6th ed. (Englewood Cliffs, N.J.: Prentice-Hall, Inc., 1965), pp. 129-45; Louis M. Smith and Bryce B. Hudgins, *Educational Psychology* (New York: Alfred A. Knopf, 1964) pp. 157-58.

11. See Abraham H. Maslow, *Motivation and Personality* (New York: Harper and Brothers, 1954), pp. 80-122.

12. See John Dewey, *Democracy and Education* (New York: Macmillan Company, 1916), chap. 14.

13. Wahlquist, *Philosophy of American Education,* pp. 99-100.

needs. Second, longer periods or blocks of time are provided for carrying out the activities which have been bilaterally agreed upon by the children and the teacher. As the student-initiated work progresses, the day's activities are adjusted so that the children can complete the work they have begun. Third, the student activities are not restricted to those suggested in the courses of study. Rather, the courses of study become resource guides or repositories of suggested activities from which the teacher and children may obtain ideas to enhance the learning experiences they mutually have planned. Fourth, the children themselves are the central focus of the child-centered school, not just books and subjects with prescribed learnings. A fifth characteristic is that activities are concerned with the problems present in everyday life rather than being concentrated on learning about the past, which is where the emphasis lies in the society-oriented school. Sixth, the children learn by doing through self-directive, purposeful activities and are not expected to assume the passive roles which exist in the traditional school.[14]

Essentialists have raised strong objections to the child-centered curriculum orientation. Some of their objections are these:[15]

First, the work of the child-centered school is frequently lacking in system and organization. Second, lacking organization, the short-lived and disconnected projects and activities of the students do little more than satisfy the children's idiosyncrasies. A third is that progressive education is largely a hit-or-miss proposition since the guidance and instructional functions of the traditional teacher are largely circumvented in the child-centered curriculum. Fourth, the absence of external restraints (imposed rigidly by teachers in traditional, society-oriented schools) results in an abuse of freedom by pupils in the child-centered schools, to the end that the children fail to develop certain personality and character traits, such as stick-to-it-iveness, which are so highly valued in America. Fifth, forsaking the scope and sequence of what is to be learned and when in the society-oriented curriculum, the child-centered school frequently permits children to spend a disproportionate amount of time studing about problems of a nonrecurring nature. Hence, they may fail to master that fund of knowledge and that set of skills which will enable them to acceptably cope with problems or situations of a recurring nature.

Much has been learned about an appropriate curriculum orientation from the successes and failures of both the child-centered and the society-oriented approaches. For example, we have learned from the essentialists who utilize the society-oriented curriculum that system and organization are important in teaching children factual information and developing their cognitive and psychomotor skills. And, for example, we have learned from the progressivists, who possess a child-centered orientation, that children will be highly motivated to learn when they have a voice in planning activities in terms of their immediate interests and needs.

In reality, the curriculum orientation issue is not necessarily an either-or proposition; that is, either a society-centered or a child-centered curriculum orientation. There is that eclectic, middle position which can

14. Ibid., pp. 94-96.
15. Pedro J. Drata, "Progressive Look At Progressive Education," *Educational Administration and Supervision* 24 (November 1938): 570-80.

bring together the strong points of both the society and child-centered orientations which we shall refer to here as the discipline-centered orientation.

Discipline-Centered Curriculum Orientation. In the 1960s, the world's fund of knowledge increased at a staggering rate. It is likely that knowledge will continue to accumulate in the future at an unprecedented rate. The notion that the school can teach children all of the factual information they will need for adult years is untenable. It is no longer feasible to hold to the notion that one can "complete" his education during school years. The rapidly increasing fund of new knowledge makes much of the present knowledge we now teach obsolete and this phenomenon will continue. These facts, coupled with our present understanding of how quickly children forget knowledge not immediately used, have raised serious questions about the justification for rote learning as practiced by the essentialists.[16]

A large segment of elementary school educators therefore have dedicated themselves to orient the curriculum so that the children can learn those knowledges, values, and skills which will enable them to continue their education on their own initiative throughout life. Furthermore, they believe that children should have those learning experiences which teach them how and where to locate information when they need it and how to assimilate, organize, and apply it.[17] The discipline-centered curriculum enables educators to accomplish these worthwhile objectives. The discipline-centered orientation focuses on the logical ordering or structuring of subject matter for the various disciplines. The new curricula are well-suited to meet the interests and needs of children. One has only to examine the new mathematics, science, social studies and English curricula, for example, to see the new materials which have been developed for children according to the structure of the subject fields or disciplines while, at the same time, appealing to the interests and needs of children.[18]

Presently, scholars in the academic fields (political science, mathematics, anthropology, geography, history and the like) are working with educationists to develop discipline oriented curricula which meet both societal needs and the individual interests and needs of children. By escaping the major shortcoming of the former society-oriented curriculum where great stress was placed upon memorizing masses of uninviting and frequently unrelated details and also by avoiding the ubiquitous pitfalls of lack of structure and organization in the child-centered curriculum, children are encouraged in the new discipline-centered curricula to use their prior knowledge of the structure of the various subject fields to discover through inquiry new knowledge about each subject discipline. In learning by discovery, the children may think intuitively and analytically, they may solve problems or experiment.[19] In short, they learn how to learn—a necessary consequence of the discipline-centered orientation in education. Of course, deduction, as a teaching strategy,

16. Elsbree, McNally, and Wynn, *Elementary School Administration,* p. 91.
17. Ibid.
18. For a brief review of some of these new curricula, see John I. Goodlad, et al. *The Changing School Curriculum* (New York: The Fund for the Advancement of Education, 1966); Glenys G. Unruh, *New Curriculum Developments* (Washington, D.C.: Association for Supervision and Curriculum Development, 1965).
19. Elsbree, McNally and Wynn, *Elementary School Administration,* pp. 90-92.

can be and is used by teachers when they deem it necessary for teaching the various subject fields of the discipline-centered curriculum.

Once the curriculum orientation has been established for an elementary school, the next major consideration is the method to be used in planning for curriculum development. A number of alternatives, useful for such planning, are discussed in the following paragraphs.

Planning for Curriculum Development

There are differing points of view about who should plan the curriculum for elementary school students. Most essentialists, possessing society-oriented leanings, traditionally opt for a curriculum that has been minutely preplanned by authorities in elementary education. Evidence of this intricate preplanning can be found in the prescribed courses of study which those of society-oriented persuasions tend to follow rigidly.

Conversely, most advocates of the child-centered oriented curriculum contend that the curriculum should be planned in broad outlines or resource units and that such planning should be done locally by the professional staff of teachers. Furthermore, these progressivists would leave the day-to-day curriculum planning of pupil learning experiences largely for the teacher and students to plan jointly. Under these circumstances, the prevailing student activities, interests and needs are the essential determinants as to what is to be taught irrespective of the suggestions included in the curriculum resource guides.

The discipline-centered curriculum orientation movement has greatly changed the planning for curriculum development. Under such orientation the community of scholars in institutions of higher education in the nation, through consultation with and advice from educationists, have developed new discipline-centered curricula according to the processes and workways of their respective disciplines. Most of these curricula, such as the elementary economics curriculum materials developed by Senesh at Purdue University and field tested in the Elkhart (Indiana) School System, though highly structured, are relevant to the interests and needs of elementary school children. When the new discipline-centered curricula materials are selected to be taught in the elementary school, the teachers and children frequently have little to say about what content is to be learned because the materials are so highly structured or programmed. The teachers and children mainly have to decide how rapidly they will cover the structured content of the new curricula and how much related material, if any, they will study in the learning situation. Some latitude is left to pupil-teacher discretion in terms of the activities they will follow in learning the structured content of the newer discipline-centered curricula.

One can turn his attention to the matter of how to organize the learning experiences for children once he has settled the matter of who should plan curriculum for elementary school pupils. Learning experiences can be planned on lecture-listen, assign-study-recite-test, or unit basis. A discussion of these alternatives follows.

Organizing for Teaching and Learning

Basically, there are three methods which teachers employ in the elementary school to organize teaching and learning situations. As suggested by Oliver, these methods include: (1) lecture-listen, (2) assign-study-recite-test, and (3) unit plans.[20] Although these alternatives are mutually exclusive, most teachers generally use some combination of them in the actual teaching-learning situation in an attempt to provide more effectual learning experiences for children. Let us briefly examine these alternatives for organizing the teaching and learning situations in the elementary school.

Lecture-Listen Method. Initially, the lecture-listen approach was used in an earlier era in our nation's history when textbooks were in short supply or altogether nonexistent. As a result of the shortage of printed materials, or in some instances the absence of them altogether, the lecture-listen model was devised as a method of **organizing for teaching and learning** whereby a knowledgeable person imparted his knowledge by telling or lecturing to others.

When a teacher employs the lecture-listen method to organize curricular experiences for children he makes **certain assumptions** of necessity. These assumptions are: (1) the content of the lecture is desirable for all pupils, (2) all children can learn the content through the uniform method of presentation at the same time and (3) the students can learn the content as passive recipients by listening to the teacher who is lecturing.[21]

Even though the lecture-listen method is the oldest way of teaching children in America's schools, it can be and still is used to a good advantage on appropriate occasions. There are certain times in teaching when it is expeditious to lecture to children in order to help them master content more readily. For example, some teachers in the social studies prefer the deductive teaching strategy whereby they set forth a generalization to children and then give them specific bits of information which support the generalization by utilizing the lecture method.[22] As another example, a teacher normally does not wait for his charges to discover all of the word recognition rules in reading—he tells his pupils some of them in order to keep learning accruing at an optimal level.

Assign-Study-Recite-Test Method. As textbooks became abundant in the nation's schools, teachers had another option in addition to the lecture-listen method for organizing the teaching and learning situations for children—the assign-study-recite-test technique. Under this plan, the teacher perfunctorily decided how much work his pupils would do daily in each text. The routine was to make basically uniform assignments to all pupils and, after a period of study, have the children recite information which they had learned through independent study. Finally, the teacher administered a test for purposes of determining how well the students had learned the content included in the textbook.

The teacher's classroom became less a lecture hall and more of a study and recitation hall when the assign-study-recite-test method came into vogue. The major purposes for conducting the recitation were to determine if the pupils had satisfactorily completed their assignments and mastered the content, and, if so, to make the next assignment.

One can still find much use being made of the assign-study-recite-test method of organizing the teaching and learning situations in the elementary school. For example, it

20. Albert I. Oliver, *Curriculum Improvement: A Guide to Problems, Principles and Procedures.* (New York: Dodd, Mead & Company, 1965) pp. 344-50.
21. Ibid., p. 345.
22. Oscar T. Jarvis, "Deduction as a Social Science Teaching Strategy: A Re-examination," *Journal of Secondary Education* 42, no. 8 (December 1967): 375-76.

is followed in a modified form in giving a directed reading lesson in the basal reader. That is, after the teacher builds readiness for reading and introduces the vocabulary, he assigns silent reading and then checks on reading comprehension through oral recitation once silent reading is completed.

Normally, when the teacher uses the assign-study-recite-test technique, the students learn the system rapidly and commit to memory certain facts from the content they are studying about "who," "what," "when," and "why" that can be recalled at recitation time. Therein lies one of the major shortcomings of the technique: learning is geared to short-range recall and, in the absence of clearly defined purposes for learning, students may become bored and frustrated in attempting to learn disjointed factual information for recall at recitation. On the other hand, this shortcoming, in large measure, can be alleviated by the teacher shifting his questioning of pupils in recitation from factual questions to thought questions. For example, the social studies teacher can ask questions in recitation which help pupils see the relationships which exist among certain facts and assist them in drawing valid generalizations from discrete bits of factual information instead of having them routinely recite esoteric and unrelated facts they have learned.

Unit Method. Spawned by disenchantment with the lecture-listen method in which the teacher was dispenser of knowledge and the students were passive listeners, and with the assign-study-recite-test approach where pupils frequently read, recalled and regurgitated facts, progressive-minded educators began to extol the merits of and practice the unit method in organizing teaching and learning situations in the elementary school shortly after the turn of the century.[23] What these educators were seeking was a way of organizing for teaching and learning which was more nondirective on the part of teachers and involved the children in such processes as planning what was to be studied, choosing appropriate activities, and evaluating learning outcomes. The unit method met these requirements.

Broadly classified, there are two types of units in the elementary school. They include the *subject matter* and *experience* units. The former is one in which the substantive content to be learned and the learning activities for pupils are directly related to a certain core of knowledge of a subject-matter field. The latter is a series of learning experiences for pupils which are developed in terms of extant student needs and interests. The subject-matter unit, therefore, stresses content and the development of cognitive skills while the experience unit places emphasis upon meeting the expressed needs and purposes of the learner. The clear distinction between these unit approaches to organizing the teaching and learning situations in the classroom has been made by the work of Mehl, Mills, and Douglass which appears in figure 4.1.

As one can infer from a perusal of figure 4.1, the subject-matter unit approach for managing the teaching and learning situation is congruent with the society-oriented curriculum discussed previously in this chapter. Also, one can infer rightly that the experience unit method is more in keeping with the child-centered curriculum orientation. The discipline-centered orientation to curric-

---

23. For a thorough discussion of unit teaching in the elementary school, see Lavone A. Hanna, et al., *Unit Teaching in the Elementary School* (New York: Holt, Rinehart and Winston, Inc., 1963).

ulum development represents an eclectic midpoint position with respect to unit teaching between the polar positioned subject-matter and experience units. That is, when the new discipline-oriented curricula, e.g., science and social studies units, are taught in the elementary school, the units are substantively oriented with respect to content to serve societal ends but many of the required and optional learning activities are more child-centered and have been planned in terms of known student interests and needs based upon commonly accepted principles of child growth and development.

Obviously, there are various teaching strategies that can be used in unit teaching such as explanation, induction, or deduction. These strategies are discussed in chapter 21 which treats classroom management.

Variant Curriculum Patterns

Since there are eighteen or more separate subjects or activities which may be included in the elementary curriculum, it is important to understand how the curriculum can be organized or designed so that teaching and learning can take place. Generally, the curriculum can be organized on a *subject, fused,* or *experience* pattern basis. A discussion of the organizational options concerning curriculum patterns is given in the following paragraphs.

Characteristics:	*Subject-Matter Unit*	*Experience Unit*
Selected by:	Teacher	Teacher and child
Purposes are:	Based upon textbook or course of study	Teacher's and child's
Plans are developed:	According to textbook	By teacher preplanning and children and teacher filling in details as unit grows
Source of content for unit is:	Textbook	Life experiences and content areas, such as social studies, etc.
Source of information is:	Textbook	Books, periodicals, community, experiences, etc.
Learning is directed toward:	Mastery of facts	Needs and interests of children and well-adjusted child
Learning experiences are:	Formal	Varied and many
Tools of learning are mastered:	Through relatively meaningless drill	Through meaningful drill and through use in solving significant problems

Fig. 4.1. Schema Contrasting Subject-Matter and Experience Units. From Marie A. Mehl, Hubert H. Mills and Harl R. Douglass, **Teaching in Elementary School**, 2d ed. (New York: Ronald Press Company, © 1958), p. 170.

Subject Curricular Patterns. When the curriculum is organized on a subject basis, the central idea is that each subject has a logic and unique organization of its own. Advocates of the subject curriculum believe that the major means to education accrues through a systematic study of the various subject fields which can be understood and mastered by the pupils. Hence, the subjects become the organizing basis of learning experiences for children.[24]

There are three distinctly different types of subject curricular patterns. These patterns include: (1) subjects-in-isolation, (2) correlated subjects, and (3) scientific subjects. Let us briefly examine the distinguishing characteristics of each.

SUBJECTS-IN-ISOLATION. A graphic portrayal of the subjects-in-isolation curriculum pattern can be seen in figure 4.2. The pattern was the first to be developed in the nation and it has many identifying characteristics. First, each subject or activity area has its own daily time period. Second, each of these areas is considered to be an entity of itself; no attempt is made to correlate or integrate learnings among the subject areas in terms of the design of the curriculum pattern. And, third, the daily schedule becomes quite rigid and unbending.

CORRELATED SUBJECTS. During the decade 1910-20 many teachers employed the correlated subjects approach to curriculum design or organization in an attempt to overcome the shortcomings of the subjects-in-isolation curriculum. The major purpose for the change to the correlated subjects design was an attempt on the part of teachers to relate the content among the various subjects for children in their graded classrooms. That is, reading materials were selected from the content fields of science, history, or geography; words for spelling were taken from subjects such as geography or arithmetic; and children wrote themes and gave oral reports in language classes from history and other subjects.[25]

Attempts at correlation were further enhanced by the manner in which the courses were sequenced. For example, if one were studying in the correlated curriculum about the history of the new world, he would also study simultaneously the geography of the new world—not the geography of the old world which might exist under the subjects-in-isolation.

It should be pointed out, however, that correlation does not reduce the number of subjects that are taught in any classroom at any grade level. Also, each subject has its own time allotment the same as in the subjects-in-isolation design.

SCIENTIFIC SUBJECTS. The scientific subjects *design is one in which* the content of the various subject fields is organized in terms of the logical ordering or structuring of each academic discipline included in the curriculum. The structuring of the content is done further in terms of what has been learned from the scientific studies of the social utility of the content and the ways in which children learn the subjects.[26] For example, the new discipline-centered curricula of the social sciences have eliminated much of the useless content of the tradi-

---

24. Hollis L. Caswell and Arthur W. Foshay, *Education in the Elementary School,* 3d ed. (New York: American Book Company, 1957), p. 258.

25. William B. Ragan, *Teaching America's Children* (New York: Holt, Rinehart and Winston, Inc., 1961), p. 103.

26. Caswell and Foshay, *Education in Elementary School,* p. 258.

understanding curriculum patterns

tional fused social studies textbooks. Furthermore, teachers have altered their methods of instruction from an overdependence on the older methods of lecture-listen and assign-study-recite-test to the unit approach in which they teach largely by induction placing great emphasis upon the processes of learning. Although most teachers still use the subject-matter or experience unit methods in teaching the new discipline-centered social science curricula daily during a specific period, the content and teaching procedures are quite different from that used in the traditional subjects-in-isolation and correlated subjects curricular designs.

The scientific subject design stresses the persistent themes and principles of each subject field so that the children can obtain a knowledge of the structure, outline or wholeness of each discipline which, in turn, will provide a framework for them whereby they can relate and organize their future

1. Arithmetic
2. Art
3. Assembly Programs
4. Civics
5. Geography
6. Handwriting
7. Health
8. History
9. Homemaking
10. Industrial Arts
11. Language
12. Music
13. Opening Exercises
14. Physical Education
15. Reading
16. Science
17. Special Interest Clubs
18. Spelling

——————— Grades 1 through 6 or 8 ———————

Fig. 4.2. Graphic Portrayal of a subjects-taught-in-isolation Type of Curriculum. From Henry J. Otto and David C. Sanders, **Elementary School Organization and Administration** 4th ed. (New York: Appleton-Century-Crofts, 1964), p. 49. Reprinted by permission of Appleton-Century-Crofts, Educational Division, Meredith Corporation.

66 understanding curriculum patterns

learning in each subject field.[27] This is in sharp contrast to other subject curriculum designs in which children are confronted with learning by rote much unrelated information of questionable value.

Fused Curricular Patterns. It is basically impossible to escape some fragmentation of learnings among the subject fields in the subject curricular patterns previously discussed. In an effort to provide more unity or wholeness among the learnings in the various subject areas, many teachers have employed fused curriculum designs such as the *broad fields* and *core* patterns in recent years. Also, these fused curriculum designs contribute towards more flexibility in daily scheduling of curricular experiences for children. Let us briefly examine the broad fields and core patterns.

BROAD FIELDS. The broad fields curriculum design is a plan in which related subjects are grouped together into large blocks of time for teaching and learning. As examples, the broad fields of language arts might consist of learnings in reading, English, spelling, handwriting, speaking, and listening; the broad fields of social studies might consist of fused learnings drawn from history, geography, political science, economics, anthropology and sociology.

A graphic portrayal of the broad fields curriculum design is set forth in figure 4.3. From a study of it, one can determine that the teacher would have far fewer time periods daily than would obtain under the subject curricular designs. Also, it is easy to infer from studying the figure that the teacher and children would likely be able to relate the learnings within the various broad fields areas to a greater extent than they would under the more traditional subject curricular patterns.

Language Arts	
Social Studies	
Arithmetic	
Science and Health	
Physical Education	Creative and Recreative Arts
Music	
Art and Handicraft	

⟵——— Grades 1 through 6 or 8 ———⟶

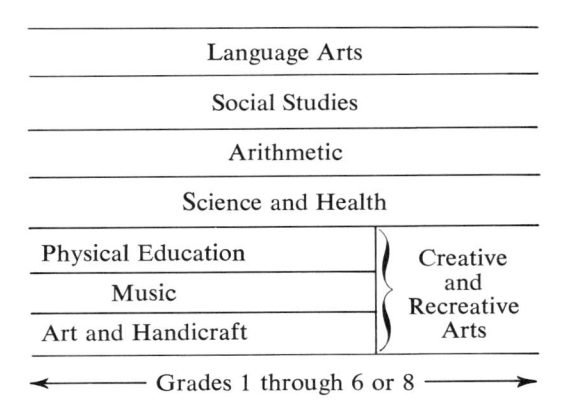

Fig. 4.3. Graphic Portrayal of a Broad Fields Curriculum Design for Elementary Schools. From Henry J. Otto and David C. Sanders, **Elementary School Organization and Administration,** 4th ed. (New York: Appleton-Century-Crofts, 1964), p. 52. Reprinted by permission of Appleton-Century-Crofts, Educational Division, Meredith Corporation.

CORE. A fused curricular pattern in which one large block of time is provided in the daily schedule wherein the language arts are integrated into the social studies program is known as the core curriculum design.[28] Or, as an alternative, the social studies can be integrated into the language arts. A graphic portrayal of the former is set forth in figure 4.4.

Much of the instruction done in the core is on a unit-of-work basis. Teachers who follow this plan can correlate the teaching and learning in the separate subjects of the noncore area with that of the unit-of-work being done in the core area wherever possible. The noncore subjects, as a general rule, are taught on a separate subjects basis.

27. Elsbree, McNally and Wynn, *Elementary School Administration,* p. 91.
28. Jarvis and Pounds, *Organizing, Supervising and Administering,* p. 51.

understanding curriculum patterns

1. Arithmetic
2. Art
3. Assembly Programs
4. Health
5. Homemaking

The Core: consisting of
History-civics-geography-literature
or
Social Studies
or
Social Studies-Science combination including full integration of reading, language, handwriting, and spelling.

6. Industial Arts
7. Music
8. Opening Exercises
9. Physical Education
10. Special Interest Clubs

⟵————— Grades 1 through 6 or 8 —————⟶

Fig. 4.4. Graphic Portrayal of a Core Type of Curriculum. From Henry J. Otto and David C. Sanders, **Elementary School Organization and Administration,** 4th ed. (New York: Appleton-Century-Crofts, 1964), p. 51. Reprinted by permission of Appleton-Century-Crofts, Educational Division, Meredith Corporation.

Experience Curricular Pattern. In an effort to break away from the subject curricular patterns and their basically subject oriented counterparts—the fused designs, teachers in the 1920s began to employ the *experience* or *activity curriculum pattern.* This movement was sparked by an attempt to more adequately provide for the learners' unique differences, purposes, interests, and needs. It also represented an attempt to make the daily schedule of learning activities more flexible.

Basically, the entire instructional day is employed to pursue studies about problems of living that are of immediate interest to the children when the experience curriculum pattern is used as figure 4.5 shows.[29] Much use of the *experience unit,* discussed earlier in this chapter, is employed to provide the unifying structure for the problems of living the pupils wish to study. For example, if the students want to learn why they should respect property rights, they will disregard the subject area boundaries in the experience curricular pattern and draw con-

29. For a thorough treatment of a type of experience curriculum known as "Persistent-Life-Situations," see F. B. Stratemeyer, et al., *Developing a Curriculum for Modern Living,* 2d ed. (New York: Teachers College, Columbia University, 1957).

68   understanding curriculum patterns

tent from any subject field such as history, geography, science, and arithmetic. Too, they will select stories for reading which bear upon the problem, write themes about property rights and the like. No specific time is provided in the daily schedule for separate subjects so that the purposes of the individual learners can be met.

In the experience curriculum, therefore, the problems of living which the children want to study are the unifying structure whereas the unifying structure for the subjects and fused curricular patterns is basically the taxonomic ordering and fleshing out of content of the separate subjects—the former being child-centered—the latter society-centered. On the one hand, the pupils and teacher jointly plan what they will study and learn. On the other hand, the teacher primarily decides what will be covered.

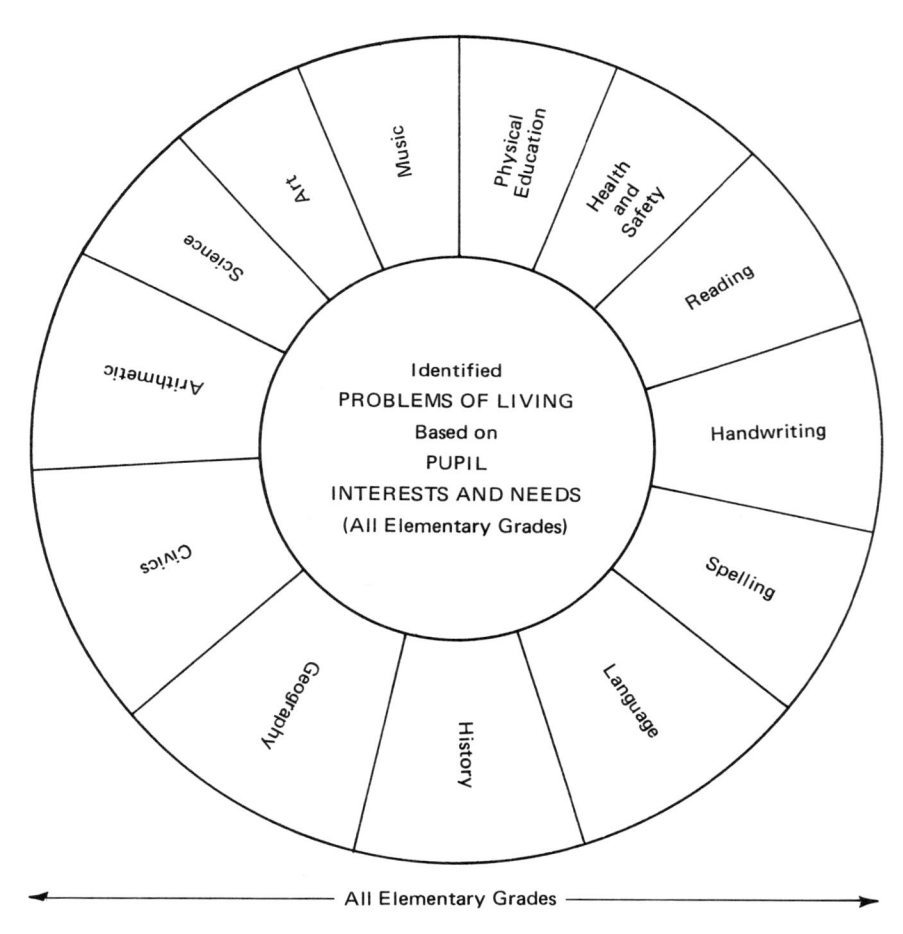

Fig. 4.5. Circle Graph Portraying the Experience Curricular Pattern. From Oscar T. Jarvis and Lutian R. Wootton, **The Transitional Elementary School and Its Curriculum** (Dubuque, Iowa: Wm. C. Brown Company Publishers, 1966), p. 76.

The experience curriculum has been used sparingly in America's schools. Most teachers employ one of the subject or fused curricular patterns.

Organizing the Daily Schedule. Obviously, the daily classroom schedules for the subjects, fused and experience curricular patterns will vary considerably. On a continuum which ranges from the rigidly set schedules of the subjects curricular design to the flexible schedule of the experience curriculum organization, these differences are easily discernible as figure 4.6 clearly shows. For example, the daily schedule of the subject patterns is divided into many separate periods daily—the end result being that it becomes rather inflexible or rigid. On the other hand, the experience design has large blocks of time daily which are quite flexible with respect to allocation of time usage.

The amount of time allocated for teaching the separate subjects or broad fields areas varies somewhat, depending upon each individual teacher. Some school systems allow each teacher to decide how much time to allocate while others prescribe time allotments by board policy.[30] A representative time allotment schedule, as practiced in the Houston (Texas) school system, is set forth in figure 4.7.

Principles for Organizing the Curriculum

Several different factors which impinge on the overall organization of the curriculum have been discussed in the preceding sections of this chapter. As a result, some of the principles of curriculum organization which logically follow are subsequently discussed.

1. AS A FIRST PRINCIPLE OF CURRICULUM ORGANIZATION, ONE MUST DECIDE ON THE CURRICULUM'S MAJOR THRUST OR ORIENTATION. For example, will it be child-centered, society-centered, or discipline-centered.

2. ONCE THE BASIC ORIENTATION HAS BEEN SETTLED, THE OBJECTIVES OF THE CURRICULUM MUST BE STATED SO THAT THEY ARE CONGRUENT WITH THE CURRICULAR ORIENTATION. That is, if the curriculum were society-oriented, the curricular objectives should be spelled out in behavioral terms which are ideally suited to equip children for effective living in adult years.

3. WHO PLANS THE CURRICULUM IS RELATIVE TO THE ORIENTATION OF THE CURRICULUM AND THE SETTING OF CURRICULAR OBJECTIVES. To illustrate, if the curriculum orientation were child-centered and the curricular objectives were specified accordingly, the teacher and children would plan the day-to-day curriculum experiences in terms of the immediate interests and needs of the learners.

4. THE PATTERN OR DESIGN OF THE CURRICULUM SHOULD BE INTERNALLY CONSISTENT WITH THE CURRICULAR ORIENTATION, OBJECTIVES, AND PLANNING PROCEDURE. That is, the design of the curriculum harmonizes these separate, yet related, aspects of curriculum. For example, if the orientation of the curriculum were child-centered with concomitant objectives and if the teacher and children jointly planned the daily teaching-learning situations, the curriculum design would have to be, quite obviously, the experience pattern. In this instance, disharmony and a lack of internal consistency would prevail if the design were, for example, subjects-in-isolation.

30. Stuart E. Dean, *Elementary School Administration and Organization* (Washington, D.C.: U.S. Department of Health, Education, and Welfare, Office of Education, 1960), p. 52.

VARIANT CURRICULAR PATTERNS

SUBJECT PATTERNS	FUSED PATTERNS	EXPERIENCE PATTERN
Subjects-In-Isolation Correlated Subjects Scientific Subjects	Core Broad Fields	Child-Centered

CORE

	Subject Patterns		Core / Broad Fields		Child-Centered
8:30- 9:00	Opening Exercises	8:30- 9:00	Opening Exercises	8:30- 9:00	Opening Exercises
9:00-10:00	Reading	9:00-11:30	Social Studies (The core of social studies, i.e., history, geography, and civics, will be fully integrated with the study of language arts, i.e., reading, handwriting, spelling and language.)	9:00-10:15	Interdisciplinary study as planned by pupils and teacher on "problems of living"
10:00-10:15	Handwriting				
10:15-10:30	Spelling			10:15-10:45	Physical Education
10:30-11:00	Physical Education			10:45-12:00	Interdisciplinary study as planned by pupils and teacher on "problems of living"
11:00-11:30	Language				
11:30-12:00	Science & Health	11:30-12:00	Physical Education		
12:00-12:30	Lunch	12:00-12:30	Lunch	12:00-12:30	Lunch
12:30- 1:30	Arithmetic	12:30- 1:30	Arithmetic	12:30- 3:15	Interdisciplinary study as planned by pupils and teacher on "problems of living"
1:30- 2:15	Music (M.W.F.) Art (T.Th)	1:30- 2:15	Music (M.W.F.) Art (T.Th)		
2:15- 2:45	History	2:15- 3:15	Science and Health		
2:45- 3:15	Geography				
3:15- 3:30	Daily Evaluation	3:15- 3:30	Daily Evaluation	3:15- 3:30	Daily Evaluation

BROAD FIELDS

8:30- 9:00	Opening Exercises	
9:00-11:00	Language Arts	
11:00-11:30	Physical Education	
11:30-12:15	Creative Arts (Music M.W.F.) Art (T.Th)	
12:15-12:45	Lunch	
12:45- 1:45	Arithmetic	
1:45- 3:15	Social Studies or Science and Health Unit Study (These areas will be alternated every 2 to 3 weeks or on a semester basis)	
3:15- 3:30	Daily Evaluation	

Fig. 4.6. Typical daily classroom schedule under different curricular patterns. Adapted from Oscar T. Jarvis and Lutian R. Wooton, **The Transitional Elementary School and Its Curriculum** (Dubuque, Iowa: Wm. C. Brown Company Publishers, 1966), p. 79.

understanding curriculum patterns

5. THE DAILY SCHEDULE FOR TEACHING SHOULD BE COMPATIBLE WITH THE CURRICULUM DESIGN. If the design of the curriculum were subjects in isolation, for example, the daily schedule should be divided into many separate periods daily.

An Appraisal of Alternative Curriculum Patterns

The literature on curriculum patterns and organization is characterized by an absence of research studies. There is little data for evaluating the relative claims of superiority made by the various curriculum advocates. There are several reasons for this. In the first place, there is no universal agreement as to what learning outcomes should be. Where the learning outcomes are somewhat different for the various forms of curriculum patterns, the question is not primarily one of difference in curriculum organization but difference in learning objectives. The question of curriculum superiority may not be subject to research proof or disproof, but may be a question of value orientation.

A second reason is the lack of agreement as to what constitutes curriculum organization. If there were agreement as to learning outcomes, the intraschool variability of curriculum organization and differences in teaching style would not make possible the comparison of different curriculum patterns. The experimental variables could not be sufficiently controlled, and the causal relationship of the experimental variable to pupil learnings would be difficult to establish if, indeed, possible at all.

And, finally, there is the nested variable of language which is the primary means of school instruction, irrespective of the pattern of curriculum organization. With some exceptions in music, art, and physical education, the evidence for learning outcomes in elementary schools are invariably expressed through language.

Subject Area	Grade 1	Grade 2	Grade 3	Grade 4	Grade 5	Grade 6
Language arts	160-180 a day	160-180 a day	130-150 a day	130-150 a day	130-150 a day	130-150 a day
Mathematics	20-30 a day	20-30 a day	50-60 a day	50-60 a day	50-60 a day	50-60 a day
History and geography	...	...	50-60 a day	50-60 a day	50-60 a day	50-60 a day
Science	50-70 a week	50-70 a week	20 a day	20 a day	20 a day	20 a day
Art	40 a week	40 a week	50-70 a week	50-70 a week	50-70 a week	50-70 a week
Music	70-80 a week	70-80 a week	80-100 a week	80-100 a week	80-100 a week	80-100 a week
Health and physical education	150 a week	150 a week	150 a week	150 a week	150 a week	150 a week
Foreign language	...	...	60 a week	60 a week	60 a week	60 a week
Length of school day (including lunch time)	5 hours	5 hours	6 hours, 10 minutes	6 hours, 10 minutes	6 hours, 10 minutes	6 hours, 50 minutes

Fig. 4.7. Time Allocations by Subject and Grade as Practiced in the Houston (Texas) Public Schools. From "Instructional Time Allotment in Elementary Schools," memo 1961-29, p. 6. Reproduced by permission of the National Education Association, Research Division.

The usual way curriculum advocates attempt to establish a position is not by research or even reasoned scholarship, but by the straw-man technique of argument. In this technique, the advocates of a particular position, such as the experience unit, describe the alternate subject matter unit in the worst possible light, as seen in figure 4.1, which was presented much earlier in this chapter. Here every virtue is attributed to the experience unit, and every vice to the subject-matter unit. Depending on the abilities and philosophical orientation of the teacher, either approach might provide excellent or very poor learning for the pupils.

Over the years, the prevailing pattern of horizontal organization for instruction in the elementary classroom has been the self-contained classroom (see chapter 19). Where a teacher, by choice or school practice, follows a subjects-in-isolation curriculum pattern approach, there is nothing to prevent him from making the appropriate correlations in subject matter. The picture of a subject matter curriculum, which was seen in figure 4.2, being composed of wholly isolated subjects is a curriculum developers point of view, not necessarily that of the classroom teacher. Even where some departmentalization horizontally exists in the elementary school, the number of different teachers is rarely too large to permit some subject integration, if it is considered desirable. The fact is we have no standard for measuring the learning outcome, so we have been unable to ascertain—merely to claim—that a correlated, fused, experience, or some other unifying type of organization is superior to subjects-in-isolation.

Notwithstanding all the advocacy about various types of alternates to subject matter, textbook instruction, it is likely that, as a teacher, you will teach in a school where the textbook will continue to be a major learning resource for the pupils and an instructional tool for the teacher. It will be organized into units. The teacher's manual will provide you with many suggestions, e.g., pupil activities, use of various media, and field trips. The possibility of extending the textbook learnings by appropriate experiences will be limited primarily by the factor of time—you will be unable to do as much as you wish.

After reviewing the various positions taken by curriculum advocates, this chapter takes an eclectic position toward curriculum organization and emphasis. The virtue is not in a society or child-centered curriculum, or a subject-matter or experience oriented curriculum. It is in the combination of those elements which facilitate teacher instruction and pupil growth. While you may have time for the development of one or two teacher-initiated units during the year, it is likely that the demands for planning, teaching, and evaluating, not to mention the myriads of other activities associated with your role as a teacher, will prevent you from developing more. If the objective is pupil growth, not teacher-developed curriculum, does it really matter if the major resources for learning are not teacher-prepared? With few exceptions, we do not allot time in schools for teachers to write and develop curriculum materials, so why should it be expected of them? Furthermore, there is no evidence that pupils learn any more from materials developed by the teacher than from materials developed by a publisher or curriculum developer.

As a teacher, you will undoubtedly do a certain amount of planning with your pupils. This helps change the pace as well as provide for some desirable learnings on the part of pupils. Pupils learn to plan by planning. But you will also wish to keep in mind the schools global curriculum objectives and your specific teaching objectives so that the learning outcomes of your students will follow some kind of sequence and provide the needed knowledge and skill development.

The point here is that there is no inherent superiority in any one curriculum design. Some are more compatible with some teachers and school system traits than are others. It is possible that in a school there should be sufficient flexibility of curriculum design to meet the various preferences of teachers. This ideal generally cannot be accommodated, however, because *administratively* a school system requires uniformity. It requires uniformity for good management as well as record keeping. Within the limits of administrative requirements, however, you may select the type of curriculum design which facilitates your most effective teaching.

SELECTED REFERENCES

CLEGG, SIR ALEC. "What Is a Humanizing Curriculum?" *National Elementary Principal* 49, no. 4 (1970): 8-12.

CROSBY, MURIEL. *Curriculum Development for Elementary Schools in a Changing Society.* Boston: D. C. Heath & Company, 1964.

ELSBREE, WILLARD S., et al. *Elementary School Administration and Supervision.* 3d ed. New York: American Book Company, 1967.

FLEMING, ROBERT S., ed. *Curriculum for Today's Boys and Girls.* Columbus, Ohio: Charles E. Merrill Books, Inc., 1963.

FRAZIER, ALEXANDER, ed. *The New Elementary School.* Washington, D.C.: Association for Supervision and Curriculum Development and Department of Elementary School Principals, 1968.

GOODLAD, JOHN I. "Directions of Curriculum Change," *NEA Journal* 55, no. 9 (1966): 33-37.

HEDGES, WILLIAM D. "Will We Recognize Tomorrow's Elementary School?" *NEA Journal* 56, no. 9 (1967): 9-12.

JARVIS, OSCAR T., and WOOTTON, LUTIAN R. *The Transitional Elementary School and Its Curriculum.* Dubuque, Iowa: Wm. C. Brown Company Publishers, 1966.

KEITH, LOWELL. *Contemporary Curriculum in the Elementary School.* New York: Harper & Row, Publishers, 1968.

LEE, J. MURRAY. *Elementary Education Today and Tomorrow.* Boston: Allyn and Bacon, Inc., 1966.

MEHL, MARIE A., et al. *Teaching In Elementary School.* 3d ed. New York: Ronald Press Company, 1965.

MEIERHENRY, W. C. "Instructional Technology: Humanizing or Dehumanizing?" *National Elementary Principal* 49, no. 4 (1970): 23-28.

MICHAELIS, JOHN U. *New Designs for the Elementary School Curriculum.* New York: McGraw-Hill Book Company, 1967.

OLIVER, ALBERT I. *Curriculum Improvement: A Guide to Problems, Principles, and Procedures.* New York: Dodd, Mead & Company, 1965.

OTTO, HENRY J., and SANDERS, DAVID C. *Elementary School Organization and Administration.* 4th ed. New York: Appleton-Century Crofts, 1964.

RAGAN, WILLIAM B. *Modern Elementary Curriculum.* 3d ed. Holt, Rinehart and Winston, Inc. 1966.

SHUSTER, ALBERT H. *The Emerging Elementary Curriculum: Methods and Procedures.* Columbus, Ohio: Charles E. Merrill Books, Inc., 1963.

WOLF, WILLIAM C., JR., and LOOMER, BRADLEY M. *The Elementary School: A Perspective.* Chicago: Rand McNally & Company, 1966.

5 the pre-primary curriculum

In this chapter, *preprimary* is used to describe institutionalized learning outside of the home in nursery school and kindergarten. The term preprimary emphasizes the continuity of early learning experiences with primary training. The more conventional term *preschool* emphasizes a dichotomy in philosophy and procedures which may be wasteful of resources and contribute to poor learning habits which may hinder rather than facilitate learning in the primary grades.

The Preschool Curriculum

By the end of the century, kindergartens were to be found throughout the world. In recent years there has been an explosion in preprimary programs and attendance in the United States. In 1966, there were about 2.5 million children enrolled in kindergarten. In the following year, there were over 3 million children enrolled in preprimary programs, with 76 percent of five year old children in attendance. The preprimary program is generally thought of as consisting of two parts—nursery school, for children ages three and four; and kindergarten for age five. Children younger than age three are infrequently found in the public school except in day care centers. It is unfortunate that the term preschool became attached to the kindergarten program. Originally started as a private venture, the kindergarten gradually became a part of the public school system. Today, less than 10 percent of the kindergarten population are in private schools.

Major Influences on Preprimary Education

The new emphasis given to early childhood education, through Headstart and related programs of federally funded compensatory education, has stimulated a great variety of programs. A convenient place to explore this diversity is to identify four major movements which have influenced preprimary education in the United States: Froebel, Montessori, child development, and the rediscovery of poverty.

Froebel and Self-Development Through Play. Chronologically and practically, the major influence affecting early childhood education was that of the Froebelian kindergarten.[1] Froebel, like other educators of his day, was strongly influenced by both Rousseau and Pestalozzi. Both of these educators sought to make learning more natural and stimulating, drawing upon the capacity of the child to grow intellectually under guidance with his physical development. Froebel's contribution was not so much to theorize about the importance of self activity and the essential factor of play in child education, but to develop an applied curriculum with accompanying methods which could be borrowed and adapted. In 1837 Froebel opened the first kindergarten in Blankenburg, Germany. Twenty years later Elizabeth Peabody opened the first English-language kindergarten in the United States in Boston, Massachusetts.

While Froebel's own theory of the kindergarten reflected his pantheistic notions of the harmony of man with nature, it was not necessary for the practicing teacher to accept those ideas to see the utility in his program. The Froebelian "gifts"—a series of toys and apparatus designed to stimulate learning through directed play—have long since been abandoned, but the demand for toys-that-teach has increased rather than diminished over the years. The Froebelian spirit continues to dominate the theory of curriculum; it might be described simply as the organization of play-interests of children to further self-development and socialization. But the legacy of Froebelian practices remain, even when the preprimary teacher is unconscious of their origin. Today, preprimary children still form circles on the floor, share their experiences (show and tell), sing songs and move to rhythmic music, play various games to increase their powers of observation, engage in arts and crafts, and listen to stories. Two of the major differences today are greater emphasis on vigorous play and the decline in nature observation and gardening as useful activities.

But the influence of Froebel extended far beyond the preschool and influenced practices in the elementary grades. Although the lines of the progressive movement and developmental psychology converged in the 1920s, the Froebelian influence is still recognized in those curriculum plans which place an emphasis on the activity of the child rather than on the transmission of information.

Montessori and Self-Development Through Work. In 1907 in the slum quarters of San Lorenzo in Rome there was opened, in connection with a new housing development, a new type of school for children age three to six. The first *Casa dei Bambini* provided the children with a prepared environment which reflected the fundamental premise of the Montessori system; children educate themselves in the execution of tasks programmed to their level of conceptual and manipulative ability. The tasks are set by the various types of instructional devices which are self-corrective. A Montessori preschool contrasts sharply with the conventional preschool in a number of ways, but one of the most striking differences is the intensity of quiet concentration by the young learners.

The story of the origin of the Montessori system has been told in a highly readable and exciting fashion by Dorothy Canfield Fisher.[2] Just as one cannot understand the

---

1. Fridrich Froebel, *Pedagogics of the Kindergarten* (New York: D. Appleton Century, 1895).
2. *Montessori for Parents.* (Cambridge, Mass.: Robert Bentley, Inc., 1965 reprint of 1912 edition), chap. 15," Dr. Montessori's Life and the Origin of the Casa dei Bambini."

spirit of the kindergarten apart from the idealism of post-Napoleonic Germany, one cannot grasp the essence of the Montessori approach apart from the personality and work of *la Dottoressa*. The Montessori system, like that of Froebel, does not reflect merely some techniques of working with children; it reflects a philosophy of the nature of man and his organic development. Just as Froebel found a key in the organizing concept of play, Montessori found her key in the organizing concept of work, work not in the sense of an adult task, but the ability of a child to apply himself diligently to some exercise, such as that of filling a pail with sand, and repeating the behavior over and over again, oblivious of other distractions.

Maria Montessori was the first woman to receive a medical degree from the University of Rome, no mean achievement in the 1890s. After a period of successful private practice and work with the Psychiatric Clinic of Rome, she served as Director of the State Orthophrenic School, an institute for feeble minded. At a time when little distinction was made between the mentally deficient and the insane, Maria Montessori devoted herself wholeheartedly to her new task. She devised methods of teaching mentally deficient children which permitted them to pass the state examinations in reading and writing set for normal school children. If deficient children could be taught to perform in such a manner, she reasoned that there must be something wrong with the usual ways of teaching children.

In 1899 she began a period of protracted study and testing to develop a sequence of self-corrective learning tasks. She was particularly influenced by two French physicians, Itard and Seguin, whose work with mental defectives in the early nineteenth century are still landmarks in the treatment and study of mental deficiency. This resulted in the conceptualization of the *Casa dei Bambini*, a place where children learn in interaction with their environment. In today's terminology, a Montessori school is first of all a place to stimulate the self-discovery of children through the execution of prepared tasks. Before the learning-as-guidance movement in American education, Montessori had moved the teacher from the center of the stage and made her an assistant to children.

The Froebelian kindergarten was over a half-century old by the time Montessori had developed her system. The tremendous interest in the United States just before World War I appears to have been interrupted by the war and a reaction in American education to anything which smacked of regimentation. While Montessori schools were privately established, pure Montessori methods never became part of the main public school kindergarten movement. However, certain Montessori ideas have been assimilated in the American kindergarten. These range from such procedures as the responsibility of children for school housekeeping to individual methods. Many of the manipulative devices produced by American manufacturers are adaptations of Montessori instructional equipment. A revival of interest in Montessori methods however, occurred in the 1960s and is now the subject of additional research, especially for use with the disadvantaged.[3]

3. See, for example, Lawrence Kohlberg, "Montessori with the Culturally Disadvantaged," in *Early Education: Current Theory, Research and Action*, ed. Robert D. Hess and Roberta Meyer Bear (Chicago: Aldine Publishing Company, 1968), pp. 105-18; and Merle B. Karnes, *Research and Development Program on Preschool Disadvantaged Children* (Urbana, Illinois: Institute for Research on Exceptional Children, University of Illinois, 1969), pp. 52, 99, 145.

The Child Development and Child Guidance Movement. A third major influence in American preschool education has been the influence of developmental psychology. In contrast to the work of Froebel and Montessori, individuals who provided systems of instruction as well as a philosophy and psychology of learning, the developmental movement has involved many different descriptive and experimental studies which have influenced the total approach to early education rather than contributing any alternative systems of pedagogy. While early educators based their conclusions and methods on shrewd observations of child behavior, the emergence of the discipline of psychology laid the basis for a more scientific study of human behavior, in which experimental variables could be controlled and results stated quantitatively, even in the application of case methods and survey techniques.

In the field of human behavior, however, it is frequently difficult to separate the values and preconceptions of the researcher from his research activity. This is one of the reasons that so much educational research presents contradictory evidence and appears merely to bolster some empirical observation or practice.

The developmental movement has not been free from these limitations. While developmental psychology has generated a wealth of descriptive information about the sequence of physiological, motor, sensory, and language development, primarily in children from middle-class backgrounds, the interpretation of this research, as well as much of its conduct, has been in the polar dichotomies of maturation versus learning. The dominant view for a period of some forty years was maturational, a position which neatly accorded with the overworked analogy of the preschool teacher as a gardener.[4] The maturational point of view was accompanied by such limiting assumptions as fixed intelligence, predetermined development, static brain functioning, unimportance of early experiences before speech, emotional reactions to instinctual needs, and a nonintellectual approach to learning.[5] Child psychology became more than anything a child biology with descriptions of typical behavior that might be expected at various chronological stages. Intervention studies dealing with experiential learning variables were seldom conducted, and the work of the Child Welfare Research Station in Iowa in the 1930s, a worthy precursor to the National Laboratory in Early Childhood Education established in 1967, was largely ignored. If the process of development was maturational, then planned intervention was not only wasteful but harmful. The experts "warned parents not to overstimulate their infants but rather to leave them alone to grow."[6]

This line of interpretation merged with the Freudian emphasis on infantile sexuality and relative interpretations of cross cultural child rearing practices to justify a permissive approach to child rearing. The essence of this approach is to reify the needs of the child and to ignore the fact that socialization and learning takes place in the context of culture.

4. Neith E. Headley, *Foster and Headley's Education in the Kindergarten*, 4th ed. (New York: American Book Company, 1966), pp. 40-41.

5. J. McVicker Hunt, "The Psychological Basis for Using Pre-School Enrichment as an Antidote for Cultural Deprivation," in *Pre-School Education Today*, ed. Fred M. Hechinger (Garden City, New York: Doubleday and Company, Inc., 1966), p. 26. This essay summarizes some of the positions Hunt presented in more detail in his monograph *Intelligence and Experience* (Garden City, New York: The Ronald Press Company, © 1961).

6. Hunt, *Intelligence and Experience*, p. 348.

This emphasis in child development had two interesting developments. It tended to separate the kindergarten from any continuity with school experiences, and it helped to develop the nursery school as part of the American preschool scene. The need to have children available for systematic scientific study led many universities to establish nursery schools as observational laboratories. Nursery schools were also established to provide girl college students with an opportunity to observe child growth and development as part of their training as future mothers, frequently as part of their training in home management. The development of the nursery curriculum was a result of the practical need to provide some kind of educational program for these young children in a laboratory setting, rather than the theory of maturation pointing toward a program of educational stimulation.

The Depression of the 1930s stimulated further nursery school development as nurseries were opened to provide work for unemployed teachers. Day nurseries were opened during World War II to provide an opportunity for mothers to work to meet manpower shortages. The cooperative nursery school movement reflects the effort to provide a parent-school partnership in child rearing. The nursery school is therefore an accepted part of the American educational scene, although it is largely privately operated except for special government and charitable efforts.

It may seem strange that little attention should be given to English influences on pre-primary education. The English infant school grew out of the eleemosynary work of Robert Owen at New Lanark, and through the work of Buchanan and Wilderspin infant education had become firmly established before Dickens introduced Froebel to England in 1854. The infant monitorial school, however, had no influence on kindergarten developments in the United States, and the kindergarten movement in the United States is a direct descendant of the Froebelian movement.

The first nursery school was established by Miss Margaret McMillan at Deptford, England in 1913. Originally, it was conceived as an alternative to the infant school, but soon developed the pattern of constituting a preinfant school for children two to five. Shortly after World War I, Americans became interested in English nursery school methods and procedures, which may be regarded as more liberal adaptations of the Froebelian kindergarten to younger learners. The rise of the English nursery school movement coincided with the general emergence of the field of child development and university-based child study centers. The English nursery school movement, therefore, lacked the clear-cut impact of earlier reformers. However, centers where English nursery school methods were introduced became leaders in nursery school education in the United States.

Rediscovery of Poverty and Early Educational Stimulation. The fourth major development in American preschool education is still very recent and still too early to assess its long-term impact. In 1964, the Economic Opportunity Act officially began the much heralded War on Poverty. One of the provisions of the act was Operation Headstart to provide entering first-graders an opportunity to make up for deficiencies in early background experiences. The first hastily organized programs in the summer of 1965 were a mixture of fervor and good intentions with a considerable lack of expertise. Since then, Headstart programs have been extended to include year-round programs, all-day programs, and prekindergarten or nursery programs. Dissatisfaction with Headstart under OEO management resulted in its transfer to the Office of Education in 1969.

The rediscovery of poverty and the relationship of early experiences to educational deprivation have given new emphasis to all phases of preschool education. But one of the most important trends has been a new emphasis of the utilization of preschool experiences to develop cognitive processes, an interest which the Sputnik blast-off in 1957 aroused in all aspects of American education. The work of Jean Piaget in intellectual development, neglected for almost thirty years, was rediscovered. While Piaget is a developmental psychologist, he had worked in an area which American psychologists and child development specialists had studiously avoided—the development of intellectual processes. Further consideration of preprimary as intellectual stimulation is postponed to chapter 23 dealing with the disadvantaged. For better or worse, the curricula of many kindergartens now not only include play and songs, but they also include formal, not simply incidental, lessons in language development, reading, and arithmetic. Throughout the preprimary years, more attention is being given to the structuring of learning to bring about specific learning outcomes.

The next section will give a brief overview of the preprimary curriculum.

Curriculum Strands in the Preprimary School

The tremendous differences in the performance characteristics and learning abilities of children of three and those of five make it difficult to generalize about the specific learnings and outcomes over this three-year age span. Three year olds will spend most of their time in play. Five year olds also spend most of their time in play if the curriculum has that emphasis, but by this age they are interested and willing to participate in more formal learning situations, despite an attention span which can be very brief or prolonged, depending on the nature of the activity. All of the activities briefly sketched in this section are used in both the nursery school and the kindergarten. However, there is a gradual increase in the task expectancies as children mature in age. Activity in the kindergarten, in contrast to that of three year olds, appears more productive and purposeful.

The preprimary curriculum attempts to bring to the child what any school curriculum seeks to achieve—a variety of experiences through which he may extend the learnings, social and intellectual, which were begun in the home. The focal point of the traditional preprimary program has been play. Most of this play is self-directed and spontaneous, utilizing the facilities provided. The play of the preprimary school, however, has a different connotation from home play. First, the environment provides a variety of alternatives through which play may be experienced. These range from playing with toys and blocks on the floor to play with animals or science apparatus. In this context, play really connotes an informal, child-centered learning situation in contrast to formal or task-centered learning. Second, there is generally some adult verbalization accompanying the play, to help the child associate verbal labels with objects or processes. While the amount of verbalization may be reduced, it is nevertheless an important part of the total learning environment.

In preprimary schools where the number of pupils is sufficiently large to have separate age groups for three, four and five year olds, age sectioning is often practiced. This permits scheduling in use of facilities as well as making adjustments in songs, stories, field trips, and other experiences so that the experience will be cumulative rather than repetitive. However, in Montessori-type preschools, where the emphasis is on the activities of the individual rather than on the group, multiage sectioning is practiced.

Health Care. The foundation of a good preprimary curriculum begins with adequate attention to the health of the children. It begins with a healthy physical environment, indoors, and out. The heating and indoor ventilation should permit sitting and playing on the floor without drafts and chills. Outside, an all-weather play area permits outside-activities the year round except in inclement weather.

Three year olds have often just been toilet trained, and toileting and washing loom as more important parts of the school day than with older children. Accidents will happen, but a straight-forward, matter-of-fact approach to man as an animal living in a cultured environment is probably as useful as any. A brief snack time for juice and cookies, followed by a brief rest or quiet period is provided in morning or afternoon programs which permit opportunities for other social learnings as well as mere feedings. In the day-care centers, the morning program may begin with breakfast, and a nap period is scheduled in the middle of the day.

Because of the susceptibility of young children to various health hazards, the teacher needs to be alert to symptoms of sickness. In day-care centers, the center may serve as a place for out-patient treatment for children requiring the attention of a nurse or doctor.

Play. The preprimary school provides a greater variety of play situations than are normally found in the home. Material and equipment are more abundant, although rarely meeting the variety and amount found in recommended lists.[7] And the child interacts with different playmates as his interests shift. A key to child development in play is the aparatus available.

Three types of play may be identified—active, manipulative, and quiet. Active play, both indoor and out, requires equipment for large muscle development, such as climbing, pulling, pushing, pedaling, balancing, running, jumping, lifting, throwing, and hauling. Outdoor play is too often neglected because of an inadequately surfaced and equipped play yard, something which even children from well-to-do suburban homes often lack, not to mention the child apartment dweller. When conditions do not permit outside play, vigorous types of activities may be planned for inside use, such as dancing, marching and running in place, crawling through barrels, even where there is no gym or large playroom available. A planned sequence of activities involving

---

7. Suggested lists of equipment and materials are given in most general texts on nursery and kindergarten education, such as: Jerome E. Leavitt, ed. *Nursery-Kindergarten Education* (New York: McGraw-Hill Book Company, Inc., 1958), chap. 12, "Plant and Equipment," pp. 268-95, or Headley, *Foster and Headley's Education,* pp. 95-126. Periodically revised lists may be obtained from the Association of Childhood Education International, Washington, D.C.

movement exploration suitable for indoor and outdoor use has been developed by Gober.[8]

Manipulative play involves beads, pegs, puzzles, sewing cards as well as nuts and bolts, screws, nails and hammers, and similar activities requiring coordination. The hardware store carries a cheaper line of smaller but durable tools, and is a neglected source of educational equipment.

Quiet play takes place on the outside as well as on the inside. Sand and water offer endless sources of pleasure to the young child, although requirements of cleanliness in a three hour program often discourage their use. Among popular quiet indoor activities are dressing up, playing house, and playing with blocks and small toys.

Language Development. Prior to the mid-sixties, little attention was given to language in the pre-school program. When it was referred to, it was invariably mentioned merely as a developmental characteristic. The work of Basil Bernstein in particular, has made educators more conscious of the importance of the relationship of limited language to all types of performance, not just cognitive. Pre-primary programs for the disadvantaged frequently name language development as a specific objective, although informal methods predominate, such as singing;[9] association with sensory experiences,[10] "sharing" or more extensive experiences with telephone conversation, dramatic play, food talk at snack time, extension of basic vocabulary development, listening and speaking activities using records and tapes and stories and talk with preschool staff.[11] Other programs make the focus of the program verbal communication and vocabulary development through assignment to sub-groups known as discussion-and-activity groups.[12] Few programs have utilized the direct verbal instruction developed by Bereiter and Engelman for kindergarten children, although their original kindergarten included some four as well as five year olds.[13] Irrespective of whether formal or informal methods are used, the teacher is expected to elicit more verbal behavior from the child. The child must not merely hear stories and talk to his playmates; he must be required to use language which will increase his perception of the real world and his capacity to deal with the world symbolically.

Reading: Books and Picture Books. Children's literature has become an educational specialty. Opinions about the suitability of books and stories are almost as varied as there are authors. One only has to compare Read's[14] stricture of *Little Black Sambo* with Arbuthnot's[15] adulatory critique to see

8. Billy Gober, *Pre-primary School Physical Education Through Movement Exploration*, mimeographed (Athens, Ga.: University of Georgia, Research and Development Center in Educational Stimulation, September 1969).

9. *Infant Education Research Project, Washington, D.C.*, Pre-School Program in Compensatory Education, Office of Education, OE-37033.

10. *Project Early Push, Buffalo, New York*, Pre-School Program in Compensatory Education, Office of Education, OE-37055.

11. *Early Childhood Project, New York City*, Pre-School Program in Compensatory Education, Office of Education, OE-37027.

12. *Pre-School Program, Fresno, California*, Pre-School Program in Compensatory Education, Office of Education, OE-37034.

13. Academic Pre-School, Champaign, Illinois, Pre-School Program in Compensatory Education, Office of Education, OE-37041; C. Bereiter and S. Engelman, *Teaching Disadvantaged Children in the Pre-School* (Englewood Cliffs, New Jersey: Prentice-Hall, Inc., 1966).

14. Katherine H. Read, *The Nursery School*, 4th ed. (Philadelphia: W. B. Saunders Company, 1966), p. 72.

15. May Hill Arbuthnot, *Children and Books*, 3d ed. (Chicago: Scott, Foresman and Company, 1964), p. 336.

that in material for young readers there can be considerable difference in likes. These likes are most often described as needs and interests of the young child. Adults write books for children, select books for children, and read and tell stories to children. Most of the time children appear to be interested in whatever the story is about, but an uninspired delivery can make even *The Three Billy Goats Gruff* as deadly as reading the telephone book. Children do not tire nearly as quickly of repetition in stories as the adult reader does, and, in fact, frequently enjoy the anticipatory response which familiarity brings.

The preprimary school should have an interesting book corner with a variety of books. Not too many should be displayed at a time; it is better to change the collection periodically than have all books available at one time. Picture books can be informational as well as fanciful. All experiences for children cannot be concrete, and much of the world of the child can expand only through language and the substitution of pictures.

In selecting stories for reading, a good rule of thumb is for the teacher to pick out books which he enjoys. Delivery is often more important than substance in maintaining interest. The stories read can often be used to extend vocabulary and dramatic play. Children may also verbalize their own interpretations. Many excellent guides for selecting books are available in addition to anthologies.[16]

Music and Songs. Singing, moving rhythmically, creating rhythms on musical instruments, listening to music, and making up musical jingles and rhymes are all parts of the music program. Singing is frequently emphasized not only for its own sake, but for the contribution it makes to language development. Songs and music may also be used not only for musical self-expression and pleasure, but to reinforce some other learning of the school day, such as a playground activity, a field trip, dramatization, or simulated work.

Preprimary teachers probably have more difficulty with singing than with any part of the school program. It is desirable that the teacher be able to play the piano, or at least to have some person available for playing the piano. Although the latter limits the flexibility of music in the program, this is a better alternative than trying to teach children to sing without a piano. The excellent record collections, such as the series *Exploring Music*[17] make it possible for the nonplaying teacher to provide the needed music for a quality program.

Development in the area of music and singing requires more structuring on the part of the teacher than do art and play activities. The words as well as the music must be taught, a repertory of rhythmic patterns elicited by the teacher, and the use of percussion and other musical instruments demonstrated. As with any other aspect of the curriculum, it is not possible to have every kind of musical experience every day or even every week. During the course of the year, however, the cycle of activities should include music for singing, music for listening, music for dramatization and movement, and music for playing, with music appropriate to holidays and other special occasions. The general references cited

16. Among these are *Bibliography of Books for Children* of the Association for Childhood Education International, and *Books of the Year* of the Children's Book Committee of the Child Study Association of America.
17. (New York: Holt, Rinehart, and Winston, Inc., 1966).

in this chapter contain extended discussions of music in the nursery program, and give extensive lists of suggested music materials. A 1960 work by Paul R. Mathews[18] provides helpful suggestions to teachers who are not specialists in music.

For the preprimary teacher, there are many practical collections of songs suitable for young children, general[19] and special for rhythms and action.[20] Many teachers develop their own collections, based on their personal likes and those of their children. Listening to music for the sake of music, however, is a liking that needs to be cultivated. If music is used too much as an accompaniment to some other activity, children may acquire the idea that music is merely a background, not to be enjoyed for its own qualities.

The relationship of the typical preprimary and elementary programs in music to the development of musicality has been questioned.[21] Part of this may result from the fact that there is less music experience in fact than in theory. There is often a hiatus in the primary program where there are no trained music teachers and the emphasis shifts to verbal subjects. Simons has suggested a more sequential approach to teaching music in the preprimary years.[22]

Art. One of the most tangible evidences of preschool growth is the ability of the child to give form and expression to his ideas and images through art. It also provides a convenient way of sharing with parents concrete examples of the youngster's behavior and growth.

A great variety of materials are sometimes included in the category of art, from building blocks to hammering with wood. Here art will be used in relation to experiences with paints, crayons, collages, papier-maché, clay, salt paste, and similar materials used in graphic and sculptural presentation.

The focus in using all of these media is on the child's own expression of creativity, and is not product or skill oriented. Generally, the child is provided with the media, simple instructions are given as to their use, and nonevaluative encouragement is given by the teacher. Patterning and modeling are discouraged, and coloring books and precut pasting are anathematized. The nondirective nature of the art program reflects the dominant maturational approach, with the expression of artistic creativity following certain stages, such as manipulative, early symbolic, later symbolic, and transitional. From this point of view, there is much talk about the need for art experiences, but very little attention to any sequencing of procedures which might facilitate art learning.[23] Sensory experiences are emphasized as a prerequisite, but the relationship of art to language is deemphasized. Art is treated es-

18. *You Can Teach Music,* rev. ed. (New York: E. P. Dutton and Co., Inc., 1960).

19. Lorrain E. Watters, *The Magic of Music: Kindergarten* (Boston: Ginn and Company, 1965); Adeline McCall, *This is Music for Kindergarten and Nursery School* (Boston: Allyn and Bacon, Inc., 1965).

20. Lois Lunt Metz, *Action Songs and Rhythms for Children* (Minneapolis: T. S. Denison and Company, Publishers, 1962); idem, *Hop, Skip, and Sing* (Minneapolis: T. S. Denison and Company, 1959).

21. U.S. Department of Health, Education and Welfare, Office of Education, *Music in Our Schools: A Search for Improvement,* Bulletin no. 28, OE-33033 (Washington, D.C.: Government Printing Office, 1964).

22. Gene M. Simons *et al., Music—A Structured Program,* mimeographed (Athens, Ga.: University of Georgia, Research and Developmental Center in Educational Stimulation, Stage 1, August 1969, Stage 2, February 1970).

23. See, for example, Herbert J. Burgart, *Creative Art: The Child and The School,* rev. ed. (Athens, Ga.: University of Georgia Press, 1964).

sentially as a nonverbal medium which language might inhibit or discourage.[24]

More recently, however, increased attention has been devoted to the sequencing of experiences, while recognizing that any progression from scribbling to symbolism will vary with individuals. Planning a scheme of media use and sequencing experiences gives a greater variety and depth to the child's artistic growth.[25] The verbal cuing which often accompanies a child's creative activity may be capitalized upon through language cuing to enhance visual perception.[26] The use of verbal cues may be used to extend a child's visual perception of real objects and his production of color, texture, pattern, variety, and composition.[27] While these methods are normally associated with primary and intermediate age children, the technique has been adapted for use with preprimary children.[28] Another adaptation for the preprimary years has been art appreciation through discovery.[29]

Most of the books on the teaching of art in the elementary grades contain selections on preprimary art. The art of entering first graders who have not had previous learning experiences is often not as developed as with children who have had previous opportunity to work with different media. The former have not had an opportunity to learn, and this is a clear indication that even in young children art is not merely a matter of exterior symbolization of covert feeling but is also a matter of learning.[30] Because of its concrete nature, the art program in the preprimary years is one of the most rewarding to teacher and pupil alike. Where art programs are the major components of remediation efforts for the disadvantaged preprimary childern, however, the results are disappointing.[31] This does not result from defects in art so much as it is an overgeneralized expectancy of development in art transferring to other areas of growth.

Science and Social Studies. The young learner has a natural curiosity as he seeks to understand the world in which he lives. But this curiosity is not very productive unless it is associated with an attempt to give meaning to the child's experiences through language. The purposes of the science and social studies program in the preprimary years are to make children more perceptive of natural and social phenomena, and to understand simple relationships. Wherever possible, experiences should be made concrete, in order for the child to associate actual phenomena with the word labels which permit him to think symbolically.

24. Helen Heffernan and Vivian Edmiston Todd, *The Kindergarten Teacher,* rev. ed. (Boston: D. C. Heath and Company. 1960), p. 258.

25. Kay Melsi, *Art in the Primary School* (Oxford: Basil Blackwell, 1967).

26. Phil H. Rueschhoff and M. Evelyn Swartz, *Teaching Art in the Elementary School* (New York: Ronald Press Company, 1969).

27. Frank Wachowiak, *Emphasis: Art* (Scranton, Pa.: International Textbook Co., 1965).

28. Robert Kent et al., *An Introductory Sequential Art Curriculum,* Parts 1 and 2, mimeographed (Athens, Ga.: University of Georgia, Research and Development Center in Educational Stimulation, September 1969).

29. Robert Kent, *Art Appreciation Through the Discovery Method,* mimeographed (Athens, Ga.: University of Georgia, Research and Development Center in Educational Stimulation, December 1968).

30. Earl W. Linderman and Donald W. Herberholz, *Developing Artistic and Perceptual Awareness* (Dubuque, Iowa: Wm. C. Brown Company Publishers, 1969).

31. See, for example, *Project Early Push, Buffalo, New York,* Pre-School Program in Compensatory Education, Office of Education, OE-37055.

At one time there was primary emphasis on the activity, with a tendency to de-emphasize verbal explanations by the teacher.[32] While there is agreement that firsthand experiences are all important, there is a new understanding of the importance of language for acquiring information[33] and providing the cognitive referents for further thought.[34] This means that the questions asked by the teacher not only supply correct terminology, but also help students to see cause and effect relationships.

In this section, science and social studies are treated together for a number of reasons. Many of the activities in which the child engages may be utilized for both science and social learnings. At this early level, the purpose is not to treat phenomena in the organized categories of disciplines, but to provide the child with an expanding and accurate knowledge system to which he can relate future experiences. Thus, a field trip to a dairy processing plant may be used for such different learnings as the relationship of pasteurization to health (bacteriology), automation of bottling process (technology), collection of milk from multiple producers (raw material supply and processing), and retailing of bottled milk to home consumers and stores (market distribution and demand). This does not mean that a unit on rain, using an actual rainy day as a take-off point for an examination of this natural phenomenon, might not be primarily concerned with naturalistic explanations. But it can also be used as basis for making social connections, as the consequences of flooding or the lack of rain to land use and cultural systems.

In addition, many science-related phenomena are maintained as part of the school apparatus. These include animals, fish, plants, rock and other collections. The extent to which animals are merely around as pets or used for science teaching depends upon the structuring the teacher gives to the learning experiences.

Work with animals is generally appealing to young children. Besides the emotional satisfaction from contact with pets, animals provide an opportunity to learn in a simple and matter-of-fact way aspects related to birth and death, the habits of animals, and the similarities and differences in the continuum of animal and human behavior. The characteristics of particular plants are not only individually interesting, but provide the basis for directed observation about the relationship of plant life to the total ecological system.

Phenomena which occur in the natural environment provide some of the most useful bases for scientific learnings. These include such forces of nature as air, wind, clouds, precipitation, electricity and magnetism, soil and erosion, and solar energy and seasonal changes, sound, and light. Mechanical phenomena may be explored through blocks, levers, pulleys, weight, motion, wheels, ramp, and friction. The technological characteristics and productive efficiency of tools and machinery are often neglected, but are a useful component for children who must live in a machine culture.

Most science teachings in the preprimary years, as social studies learnings, are adaptations of the primary program, and preprimary teachers will find these references

32. Denise Farwell, "Science and Social Science," in *Nursery-Kindergarten Education* Jerome E. Leavitt, ed. (New York: McGraw-Hill Book Company, Inc., 1958), p. 233.

33. Headley, *Foster and Headley's Education*, pp. 368-69.

34. Read, *Nursery School,* p. 72.

useful. It will be necessary, however, to make modifications, especially in the nursery school, due to greater differences in language development.

The usual approach to incidental science in the preschool years, like other traditional approaches, is now being questioned. According to Zeitler,[35] preprimary science experiences can be taught in an articulated, sequential manner which stress scientific behavior consistent with the capabilities of children of ages three, four, and five. The program is highly perceptual; however, children investigate, manipulate equipment, and test their ideas as they move through the program. An alternative approach now being investigated is the integration of three recent science curriculum studies—"Science, A Process Approach;" "Elementary Science Study;" and "Science Curriculum Improvement Study"—into one science program beginning with children age four. Modifications are necessary but the teaching content is the same. Teachers also have available a variety of commerical programs, which vary from a few experiences with the senses to a completely organized program.

Comparatively speaking, the quality of material for preprimary science instruction is superior to that for social studies instruction. This results from the fact that a natural phenomenon lends itself much more readily to acquisition of insights. In contrast, the explanations which make social phenomena meaningful are usually symbolic and abstract, and regarded as beyond the capabilities of the very young. Hence, social studies often becomes little more than a series of visits, real or vicarious, to certain institutions in which there is merely a simple description of activities with no attempt to relate them in a meaningful way to broader social concepts. Often suggested social studies learnings dealing with the home, grocery store, gas station and other such social phenomena appear to add little to what the normal child acquires, both in terms of experience and symbolic relationships, in the normal process of rearing.[36]

A number of more abstract verbal units in the social studies have been developed at the kindergarten level at the University of Georgia by the Anthropology Curriculum Project[37] and the Geography Curriculum Project[38] directed by Rice. Although the organization of these various units is somewhat different, they share in common the premise that the cognitive interests and capacities of young learners have been underestimated and that more distant and abstract phenomena are of interest to young learners. Although field trial of these units has generally substantiated the assumptions of the Anthropology[39] and Geography[40] projects, the more formal nature of these

35. W. R. Zeitler, *Pre-Primary Science Program*, mimeographed (Athens, Ga.: Research and Development Center in Educational Stimulation, University of Georgia, 1969).
36. See, for example, Heffernan and Todd, *Kindergarten Teacher*, pp. 138-47.
37. Anne Hunt, Jean Blackwood, and Frances Emmons, *Concept of Culture: An Introductory Unit* (Athens, Ga.: Anthropology Curriculum Project and Research and Development Center in Educational Stimulation, 1968). Teacher Manual, publication no. 51; Pupil Activity Book, publication no. 51a.
38. William A. Imperatore, *Earth: Man's Home: A Beginning Geography Unit* (Athens, Ga.: Geography Curriculum Project, 1968). Teacher Manual, publication 1A: Pupil Workbook and Pictorial Test, publication 1BC.
39. Anne Johnson Hunt, "Anthropology Achievement of Normal and Disadvantaged Kindergarten Children" (doctoral diss., University of Georgia, 1969).
40. William A. Imperatore, "Evaluation of a Conceptual Geography Unit for Kindergarten." Geography Curriculum Project (doctoral diss., University of Georgia, 1969).

units is not generally accepted by most preprimary teachers who still reflect the incidental learnings approach to outcomes of the preprimary curriculum.

The supply of picture books and simple informational books in science and the social studies suitable for the preprimary years is almost unlimited. Information books should be a part of the preprimary library, whether housed in interest centers or in a section of the library area. Most of the filmstrips and other audio-visual material suggested for use in connection with science and social studies are materials originally developed for primary use. This is no limitation as to use, however, since the explanations are given in a simple fashion. The teacher may make the necessary verbal explanations. As a teacher develops a science and social studies sequence with respect to content and timing, he will also wish to develop his own file of flat pictures.

Field Trips. Field trips are frequently made in connection with science and social studies experiences. This time may therefore be convenient for the discussion of some fundamental procedures, irrespective of age level or subject area, which will make the field trip more meaningful.

It is convenient to think of the field trip as consisting of three distinct phases—briefing, execution, and debriefing. Briefing is the preparatory stage in which the trip is planned with the students. Things to look for should be carefully noted and the correct labels learned. When an appropriate filmstrip or pictures are available, these visual aids may be profitably utilized. From the standpoint of learning psychology, the briefing stage is one in which a perceptual cognitive set is developed. Older children may actually plan many of the mechanics of execution. (It may be appropriate at this stage to caution children about some of the odors or noises which they may encounter. Many a field trip to a barnyard has proved disappointing because the aversive reaction of children to manure and animal smells did not permit them to observe the work cycle.)

Safety precautions and requirements should be outlined during the briefing phase. These safety precautions should be made specific both as to mode of transportation and to the nature of the field trip. They may be reviewed just before embarking on the trip.

The execution of the field trip should focus on the major learnings and not the incidental learnings. If the trip is not conducted in a manner to meet the stipulated learning objectives, there is no way to measure its effectiveness. While children learn different things on a field trip—each learner brings to a learning task his own background—the purpose in having a field trip is to develop common learning outcomes.

The third phase of a field trip is debriefing. After the field trip, the experience is discussed in class, an experience chart developed, and other appropriate activities are engaged in, such as locating the place on a map, drawing a picture, or making up a story. Often thank-you letters are written. The field trip is sometimes used to initiate a new learning activity and the debriefing sets the stage of transition to acquiring additional information from books and other sources. The debriefing activities help tie in the concrete experience to abstract symbols and generalizations.

Any community, large or small, is a teaching resource frequently recommended but infrequently utilized. Some places are just too dangerous to take children and there is also a limited amount of time which can be devoted to extended field trips requiring transportation. Theoretically, the most profitable field trips in science and social studies are those devoted to the introduction of major and continuing ideas. As an actual fact, however, preprimary children will be excited about a visit to a fire station and somewhat mystified by a visit to a garbage landfill. The fire station experience is exciting and concrete; on the other hand, the landfill only provides an unpleasant olfactory stimulus; the social learning is embedded in the abstraction of social organization.

Field trips are difficult at best. The sheer mechanics of shepherding three- and four-year-olds frequently counsels the most ambitious teacher to leave them to the safety of the play yard.

Mathematics. Concepts of space and quantity are fundamental understandings prerequisite to comprehension of both natural and social phenomena. Many of these concepts are taught incidentally in connection with other activities—counting numbers in stacking blocks, learning numerals with the days on the calendar, measurement of volume in the sandpile with units of different size, using rulers and yardsticks to measure the children's heights, the area needed to play in, or the height of the slide. As with other areas of learning, however, the relations must be put into words and made explicit; they are acquired in learning situations, and are not inferred merely from the opportunity to use different sets or items which reflect different mathematical properties. Among some of the space and number relations suitable for preprimary development are: using money; age, house and telephone numbers; numerals on clocks; calendars, scales, rulers; use of form puzzles to manipulate geometric variations; and matching sets.[41] Generally speaking, however, there is less emphasis on space and number relations in preprimary programs than on almost any other type of learning. In the 1950s, references to number relations in books were often simply omitted[42] or briefly treated as a foundation for first-grade learning.[43]

The decade of the 1960s found an increased interest in mathematical learning among young children as a by-product of the increased American interest in the work of the Swiss psychologist Piaget. Among Piaget's many facets of interest in logical thought processes was that devoted to the developmental processes relating to conservation of number, relations, length, and other mathematical properties. Preprimary mathematics units, such as that developed by Carey and Steffe,[44] not only teach young children mathematical ideas but teach these ideas in the context of mathematical thinking. The work of Carey and Steffe suggests the importance of establishing at an early age certain relationships explicitly through

---

41. Office of Education, *Educating Children in Nursery Schools and Kindergartens,* Bulletin OE-20054 (Washington, D.C.: Government Printing Office, 1964), pp. 40-43.

42. See, for example, Leavitt, *Nursery-Kindergarten Education.*

43. See, for example, Headley, *Foster and Headley's Education.*

44. Russell L. Carey and Leslie P. Steffe, *An Investigation in the Learnings of Equivalence and Order Relations by Four- and Five-year Old Children,* Research Paper no. 17 (Athens, Ga.: Research and Development Center in Educational Stimulation, December 1968). Appendix 2 of this publication contains the instructional units dealing with length comparisons and conservation of length relations.

concrete manipulation and verbalization to facilitate understanding of numbers and measurement.

The traditional type of mathematics learning in the kindergarten, however, is usually an extension of the readiness activities typical of the first months of the first grade.

Teaching Reading as a Skill. It has been repeatedly demonstrated that children younger than age six can be taught to read. Conventional preprimary programs typically exclude formal teaching of reading, although some incidental skills, such as letter recognition, may be acquired incidentally or as part of language arts activities. The research of Durkin has dispelled the assumption that early reading is harmful.[45] A longitudinal study has demonstrated that students in the middle grades who learned to read in kindergarten maintained their reading superiority where there was an adjustment in the reading program, but that initial advantages were lost when no adjustment was made.[46] However, teaching of reading in the first grade continues to be the division of labor that sets off the preschool world from the school. The orthodox preprimary view asserts that although children can be taught to read earlier, they should not be taught.

Assumptions about the cruciality of the early years have nevertheless raised questions about the possibility of early reading and its effect upon intellectual development. Preprimary reading is now found in two extreme types of programs—compensatory education and middle class suburban. Among the planned programs to stimulate early reading is the sequence developed at the former Research and Development Center in Educational Stimulation at the University of Georgia.[47] Preprimary programs which move in the direction of greater cognitive emphasis frequently find that the learning interests of children shift from exclusively oral interests to reading interest. Preprimary reading will be discussed in more detail in the chapter on reading.

Socialization. The preprimary, like any other organization for training the young, performs a dual function. On the one hand it serves as a means for stimulating the development of the intellect; on the other it serves as an agency of socialization. Typically, any group socializes its members through informal rather than formal means, and for this reason this important idea is not subsumed under social studies with which it is frequently identified. The organization and management of the preprimary rather than any formal curriculum, are the vehicles through which socialization takes place. The pattern of adult behavior with children, shown in the organization and management structure, in turn, reflects the values of the culture, which are often contradictory. Thus it is expected that the young child become self-reliant and at the same time work cooperatively; be an individual and yet share in the responsibilities of the group; work and play alone and yet work and play with others; share use of the school property and equipment but protect his own property; defend himself and not be aggressive. The

45. Dolores Durkin, *Children Who Read Early* (New York: Teachers College Press, Columbia University, 1966).

46. Paul McKee and Joseph E. Brzeinski, *The Effectiveness of Teaching Reading in Kindergarten* (Denver: The Denver Public Schools and the Colorado State Department of Education, 1966).

47. Robert L. Aaron and George E. Mason, *Language Arts and Verbal Learning Program: part 2. Introductory Exercises in Reading; part 3, Introductory Exercises in Writing* (Athens, Ga.: University of Georgia, Research and Development Center in Educational Stimulation, 1968).

very process of putting children into a group creates behavioral problems of insecurity, isolation, hostility, aggression, rivalry, and other types of conflict and tension. Much of the energy of the teacher is directed toward creating the social environment in which positive growth takes place, friendships are created, and a sense of group solidarity emerges.

One of the great contradictions in the American child literature is the parallel emphasis on permissive self-development and working in a group. In practice, the individual teacher and his interactions with the children of a particular group create the social climate of the classroom in which socialization takes place. Thus, the preprimary learning environment epitomizes the personality and character of the teacher more than any other subsequent stage in group training. This results largely from the fact that much of the significant preprimary learnings take part in interaction with adults, in the course of which the task resolution is subordinate. In the voice and gesture of the teacher who sets goals, offers encouragement, proffers guidance, and makes admonitions are embodied one of the means by which norms of the culture are imparted to the young. In turn, the peer group at any age acts as a means of socialization, for children also interact and learn from children.

Among the social learnings are recognizing limits, setting and following procedures, observing rules, sharing responsibilities, carrying out obligations, and participating in common work tasks. Thus the routines of good housekeeping not only provide a safe environment and facilitate learning, but are beginning ways of learning how to live in the social order.

Children are quick to perceive differences in talk about desirable democratic values and the actual behavioral patterns in the group structure. One of the dichotomies in American culture today is the verbalization of democratic ideals without structuring in the schools the behavioral context in which such ideals must function. To help make real the objective of democratic equality in a multi-ethnic society, it is incumbent upon the schools to structure multi-ethnic groups, and not take refuge in defensive values such as the neighborhood school. The place to provide for socialization in democratic behaviors is in the preprimary school and at home.

Health and Safety. The survival of the species depends upon the survival of the young. Every culture attempts to protect its young from harm. Three ways, common to all cultures, are to provide supervision, to keep harmful things away from the child, and to provide powerful taboos which protect the child. Contradictory as it may sound, cultures institutionalize the sentiment of fear as a protective device for its young members for their own safety.

In addition to a healthful environment and proper medical supervision, the preprimary ritualizes certain health care habits which are important to personal health, and for group acceptability. These include washing hands, brushing teeth, combing hair, wearing proper clothes, and other aspects of grooming. Other helpful habits may be talked about and demonstrated, such as getting enough sleep and eating proper foods.

A technological society offers special hazards to the young child. Hazards involving fire, guns, moving vehicles, power machinery, and electricity must be emphasized in addition to the potential dangers of medicines, poisons, and cleaning agents. Even the air, water, plants and animals which surround children in their every day living may be potential dangers. Every year many children die from playing in old refrigerators or putting plastic bags over their heads. Some of these health and safety understandings may be taught in connection with the science program and the use of school and playground equipment. But the desired outcome of the science program is knowledge, whereas the objective of the safety program is to routinize positive and aversive behaviors which are helpful to the health and safety of the child. These include commonplace amenities of socialization such as sharing and taking turns but which also may serve as important survival traits.

Time Schedule in the Preprimary Program. A variety of combinations in use of time may be followed to encourage different experiences which stimulate both social and intellectual growth. While most programs are kept fairly flexible, some structuring is nevertheless important to provide for both good management and sequencing of experiences.

In preprimary programs where the staff is responsible for both morning and afternoon groups, it is common to have programs of two-and-a-half hours. Allowing for arrival and departure time before and after the set periods requires a total of six hours. In those programs which are offered only in the morning, it is not unusual for the length to be three hours. Additional variations are found where three-year-olds come twice a week, alternating with four-year-olds who attend three days a week, while five-year-olds attend daily. The program for three-year-olds is largely devoted to free or guided play activities, with the amount of teacher direction increasing with the age of the child and more definite outcomes anticipated, as in the kindergarten year.

In those preprimary programs which function as day centers, the enlarged amount of time requires a greater variety of activities and time allocations for feeding and sleeping.

A three hour program for four-year-olds might have elements of the following:

8:45- 9:00	Pupils arrive. Free quiet play or self-selected activity.
9:00- 9:10	Good morning circle. Group singing and rhythms or group discussion.
9:10- 9:30	New concept learning from science or social studies.
9:30-10:00	Vigorous play (outside, weather permitting).
10:00-10:10	Toilet and wash hands.
10:10-10:20	Snack of juice (milk) and crackers.
10:20-10:30	Rest.
10:30-11:00	Art, craft, or other quiet play activity. May alternate with dancing and singing.
11:00-11:20	Outside play (weather permitting); toilet and wash.
11:20-11:40	Story or Music.
11:40-11:50	Clean up.
11:50-12:00	Dress.
12:00-12:15	Children Leave.

Cooperation With Parents. In the preprimary years, parents are more involved in the care and rearing of children than in later years. In the biological and social dependency of the child on his parents lies the basis of preprimary school and parent cooperation. This school-parent cooperation may be either formalized or rather informal. In cooperative preprimary programs, parents sometimes serve as members of the teaching staff, under the direction of the lead teacher. Cooperative programs frequently involve parent education sessions, in which parents study together such matters as child care and learning. Discussion with parents serves as an informal means of reporting to parents on their child's growth. The degree of parent involvement in any preprimary program depends upon the interests of the parents and the work styles of the teachers.

Summary. Preprimary programs are now regarded as desirable experiences for young children. Programs with different emphasis, reflecting differing points of view pertinent to desirable learning experiences for children, are available. Most preprimary programs continue to emphasize a fairly permissive play environment, although there is increasing emphasis on cognitive development through more structured programs in the kindergarten years.

An Appraisal of Preprimary Programs

A more extensive appraisal of preprimary programs will be made in chapter 23—"Culturally Disadvantaged." It should nevertheless be noted here that there is little articulation today between preprimary and primary experiences. The available evidence does not show that traditionally operated preprimary programs, with their emphasis on incidental learning in connection with play, contribute to any long-term advantage in school. By the end of the first year, the advantages which preprimary students hold over first year starters have largely washed out. The case for increased learning in the school years is not substantiated. This may result from the failure to dovetail preprimary and primary programs in such a way that the learning of the primary grades would be sequential rather than repetitive; early advantages are simply not maintained through additional learning. The traditional American programs, however, rest their claims on contributions to child development rather than to some subsequent advantage in schooling. The more recent claims to the importance of early intervention follow a different rationale.

By way of contrast with European schools, American preprimary programs, except for kindergarten, do not enjoy comparable public support. In England the infant school begins with children of five years of age. The impact of Froebel and Montessori on the English infant school was to liberalize the beginning years of school from the formal methods of instruction rather than to develop new frontiers in child education.[48] Nursery programs have more extensive public support on the Continent. This reflects in part the influence of socialism and recognition of the need to provide working mothers with more wholesome care facilities for their children than were available through private efforts alone. While nursery education is not universal, it is more generally accessible in Europe to parents who need or desire this type of education.

In recent years perhaps no country has placed such an emphasis on preprimary education as the USSR, where a sequential curriculum under government auspices has been prepared for children from two months to

---

48. P. B. Ballard, ed. *The Practical Infant Teacher* (London: New Era Publishing Co., Ltd., n.d.), i, 5, gives a contrasting picture of an Infant Class, Oratory School, Chelsea, in 1905 and 1925.

seven years of age.[49] However, in rural areas preprimary education is almost entirely lacking, and even in Moscow only about 50 percent of the children of kindergarten age are enrolled in preschool programs. The major outlines of Soviet preschool education parallel those in western countries. There are two important differences, however, which stand in marked contrast to the American kindergarten. In the American preprimary program, there is such an emphasis on child self-direction and permissiveness that the old concept of manners or etiquette with respect to correct behavior toward one's elders has almost completely disappeared. In contrast, it would seem that these are regarded as desirable traits which are to be developed in the Soviet preschool. In the American preprimary program, there are vague statements about democratic values and democratic living, but the emphasis is child-centered. Patriotism and citizenship are somewhat remote, and national holidays and birthdays of famous Americans as the entry point into our historical heritage are not emphasized. The Soviet preschool program, however, is definitely slanted to the context of the Soviet system. The making of good Soviet citizens begins in the preschool.

These differences do not mean that the conception of the Soviet preschool system is superior to that of the United States. It may be that in our preoccupation with the child we have overlooked the fact that any child must always be reared in the context of a particular culture, usually the culture into which he is born. A comparison of preprimary practices in the United States with other countries serves as a useful reminder that while there is a commonality in preprimary procedures, because of the biological nature of humanity, there are also differences which reflect the values of a culture. In the past four decades these values have reflected, in the name of psychology, a maturational view of child development. In the coming decades it will be necessary to emphasize the cultural view that patterns of behavior are learned. From this fusion might develop a greater articulation between preprimary and primary schooling and a greater sense of purpose in the continuity of learning.

As a prospective teacher, you will wish to review the opportunities for teaching young children. Many teachers find work with preprimary children exceptionally rewarding. From the professional standpoint, the lack of emphasis on subject matter does not make the work less demanding. The personal, emotional, and behavioral problems of young learners in their first steps away from home require not only a respect for young learners but many different abilities in working with children. As you explore both the historic and contemporary literature on early childhood education, both in the United States and abroad, you will become more deeply aware of different points of view and similarities in child education theory and practices. You will want to broaden your horizon by looking at child rearing practices in nonwestern countries which do not share common cultural roots with the United States and which are quite different in their assumptions about life and death. These, in turn, have different implications relating to the nature of man and the rearing of the young.

Even male teachers are now looking more

49. Educational Testing Service, *Soviet Pre-School Education* (New York: Holt, Rinehart and Winston, Inc., 1969).

closely at early childhood education. They are not, however, breaking new ground. As we have seen, the early infant educators were men—Buchanan, Wilderspin, and Froebel.

As you look toward your own teaching career, you will want to know more about early childhood education, even if you do not teach the preprimary years. You will want to know simply because you cannot be a good primary or intermediate grade teacher if you do not know how your teaching fits into the child's previous experiences.

SELECTED REFERENCES

Educational Testing Service. *Soviet Preschool Education.* New York: Holt, Rinehart and Winston, Inc., 1969.

FROEBEL, FRIEDRICH. *Pedagogics of the Kindergarten.* New York: D. Appleton Century, 1895.

HEADLEY, NEITH E. *Foster and Headley's Education in the Kindergarten.* 4th ed. New York: American Book Company, 1966.

HEFFERNAN, HELEN, and TODD, VIVIAN EDMISTON. *The Kindergarten Teacher.* Rev. ed. Boston: D. C. Heath and Company, 1960.

HUNT, J. MCVICKER. *Intelligence and Experience.* Garden City, New York: Ronald Press Company, 1961.

HUNT, J. MCVICKER. "The Psychological Basis for Using Pre-School Enrichment as an Antidote for Cultural Deprivation," In *Pre-School Education Today.* Edited by Fred M. Hechinger. Garden City, New York: Doubleday and Company, Inc., 1966.

LEAVITT, JEROME E., ed. *Nursery-Kindergarten Education.* New York: McGraw-Hill Book Company, Inc., 1958.

LINDERMAN, EARL W., and HERBERHOLS, DONALD W. *Developing Artistic and Perceptual Awareness.* Dubuque, Iowa: Wm. C. Brown Company Publishers, 1969.

Montessori For Parents. 1912; reprint ed. Cambridge, Mass.: Robert Bentley, Inc., 1965.

READ, KATHERINE H. *The Nursery School.* 4th ed. Philadelphia: W. B. Saunders Company, 1966.

the primary school program

6

Two terms are used throughout the world to denote fundamental education below the secondary level with an emphasis on the basic skills—primary, as in England, and elementary, as in the United States. In the historical development of the elementary school, a distinction was made in the grades where English grammar was emphasized, roughly equivalent to the intermediate grades, and the label primary applied to the lower grades which taught reading. Eventually, primary and grammar grades were placed under a single management with a vertical curriculum, and the present elementary school developed.

Today separate primary schools are rare, and primary most frequently is used to refer to grades one through three or four, and includes preschool grades when attached to the school. One of the recent developments is the revival of the years of the grammar school in age if not in emphasis, and is the subject of the next chapter, "The Intermediate School." This kind of organization naturally implies the existence of "The Primary School" with a distinct spirit, purpose, and organization, and is the subject of this chapter.

History of the Primary School

There is no adequate history of the development of the primary school in the United States;[1] the most adequate documentation available is for primary schools in Boston. Here early childhood education began at the age of four as a part of the public school system, some forty years before the first English-speaking kindergarten was opened in Boston in 1860 by Miss Elizabeth Peabody. The primary schools reflect an English tradition of social amelioration; the kindergarten, German idealism. Since the kindergarten and early childhood education movement presently enjoy popularity, it is significant that the primary school was originally conceived to serve the very purpose for which kindergartens are advocated today—to facilitate the learning of poor children.

In the early nineteenth century in Boston, children were not admitted to the public school until they had learned simple read-

1. Adolph E. Meyer, *An Educational History of the American People,* 2d ed. New York: McGraw-Hill Book Company, 1967, p. 441.

ing.[2] As a result, most poor children were never qualified for admission, since they were not taught at home and the colonial dame school system had collapsed. The moving reform spirit was Elisha Ticknor, a former principal of the Free Grammar School, who as early as 1805 began calling the attention of his friends to the neglect of the education of young children, especially among the poor. At the June 11, 1818 meeting of the Boston select-men, two years after Robert Owen opened his Infant School at New Lanark, $5,000 was voted for the education at public expense of children four to seven years of age. In 1818-19, eighteen infant schools were established. Ten years later the number had increased to fifty-six schools with an enrollment of over three thousand children. Eventually, the name was changed to primary.

The curriculum of the primary school consisted of easy reading, spelling, nature study, introductory writing, and singing. The teachers were all female, in contrast to the prevailing practice of male teachers. There were two yearly promotions to the grammar school, in April and in October, on certificate by the principal of the grammar school, who conducted examinations in simple reading, spelling, and punctuation.[3]

Management of the primary schools was separate from the grammar schools. Originally entrusted to a Primary School Committee of 36 members, the number was subsequently increased to 72. While the primary schools in Boston enjoyed a substantial development under this arrangement, there was growing concern about the separate organization and lack of articulation with the grammar school. The grammar principal examined for promotion, but he had no supervision over the primary curriculum. In the school reorganization of 1854, the separate Primary Committee was abolished, and management was entrusted to the City Board of Education. Finally, in 1866, almost forty years from the establishment of the first primary schools, the city regulations were amended to provide that the grammar school principals should also act as principals of the primary schools within their respective districts, allotting time as necessary to secure the best interests of the pupils.[4] This arrangement combined uniform supervision with small schools which pupils could attend in their own neighborhood.

Another change was made in the age of admission of the primary schools in 1862-63, when the school entering age was changed from four to five years of age. This was primarily done to reduce the pressure on facilities and teachers, which did not expand with the increase in population, but the argument was also advanced that children spent too much time working at unhealthy tasks and did not have enough time for play. This attitude may reflect both a formalization of the primary program, and the influence of the new kindergarten movement.[5]

2. Very young children frequently attended school with their older brothers and sisters in rural areas, where there was a common lament that they were the cause of much disturbance. "Hints" concerning the teaching of infants included the provision of lower benches and work suited to them, such as healthful and pleasant exercises singing of hymns and moral songs, study of natural history and other useful objects, writing and drawing, and the use of milder discipline See *Connecticut Common School Journal* 1, no 1 (August 1838): 3; Ibid., no. 2 (1 September 1838).
3. Ibid., 3, no. 12 (May 1, 1841): 156.
4. *Thirty-first Annual Report of the Massachusetts Board of Education* School Committees' Reports (Boston: Wright and Potter, 1868), p. 17
5. *Twenty-sixth Annual Report of the Massachusetts Board of Education,* School Committees Reports (Boston: Wright and Potter, 1863), p. 8

From Boston the primary school movement spread rapidly to other parts of the country, and was especially strong in New England. The first Infant School was established in New York in 1827, and in 1830 the name was changed to Primary Department. Where possible, these departments were combined with existing schools of the Public School Society. In 1832 it was decided to replace the Lancastrian monitorial schools with primary schools, modeled on the Boston plan.[6] In 1833 an Infant Model School was established in Philadelphia. In 1836, after a committee visit to schools in New York and Boston, 26 primary schools were established in place of the juvenile monitors of the Lancastrian system. In 1837 there were 60 primary schools in Philadelphia.[7]

In Boston, the primary school was a new creation; in other parts of New England, it took over the functions of the old dame school; and in cities such as Philadelphia and New York, it replaced the existing monitorial schools.

But the primary schools were not simply ABC schools, as were the older dame schools. They reflected a new conception of a curriculum for young children, as indicated in the recommendations of the Board of School Visitors of Hartford.[8]

First. Primary Schools to be located in different parts of the district for young children, where all the arrangements of the school room, the playground, and the exercises shall be adapted to promote the health, manners, moral culture, and the gradual and harmonious development of the young. The alphabet, easy lessons in reading, oral instruction in respect to real objects, maps, and figures, habits of observation, vocal music, and drawing on the slate would form the course of instruction for these schools.

They are to be taught by females, and we would add, they should be under the supervision, in part at least, of the mothers of the district.

Everywhere the curriculum emphasized, "real objects and visible illustration" and a deemphasis of lessons in books. Equally important was the health, manners, and the habits of the primary child.[9]

American historians give credit to the formation of primary schools in the United States to the English Infant School movement,[10] the founders of which were Robert Owen, James Buchanan, and Samuel Wilderspin.[11] James Buchanan was selected by Robert Owen to teach in the infant school of New Lanark, which opened in 1816. Here there was an emphasis on order, cleanliness, and kindliness, and the curriculum consisted of childish games, dancing, stories, and lessons consisting of conversation and talk based on pictures and field trips. ". . . there was nothing formal, no tasks to be learned, no readings from books."[12] Owen and his Quaker partner William Allen disagreed on the informal curriculum, especially dancing. In 1824 changes in curriculum were forced on Owen, and he resigned from active management. The Owenite school, imaginative and radical for its day, was over.

6. Ellwood P. Cubberley, *Public Education in the United States* (Boston: Houghton Mifflin Company, 1934), pp. 140-41.
7. *Connecticut Common School Journal* 4, no. 1 (December 1, 1841): 16.
8. Ibid., p. 6.
9. Ibid., p. 14.
10. Cubberley, *Public Education,* p. 137-38; Meyer, *An Educational History,* p. 145.
11. W. A. C. Stewart and W. P. McCann, *The Educational Innovators* (London: Macmillan & Company, 1967), pp. 53-74, 241-67.
12. Robert Dale Owen, *Threading My Way* (London: Trübner, 1874), p. 90, cited in Ibid., p. 67.

Expansion of the infant school movement in England depended first on philanthropic support and encouragement. James Mills, leaders of a group of Whigs and Radicals, were concerned in the post-Napoleonic period with the problem of delinquency in young children and the lack of suitable educational arrangements. In 1818, two years after the opening of the New Lanark school, they brought (with Owen's encouragement) James Buchanan to Brewer's Green where he conducted a school until 1839. While Buchanan developed many new and appropriate methods for working with young children, he was a very self-effacing person. As a result, his informal methods, so like those of Pestalozzi, failed to gain wide attention.[13]

Wilderspin was quite the opposite of Buchanan. While Owen was the philosopher and Buchanan the first teacher, Wilderspin was the great popularizer of infant schools, to which he devoted his life from 1820 to his death in 1866. He used his experiences at Spitalfields, to which he was brought in 1820, to systematize the process of infant education, and, largely due to his efforts, infant education received an enthusiastic reception and has since remained a part of the English system of public education. In less than fifteen years over 2,000 infant schools were established.

Wilderspin developed many ways of working with children in a simple and concrete fashion, particularly devising various types of apparatus to stimulate the use of the senses. Thus large blocks with letters were used in teaching reading, pictures in science, and the arithmeticon, a special counting device of his invention, for the teaching of arithmetic. Although the conventions of the regular day school eventually reduced many infant school procedures into parrot-like repetition, the original conceptions, worked out independently, are Pestalozzian in character. The formalization of infant procedures did not result from Wilderspin's methods, but the inevitable tendency in an institutional setting for more formal and rote methods to replace those which attempt to develop the growth of the child, through the use of the senses, did inevitably develop.[14]

The lack of American professional journals in education prior to the middle of the 1830s makes it difficult to document the impact of Owen and Wilderspin on American schools. General accounts of infant school practices in England, however, were published in the United States. One of these early reports included a description of the infant school at Spitalfields.[15] Wilderspin was a prolific writer, and set forth his conception of the infant school in a number of publications, particularly *The Infant System* which went through many editions.

The importance of the primary school does not depend so much on its origins— any country will adapt approved practices to its own particular needs. The development of early primary schools indicates that the attempt to find a more rational and appropriate means for educating very young children in the United States antedated the general establishment of public education and the kindergarten movement. Thus, early childhood education was conceived, from the beginning, as a public responsibility for the mass of children, and not as a privilege for a few. The primary school also

---

13. Stewart and McCann, *Educational Innovators*, p. 253.

14. Ibid., p. 267.

15. *Connecticut Common School Journal 2*, no. 14 (July 1840): 267-68.

avoided the philosophical and psychological discontinuity that the later kindergarten movement created, because the primary school was a school, although adjusted to the development of young children.

William Lowell, lecturing before the American Institute of Instruction in 1830, gave the following description of the infant school:

> A well-regulated Infant School furnished a happy contrast to the defects of the elementary school [i.e. the grammar grades]; it exhibits a spacious, airy, cheerful and comfortable apartment, prepared expressly for good influence on the infant being; a frequent change of attitude and employment; the presence of pictures and other objects as calculated to inspire the mind with activity and delight, or to diffuse tranquility and tenderness of feeling; mental employments interspersed with appropriate juvenile exercises, or judicious intervals of entire rest; lessons adapted to the capacities and desires of infancy; mental exertion rendered agreeable and voluntary; discipline consisting chiefly of rational and affectionate measures addressed to sympathy and moral feeling, and, as far as practical, to reason, and turning upon the incidents arising from the pupils' intercourse with each other.[16]

The American concept of the infant school, later the primary school, thus lays an approach for the education of young children which unites useful instruction without the excesses of child-centered play which later came to dominate the kindergarten. This issue is one of practical utility today, as more and more states include children of less than six years of education in provisions for public support.

Historical Development of the Primary Curriculum

In the colonial period, the primary curriculum was mainly a language arts curriculum, with an emphasis on reading and religion, with some attention to writing and less to arithmetic.

By the first quarter of the nineteenth century, however, it was necessary to distinguish between the traditional curriculum, and the influence brought with the establishment of the infant schools, which later became the primary grades of the elementary school. The traditional curriculum continued the emphasis on the language arts, especially reading; good behavior, manners, and a secular morality replaced the religious emphasis; and arithmetic became for the first time a subject of major importance. The infant schools brought a less bookish emphasis; a methodology which utilized the senses and inductive reasoning; greater use of pictures and apparatus, and recourse to nature for science lessons; such diversions as songs, games, and play; and more attention to the health of the child. Since he was no longer conceived as a miniature adult, wayward and sinful, he could be treated in mind and discipline more for what he was, a person of tender years.

These innovations of the early primary schools rarely extended to the rural areas, and in time procedures in the cities became more formal, particularly as the admission ages were changed from four to five and then six. Without the time for the development of the senses, and activities which have long been denominated as readiness, the shortened primary school became more like the grammar grades, a trend accelerated by common administration. In the twentieth century an attempt was again made to provide less formal methods of education for primary children. Many of these efforts failed to take into account some of the early

---

16. Cubberley, *Public Education,* p. 139.

successes the country had had with early childhood education.

While the traditional primary curriculum may seem unduly narrow, there was less emphasis in the reading selections on story content than on selections which would help form correct historical attitudes and impart other useful information. Reading thus served more than an exercise in skill; it was a vehicle for content. And the object lessons provided a rudimentary science which, as in so many other matters, varied widely with the knowledge of the teacher.

In subsequent years, geography and history in varying degrees became a part of the primary curriculum, especially by the third and particularly the fourth grade. Later these became more or less correlated in some type of social studies offering. Music, art, and health and physical education, originally introduced with the infant school movement, regained their importance after the turn of the century, at least in official descriptions of primary programs. Thus by the end of the nineteenth century, in theory if not in practice, the primary curriculum corresponded to the nine areas discussed in the next section.

Curriculum Strands in the Traditional Primary Grades

There are normally nine content areas in primary school learning—reading, language arts (writing, spelling, listening, speaking, syntax and grammar, drama), arithmetic, science, social studies, health, music, art, and physical education. It is rare that foreign language instruction is begun at the primary school level. Each of the major curriculum strands are discussed in separate chapters, and this chapter merely presents an overview of the primary curriculum.

Reading and language arts dominate the primary curriculum, and it is not unusual to find 50 percent or more of primary time devoted to these two subjects. However justified this emphasis, it must be recognized that such an allocation leaves little time for other instruction. Common casualties are science and social studies, particularly in the first and second grades, since a common practice is to schedule language arts and arithmetic before noon and music, art, and physical education in the afternoon. An alternate arrangement is the "broad fields" approach, i.e., reading and language arts; mathematics, science, and social living; and appreciative and recreative arts. The advantage of this schedule is that it provides flexible blocks of time; the disadvantage is that it offers little control over sequential development. Specific subject and broad field scheduling are represented in figure 6.1.

Reading. The sequence of skills vary with the reading series in use. While there are common approaches in the sequence of basal or sight word reading, there are substantial differences in linguistic and other structural approaches (see chapter 10).

By the end of the third grade, however, it is the object of all reading programs to develop an independent reader. An independent reader is one who is efficient in both word recognition and comprehension skills, so that he not only recognizes words but is able to derive meaning from written discourse. An independent reader is thus one who can use reading for study and for pleasure.

Since reading involves the decoding of written symbols into speech, reading is fre-

the primary school program

Subject Curriculum		Broad Field Curriculum	
8:00- 8:10	Opening Activities	8:00- 8:10	Opening Activities
8:10- 8:40	Reading	8:10- 9:10	Language Arts
8:40- 9:10	Math		
9:10- 9:30	Recess—Snack	9:10- 9:30	Recess—Snack
9:30-10:00	Science	9:30-10:30	Soc. St., Science and Health
10:00-10:30	Social Studies		
10:30-11:00	Language Arts	10:30-11:00	Arithmetic
11:00-11:30	Lunch	11:00-11:30	Lunch
11:30-12:00	Recess—Free Play	11:30-12:00	Recess—Free Play
12:00- 1:00	Art MW	12:00- 1:00	Art, Music
12:00-12:30	Music TTF		
12:30- 1:00	Health TTF		
1:00- 1:10	Recess	1:00- 1:10	Recess
1:10- 1:40	Reading	1:10- 1:40	Language Arts
1:40- 2:20	P.E.	1:40- 2:20	P.E.
2:20- 2:30	Closing Activities	2:20- 2:30	Closing Activities

Fig. 6.1. Comparisons of time allocations for subject and broad field curriculum alternatives, holding lunch, recess, and opening and closing times constant, in ten-minute modular blocks.

quently emphasized as an important element within a comprehensive language arts program. Reading involves sound discrimination, in order that appropriate phoneme-grapheme associations may be made. And one way to learn the alphabet, knowledge of which facilitates reading, is by writing. Thus, the teaching of reading does not merely involve visual discrimination, but involves listening, speaking, and writing. As one teacher explained, "We listen to the sounds of the word; we see how the sounds look in writing; we say the words out loud from print; and we write and spell what we hear, see, and say." Many primary teachers nevertheless find it useful to distinguish between reading and language arts, since the latter is so often associated with stories for pleasure and dramatic play.

Most of the words primary children encounter in the graded reading materials are within their spoken vocabulary. All subject areas, however, offer the opportunity to develop new vocabulary and concepts.

The development of word power—written, spoken, and in spelling—is not restricted to the formal reading lesson but is part of all instruction, whether in science or in art.

By the end of the primary period the child who is making normal reading progress should be expected to have mastered the phoneme-grapheme skills of decoding and encoding; read in a steady, rhythmic manner both orally and silently; derive informational and appreciative meanings from phrases and sentences as well as words; and display skill in content reading. Practice is required to develop skill in reading for information, and the wise teacher will have reading lessons using science, social studies, and other material as well as literary material emphasizing a story.

A comparison of primary texts with intermediate texts indicates that in the intermediate school reading for information will become an increasingly important source for learning. It is therefore important that every effort be made to prevent reading failures from occurring in the primary grades. The primary student who begins the intermediate school unable to read efficiently is not merely a poor reader—he is a disabled learner.

Language Arts. Language is the vehicle of thought and communication, and underlies all school instruction. The language arts program is designed to provide the primary child with experiences in eight related areas —listening to and speaking English, reading, learning to write and to spell, written composition, creative dramatics, and English usage.

The foundation of the language arts program is oral language. Language is an arbitrary system of vocal symbols that the child acquires through imitation, i.e., listening and speaking. Oral communication is based exclusively on sounds, and any deficiencies in speech which a child brings to the primary school requires correction by practicing good speech. Good speech is important to success in reading and writing, which is the graphological means of recording sound.

But a language is not only a system of arbitrary vocal symbols. It has a structure which prescribes a particular word order, sentence form, and use of function words. The child entering school brings with him a functional syntax, which may or may not conform to approved English usage. Acquisition of correct syntax is important to success in reading, since the written language is expressed formally. Practice in correct syntax, however, does not require study of the rules of grammar.

By the end of the primary school, it is expected that the child will be able to express himself orally in a variety of situations, ranging from creative dramatics to storytelling; be able to distinguish the phonemes required for correct spelling, be able to write legibly in cursive; write functional paragraph reports and short creative compositions; and to use the correct patterns of standard oral English.

Children vary widely in English usage by socioeconomic condition, and English deficiencies may range from the slurring of word endings to dialectical handicaps. Instruction in appropriate English usage will therefore vary from class to class. The formal study of grammar is an inefficient means of improving English usage, and has no place in the language arts program of the lower intermediate school, much less that of the primary school.

The development of effective language, however, is not restricted to the formal language arts program. The basic purpose of language arts instruction is to facilitate more efficient and complex communication. All school experiences, formal and informal, may therefore be used to develop language arts competencies.

Mathematics. One of the most extensive curriculum reforms of the 1960s was the replacement of arithmetic by mathematics in the elementary schools. This reform was based on the recognition of mathematics as an arbitrary symbol system with rules of construction and interpretation based on logic, rather than a graded system progressing from arithmetic to algebra, trigonometry, and geometry.

Older primary mathematics programs concentrated on the fundamental arithmetic skills of simple addition, subtraction, multiplication, and division, and the application of these skills to simple problems.

A great variety of topics are included in the new mathematics for the primary grades. Some of the topics of the School

Mathematics Study Group (SMSG) include sets, geometric shapes, fundamental operations, linear measurement, length and area, and sets of points. The Stanford Project also teaches geometry in the primary grades.

The "new math" naturally includes much "old math," and in the primary grades much of the emphasis is not so much on new content but on teaching methodology—teaching for meaning through inquiry rather than by rote. New content as well as new procedures require teachers with more knowlege and skill in mathematics.

Chapter 12 of this text not only describes the various new projects and new teaching procedures in mathematics, but gives a detailed grade-level sequence.

Natural Science. One of the most neglected areas of the primary school curriculum is the teaching of natural science. This probably reflects the fact that most primary teachers are women, and women characteristically express a low interest in science and mathematics (sometimes called the language of science). The science preparation of elementary teachers rarely extends beyond the hours required as a part of general education, except for methods in science education. Hence, the teachers bring to the classroom not merely slight knowledge, but low interest as well. Many primary science programs, where they exist, take the form of ad hoc units built around some practical theme, such as "How We Get Our Water," and are frequently indistinguishable from social studies units. They lack sequence and certainly have not developed any systematic body of scientific principles or processes. Planned programs usually emphasize plants, animals, and human health.

Curriculum reform in science (see chapter 13) has developed some challenging new programs for the primary grades, but they have been less successful than the new mathematics programs. *Science—A Process Approach,* as the name implies, emphasizes and organizes science instruction around the process skills. Eight processes are emphasized in the primary program—observation, numeration, measurement, relationships of time and space, classification, communication, inference, and prediction. In addition to cognitive processes and outcomes, attention is also given to the affective aspects of science—development of a scientific attitude and recognition of the ways science serves mankind.

One of the most popular approaches to teaching science is organization by selected topics on the basis of grade level within science areas. For example, primary units in astronomy might include the solar system, interstellar space, and earth-sun-moon relations; primary units in geology and physical geography might include atmosphere and weather, seasons and climate, and morphology and changes.

In a topical approach, more abstract topics are placed in higher grades, but almost any topic may be studied at any grade level. The criterion for placement is not so much the topic as it is the complexity of treatment.

Just as important as the systematic content of the new sciences is the emphasis on the methodology of the sciences. While all programs do not agree with the categories of *Science—A Process Approach,* there is general agreement that science training should emphasize methods of teaching which require exploration, experimentation, inquiry, and discovery. In the primary grades, there is much emphasis on field observations, as well as demonstrations, to corroborate textual explanations. Because the world of science contains concrete referents, science is ideally suitable to the development of concepts, and provides a basis for the growing power of understanding abstract cause-effect relationships through growth in scientific language.

Social Studies. As in science and mathematics, social studies curriculum projects have developed new content and provided new emphasis on social science methodology (see chapter 14).

Social sciences which have been increasingly used for primary social studies content include economics and the behavioral sciences—cultural anthropology, sociology, and social psychology—while content drawn from history and geography has declined. Political science has never been important as a source of subject matter in the primary grades.

Curriculum development at the elementary level in social studies was under the aegis of the U.S. Office of Education. In contrast to the mathematics and science curriculum development, which involved national panels of scholars in the disciplines, social studies curriculum development was characterized by a multiplicity of projects, usually spearheaded by social studies educators with members of the disciplines involved largely as consultants. Notwithstanding the quality of most of the new social studies, the result has been an increase in social studies diversity.

Many of the projects developed material at the primary level. In general, a multidisciplinary approach was utilized, as in the Taba-Contra Costa and Minnesota Projects, although one alternative was the use of one discipline as an organizing core, the best example of which is the Senesch-Indiana economic materials, now published by Science Research Associates. Another alternative was the development of single discipline units to be introduced by grade level into the existing social studies program, as with the Georgia Anthropology Curriculum Project.

The two dominant characteristics of the new primary social studies material are the emphasis on structure and inquiry-discovery methodologies. Related clusters of concepts and generalizations were selected to emphasize the organization of knowledge in relation to the underlying structure of the discipline. Teaching strategies emphasize inquiry methods designed to develop fundamental concepts and generalizations and competency in the use of research methods, such as making field observations, doing case studies, using questionnaires, and interpreting data.

The new social studies methodology is compatible with the older project or activity methodology used in the primary grades but with an important shift in emphasis from description to analysis and synthesis. This means that the emphasis is on the intellectual inferences which can be drawn from the activity, not the activity for the mere sake of involving children.

Because of the diversity of content, it is not possible to outline a sequence of social studies experiences by grade level. In general, however, the organization of topics by grade level continues to follow a sequence from family to community study, with the selection of families and communities in different parts of the world varying from project to project. There is less emphasis on expanding environment organization and regional communities to the study of families and communities in depth. More detailed explanations of social science content are given in chapter 14.

Health Education. Concern for health and health education is important in the primary grades. From the standpoint of sickness, children are still subject to childhood diseases; from the standpoint of safety, they must learn to be responsible for their actions away from home. Instruction in health practices is also important, for many children come to school from homes in which they do not have the opportunity to learn about and practice good health habits.

Most of the various areas of health education (see chapter 15) are introduced in the primary grades. In the first grade, there is an emphasis on good health habits and safety, with a gradual emphasis on more substantive aspects of health in the third grade. Health education is no longer narrowly interpreted simply to mean care of the physical body, but also includes aspects of family and mental health.

The provision of health services is related to health education, but has a different objective—providing direct health care for the child. In general, health care is provided only to a limited extent, except to children from poor families, and is not regarded as a major responsibility of the school, except in Title I programs.

Physical Education. The program of physical education in the primary grades does not merely serve objectives of physical fitness, but broader ranges of social and personal development through physical activity (see chapter 18). In the popular mind, physical activity is separated from mental development, a separation which naturally results from the emphasis on competitive sports in high school and college.

In the primary grades, the objective is education through physical activity. For this reason, a variety of activities are emphasized such as play, rhythms and dances, simple games of low organization, motor skill development, and individual activities. The newer approach to physical education, however, is on movement exercises and exploration rather than skill development. Notwithstanding the adaptation of the inductive approach to teaching physical education, there is still considerable emphasis on demonstrations and following correct procedures. This results from the fact that performance substantially improves with training.

Art. From the earliest primary schools, drawing on slates was recognized as a means of exercising the senses, and was emphasized in the schools of Colonel Francis Parker in Quincy, Massachusetts and Chicago in the late nineteenth century. But art in the primary schools really found itself with the creative-expressionistic movement of the 1920s. Some of the most exciting school achievements of the period were the development of a new style of art for children —individual expression, which persists to this day as the distinctive characteristic of art in the primary school.

The symbolic stage characterizes the visual art of the primary school, in which the use of conventional representation facilitates economy of expression. The most common media of this age are crayons, tempera, and clay. An increase in manual dexterity in the upper primary grades presents the introduction of printmaking, weaving, and simple construction.

Often art is used in the primary grades as an illustrator's adjunct to social studies, or some other activity. While all children will not find the same degree of pleasure in art, experience with a variety of media and different techniques offers opportunities for more children to achieve satisfaction within the art program.

A regular schedule, often alternating with music, is frequently utilized to provide systematic experiences for children in both art and music.

Music. The objective of primary music education is to lay the foundation for the development of musicality, which may be simply defined as the capacity to enjoy and express oneself in music. Music is a curriculum of tones, expressed by voice or instrument. Just as the elements of line, form, texture, space, color, and movement assist the artist in creating a visual expression, the elements of melody, harmony and rhythm are combined by the musician into the form of the composition.

A complete program for the development of musicality includes listening, moving, performing, and composing. Because of the technical nature of music, children in primary grades who do not have a special music teacher will primarily listen and move to music, with performance restricted to singing and the use of simple rhythm instruments (see chapter 16).

In primary singing, children are introduced to a repertory of songs which permits them to extend the range of their singing voice and develop sensitivity to changes in tone, pitch, volume, melody, and rhythm. In primary listening, they identify sounds and tones that are high, low, soft, loud, fast, and slow and recognize simple rhythmic patterns. In rhythm activities, they are able to respond to the mood and rhythm of the music by walking, running, skipping, galloping, and the use of other fundamental movements. They also begin to verbalize the affective interpretation of music, and are progressively introduced to the great compositions of music.

Teaching in the Primary School

The beginning years of schooling have always offered the greatest opportunities and challenges to educators to explore new ways of teaching. In contrast to the professional schools, concerned with developing expertise, and the secondary schools, devoted to preparation for college, the lower grades have often reflected, even within somewhat conventional settings, a great variety of approaches towards the education of the young learner. This may result from the nature of primary education itself as well as the nature of the learner. The purpose of primary education is not merely to develop the fundamental skills of literacy, but to develop intellectuality which results from the use of the senses in conjunction with language. The primary learner is not committed to learn anything in particular as much as he is committed to the general principle of learning. It is therefore useful to mention some of the different approaches which have been used, at various times, to achieve this objective.

The Nongraded School. A nongraded school is one in which pupils progress from learning task to learning task, not from one grade to another.[17] A nongraded school organization naturally carries with it several adjunct practices: multiage sectioning, performance objectives, individualization of instruction, and small group work. So accustomed are we to the pattern of the graded

---

17. James Lewis, Jr., *A Contemporary Approach to Non-graded Education* (West Nyack, N.Y.: Parker Publishing Company, 1970).

school that the concept of the nongraded school always seems radical. At one time, in the pristine days of teaching children, grading was radical and nongradedness traditional. Ever since graded schools were introduced, many educational reformers have been trying to reestablish nongraded schools.

Multiage Sectioning. This is simply a device in which children of several ages, e.g., five, six, and seven, are grouped together in a class. In England, this is called "family" grouping, on the assumption that it more naturally reflects the membership of children in a social group. Children work at tasks suitable to their level of performance, based on previous learning, but the older children act as socializers for the group.

Performance Objectives. The specification of performance objectives has three principal aspects—breaking down learning tasks into small steps, stipulating the conditions for learning, and establishing the acceptable attainment level. Performance objectives are characteristic of a sequential curriculum, and imply a curriculum which is neither pupil- nor teacher-centered. Instead, performance objectives imply learning outcomes which have been previously planned, so that the sequence provides for the needed continuity. One of the criticisms of the child-centered school, in which learning outcomes were planned to meet the interests of the pupils, was the lack of continuity, and the pursuit of activity for its own sake without regard to sequential learning outcomes.[18]

Individualized Teaching. In an attempt to provide for the specific learning needs of different pupils in the nongraded school, more attention is given to individualized instruction. One way of individualization is to provide different learning tasks. Different learning tasks can be provided in individual expressive or manipulative activities in which a common base of knowledge or experience is not necessary, as in a construction project, a report, or a paper. Where common learning is necessary, as in a sequential curriculum, one of the ways of individualization is to vary the time required to perform the task or terminal behavior. Students are expected to perform the same tasks, but some attain the desired performance criterion quickly while others take longer.[19]

Programmed Instruction. Programmed instruction consists of carefully structured learning sequences in which information is presented in a series of narrative frames. Each narrative frame develops a complete idea, and corresponds to a short paragraph. Within sentences in the frames, blanks indicate the items to be learned. The item is explained in the preceding part of the frame, and the student fills in the blank from the previous information. He can check his response, and ascertain the correctness of the item, thus receiving immediate positive reinforcement or corrective feedback. The program can either be presented by a teaching machine or in the form of a text.

Programmed texts are demonstrably efficient teachers, and are easy for many pupils to use. Programmed texts are particularly adaptable to individualizing instruction in the nongraded school, and have

18. Harold Rugg and Ann Shumaker, *The Child-Centered School* (Yonkers-on-Hudson, N.Y.: World Book Company, 1928), p. 125.
19. Donna K. Stahl and Patricia M. Agalone, *Individualized Teaching in Elementary Schools* (West Nyack, N.Y.: Parker Publishing Co., 1970).

the additional advantage of freeing the teacher of much of the time needed in drill teaching. This allows the teacher to spend more time working with pupils individually or in groups.[20]

Integration. As an alternative to instruction in separate subjects, one of the watchwords of progressive education was an integrated curriculum and teaching. Pedagogically, integration (not to be confused with racial integration) is the arrangement of subject matter or experiences in such a manner as to constitute a unit of study or a problem-solving situation.[21]

There are various degrees of integration. One is correlation, in which the identity of the various subjects is maintained, as in geography and history, but the subject matter is related by a common theme, as in "Our Colonial Heritage." Another step is fusion, in which a broad curriculum area, such as the social sciences, are called upon to provide relevant information centered about a problem, theme, or unit that crosses several disciplines, such as "The Family," utilizing data from anthropology, sociology, psychology, economics, and history. A third variation is the core curriculum, often combining language arts and social studies, so that a correlated or fused unit, such as "Our Colonial Heritage," is used as a vehicle for the study of relevant subject matter from the social sciences and literature. A final step is the integrated day, which permits the pursuit of all aspects of the curriculum around a focal point, one central theme, organized into large units.

The integrated day has recently become the subject of new interest via the British primary school.[22] A comparison of this point of view with the American progressive school literature indicates their kinship.[23]

The integrated day is not an innovation; it is an exhumation.

Project and Activity. One of the first terms used to indicate the organization for simultaneous learning was that of project, used by Kilpatrick to apply to four different types of learning experiences: a producer's project, as in an artist painting a picture; a consumer's project, as in a person enjoying the visual stimulation of an artist's product; a problem project, to solve a problem or clear up a difficulty, as "What technological development had occurred which permitted initiation of the age of exploration and discovery?"; and the drill or specific learning project, as the need to learn fractions or decimals in connection with another project involving measurement, but only after the need arises.[24] The key to the Kilpatrick project was purposeful pupil activity, a difficulty which he never successfully solved in connection with knowledge acquisition.

McMurray was another early project advocate. He defined a project as the organization of knowledge into complete wholes to achieve purposive ends, and to facilitate

20. Frances Olsen, "Programmed Learning in the Nongraded School," in *Programmed Instruction,* ed. Allen D. Calvin (Bloomington, Ind.: Indiana University Press, 1969), pp. 181-92.
21. L. Thomas Hopkins, *Integration: Its Meaning and Application* (New York: D. Appleton-Century Company, Inc. 1937), p. 21.
22. Mary Brown and Norman Precious, *The Integrated Day in the Primary School* (New York: Agathon Press, Inc., 1969).
23. Robert Hill Lane, *The Progressive Elementary School* (Boston: Houghton Mifflin Company, 1938).
24. William Heard Kilpatrick, *Foundations of Method* (New York: Macmillan Company, 1926), pp. 346-48, 355. This book is not only a classic in American education because of the point of view of the leading exponent of progressive education, but because it is written in the form of a dialogue.

the growth of ideas. He admitted two types of projects. The child-initiated project was something the child undertook to meet a felt need, such as building a birdhouse, and corresponds to Kilpatrick's producer's project. The child-appropriated project was one into which the child was easily engrossed and to which he gave his undivided attention. Examples were the invention of the cotton gin or planning of a canal lock. This second category embraced Kilpatrick's problem and consumer projects. Like Kilpatrick, however, McMurray never made it clear how such remote topics as the invention of the cotton gin were to become "appropriated" by the child.[25]

One of the earliest large scale curriculum experiments was with a school conducted on a project basis by Ellsworth Collings, a doctoral student of Kilpatrick. Like the more famous Eight Year Study of progressive secondary schools, this study indicated that project taught pupils achieved as well on subject matter tests as conventionally taught students, while outperforming control students in the affective domain.[26]

Subsequently, the term "activity" became one of the preferred terms to denote the method of organizing the school day. The term activity was considered more dynamic and expressive of the nature of the young learner, and more accurately described a curriculum which should be characterized by the behavior of "being, doing, and acting, of things on the move."[27] The term "activity" was often merely an alternate label for unit of work. Melvin tried to distinguish between a unit of study and a major activity by calling the unit subject a "realm," e.g., "Study of Comparative Cultures," whereas a museum visit or a dramatic presentation of comparative cultures would be a major activity. If such major activity took place in the fall, other activities, such as collecting leaves and having a Halloween party, might be carried on as minor activities. While many teachers accept the principle of activity as a method of subject matter reinforcement, the activists insisted the contrary: "Activities stand alone as a part of life, not to buttress subject matter."[28]

As with the earlier definition of the project method by example, an attempt to define activity pragmatically indicated that any, and everything, that went on in the school was identified as an activity. The crucial element in an activity program, however, appeared to be active interaction of the child with the physical or social environment.[29]

Unit of Work. The unit of work is similar in definition to the McMurray definition of project—the organization of experiences to provide for meaningful learning. At one time it implied a way of organizing an integrated day through a series of related activities, as indicated by the published units of the Lincoln School of Teachers College. In one second grade unit, carrying the mail is used as a center of interest around which many experiences were pro-

25. Charles A. McMurray, *Teaching by Projects* (New York: Macmillan Company, 1921), pp. 1-2.

26. Ellsworth Collings, *Experiment with a Project Curriculum* (New York: Macmillan Company, 1923).

27. A. Gordon Melvin, *The Activity Program* (New York: John Day, 1936), p. 17.

28. Ibid., p. 152.

29. William Heard Kilpatrick, "Definition of the Activity Movement Today," in *The Activity Movement: The Thirty-third Yearbook of the National Society for the Study of Education, Part 2*, ed. Guy Montrose Whipple (Bloomington, Ill.: Public School Publishing Company, 1934), p. 55.

vided in the city and to which science, language, and other learnings were attached.[30]

In the extreme form, a unit has been used as a means of relating everything to a "center of interest." Washburne is cited as telling a "fishy" story in which the center of interest for the month was fish, and all learning involved the study of fish—the history of fishing, the geography of fisheries, the reading was on fishing and fishermen, the spelling words related to fishing and fish, compositions were written about fishing, and the arithmetic had to do with the price, weights, and quantities of fish.[31]

As the emphasis on activity and the integrated day waned, the concept of unit shifted. Today a unit may be multidisciplinary or single disciplinary, and can be rather long or fairly short—it does not have to be an endless wandering. The unit is simply a logical way of organizing a coherent and systematic sequence of learning, and it may or may not involve projects or activities. The nature of the unit depends upon the learning tasks, and units are not deliberately selected for the purpose of fostering muscular activity. An English writer has described this unit approach as "topic teaching."[32]

Creative Teaching. Like many other terms in the educational repertory, this term has no precise meaning. It ranges from an emphasis on individual expression in the arts and humanities[33] to problem solving and related discovery and inquiry methods.[34] The concept of creativity is merely another way of emphasizing some aspects of working with children—children should be encouraged to ask questions and to seek answers, to express their ideas verbally, and in arts and crafts to become actively involved in learning, to assert their individuality, and to make use of their power of observation and analysis.

Observation and Environmental Studies. For over 200 years it has been a standard recommendation that teachers involve young children in learning with the use of their senses. Observation and field study was one of the key Pestalozzian principles, and was vigorously pursued by Francis W. Parker in his methods of teacher training.[35] The psychological principle of teaching by observation is associational—through a combination of the experience with language the pupil may form more accurate concepts more efficiently. In a day when the school playground may offer little more of promise than a beaten tenement, references to fields, woods, and the countryside seem remote and unreal. The principle is just as valid today as it was over a hundred and fifty years ago when Pestalozzi taught geography lessons from a hilltop.[36] Where it is difficult to have access to the real environment, pictures—flat, filmstrip, and moving—afford a vicarious way of exercising the powers of observation of the environment.

30. Avah W. Hughes, *Carrying the Mail* (New York: Bureau of Publications, Teachers College, Columbia University, 1933).
31. Lane, *Progressive Elementary School*, p. 83.
32. Peter Rance, *Teaching by Topics* (London: Ward Lock Educational, 1968).
33. Gertrude Hartman and Ann Shumaker, *Creative Expression: The Development of Children in Art, Music, Literature, and Dramatics* (New York: The John Day Company, 1932). In this publication are brought together the issues of *Progressive Education* from the 1920s devoted to creativity.
34. Mary Lee Marksburry, *Foundations of Creativity* (New York: Harper and Row, Publishers, 1963).
35. Francis W. Parker, *Talks on Pedagogics* (New York: E. L. Kellogg & Co., 1894).
36. Muriel F. S. Hopkins, *Learning Through the Environment* (London: Longmans, Green & Co., Ltd., 1968.)

Separate Subjects. The dominant method of teaching in the primary school has been a separate subject organization, in practice if not in theory. The curriculum reform era of the 1960s was a separate subjects approach, even though some of the curricula, as in social studies and science, include broad fields. Notwithstanding the frequent criticism of subjects, the fact remains that subject organization persists because it affords a manageable way for teachers to help young children acquire many of the fundamentals needed for learning. As Washburne pointed out many years ago, there are differences in subject matter—social science is different from arithmetic, and the creativity desired in art would be disastrous for spelling.[37] There is no need for a primary teacher to have to apologize for developing a subject in a systematic, orderly manner. At the same time, there is no need to always require a rigid demarcation of subject matter.

This review of various approaches to teaching in the primary school was not intended to be exhaustive. Team teaching, for example, is not discussed.[38] It has been designed to indicate some of the many different practices, and show that in the primary school it is possible to follow different educational alternatives—the emphasis of the next section.

Educational Alternatives in the Small Primary School

Most teachers who teach in the primary grades will teach in an elementary school. The elementary school will tend to have a large enrollment and many teachers under the supervision of a building principal, except in small school districts. In large school districts, the requirements of administrative uniformity limit the number of educational alternatives. The purpose of this section is to indicate that the *small* primary school offers the opportunity for teachers and parents to pursue educational alternatives which is difficult to do within the organizational patterns of those *large* elementary schools which include primary grades.

Today parents and teachers are concerned about the kinds of educational experiences children receive in school, and many are frustrated because they find it difficult to pursue educational alternatives. The organization of separate primary schools offer a number of advantages. In the first place, a primary school can be small, because the educational experience level of the students does not require a high degree of specialization. From this important attribute of smallness, a number of other attributes are subsumed. It can be a neighborhood school in fact and not in theory, because the children can come from within walking distance. Because it is small, it is forced to use multiage sectioning, with only a few pupils at the various performance levels within the ranges represented by K-4. Hence, it is possible to have an enrollment of about fifty to sixty pupils. The number of full time teachers need not exceed two or three. Teachers are thus free to innovate, and their direct face-to-face relationships permits the type of interaction needed for cooperative team teaching.

37. Carleton Washburne, "The Case for Subjects in the Curriculum," *Journal of the National Education Association* 26, no. 1 (January, 1937), p. 5.

38. Judson T. Shaplin and Henry F. Olds, eds., *Team Teaching* (New York: Harper and Row, Publishers, 1964).

More direct parental involvement is encouraged. The small size of the school encourages them to relate to it in a more personal manner. The program can be a very flexible one and the limitations on beginning at a particular age by a fixed date can also be lifted. In fact, it is envisaged that children would be permitted to begin any month, because the arrangements for group and individual instruction could readily be changed to accommodate to different performance levels, including beginners.

Because the school is small, it can be housed in regular housing in the neighborhood, a matter which might run into regulatory difficulties with zoning and school building requirements. But some of the best private schools are located in buildings originally built as residences.

One objection to the small primary school might be the absence of media centers and special centers. The former could be made available on a satellite basis, a number of primary schools drawing on the services of a designated media center. It is emphasized, however, that this pattern is not conceived as a fixed administrative pattern, in which a number of primary schools are feeders to an intermediate school. This administrative uniformity would, as it did with the earlier primary schools, tend to require curriculum uniformity and eliminate the possibility of teacher-parent initiated educational alternatives.

If there were a sufficient number of primary schools, certain teachers with special skills could be made available on a rotating basis. More desirable, however, would be the recruiting of part-time teachers, especially mothers or fathers of the children in the neighborhood. They would assist with specialized aspects of the program, whether art, science, math, or some other subject, according to the need to supplement the strengths of the regular teachers.

The small primary school is not inconsistent with defined learning outcomes and performance criteria. It simply opens the way for teachers and parents to exercise more options in working with children to achieve those ends. Thus one primary school might appear to be extremely child centered and permissive, and another more formal and structured. Both would be acceptable alternatives, emphasis being on the attainment of performance levels needed for success in the intermediate school rather than on the standardization of instructional procedures.

At the same time, the primary schools could have certain curriculum variations. One school might prefer to give added emphasis to science, another to the humanities, and another to social studies. Each would have the option to emphasize its area of excellence, without neglecting the minimal performance criteria of the established curriculum. Such schools could thus combine both the aspects of the traditional school, with competence in the fundamental skills, and aspects of the experimental school with an emphasis on creativity and innovation.

Larger primary schools could, of course, be organized, with more pupils, more teachers, and more sections, and some might hold that a larger primary school is necessary for purposes of cross-class socialization. This inevitably involves bussing of children between high and low income areas, and there is no evidence to indicate that such strategies offset the inconvenience, added expense, and lack of pupil and parental identity with the school. Size in itself is no guarantee against provincialism, however, and the conceptualization of a small primary school that reflects in its size the growth of the child appears to offer a means to return the primary school to the children and to the teachers. The mania for large schools appears to conform more to the niceties of hierarchical administrative plans than to educational needs, especially for young children.

A small primary school would not require a building principal, and the size of staff, pupils, and parents would encourage the use of direct contacts for the paper control of large organizations. The responsibility for administration and supervision would rest on the staff as part of their teaching function, but a head teacher, first among equals, might act as the channel of administrative communication, for which extra compensation would be paid.

The risk of small schools are fraught with dangers. One of the great strengths is the identification of the school with its teachers, which can be a vice, equally great, if the teachers are mediocre. Pupils are trapped, but no more so than in a large school where the regime of the self-contained classroom prevails. Parental involvement, which can be an asset when teachers and parents are bound together, in a mutual educational enterprise, can become a liability when there is parent-teacher conflict or even parental division. Popular will in a small community can often be as abrasive as tyranny in a large community.

It is thus not suggested that any school system abandon its regular elementary buildings, even after the establishment of intermediate schools, and replace them with a complete number of small neighborhood primary schools. This organization should rather be regarded as one of the alternatives that are available to a school system in meeting the needs of children and providing ways in which parents can relate more directly to the school. And this is the advantage of the use of private dwellings for small primary schools. They can be used for this purpose so long as the school exists to meet a particular need, and then released when needs and interests change. But the erection of a school building implies a sense of permanence. The solidity of the building is reassuring, but the building often perpetuates programs or restricts change because of the traditions represented by the building.

The small primary school, with its multiage nongradedness, recreates the intimacy of The Little Red School House. If a child of four wishes to start, it would not be necessary to send him to some central office for a battery of psychological tests. He could be placed in the learning environment, and his performance observed in terms of actual behavior, not predicted behavior. It affords an opportunity for younger and older children to learn together and help each other, and avoid the creation of the artificial peer groups that come with uniform ages in fixed classes. In England this is called family grouping.[39] It is, as indicated in the Prologue, as old as education, and was the standard way of organizing schools until the invention of the graded school.

The use of multiage grades in the small primary school does not preclude group instruction and drill for skill development, where appropriate. It does mean that on the

---

39. Lorna Ridgway and Irene Lawton, *Family Grouping in the Primary School* (New York: Agathon Press, Inc., 1969).

basis of performance criteria the teacher will need to be more careful in assessing pupil learning, so that group work is appropriate to a particular group, and not too easy or too difficult, as is so often the case with large group instruction. The small primary school will require that more attention be given to individual instruction. One of the first consequences is that for a student to become an independent learner, he must acquire the skills of information gathering early. This in turn requires that he become an efficient reader quickly. In order for the teacher to check the progress of pupils, they must also become efficient in writing-up and making inferences from data. Consequently, the pupil in the small primary school must become efficient not merely in the mechanics of writing, but in written composition. The primary school thus demands that pupils become self-directing as early as possible, and thus the organization of the primary school requires an attention to competence in the skill subjects. This procedure is a departure from the project-, child-centered schools of the 1920s and 1930s which made very little change in the organizational structure and placed most of their emphasis on changes in tasks and methods.

The proposed primary school would attempt to hold tasks constant, and permit children to have the needed time to attain proficiency. This kind of organization, which emphasizes a return of the school to children, teachers, and parents, provides the framework in which many different educational alternatives may be tried.

This sketch of a small primary school has not been given as a description of reality. It is merely suggested as a possible way in which teachers and parents may provide some educational alternatives to the uniform type of instruction given in the larger school units.

Evaluation of the Primary School

Whether a school boy is in Mwanza or in Cedar Falls, he will find a primary school. They share this common heritage which is the initiation into a literate culture through mastery of the fundamental skills of reading and writing, and numbers. On mastery of these skills is erected the rich structure of formal learning, whether in history, chemistry, law, or medicine. On the strength of this foundation is built the subsequent years of intellectual growth.

In the past century, the primary curriculum has been expanded to include scientific and aesthetic experiences; organization and teaching methods have been adjusted to the active, sensory nature of the child; discipline rendered mild and persuasive rather than punitory; and the conception of the child changed from an incipient monster to an angel. But in the primary school of tomorrow, no less than in the scribal school of ancient Sumer, a major objective will be to teach the child to read, to write, to cipher, and to express and understand communications in formal language. For many a child in underdeveloped countries, primary education provides a scant literacy; in the United States, it lays the foundation work for the intermediate school which embraces a rich and complex curriculum.

The development of the intermediate school naturally implies the development of the primary school. What could result is simply a truncated elementary school of three or four grades, residue of the separation. In an age where there is a demand for more involvement, more accountability, a greater identity with parents and the neighborhood, and more educational alternatives, it appears that the organization of the nongraded primary school offers to parents, teachers, and children the option to create smaller schools more responsive to their wishes.

In England, the methods of the infant school, for children ages five, six, and seven, have progressively influenced changes in the upper primary grades, known as the junior school. Most of these methods and arrangements attempt to follow procedures and techniques which in the twentieth century were called "progressive" and which in the nineteenth century were invariably described as Pestalozzian. What the English have appeared to do, at least in the better schools, is to utilize many of the natural, informal, and ingenious methods of teaching in large classes with a high degree of individuality without neglect of basic skills.

The history of American education indicates that two of the ideas of the British primary school—family, i.e., multiage sectioning, and the integrated day—are no novelty.[40] These are a half-century older than the progressive movement, with its emphasis on informal methods.

But informal methods of teaching have always placed a greater premium on individual teacher competency, because there is no recipe or formula. Herein lies its strength and its weakness. Most teachers are like the run of ordinary mortals, and possess adequate but not extraordinary talents. In the hands of a master teacher, informal methods lead to an exciting interaction between teacher and pupil, a high degree of aesthetic originality, a capacity to work individually, and a sense of pupil purpose. It is not clear from the record in the United States, however, if these results came about as a result of the school, or was the happy combination of children matched to a school with a particular parental clientele which supported the school.

All too often informal methods had the opposite results, and led to their discredit: license was misconstrued as liberty; aimlessness as pupil planning; shoddy work as individuality; and mere divergence as creativity. For informal methods to become institutionalized, it is not enough for a few teachers to have a messianic fervor. The procedures must be susceptible to rational transmission through training. This may eventually be the major contribution of the current interest in the British primary school, for neither the philosophy nor the methods are new.

In recommending the permissive organization of small, nongraded primary schools, it is emphasized that this approach is not regarded as a panacea. One of the major advantages is that it permits the exploration of educational alternatives within the framework of the public school system. Without the creation of these alternatives, it is inevitable that more and more attention will be given to the creation of private schools by parents concerned with the kind of education they are getting in the public schools.[41]

Most of these will fail because of lack of financing and organization, but their existence indicates a discontent of parents with the available public education. This discontent is reflected in a lower level of school support, and a lack of moral support

---

40. Robert Hill Lane, *The Progressive Elementary School* (Boston: Houghton Mifflin Company, 1938).
41. Jane Howard, "Free Schools," *Life,* 8 January 1971, pp. 45-51, 54.

which is essential to the public education commitment. The opportunity to organize small, nongraded primary schools therefore not only offers a useful means to foster creativity within education, but an avenue through which parents may express their continued support of public education.

SELECTED REFERENCES

BASSETT, G. W. *Innovation in Primary Education.* London: John Wiley and Sons, Ltd., 1970.

BROWN, MARY, and PRECIOUS, NORMAN. *The Integrated Day in the Primary School.* New York: Agathon Press, 1969.

CUBBERLEY, ELLWOOD P. *Public Education in the United States.* Boston: Houghton Mifflin Company, 1934.

DAVIS, DAVID C. *Patterns of Primary Education.* New York: Harper and Row, Publishers, 1963.

JONES, OWEN R. *The Primary School.* Melbourne, Australia: F. W. Cheshire, 1966.

HUEY, J. FRANCIS. *Teaching Primary Children.* New York: Holt, Rinehart and Winston, Inc., 1965.

IMHOFF, MYRTLE. *Early Elementary Education.* New York: Appleton-Century-Crofts, Inc., 1959.

LAMBERT, HAZEL M. *Early Childhood Education.* Boston: Allyn and Bacon, Inc., 1960.

LOGAN, LILLIAN M. *Teaching the Young Child.* Boston: Houghton Mifflin Company, 1960.

MEYER, ADOLPH E., *An Educational History of the American People.* 2d ed. New York: McGraw-Hill Book Company, 1967.

MICHAELIS, JOHN U.; GROSSMAN, RUTH H.; and SCOTT, LLOYD F. *New Designs for the Elementary School Curriculum.* New York: McGraw-Hill Book Company, 1967.

RIDGWAY, LORNA, and LAWTON, IRENE. *Family Grouping in the Primary School.* New York: Agathon Press, Inc., 1969.

ROGERS, VINCENT R. *Teaching in the British Primary School.* London: Macmillan & Company, 1970.

STEWART, W. A. C. and MCCANN, W. P. *The Educational Innovators.* London: Macmillan & Company, 1967.

WOLF, JR., WILLIAM C., and LOOMER, BRADLEY M. *The Elementary School: A Persspective.* Chicago: Rand McNally and Company, 1966.

the intermediate school program

7

A school which occupies a position between the conventional elementary school and the high school is the intermediate school. The term "intermediate school" is used here to refer to both the traditional "junior high school" and the newer "middle school." The intermediate school is a bridge connecting the elementary school with the senior high school. In its bridging capacity, it reputedly helps children make the transition from the organization and program of the elementary school to that of the high school. We will investigate this bridging effect in greater depth in a later section of this chapter.

The organization of the intermediate school is significant to prospective elementary teachers because there is no fixed elementary grade organization or certification. A prospective elementary teacher might teach from grade one to eight, depending upon job opportunities in a school system at a given time.

Now, let us briefly examine the emergence of the junior high school and the middle school in the nation.

Intermediate School in Historical Perspective

When one uses the terms "junior high school" and "middle school" he is referring to two different and distinct organizational arrangements. Normally, the junior high school is an organizational arrangement which incorporates grades 7 and 8; or most frequently, grades 7, 8, and 9. The organizational plan of the middle school includes grades 5, 6, 7, and 8; or most frequently, grades 6, 7, and 8.

Development of the Junior High School. In 1888, Charles W. Eliot, President of Harvard University, stated in a speech at the National Education Association that if secondary education could begin before the ninth grade, students could finish high school a year earlier and enter college at a younger age.[1] To accomplish this he

---

1. For comprehensive discussions of the development of the junior high school, see: Leslie W. Kindred and Associates, *The Intermediate Schools* (Englewood Cliffs, New Jersey: Prentice-Hall, Inc., 1968), pp. 18-33; Theodore C. Moss, "The Middle School Comes—and Takes Another Grade or Two," *National Elementary Principal* 48, no. 4 (February 1969): 37-41.

recommended shortening the elementary and high school programs, which had an 8-4 organizational arrangement. Subsequently, NEA appointed the "Committee of Ten on Secondary School Studies" which recommended in 1893 that high school subjects be taught in late elementary school years. This was equivalent to a reorganization of the school to accommodate a six-year high school. The end result, however, was the establishment of a 6-6 organizational plan for the elementary and high school with the elementary school losing two years to the high school. The economy of time idea suggested by Eliot, therefore, did not materialize and students continued to enter college at the same age under the new 6-6 organizational arrangement.

Within the first decade of the twentieth century two major educational happenings shifted the 6-6 organizational plan to a 6-2-4, 6-3-3 or other arrangements. First, G. Stanley Hall published a two-volume work, *Adolescence,* in which he showed that the psychologists believed that twelve year olds who normally would be seventh graders represented the turning point for entrance into adolescence rather than fourteen year olds as formerly thought. Therefore, it was suggested that twelve year olds should be placed with their peers in either a three-year organizational unit or with older students in a six-year high school. Second, there was a great deal of unhappiness with the content of the upper elementary grades. It was suggested by prominent educators of the time, such as William R. Harper, President of The University of Chicago, that the apparently fruitless studies in subjects like grammar, reading, penmanship, and spelling should be dispensed with in grades 7 and 8. It was recommended that they should be replaced by the addition of vocational courses and broadened offerings of an extracurricular nature designed to appeal to and meet the interests of children who were dropping out of school at the end of eighth grade. Furthermore, it was suggested that the addition of these courses be coupled with a reorganization of the schools from the traditional 8-4 plan to a 6-6, 6-2-4, 6-3-3, or some other in order that the students, who were potential dropouts, could study with peers of the same age and in courses which were more compatible with their educational needs and interests. Too, during this time, studies by Thorndike, Ayers, and Strayer showed that the holding power of the schools with respect to lessened dropouts was directly related to the nature and quality of the curriculum.

Thus, the events of the time from about 1888 to 1910 appear to have justified the establishment of the junior high school. In sum, these events involved: (1) a desire to economize on time (which did not materialize), (2) a changed belief that the age of adolescence began at 12 rather than 14 years, (3) that secondary education should cover six years of schooling in either a six year block or, more preferably, with a junior high school of two or three years beginning at grade seven to bridge the gap between elementary and high school, and (4) that the curriculum offerings in grades 7 and 8 should be made more relevant to the needs of the youth.

The predominant organizational plan for school systems having 25,000 or more students in 1966 was the 6-3-3 plan, as table 7.1 shows. Even in smaller systems (3,000 to 24,999 students) approximately 50 percent employed the 6-3-3 plan. It seems

Table 7.1. *Organization by Grade, 1966 as Found in Selected School Systems Enrolling 300 or More Pupils. From: "Public School Programs and Practices,"* NEA Research Bulletin *45, no. 4 (December 1967): 118.*

Type of grade organization	Estimated total, systems enrolling 300 or more pupils (percent)	Systems grouped by enrollment 25,000 and over (percent)	3,000-24,999 (percent)	300-2,999 (percent)
6-3-3	21.5	75.8	49.1	12.6
8-4	21.4	10.1	13.7	23.8
6-6	22.4	0.7	3.8	28.1
6-2-4	11.9	6.7	14.5	11.3
7-5	3.4	2.7	4.7	3.0
5-3-4	3.3	1.3	3.0	3.5
4-4-4	1.1	0.0	0.4	1.3
Other	15.0	2.7	10.7	16.5
Number of systems	12,130	150	234	232

clear, therefore, that the junior high school, which first emerged in Berkeley and Los Angeles (California) and in Columbus (Ohio) from 1909 to 1911, was rather firmly entrenched in grades 7-9 in 1966, particularly in the larger school systems.

Development of the Middle School. There has been a rapid growth in the number of middle schools organized in the last half of the 1960s. In a 1967-68 survey, Alexander found 1,101 middle schools with grades 5-8 or 6-8 as the basic arrangement. These middle schools were reorganized in systems formerly having the 6-3-3, 6-2-4, or 6-6 arrangement.[2] Hines and Alexander, two of the leaders in the middle school movement, have predicted that this reorganization movement will expand geometrically.[3]

The question can be raised: "Why is the middle school recommended as the intermediate unit in lieu of the junior high school?" A number of reasons have been advanced by Kindred and his collaborators.[4] Some of the more important ones appear to be the following.

First, the traditional junior high school, i.e., grades 7, 8, and 9 interrupts the curriculum cohesiveness of the high school since the high school uses the Carnegie Units which are predicated on a four-year sequence of courses. When the ninth grade is housed in the junior high school under the 6-3-3 plan, the ninth grade is actually the first year of high school. By reorganizing the grades into a middle school as the intermediate unit, the ninth grade is returned to the high school where it rightly belongs as long as its program is fixed to Carnegie Units. Also, ninth graders are more like tenth graders than they are like eighth graders, a fact which subsequently will be documented.

A second reason for the emergence of the middle school plan is a desire on the part of some educational authorities to avoid

2. William M. Alexander, *A Survey of Organizational Patterns of Reorganized Middle Schools.* (Gainesville: University of Florida, Final Report, Project No. 7-D-026, July 1968).

3. Vynce A. Hines and William M. Alexander, "Evaluating the Middle School," *National Elementary Principal* 48, no. 4 (February 1969): 32-36.

4. Kindred and Associates, *The Intermediate Schools;* Moss, "The Middle School Comes."

such practices as departmentalization for instruction and the emphasis on many activities of questionable value such as interscholastic sports and marching bands. In short, the junior high school in too many instances is a miniature high school. Many educators now believe the junior high school to be less suited to the intellectual, emotional, social, and physical development of children who are of later childhood or early adolescent years.

The first two major objections to the extant junior high school were largely matters of organization as related to programs and activities. The third and major objection to the junior high school, however, is concerned with the changed maturational development of the students. Puberty now begins earlier as a result of improved health standards and nutrition. Today, children who are 11 years old have reached approximately the same developmental level as the 12 year old for whom the junior high was established some 60 years ago. Dacus has found, for example, that on measures of social, emotional, and physical maturity and opposite sex choices among pupils in grades 5 through 10 that there were less difference between students of grades 6 and 7 than among other grades comparisons.[5] Jones found in studying the attitudes and interests of ninth graders that they were more like tenth graders than they were like eighth graders.[6] It would appear, therefore, that sixth graders can be cared for better in an intermediate school and the ninth graders can receive more suitable instruction in the four-year high school.

The criticism of the junior high school with respect to its program and activities as well as newer evidence about maturational changes in children's growth seems to indicate that a feasible organizational arrangement for a school system would be a 5-3-4 plan. This seems to be congruent with the findings in an NEA Research Bulletin survey report on 154 middle schools in 51 school systems which enrolled over 12,000 pupils during 1968-69, as shown in table 7.2. Only 20 of the 154 middle schools incorporated grade 5 in the middle school. Why then does it appear that there is some reluctance to adopt an organizational arrangement of 4-4-4 system wide which would make grade 5 part of the middle school?

First, 10 year olds are not as noisy and boisterous as the 11 year old sixth graders tend to be. They are friendly, straightforward, and desirous of pleasing adults and gaining their approval. They tend to show more of the traits of children than of early adolescents. It is also alleged that if the conventional departmentalized program of the traditional junior high school is incorporated into the middle school, serious questions can be raised about the educational benefit which would accrue for the 10 year old fifth grader—for that matter, the 11 year old sixth grader.[7]

As can be seen in table 7.2, the middle school serves the bridging effect mentioned earlier in this chapter between the elementary school and the high school. It provides for a gradual transition from the self-contained classroom in grades 5 and 6 to a predominant departmentalized arrangement dur

---

5. W. Pence Dacus, *A Grade Structure for the Early Adolescent Years*, (Houston: Bureau of Educational Research and Services, University of Houston, 1963).

6. Mary C. Jones, "A Comparison of the Attitudes and Interests of Ninth-Grade Students Over Two Decades," *Journal of Educational Psychology* 51 (August 1960): 178-79.

7. Moss, "The Middle School Comes," p. 40.

Table 7.2. *Instructional Organization and Practices in 154 Middle Schools in 51 Systems Enrolling Over 12,000 Pupils, 1968-69.* From: "Middle Schools in Theory and in Fact," NEA Research Bulletin 47, no. 2 (May 1969): 51.

Number and percent of schools by grade level[a]

Instructional organization and practices	Grade 5 (20 schools) Number	Grade 5 Percent	Grade 6 (146 schools) Number	Grade 6 Percent	Grade 7 (154 schools) Number	Grade 7 Percent	Grade 8 (148 schools) Number	Grade 8 Percent
ORGANIZATION								
Self-contained classrooms	10	50.0	31	21.2	3	1.9	3	2.0
Partial departmentalization	7	35.0	74	50.7	55	35.7	36	24.4
Total departmentalization	3	15.0	35	24.0	91	59.1	105	70.9
No reply	...	......	6	4.1	5	3.3	4	2.7
PRACTICES								
Subject area teams	4	20.0	45	30.8	51	33.1	52	35.1
Interdisciplinary teams	2	10.0	19	13.0	29	18.8	25	16.9
Small group instruction	7	35.0	55	37.7	63	40.9	66	44.6
Large group instruction	4	20.0	35	24.0	45	29.2	47	31.8
Flexible scheduling	5	25.0	39	26.7	44	28.6	43	29.1
Closed-circuit TV	1	5.0	22	15.1	25	15.6	25	16.9
Independent study	3	15.0	30	20.5	39	25.3	40	27.0
Individualized instruction	4	20.0	39	26.7	47	30.5	48	32.4
Tutorial programs	3	15.0	32	21.9	33	21.4	31	20.9

[a]Percentages are based on the total number of middle schools in the survey which include each of the grades. The number of schools with each grade is shown in the column headings.

ing the last year or grade 8. Most children come to the middle school having studied in self-contained classrooms and a gradual transition is effected during middle school years toward departmentalization—the organizational arrangement of most high schools.

The middle school characteristically is more than a mere grouping of grades. Its identifying characteristics, some of which are spelled out in Table 7.2, have been suggested in an NEA Research Bulletin as follows:[8]

1. A span of at least three grades to allow for the gradual transition from elementary- to high-school instructional practices (must include grades 6 and 7 and no grades below 5 or above 8).
2. Emerging departmental structure in each higher grade to effect gradual transition from the self-contained classroom to the departmentalized high school.
3. Flexible approaches to instruction—team teaching, flexible scheduling, individualized instruction, independent study, tutorial programs—and other approaches aimed at stimulating children to learn how to learn.
4. *Required* special courses, taught in departmentalized form, such as industrial arts, home economics, foreign language, art, music, typing; frequently an interdisciplinary or multidisciplinary approach is used, e.g., "unified arts," "practical arts," "humanities," "performing arts," "exploratory," "urban living."
5. Guidance program as a distinct entity to fill the special needs of this age group.
6. Faculty with both elementary and secondary certification, or some teachers with each type (until special training and certification are available for this level).
7. Limited attention to interschool sports and social activities.

Program of the Intermediate School

There appears to be little difference in the basic courses of study included in the intermediate school irrespective of whether it is a middle school (grades 5-8, 6-8) or a junior high school (grades 7-9, 7-8). A typical program of studies for the intermediate school has been outlined by Coplein as shown in figure 7.1.

The major difference in the junior high school and the middle school seems to reside in how the courses are taught as dictated by the curriculum design.[9] In the junior high school, the traditional curriculum design has been subjects-in-isolation and the typical organizational plan for instruction horizontally has been departmentalized classrooms. In the middle school, however, it appears that there is widespread use of the broad fields and core curriculum patterns. Grooms, who has been very active in the middle school movement, has said, for example, that the curriculum of the middle school consists of social science, science, mathematics, and language arts while also including the related areas of unified arts, foreign language, and physical education.[10] In this instance, the offerings in social science, language arts, and unified arts would most likely be taught in a broad fields curriculum pattern.

The core is used in some schools in which the language arts or social studies becomes the core and the other broad fields area is integrated or fused into the core. A newer version of the core curriculum for the middle school is the *unified studies* approach, which can be seen in figure 7.2.[11] In this approach,

8. "Middle Schools in Theory and in Fact," *NEA Research Bulletin* 47, no. 2 (May 1969): 49.
9. See chapter 4 of this text for a discussion of curriculum patterns.
10. M. Ann Grooms, *Perspectives on the Middle School* (Columbus, Ohio: Charles E. Merrill Books, Inc., 1967), p. 75.
11. Kindred and Associates, *The Intermediate Schools*, pp. 126-27.

a unifying theme becomes the central focus in which children assigned to the separate subjects of social studies, science, English, and mathematics also meet in a "core" class where the theme is identified and studied. Such a unifying theme might be "Building a Model Community"—and pupils in the "core" class might address themselves to such problems as: "What constitutes a community?" "How is it governed?" "What services does it provide for its constituents?"

Teachers of the subject areas are known as resource teachers to the core class and they follow up in their regular classrooms a study of the problems which arise in the core class by teaching related information and skills. Stated another way, the subject teachers, in their regular subject area classrooms which are known as resource classes, teach from their individual subject fields whatever the students need to know about the extant unifying theme. The subject teachers pursue their individual programs in the resource classes when the students do not need to work on the problems of the unifying theme. The problems identified in the core class are also resolved finally in the core class.

In the unified studies approach, the core teacher is also one of the subject area teachers. The core teacher likewise serves as team leader. Under the leadership of the core teacher, therefore, the teaching team can unify the classwork of the resource classes and the core class and they can provide systematic and meaningful guidance to the students, both of which are essential aspects of the middle school concept.

The limited extent to which such inter-

	Grades				
Subjects	5	6	7	8	9
Language Arts	***	***	***	***	***
Reading	***	***	**	**	*
Mathematics	***	***	***	***	**
Science	***	***	***	***	**
Social Studies	***	***	***	***	**
Music	***	***	**	**	*
Art	***	***	**	**	*
Physical Ed.	***	***	***	***	***
Health	**	**	**	**	**
Foreign Language	*	*	*	*	*
Business Ed.					*
Agriculture					*
Vocational Ed.					*
Homemaking-Ind. Arts			**	**	*

*** Required
 ** Generally required
  * Elective or limited amount.

Fig. 7.1. Typical Program of Studies for the Intermediate School. From: Leonard E. Coplein, "Program of Studies," in Leslie W. Kindred and Associates, **The Intermediate Schools** (Englewood Cliffs, New Jersey: Prentice-Hall, Inc., © 1968), by permission of Prentice-Hall, Inc., p. 139.

disciplinary teaching teams are used, as in the case of the unified studies approach, can be approximated by studying the figures presented in Table 7.2. There it can be seen that this approach is used more sparingly in grades 5 and 6 (10 and 13 percent) than it is in grades 7 and 8 (18.8 and 16.9 percent). Actually, team teaching by subject area in the middle school seems to be a frequent practice. Table 7.2 depicts this to occur in about one-third of the surveyed middle schools at the sixth-, seventh-, and eighth-grade levels.

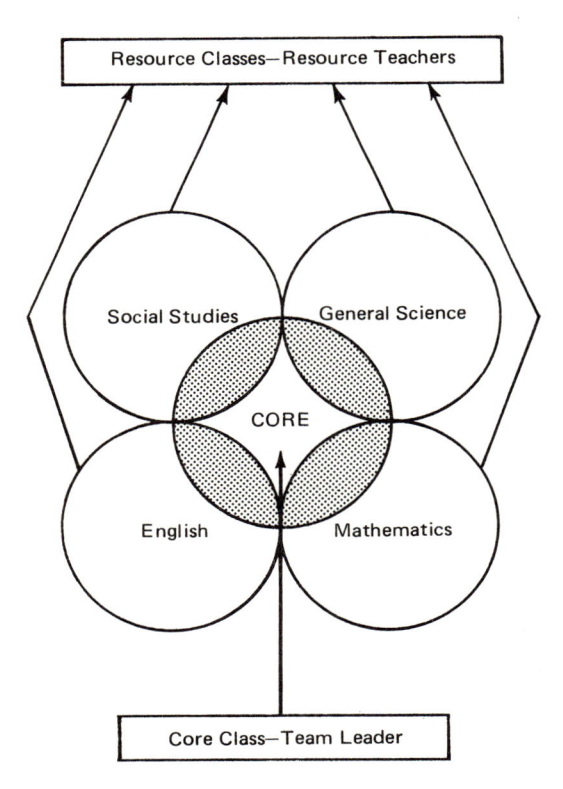

Fig. 7.2. Model of a Unified Studies Program. From: John M. Mickelson, "Curriculum Designs," in Leslie W. Kindred and Associates, **The Intermediate Schools** (Englewood Cliffs, New Jersey: Prentice-Hall, Inc., © 1968), by permission of Prentice-Hall, Inc., p. 126.

Major Functions of the Intermediate School

There appear to be four major functions for the intermediate school whether it is to be the more traditional junior high school or the new middle school.[12] These functions are: (1) a transitional bridge linking elementary and high school, (2) a special program for preadolescent and early adolescent students, (3) increased opportunities for exploratory experiences, and (4) a continuation of general education. Let us examine these functions individually.

Transitional Bridge Linking Elementary and High School. A reputed strength of the intermediate school is a bridging function. Gradually, children in the middle school, for example, move from organizational arrangements of a self-contained classroom nature in grade 5 to a departmental plan in grade 8. Table 7.2 clearly shows this point. During this time, they must make the transition from childhood to adolescence. Thus, the beginning phases of the middle school are akin to those programs and organizational arrangements of the elementary school. Systematically and slowly, the programs and organizational arrangements for the students are changed in the middle school as they leave the childhood years and move into the adolescent years. Finally, the program and organizational arrangements in the ending phases of the middle school are much like that of the high school. Hence, the middle school serves its bridging function.

Special Program for Preadolescent and Adolescent Students. Many educators in

---

12. William M. Alexander, "The Junior High School: A Changing View," in *Readings in Curriculum*, eds. Glen Hass and Kimball Wiles (Boston: Allyn and Bacon, Inc., 1965), 418-25.

the more modern intermediate schools have forced program revision by utilizing broad fields or some version of the core curriculum patterns to escape some of the shortcomings of the subjects-in-isolation curriculum pattern formerly used in the traditional junior high school. In so doing, they create larger block-of-time arrangements, particularly in the earlier grades, which permit more flexible curriculum alternatives. Too, team teaching by subject area and on an interdisciplinary basis, flexible scheduling, independent study, individualized instruction, and tutorial programs are other adjustments which have been made for children of intermediate school years (see table 7.2).

Guidance is one of the important aspects of the special program for the preadolescent and adolescent. One survey showed that 92 percent of the 154 middle schools enrolling over 12,000 pupils in 1968-69 had the services of a full- or part-time guidance counselor.[13] The guidance counselor plays a vital role in seeing that special provisions are made for the intermediate school children. For example, he assists in planning a curriculum sensitive to the needs of the students, makes pupil assessments, coordinates the use of municipal and private counseling services beyond those that he can provide, helps teachers and administrators with the task of pupil placement, and counsels students on a group and individual basis.

Increased Opportunities for Exploratory Experiences. A more flexible curriculum in the modern intermediate school should include a provision whereby students can investigate prevocational opportunities in depth. Other exploratory experiences might include the practical arts, such as industrial arts and home economics. A few middle schools are presently requiring that all students take the practical arts in grades 7 and 8 on a coeducational basis. Some middle schools that require music and art at every grade do so on an exploratory basis in a unified arts program. Other opportunities are provided in some middle schools such as instrumental and vocal music, Spanish, French, and speech.[14]

Continuation of General Education. One of the most important functions of the intermediate school is to hold back the development of interscholastic sports, dances, marching bands, and other activities of that nature which are highly competitive and frequently disruptive of the intellectual activities which the school conducts. At this point, the junior high school seems to have failed to sidestep these developments since, in many instances, it tends to be a miniature high school. The middle school, newer in origin and not hemmed in by established programs and traditions, appears to be avoiding this pitfall better than the junior high. This is true particularly at the fifth and sixth grade levels.[15] It would appear, therefore, that the continuance of general education which emphasizes the intellectual development of students patterned after the elementary school should be a major function of the intermediate school—at least through grade six or seven.

Evaluating the Intermediate School

There are many unanswered questions that must be investigated in the near future in an effort to determine whether the estab-

13. "Middle Schools in Theory," p. 51.
14. Ibid.
15. Ibid., p. 52.

lishment of the new intermediate school is justified.[16] A listing of some of the more important questions that should be answered is the following:

1. Will intermediate school children have improved self-concepts in comparison with their age-mate counterparts in schools having other organizational and instructional arrangements?
2. Are students of the intermediate school more autonomous than their counterparts in other types of schools?
3. Do students of the new intermediate school succeed better in high school than do their peers in more conventional schools?
4. Are pupils of the modern intermediate school more creative than their peers in other types of schools?
5. Will there be fewer discipline problems among students in the newer intermediate school than among pupils in more conventional schools?
6. What grades should be included in the intermediate school so that its program will be the most beneficial in moving children into adolescence gracefully—grades 5-8, 6-8 or some other arrangement?
7. Are there fewer dropouts at the end of the compulsory attendance years among students who studied in the modern intermediate school than among pupils in other types of schools?
8. Do students in the newer intermediate school more nearly work up to expectancy as individuals than do their age-mates in more conventional schools?

The modern intermediate school appears to be founded on sound premises. Until the questions posed under the section on evaluation are answered, the following points which presently seem to justify its establishment are adduced.

1. Children enter pubescence earlier now than formerly—at about eleven years of age. Why not place eleven year olds in the intermediate school?
2. It appears that sixth graders are more like seventh graders than fifth graders, and ninth graders are more like tenth graders than eighth graders. Why not create an intermediate school housing grades 6-8?
3. The ninth grade program of study is affected greatly by the Carnegie Units which cover a four-year high school program. Why not place the ninth grade in a four-year high school?
4. Children enter the intermediate school accustomed to the organizational plan and instructional arrangement of the elementary school. Why not create an intermediate school program that gradually bridges the gap between the procedures and program of the elementary school and that of the high school?
5. There appears to be enough pressures on children of early adolescent years, e.g., private music lessons, boy or girl scout activities, little league baseball, church activities. Why not create an intermediate school which does not have interscholastic sports, marching bands, and social functions such as school dances in an effort to lessen pressure during early adolescent years and which prolongs an emphasis on general education?

The new intermediate school movement in the nation can be one of the most important changes in education in recent years. It seems to be founded on sound premises and objectives. It must be pointed out, however, that simply changing the name of the junior high school to the middle school

16. Hines and Alexander, "Evaluating the Middle School," pp. 35-36; for an extended list of questions to be answered, see William M. Alexander, et al., *The Emergent Middle School* (New York: Holt, Rinehart and Winston, 1968), pp. 139-45.

without revising the program and procedures discussed in this chapter will accomplish little. The name of the intermediate school unit, therefore, is unimportant. What is important is the nature of the program and the nature of the students included in the modern intermediate school unit.

An Appraisal of the Intermediate School

In the United States, the demarcation in school organization between elementary and secondary grades is not precise. According to the size of the school system, conventional arrangements, and exigencies of school enrollment, elementary schools may embrace six, seven, or eight grades. State certification practices usually permit grade overlap in the intermediate years, so that whether teaching at the seventh or eighth grade is elementary or high school depends upon a point of view more than it does upon a substantive difference in curriculum or certificate. Since over 40 percent of the school systems utilize either 6-3-3 or 6-6 grade organization plans, it may be inferred that the first six years are elementary and the last six years are secondary. Here the break conforms to the distinction between elementary and secondary at the end of grade six which is characteristic of school systems in other parts of the world.

At the present time, the middle school of grades 6, 7, and 8, sometimes including grade 5, is proposed as an alternative to the pattern of the junior high school of grades 7, 8, and 9. To justify the middle school alternative, many advantages are claimed which are not unique to this type of organization. Some of these alleged advantages over the junior high type of intermediate school include a gradual shift from the self-contained classroom to departmentalization, core subject teaching, more flexible approaches to instruction, special courses, flexible scheduling, and guidance services. These practices are not peculiar to any type of grade organization, and may be conducted by teachers in a variety of grade organizational patterns.

Some of the alleged advantages are a peculiar form of special pleading. In view of the increase in departmentalization in lower elementary grades, the need for a "bridging" organization to provide for an easier transfer from the self-contained classroom to departmentalization in the upper middle grades is inconsistent with school trends. Furthermore, the increase in the use of teacher aids and other supportive personnel in the elementary school exposes the elementary student to work with a variety of adults so that the need for a cushion between the self-contained and the departmentalized classroom is probably imaginary.

In historical perspective, there has always been a shift in emphasis as elementary practitioners attempted to prolong the elementary school experience and as secondary practitioners attempted to emphasize earlier secondary training. Often these shifts are a matter of values and philosophy and are associated with changes in teacher expectancy and school climate more than formal changes in curriculum. In fact, it is frequently impossible to ascertain, on the basis of material studied, any difference in curriculum at the eighth grade in schools organized under such diverse plans as 8-4, 6-3-3, 6-6, 7-5, 4-4-4, and 5-3-4. The language of the middle school advocates, however, is closer in spirit to the language of progressive elementary educators of the thirties than it is to the subject orientation of secondary educators of the sixties. In fact, if it were not for advocacy of the middle school as a form of organization, a reader might think he was reading a justification for such plans as mere nongradedness or activity teaching.

The concept of the junior high school, as its name implies, is more clearly identified with secondary schooling, while the focus of the middle school is not yet clear. Since high school academic counting is tied to a four year sequence of academic units, there is good logic backed by an established behavior pattern to placing the ninth grade in a senior high school. On the other hand, such a shift overlooks the opportunities for individual excellence which the junior high affords to ninth graders—the seniors of a junior high—compared with their role as freshman in a four-year senior high school. However, similar opportunities would likewise be available to them as eighth graders in a middle school, just as it would pass from sixth to fifth graders in a five-year elementary school. Since behavior is not merely maturational but reflects the social context as well, any arguments based on optimum age placement are tenuous, particularly in view of the fact that individuals mature at different ages. Claims of optimal maturational fit are based on means, and do not take into account individual differences which occur at all ages. If the question of academic bookkeeping is important, the expedient of merely requiring Carnegie units for the last three years of senior high school would be as logical, though perhaps more difficult, as placing the ninth grade in the senior high school.

Most recommendations concerning school organization, as with the new emphasis on the middle school, represent ideological preferences without substantiating evidence. There is little or no evidence to substantiate any claim made for the advantages of any competing plan. In view of the many variables involved, the question of optimal organization is probably not researchable.

What is seldom emphasized is that school organization is a function of pupil number rather than of grand educational design. When the number of children in a school system was very small, it was not uncommon for all grades to be housed in a 1-11 or 1-12 organizational plan. As school districts increased in enrollment and required new housing, it appeared expedient and logical to house high school students in a grade organization separate from younger students. The popularity of the junior high school in larger school districts reflects the need for additional secondary housing.

In the concern for the "bridging" effect, the philosophy of both the junior high and of the middle school overlook the socializing effect of younger students coming into contact with older students. Many of the behavior and emotional problems associated with the pre- and early teens may reflect the isolation of these students from older students and the absence of models of more mature forms of behavior and expectancies. The use of a socializing model, rather than a maturational model, might suggest the 1-12 or 6-6 plan as a desirable form of grade organization. If a maturational thesis were logically followed, it might even suggest that the number of years spent in school be shortened. Some of the behavior problems associated with students of all ages, whether they are sixth graders or college seniors, might indicate that students are kept too long in a role from which they aspire to escape, even if it is to another level of education.

Since the disillusionment with the Prussian idol that came with World War I, American educators have seldom looked abroad for comparison except with jaundiced eye. The term "middle school" is similar to the pre-Weimar *Mittelschule* or the Italian *Scuola Media* in number of years if not in function. The former was a terminal school, and the latter could be terminal or bridging, according to the aspirations of the students. Current school organization in England divides schooling into primary and secondary, each of about six years. The primary school is divided into an infant school for grades 1-2, junior school for grades 3-6, lower secondary for grades 7-9, and grammar, technical, or comprehensive for the upper secondary grades. But there grade divisions are not always fixed.

In France, the first five grades are classified as primary and the others secondary. The sixth and seventh grades are orientation grades, not unlike grades 7 and 8 in the 6-2-4 plan in the United States. Grades 8 and 9 are upper secondary, and grades 10, 11, and 12 are terminal classes—grades which lead to the baccalaureate. In Russia, grade organization in ten-year schools tend to follow a 4-4-2 pattern, in which students do not begin the first year of formal schooling until age 7.

In all of these arrangements, as in the United States, it will be seen that a variety of patterns may be used. What the best pattern is probably must be judged in terms of local conditions and national expectancies. In the long run, it probably makes little difference if the intermediate school in the United States reflects the 6-3-3 plan with the junior high school or the 5-3-4 plan with the middle school. There will always be as much variation from the dominant pattern in percentage spread as there will be in percentage adherence to major patterns. It is possible to have many different combinations of grades making up schools, such as preprimary, primary, elementary, lower secondary, and upper secondary. These can be housed in one building, in separate buildings, or in building combinations. While the climate of the school may differ somewhat according to the housing pattern, the final product of the school, both in terms of graduates and those who drop out, will probably differ little as a result of different organizational patterns. It will depend more on the curriculum of the school and what the children are taught.

As a prospective teacher, you will have to be able to teach in whatever organizational arrangement exists in the school system in which you are employed. Whatever your own preferences, they will have to be adjusted to the organization of your school system. Children will probably learn more or less not because of the organization, but because of the way they are taught. Your own clarity of teaching goals and efficiency in the classroom is more important to their learning than the organizational pattern of the school district. After all, enrollment shifts and local variations have frequently required adaptations within a particular school district, so that rarely are all children in a school system housed or organized according to one educational plan. Frequently, decisions to put all sixth grade children in a school system together, or all ninth grade children together, appear to be no more than the need to do something to take care of enrollment and housing requirements. And still children learn. In view of the many different intra- and interclass organizational patterns in the elementary school used for instruction today, the question of the middle versus the junior high school is perhaps irrelevant. We should attempt to increase the school performance level of our pupils, and this can be done under a variety of organizational arrangements.

In theory, the development of an intermediate school which excludes the ninth grade would contribute to stronger teacher preparation programs by differentiating in the performance requirements of prospective primary and intermediate teachers. Undoubtedly, the span of performance behavior for prospective teachers of grades 1-8 is now too broad. If you plan to teach at the lower elementary grades, you should probably emphasize reading and language arts. If you wish to teach in the upper elementary grades, more subject matter preparation appears appropriate. With the newer emphasis on the intermediate school, colleges of education should design special training programs for prospective teachers of the intermediate school, provided, of course that the movement becomes widespread.

SELECTED REFERENCES

ALEXANDER, WILLIAM M. *A Survey of Organizational Patterns of Reorganized Middle Schools.* Final Report, Project No. 7-D-026. Gainesville: University of Florida, July 1968.

ALEXANDER, WILLIAM M., et al., *The Emergent Middle School.* New York: Holt, Rinehart and Winston, 1968.

BOSSING, NELSON L. and CRAMER, ROSCOE V. *The Junior High School.* Boston: Houghton Mifflin Company, 1965.

BRIM, R. P. *The Junior High School.* Washington, D.C.: The Center for Applied Research in Education, Inc., 1963.

EICHHORN, DONALD H. *The Middle School.* New York: The Center for Applied Research in Education, Inc., 1966.

GROOMS, M. ANN. *Perspectives on the Middle School.* Columbus, Ohio: Charles E. Merrill Books, Inc., 1967.

KINDRED, LESLIE W. and ASSOCIATES. *The Intermediate Schools.* Englewood Cliffs, New Jersey: Prentice-Hall, Inc., 1968.

MURPHY, JUDITH. *Middle Schools.* New York: Educational Facilities Laboratory, 1965.

POPPER, SAMUEL H. *The Middle School: An Organizational Analylsis.* Waltham, Mass.: Blaisdell Publishing Co., 1967.

instruction for exceptional children

8

There are many types of exceptional children. Broadly, they include the intellectually exceptional, creative, physically handicapped, emotionally disturbed and socially maladjusted. The term "exceptional children" refers to pupils who differ significantly from "average" or "typical" children to the degree that program modifications need to be made for them in either special classes or within the regular classroom.[1]

On the average, about one in every eight children in the elementary school is exceptional. According to Mackie, Hunter, and Neuber, the incidence of exceptionality extant among children ranging in age from five to seventeen years is as follows:[2]

Area of Exceptionality	Percent of Incidence
Visually handicapped (blind and partially seeing)	0.09
Crippled	1.00
Special health problems	1.00
Deaf and hard of hearing	0.58
Speech impaired	3.50
Socially maladjusted and emotionally disturbed	2.00
Mentally retarded	2.30
Gifted	2.00
TOTAL	12.47

Children who are exceptional fall into one of two groups—those who are incapable of performing at the level of the average and those who perform well above the average. Furthermore, the program modification for some of the exceptional children will be quite pronounced and may be required throughout their schooling while others will need only minor adjustments in programs for a short duration.[3] Let us examine the various types of exceptionality extant among elementary school children.

Intellectually Exceptional

The intellectually exceptional children can be classified into two groups—gifted and mentally retarded. How these children are identified and some suggestions about program modifications for them are included in the following sections.

1. Walter B. Barbe, *The Exceptional Child* (Washington, D.C.: The Center for Applied Research in Education, Inc., © 1963), p. 2.
2. Romaine P. Mackie, Patricia P. Hunter, and Margaret A. Neuber, *College and University Programs for the Preparation of Teachers of Exceptional Children* (Washington, D.C.: U.S. Office of Education, 1961-62), p. 125.
3. Barbe, *Exceptional Child.*

Gifted

The intellectually able children in the elementary school may be classified into two groups—*extremely gifted* and *gifted*. The *extremely gifted* children are those students who possess I.Q.'s of 170 or more. Generally, only one child in every ten thousand to one hundred thousand children is extremely gifted. Such a child possesses the potential for making significant contributions to his generation as well as to succeeding ones.[4]

The *gifted* children are those who possess I.Q.'s that range from 130 to 170.[5] About one child in every 40 to 160 children is gifted. These children have the ability to make contributions of a higher order to their own generation.[6]

All gifted children, i.e., extremely gifted and gifted, may display certain positive characteristics and negative characteristics on occasion. As outlined by Dunlap, these characteristics include the following:[7]

Positive Characteristics. As a group, gifted children tend to be strong and healthy, well-adjusted, friendly, understanding, and alert. In a congenial setting, they are likely to:

1. Learn rapidly and easily
2. Retain what they learn without much drill
3. Show much curiosity as indicated by the kinds, depth, scope, and frequency of their questions
4. Have rich vocabularies marked by originality of thought and expression
5. Enjoy reading, usually at a mature level
6. Show interest in words and ideas as demonstrated by their frequent use of dictionaries, encyclopedias, and other source books
7. Reason things out, think clearly and precisely, be quick to comprehend
8. Have the ability to generalize, to see relationships, to make logical associations
9. Examine, tabulate, classify, collect, and keep records
10. Know and appreciate many things of which other children are unaware
11. Be interested in the nature of man and his universe at an early age
12. Seek older companions among children and enjoy adults
13. Possess a good sense of humor and be cheerful
14. Have a strong desire to excel

Negative Characteristics. Not all symptoms of giftedness are welcomed by teachers or by parents. Characteristics that are negative or unacceptable from an adult's point of view often tend to overshadow more positive signs of ability. Gifted children may be:

1. Restless, inattentive, disturbing, or annoying to those around them, like many children who have unmet needs
2. Poor in spelling, careless in handwriting, or inaccurate in arithmetic because they are impatient with details requiring rote learning or drill
3. Lackadaisical in completing or handing in assignments, and indifferent toward classwork when uninterested
4. Outspokenly critical both of themselves and of others, an attitude which often alienates adults as well as children

Generally, there are three ways of meeting the needs of all gifted children in the elementary school. These methods include:

---

4. James M. Dunlap, "The Education of Children with High Mental Ability," in *Education of Exceptional Children and Youth,* 2d ed., eds. William M. Cruickshank and G. Orville Johnson (Englewood Cliffs, New Jersey: Prentice-Hall, Inc., 1967), pp. 148-49.
5. Barbe, *Exceptional Child,* pp. 31-38.
6. Dunlap, "Education of Children," pp. 148-49.
7. Ibid., p. 154.

(1) acceleration, (2) special classes, and (3) enrichment in regular classrooms.[8]

For many years, *acceleration* has been employed as a strategy for meeting the needs of gifted children. Acceleration works in one of two ways as a general rule. First, certain gifted children are allowed to enter school a year early and progress through school with students who are a year older than they are. Second, gifted children are permitted to double-promote or skip a grade in order to be placed in appropriate teaching and learning situations which are commensurate with their abilities. When the latter method of acceleration is practiced, care should be taken to see that each child properly adjusts socially and emotionally to working with an older group of students.

Special classes have been utilized in working with gifted children in metropolitan areas where enough children are available to form such classes. The Major Work Program in the Cleveland Public Schools is illustrative of the special classes approach. In their plan, children with I.Q.'s of 125 and above are selected to attend special classes for the gifted with other pupils of their approximate age. The special classes in this instance are provided in the regular school and the gifted children participate in all school activities.[9]

Another plan of special classes to meet the educational needs of gifted children is that practiced in Pittsburgh's Colfax School. Under the Colfax Plan, gifted children are placed in regular classrooms for one-half of each school day to study with average students in art, music, and physical education. The other half day they pursue academic studies employing workshop activities in special classes limited to the gifted, where individual and group projects are conducted in an experimental laboratory setting.[10]

Enrichment in regular classrooms is another method for meeting the educational needs of gifted children. For example, teachers form appropriate intraclass groupings of gifted students to work on their unique needs or else they give them as much individualized instruction as possible while the pupils pursue independent study projects in the regular classroom. In all likelihood, enrichment in regular classrooms is the most frequently utilized plan for educating gifted students in the nation's elementary schools.[11]

Mentally Retarded

Another group of intellectually exceptional children is the mentally retarded group. Those children which can be classified as being mentally retarded may be placed into one of three categories: (1) educable mentally retarded, (2) trainable mentally retarded, and (3) severely mentally deficient. Let us examine some of the characteristics of these mental retardates and some of the issues involved in educating them.

Educable Mentally Retarded. Those children who possess I.Q.'s which range from

8. See Oscar T. Jarvis and Haskin R. Pounds, *Organizing, Supervising, and Administering the Elementary School* (West Nyack, N.Y.: Parker Publishing Company, 1969), pp. 114-15.
9. Norma E. Cutts and Nicholas Moseley, *Teaching the Bright and Gifted* (Englewood Cliffs, N.J.: Prentice-Hall, Inc., 1957), pp. 95-96.
10. Hedwig Pregler, "The Colfax Plan," *Exceptional Children* 20, no. 5 (February 1954): 198-201, 222.
11. For suggestions on methods of teaching the gifted, see: E. Paul Torrance, *Gifted Children in the Classroom* (New York: Macmillan Company, 1965), pp. 38-45; Joan B. Nelson and Donald L. Cleland, "The Role of the Teacher of the Gifted," *Education* 88, no. 1 (September-October 1967): 47-51.

50 to 75 may be classified as being educable mentally retarded. Many school systems follow the practice of educating this group of mental retardates through the medium of special classes in the regular school; a practice questioned by some.[12] When this practice obtains, the EMR students are not completely isolated from other children in that they participate in all of the school's activities of an extra-class nature.

Barbe has cautioned that the educable mentally retarded child will not excel the sixth grade level by much in academic achievement on reaching his full mental development. Further, he has pointed out that both his learning rate and capacity for learning are one-half to three-fourths of that possessed by the average child.[13]

EMR special classes in the elementary school are multiaged and ungraded in nature more often than not. That is, children ranging in chronological age from 6 to 10 years are placed in a primary section and pupils ranging in age from 9 to 13 years are sectioned into an intermediate section. Usually, the pupil-teacher ratio is 15 to 1, in these sections.[14] Beyond this special training, the EMR students normally enter a prevocational program which is followed by a work-school training phase.[15]

Children in the EMR classes should be taught by teachers who have had special training. Likewise, they require a special curriculum whose purposes are primarily social, personal, and occupational.[16] In addition to special teachers and curriculum, EMR children require special instructional materials suited to their unique educational needs; particularly do they need an abundance of manipulative aids such as the abacus or place value board in arithmetic to assist them in learning concretely.

Other plans for educating EMR children involve such practices as placement in the regular classroom with assistance from a special itinerant teacher, placement in a special class for part of the day and in the regular classroom for the remainder of the day for such subjects as art and music.[17]

Trainable Mentally Retarded. Children who range in I.Q.'s from 30 up to about 50 may be classified as trainable mentally retarded. One may expect to find two or three TMR children in every 1,000 pupils.[18]

TMR children can profit from a training program geared to meet their special needs. With proper training, the TMR children can learn to care for themselves personally with respect to eating, dressing, and safety.[19] Also, some of them can learn through sheltered workshops provided in some elementary schools, for example, to develop a degree of vocational competency that will enable them to perform certain routine tasks and thereby become partially self-supporting. Such training and vocational pursuits are very carefully supervised.[20]

There are many agencies which attempt to provide training programs for TMR chil-

12. For a provocative paper concerning this point, see: G. Orville Johnson, "Special Education for the Mentally Handicapped," *Exceptional Children* 29, no. 1 (October 1962): 62-69.
13. Barbe, *Exceptional Child,* p. 15.
14. Ibid., p. 18.
15. Leon Charney and Edward LaCrosse, *The Teacher of the Mentally Retarded* (New York: John Day Company, 1965), p. 66.
16. Marie A. Mehl et al., *Teaching in Elementary School,* 3d ed. (New York: Ronald Press Company, © 1965), p. 309.
17. Samuel A. Kirk, *Educating Exceptional Children* (Boston: Houghton Mifflin Company, 1962), p. 132.
18. Barbe, *Exceptional Child,* p. 22.
19. Mehl, et al., *Teaching in Elementary School,* p. 308.
20. Barbe, *Exceptional Child,* p. 24.

dren: (1) state residential schools, (2) day care programs sponsored by civic or religious groups, and (3) the public school. If the individual child's mental deficiency is not such that he must be institutionalized in a state residential school or be confined to his own home, the public school is most likely the best agency in our society to provide effectual training for the trainable mentally retarded. This practice has the salutary effect of maintaining the total family unit together which provides a strong supportive base for the TMR child.[21]

Severely Mentally Deficient. The group of children who possess I.Q.'s which range from 0 to about 30 are classified as the severely mentally deficient. These children cannot be trained to care for themselves, hence are custodial cases. Since they are not trainable, there is no provision for them in the public school. Severely mentally deficient children are cared for by their parents at home or else they are institutionalized. They are infrequently, if ever, seen in our society.[22]

Creative Children

Creative children are capable of contributing new ideas, solutions, symbols, interpretations, and implications.[23] Torrance views *creativity* as a process when he states that it is ". . . the process of sensing problems or gaps in information, forming ideas or hypotheses, testing and modifying these hypotheses, and communicating the results. This process may lead to any one of many kinds of products—verbal and nonverbal, concrete and abstract."[24]

In summarizing the identifying characteristics studies of creative children, Mehl, Mills, Douglass, and Scobey have listed twenty-five distinguishing characteristics of the typical creative child. These characteristics are that he:[25]

1. Is intelligent beyond the average, but not necessarily gifted
2. Is not necessarily interested in I.Q. scores or high marks in school
3. Is not a satisfactory student
4. Is persistently discouraged by parents, teachers, and classmates and sometimes is a problem to them
5. Is less concerned about financial success; has low interest in economic values
6. Is energetic
7. Is independent in thought and action
8. Is flexible, permissive, and tolerant
9. Tends to be a non-conformist
10. Is non-authoritarian and does not need to impose order
11. Accepts innovation and challenge presented in apparent imperfections
12. Turns disorder into meaning
13. Is rather intuitive, achieving perception through intuition rather than senses
14. Is sensitive to things but not with hurt feelings
15. Is more imaginative than the average person
16. Is humorous and playful
17. Has a mind that moves rapidly from one thing to another
18. Is original
19. Prefers complexity

21. Elmer W. Weber, *Mentally Retarded Children and Their Education* (Springfield, Illinois: Charles C Thomas, 1963), p. 69.
22. Mehl et al., *Teaching in Elementary School,* p. 308.
23. Ibid., p. 294.
24. E. Paul Torrance, *Creativity* (What Research Says to the Teacher, Bulletin no. 28. Washington, D.C.: Association of Classroom Teachers, a Department of the National Education Association, 1963), p. 4.
25. Mehl et al., *Teaching in Elementary School,* pp. 295-96.

20. Enjoys risks and uncertainty
21. Has a strong sense of destiny
22. Is likely to possess high opposite-sex characteristics
23. May be a slow starter but a quick finisher
24. Blooms in different ways at different times
25. Is troubled by things generally but handles his own troubles adequately

There appear to be many blocks to the releasing of creativity in the classroom, such as emphasis on pupil conformity to peer-group norms in behavior, undue rewards for "success" which makes children fearful of trying new approaches that may fail, and authoritarian teaching which may impede student questioning and exploration.[26] Teachers can release creativity and assist children to learn in creative ways by developing teaching and learning situations in which the pupils have ample opportunities to explore, manipulate, question, experiment, take risks, test hypotheses, and modify ideas; in short, to inquire.[27] Such teaching and learning situations will be facilitated if the teacher can establish a friendly classroom environment, lessen interpersonal competition among children, become more accepting of extant pupil differences, and provide opportunities throughout the week for creative pursuits rather than at stipulated time periods such as in music, art or English classes.[28]

Physically Exceptional

There are a number of physically exceptional children in the elementary school who, for the most part, receive their education in the regular classrooms.[29] These children include the visually, aurally, speech, orthopedically, and special health handicapped. Let us examine the characteristics of each group and explore the program modifications that customarily are made for them.

Visually Handicapped

Children who are visually handicapped are classified as being either blind or partially sighted. Technically, a blind child has a visual acuity of 20/200 or less in his better eye with corrected vision. On the other hand, a partially-sighted child has a visual acuity, after visual correction, of between 20/70 and 20/200 in his better eye.[30] This means that a partially-sighted child possessing visual acuity of 40/100 can see at 40 feet what an average child could see at 100. The incidence of blind children is one child in every three thousand and only about one child in every five hundred children is partially sighted according to the foregoing definitions.[31]

Approximately 25 percent of the children in the elementary school have minor vision defects which, because they are correctable, do not result in an educational handicap. Others with uncorrected vision problems, however, are easily identifiable by the classroom teacher. For example, they frequently

26. Torrance, *Creativity,* pp. 21-22.
27. Ibid., pp. 12-14.
28. See: Albert H. Shuster and Milton E. Ploghoft, *The Emerging Elementary Curriculum: Methods and Procedures* (Columbus, Ohio: Charles E. Merrill Books, Inc., 1963), p. 336.
29. See Dorothy Waleski, "The Physically Handicapped in the Regular Classroom," *NEA Journal* 53, no. 9 (December 1964): 13-16.
30. Charles W. Telford and James M. Sawrey, *The Exceptional Individual: Psychological and Educational Aspects* (Englewood Cliffs, N.J.: Prentice-Hall, Inc., 1967), pp. 271-72.
31. Ibid., pp. 275-76.

rub, squint, or blink their eyes and while reading they may hold the book very close or far away.[32] When children suffer from uncorrected vision problems, they should be referred to an ophthalmologist for examination to see if their problems are correctable and whether or not special program provisions need to be made for them.

Generally, it is considered best by most authorities to place partially sighted children in regular classrooms and let the teachers make whatever adjustments are necessary such as those in program, seating arrangements, and materials which will provide effectual teaching and learning situations for them. The education of blind children, however, cannot be handled quite that easily since they must learn to read and write in braille. They can learn the braille in special classes while, at the same time, spending part of the school day in regular classrooms. Or, as practiced in some schools, they can be assigned primarily to regular classrooms and receive specialized instruction from a special itinerant teacher of the blind in another room.[33]

Aurally Handicapped

The aurally handicapped children may be placed in one of two groups—deaf and hard-of-hearing. The former have hearing losses ranging from 60 to 100 decibels and the latter 20 to 60 decibels.[34]

Generally, the deaf children are educated in residential schools, in special classes of the regular school, or in day schools. Instruction is administered through either the manual alphabet, sign language, or lip reading methods. Sometimes a combination of these, e.g., lip reading and sign language, is used conjointly.[35]

There are far more hard-of-hearing children than there are deaf children. Those children with mild hearing losses, i.e., 30 to 40 decibels, are educated in the regular classroom. In this instance, the classroom teacher must see that they are seated where they can hear adequately. The children who have moderate hearing losses, i.e., 40 to 60 decibels, can most likely perform acceptably in the regular classroom when they are fitted with a hearing aid. Hearing therapists are available in many schools to assist hard-of-hearing children develop such special skills as lip reading and speech. The classroom teacher can help the hard-of-hearing child who needs this special instruction by cooperating with the hearing therapist.[36]

Speech Handicapped

There are several categories of speech defects such as problems of: (1) speech development, (2) articulation, (3) voice, and (4) stuttering.[37] The usual practice in educating the speech defective children is to place them in regular classrooms although special classes are provided in some large school systems.

32. Ibid., p. 273.
33. Barbe, *Exceptional Child*, pp. 47-48. Anthony J. Pelone, *Helping the Handicapped in a Regular Class* (New York: Bureau of Publications, Teachers College, Columbia University, 1957) pp. 8-9.
34. Telford and Sawrey, *Exceptional Individual*, pp. 298-99.
35. Barbe, *Exceptional Child*, p. 52.
36. Mehl et al., *Teaching in Elementary School*, pp. 299-300.
37. Stanley H. Ainsworth, "The Education of Children with Speech Handicaps," in *Education of Exceptional Children and Youth*, 2d ed., eds. William M. Cruickshank and G. Orville Johnson (Englewood Cliffs, N.J.: Prentice-Hall, Inc., 1967), pp. 390-407.

When children with speech disorders are placed in the regular classroom, the teacher can help meet their educational needs in various ways. He can: (1) screen children suffering from speech impairments and make appropriate referrals to such persons as the school psychologist or speech correctionist, (2) work cooperatively with the speech correctionist in providing prescribed individual instruction in the classroom as time permits, and (3) create an atmosphere in the classroom in which the speech deviates have opportunities to practice the use of correct sound.[38]

Orthopedically Handicapped

Children who are orthopedically handicapped, e.g., those who have been crippled by osteomyelitis, cerebral palsy, and poliomyelitis, are generally placed in the regular classroom for instruction. When this obtains, the classroom teacher should adapt the instructional program for the orthopedically handicapped children insofar as possible and also involve them in the ongoing or typical classroom activities. Such a practice contributes towards peer acceptance of the orthopedically handicapped and helps them develop positive self-concepts as well.[39]

One of the major purposes in educating the orthopedically handicapped children is to help them learn to live as normal a life as is possible given their physical impairment. The teacher, in endeavoring to achieve this goal, should attempt to prevent other children from calling special or undue attention to the orthopedically handicapped child. Also, the school facility can be modified slightly to aid the orthopedically handicapped children to become more autonomous and self-reliant. For example, ramps, rails, and less slippery floor surfaces can be installed which will enable many orthopedically handicapped children to be more ambulatory in the facility.[40]

When the severity of the physical impairment is extreme, e.g., severe ambulatory or palsy problems, special classes and schools where specialized service and equipment are available may be compulsory. This practice obtains where physically handicapped children cannot cope successfully with an adjusted program in the regular classroom.[41]

Special Health Handicapped

Since many children who are the special health handicapped, e.g., those affected by rheumatic fever, epilepsy, diabetes, and malnourishment, are placed in the regular classroom for instruction, the teacher must learn how to make minor program adjustments for them, such as extended rest periods and reduced work loads. Actually, the curriculum for the special health handicapped children does not vary from that of the average students (with the exception of the refraining from participation in strenuous activities in some cases, such as those occurring in physical education).[42]

Some special health handicapped children, depending on the type and severity of their problems, are placed in special classes for instruction. Others, such as those who are hospitalized or are convalescing at

38. Mehl et al., *Teaching in Elementary School*, p. 299.
39. R. Murray Thomas and Shirley M. Thomas, *Individual Differences in the Classroom* (New York: David McKay, Inc., 1965), pp. 531-32.
40. Mehl et al., *Teaching in Elementary School*, p. 302.
41. Benjamin Spock and Marion O. Lerringo, *Caring for Your Disabled Child* (New York: Macmillan Company, 1965), pp. 121-23.
42. Barbe, *Exceptional Child*, p. 65.

home, receive instruction or tutoring from a "generalist" teacher, provided by the school for a few hours each week.[43] Those special health handicapped children who are bedridden for extended periods of time beyond normal convalescence receive instruction from a homebound teacher. Teleteaching—intercommunications equipment and portable audiovisual equipment used to connect the convalescent child with the classroom—has been used effectively in recent years to enrich the homebound and hospitalized student's program.[44]

Emotionally and Socially Handicapped

Perhaps less is known about how to work effectually with the emotionally and socially handicapped than with other groups of exceptional children.[45] Problems involving appropriate methods of identification, placement, therapy, and education have been complicating factors in successfully coping with the emotionally and socially handicapped children.[46]

Technically, a child is *emotionally disturbed* if he is maladjusted in relationship to himself; whereas a *socially maladjusted* child is maladjusted in his relationship with others.[47] Emotionally disturbed children may demonstrate such observable behavior as hostility, defiance, aggressiveness. Conversely, they may become overly passive. Also, they may be accident-prone, frequently sick and complain of minor aches, pains, or fatigue. Unconscious internal tension and conflict may result in the emotionally disturbed child displaying fears, guilt, anxieties, or frustrations.[48] The problem with the socially maladjusted child is somewhat different. As a general rule, he has little, if any, concern for others. Because he has a restricted conscience limiting his ability to feel sorry or guilty, he is unable to control his actions like the socially well-adjusted child. As a result, oftentimes his behavior is viewed as not being socially acceptable.[49]

There are a number of ways to provide programs for the emotionally and socially handicapped children. They include placement in special classes, special schools, day care centers, psychiatric hospitals, residential schools, and in the regular classrooms of the elementary school.[50] Most emotionally and socially handicapped children, however, are placed in the regular classroom for instruction. There appear to be three good reasons for this practice: (1) many school systems do not have the financial resources to provide special classes for the emotionally and socially handicapped children, (2) these children can be best helped when they associate with well-adjusted children in the regular classroom provided, of course, that their maladjustment is not too

---

43. Leo E. Connor, *Administration of Special Education Programs* (New York: Bureau of Publications, Teachers College, Columbia University, 1961), pp. 37-39.

44. Dorothy Carr, "Teleteaching—A New Approach to Teaching Elementary and Secondary Homebound Pupils," *Exceptional Children* 31, no. 3 (November 1964): 118.

45. See: Herbert C. Quay, "Some Basic Considerations in the Education of Emotionally Disturbed Children," *Exceptional Children* 30, no. 1 (September 1963): 27-31.

46. See Barbe, *Exceptional Child*, pp. 85-92.

47. Ibid., p. 85.

48. Mehl et al., *Teaching in Elementary School*, p. 305.

49. William C. Morse, "The Education of Socially Maladjusted and Emotionally Disturbed Children," in *Education of Exceptional Children and Youth*, 2d ed., eds. William M. Cruickshank and G. Orville Johnson (Englewood Cliffs, N.J.: Prentice-Hall, Inc., 1967), p. 582.

50. Ibid., 615-19; Barbe, *Exceptional Child*, 85-92.

severe, and (3) rehabilitation of the maladjusted children and their reintegration into the regular classroom might be more difficult if they were educated elsewhere.[51]

There are some things which the regular classroom teacher can do to help emotionally and socially handicapped children become better adjusted. For example, he can: acquire as much knowledge as possible about the identifying characteristics of each; screen those in need of special help and make appropriate referrals; be patient, understanding, and mature in dealing with them; show that he has a genuine interest in helping them; work closely with available specialists by providing them with information and support; maintain open lines of communication with parents; and help the handicapped children develop positive self-concepts.[52]

Disadvantaged Children

In recent years, a new group of children referred to by various names such as the economically deprived, the culturally disadvantaged, the culturally different, the socially disadvantaged and the like have received much attention and can be added to the ranks of exceptionality.[53] Presently, it appears that the best term that can be used to identify this group of children is *disadvantaged*. This generic term covers all children who do not achieve well in school because of deprivation resulting from economic or cultural limitations which have had deleterious effects upon their environment and experiences.

Because the large numbers of children in the nation which presently can be classified as being disadvantaged represent such a formidable problem in education, chapter 23 is devoted exclusively to an examination of this issue.

The Classroom Teacher and Exceptional Children

The teacher in the regular classroom is in most instances a key person in helping to meet the instructional needs of exceptional children in the elementary school. This is particularly true when exceptional children are placed in the regular classroom for all or part of their instruction.

There are a number of things which the regular classroom teacher can do in developing viable educational opportunities for exceptional children who are totally or partially integrated into his classroom for instruction. First, he can familiarize himself with the nature of exceptional children which are to be found in the elementary school. This would include a knowledge of the types and incidence of exceptionality in children and the characteristics of the different categories of exceptional children. Second, he can become knowledgeable about the school's policies, procedures, and programs for educating the exceptional children. Third, the regular classroom teacher can become accepting of exceptional children with whom he works. Fourth, he can cooperate fully with specialists employed by the school in the field of special education. For example, he can provide learning experiences recom-

---

51. Jarvis and Pounds, *Organizing, Supervising*, p. 122.

52. See Pearl H. Berkowitz and Esther P. Rothman, *Public Education for Disturbed Children in New York City* (Springfield, Illinois: Charles C. Thomas, 1967).

53. For a discussion of disadvantaged children see: Lester D. Crow et al., *Educating the Culturally Disadvantaged Child* (New York: David McKay Company, Inc., 1966); Frank Riessman, *The Culturally Deprived Child* (New York: Harper & Row Publishers, 1962). A. Harry Passow et al., eds., *Education of the Disadvantaged: A Book of Readings* (New York: Holt, Rinehart and Winston, Inc., 1967).

mended by the speech correctionist for speech handicapped children who have been placed in his room for instruction. And, fifth, the regular classroom teacher can make certain adaptations in his instructional program and teaching-learning situations for exceptional children placed in his classroom. Some examples of this point include (1) seating hard-of-hearing children in the front of the room where they are likely to be able to hear class discussion better, (2) providing enrichment experiences for gifted children such as independent study or programmed materials, and (3) being supportive of physically handicapped children by creating a classroom environment which is not patronizing or overly sympathetic while, at the same time, it is free of ridicule.

The role that the regular classroom teacher plays in helping to meet the educational needs of exceptional children cannot be overemphasized. Some authorities, for example, believe that exceptional children should have some portion of their schooling with more typical children in order that all children can learn to identify with one another.[54] When this exists, quite obviously, the regular classroom teacher is a vital element of the total program for exceptional children in the elementary school.

An Appraisal of Instruction For Exceptional Children

It is a commentary on our preference for educational euphemisms that in the one category of exceptional children American educators embrace with the halt, the maim, and the blind both the genius and the idiot. Comparatively speaking, tremendous strides have been made in the education of the handicapped, whether resulting from physical or mental deficiency. The fact that we teach the deaf to speak and the blind to read are but two indications of the extent to which the capacity of man to train and educate overcomes limitations of organic inadequacy. While the mentally deficient are more humanely treated than in former years and specialized training offers some hope of small success, the fact that a large part of the disadvantaged school population has the characteristics of the educationally retarded highlights the inadequacies of our treatment in this area.

Unless a person deliberately chooses a career of teaching the severely physically handicapped, for example, it is likely that he will not encounter these children. Most frequently they are placed in special classes. The milder degrees of mental deficiency, however, often occur in the school, where the actual condition may not be diagnosed by the teacher, unless there is referral to trained psychometrists. While the number of mentally deficient are small, there is a much larger number of disadvantaged children whose performance levels in school are similar to those of the retarded.

The regular classroom teacher, however, should always keep in mind some generalizations relating to the diagnosis of mental deficiency. Mental retardation is relative, not absolute, and is subject to change with education. The diagnosis which comes from individual testing is not so much a description of capacity as it is of previous experience and opportunity to learn. The only certain way to determine the degree of mental retardation is to place a child in an instructional situation and make observations of actual task performance. Generally, real task performance of educable and trainable mental retardates exceed the level of per-

---

54. Henry J. Otto and David C. Sanders, *Elementary School Organization and Administration*, 4th ed. (New York: Appleton-Century-Crofts, Inc., 1964), pp. 89-90.

formance predicted from IQ measures. This results from the fact that the IQ test primarily measures abstract and symbolic skills used in schools, which in many cases are only slightly related to real job tasks. As adults, mental retardates most often blend imperceptibly into the general population where their functional characteristics make them indistinguishable from other adults.

Most mentally retarded children do not suffer from organic impairment as much as they do from cultural deprivation, but it is rare that the institutional setting provides conditions of learning which deliberately increase response levels. Today, interest in the problems of the culturally disadvantaged and the slow learner overlap with the area of the mentally retarded. They all have similar indices of learning difficulty. Notwithstanding the fact that the costs per pupil of training the mentally retarded are higher than the costs of training the normal population, the long term costs of education are much less than the costs of institutionalization or welfare support. Education of the mentally retarded is not only a matter of eleemosynary concern but one of manpower utilization which brings social as well as individual benefit.

It is nevertheless striking that while we have a number of specialists and programs relating to the handicapped, such as the Handicapped Children's Act of 1968, the special research efforts of the National Institute of Health, and the special state programs, there are no comparative programs to develop the talents of the gifted. After the advent of Sputnik, increased interest was shown in special programs for the gifted, for example, the Merit Scholarship Program for high school students which seeks to recognize unusually able students. Some states, such as North Carolina and Georgia have financed Governor's Honors Programs for selected gifted students. At the elementary level, however, no comparable programs have been offered, except in isolated instances.

Even more striking in the concept of exceptionality is the exclusion of those rare traits in the population associated with the development of artistic, music, and dance skills. While the elementary school gives lip service to the development of skills in these areas, the fact is that the acceptance of a philosophy of child self-expression is a negation of the rigorous training which is a prerequisite to the attainment of these skills, at least in music and ballet. It is not uncommon to find adults providing, through the Little Leagues, the Y, and boys' clubs, the specialized training that develops athletic ability. While some boys and girls have the physique and motor coordination which helps them to excel in sports, the eventual excellence inevitably comes with practice. If one day most of the musicians in the United States are Japanese, it may reflect the fact that we are unwilling to identify through training the potential for excellence, whereas the Japanese have deliberately stimulated it, even among preschoolers, through training.

An earlier section in this chapter has indicated that children who are described as creative are different in their behavior patterns from their more conventional classmates. Longitudinal studies of the relationship of childhood creativity to adult creativity are lacking. At the present time, it is impossible to say with certainty that the creative child will be a creative adult. One of the basic problems relating to psychological investigations of creativity is the lack of precise and objective definitions of creativity.

In children, it would appear that creativity is almost synonymous with divergence. In the adult world, however, creativity is more than divergence—it implies productive originality, whether in the form of art, music, literature, architecture, science, or some other field. Also, in the adult world it is hard to differentiate between creativity as the fruitful product of knowledge—convergent thinking—and pristine originality. Too little is known about the relationship and comparison between disciplined research to productivity and the contribution of the creative dilettante. It may be that the plodding pace of the former creates little enthusiasm whereas the apparent luck or adventuresomeness of the latter appeals to the romantic strain within all of us. Until more is known, however, good classroom pedagogy would seem to require the teacher to attempt to capitalize on whatever divergent urges his charges may have to further their schooling and perhaps cultivate some hidden talent. Only time and age can reveal each child's long term creativity.

As a teacher you will come into contact with many kinds of pupils. Some will be so bright that only the faintest clue will help them make connections and see relationships; others will apparently learn little from the exercise of all your teaching strategies. As you prepare to become a teacher, you will need to find more about the types of deviations described under the global rubric of exceptionality. You will need to do this so you can assist children with their learning problems, if not directly, at least by referral to the specialists who have these competencies. You may also wish to decide to become a teacher of exceptional children, a decision which would require you to take special training not included in the preparatory program of general elementary teachers. One of the dangers you will need to guard against is making premature judgments about children on the basis of a few observations. Also, refrain from making over-generalizations about the exceptionality of your children from inadequate data. Consult your specialists. They are in the school system to assist you with the educating of exceptional children.

SELECTED REFERENCES

BARBE, WALTER B. *The Exceptional Child.* Washington, D.C.: The Center for Applied Research in Education, Inc., 1963.

BLOOM, BENJAMIN S. et al. *Compensatory Education for Cultural Deprivation.* Chicago: University of Chicago Research Conference on Education and Cultural Deprivation, 1964.

CHARNEY, LEON, and LA CROSSE, EDWARD. *The Teacher of the Mentally Retarded.* New York: John Day Company, 1965.

CONNOR, FRANCES P. *Education of Homebound or Hospitalized Children.* New York: Bureau of Publications, Teachers College, Columbia University, 1964.

CRAWFORD, FRED L. *Career Planning for the Blind.* New York: Farrar, Straus and Giroux, 1966.

CRUICKSHANK, WILLIAM M., and JOHNSON, G. ORVILLE, eds. *Education of Exceptional Children and Youth.* 2d ed. Englewood Cliffs, N.J.: Prentice-Hall, Inc., 1967.

DAVIS, HOLLOWELL, and DAVIS, S. RICHARD, eds. *Hearing and Deafness.* New York: Holt, Rinehart and Winston, 1966.

DUNN, LLOYD M., ed. *Exceptional Children in the Schools.* New York: Holt, Rinehart and Winston, Inc., 1963.

GRIFFITHS, CIWA. *Conquering Childhood Deafness.* New York: Exposition Press, Inc., 1967.

GALLAGHER, JAMES J., ed. *Teaching Gifted Students.* Boston: Allyn and Bacon, Inc., 1965.

JENKINS, GLADYS G. et al. *These Are Your Children*. Chicago: Scott, Foresman and Company, 1966.

KARLIN, ISAAC et al. *Development and Disorders of Speech in Childhood*. Springfield, Illinois: Charles C Thomas, 1965.

LONG, NICHOLAS J. et al., eds. *Conflict in the Classroom: The Education of Emotionally Disturbed Children*. Belmont, California: Wadsworth Publishing Company, 1965.

MEHL, MARIE A. et al. *Teaching in Elementary School*. 3d ed. New York: Ronald Press Company, 1965.

RIESSMAN, FRANK. *Helping the Disadvantaged Pupil to Learn More Easily*. Englewood Cliffs, N.J.: Prentice-Hall, Inc., 1966.

TELFORD, CHARLES W., and SAWREY, JAMES M. *The Exceptional Individual: Psychological and Educational Aspects*. Englewood Cliffs, N.J.: Prentice-Hall, Inc., 1967.

THOMAS, R. MURRAY, and THOMAS, SHIRLEY M. *Individual Differences in the Classroom*. New York: David McKay Company, Inc., 1965.

TORRANCE, E. PAUL. *Creativity*. Bulletin no. 28. Washington, D.C.: National Education Association—Department of Classroom Teachers and American Educational Research Association, 1963.

TORRANCE, E. PAUL. *Guiding Creative Talent*. Englewood Cliffs, N.J.: Prentice-Hall, Inc., 1962.

SHUMSKY, ABRAHAM. *Creative Teaching in the Elementary School*. New York: Appleton-Century-Crofts, 1965.

SPOCK, BENJAMIN, and LERRINGO, MARION O. *Caring for Your Disabled Child*. New York: Macmillan Company, 1965.

WITTY, PAUL A., ed. *The Educationally Retarded and Disadvantaged, The Sixty-sixth Yearbook of the National Society for the Study of Education*. Chicago: University of Chicago Press, 1967.

the school's media center

9

The media center has been defined as a "learning center in a school where a full range of print and audiovisual media, necessary equipment, and services from media specialists are accessible to students and teachers."[1] To gain an adequate understanding of the media center's vital role in the instructional program of the elementary school, one must understand its purposes, the characteristics which make for an effectual media program, the roles of the media specialist and the teacher as their roles relate to the center's program and services, and pupil use of the media center. A discussion of these important aspects of the media center's functioning is set forth in the following paragraphs of this chapter.

Purposes of the Media Center

The purposes of the library in the elementary school have been well-known for many years.[2] Presently, the purposes of the modern media center, progeny of the library, can be reduced to two in number, and are: (1) it serves as a learning or resource center for pupils and teachers, and (2) it services classrooms with the instructional media required by teachers so that optimal teaching and learning can be accomplished. Now, let us examine these purposes.

Learning or Resource Center. It has been suggested that by the year 2000 the media center will replace classrooms as the primary center of learning.[3] While this prediction appears to be somewhat exaggerated, it illustrates dramatically the new-found role of the media center in the elementary school as that of a learning or resource center. One has only to understand the changed use of what was once known as the library, which served primarily as a repository for a limited array of books, to that of the modern media center where a plethora of books, tapes, discs, magazines, slides, transparencies, almanacs, atlases, maps, globes, newspapers, dictionaries, encyclopedias and the like is available. Also, the media center provides individual study carrels, acoustically treated conference

1. *Standards for School Media Programs* (Chicago: American Library Association—Washington, D.C.: National Education Association, 1969), p. xv.
2. American Library Association, Committee on Post-War Planning, *School Libraries for Today and Tomorrow* (Chicago: American Library Association, 1945), pp. 9-10.
3. Louis Shores, "The Medium School," *Phi Delta Kappan* 47, no. 6 (February 1967): 285.

rooms for typewriters and for small group viewing and listening, and a flexible space the size of a regular classroom which is equipped to meet the instructional needs of students growing out of such activities as group projects.[4] Other illustrations could be given to show how the media center serves as a learning or resource center in the elementary school, such as the instruction the media specialists provide for children concerning how to use the media center, but these suffice to make the point. In short, the media center provides a learning or resource center where materials, professional assistance, technology, and facilities are available for large and small group work or for independent study.[5] Furthermore, as a learning or resource center, the media center is available for use on an extended-hour basis before and after school, on certain evenings and over weekends in addition to the customary hours of the regular school day. Also, it should be open to pupils, teachers, parents and other citizens during vacation periods.[6]

Service to Classrooms. The second major purpose of the elementary school media center is to provide teachers with necessary media for the instructional program extant in each of the individual classrooms. Implicit in this purpose is the providing of long- or short-term loans of media collections, selected by the teachers and the media specialists for the classrooms, which are appropriate to the individual abilities, interests, and needs of the children. Likewise, the media center can provide many corollary services to teachers as well as classrooms, such as having a systematic program for informing the staff about new materials which have been received, conducting in-service programs which alert the staff to the full range of media available and how to use them, producing instructional materials which supplement available commercial materials, and making the services of the media staff available to classroom teachers as resource consultants.[7]

Facets of an Effectual Media Program

The media program has been defined as all of "the instructional and other services furnished to students and teachers by a media center and its staff."[8] There are, therefore, many facets of an effectual media program, including: (1) organizing, (2) scope of collection, (3) staffing, (4) facilities, and (5) scheduling. Let us examine each of these facets in turn.

Organizing the Media Program. There appears to be little question that the best method for organizing the media program is to have a centralized media center with satellite classroom collections. This plan of organization makes all of the media, i.e., "printed and audiovisual forms of communication and their accompanying technology,"[9] available to everyone in the school. As a learning or resource center, a broad array of media becomes available to individuals and groups who wish to study and work or receive instruction in the media center. As a service center to the class-

---

4. *Standards for School Media Programs,* pp. 40-43.
5. For a discussion of how the media center enhances independent study, see: Robert S. Gilchrist and Willard G. Jones, "The Instructional Program and the Library," *Theory Into Practice* 6, no. 1 (February 1967): 5-7; Mildred L. Krohn, "Learning and the Learning Center," *Educational Leadership* 21, no. 4 (January 1964): 217-22; Leila Ann Doyle, "Something New Has Been Added to the Library," *Childhood Education* 43, no. 2 (October 1966): 64-68.
6. *Standards for School Media Programs,* pp. 22 23.
7. Ibid., pp. 8-9.
8. Ibid., p. xv.
9. Ibid.

rooms, appropriate collections of media which are relevant to teachers' individual instructional programs can be withdrawn by the teachers from the centralized media center. For example, each teacher makes periodic withdrawals of media concerned with topics or units he is teaching, for the classroom collection, and then returns such media to the centralized media center once the topic or unit work is completed. As a result of this plan, the satellite classroom collection is not displaced by the centralized media center. Rather, the individual classroom collection becomes more functional as a circulating part of the centralized media center's collection—a larger collection that is available to all.[10]

Scope of the Media Collection. Excluding professional materials for the school faculty, the textbook collection, and materials acquired exclusively for classroom use such as dictionaries, encyclopedias, magazines, and newspapers, the basic collections of the media center for the elementary school of 250 students or more, as recommended by the American Library Association and the National Education Association, can be seen in figure 9.1. The basic collections stipulated by the regional accrediting associations, e.g., the Southern Association of Colleges and Schools, are less than those suggested by ALA and NEA.

In order that the classroom teachers, media specialists and administrators can keep abreast of the latest developments in elementary education, an extensive and up-to-date professional materials collection is needed in the school's media center. The professional collection, according to the recommendations of ALA and NEA, should include from two hundred to one thousand titles of books, from forty to fifty professional magazines, and *Education Index.*

Also, the professional collection should include such materials as curriculum guides, courses of study, units of work, and the like.[11]

Staffing the Media Center. If a viable program is to be provided in the media center, it must be appropriately staffed.[12] At least three types of staff members can be found in elementary school media centers: (1) media specialist, (2) media technician, and (3) media aide. The definitions of each, according to the ALA and the NEA, are:[13]

Media specialist—An individual who has broad professional preparation in educational media. If he is responsible for instructional decisions, he meets requirements for teaching. Within this field there may be several types of specialization, such as (a) level of instruction, (b) areas of curriculum, (c) type of media, and (d) type of service. In addition other media specialists, who are not responsible for instructional decisions, are members of the professional media staff and need not have teacher certification, e.g., certain types of personnel in television and other media preparation areas.

Media technician—A media staff member who has training below the media specialist level, but who has special competencies in one or more of the following fields; graphics production and display, information and materials processing, photographic production, and equipment operation and simple maintenance.

Media aide—A media staff member with clerical or secretarial competencies.

10. Williard S. Elsbree, Harold J. McNally, and Richard Wynn, *Elementary School Administration and Supervision*, 3d ed. (New York: American Book Company, 1967), p. 424.
11. *Standards for School Media Programs*, pp. 33-34.
12. For a thorough discussion of staffing the media center, see Ibid., pp. 7-17.
13. Ibid., p. xv.

the school's media center

Books	At least 6000-10,000 titles representing 10,000 volumes or 20 volumes per student, whichever is greater
Magazines	
Elementary school (K-6)	40-50 titles (includes some adult non-professional periodicals)
Elementary school (K-8)	50-75 titles
Newspapers	One local, one state, and one national newspaper to be represented in the collection
Elementary school	3-6 titles
Pamphlets, clippings, and miscellaneous materials	Pamphlets, government documents, catalogs of colleges and technical schools, vocational information, clippings, and other materials appropriate to the curriculum and for other interests of students
Filmstrips	500-1000 titles, representing 1500 prints or 3 prints per pupil, whichever is greater (the number of titles to be increased in larger collections)
Globes	
Elementary school	1 globe in each teaching station and 2 in the media center In addition, special globes to be available in the media center
Maps	1 map for each region studied and special maps (economic, weather, political, historical, and others) for each area studied
	Duplicate maps available for each class section requiring maps at the same time, the number of duplicates to be determined by sections of students and the availability of maps on transparencies and filmstrips
	Wall maps for teaching stations
Microform	To be purchased as available on topics in the curriculum. All periodical subscriptions indexed in *Reader's Guide* and newspaper files should be obtained as needed for reference
Slides	2000 (including all sizes of slides)
Transparencies	2000 transparencies, plus a selection of subject matter masters

Fig. 9.1. The Basic Collections of the Media Center. Reproduced from: **Standards for School Media Programs** (Chicago: American Library Association—Washington, D.C.: National Education Association, 1969), pp. 30-33.

Tape and disc recordings (excluding electronic laboratory materials)	1000-2000 titles representing 3000 records or tapes or 6 per student, whichever is greater (the number of titles to be increased in larger collections)
8mm films Single concept Regular length[1]	1½ films per student with at least 500 titles supplemented by duplicates
16mm films	Acquisition of 16mm films at the building level would depend upon extent and frequency of use of individual film titles in the school, upon the availability of a system media center and its collection of film resources and upon other factors.[2] Whatever the source, the films must be quickly and easily accessible to the students and teachers requiring them. The recommendation given below is stated in terms of accessibility
	Recommended: access to a minimum of 3000 titles supplemented by duplicates and rentals
Graphic materials Art prints (reproductions)	1000 with duplicates as needed
Pictures and study prints	Individual study prints and pictures for the picture and vertical file collections; in addition to individual prints, access to 15 sets per teaching station plus 25 sets available from the media center
Other graphics[1]	Posters, photographs, charts, diagrams, graphs, and other types
Other materials[2] Programed instructional materials	Printed, electronic, and other forms of programed materials
Realia	Models, dioramas, replicas, and other types of realia
Kits	
Art objects	
Video tape recordings	
Remote access programs	
Resource files	

1. Because of the nature of certain media forms and the evolving or transitional development of others, quantitative recommendations cannot be given. Nevertheless, these materials make a unique contribution to the instructional program and provide resources for the academic needs and general interests of students. An abundant number should be available in the media center.
2. Absence of a quantitative recommendation should not be interpreted as meaning that it is not desirable for the media center in the individual school to have 16mm films in its collection. Former standards have indicated that a school should purchase films used six or more times a year, and that an annual rental fee for a film totaling from one-fifth to one-seventh of its purchase price generally indicates the feasibility of permanent acquisition. In at least one large metropolitan school system, experience indicated the value of a basic elementary school building collection of 300-400 film titles, with access to a central collection on a daily delivery basis.

Fig. 9.1. (Cont'd)

If there are two or more media specialists staffing the media center, one of them is designated as head of the center. The media specialists should be employed on a ratio of one full-time position for every two hundred fifty students or major fraction thereof. The media technicians and media aides perform their duties under the supervision of the professional media specialist. Generally, there should be a minimum of one media technician and one media aide staffing the media center per professional media specialist in schools having two thousand or fewer students enrolled.[14]

Facilities for the Media Center. Information concerning the facilities and arrangements of the media center, e.g., shelving, tables and chairs, circulation and distribution areas, reading and browsing areas, stacks, and such are readily available from many sources.[15] The equipment available to students and teachers from the media center of the elementary school, however, is of such proportions that it should be examined in detail here.

The multimedia equipment recommended by the ALA and the NEA for use in the elementary school media center and classrooms to complement teaching and learning can be seen in figure 9.2. The *basic* specifications are for more traditionally oriented programs while the *advanced* recommendations are for elementary schools utilizing innovative instructional approaches such as independent study. As one can rightly infer from perusing figure 9.2, the elementary teacher must have an understanding of the use of multimedia and be able to operate many different types of equipment if he is to use these aids effectively in teaching.

Scheduling the Media Center. It was thought formerly that every classroom of children in the elementary school should have one regularly scheduled period weekly in the media center. Aside from the scheduled periods in which the media specialist annually orients children who need to know about how to use the center and what services it provides, it presently is believed by most authorities that individual students or small groups of pupils should have access to the elementary school media center at any time during the school day. This system of basically open scheduling facilitates both of the major purposes of the media center, i.e., its purposes as a teaching or resource center and as a service agency to the classrooms purveying appropriate multimedia to teachers and children.

As previously mentioned, the media center should be scheduled to remain open before and after school hours, on given evenings, and over weekends. Likewise, it should be kept open during vacation periods so that children can have ready access to its materials for leisure time or informational reading.

Roles of the Media Center's Staff

Each staff member in the media center assumes a given role in the total media program of the elementary school. A discussion of the various roles the media staff members assume is set forth in the following paragraphs.

14. Ibid., pp. 10, 12, and 15-17.
15. See: *Standards for School Library Programs* (Chicago: American Library Association, 1960), pp. 119-28; *Standards for School Media Programs*, pp. 40-43; Peggy Sullivan, "Facilities and Arrangements of the Elementary School Library," *Childhood Education* 43, no. 2 (October 1966): 76-79; Marvin R. A. Johnson, "Facilities and Standards," *Library Trends* 17, no. 4 (April 1969): 362-73.

	Basic	*Advanced*
16mm sound projector	1 per 4 teaching stations plus 2 per media center	1 per 2 teaching stations plus 5 per media center
8mm projector (only equipment for which materials exist at the appropriate school level should be procured)	1 per 3 teaching stations plus 15 per media center	1 per teaching station plus 25 per media center
2 x 2 slide projector remotely controlled	1 per 5 teaching stations plus 2 per media center	1 per 3 teaching stations plus 5 per media center
Filmstrip or combination filmstrip-slide projector	1 per 3 teaching stations plus 1 per media center	1 per teaching station plus 4 per media center
Sound filmstrip projector	1 per 10 teaching stations plus 1 per media center	1 per 5 teaching stations plus 2 per media center
10 x 10 overhead projector	1 per teaching station plus 2 per media center	1 per teaching station plus 4 per media center
Opaque projector	1 per 25 teaching stations or 1 per floor in multi-floor buildings	1 per 15 teaching stations plus 2 per media center
Filmstrip viewer	1 per teaching station plus the equivalent of 1 per 2 teaching stations in media center in elementary schools	3 per teaching station plus the equivalent of 1 per teaching station in media center in elementary schools
2 x 2 slide viewer	1 per 5 teaching stations plus 1 per media center	1 per teaching station plus 1 per media center
TV receiver (minimum 23 in. screen)	1 per teaching station and 1 per media center where programs are available	1 per 24 viewers if programs are available, in elementary schools 1 per media center
Microprojector	1 per 20 teaching stations	1 per 2 grade levels in elementary schools 1 per media center
Record player	1 per teaching station, K-3 1 per grade level, 4-6 3 per media center 1 set of earphones for each player	1 per teaching station, K-6, plus 5 per media center 1 set of earphones for each player
Audio tape recorder	1 per 2 teaching stations in elementary schools plus 2 per media center 1 set of earphones for each recorder	1 per teaching station plus 10 per media center in elementary schools 1 set of earphones for each recorder

Fig. 9.2. Multimedia Equipment Available from the Media Center. Reproduced from: **Standards for School Media Programs** (Chicago: American Library Association—Washington, D.C.: National Education Association, 1969), pp. 45-49.

the school's media center

	Basic	*Advanced*
Listening station	A portable listening station with 6-10 sets of earphones at the ratio of 1 per 3 teaching stations	1 set of 6-10 earphones and listening equipment for each teaching station and media center
Projection cart	colspan: 1 per portable piece of equipment, purchased at the time equipment is obtained	
Projection screen	colspan: 1 permanently mounted screen per classroom plus additional screens of suitable size as needed for individual and small group use. The permanent screen should be no smaller than 70 x 70 with keystone eliminator.	
Closed-circuit television	All new construction should include provisions for installation at each teaching station and media center. Older buildings should be wired for closed-circuit television with initiation of such programs.	
Radio receiver (AM-FM)	1 per media center plus central distribution system (AM-FM)	3 per media center plus central distribution system (AM-FM)
Copying machine	1 per 30 teaching stations plus 1 per media center	1 per 20 teaching stations plus 1 per media center
Duplicating machine	1 per 30 teaching stations plus 1 per media center	1 per 20 teaching stations plus 1 per media center
Micro-reader (some with microfiche attachment)	Equivalent of 1 per 10 teaching stations to be located in the media center	Equivalent of 1 per 5 teaching stations to be located in the media center
Micro-reader printer	1 per media center	3 per media center
Portable video tape recorder system (including cameras)	1 per 15 teaching stations with a minimum of 2 recorders per building	1 per 5 teaching stations with a minimum of 2 recorders per building
Light control	Adequate light control in every classroom and media center to the extent that all types of projected media can be utilized effectively	

Fig. 9.2. (Cont'd)

the school's media center

Local production equipment	Per building Dry mount press and tacking iron Paper cutters Two types of transparency production equipment 16mm camera 8mm camera Rapid process camera Equipment for darkroom Spirit duplicator Primary typewriter Copy camera and stand Light box 35mm still camera Film rewind Film splicer (8 mm and 16 mm) Tape splicer Slide reproducer Mechanical lettering devices Portable chalkboard
Items for special consideration	Large group instruction The following equipment should be available for each large group instructional area: 10 x 10 overhead projector, auditorium type; large screen with keystone eliminator; 16mm projector, auditorium type (consideration should be given to possible use of rear screen projection) Television A complete distribution system of at least six channels should be available in a building so that: broadcast TV 2500 MHZ, UHF, or VHF can be received; signals can be distributed to each room from the central TV reception area and/or from a central studio; signals can be fed into the system from any classroom; signals are available simultaneously 3¼ x 4 projectors If still used by teachers at the school building, there should be 1 per school building plus 1 auditorium type per each large group instructional area. Equipment to make tele-lecture available

Fig. 9.2. (Cont'd)

Media Specialist's Role. The professional media specialist assumes a diverse role in the elementary school media center and in promoting its program. Although it is virtually impossible to list a complete set of the responsibilities the media specialist assumes, some of the more important functions appear to be the following:

First, he sees that maximum use of the various media collections is made by faculty and students. Second, he offers guidance to children in learning how to use the media center so that their educational needs will be effectively met. Third, he consults with teachers and assists them in evaluating and selecting media for the instructional program. Fourth, he serves as a resource consultant on many committees such as the system-wide curriculum development committee and the textbook committee. Fifth, the media specialist administers the operation of the media center. Sixth, he sees that all media are easily accessible to faculty and students. Seventh, he assists faculty, students, and media technicians in producing materials to supplement those which are available to the school. Eighth, he serves as a resource person in the classrooms upon request of the teachers.[16]

Media Technician's Role. The media technician renders a specialized service to the elementary school media center. Some of his most important responsibilities include: (1) assisting media specialists and teachers in the production of graphics such as transparencies, posters, and charts; (2) assisting teachers and students in locating necessary media, bibliographic searching, manning the circulation desk, and the like; (3) making photographic productions such as developing publicity pictures, serving as a cameraman in the making of films or the photographing of items for slides, resource files, etc. and (4) repairing and maintaining audiovisual equipment. Of necessity, he must have specific skills and special abilities which are unique to his role in the total media program of the elementary school.[17]

Media Aide's Role. The responsibilities of the media aide primarily involve clerical and secretarial work. That is, he does routine typing and record keeping including routine circulation work. Additionally, he sees that materials are properly shelved and filed and that the media center is kept neat and orderly.[18]

The Teacher and the Media Center

In reviewing the research on the elementary school library, precursor of the modern media center, Willson concluded that the one factor which contributed most to the success of the library program was the degree to which students were motivated by their teachers to use the library and its resources.[19] Her review also showed that when a teacher has significantly low reading habits and library background, there is a corresponding low mastery of reading and library skills among his students. Conversely, when a teacher rates high in reading habits and library background, his students also rank high in reading and library skills attainment.[20]

16. For comprehensive discussions of the media specialist's role in the program of the media center, see: Alice Brooks McGuire, "The School Librarian: A New Image," *Educational Leadership* 21, no. 4 (January 1964): 227-39; Helen F. Rice, "Changing Staff Patterns and Responsibilities," *Library Trends* 17, no. 4 (April 1969): 401-9; *Standards for School Media Programs,* pp. 8-12; Valerie Melnick, "The Librarian's Role," *Theory Into Practice* 6 no. 1 (February 1967): 40-44.
17. *Standards for School Media Programs,* pp. 15-16.
18. Ibid.
19. Ella Willson, "Research on the Elementary School Library," *Theory Into Practice* 6, no. 1 (February 1967): 34.
20. Ibid.

Obviously, the dramatic change from viewing the library as a quiet and isolated study area in which a limited array of books, magazines, and newspapers were housed to the contemporary media center in which a broad array of multimedia is available for teaching and learning has imposed new roles upon the elementary classroom teacher. For example, in schools equipped with the modern media center, the classroom teacher is freed somewhat from the textbook in preparing his lesson plans. He can enlist the help of the media specialist in planning an appropriate learning experience for boys and girls, such as independent study or small group research projects in the media center as an extension of the children's classroom study. Or, the teacher and media specialist can team teach research skills in the media center when appropriate, including such elements as: (1) outlining, (2) notetaking, (3) using the card catalog, (4) locating and using the stacks, and so on.[21]

Essentially, the teacher now has a resource center from which he can secure the media he needs for effectual teaching. Also, he can find in the media center a production laboratory and a media technician to help him make the instructional materials, e.g., transparencies, graphs, and posters, he needs to supplement available commercially prepared materials for classroom use. In short, the teacher must work cooperatively with the media center staff in order to derive the greatest educational advantages for his pupils in the use of the media center as a teaching and resource center and as a service agency to his classroom.

The Pupil and the Media Center

The media center serves pupils' educational needs in many ways in the contemporary elementary school.[22] It provides opportunities for them to do individual or group viewing, listening, or recording. A materials preparation area is provided where they can make such things as transparencies, charts, posters, dioramas, and graphs for their study projects. Private study carrels are available for independent study. Systematic programs providing instruction in how to use the media center and how to benefit most from its program are provided by the media specialists. A vast array of media is available for use within the media center and the media staff encourages the children to use the media in their classrooms or at home whenever it enhances their studies. The reading and browsing areas are frequented by the pupils and the "storytelling corner" is well-known to the students.

These are only a few examples of how the media center serves pupils as a learning or resource center and as a service agency to their classrooms. Essentially, pupils are introduced to the media center upon their initial enrollment in school, i.e., nursery, kindergarten, or first-grade, and they are taught certain skills at an early age which enable them to learn to use the media center and profit from its program throughout their years in school.

An Appraisal of the Media Center

The terms learning center or media center have recently emerged to replace the traditional term library. These terms are supposed to reflect more adequately the combination of media — print, visual, and audio — which are now recommended as essential to

21. Anna Bertrand Beachner, "The Teacher's Role," *Theory Into Practice* 6, no. 1 (February 1967), 37-39.
22. See Doyle, "Something New Has Been Added" pp. 64-68.

learning. Standards of the American Library Association, as you previously read, now list in detail minimum standards not only for books, magazines, and pamphlets, but also films, filmstrips, transparencies, tape and disc recordings, and other communication means. Paralleling the increased emphasis on media use is also an increase in the function of the media center as a producer of original curriculum materials. All of these recommendations require more space, more equipment, and more personnel, notwithstanding the fact that few elementary schools in the country actually achieved the minimum standards formerly recommended for the traditional library.

This chapter has described the idealized learning center as conceived by media specialists. You may not ever find such facilities available in your immediate teaching career. If you are not blessed with abundant media and facilities, this does not necessarily mean that teaching need be less effective, for a teacher's voice and actions may be the most enduring audio-visual ever put before children. You communicate not only in language but with your face and expression. And you can give your pupils what no picture or record can ever impart—feedback, reinforcement, and correction.

Even if funds were available to provide facilities such as a media center, a school might wish to weigh other alternatives for improving instruction. While the research evidence indicates that children learn from a great variety of media, there is little evidence that the achievement of children is increased significantly by the use of visual and audio materials over conventional classroom materials. Characteristically, school systems which have outstanding media facilities generally have good student performance. The good student performance, however, can seldom be attributed causally to media use. Such school systems frequently have populations with middle and upper class structures, higher salaries for teachers, and higher levels of certification. They tend to have more of everything that money can buy. Media centers alone, however, appear to have had little impact on achievement in school districts where there is a disadvantaged population and the total educational effort is low.

The educational technology that can be housed in a media center is very impressive —and Americans are very impressed with educational hardware. At a given time, however, a learner can use only one communication medium—he cannot, concurrently, be reading a book, viewing a filmstrip, listening to a record, and manipulating a teaching machine. In any given learning task, the teacher or the teacher and the student need to select the most economical and efficient medium to facilitate pupil learning. While the emphasis on pupil use of the learning center is consistent with current advocacy of independent study, there is a body of research literature which clearly suggests that such means are inappropriate for the disadvantaged student who may require more directed teaching in a structured program. The media center, therefore, is not a panacea to the improvement of instruction. It is merely a resource. And many individual teachers long ago found, for example, that their own carefully clipped and indexed picture files often provided one of the most economical and easily accessible visual supplements.

The somewhat cautious comments in this survey are not intended to discourage the use of newer media or the media center.

They are intended, however, to put the newer media and media center into their proper educational perspective.

SELECTED REFERENCES

BAKER, W. B. "Place of School Libraries Today," *Education* 76, no. 1 (1965): 44-48.

CAMPBELL, EDWARD A. "A Guide for Evaluating and Using 'Free Materials'," *Clearing House* 39, no. 9 (1965): 557-59.

CYR, HELEN W. "Library for Every Elementary School," *California Education* 3, no. 7 (1966): 18, 20.

ELLSWORTH, RALPH E. *The School Library*. New York: The Center for Applied Research in Education, Inc., 1965.

GRAHAM, MAE, ed., "The Changing Nature of the School Library," *Library Trends* 17, no. 4 (1969): entire issue.

LOWRIE, JEAN E. *Providing School Library Service for the Culturally Disadvantaged*. Chicago: American Library Association, 1965.

MAHAR, HUBERT H., ed. *The School Library as a Materials Center*. U.S. Office of Education, Circular no. 708. Washington, D.C.: Government Printing Office, 1963.

McALLISTER, CARLYNE. "Teacher Contacts With Library Important," *Education* 86, no. 7 (1966): 408-11.

MILLER, W. R., and BERRY, ROBERT H. "Adopting the Right Textbook," *Clearing House* 37, no. 1 (1962): 18-23.

PALOVIC, LORA, and GOODMAN, ELIZABETH B. *The Elementary School Library in Action*, West Nyack, N.Y.: Parker Publishing Company, Inc., 1968.

SAUKKONEN, MIRJAM A., and CASE, ROBERT N. "Providing the *Right Material*," *Theory Into Practice* 6, no. 1 (1967): 48-51.

School Library Services, *The Media Centered Library*. Atlanta: Georgia Department of Education, 1969.

Standards for School Library Programs. Chicago: American Library Association, 1960.

Standards for School Media Programs. Chicago: American Library Association—Washington, D.C.: National Education Association, 1969.

TANNER, CLARABEL. "How ALA Standards Help School Libraries," *Education* 86, no. 7 (1966): 395-97.

PART THREE

teaching the skills subjects

Photo: Courtesy of El Paso (Texas) Independent School District.
Photography: Seth J. Edwards, Jr.

reading: key to man's cultural heritage

10

The most important task the elementary school student undertakes is to learn to read. The most important task of the school is to help pupils learn to read efficiently.

The great importance of reading derives from the nature of literate cultures and of schooling. In a literate culture, the written tradition is the most important means of cultural accumulation, preservation, and transmission. Unless a person is an efficient reader, he does not have access to the cultural heritage.

Reading is so important in the school because reading and writing must be taught formally. In contrast to oral language, acquired through enculturation, reading and writing require knowledge of the code, the relationship of language sounds to written symbols. Acquisition of the code is facilitated by the assistance of a teacher.

Even more important, however, is the development and extension of man's cognitive and intellectual capacity through reading. While the language of colloquial communication supplies the basic lexical and syntactic features of any language, writing and reading provide more formal, complex, and systematic modes of expression. Reading is not a fetish, as Huey and Dewey believed over half a century ago.[1] It is a means by which man develops his human nature.

This chapter is not a general survey of reading. The emphasis is on methods of teaching beginning reading which contrasts the *code* and *meaning* approaches. This approach is taken because public[2] and scholastic[3] differences in the teaching of beginning reading have long centered on the relative merits of these two approaches. The social and emotional aspects of reading[4] are not considered because of the tendency to use correlations as causal explanations of reading failure.[5] In addition to code-meaning methods, the chapter indicates some of the special approaches to reading with compensatory, bilingual, and remedial groups

1. Edmund Burke Huey, *The Psychology and Pedagogy of Reading* (New York: Macmillan Company, 1908), pp. 302-4.

2. Rudolph Flesch, *Why Johnny Can't Read—And What You Can Do About It* (New York: Harper & Brothers, 1955).

3. Jeanne Chall, *Learning to Read: The Great Debate* (New York: McGraw-Hill Book Company, 1967).

4. Helen Robinson, *Why Pupils Fail in Reading* (Chicago: University of Chicago Press, 1946).

5. Ronald Wardhough, *Reading: A Linguistic Perspective* (New York: Harcourt, Brace & World, Inc., 1969), pp. 2-3.

and the approach to teaching reading in the intermediate grades where reading merges with study skills. The chapter begins with a discussion of three levels of reading.

What Is Reading?

Reading may be parsimoniously defined as the meaningful decoding of a message. Reading also may be defined in such a global manner that it becomes synonymous with education[6] or in such a complex manner[7] that the definition is functionally meaningless for reading instruction. The multiple definitions of reading[8] indicate the futility of a single definition.

An observation of reading behavior indicates that there are different behaviors manifested by a beginning reader and a skillful reader. A comparison of the content of beginning reading with advanced reading indicates a shift in simple words already in the vocabulary of the child to new and more complex words which require not merely decoding but study. It is therefore proposed that reading be considered from the standpoint of three levels.

Level 1: Decoding. The first and basic level is the level of *code* mastery and is the most important aspect of beginning reading. It is characterized by two emphases—mastery of sound-letter (phoneme-grapheme relations) and acquisition of a sight vocabulary of high frequency words.[9] The simple, monosyllabic words at this level are characteristically already in the verbal repertory of the child, whether based on phonemic regularity[10] or usage frequency,[11] and consequently the development of word recognition may proceed with a minimal attention to meaning.[12] The following are examples of Level 1 reading:

Gus drops his gun in the mud.
Men dig in the mud.
Men must dig for the gun.
The gun is in the mud.
The gun rests in the mud.
The gun rusts in the mud.[13]
Look here, Janet.
I can ride on a pony.
I can have a pony ride.
I like to ride on a pony.
Come on, Janet, come on.[14]

Level 2: Information. The informational level of reading begins when the pupil becomes sufficiently skillful in Level 1 skills to read for information. Level 2 reading continues throughout schooling, and is the

6. Arthur I. Gates, "Character and Purposes of the Yearbook," in *Reading in the Elementary School,* Forty-eighth Yearbook of the National Society for the Study of Education, part II, ed. Nelson B. Henry (Chicago: University of Chicago Press, 1949), p. 4.
7. Theodore Clymer, "What is 'Reading'?: Some Current Concepts," *Innovation and Change in Reading Instruction,* Sixty-seventh Yearbook of the National Society for the Study of Education, part II, ed. Helen M. Robinson (Chicago: University of Chicago Press, 1968), chap. 1.
8. *Webster's Third New International Dictionary.*
9. For lists of high frequency words, as compiled by Dolch, Stone, and Fry, see: Miles V. Zintz, *The Reading Process* (Dubuque, Iowa: Wm. C. Brown Company Publishers, 1970), pp. 59-60, 145-50.
10. e.g., "Nat is a fat cat." Charles C. Fries et al. *Merrill Linguistic Readers,* Reader 1 (Columbus, Ohio: Charles E. Merrill Books, Inc., 1966), p. 6.
11. e.g., "Then the bus went fast." Ira E. Aaron et al., *The Bus Ride, Level 2, Book 1, Scott, Foresman Reading Systems,* ed. Helen M. Robinson (Glenview, Ill.: Scott, Foresman and Company, 1971), p. 3.
12. This position follows that of the structural linguists, such as Bloomfield and Fries, but would be rejected by the semantic linguists, such as Goodman.
13. Glen McCracken and Charles C. Walcutt, *Reading Goals: Extended Readers for Basic Reading,* The Red Book (Philadelphia: J. B. Lippincott, 1966), p. 27.
14. Mabel O'Donnell and Byron H. VanRoekel, *Outdoors and In,* The Harper & Row Basic Reading Program (Evanston, Ill.: Harper & Row. Publishers, 1966), p. 29.

most important type of reading in the subject matter courses. Level 2 reading compares generally with procedures which are frequently described as comprehension and study skills, and is the characteristic focus of intermediate reading. Systematic vocabulary development is a continuing part of Level 2 reading. An example of Level 2 reading follows:

> *Language and Thought.* In the first chapter it was said that only humans possess true language. It probably is equally correct to say that because we have language we are truly human. One important asset that man possesses is his ability to reason. It is safe to say that without language man would not be able to reason as he does. The ideas and concepts he deals with are given verbal labels, and he must express his ideas by using these labels.[15]

Level 3: Aesthetic-Appreciative. This level is especially characteristic of literary study in which conventional words have figurative meanings. The development of an aesthetic appreciation of prose and poetry requires the same careful attention to the study of words and their use as does Level 2, which is concerned with scientific subject matter. In addition to literature, Level 3 involves reading about art, music, dance, drama, and all forms of expression in which language is used as a surrogate and interpretive channel of communication. The following is an example of Level 3 reading:

> All the greatest exponents of civilization, from Dante to Goethe, have been obsessed by light—perhaps one could take it as the supreme symbol of civilization. But in the seventeenth century light passed through a crucial stage. The invention of the lens was giving it a new range and power. Vermeer used the utmost ingenuity to make us feel the movement of light. He loved to show it passing over a white wall, and then, as if to make its progress more comprehensive, passing over a slightly crinkled map. And yet the scientific approach to experience ends in poetry and I suppose that this is due to an almost mystical rapture in the perception of light.[16]

The three reading levels overlap and are not mutually exclusive. Even mature readers encounter unfamiliar words which require decoding, while prereaders can enjoy the alliterative quality of poetry. An emphasis on Level 2 and 3 reading for a beginner nevertheless confuses the initial techniques of reading instruction with the subsequent levels of study and interpretation.[17]

These distinctions by level are followed by those who emphasize a code or structural approach to beginning reading,[18] but are not followed by those who emphasize a meaning approach.[19] It is nevertheless thought that a recognition of different levels of reading serves to remind the teacher of

---

15. Albert J. Kingston and Marion J. Rice, *Language,* Pupil Text, Publication no. 44 Anthropology Curriculum Project (Athens, Ga.: University of Georgia, 1968), p. 7.
16. Kenneth Clark, "Civilization—A Personal View," a film produced by the British Broadcasting Corporation for television, quotation from *Guide to Civilization: The Kenneth Clark Films on the Cultural Life of Western Man,* National Gallery of Art, Washington (New York: Time-Life Films, Inc., 1970), p. 68.
17. The preceding discussion parallels Charles C. Fries's three stages of reading: the beginning or transfer stage of learning letters and spelling patterns; productive reading stage of instantaneous comprehension; and vivid imagination realization stage in which reading is more effective than speech for obtaining new experiences. See his *Linguistics and Reading* (New York: Holt, Rinehart and Winston, Inc., 1963), pp. 186-215.
18. Glenn McCracken and Charles C. Walcutt, "A Message to the Teacher from the Authors," *Basic Reading, Teacher's Edition, Readers 1-8* (Philadelphia: J. B. Lippincott, 1964).
19. Kenneth S. Goodman, "The Search Called Reading," *Coordinating Reading Instruction,* Scott, Foresman Reading Systems, ed. Helen M. Robinson (Glenview, Ill.: Scott, Foresman and Company, 1971), pp. 10-14.

reading instruction that the behavior of beginning readers is not like that of skillful readers, and consequently beginners must be taught the simple, less complex steps which enter into skillful reading. The newer approaches to reading, however, indicate more emphasis on code mastery in Level 1 reading.

Level 1 reading is the major task of the primary school. More able students will complete Level 1 in the first year (if they are provided a suitable program); slower students may take three or four years with the best instruction under able teachers. But students who do not acquire Level 1 skills soon become disabled readers.[20] It should be emphasized, however, that all Level 1 is not concerned with phoneme-grapheme relationships. This is a matter of emphasis, not the whole method. Because of the importance of phonics and linguistics to Level 1 skills, the next section will deal with these aspects.

Phonetics, Phonics, and Linguistics

This section is important because the advocates of teaching beginning reading as a code justify their position on the basis of phonetics and linguistics. Furthermore, confusion has frequently resulted from the interchangeable use of phonetics and phonics.[21]

Phonetics is the scientific study of the sounds of language, including their physiological production and their acoustic qualities. The standard scientific orthography for the representation of the sounds of language is the Internationl Phonetic Alphabet, which is an articulatory method for describing speech sounds. A modified form of the IPA is given in figure 10.1, with a transcription of "Twinkle, Twinkle, Little Star." A cursory examination of figure 10.1 indicates that the teacher of reading instruction is not concerned with phonetics.

Phonics is concerned with the relationship of the sounds of language to conventional spelling. Almost every language, including English, has more sounds than it has letters in its alphabet. English has 44 sounds and 26 letters in its alphabet. The fact that the letters c, q, and x are not included in the phoneme list in figure 10.2 results from the fact that these letters, while used in spelling, have no distinctive sounds. A comparison of the spelling of phonemes in figure 10.2 with the IPA in figure 10.1 indicates why reading teachers are concerned with phonics, but not with phonetics.

A teaching of phonics, however, requires far more than a knowledge of the phonemes. This results from the fact that the phonemes do not appear in isolation but as parts of words. The sounds of phonemes shift somewhat as they appear in words, and the number of allophones is greater than the number of phonemes. The allophone of "p" in *pan* is different from that of "p" in *span*. Thus a large part of phonics is concerned with two and three letter initial blends, e.g., *clap, scrap;* terminal endings, e.g., *bend, milk;* doubling of consonant when preceded by short vowel when adding *ing,* e.g., run, ru*nning;* dropping of *e* when consonant preceded by long vowel, as ride, ri*ding;* when letters are silent, as in si*gh*t and *w*reck; and similar orthographic representations of sounds.

20. Irving H. Anderson and Walter F. Dearborn, *The Psychology of Teaching Reading* (New York: Ronald Press Company, 1952), pp. 212-57.
21. Anderson and Dearborn, *Psychology of Teaching Reading,* passim; Jullie Hay and Charles E. Wingo, *Reading with Phonics, Teacher's Edition,* rev.ed. (Philadelphia: J. B. Lippincott Company, 1960).

Characteristically, some 140 phoneme-grapheme sequences are used, as shown in figure 10.3. There is no scientific evidence concerning the sequence in which phoneme-grapheme sequences are introduced. In a departure from most programs, the Scott Foresman Reading Systems, to be discussed later, begin with consonants but teach all the sounds of one vowel before proceeding to the next vowel.

Newer books now include strong sections on phonics.[22] In addition, there are many specialized books for supplemental phonics teaching. One of the best known and most widely used is that of Durrell.[23] There is no shortage of material. Dechant lists 114 separate items by program and publisher for teaching phonic-linguistic skills.[24] The major deficiency lies in the failure of teachers to acquire mastery of phonic principles and to use them as a part of their teaching.

Linguistics is a branch of anthropology concerned with language as a form of human communication. Linguistics is divided into many special branches, but the branch that has made the most impact on reading teaching is structural linguists. Structural lin-

22. Dolores Durkin, *Teaching Them to Read* (Boston: Allyn and Bacon, Inc., 1970), pp. 233-94.
23. Donald D. Durrell and Helen A. Murphy, *Teacher's Manual for Speech to Print Phonics* (New York: Harcourt, Brace & World, Inc., 1964).
24. Emerald Dechant, *Linguistics, Phonics, and the Teaching of Reading* (Springfield, Ill.: Charles C. Thomas Publisher, 1969), pp. 135-49.

IPA Alphabet

IPA Symbol	Sound	IPA Symbol	Sound
æ	at	ɔ	raw
eɪ	ate	u	boot
ɛ	bet	ʊ	pull
ɑ	cart	ɔi	toy
b	bat	aʊ	out
tʃ	check	p	pot, top
dʒ	do	r	rock, borrow
i	see	s	see, toss
f	fat	ʃ	ship
g	go	t	top
h	hit	θ	thick
ɪ	it	ð	the
aɪ	pie	ʌ	stuck
d	just	ju	you
k	keep	ɜr	her
l	let, ball	v	vain, ever
m	man, ham	w	wish
n	name, can	j	yet
ŋ	tank, sing	z	zone, has
ɒ	top	ʒ	azure, vision
oʊ, o	so	ə	about, likable

Phonetic Transcription of "Twinkle, Twinkle, Little Star"

GENERAL AMERICAN	EASTERN—NEW ENGLAND	SOUTHERN
[twɪnkl twɪnkl lɪtl stɑr haʊ aɪ wʌndə whʌt ju ɑr ʌp əbʌv ðə wɜld so haɪ laɪk ə daɪmənd ɪn ðə skaɪ]	[twɪnkl twɪnkl lɪtl stɑ haʊ aɪ wʌndə whʌt ju a ʌp əbʌv ðə wɜld so haɪ laɪk ə daɪmənd ɪn ðə skaɪ]	[twɪnkl twɪnkl lɪtl stɑ haʊ a wʌdə whʌt ju ɑ ʌp əbʌv ðə wɜld so haɪ laɪk ə daɪmənd ɪn ðə skaɪ]

Fig. 10.1. Modified IPA Alphabet, with Phonetic Transcription of "Twinkle, Twinkle, Little Star" in Three Regional Dialects. From: Albert J. Kingston and Marion J. Rice, **Language**, Pupil Text, Publication no. 44 (Athens, Ga.: Anthropology Curriculum Project, University of Georgia, 1968), p. 24.

guists and phoneticists agree that the written phoneme is a grapheme, i.e., the sounds are represented by letters of the alphabet. But they differ in their approach to teaching reading. Phonicists not only sound the letters, e.g., b /b/, but blend letters to form whole words, *ba, bat, brat*. Linguists, however, only sound the letter in the context of the total word, e.g., /b/ in *bat* but never b/b/ or *ba*. In a strict linguistic approach the *name* of the letter only is used; it is never sounded.[25] This distinctive emphasis should be kept in mind whenever the term *linguistic* is used. On the other hand, features of phonics (sounds in isolation and blending) and linguistics (regular whole words) can be so combined that it is appropriate to label the approach as phonic, linguistic, or phonic-linguistic.[26]

25. Ibid., p. 7
26. As an example, see: Glenn McCracken and Charles C. Walcutt, *Phonics Guide to Basic Reading* (Philadelphia: J. B. Lippincott, 1965).

BASIC PHONEMES OF THE ENGLISH LANGUAGE

Unvoiced Consonants		Voiced Consonants	
f	fat	b	bat
h	hat	d	dig
k(c)	kit cat	g	get
p	pan	j(dg)	jet edge
s	set	l	lad
t	ten	m	man
ch(tch)	chin match	n	net
sh	ship	ng	sing
th	thin	r	ran
wh	when	th	then
		v	van
		w	wet
		y	yes
		z	zoo
		zh	measure

Pure Vowels		Diphthongs	
a	bat	a	hate
a	father barn	ou-ow	out cow
a	ball saw water	oi-oy	soil boy
a	chair dare wear	i	time
e	bet	o	go
e	Pete theme	u	use mute few
i	sit		
o	got		
u	cut		
u	put book		
u	boot		
a	above		
er	cedar her third word burn		

Fig. 10.2. Basic Phonemes of English. From: Glenn McCracken and Charles C. Walcutt, **Teacher's Edition, Lippincott's Basic Reading Book D** (Philadelphia: J. B. Lippincott Company, 1969), p. 140.

The next section deals with approaches to teaching reading. Because of the previous discussion of phonics and linguistics, more attention is given to the sight-meaning approach.

Approaches to Teaching Beginning Reading

The purpose of this section is to indicate the distinctive characteristics of several current approaches to teaching reading: sight-meaning (look and say), phonic supplemental, phonic-linguistic, linguistic, language experience, programmed text, and modified alphabet. Interesting experimental variants, such as computer-assisted instruction,[27] are too limited in application to merit discussion at this point.

At the present time, reading specialists continue to emphasize the importance of the teacher and to deeemphasize methods in the teaching of reading.[28] The position is logically self-contradictory. To improve the training of teachers, there must be improvement in training method. The present global or survey approach to beginning reading fails to *train* the prospective teacher. As a result, he invariably teaches himself on-the-job, using the manuals of the reading series used in the school system. The improvement of the training of reading teachers requires the improvement of training in *methods*.

Sight-Meaning. Sight-meaning has been the dominant approach to the teaching of reading for the past four decades. In definition, this approach defines the problem of reading as primarily one of reading comprehension (Level 2) and appreciation (Level 3). In methodology, it emphasizes new words as wholes rather than as parts, and sound-symbol relationships are taught incidentally and not explicitly (Level 1). In type of reading, more emphasis is placed on silent than on oral reading.

The vocabulary of sight-meaning books is based upon *use frequency*. As a result, the vocabulary is highly irregular in spelling. Many different ways of recognizing new words are used, such as picture clues, context clues, structural analysis, word shape, and phonics. Phonics is regarded, however, merely as one of the methods used in word recognition, and is taught in an extensive rather than intensive manner.

Because the emphasis is on the meaning of a story rather than word recognition skills, the sight-meaning emphasis using a frequency vocabulary neccessitates a limited vocabulary. In the Scott, Foresman New Basic Reader series, 72 words are introduced in the preprimers and 101 new words in the primer.[29] As a result, the sight-meaning approach requires much repetition for word mastery.

In the sight-meaning approach, there is less emphasis upon the grapheme-phoneme relationships. For example, in the first story of the Scott Foresman New Basic Readers primer, the new word *hat* is introduced. There is much talk about the story, but

27. Mildred Letton Wittick, "Innovations in Reading Instruction," *Innovation and Change in Reading Instruction,* Sixty-seventh Yearbook of the National Society for the Study of Education, part II, ed. Helen M. Robinson (Chicago: University of Chicago Press, 1968), pp. 94-95.

28. Helen M. Robinson, "The Next Decade," *Innovation and Change in Reading Instruction,* Sixty-seventh Yearbook of the National Society for the Study of Education, Part II, ed., Helen M. Robinson (Chicago: University of Chicago Press, 1968), p. 399.

29. Helen M. Robinson, Marion Monroe, and A. Sterl Artley, *Fun With Our Friends,* Teacher's Guidebook, The New Basic Readers (Chicago, Ill.: Scott, Foresman and Company, 1962), pp. 10, 158.

168   reading: key to man's cultural heritage

PHONEME-GRAPHEME SEQUENCES

Lippincott		Hay-Wingo	
a, short	sh	a, short	a, long
e, short	ch, tch	e, short	i, long
i, short	th	i, short	o, long
o, short	wh	o, short	o, i, irregular long,
u, short	qu	u, short	as in gold, wild
m	x	s	br, cr, dr, fr, gr,
n	y	m	pr, and tr
r	z	f	run, running rule
s	ng	r	hide, hiding rule
d	-ing	n	ar
nd	-ed	g, hard	or
t	er as er	b	er, ir, ur
st	ar as er	t	sit, sitter rule
nt	ir, or, ur as er	p	help, helper rule
g, hard	-y, -ay	d	ride, rider rule
p	-ey	s blends, nd	ai as in rain
gr	c, soft	m blends, ss and st	ay as in lay
dr	g, soft	f blends	ee
sp	dg, dge	r blends	ea as in sea
mp	-tion, -sion	n blends, ft	ie, y, lie, fly
c, hard	oo (cook)	b blends	ow, oe, ow
h	oo (food)	t blends	low; hoe; load
f	ow (snow)	review	ea as short e, bread
ar	ow (cow)	p blends, mp, ff	ie as long e, brief
er	ou	d blends	a as short u, away
ed	oi, oy	c as in cat	c as s, -ce as -s
w	u, long	ck as in sock	ou, ow: house, how
ow (cow)	ue, long	k as in kid	oi, oy: toil, toy
l	ui, long	k and c (k) blends	-y as short i: funny
ll	ew, eau	-ck blends	gh silent: sigh, sign
b	aw, au	l blends	-ies as plural
le	ph, as f	-ll blends	k silent: knife
k	ch, hard	h	w silent: wreck
ck	ch, as sh	-nt, -mp, -ll,	t silent: often
nk	wr, kn	-lk, lt, st, lf, nd,	b silent: limb
e, signal	b, silent	-lm, -ft, -lp, ld, sk, pt	j
a, care	l, silent	j blends	je as j in change
a, long	g, silent	w blends	dge as j in edge
e, ee long	h, silent	v, qu, y, z,—zz blends	oo as in cool
ea	gh, silent	sh, -sh	oo as in cook
ai	gh as f	ch as in chick	ew as in blew
i, long, ie	ea as short e	tch as in witch	ue as in blue

Fig. 10.3. Phoneme-Grapheme Sequence from Two Phonic Series: Complete and Supplemental. From: Glenn McCracken and Charles C. Walcutt, **Lippincott's Basic Reading, Books A, B, C, D, Teacher's Edition** (Philadelphia: J. B. Lippincott Company, 1969), Book D, p. 139; and Julie Hay and Charles E. Wingo, **Reading with Phonics,** rev. (Philadelphia: J. B. Lippincott Company, 1960).

reading: key to man's cultural heritage   169

Lippincott		Hay-Wingo	
ir	ea as long a	-nch	aw as in saw
o, long	ear	-tch	au as in haul
ore, or	ie as long e	-ng, -nk, th, wh	al as in halt
oa	ei as long e	x as in tacks	all as in ball
oe	ei as long a	-s plural and poss.	bends - se as z in wise
j	eigh as long a	bl, cl, fl, gl, pl, sl	blends
v	ey as long a	sc, sm, sn, sp, st, sw	ph as f in telephone
	ough	a, long	-le as in apple
			scr, spr, str, spl, thr
			-tion, sion as shun
			or as er sound: visitor
			ed as second syllable: tasted
			ed as d sound: named
			ed as t sound: kissed
			a as in bare, air
			two syllables
			three syllables
			vowel review

Fig. 10.3. (Cont'd)

there is no reference anywhere in four pages of guided teacher talk to the sound of hat, the spelling of hat, or words which might rhyme with hat.[30] In contrast, in the Merrill Linguistic readers (discussed later), there are twenty-three teaching pages which develop the *at* sound in nine words: *cat, fat, Nat, pat, mat, sat, hat, rat, bat.* Six sight words are introduced: *is, a, the, on, not, look.* Sight words facilitate the reading of words in sentences, such as "Is the cat on the hat? The cat is on the mat." In contrast, the beginning primer sentence in Scott, Foresman is "Dick said, 'Look at the hat!'" There can be little practice with the sound *at,* however, because it occurs only four times in *hat* and twice in *at* in 58 running words. No mention is made in the teacher guide of *at* and *hat.*

The sight-meaning approach is characteristic of most basal reader programs. Difference in the programs are incidental and not substantive; there is a different list of sight words used and a different set of pictures.

The emphasis on the sight-meaning approach coincided with the interest in silent reading and the development of standardized tests.[31] Studies, although poorly controlled and lacking in experimental rigor, were cited as authoritative sources for emphasizing silent reading and reading for meaning. Gray, as early as 1919, set the stage for subsequent developments when he wrote that "the word should be accepted as the unit of recognition at the outset and that analysis or phonetic training should be introduced later when it is needed to keep the word units clear."[32] Since that time the sight-meaning approach has not excluded

30. Ibid., pp. 28-33.

31. Nila B. Smith, *American Reading Instruction* (New York: Silver Burdett and Company, 1934), pp.153-84.

32. William S. Gray, "Principles of Method in Teaching Reading, As Derived from Scientific Investigation," *Fourth Report of the Committee on Economy of Time in Education,* The Eighteenth Yearbook of the National Soceity for the Study of Education, part II (Bloomington, Ill.: Public School Publishing Co., 1919), p. 33.

any consideration of phonics, but phonic applications are both analytical and incidental. The analytical approach begins with a word, and separates it into its components, in contrast to the synthetic method, which begins with the sounds represented by letters which are combined to form a word. The incidental approach emphasizes that when phonics is undertaken, it is undertaken only as a result of the appearance of a word in a story.

However, the extreme sight-meaning emphasis was really a product of the 1920s, and is highly related to silent reading. In 1919, Gray was writing that oral reading is the "natural" form of primary reading; that much oral reading in the first grades facilitates efficient silent reading in the upper grades; that special word analysis drill periods should be used, including syllabification; and that by the end of the second month of the first grade pupils should learn a sufficient vocabulary so that phonetic analysis of such words as *ran* and *can, cat* and *sat* could begin.[33] Programs in the 1970s will probably be more like reading programs before 1920 than in the period 1930-60.

In 1919 there was a much higher expectancy of reading performance than came to prevail later. As the sight-meaning approach grew, the level of reading expectancy progressively declined. Thus the primer vocabulary count declined from an average of 406 words in 1962 to 378 in 1931 and 289 in 1931.[34] The Scott, Foresman primer of 1962 (New Basic Readers) included 173 words. Assuming that later teachers and pupils were equal to pre-1920 teacher and pupils, it would seem that the decline in reading performance, as measured by number of words, was related to the method of instruction. The trend toward learning by repetition also accompanied vocabulary reduction.

Other characteristics are found in the development of sight-meaning readers during the 1920s. In content, material shifted from literature to real life situations; teachers manuals became more elaborate; and reading definitions and objectives more and more complicated. In 1919, it was not necessary for Gray to define reading. He could address his readers on the assumption that they understood what he was talking about. Almost twenty years later, however, reading had lost its specific implication. Gray defined reading broadly not only to mean a synonym for critical thinking but also for problem solving.[35] As one looks at the reading literature in retrospect over these years, it is no wonder that reading as a skill subject declined. The reading experts were no longer talking about reading—they had made it synonymous with education. As a result, reading methodology became diffuse and the most practical guides for the teaching of reading became the manuals prepared by the publishers of the various basal series.

The approaches of basal readers are frequently characterized as eclectic approaches, because a variety of methods are used.[36] However, the method of the basal series into the 1960s was so dominated by the whole-

33. Ibid., p. 33.
34. Smith, *American Reading Instruction*, p. 204.
35. William S. Gray, "The Nature and Types of Reading," *The Teaching of Reading: A Second Report*, The Thirty-sixth Yearbook of the National Society for the Study of Education, part I Bloomington, Ill.: Public School Publishing Company, 1937), pp. 23-38.
36. Zintz, *Reading Process*, p. 138; Durkin, *Teaching Them to Read*, p. 13, Wittick, "Innovations in Reading Instruction," p. 76.

word approach that it obscures the differences in approaches to beginning reading if basal methods are merely described as eclectic.

Supplemental Phonics. A supplemental phonics program is one in which systematic phonics instruction supplements a basal reading series. Phonics principles are taught systematically rather than incidentally in a planned progression which is not dependent on a story; phonics is taught as a part of specific reading skills; and the introduction of phonics comes early rather than late.

Examples of supplemental phonics programs previously referred to are those of Hay-Wingo and Durrell. Hay-Wingo is one of the oldest, and incorporates systematic sound-letter discrimination, consistent left and right blending, and begins with short vowel sounds in three letter words.

Phonic-Linguistic Basal Readers. A phonic-linguistic basal reader program has the usual array of readiness, workbooks, guides, preprimers, and primers. The main difference in such readers with sight-meaning basal readers is the early, heavy, and concentrated emphasis on phonics. The best example of a complete phonic-linguistic basal reading program is the Lippincott series. Because of the heavy emphasis on decoding rather than look-say, this series has about two thousand words in the first grade program compared to about three hundred fifty words in sight-meaning basal sequences.[37] Further discussion of the phonic-linguistic approach is given in the section on reading research.

A characteristic of the Lippincott series, which has nothing to do with the method, is the emphasis on the literary nature of the reading selections compared with the stories of social realism which characterize most basal series.

Linguistic Approaches. As indicated previously, in a linguistic approach the sounds of letters are inferred from words. In a phonic approach, short *a* (apple) is taught explicitly, and then the rule is applied in short *a* monosyllables—*mat, man, ram, pad*. In a linguistic approach, the rule for short *a* is derived from *at, mat, pat, sat, cat*. Another explicit difference is in the handling of certain other orthographic rules, such as silent *w*. In figure 10.3, silent *w* appears, and the rule is taught that in words which begin with *wr* the *w* is silent, e.g., *wreck, write, wrap*.[38] In a pure linguistic approach, the rule is very explicit "Do not discuss 'silent' w."[39]

Two of the best known examples of linguistic approaches are those of Bloomfield[40] and Fries.[41] Both of these exclude pictures, on the grounds that deriving meaning from picture clues encourages guessing.

There are many variations of linguistic approaches, and there is no such thing as *a linguistic method* of teaching reading.

Programmed Reading. A programmed reader is one which breaks down the learn-

37. Glenn McCracken and Charles C. Walcutt, *Lippincott's Basic Reading*, Teacher's Edition, Books A-H, Grades 1-3, (Philadelphia: J. B. Lippincott Company, 1969).
38. McCracken and Walcutt, *Lippincott's Basic Reading*, Book D, pp. 34 and 26. Hay and Wingo, *Reading With Phonics*, pp. 157 and 98.
39. Charles C. Fries et al., *Merrill Linguistic Readers, Reader 6*, Teacher's Edition (Columbus, Ohio: Charles E. Merrill Books, Inc., 1966), p. 60.
40. Leonard Bloomfield and Clarence L. Barnhart, *Let's Read* (Detroit: Wayne State University Press, 1961).
41. Fries was senior author of the Merrill Linguistic Readers, which may be regarded as a linguistic basal series.

ing sequence into many small tasks, operationally defines the learning steps, and provides repetitive practice and immediate feedback in which the student monitors his own progress. Programmed readers tend to combine phonic and linguistic principles, and emphasize the teaching of beginning reading as the acquisition of a code. The approach is very straightforward, and may proceed directly to teaching letters to teaching sounds to writing words and to saying words. Because of the nature of programming, the forced discrimination response is frequently used, e.g., *I am / a mat / a cat.* In the beginning stages, programmed reading requires as much teacher monitoring as in other approaches. The student, however, becomes an independent worker at an earlier stage and is able to monitor his own progress with less dependence on the teacher.

Examples of programmed readers are the Michigan[42] and Sullivan[43] programs.

Modified Alphabet. The spelling approach to the improvement of teaching reading through increasing the number of characters to provide a phonetically regular alphabet is not new.[44] The best known modern version, of which there are British and American[45] interpretations, is the Initial Teaching Alphabet, developed in 1959 by Sir James Pitman. Figure 10.4 is an example of ITA. ITA is designed to facilitate the beginning teaching of reading. After relative efficiency is acquired, the reader gradually shifts to conventional writing and spelling.

Language-Experience. The chief difference between the sight-meaning approach and the language experience (L.E.) approach is in the source of material used for reading. In L.E., the language for instruction comes from stories dictated by the pupil, not from a basal reader. The L. E. approach is based upon the premise that the language of each individual child is the natural language to begin the teaching of reading. There is no one L. E. approach. Some, like Stauffer,[46] are staunch sight-meaning advocates and word recognition skills are always taught in context. In other L. E. programs, basal readers and phonic drills are used in addition to pupil stories.[47]

L. E. teachers usually emphasize pupil creativity in writing. L. E. is thus just as much a written composition method as it is one for teaching reading.

Free Reading. In a free reading approach, pupils select materials which they think will be of interest to them. Such an approach is based on the assumption that pupils will be more interested in learning to read if they select their own material from a wide variety of offerings.[48] It is likely that both free and language-experience approaches are too complicated for the novice teacher to implement successfully.[49]

42. Donald E. P. Smith and Judith M. Kelingos, *Michigan Successive Discrimination Reading Program* (Ann Arbor, Mich.: Ann Arbor Publishers, 1964).
43. Sullivan Associates, *Programmed Primer 1* (St. Louis: McGraw-Hill Book Company, 1963).
44. Charles C. Fries, *Linguistics and Reading* (New York: Holt, Rinehart and Winston, Inc., 1965), pp. 8-9; Maurice Harrison, *Instant Reading: The Story of the Initial Teaching Alphabet* (London: Sir Isaac Pitman & Sons, Ltd., 1964), p. 46.
45. Albert J. Mazurkiewicz and Harold J. Tanyzer, *Early-to Read I/T/A Program,* rev. ed. (New York: Initial Teaching Alphabet Publications, Inc., 1965).
46. Russell G. Stauffer, *The Language-Experience Approach to the Teaching of Reading* (New York: Harper & Row, Publishers, 1970), p. 177.
47. Chall, *Learning to Read,* p. 43.
48. Roland West, *Individualized Reading Instruction* (Port Washington, N.Y.: Kennikat Press, 1964), pp. 40-41.
49. George D. Spache, *Toward Better Reading* (Champaign, Ill.: Garrard Publishing Company, 1966), pp. 150-61; Chall, *Learning to Read,* pp. 41-42.

The Initial Teaching Alphabet

Number	Character	Name in T.O. letters	Example	Traditional spelling	Number	Character	Name in T.O. letters	Example	Traditional spelling
1	æ	ae	ræt	rate	22	w	wae	will	will
2	b	bee	big	big	23	y	yae	yell	yell
3	c	kee	cat	cat	24	z	zee	zoo	zoo
4	d	dee	dog	dog	25	ʐ	zess	rœʐ	rose
5	ee	ee	meet	meat	26	wh	whae	when	when
6	f	ef	fill	fill	27	ch	chae	chick	chick
7	g	gae	gun	gun	28	th	ith	thin	thin
9	h	hae	hat	hat	29	th	thee	then	then
9	ie	ie	tie	tie	30	ſh	ish	ſhip	ship
10	j	jae	jig	jig	31	ʒ	zhee	viʒon	vision
11	k	kae	kit	kit	32	ŋ	ing	siŋ	sing
12	l	el	lamp	lamp	33	a	ah	father	father
13	m	em	man	man	34	au	au	taut	taut
14	n	en	net	net	35	a	at	appl	apple
15	œ	oe	tœ	toe	36	e	et	egg	egg
16	p	pee	pig	pig	37	i	it	dip	dip
17	r	rae	run	run	38	o	ot	hot	hot
18	s	ess	sad	sad	39	u	ut	ugly	ugly
19	t	tee	tap	tap	40	ω	oot	bωk	book
20	ue	ue	due	due	41	ω	oo	mωn	moon
21	v	vee	van	van	42	ou	ow	vou	vow
					43	oi	oi	oil	oil

Fig. 10.4. The Initial Teaching Alphabet. From John Downing, *Initial Teaching Alphabet* (New York: Macmillan Company, 1964), pp. 16-17. Reprinted with permission of the Macmillan Company.

173

Free reading is sometimes called individualized or personalized reading instruction. Since the term "individualized" has the more general connotation of working with pupils according to their performance level, the older term of "free reading" from the 1920s is preferred to describe this methodological emphasis.

Systems Approaches. Two reading programs using the terminology "system" have been introduced. One is DISTAR, discussed under compensatory approaches, and the second is the Scott, Foresman Reading Systems, introduced in 1971,[50] discussed here.

Studious effort is made by the publishers to avoid any comparison of Reading Systems with the New Basic Readers,[51] but some comparisons are essential in order to indicate the new shifts in emphasis in readiness, use of natural language, and development of skills sequences, which are more significant than the multiplicity of coordinated materials provided the teacher.[52] The Reading Systems format consists of core or minimum materials for teacher and pupil use, with a variety of visual, audio, and kinesthetic material to develop "systems" to personalize instruction for pupils needing special assistance.

The concept of readiness is still recognized, but the emphasis has shifted to skills necessary for reading. After children are taught the first steps of oral language and word awareness, they begin learning the names and letters of the alphabet simply as an initial skill used in reading. And there is an *earlier* emphasis. At the end of Level 1 (former readiness level), learning tasks have included learning to name and write the alphabet. And use is made of such old props as "The Alphabet Song."[53] While letters are taught in *Learn to Listen, Speak, and Write,* there is a tendency in the New Basic Readers to deemphasize letter names. Thus, in word recognition directions, attention is invited to the visual shape of letters such as *h, m,* and *n* not by name but by such characteristics as "tallest" and "widest."[54]

Not only are *letter names* taught earlier and more systematically but *letter sounds* also. The sequence is as follows: Level 1, recognize and write letters; Level 2, initial consonants, b, g, f, h, r, t, l, m, s, d, n, p, w, y, k, c, v, z, j, ch, sh, th, qu, kw; and Level 3 vowel sounds:

a as in sat, ball, cart, rake, saw, pail, play
e as in left, sheep, her, few, eat
i as in big, dime, girl
o as in mom, nose, torn, soak
u as in cup, curb, use.

The *Studybook* provides for specific development of word recognition skills as sequentially introduced in the readers. For example, the first story is *The Bus Ride.*[55] From this story the two initial consonants *b* and *g* are selected for skill development. Although only three words in the story begin with *b/b/* and three with *g/g/,* the *Study-*

50. Ira Aaron et al., *Scott, Foresman Reading Systems, Primary Levels 1-12* (Glenview, Ill.: Scott, Foresman and Company, 1971).
51. Helen M. Robinson, Marion Monroe, and A. Sterl Artley, *The New Basic Readers* (Chicago: Scott, Foresman and Company, 1962).
52. The New Basic Readers were coordinated with *Learn to Listen, Speak and Write.* Components such as *My Practice Pad* antedate Reading Systems components, such as *Independent Practice Pad,* Level 1. See Marion Monroe, Ralph G. Nichols, and W. Cabell Greet, *Learn to Listen, Speak, and Write,* Teacher's Edition, Levels 1-1 and 1-2 (Chicago: Scott, Foresman and Company, 1960).
53. *The Alphabet Book,* Level 1 (Glenview, Ill.: Scott, Foresman and Company, 1971).
54. Robinson, Monroe, and Artley, *Fun with Our Friends,* Guidebook (Chicago: Scott, Foresman and Company, 1971).
55. Aaron, et al., p. 3.

book[56] uses 12 words with initial $b/b/$ with 29 repetitions and 6 words with initial $g/g/$ with 22 repetitions. This direct practice in phoneme-grapheme skills of words in sentences is a feature of the *Studybook*.

There is a use of more natural language. One of the Reading Systems stories begins (former preprimer level):[57]

Let's play follow the leader.
Everybody line up.
Do what I do.

In contrast, an older story (primer level) begins:

"I like this new game," said Susan.
"It is easy to make the clowns go down."
"I got all but three."[58]

The language of the former makes sense without the pictures; the older story gets its meaning from the picture—children bowling with clown pins.

Rigid vocabulary control has been reduced but it has not been eliminated. Any beginning reading system controls vocabulary either on the basis of word frequency or word similarity. In *The Bus Ride* there are 26 words in 33 lines with service words repeated from ten to 40 times.

Many of the characteristics of the older Scott, Foresman materials are continued in Reading Systems. Some of the more obvious ones are the elaborate teacher manuals with a plethora of teacher talk and directions, the profuse and colorful (but more realistic) illustrations, multiple objectives for each learning task, and the continued emphasis on reading for meaning and the use of multiple word recognition cues. Reading Systems is nevertheless a significant departure from the older basal reading programs which dominated the 1960s and incorporates the following trends in the teaching of reading which will be more prominent in the 1970s: more emphasis on initial reading skills and less emphasis on generalized readiness, early learning of the alphabet, early learning of sound-letter relationships, use of more natural language, the provision of a greater variety of material, more emphasis on moving able children faster, more emphasis on teaching reading skills to prevent remedial reading cases, and realistic, multi-ethnic illustrations.

Special Purpose Reading Approaches

The reading approaches described previously are designed for all types of children. Those who encounter particular difficulty are cycled into supplementary work. This section is concerned with special programs for the disadvantaged, Spanish-speaking children, and remedial work.

Compensatory Reading. The direct verbal approach of Siegfried Engelmann[59] is predicated on the assumption that pupils fail in school because they are not taught skills essential to success in school. Instead of defining handicaps of disadvantaged children globally, the handicaps are defined specifically as a lack of sound-word discrimination and inadequacy in syntactic rather than lexical language elements. In contrast with most reading programs which begin with letter names, DISTAR (Direct Instructional System for Teaching Arithme-

---

56. Aaron, et al., *Studybook, Scott Foresman Reading Systems, Level 2* (Glenview, Ill.: Scott, Foresman and Company, 1971).
57. Charlemae Rollins, "Follow the Leader," *Let's Play,* Level 2, Book 2 (Glenview, Ill.: Scott, Foresman and Company, © 1971), p. 6. Reprinted by permission.
58. Robinson, Monroe, and Artley, *Fun With Our Friends,* © p. 104. Reprinted by permission.
59. Siegfried Engelmann, *Preventing Failure in the Primary Grades* (Chicago: Science Research Associates, Inc., 1969).

tic and Reading) begins with letter sounds. A modified initial teaching alphabet is used in Level 1, with traditional orthography in Level 2. Level 1 (Kindergarten or first grade) emphasizes decoding in a structured sequence. After nine letter sounds are introduced, regular word reading is begun. Later take-home stories are introduced, one of which begins:

> A girl had a little cat. She loved her little cat. She walked with her cat and she talked to her cat. She went to the park with her cat. She loved her little cat.[60]

The DISTAR system is highly structured with specific learning tasks, and requires intensive direct verbal instruction by a teacher. The lessons are designed to be taught in small groups of about ten students each for thirty minutes daily. There are 159 lessons in the reading program, to be taught daily. Comparative research with the preliminary version of these materials indicated the relative success of this structured compensatory approach compared to traditional approaches. More follow-up work was needed, however, to prevent the loss of early gains.[61] Since that time, Level 2 material, emphasizing comprehension skills, has been developed and Level 3 material is under development.

Spanish Language Background. Children who learn to read in English as a second language are not only faced with the difficulty of reading; they are faced with the difficulty of learning a second language.[62] Reading programs for such children now generally assume that a child should be taught English as a second language before he is taught to read. One of the most effective reading programs for children with a Spanish language background are the *Miami Linguistic Readers.*[63] These readers incorporate the aural-oral approach of TESL (Teaching English as a Second Language) to develop sound contrasts between English and Spanish, vocabulary and grammar is controlled, sound-symbol relations are presented systematically, and the child can understand and speak what he is expected to read.

Eventually, the time may come in the United States when children who speak Spanish and Indian in the home are schooled in the primary years in their family tongue and are then taught to read and write English in the intermediate years. In a true bilingual model they would be taught concurrently in Spanish and English. There is some research to indicate that teaching a child to read in his native tongue is a more effective approach than instruction in a second language.[64] Bilingualism is no longer regarded as an educational handicap.[65]

Corrective and Remedial Reading. For various reasons, many children learn to read with such extreme difficulty that they become slow, deficient, or retarded readers. Corrective work is normally undertaken by the teacher within regular classroom instruc-

60. *DISTAR Orientation* (Chicago: Science Research Associates, 1970).
61. Merle B. Karnes, *Research and Development Program on Preschool Disadvantaged Children Final Report,* Project No. 5-1181, Contract No. OE 6-10-235 (Urbana, Ill.: Institute for Research on Exceptional Children, University of Illinois 1969), pp. I, 13, 18, 23.
62. Zintz, *Reading Process,* chap. 14, "Teaching Reading to the Bilingual Child."
63. *Miami Linguistic Readers* (Boston: D. C Heath, 1965).
64. Nancy Modiano, "A Comparative Study of Two Approaches to the Teaching of Reading in the National Language," New York University School of Education, 1966, cited in Zintz, *Reading Process,* p. 350.
65. Elizabeth Peal and Wallace Lambert, "The Relationship of Bilingualism to Intelligence," *Psychological Monographs: General and Applied* no. 76 (Washington: American Psychological Association, 1962): 1-23.

tion; remedial work may involve work outside the classroom in special reading classes.

Two approaches are used in remedial reading. In the counseling approach, the teacher is primarily a therapist. The counseling approach is based on the point of view that reading disabilities are primarily emotional, and that corrective procedures must begin with an improvement in personal adjustment of the individual.[66] In the teaching model, the teacher is primarily a reading teacher. The teaching approach is based on the assumption that personal maladjustment is primarily a function of lack of success in learning to read, and that corrective procedures must emphasize making the pupil a successful reader.[67] There is no research evidence concerning the relative efficacy of the two approaches.

There are no distinctive approaches to remedial work compared to regular reading instruction. Older approaches tended to follow the counseling model.[68] A compilation of remedial approaches reported by Harris in 1968 indicates a heavy emphasis on learning the "code," using such procedures as phonic, linguistic, multisensory, and modified alphabets.[69] Remedial techniques have long been interpreted by some to justify a heavier code emphasis in beginning reading. The most promising development in reading is the new emphasis on the prevention of reading failures by giving more emphasis to word recognition skills and earlier corrective practices.

A limited number of severe cases of reading disability resulting from neurological and related medical causes require the help of clinically trained reading teachers, who also have a background in special education. In many cases, much more structured teaching is required than is found in the typical reading class. The field of dyslexia is a highly specialized field in which only trained specialists are competent to pass judgment. In particular the tendency should be avoided to ascribe all reading problems to dyslexia, a term developed by medical specialists to describe reading disabilities associated with the development of the central nervous system.[70]

Efficiency of Various Approaches To the Teaching of Beginning Reading

The history of reading instruction has been largely a history of improvements in methods of beginning reading instruction. Prior to the scientific testing movement, most judgments of superiority were based on logic and personal preference. For the last fifty years, there have been numerous studies which have "proved" the superiority of Method A over Method B. The result of this research, on the whole, has been contradictory and inconclusive, poorly designed and lacking in control of the ex-

66. Arthur W. Heilman, *Principles and Practices of Teaching Reading* 2d ed. (Columbus, Ohio: Charles E. Merrill Publishing Company, 1967), pp. 461-67; George D. Spache, *Toward Better Reading* (Champaign, Ill.: Garrard Publishing Company, 1963), pp. 298-99.

67. Emerald Dechant, *Diagnosis and Remediation of Reading Disability* (West Nyack, N.Y.: Parker Publishing Company, 1968), pp. 70-71.

68. Emmett Albert Betts, *Foundations of Reading Instruction* (New York: American Book Company, 1954), pp. 54, 482; Miles A Tinker and Constance M. McCullough, *Teaching Elementary Reading* 2d ed. (Appleton-Century-Crofts, Inc., 1962), p. 548.

69. Albert J. Harris, "Diagnosis and Remedial Instruction in Reading," *Innovation and Change in Reading Instruction*, The Sixty-seventh Yearbook of the National Society for the Study of Education, part II, ed. Helen M. Robinson (Chicago: University of Chicago Press, 1968), pp. 159-94.

70. Students interested in dyslexia are referred to publications cited in Harris, "Diagnosis and Remedial Instruction."

perimental variables, and especially lacking in control of long term effects.[71] As a result, there is some tendency to shift all emphasis to the teacher and to say that no differences result from method, that research is merely a form of special interest pleading, or reflects a spirit of the times. Methods of teaching reading have been developed by practitioners over long periods of time, and in looking at research results it is well to remember the caveat of Fries that there is little relationship of reading practice to educational research.[72]

With these precautions, it is nevertheless useful to look at the report of the Coordinating Center for First Grade Reading Instruction and the synthesis of Chall which indicate that in beginning reading instruction a heavier code emphasis facilitates learning to read.

Coordinating Center for First-Grade Reading Instruction. The Coordinating Center involved the comparison of six methods in 15 projects utilizing the same educational measurements. The six methods were basal, basal plus phonics, I.T.A., linguistic, phonic-linguistic, and language experience. The principal investigators drew the following conclusions from the analysis of methodology:[73]

1. Word study skills must be emphasized and taught systematically regardless of what approach to initial reading instruction is utilized.
2. Combinations of programs, such as a basal program with supplementary phonics materials, often are superior to single approaches. Furthermore the success of such methods as the Language Experience approach indicates that the addition of language experiences to any kind of reading program can be expected to make a contribution.
3. Innovative programs such as Linguistic readers are especially effective in the word recognition area. The superiority of these programs to Basal programs is not as evident in the area of comprehension. It is likely that Basal programs should develop a more intensive word study skills element, while programs which put major emphasis on word recognition should increase attention paid to other reading skills.
4. It is necessary for teachers to make differential expectations concerning mean achievement of boys and girls. On the average, boys cannot be expected to achieve at the same level as girls, at least with the materials, methods, and teachers involved in this investigation. A probable explanation from the data of this study is that boys are less ready to read when they enter school.
5. Boys and girls do not profit uniquely from any of the programs utilized in this investigation. On the average, girls' achievement is superior to boys' no matter what approach to beginning reading is used.
6. Reading programs are not equally effective in all situations. Evidently factors other than method, within a particular learning situation influence pupil success in reading.
7. Reading achievement is related to characteristics in addition to those investigated in this study. Pupils in certain school systems become better readers than pupils in other

71. Guy L. Bond and Robert Dykstra, *Final Report, Coordinating Center for First-Grade Reading Instruction Programs,* Project No. X-001 Contract No. OE-5-10-264 (Minneapolis: University of Minnesota, 1967), p. 4; Chall, *Learning to Read,* pp. 80-85; Robinson, "The Next Decade," pp. 410-15.
72. Fries, *Linguistics and Reading,* p. 29.
73. Bond and Dykstra, *op. cit.,* pp. 210-212.

school systems even when pupil characteristics are controlled statistically. Furthermore, these differences in achievement from project to project do not seem to be directly related to the class, school, teacher, and community characteristics appraised in this study.

8. Pupils taught to read by means of a transitional alphabet such as I.T.A. may experience greater difficulty making the transition to traditional orthography in spelling than they do in reading. Longitudinal information is necessary to study this problem.

9. Future research might well center on teacher and learning situation characteristics rather than method and materials. The tremendous range among classrooms within any method points out the importance of elements in the learning situation over and above the methods employed. To improve reading instruction it is necessary to train better teachers of reading rather than to expect a panacea in the form of materials.

10. Children learn to read by a variety of materials and methods. Pupils become successful readers in such vastly different programs as the Language Experience approach with its relative lack of structure and vocabulary control and the various Linguistic programs with their relatively high degree of structure and vocabulary control. Furthermore, pupils experienced difficulty in each of the programs utilized. No one approach is so distinctly better in all situations and respects than the others that it should be considered the one best method and the one to be used exclusively.

11. The expectation of pupil accomplishment in initial reading instruction probably should be raised. Programs which introduced words at a more rapid pace tended to produce pupils with superior word recognition abilities at the end of the first grade. Children today tend to be better equipped for reading instruction when they enter first grade than they were some years ago and are probably prepared to learn more words and develop more mature study skills than are currently expected of them in many programs.

12. Indications are that the initial reading vocabulary should be selected with a greater balance between phonetically regular words and high utility words. It is likely that introducing words solely on the basis of frequency of use presents an unusually complex decoding task for the beginning reader. On the other hand, it appears that presenting only phonetically regular words makes it very difficult to write meaningful material.

13. A writing component is likely to be an effective addition to a primary reading program. In the first place, the Language Experience approach which involves considerable written expression, was an effective program of instruction. In addition, programs such as I.T.A. and Phonic/Linguistic, both of which were relatively effective, encourage pupils to write symbols as they learn to recognize them and to associate them with sounds. This appears helpful to the pupil in learning sound-symbol relationships. Furthermore, it is likely that writing such common but irregular words as "the" helps the child to commit them to his sight vocabulary.

14. It is impossible to assess the relative effectiveness of programs unless they are used in the same project. Project differences are so great even when pupil readiness for reading is controlled that a program utilized in a favored project would demonstrate a distinct advantage over one used in a less favored project regardless of the effectiveness of the program.

15. The relative success of the non-basal programs compared to the basal programs indicates that reading instruction can be improved. It is likely that improvement would result from adopting certain elements from each of the approaches used in this study. The first step would be to determine the elements within the various approaches most important to the success of that program. For example, the I.T.A. and Phonic/Linguistic programs, both of which were relatively effective, have in common a vocabulary controlled on sound-symbol regularity, introduction of a relatively large reading vocabulary, and emphasis on writing symbols as a means of learning them. It would be interesting to know which of these elements, if any, is primarily responsible for the effectiveness of the program. Perhaps an instructional program which incorporated the most important elements of all of the approaches used in the study would be a more effective method of teaching than any currently in use.

The research of the Coordinating Center was continued through the second grade. The findings at the end of the second grade confirmed the findings at the end of the first grade: high correlation of knowledge of letter names and sounds with reading success; high correlation between word recognition and comprehension; phonics highly related to word recognition; differences in school systems are more important in accounting for differences in achievement than differences in method; girls exceed boys irrespective of the method used; a heavier vocabulary and acceleration of phonic skills contribute to independence in reading; and direct instruction in comprehension is desirable.[74]

The Chall Review of Research. In contrast to the research coordinated by the Coordinating Center for First-Grade Reading Instruction, Jeanne Chall undertook to review and synthesize reading research for the period 1910-65 in the focus of two approaches to reading: the sight-meaning approach of basal readers and the code acquisition approach of phonic, linguistic, and other teaching methods. Her synthesis of the results of experimental and correlational studies are similar in most respects to the findings of the Coordinating Center. Chall's conclusions are summarized below:[75]

1. A code (phonic/linguistic) emphasis is related to better overall early reading achievement.
2. Reading skills development under the two approaches are somewhat different:
   a. *Code* emphasis gives an early initial advantage in word recognition and oral reading, which is not necessarily related to an advantage in reading-for-meaning on silent tests. However, by the end of the first or sometimes during the second grade, this early recognition advantage becomes related to better comprehension.
   A code emphasis appears to contribute to slower initial reading because of early emphasis on accuracy. This initial deficit appears to disappear by the third or fourth grade.
   b. *Meaning* emphasis gives an initial advantage in reading-for-meaning about the middle of the first grade, but the deficit in reading recognition skills eventually depresses word comprehension toward end of first or in second grade.

74. Robert Dykstra, *Final Report of the Continuation of the Coordinating Center for First-Grade Reading Instruction Programs,* Project No. 61651, Contract No. OEC3-7-001651-0472 (Minneapolis: University of Minnesota, 1967), pp. 129, 153, 156, 157, 162.

75. Chall, *Learning to Read,* pp. 137-39, 149-50.

The initial advantage in rapid reading is lost by the fourth grade.

3. Code learning is facilitated by both phonic (direct teaching of sound-symbol relationships); linguistic (inference of letter-sound correspondence); and modified alphabet systems, all of which reduce the ratio of irregular to regularly spelled words. However, both linguistic and modified alphabet approaches seem to benefit from direct teaching of sound-letter correspondence.
4. Individual differences appear to be related to differences in method as follows:
    a. Children of lower intelligence and socioeconomic background eventually learn better from a code emphasis, but this advantage does not show itself initially.
    b. Children of high ability and socioeconomic background gain an immediate advantage from phonic-linguistic teaching. However, the difference in the code vs. meaning approach is not as crucial, since they work out sound-letter relationships when these are not immediately taught.
5. Knowing the *names of letters* before learning to read helps a child learn to read, irrespective of method.
6. Knowing *sounds of letters* before learning to read helps a child learn to read, irrespective of method.
7. Letter and phonics knowledge is more closely related to reading success in the primary grades than is mental ability.
8. A low level of phonics knowledge is related to low reading achievement beyond the third grade.
9. As children progress in school, there is a higher correlation between intelligence and reading achievement. Consequently, a high level of phonics knowledge may not necessarily be associated with a high level of reading achievement in the upper grades.

The research of the Coordinating Center for First-Grade Reading Instruction has been the subject of criticism.[76] The reports of the Center and Chall synthesis nevertheless indicate the need to supplement traditional basal materials with a greater phonic or linguistic emphasis, and show that the exclusive pursuit of one method is not desirable. Anderson and Dearborn twenty years ago indicated the need for a mix in reading programs, cautioning that a method mixes "the bitter and the sweet."[77] It is anticipated that there will be a revival in eclectic methods under the vague concept of balance, as recently stated by McCullough.[78] This concept, however, makes a specific place for a heavier code emphasis.

Readiness and Beginning Reading

For many years, one of the major concepts in beginning reading has been that of reading "readiness." Betts in 1954 devoted over a hundred pages in six chapters to aspects of readiness.[79] The concept is still very much a part of beginning reading.[80] The concept of readiness has many facets, but may be simply stated as follows: There is a point in the biological and psychological maturation of the child at which formal reading instruction should be begun.

76. See, for example, Russell G. Stauffer, "The Verdict: Speculative Controversy," in *Issues and Innovations in the Teaching of Reading,* ed. Joe L. Frost (Glenview, Ill.: Scott, Foresman and Company, 1967), pp. 343-45.
77. Irving H. Anderson and Walter F. Dearborn, *The Psychology of Teaching Reading* (New York: Ronald Press Company, 1952), pp. 256-57.
78. Constance M. McCullough, "Balanced Reading Development," *Innovation and Change in Reading Instruction,* The Sixty-seventh Yearbook of the National Society for the Study of Education, part II, ed. Helen M. Robinson (Chicago: University of Chicago Press, 1968), pp. 320-56.
79. Emmett Albert Betts, *Foundations of Reading Instruction* (New York: American Book Company, 1954).
80. Zintz, *Reading Process,* chap. 16, p. 373.

This point of view completely neglected learning as a part of the readiness component. Consequently, the remedy for the lack of readiness was not teaching, but the delaying of instruction. In one of the best critiques of the concept of readiness, Durkin points out that even in the 1960's traditional practices relating to readiness were emphasized, especially by the Association for Childhood Education International which "continued to show allegiance to the 'let them grow into it' philosophy."[81]

While the maturational point of view will persist for a long time, particularly in early childhood education,[82] there is a new tendency to emphasize readiness to read as a function of previous learning.[83] Furthermore, experiments with young children, such as O.K. Moore's talking typewriter,[84] Durkin's reports of children who learn to read before they come to school,[85] and newer conceptions of the potentialities of the early years for intellectual development[86] have changed the conception of readiness. It is significant that not only the DISTAR materials of SRA but also the Scott, Foresman Reading Systems have abandoned the concept of reading readiness. While the emphasis at the research level has shifted from nature to nurture, the delaying tactic of readiness is still all too common in the schools. The way to get children ready to read is to teach them skills used in reading. These include such skills as mastery of the language, knowledge of letters and knowledge of sounds. If the long term aim is to have children "go to school at public expense beginning at the age of four" it is mandatory that consideration be given to earlier teaching of reading.[87]

While the emphasis on the age of beginning reading is usually focused on *delaying* reading for some students, there is an accumulating body of evidence that formal reading experience may even be desirable for children below six. In the reports of the Coordinating Center for First-Grade Reading Instruction previously referred to, one of the findings was that younger children on the whole did better than older children. This might indicate that the association of sounds with the alphabet and the learning of the alphabet may be routine tasks which are actually more appropriate for younger than for older children.

One of the few longitudinal reading studies concerning the long term effectiveness of beginning the teaching of reading in kindergarten was conducted in the public schools of Denver during the period 1960-66.[88] Space

81. Durkin, *Teaching Them to Read*, p. 29.
82. A good example of the maturational point of view is given by Frances Ilg, "The Child from Three to Eight, with Implications for Reading," *Teaching Young Children to Read*, U.S. Office of Education Bulletin no. 19, ed. Warren G. Cutts (Washington, D.C.: Government Printing Office, 1964), pp. 21-30.
83. J. McVicker Hunt, *Intelligence and Experience* (New York: Ronald Press Co., 1961).
84. Omar K. Moore, *Autotelic Responsive Learning Environment*, Working Paper No. PITT R/D40 (Pittsburgh: Learning Research and Development Center, University of Pittsburgh, April 1967).
85. Dolores Durkin, "A Study of Children Who Learned to Read Prior to First Grade," *California Journal of Educational Research* 10 (May 1959) 109-113; idem, *Children Who Read Early* (New York: Teachers College Press, Columbia University, 1966).
86. Benjamin S. Bloom, *Stability and Change in Human Characteristics* (New York: John Wiley and Sons, 1964).
87. Educational Policies Commission, *Universal Opportunity for Early Childhood Education* (Washington: National Education Association, 1966), p. 1.
88. Paul McKee and Joseph E. Brzeinski, *The Effectiveness of Teaching Reading in Kindergarten*, Cooperative Research Project No. 5-037 (Denver, Colorado: The Denver Public School and the Colorado State Department of Education, 1966).

does not permit a description of the various treatment groups and different findings. It was found, however, that children who were formally taught reading skills in kindergarten,[89] in contrast to those who merely experienced readiness activities, not only performed better in the first grade but maintained their reading and academic superiority throughout the fifth grade without adverse side effects. It was necessary, however, to adjust the reading program at the first grade and subsequent levels to the performance level in order to maintain the gains. In those treatment groups where the children went into the regular reading program not adjusted to their previous level, the advantages of learning early to read had disappeared by the end of the second grade. This finding is consistent with other research on compensatory or early training programs that the early training gains are lost where there is no modification to sustain the higher performance level of the children.[90]

As noted in chapter 5 dealing with the preschool, the distinction between kindergarten and school experiences is entirely arbitrary and violates the principles of individual differences and fitting instruction to the performance level of the child. The convention that reading should not be taught in kindergarten is a *modus vivendi* that protects the special privileges of the kindergarten and first grade teacher in total disregard of the performance abilities of the child.

A common way to ascertain the appropriate time to begin reading is the administration of a readiness test. If readiness is a function of previous learning, the administration of readiness tests further penalizes disadvantaged children who have lacked the opportunity to learn the skills necessary to begin reading activities. It is therefore suggested that the teacher of beginning reading initiate reading instruction, consisting of letter identification, letter names, and letter sounds from the very beginning. Success in letters and sounds are highly specific to success in reading. Those children who already know their letters and sounds may be grouped according to their performance level. In this way, neither the slow nor the advanced child is penalized. Both are taught according to their performance level, not according to some arbitrary conception of readiness.

Many reading activities may be initiated in the kindergarten, and may range from informal reading activities to highly structured reading activities. Many of the new materials are eminently suitable for use with five-year-old and younger children.

Teaching Reading in the Middle Grades

There has been little change in the approaches or the emphasis in teaching reading in the middle grades for the past thirty years. The research emphasis and controversy over approaches to teaching reading have been largely concerned with beginning reading, not the extension of reading skills with students who have already learned the basic skills of word recognition. Huus, in 1968, identified children's improvement in word recognition and comprehension, vocabulary development, and individual work emphasis through trade books and programmed instruction as some of the changes in

89. The methods used are described in Paul McKee and M. Lucille Harrison, *Program in Skills Basic to Beginning Reading* (Boston: Houghton Mifflin Company, 1960).

90. Karnes, *Research and Development Program,* p. 23.

reading in the middle grades. These hardly can be called changes or innovations.[91]

Reading in the upper grades is primarily a matter of general intellectual development and study, and the emphasis on reading shifts from Level 1 to Level 2 and 3, as previously described. There must be a program to maintain word recognition skills, but most of the emphasis shifts to vocabulary development, locating information, evaluating material, organizing and summarizing data, identifying and retaining major concepts and supporting data, and adjusting the rate of reading to the purpose.

There is nothing distinctively "reading" in the development of these skills, and they are just as applicable to social science and science and other areas of study requiring the acquisition of information from books. However, a traditional division of labor has assumed that students acquire these basic study skills as part of the language arts program. The language of each discipline tends to be more technical and specific as students progress in school. The literary language of stories and poetry common to reading seldom has the technical characteristics necessary to develop vocabulary and comprehension skills in the content areas. One example of an attempt to provide a greater content variety in reading materials is represented in the O'Donnell-Cooper subject matter emphasis in basic readers.[92]

In the middle grades, the two major emphases in reading are vocabulary development and study skills. Zintz provides detailed chapters on comprehension development, study skills, critical reading, oral reading, and use of library.[93] These upper grade reading skills are similar to subject matter skills.[94] Reading meaningfully to acquire, interpret, and evaluate information is a responsibility of teachers in all fields, not merely that of the "reading" teacher.

Tests in Reading

Measurement of reading achievement in the public schools typically utilizes standardized achievement batteries, such as the Gates, Metropolitan, Stanford, and California reading tests.[95] It is now increasingly recognized that there are no suitable tests for use at the primary level because of lack of content validity, that is, there is too much difference between what is actually taught in a reading program and what is found on the tests. Hobson has flatly stated that there are no suitable tests for measuring reading skills acquired in the first grade.[96]

Only one illustration can be given, involving the use of the Merrill Linguistic Readers 1-3. Of the 35 keyed responses on the Metropolitan Achievement Test, Primary

91. Helen Huus, "Innovations in Reading Instruction: At Later Levels," *Innovation and Change in Reading Instruction,* The Sixty-seventh Yearbook of the National Society for the Study of Education, part II, ed. Helen M. Robinson (Chicago: University of Chicago Press, 1968), pp. 126-58.

92. Mabel O'Donnell and J. Louis Cooper, *From Codes to Captains,* Teacher's Edition, Basic Fourth Reader Strand 2, How to Read in the Subject-Matter Areas (New York: Harper and Row, Publishers, 1963).

93. Zintz, *The Reading Process,* chaps. 8-12.

94. Helen McCracken Carpenter, ed., *Skill Development in the Social Studies,* Thirty-third Yearbook of the National Council for the Social Studies (Washington: NCSS, 1963).

95. A description of the characteristics of standardized reading tests are given in various editions of the *Mental Measurements Yearbook.* See also brief references in Zintz, *The Reading Process,* pp. 492-99.

96. J. R. Hobson, "Stanford Achievement Test," *The Fourth Mental Measurements Yearbook,* O. Buros (ed.) (Highland Park, N.J.: Gryphon Press, 1953), p. 592.

Battery, Form A,[97] only three responses on the word recognition test fall within the Merrill matrices, all in Reader 3. Of the 33 keyed responses on the Stanford Achievement Test, Primary I Battery,[98] none appear in Merrill Readers 1-3. Irrespective of the reliability of these standardized tests, they are not valid measures for the *Merrill Linguistic Series*. This results from the fact that the linguistically regular words of the Merrill series are not included in the irregular words of the two tests.[99]

To meet the lack of content-valid tests, publishers are developing content-specific tests to accompany their own reading programs. A feature of such programs as the Scott, Foresman Reading Systems and DISTAR, previously described, are the special tests to assess progress within those programs. General reading tests should probably not be used until the end of the third grade, when it is expected that most pupils will have achieved independence in reading in any program.

Learning to Teach Reading

As a prospective elementary teacher, you will most likely take a minimum of one specialized course in reading. You will undoubtedly find this experience will not adequately train you to teach reading. This results from the survey nature of most introductory reading courses and their lack of emphasis on training in methods of teaching. Also, *knowing about reading* is not the same as *skill in teaching*. Skill is acquired by practice, and few colleges of education provide the training situations with pupils to practice either the teaching of beginning reading or the study and comprehension skills of the middle grades. You will learn to teach reading on-the-job, and there are a number of things you can do to make this experience more effective for you and your pupils.

The first thing to do is to study and *know* the sequence of reading skills in the program of the school in which you teach. Notwithstanding criticism of basal readers, they are nevertheless much better programs than an experienced teacher, much less a novice, can create *de novo*. You should know the reading *objectives* and *content* so well that you can teach without a crutch. Use the teacher's manual to plan your teaching, not as a script to be literally followed. You will also need to know more than the reading skills of your grade level. Children will differ in their performance levels. To adjust your teaching to their needs, you should have a complete conception of the reading program. This means that you must be alert to get materials above grade level for your abler pupils, and below grade level for slower pupils.

As you work with your pupils, you may find it desirable to supplement the program with systematic work in phonics and linguistics. If there is a need for this kind of work, you can assist your pupils with systematic drills which you direct. A modest investment—less than ten dollars—will provide you with a teacher-directed program you can implement. If your program appears strong in phonics and linguistics but somewhat short in meaningful reading material, you can ask pupils to bring material from home to read (see "Free Reading"). The interrogatives *Who? Where? What?*

---

97. Harcourt, Brace & World, Inc., 1958.
98. Harcourt, Brace & World, Inc., 1964.
99. Molly M. Rice, "Measuring Reading Achievement . . . in a Linguistic Program," unpublished Master's thesis, University of Georgia, 1971, p. 13.

When? Why? provide endless cues to elicit meaning from simple as well as complex stories.

If you initiate the teaching of reading, you can find out what knowledge your pupils have of letters and sounds by devising a simple letter and sounds test, if none is available. Differentiate your instruction from the beginning, adjusting your teaching to various performance levels.

If you are a middle grade teacher, most of your emphasis should be on study and comprehension skills. But you cannot take for granted that all students have mastered word recognition skills. If students call *toy* for *boy* and *sam* for *was,* systematic attention to phoneme-grapheme correspondence may be required. If students call words hesitatingly and slowly, they may need practice in mastering sight words (see "service words") and oral reading with attention to phrasing and intonation. In the middle grades, a variety of subject matter should be utilized in reading instruction, not merely literature. But whatever you do should relate to pupil performance needs and reading skills, not to an arbitrary grade performance level.

As you learn to teach reading, you should also analyze and study the components of various reading programs. In this way you can work more intelligently with the reading consultant in obtaining materials to suit particular pupil needs and to obtain needed assistance. And if you have the opportunity to participate in any kind of special reading program, avail yourself of that opportunity. The opportunity to obtain special help and materials as well as to be stimulated by the enthusiasm of your colleagues will be of great value in learning how to teach reading in school.

An Appraisal of Reading Instruction

The history of American reading instruction has seen many changes in emphasis. Methods utilized have included, in historical sequence, the alphabet method (letters blended to form words, *c-a-t*), the phonic method (sounds blended to form words, *ka-t*), the word method (look and saying whole words, cat), phrase method (on the erroneous assumption that mature readers read in phrases), sentence method (a combination of the word and phrase method), changes in orthography (using a constant sign for the phoneme, as in *kat*), experience method (children dictating stories), and linguistic method (using regular rhyming words, *cat, bat, sat*). To a certain extent, all reading teachers use look-and-say, even if it is to supply the needed word.[100] All methods tend to have certain drawbacks, and some children tend to have difficulty in learning to read no matter what methods are used. After a period of relative neglect of emphasis on the code aspects of reading, decoding will undoubtedly receive new impetus without sacrificing the gains which have been made in teaching reading as a meaningful activity and not merely as a mechanical skill.

Children need to become efficient readers because their success in school depends largely on their ability to get information by reading. During the past decade, most of the criticism of reading was focused on the materials and methods of instruction used. In particular the basal readers were under attack, with their over-emphasis on sight-meaning approaches using irregular

100. Anderson and Dearborn, *Psychology of Teaching Reading,* p. 212.

words of high frequency. The evidence indicates that many of these deficiencies are being corrected, either by the use of supplementary materials or the design of new reading programs which incorporate many of the new emphases of reading instruction.

As many of the improved materials are adopted, the question of teacher efficiency will become more and more prominent. While there will never be a teacherproof system, there are already available materials which produce effective readers when properly used by the teacher. Proper use depends on specific lesson planning and general efficiency in classroom management. In the 1970s, it is likely that more and more emphasis will be shifted to the performance of the teacher, irrespective of the method used. Because of the short period of time in which most prospective teachers engage in student teaching, few new teachers have had adequate classroom experience in teaching reading. They must learn to teach on the job. Consequently, a clear conceptualization of reading objectives and the procedures to attain them is a prerequisite to good reading instruction. It is for this reason that we have so strongly emphasized teacher planning and mastery of the content of the teaching act, and knowledge of tested procedures which facilitate pupil learning.

Selected References

Anderson, Irving H., and Dearborn, Walter F. *The Psychology of Teaching Reading.* New York: Ronald Press Company, 1952.

Bond, Guy L., and Dykstra, Robert. *Final Report, Coordinating Center for First-Grade Reading Instruction Programs,* Project No. X-001, Contract No. OE-5-10-264. Minneapolis, Minn.: University of Minnesota, 1967.

Chall, Jeanne. *Learning to Read: The Great Debate.* New York: McGraw-Hill Book Co., 1967.

Dechant, Emerald. *Diagnosis and Remediation of Reading Disability.* West Nyack, N.Y.: Parker Publishing Company, 1968.

Durkin, Dolores. *Teaching Them to Read.* Boston: Allyn and Bacon, Inc., 1970.

Dykstra, Robert. *Final Report of the Continuation of the Coordinating Center for First-Grade Reading Instruction Programs,* Project No. 61651, Contract No. OEC 3-7-001651-0472. Minneapolis, Minn.: University of Minnesota, 1967.

Fries, Charles C. *Linguistics and Reading.* New York: Holt, Rinehart and Winston, Inc., 1963.

McKee, Paul, and Brzeinski, Joseph E. *The Effectiveness of Teaching Reading in Kindergarten,* Cooperative Research Project No. 5-0371. Denver, Colorado: The Denver Public Schools and the Colorado State Department of Education, 1966.

National Society for the Study of Education. *Innovation and Change in Reading Instruction,* The Sixty-seventh Yearbook, part II. Edited by Helen M. Robinson. Chicago: University of Chicago Press, 1968.

Smith, Nila B. *American Reading Instruction.* New York: Silver, Burdett and Company, 1934.

Spache, George D. *Toward Better Reading.* Champaign, Ill.: Garrard Publishing Company, 1966.

Wardhough, Ronald. *Reading: A Linguistic Perspective.* New York: Harcourt, Brace & World, Inc., 1969.

Zintz, Miles V. *The Reading Process.* Dubuque, Iowa: Wm C. Brown Company Publishers, 1970.

language and communication

11

The language arts is the general term used in the elementary school to describe the communication skills of speaking, listening, reading, and writing in the English language. Writing is a broad area in itself which subsumes penmanship, spelling, written composition, and syntax. Creative dramatics and drama are frequently classified with visual art and music as an affective-expressive art, but in this book creative dramatics and drama are treated as a part of the language arts program. Foreign or second language learning is sometimes classified with the language arts, but the acquisition of a second language has learning characteristics different from the regular language program. It is for this reason that special attention will be given to TESL (Teaching English as a Second Language) to children with severe dialectical handicaps or who come from non-English speaking homes.

The authors' point of view is that the four major aspects of communication are interrelated. A comprehensive language arts program therefore will involve speaking, listening, reading, and writing in a complementary rather than isolated fashion. However, each aspect requires specific skill development, and a high level of performance in one does not automatically assure facility in the other, especially in the lower grades. Systematic and sequential development in the various communication skills is required. Formal grammar training, whether of the traditional, structural, or transformational generative types is not necessarily recommended. Correction of inhibiting dialect deficiencies is treated simply as a matter of direct verbal training, rather than as a matter of grammar or linguistic science. The channel of oral and visual communication, however, imposes different kinds of learning tasks, notwithstanding the fact that the written marks stand for the same arbitrary code. A separate chapter was therefore devoted to reading. This chapter begins with a discussion of the importance of language.

The Importance of Language

Language is the distinctive form of human communication. Like the air, language is so ubiquitous and pervasive that it is taken for granted. First grade teacher and college professor alike base their teaching upon a common assumption—that the learner can receive and send a message in language. All types of classroom transactions and teaching strategies—from a class in English to coaching football, from the management of classroom behavior to the administration of the total school—involve the use of language. Not only does the human animal send and receive messages, but he uses language to give directions to himself. The process of thought is inextricably bound up with language. Words, ideas, concepts, statements, generalizations, inferences, conclusions, propositions—all of these terms imply language, the unique human capacity of man to communicate through sound symbols.

The development of intellectuality and the transmission of knowledge through language is the primary function of the school. The learning of specific subject matter, from Art to Zoology, involves in a large part the acquisition of the arbitrary system of vocal signs peculiar to that subject. Even where many concrete experiences are utilized to facilitate the association of things and words, a premium is placed upon the correct use of language. Without language there would be no school.

The emphasis thus far has been on language and schooling. But language existed long before the invention of writing and the invention of the school. All preliterate societies have language, belong to a particular speech community, and are able to carry on all transactions which involve face to face communication. The functions of language in preliterate societies help us appreciate even more fully the significance of language as the most important part of man's culture.

Everywhere men live, they live in groups. Group living is a prerequisite to rearing the young and transmitting the practices of the group through which they survive. However large or small, the people of the group share a common language which helps bind the group together. It not only helps members to communicate, but in the communicative acts helps each member fulfill personal survival needs.

Language helps each member of the group to understand his role and status; the interlocking nexus of prohibitions, customs, commands, and expectancies; the nature of the social structure; and the way the members of the group must cooperate to achieve common goals. But just as language binds together the members of a group, creating an in-group sentiment, language also serves the opposite function. It serves as a barrier to those who do not speak the same langauge, and sets them apart. By analogy, the teacher can see how a common language functions to socialize and solidify activity within his class, a microcosm of the social order. He also can see how the occurrence of different languages or dialects in the class serve not merely as barriers to communication but as barriers to collaboration and group action.

The language of a group not only serves as a means of communication, but it expresses the artifact, ideational, and behavioral content of a culture. While there has been no substantiation of the Whorf hypothesis that language reflects different thought categories,[1] it is generally recognized that a people who have made great progress in science will have many words relating to science and technology; one

1. B. L. Whorf, *Language, Thought, and Reality: Selected Writings of Benjamin Lee Whorf,* ed. John B. Carrol (Cambridge, Mass.: M.I.T. Press, 1965).

which prizes control over the occult and the supernatural will have many words relating to religion; and one which emphasizes kinship relations will have many words to define lineage. In the Hawaiian language the multiplicity of terms relating to the following ideas are an indication of cultural interest: rain, 64; lazy, 39; cloud, 33; taro, 225; house, 133; feast, 23; document, 63.[2] Such examples could be repeated many times, including in American English the many labels relating to car.

Language is a means of socializing the young and transmitting the culture of a group from one generation to another. Without language, much of our culture would cease to exist. The hominoid man would probably become no more than an agile pongidae or more mobile ape. Although anthropologists distinguish the emergence of hominidae from pongidae primarily on the basis of tools, the real basis is never found in a fossil site. Man probably became human and intelligent through his use of language.[3]

The Nature of Language

Just as the use of language is taken for granted, the teaching of language arts to young learners is generally undertaken without any consideration of the nature of language as reflected in anthropological studies. Many errors in practice and emphasis grow out of this neglect. It is therefore important to say a few words about the nature of language.[4]

Language is, first of all, *species specific*. Only man has language. Both a dog and a boy can give a yelp of pain, but only the boy can tell what he did yesterday, what he thinks about love or God, or tell about his plans for the future. Man communicates with gestures and signs as well as sounds, but these means pale in comparison with the complex and facile means of auditory communication.

Not only is language species specific, but all men have language. No group of men have been found living at any time in any part of the world who do not use language. The size of some speech communities may number only a few individuals; others may number millions. But the purpose of language is the same for all groups—to communicate with other men.

There is no such thing as a primitive language. There are groups of people without writing, a relatively late and independent invention, but the language of any group is completely adequate to reflect the culture and the needs of those who speak it. All languages have equal potentiality to develop from their phonemic structures language reflections of changes in the culture.

The origins of language are unknown. Man lived thousands of years before there were written records. Various theories have been advanced as to the origin of language, but there is no way to test these ideas.

Language is learned. While every healthy child has the latent structure for language.

2. Mark K. Pukui and Samuel H. Elbert, *Hawaiian--English Dictionary* (Honolulu: University of Hawaii Press, 1957).
3. Lenneberg proposes a different explanation that language is a manifestation of species-specific cognitive capacity which is the consequence of certain biological peculiarities. This makes the temporal order of intelligence prior to language Erich H. Lenneberg, *Biological Foundations of Language* (New York: John Wiley and Sons Inc., 1967), pp. 374-79.
4. See Albert J. Kingston and Marion J. Rice *Language*, Pupil Text, Publication no. 44 (Athens Ga.: Anthropology Curriculum Project, University of Georgia, 1968); Alexandra Ramsay, *Language Anthropology and Communication*, Publication no 45 (Athens, Ga.: Anthropology Curriculum Project, University of Georgia, 1968).

no human infant is born with language. He can neither produce words himself nor understand those of his parents. He learns to make speech sounds in interaction with people. Language is learned as a part of growing up. Every activity that a child participates in and every experience he has is accompanied by opportunities to learn and use language.

By the time any normal child enters school, he has achieved a fantastic accomplishment. Not only has he learned thousands of words and their meaning, but he has learned the word order and structure of his language. He has learned its syntax. He has learned this without formal lessons in grammar, but through normal everyday activities with which language is associated. Throughout the rest of his life, in school and out, he will acquire better language usage. He will continue to add to his vocabulary and to construct new sentences as he studies new subject matter and has new experiences. In literate cultures, he will learn to read and to write as well as speak his language.

The language learned by children is typically the language of the parents and other adults who rear them. This fact has tremendous pedagogic implications for children from non-English speaking homes and from homes where the language is very deviant from the standard English of educated people.

Irrespective of the language spoken in a home, children learn the language of their primary culture easily and without difficulty because it is a central part of their lives. From the day a child is born, he is reared in a particular language. But any language can be learned. Second language learning, however, is usually more difficult than primary language learning because the learner has already developed a set of communication expectancies. He not only has to adjust the organs used for speech to develop new sounds, but he has to develop a new morphology and syntax. Thus a child who has learned to speak only Spanish at home and who attends a school where instruction is in English not only has the problem of learning an alternate lexicon but an alternate grammar. The lack of opportunity to use the language in the natural context of enculturation makes practice difficult. Where two languages are spoken interchangeably in a bilingual home, however, the learning of more than one language is acquired with the same facility as learning one.

Uniform languages are usually found only in small, nonliterate societies with simple cultures. In larger and more complex societies, as in the United States, instead of a language common to all speakers there are many variations which reflect regional, educational, and social class differences. A dialect of a language is simply a variation of the language. The standard language of a country is simply the dialect spoken by educated people in the nation's capital and used for broadcasting, as the Italian of Rome or the French of Paris. In the United States, there is no standard American English, although what is called Chicago English has become a standard for broadcasting. There are many acceptable regional variations in the United States which contrast in phonology, vocabulary items, and the pronunciation of whole sentences.

Unacceptable dialects in the United States are generally dialects which reflect nonliterary grammar usage. *He done gone* is grammatically unacceptable and reflects the educational level of the speaker, although it communicates past action just as effectively as *he has gone*. There is nothing inherently wrong in the use of such expressions as *I ain't got none* or *He been here*. Because such expressions are socially unacceptable, however, a failure to acquire standard English handicaps a person in job opportunities and in social relations.

Severe dialectical deviations, however, can also handicap a person in schooling. Schooling, it has been repeatedly emphasized, is concerned with the transmission of culture. While dialects may be perfectly satisfactory for ordinary face to face communication, dialectical deviations often handicap formal communication for the transmission and reception of knowledge. Many disadvantaged children come to school with the failure to clearly articulate word endings and to clearly differentiate words into sentences. A child who mumbles *Disabaw* for *This is a ball* or *Gimebuk* for *Give me those books* is not merely deficient in lexical phonology but does not manifest control over the syntax of language which makes it possible to generate sentences. In such cases, teaching English as a second language in a very structured manner is often a prerequisite to success in school. This subject will be discussed in more detail in connection with the implementation of language arts training.

Thus far the nature of language has been discussed in a very general manner. It is now appropriate to discuss language in a more specific manner based upon its attributes.

Attributes of Language

Language may be defined as an arbitrary system of vocal signs used by men to communicate with each other. Each of these attributes is important for understanding language and for language arts instruction.

Arbitrary system refers to the fact that the sounds used in speaking have meaning only because men have agreed that a certain sound means a specific thing. In English, the sound *dog* evokes the image of a particular kind of animal with certain characteristics. But there is nothing inherent in the animal that requires the sound *dog*. In French, the arbitrary sound for the same animal is *chien;* in Spanish, *perro*. The way sounds are put together in a language have meaning because over long periods of time the meanings were fixed by chance or custom. Consequently, the school expansion of language normally proceeds through systematic vocabulary development in which labels and referents are arbitrarily learned.

The fact that language is an arbitrary system does not mean there is never any change in sound and referent. Language is always changing. Discoveries of new inventions bring new labels into a language. New words are invented and words are borrowed. Pronunciations change and word meanings change. Many irregularities in English writing result from a change in sound after the orthographic representation was fixed. But whatever changes take place, the sound-meaning relationship is always arbitrary. There are certain conventions in the use of prefixes and suffixes in English words which are sometimes helpful to a student in learning a new word, but these morphological components are phonologically arbitrary. The pedagogic implication is quite clear—children acquire a vocabulary; they do not contrive it. Something that is arbitrary and conventional is learned by reception and not by discovery. The fact that language is about fifty per cent redundant nevertheless provides the opportunity for students to infer new arbitrary meanings from context, but the meaning is previously existent and given in the language used.

System in the definition refers to the fact that language has a particular structure. The components are related in a definite and systematic manner. The dual concept of *phoneme* and *morpheme* provides a basis for the analysis of language structure. More will be said about phonology, morphology, and syntax later. At this point it is sufficient to point out that in English the arrangement *the dress is red* conforms to accepted structure whereas *the red is dress* does not. Grammar is predicated upon the principle of structure, and because the child learns the structure of language as well as the vocal signs he is able to generate spontaneously an infinite number of new statements.

The word sign in the definition is important. Sign is another way of emphasizing that the sounds used in language have meaning. In order for two men to communicate, the sender and the receiver must know the meaning of the signs which make up the code. If you read *Ha zoa goomed ha tor* you may elicit sounds but you do not receive a message, because the sounds do not function as signs. But if you are told *ha* is *the,* *zoa* is *ox,* *goomed* is *gored,* and *tor* is *matador* you are immediately able to substitute the signs and receive a message. Some teachers of the language arts find it useful to think of language as a code. This emphasizes the reciprocal interaction of symbols and their meaning, a prerequisite to communication and the acquisition of information. Much faulty classroom instruction occurs when this principle is violated; to learn, the pupil must know the meaning of the signs (see "Vocabulary Development").

This discussion of language has implications for language arts instruction in a number of ways. Emphasis has been repeatedly placed on the word *vocal*. Real languages develop in the speech of a particular group of people. Artificial languages, such as Esperanto, may be contrived but they never operate as functional languages. The vocal nature of language provides the pedagogic basis for intensive oral language development with retarded or disadvantaged children prior to instruction in reading and writing.

The relationship of writing to speech is also instructive. While the origins of speech are unknown, the diffusion of writing and literacy to preliterate cultures using the Roman alphabet is largely a product of nineteenth and twentieth century missionary activity.[5] The planned introduction of writing and reading involves the study of the sounds and syntax of the language, the construction of an alphabet in Roman orthography to represent the sounds, the use of the new code to translate portions of the Bible, and teaching the people the new code to read the translation in their own language. Many people read and write in their own language today as a result of these planned efforts to provide Bible trans-

---

5. See, for example, the work of the Baptist missionary Loughridge among the Creek. R. M. Loughridge and David M. Hodge, *English and Muskokee Dictionary* (Okmulgee, Oklahoma: Baptist Home Mission Board, 1964). This is a reprint of a dictionary compiled in 1854.

lations. This work goes on, especially under the auspices of the Wycliffe Bible Society, and continues to be a principal means of bringing literacy to preliterate peoples.[6] The construction of a written from an oral language indicates the importance of phoneme-grapheme correspondence in teaching reading and writing.

And finally, it must be remembered that the purpose of language is for men to communicate. There can be no communication unless the material used in language arts instruction makes use of signs in English. The concept of arbitrary vocal sign indicates the importance of using meaningful rather than nonsense words in language arts instruction. This does not imply, however, that the word must be treated as a unit independent of phonological components and graphological equivalents.

Structure of Language

In an overview of the language arts, only a few words can be said about the structure of language from the standpoint of modern linguistics. The three key ideas are phonemics, morphology, and syntax.

All languages use a limited number of sounds, called *phonemes*. These sounds, for the most part, are made up of vowels and consonants, but they have no meaning in themselves. Man is able to produce an infinite variety of sounds, but no language uses anywhere near this number. Generally, the range of phonemes found in languages is from 15 to 85. Counts of the number of phonemes in English vary, but in figure 10.1 in chapter 10 the number 44 is used. Phonemes are the sound building blocks of language.

Phonemes do not occur in isolation, but are put together in particular combinations to convey meaning. The phoneme is the unit of sound, and the *morpheme* is the smallest portion of sound that conveys meaning. Some morphemes stand alone as words and others must be used in conjunction with other morphemes. In English, less than 50 phonemes are used to build the thousands of words that constitute the English language, some 450,000 of which are included in *Webster's Third New International Dictionary*.

A consideration of phonemes, syllables, and morphemes sheds light on the concept of morpheme. Phonemes do not occur in isolation, but in either monosyllabic or polysyllabic words. In the monosyllable *pan,* the three phonemes /p/ /a/ /n/ appear in sequence. In *pane,* /p/ /ā/ /n/, however, the last letter *e* carries the symbol for a phonemic shift from short *a* to long *a*. While exceptions can be cited to most phonemic rules, knowledge of spelling patterns such as *hit, hitting* and *hike, hiking* are semantically as well as orthographically useful—meaning is conveyed by the correct spelling which permits pronunciation of the vocal sign.

A syllable is a word or group of letters that makes a distinctive sound. The loud part or nucleous is made up of a vowel, and the less loud parts or margins are made

---

6. One of the major exceptions is the development of the Cherokee syllabary by Sequoia, a rare example of a native devising a new orthography for a language. George E. Foster, *Story of the Cherokee Bible* (Ithaca, N.Y.: Democrat Press, 1899); Jack Frederick Kilpatrick and Anna Gritts Kilpatrick, eds., *New Echota Letters: Contributions of Samuel A. Worcester to The Cherokee Phoenix* (Dallas, Texas: Southern Methodist University Press, 1968). For a brief discussion of the Cherokee syllabary as an example of stimulus diffusion see, Marion J. Rice, *The Concept of Culture,* Pupil Text, Publication no. 46 (Athens, Ga.: Anthropology Curriculum Project, University of Georgia, 1966), p. 47.

up of consonants. Because of the complex blending of consonants, English does not have a simple but a variety of syllable patterns, as vowel only in *a/bout,* vowel-consonant in *em/ploy,* consonant-vowel in *no/ble,* and consonant-vowel-consonant in *fif/teen.* Encoding and decoding is facilitated by syllabification, whether dealing with polysyllabic words such as *milktruck* or *australopithecines.* Exaggerated pronunciation in connection with syllabification can often be misleading, however, particularly with the schwa sounds in such words as *away* (uh/way, not ay/way) and *laborer* (lābohruh). Auditory discrimination in relation to syllabification is found in connection with phonic programs. A number of simple rules of spelling assists with syllabification.

The third structural part, morpheme, may be a monosyllable or a polysyllable, but a morpheme is not a syllable. *Mississippi* is composed of four syllables, but it is only one morpheme. It takes all those letters in syllables to convey the idea of one river with that name. In contrast, cats is a one syllable word, but it is composed of two morphemes, *cat* plus *s,* which in English is added to mean more than one, or plural, as *dogs, fights, houses,* and *winches.* A number of spelling irregularities result from the morphology of plurals, e.g., *child, children.* Walked is composed of two morphemes; the addition of *ed* to *walk* means past tense. Run is a morpheme; the addition of other morphemes, as *er* in *runner* and *ing* in *running* make up additional words. The way morphemes are used in groups becomes the grammar of the language. Morphemes which are only used in combination with other morphemes are called bound morphemes. Some examples of bound morphemes are *s, er, ed, ing, ful* and *ly* as in *boys, walker, hearing, winner, thoughtful,* and *slowly.*

Since bound morphemes can be added to stable morphemes to create new words—cat, cats; thought, thoughtful—the number of vocabulary items greatly outnumbers the morphemes. In turn, morpheme constructions are combined into sentences to express ideas. The number of possible combinations is infinite, without limit. The complexity of language usage is expressed primarily at the sentence level where morphemes are arranged sequentially in accordance with the rules of grammar.

In the preceding section, it was emphasized that sentence structure is not random, but grammatical. The combination of morphemes to express complex thoughts conforms to regularities. The child acquires the syntax of his language with no more difficulty than he acquires the phonological and morphological components. Although he may lack grammatical descriptors, such as noun and verb, the beginning elementary child has learned through practice and experience the nuances in such sentences as:

Jim is happy to go.
Jim is happy I came.
Jim is happy he went.

Children who acquire standard morphology in the home have little difficulty with the standard English of school usage and language arts instruction, even though few will ever conform to the grade "A" expectancies of professional English teachers. Much of this results from the fact that a considerable amount of formal English has nothing to do with usage or the expression of ideas, but with the acquisition of a system of labels to describe grammar. Students can use a nominative absolute without ever being able to conjure up an example, just as a first grader happily makes use of definite and indefinite articles and of subjects and predicates without knowing they exist. The grammar problem for most students is not in the use of language. The grammar problem largely exists because formal English grammar, based on the Latin model, became a school screening device before the era of scientific knowledge. The continued emphasis on descriptive grammar rather than language usage is an anachronism in a scientific age.

Normal children do not have to be taught language in school. They need to experience use of the language. Where dialectical deviation requires special treatment, the treatment must be prescriptive and not global to be effective.

Speaking

All discussions of the language arts emphasize the importance of speech and the development of oral communication skills. The teacher, whether primary or intermediate, who takes this admonition seriously, will nevertheless be disappointed to find little sequentially planned material for systematic oral communication development. In contrast to the teaching of reading and English grammar the assistance to language arts teachers to improve speaking generally consists of little more than exhortations about the importance of oral language, statements of general objectives, and suggested types of experiences which range from show and tell to creative dramatics and oral discussion.[7]

This deficiency results from the fact that oral language is learned as a process of enculturation, that reading and writing as well as oral language activities enter into the extension of speech in the school, and, more important, the failure to diagnose specific language deficiencies and prescribe specific types of treatments. Thus, while creative dramatics is an accepted method of oral language development in the language arts program for the normal child, the use of creative dramatics as a means to improve dialectically deficient oral language traits is not treatment specific to the deficiency.[8] The phonology, morphology, and syntax of language not only characterizes aspects of school subject matter denominated "language arts," but is inherent in all school instruction, whether the subject is social studies or art.

The learnings which are so meticulously stipulated as specific learnings in the typical English curriculum are inherent in the nature of language. For example, in the process of schooling a student will use kernel sentences, expand kernel into more complex sentences, use nominals, verbs, and adjectives, apply different levels of abstraction, use inflectional forms of verbs to indicate tense, use vowel digraphs and diphthongs in words, to mention a few of the language learnings.[9]

What is needed is a clear differentiation of pupil performance abilities so that the

---

7. Some examples of good treatments of the general type are Pose Lamb, ed., *Guiding Children's Language Learning* (Dubuque, Iowa: Wm. C. Brown Company Publishers, 1967); Carrie Rasmussen, *Speech Methods in the Elementary School* (New York: Ronald Press Company, 1949).

8. *Hancock County School Improvement Project, Second Annual Report* (Sparta, Ga.: Hancock County School District, 1968).

9. Division of Curriculum Development, *A Design for an English Curriculum* (Atlanta, Georgia: Georgia State Department of Education 1968), pp. 115-16.

training is specific to his needs. Time is limited in school. If it is to be used wisely for the training of the student, the program must have particular rather than global performance needs. It is therefore useful at this point to differentiate the discussion according to pupil performance levels.

It should be first emphasized, however, that any oral language program in the school should take into account regional characteristics of the educated adult speech community. If not, the teacher may find himself trying to correct "errors" which are merely accepted dialectical deviations. For example, in Georgia dialects there is frequently little differentiation between *en* and *in* sounds, the allophonic shift causing the short *e* to be pronounced as short *i*.[10] Thus words such as *pen* and *pin* are both pronounced as /pin/. Short *e* phonic discrimination using *en* words in the Scott Foresman Reading Systems, the Lippincott Basic Readers, and the Merrill Linguistic Readers[11] are inapplicable to sections of the country where *en* words are pronounced as *in*. Children nevertheless are expected to learn the correct spelling. Material developed by publishers for a national market cannot, of course, reflect these regional variations and the appropriate modifications must be made by teachers. Since most teachers teach in their native region, they generally make the modifications with little effort. However, where a teacher from another dialect area moves into a community, lack of proper consideration of accepted speech variations can often lead to much misspent language development effort.

This section is concerned with three specific types of speech improvement—articulation, substandard speech as dialect, and teaching English as a second language to non-English speakers.

Articulation. Articulatory disorders account for about three-fourths of defective speech and are primarily the result of oral inactivity, sound substitutions, and dialectical deviations. Consequently, articulatory disorders are subject to correction within the general school program, provided articulation is made a specific part of corrective training.[12] Articulatory disorders which result from structural deficiencies, however, normally require correction by speech therapists.

Articulation may be simply defined as the formation of speech sounds. Accurate articulation is learned, as with all other language behavior. Thus articulatory disorders may range from indistinct enunciation, resulting from simple carelessness in speech, to speech patterns which are almost unintelligible. Since reading and spelling also involve the correct encoding and decoding of sounds, articulatory training in listening to and producing the correct spoken sounds also contributes to these aspects of the language arts program.

There are two approaches to articulatory training. One is the general approach, in

10. *Language: Record Narration Guide,* Publication no. 47 (Athens, Ga.: Anthropology Curriculum Project, University of Georgia, 1968).
11. Ira E. Aaron et al., *Studybook, Level 3,* Scott Foresman Reading Systems (Glenview, Ill.: Scott, Foresman and Company, 1971), fence, pp. 26, 32; hen, p. 31; went, p. 34; bench, p. 35; Glen McCracken and Charles C. Walcutt, *Lippincott's Basic Reading, Workbook A, Teacher's Edition* (Philadelphia: J. B. Lippincott, 1969), engine, p. 6; end, enter, envelope, p. 7; *Merrill Linguistic Readers, Reader 3, Teacher's Edition* (Columbus, Ohio: Charles E. Merrill Publishing Co., 1966), ten, men, pen, hen, Ben, pens, hens, p. 19; pigpen, p. 21.
12. Virgil A. Anderson, *Improving the Child's Speech* (New York: Oxford University Press, 1953), p. 47.

which all children participate systematically in speech development activities which involve auding and articulatory discrimination. An example of this approach is *The Child Speaks,* a manual consisting of nineteen units with daily lessons of twenty to thirty minutes to develop phonemic speaking discrimination.[13]

The major difference between such a manual, and the phonic books used in connection with reading, is in the selection of the words. In a speech development program, the words selected for discrimination are not controlled for word length or regularity, but are designed to develop facility in oral usage only. In a reading phonics program, on the other hand, phonemic discrimination is also tied to grapheme identification and discrimination, but it serves a similar function. A child who can decode *robbin* may still say *wobbin* if the oral training in the use of *r* instead of *w* has been inadequate to extinguish the incorrect articulatory substitution. General articulatory training, which is based upon the use of the correct phonemes of the language, is beneficial not merely to the remediation of articulatory disorders but to the entire language arts program.

Speech training is generally most effective when it is done in small groups, not with the entire class. It is therefore suggested while the whole class may benefit from general articulatory training, especially from the standpoint of phoneme-grapheme correspondence, intensive articulatory training be restricted to the pupils in the class who specifically require this type of training. It is recognized, however, that in certain classes collective speech may be so substandard that the only alternative is to conduct programs on a class basis, or on a small group basis for the entire class.

Intensive articulatory training should be preceded by testing to determine the type of articulatory disorders which are most serious and which need correcting. Two simple articulatory tests which a regular elementary teacher may administer are the *Developmental Articulation Test*[14] and the *Photo-Articulation Test.*[15] These tests, as well as the more complex research diagnostic measurements, such as the *Templin-Darley Tests of Articulation,*[16] are based on the principle of picture stimulus to elicit the articulation of the desired sound. Such tests can be used with young children who have not yet learned to read, provided they know and can say the correct label for the pictures, e.g., "/v/ These cards are *valentines.*" In the case of disadvantaged children, it is frequently necessary to have alternate pictures or even to cover the mouth and elicit

---

13. Margaret C. Byrne, *The Child Speaks* (New York: Harper & Row, Publishers, 1965). Another example of a general text useful for general articulatory development is: Louise Binder Scott and J. J. Thompson, *Phonics: In Listening, In Speaking, In Reading, In Writing* (St. Louis: Webster Division, McGraw-Hill Book Company, 1962). Two other books widely used in general programs are: Louise Binder Scott, *Learning Time with Language Experiences for Young Children* (St. Louis: Webster Division, McGraw-Hill Book Company, 1968) and Louise Binder Scott and J. J. Thompson, *Talking Time,* 2d ed. (St. Louis: Webster Division, McGraw-Hill Book Company, 1966).

14. Robert F. Hejna, *Development Articulation Test,* rev. ed. (Ann Arbor, Mich.: Speech Materials, 1959).

15. Kathleen Pendergast et al., *Photo-Articulation Test* (PAT) (Danville, Ill.: Interstate Printers and Publishers, 1969).

16. Mildred C. Templin and Frederic L. Darley, *The Templin-Darley Tests of Articulation: Manual,* 2d ed. (Iowa City, Iowa: Bureau of Educational Research and Services, 1969).

the desired sound by speech stimulus.[17] Since there are already known deficiencies in certain types of speech, such as rural southern Negro,[18] it is frequently more economic to proceed directly with articulatory training because the types of deficiencies are not unique but fairly general. The collection of test data, however, provides a more concrete base for measuring progress.

Other types of tests widely used are speech tests consisting of paragraphs, sentences, or words which require use of consonants in initial, medial, and terminal positions, and vowels and dipthongs. These tests can only be used with readers.[19] All of these tests are based on precise phonetic discrimination, and while a reading teacher does not require a knowledge of phonetics for phonics teaching, a knowledge of phonetics is useful to the language arts teacher who attempts any systematic speech improvement.[20] This is owing to the fact that whereas most articulatory treatment requires merely an acoustic approach, some cases require a phonetic placement approach utilizing correct placement of the tongue and lips to produce the necessary sounds.[21]

There are a number of articulatory error patterns which help the teacher in identifying articulatory errors. Typical consonantal substitutions include: *w* for *r* and *l*, as in *red* and *lamp;* voiceless *th* for *s*, as in *sun;* voiced *the* for *z*, as in *zebra; f* for the voiceless *th*, as in *thumb; d* for the voiced *the* and *g*, as in *this* and *get; b* for *v* as in *valentine; s* or *ch* for *sh*, as in *shoe;* and *t* for *k*, as in *candy*.[22] In substandard speech, a particular type of articulatory defect is associated with the morphology of inflection related to the omission of *s* to denote plural and *ed* to denote past tense. The terminal consonant is generally weaker than the initial consonant, and is only exaggerated in attempts to correct terminal omissions. However, omission of terminal consonants is one of the major problems in the lack of word differentiation associated with substandard speech.

Space will only permit brief consideration of training sequences. After the particular articulatory problem is identified, a period of intensive ear training follows in which the teacher models the correct sound acoustically. Anderson[23] recommends the use of completely new words for consonant substitution training rather than the use of familiar words, since the modeling of *red* for a child who says *wed* still evokes the response *wed*. This may involve the use entirely of new syllables which he has not learned incorrectly. Ear discrimination with the new sound utilizes words, poems, stories, and songs.[24] The next step after auditory

17. Myrna Smith, "Articulation Evaluation," *Hancock County School Improvement Project, Second Annual Report* (Sparta, Ga.: Hancock County School District, 1968), p. 95.
18. Joan C. Baratz and Roger W. Shuy, eds., *Teaching Black Children to Read* (Washington: Center for Applied Linguistics, 1969). See especially Raven I. McDavid, Jr., "A Checklist of Significant Features for Discriminating Social Dialects," in *Dimensions of Dialetc*, ed. E. L. Everetts (Champaign, Illinois: National Council of Teachers of English, 1967), pp. 7-10.
19. Virgil A. Anderson, *Improving the Child's Speech*, pp. 50-62; Scott and Thompson, *Talking Times*, pp. 108-10.
20. Wilbert Provonost, *The Teaching of Speaking and Listening in the Elementary School* (New York: David McKay, Inc., 1959), p. 156.
21. Virgil A. Anderson, *Improving the Child's Speech*, p. 148.
22. Byrne, *The Child Speaks*, pp. 1-2.
23. Virgil A. Anderson, *Improving the Child's Speech*.
24. A description of the many kinds of objects, games, pictures, and other devices which facilitate ear training is given in Charles Van Riper, *Speech Correction: Principles and Methods* (New York: Prentice-Hall, Inc., 1947), pp. 160-84.

discrimination is to provide exercises in which the child pronounces the sound. This involves repeating specially prepared sentences and poems which require articulation of the correct sound. An older child who can read and write will be expected to use these methods to help fix the correct sound. During this time it is always desirable to emphasize the optimum articulation, and not accept an imperfect compromise. The ultimate objective, of course, is to eventually have the child use the correct articulation in ordinary speaking situations—in the home and on the playground as well as in the classroom.

In articulation training, it is desirable that the teacher establish an efficient, systematic sequence and adhere to it. This facilitates the use of limited classroom time and permits the child to concentrate on the articulation drills without the distraction of novel teaching situations. One of the characteristic features of articulation training is the use of paired words and the particular emphasis on sounds. With younger children, it is often desirable to train directly without any emphasis on the defect. With older children, however, specific awareness of the defect and the desire to improve the defect through rigorous training often facilitates retraining.

Articulation training is not generally discussed in the typical book on language arts in the elementary school. Such general language arts methods as oral reading, choral reading, creative dramatics, and general oral language stimulation only contribute to articulation improvement *after* there is specific improvement in the *sounds* which are causing the difficulty. Articulation problems are subject to general remediation within the classroom program and are too extensive to be left to treatment by the limited number of speech therapists. The services of the speech therapists should be utilized on a consultative basis (see chapter 8), but his special training should be reserved for the difficult cases which require clinical training.

Materials previously listed in connection with general speech development are frequently used in more intensive articulatory training. However, the organization of these materials for use by the general classroom teacher are sometimes less specific than are materials developed for articulatory correction.[25] The general elementary teacher may often find that the speech therapist can make specific suggestions concerning the selection of specific articulatory training materials, including the use of records.

Substandard Speech. Substandard speech is speech so deviant from the norm of cultivated speech of a region that it interferes with communication and learning. Substandard speech is deficient not because of some articulatory differences but because it is linguistically defective for formal communication. A child is at no great handicap if he cannot conjugate a verb on an English test, but he is at a distinct disadvantage, as far as benefiting from schooling is concerned, if his oral language control does not permit him to emit distinct words arranged in sentences according to the rules of grammar.

There are two major types of substandard speech. One is the English dialectic deviant, in which English is the native language but

---

25. For example: Lucille D. Schoolfield, *Better Speech and Better Reading* (Magnolia, Mass.: Expression Company, 1951); Edgar L. Lowell and Marguerite Stoner, *Play It by Ear: Auditory Training Games* (Los Angeles: Wolfer Publishing Co., 1960); Marilyn Tayler, Karen Hermon, and Katherine Bruton, *Improving Oral Communication* (Salina, Kansas: United Educational Enterprises, 1966).

defective for formal communication. The second is the foreign dialect deviant, in which English is imperfectly learned as a second language. In both cases, the language defect is culturally transmitted by the environment of primary learning, and is invariably associated with low socio-economic status. An explanation of the origin of the defect is not sufficient to remove the deficiency. Substandard speech is subject to corrective and preventive training, but requires systematic, prolonged, and concentrated effort. The typical language arts program, designed for middle class children who learn standard English in the homes, is completely inadequate for substandard speech remediation.

Two types of language training will be emphasized in this section. The first deals with English dialectical correction; the second, with preventing foreign language dialect development through the correct teaching of English as a foreign language (TESL).

The most extensive and deviant English dialect in the United States is rural southern Negro, sometimes referred to as "Black English." While variations have developed in parts of the country, the dominant characteristics of Negro substandard English are found throughout the country, whether in New York or Los Angeles. This results from the simple fact that since World War I southern Negroes have moved to all parts of the country, and carried with them their regional dialect. Some of the more common characteristics of this regional dialect are omission of the noun plural ending, as *two boy;* omission of the noun possessive ending, as *John hat;* use of *ourn, yourn, hisn, hern,* or *therein;* use of *hisself, theirselves;* and omission of terminal consonant endings, so that words such as *book, cup,* *hit* do not convey the sound of distinct words, but rather partial words, i.e., *buh, kuh, hi.*

In verb inflection some common deviations are use of one form of *to be* with all persons, as *I is, you is, we is;* nonagreement of verb and subject, as *I were* and *We was, I does* and *he do;* omission of *t, d,* and *ed* from the past tense or past participle of verbs, as *yesterday he talk* or *I were burn yesterday;* omission of the verb *to be* before predicate nouns or adjectives, as *he a good boy;* omission of auxiliary *has* with *been,* as *he been working;* and substitutions of *been, done,* or *done been* for *have,* as *they done finished.*[26]

There are several different approaches to the issue of substandard English among black speakers. One is the relativistic approach, best exemplified by the Center for Applied Linguistics at Washington. In one of their most recent collection of essays, all of the authors contend that "Black English" is a well developed language system, that it presents a regular sequence and structure, and is quite adapted to the expression of ideas. Hence, these authors conclude that *no* attempts should be made to change the language of the elementary child, but rather that the child should be taught to read in his dialect. They conceive the major problem of reading as that of training teachers to distinguish when the child is correctly decoding, but orally responding in his dialect.[27] These linguistic relativists place almost all of their emphasis on language as

26. L. Ramon Veal, "Elementary English," *Hancock County School Improvement Project: Second Annual Report* (Sparta, Georgia: Hancock County School District, 1968), pp. 11-12.
27. Baratz and Shuy, *Teaching Black Children.* Essayists include: Raven I. McDavid, Jr., Kenneth S. Goodman, William Labov, Ralph W. Fasold, Joan C. Baratz, Roger W. Shuy, Walter A. Wofram, and William A. Stewart.

a phonological system. They have conducted no research to substantiate their premise that more effective teaching of reading would occur if taught in dialect, and argue only by analogy.[28] No educational system in any country at any time has ever tried to teach in a dialect which was considered as substandard.

Space does not permit a critical examination of the position of the relative linguists. It will be sufficient to point out here that their approach is primarily based on colloquial communication and they tend to ignore language as a formal learning tool. Hence, they take a more optimistic impression of dialect usage than a teacher would infer in an instructional setting where the acquisition of new and formal language is a means of acquiring new knowledge. They also tend to ignore the most severe kind of language deficiency, in which the lack of lexical content and articulatory-inflectional deviations add up to a language deficit when comparison is made with speakers of standard English. The relative linguists start and end with a premise as to the adequacy of the spoken language. However correct from an anthropological-linguistic point of view, it is not very helpful pedagogically.[29]

A second approach to substandard English might be called the quantity-lexical model. This approach is based on the premise that the nonverbal responses of the child in a test situation are based upon a language deficiency in terms of labels which stand for ideas. Hence, a large part of an oral language training program is to provide the child with verbal labels.[30]

Among the best known and widely used sets of materials which follows the lexical model are the Peabody Language Development Kits. There are two levels—Level P for children ages 3-5,[31] and Level 2 for children 6-8.[32] The manual for each level includes 180 daily lessons covering some twenty or more different kinds of activities, ranging from rhyming to vocabulary building. The kits include a variety of concrete objects to elicit and stimulate the use of oral language. Because of the explicit nature of the lessons, the untrained classroom teacher finds PLDK materials relatively easy to teach. These materials provide specific lessons with which the teacher can conduct a program in oral language development, and are not intended to replace the regular language arts work in reading, writing, English, and spelling.

Variations of the PLDK materials have been developed by various projects under

28. It is one thing to teach a child in a vernacular which is standard, and then make a transition to a second language. This is quite different from teaching a child in a dialect which is regarded as substandard, and equating it to a vernacular.

29. Stewart, in Baratz and Shuy, *Teaching Black Children*, correctly points out that the use of Joel Chandler Harris stories, however appropriate as of the nineteenth century, is inappropriate for use today. This results from the fact that most Negroes today are urban Negroes living in the twentieth century, and, notwithstanding phonological similarities, the world of *Uncle Remus* is just as remote from the Negro child as from the white child. These white linguists, however, also miss the point that a twentieth century urban Negro dialect is equally unacceptable to educated Negroes.

30. The writings of Martin and Cynthia Deutsch particularly are identified with this point of view. For example, see M. Deutsch et al., *Communication of Information in the Elementary School Classroom*, Cooperative Research Project No. 908 (Washington: U.S. Office of Education, 1964); C. Deutsch, "Auditory Discrimination and Learning: Social Factors," *Merrill Palmer Quarterly* 10 (1964): 277-96.

31. Lloyd M. Dunn, Kathryn B. Horton, and James O. Smith, *Peabody Language Development Kits: Manual for Level P* (PL DK-P) (Circle Pines, Minn.: American Guidance Services, Inc., 1968).

32. Lloyd M. Dunn and James O. Smith, *Peabody Language Development Kits: Manual for Level 2* (Circle Pines, Minn.: American Guidance Services, Inc., 1966).

U.S. Office of Education contracts. Among these are the Multisensory Language Development Project (MULDIP) of the Southeastern Education Laboratory.[33] As may be inferred from the title, this particular program makes extensive use of various objects which can be touched, smelled, tasted, and manipulated.

A third approach to substandard language is the structural-syntactic approach. In contrast with the lexical, this approach is more concerned with the correct use of structural words in order to make correct statements to represent reality than it is with the mere increase in the use of nouns and verbs. In contrast with the relative linguistic approach, emphasis is placed on the correct use of postive and negative statements using language as a basic teaching tool. This approach leaps both the arguments of environmental deprivation and regularity of structure and simply asserts that, for whatever reason, if a child cannot use language as a surrogate for reality he has a language deficiency insofar as schooling is concerned.

Among the most persuasive exponents of this approach are Bereiter and Engelmann.[34] According to their analysis, the language of many dialectically deficient speakers, particularly the Negro, is in the inability to differentiate sentences into the meaningful components, i.e., words. Thus a sentence "It says there that he came" may be rendered "Ih say dar he cum" or, even more pronounced, the run-on of words together so that "This is a book" is rendered "Diuhbuh." Language training, therefore, is not conceived merely as a means of speech improvement in the conventional language arts sense. Language training becomes a fundamental point of training in order to teach the child in school.

The method of instruction is a direct verbal model, similar to that used in teaching a foreign language. The teacher works with small groups from eight to twelve children. The core of the model is the statement as a description of reality, i.e., "This is a dog." This simple statement is called a first order statement, because it merely points and asserts a fact. Second order statements are those which convey information about an object. Basically, second order statements are used to teach a polar concept, a nonpolar concept shared by some members of the identity class, and nonpolar concepts shared by all members of the identity class. Thus while negations may be made concerning the first three statements in the four-statement hierarchy, it is not possible to make a negation about the fourth statement and have the statement conform to reality as expressed by the categories of language. The form of the four-statement hierarchy is:

This is a dog.
This dog is fat.
This dog is brown.
This dog is an animal.

Elements of the program include: the single identity statement; the plural identity statement; the not statement, polar discrimination, multiple polar discrimination e.g., (fat and long); special polars e.g., (next to); second order statements with nonpolar attributes; the concepts *and, only, or, some, if-then,* verb inflections, comparisons, and expansion of concepts introduced earlier.[35] A commercial form of the program is now

33. Azalia S. Francis, *Multisensory Language Development Project, Various Levels* (Atlanta, Ga.: Southeastern Education Laboratory, 1969-).
34. Carl Bereiter and Siegfried Engelmann, *Teaching Disadvantaged Children in the Preschool* (Englewood Cliffs, N.J.: Prentice-Hall, Inc., 1966); Siegfried Engelmann, *Preventing Failure in the Primary Grades* (Chicago: Science Research Associates, Inc., 1969).
35. Bereiter and Engelmann, *Teaching Disadvantaged Children,* pp. 122-208.

available as part of the DISTAR series, integrated with the teaching of reading and arithmetic.[36]

Teaching English as a Second Language (TESL). The programs previously described are designed primarily for children who have learned English as their native language, but have learned it imperfectly for purposes of formal schooling. A different problem exists for children who learn to speak one language at home, and who must learn English as a second language in school. While the problems of the former are largely associated with children of lower socio-economic status, teaching English as a second language is primarily concerned with providing the student with an alternative communication system. Here the problem is to develop a bilingual child, one who can use English effectively in the school and other English language situations while retaining his original language for family and other personal contacts.

In teaching a second language, there are two paramount considerations. The first and major task is to impart the linguistic patterns of the new language. Teaching English as a second language is therefore modeled upon the techniques of good foreign language teaching. Talk about language is kept to a minimum; the emphasis is upon the use of spoken language.[37] At the elementary level, it is particularly important to develop the skills of recognizing and imitating the new language patterns. Much effort of TESL for elementary students is concerned with pattern drills, in which the teacher provides an accurate model for the students. The sequence in teaching should be based on the development of accuracy and fluency of limited materials, and errors should be promptly corrected.

The second task in TESL instruction is a careful analysis of the phonological difficulties which the students experience in learning English, because of the interference of the primary sound system with second language learning. This aspect of teaching requires that a teacher have a good "ear" and thus a command of American English phonology is important to the TESL teacher.[38] While each foreign language imposes individual problems,[39] it is possible to analyze the major difficulties of a native speaker of one language learning English. Thus a knowledge of the contrastive patterns of Spanish and English is very useful in helping a TESL teacher of Spanish children be alert to the particular problems which Spanish children face. These range from contrasts in structure, such as *no* for negation in place of *not,* and differences in vowels. A brief summary of these differences is given in Zintz.[40] Because of the fact that the student has learned both a different structural and phonological system, much repetition and practice in speaking English is required. The Center for Applied

36. For a brief overview of the DISTAR Language System, see *DISTAR Orientation* (Chicago: Science Research Associates, Inc., 1970), pp. 49-51.
37. Betty W. Robinett, "Applications of Linguistics to the Teaching of Oral English," *On Teaching English to Speakers of Other Languages,* series 2, ed. Carol J. Kreidler (Champaign, Ill.: National Council of Teachers of English, 1966).
38. Sarita G. Schotta, *Teaching English as a Second Language* (Davis, Calif.: University of California, 1966), p. 14.
39. Virgil A. Anderson, *Improving the Child's Speech,* p. 195.
40. Miles V. Zintz, "Contrastive Analysis of Spanish and English," *The Reading Process* (Dubuque, Iowa: Wm. C. Brown Company Publishers, 1970), pp. 314-17, adapted from *Teaching English as a New Language to Adults,* Curriculum Bulletin no. 5 (New York: Board of Education of the City of New York, 1963-64), pp. 7-9.

Linguistics has a useful film series related to TESL teaching, especially Film 5 which shows English taught to a third and ninth grade class of Spanish speaking children.[41]

In the last decade, many TESL text materials have been published.[42] Four of these have been specifically designed for native Spanish speakers.[43] Other materials are being developed. Among those being given extensive testing is the Oral Language Program of the Southwestern Cooperative Educational Laboratory, Albuquerque.[44] Each lesson is concerned with a specific learning task, and the teaching procedures are given in detail. The material has been successfully piloted with many Spanish-speaking children. Its effectiveness with Indian children is not known. The development of material particularly suited to the needs of Indian children has lagged behind the development of material for Spanish-speaking children. One reason is that there are many Indian languages, not just one, each of which requires the same contrastive study as has been made with Spanish if the specific TESL needs are to be met. English second language programs geared to Spanish do not match Indian language needs.[45]

The foregoing discussion has been concerned with particular needs for articulatory training, improving the English of Negro speakers, and teaching English as a second language. In schools where these special oral language problems do not exist, the general language program with either an English or reading emphasis are most frequently used for speech improvement. These general language arts activities include storytelling, talks, conversation, discussion, rhythms, creative dramatics, dramatization with puppets, oral reading, choral reading, club meetings, and other occasions where language is used. These methods are not specifically corrective or remedial, and are simply a part of the experience of the normal child in school.[46] The methods do not hurt dialectically deviant children, either English or foreign speaking, but such activities should not be expected to correct dialect deficiencies.

Listening

The physical properties of sound and the physiological structure of the receptor, the ear, provide the mechanical basis for hearing. Listening, however, always connotes attention, discrimination, and an intellectual attempt to apprehend. Teachers, children, husbands and wives frequently lament "He hears but he does not listen." While the term auding[47] has been used in the past

41. Theodore B. Karp, Patricia O'Connor, and Betty Wallace Robinett, *Principles and Methods of Teaching a Second Language: A Motion Picture Series for Teacher Training-Instructor's Manual* (Washington: Center for Applied Linguistics of the Modern Language Association of America, 1963).
42. See Zintz, "Contrastive Analysis," p. 323, for a list of twelve publications.
43. Louise Lancaster, *Introducing English: Oral Pre-Reading Program for Spanish-Speaking Primary Pupils* (Boston: Houghton Mifflin, 1966); *Miami Linguistic Readers,* fifty-three booklets, (Boston: D. C. Heath, 1964-66); *Teaching English to Puerto Rican Pupils* (New York: Board of Education of the City of New York, 1957); Puerto Rico, Department of Education, *American English Series: English as a Second Language* (Boston: D. C. Heath, 1965-67).
44. Robert T. Reeback et al., *Oral Language Program* (Albuquerque, N.M.: Southwestern Cooperative Educational Laboratory, Inc., n.d.)
45. Yvonne Weaver, "A Closer Look at TESL on the Reservation," *Journal of American Indian Education* 6 (January 1967): 28.
46. See Carrie Rasmussen, *Speech Methods in the Elementary School* (New York: Ronald Press Company, 1949).
47. Don Pardee Brown, "Auding as the Primary Language Ability" (doc. diss. Stanford University, 1954); abstract, *Dissertation Abstracts* 14 (1954): 2281-82.

two decades to refer to the process of recognizing and interpreting spoken symbols, this unpleasant looking and sounding word adds nothing to the analysis and improvement of listening skills. To listen, one must first hear.

The general language arts literature on listening makes a sweeping bow in the direction of listening, but is invariably weak on prescription. This results from the failure to recognize that listening is not a gross process, but is somewhat specific, as indicated by the prepositions *to* and *for* so frequently used with the verb. Furthermore, there is a general tendency to associate listening with the process of deriving meaning from oral discourse. In this connection, listening becomes a general synonym for study.[48]

Speaking and Listening. One of the primary purposes of any listening program is to discriminate between spoken sounds. Thus one type of listening requires discrimination to reproduce the sound orally, as described in the preceding section relating to speaking. Another type of listening emphasis relates to visual discrimination, and is used in connection with spelling and reading. Auditory discrimination is thus involved in programs to improve speech, reading, and spelling. Thus, while there are books which specifically use listening as a key word in the title,[49] programs to improve listening are also programs to improve talking.[50] Structured programs to help deaf and hard-of-hearing children learn to talk contain excellent sequential plans for the development of listening skills.[51]

Listening and Comprehension. Listening by its very nature involves comprehension. In this section, however, it is assumed that the listener, irrespective of his age, uses normal language, and the function of listening experiences is to further his appreciation or knowledge through deriving more meaning from oral discourse or talk.

Practices used to increase listening comprehension range from the discrimination of distinctive sounds and animal cries in kindergarten, to first grade show and tell, to listening to oral discourse to answer such questions as: What is the purpose of the speaker? What evidence does he present? What is his conclusion? What is the relationship between his evidence and his conclusion? How does he handle arguments? Does he appeal to reason or to emotion? What new words were introduced?

A comparison of these types of questions to extend listening comprehension indicate that the same intellectual processes are also involved in increasing comprehension from reading (see chapter 10, "Teaching Reading in the Middle Grades"). There is a difference in channel, but to derive meaning from the message requires the same knowledge of the code.

Whether measures of listening comprehension actually measure listening or vo-

---

48. Ruth G. Strickland, *The Language Arts in the Elementary School* 3d ed. (Lexington, Mass.: D. C. Heath and Company, 1969), pp. 127-41; Ralph E. Kellogg, "Listening," *Guiding Children's Language Learning,* ed. Pose Lamb (Dubuque, Iowa: Wm. C. Brown Company Publishers, 1967), pp. 117-36; Paul S. Anderson, *Language Skills in Elementary Education* (New York: Macmillan Company, 1964), pp. 81-87.

49. D. H. Russell and E. F. Russell, *Listening Aids Through the Grades* (New York: Bureau of Publications, Teachers College, Columbia University, 1959); R. G. Nichols and Leonard A. Stevens, *Are You Listening?* (New York: McGraw-Hill Book Co., 1957).

50. Louise Binder Scott, *Learning Time with Language Experiences for Young Children* (St. Louis: Webster Division, McGraw-Hill Book Company, 1968), p. 71.

51. Tina E. Bangs, *Language and Learning Disorders of the Pre-Academic Child, with Curriculum Guide* (New York: Appleton-Century-Crofts, 1968), pp. 191-333.

cabulary is now questioned. Studies of the Sequential Tests of Educational Progress: Listening (Form 4) by Anderson and Baldauf,[52] of the Brown-Carlsen Listening Comprehension Test by Langholz,[53] and of both tests by Kelly[54] raise doubts about the reliability and validity of these tests as measures of listening. This naturally results from the fact that while an audiometer can be used to measure hearing threshold in terms of decibels, a listening test involves meaning. Students who have acquired a large vocabulary through family background or reading are hence better equipped to listen than are students with a limited vocabulary. While many studies have been undertaken which show the beneficial effect of training in listening, there is some question as to what the students were actually trained in. This results from the fact that there is no overall theory which ties listening research together.[55]

Listening and Classroom Behavior. Paying attention is a pupil attribute highly desired by teachers, and is a prerequisite to learning. Most of the time the pupil is engaged in hearing rather than talking behavior, but if he does not listen he cannot differentiate the learning message from the noise.

The teacher can do many things to help children to listen more effectively. This begins with some rules of common courtesy, such as taking turns in talking and not interrupting others while talking. These should be practiced, and not just talked about. In time, other characteristics of good listening are added. Do I listen to directions? Do I listen carefully to the assignment? When an explanation is given, do I get the facts? Do I try to follow the thought of the person speaking?

In developing good listening habits, it is desirable that teachers strive to reach the point where they speak clearly but quietly, give directions but once, and give children practice in summarizing, reviewing, answering thought questions, and taking tests orally. Listening is not a passive activity, but the only way that listening can be evaluated is in terms of performance. Consequently, the development of listening eventually blends into the development of study habits and classroom behaviors related to various aspects of learning.

Spelling

Accurate spelling is an important part of the language program for several reasons. Correct spelling facilitates precise, written communication and reduces the ambiguity which comes from nonstandard orthographic representation. Spelling facilitates encoding and written expression. And, finally, spelling is one of the objective marks of literacy.

Spelling is nevertheless a difficult part of the language arts program. This results from the fact that spelling involves not only an alphabetic interpretation of words, but rendition in writing as well. While oral spelling bees have long been part of the American educational scene, spelling is not orally functional. The purpose of teaching spelling

52. Harold M. Anderson and Robert J. Baldauf, "A Study of a Measure of Listening," *Journal of Educational Research* 57 (December 1963): 197-200.

53. Armin P. Langholz, "A Study of the Relationship of Listening Test Scores to Test Item Difficulty" (doc. diss. Ohio State University, 1965): abstract, *Dissertation Abstracts* 26 (1966): 6912.

54. Charles M. Kelly, "An Investigation of the Construct Validity of Two Commercially Published Listening Tests," *Speech Monographs* 32 (June 1965): 139-43.

55. Thomas G. Devine, "Listening," *Review of Educational Research* 37 (April 1967): 152-58.

is to help the child acquire facility in the use of graphemes—written signs—to stand for phonemes—speech signs. Spelling may thus be defined as the alphabetic, written rendition of vocal signs. The selection of a written channel for the transmission of a message involves kinesthetic, auditory, and visual discrimination.

At the outset, it is important to refute the overemphasized problem of irregularity in English spelling. Linguists agree that English is not as phonetic as some of the Romance and other languages, but the emphasis on irregularities, such as the variety of sounds represented by *ough* and the many different renditions of *e* as in *me* merely tend to obscure the regularity which exists in English. For various reasons, which cannot be discussed here, *ough* came to represent such diverse sounds as *dough, cough, through, hiccough, bough;* and long *e* variants appear in such words as *we, mete, seize, key, meat, machine, meet, field, people*.[56] Other irregularities in phoneme-grapheme correspondence result from the orthographic changes which come from the adding of morphemes, e.g., *run, runnning, talk, talked, ed /t/; named, ed /d/; act, actor, or /er/.*

Notwithstanding these apparent inconsistencies, which in the large part conform to rules, English spelling is not the chaos that the whole-word advocates of yesterday portrayed. English is fundamentally *phonemic* in the written form. Instead of single letters, however, it uses *patterns* of letters as the functional units of representation.[57] Pronunciation variations resulting from differences in educated regional dialects is a far greater spelling problem than the irregularities in grapheme-phoneme correspondence. There has been no resolution of this problem.[58] Fasold, however, concludes that because of the regularity with which certain dialectical shifts are made in Black English, no special orthographic representation is needed.[59] If this is the case with one of the most deviant types of dialects in the United States, regional rule substitution poses no insuperable spelling problem.

The Initial Teaching Alphabet, however, was an attempt to improve the teaching of reading by orthographic changes. One of the unexpected byproducts of ITA is that it appears to greatly facilitate the written expression of young children.[60] Preoccupation with ITA as merely a reading system, rather than as a means of facilitating language arts development, has generally restricted comparisons of ITA to other methods of teaching reading. The results have not been encouraging. Such comparisons, however, ignore the free writing aspects of ITA, which may be its greatest advantage.[61] This suggests that the early teaching of spelling, with careful attention to spelling patterns, might have the same advantages for traditional orthography.

56. Charles C. Fries, *Linguistics and Reading* (New York: Holt, Rinehart and Winston, Inc., 1963), p. 161.

57. Ibid., p. 169.

58. Thomas D. Horn, "Handwriting and Spelling," *Review of Educational Research, Language Arts and Fine Arts* 37 (April 1967): 172.

59. Ralph W. Fasold, "Orthography in Reading Materials," in *Teaching Black Children to Read*, ed. Joan C. Baratz and Roger W. Shuy (Washington: Center for Applied Linguistics, 1969), p. 85.

60. Maurice Harrison, *Instant Reading: The Story of the Initial Teaching Alphabet* (London: Sir Isaac Pitman and Sons Ltd., 1964), pp. 148-56.

61. See chapter 10. Also, James J. Ryan and Nathan W. Gottfried, "A Comparison of Beginning Reading Achievement for Pupils Instructed with Materials Using ITA and Traditional Orthography: Interim Report," Technical Report no. 67-2, mimeographed (Minneapolis, Minn.: Minnesota State Department of Education, March 1967).

Phonic advocates have long contended that about 85 percent of English spelling is regular.[62] Research at Stanford using computer analysis has recently demonstrated that individual grapheme-phoneme relationships could be predicted with an accuracy of almost 90 percent, but not in terms of whole words.[63] Hay and Wingo have pointed out that there are 3,378 monosyllables in English that contain vowel elements. The purely phonetic monosyllables number 2,931. There are only 447 monosyllables which are unphonetic and which must be taught as sight words.[64]

Fries has indicated that there are three major spelling patterns with fourteen sub-variants.[65] These are illustrated below:

The most common spelling pattern is the monosyllable CVC pattern with a short vowel sound. There are a number of variants of this pattern:

initial consonant, e.g., *bat, cat, fat*
terminal consonant, e.g., *mat, mad*
vowel, e.g., *bag, big, beg, bog, bug*
initial consonant digraph, e.g., *than, shad, chap*
terminal consonant digraph, e.g., *bath, ash, gush*
initial consonant clusters, e.g., *span, blot, splash*
terminal consonant clusters, e.g., *disk, grand, gulp*
terminal double consonants for phoneme, e.g., *back, lugg, kiss, ball*

Another significant set of spelling patterns follows the CVC model with a terminal *e* to indicate a shift to the long vowel sounds. Variants of this pattern are:

CVC pattern, e.g., *mad, made; dim, dime; hop, hope; tub, tube*
initial consonant clusters, e.g., *grip, gripe; slop, slope*
terminal consonant clusters, *back, bake; chaff, chafe; rill, rile*

Three other major spelling patterns are medial vowel combinations which signal the long vowel sound:

bet, beat; fed, feed
mall, mail; pry, pray
rod, road; got, goat; prod, proud

The object in teaching regular words in reading is to develop the capacity for instantaneous recognition so that eventually most words function as sight words for a skillful reader. A similar objective is sought in spelling. Spelling patterns are over-learned so that the thought of the word becomes a cue for automatic letter representation. The problem of correct representation of the *schwa* sound in unstressed syllables is a more difficult one for the speller. The *schwa* sound is like a deemphasized short *u* sound, and may be represented by all vowels and a number of terminal endings, i.e., *local, secret, imitate, polite, column, table, stencil, pestle, renewable, corruptible*.[66] The speller must learn the sequence of letters needed to produce this sound.

In addition to learning regular spelling patterns of the reading program, the primary student must also learn irregular words of common usage, commonly called sight

62. Glenn McCracken and Charles C. Walcutt, *Lippincott's Basic Reading, Book D, Teacher's Edition* (Philadelphia: J. B. Lippincott Company, 1969), p. ix.

63. See especially Richard E. Hodges, "The Case for Teaching Sound-to-Letter Correspondences in Spelling," *Elementary School Journal* 66 (March 1966): 327-36; National Conference on Research in English, *Research on Handwriting and Spelling*, ed. Thomas D. Horn (Champaign, Ill.: National Council of Teachers of English, 1966).

64. Julie Hay and Charles E. Wingo, *Reading with Phonics, Teacher's Edition*, rev. (Philadelphia: J. B. Lippincott Company, 1960), p. v.

65. Fries, *Linguistics and Reading*, pp. 169-82.

66. Dolores Durkin, *Teaching Them to Read* (Boston: Allyn and Bacon, Inc., 1970), p. 243; Fries, *Linguistics and Reading*, p. 184.

words. These words should not be learned from an arbitrary list, but simply as they are introduced into the reading program.

In teaching spelling, the elements of seeing, saying, hearing, and writing must be always emphasized. A multisensory approach to spelling is generally recommended.[67]

Spelling today, in comparison to half a century ago, is little emphasized. In the nineteenth century, much attention was given to the spelling of difficult, obscure, and infrequently used words. After Rice demonstrated the futility of mechanical spelling drills,[68] there was a shift in emphasis to spelling of words of high frequency common usage. Other changes in spelling emphasis in the early twentieth century were a rapid development of spelling scales,[69] word lists,[70] and analysis of spelling errors.[71] There were also efforts to improve the efficiency of spelling utilizing experimental techniques. Among some of the findings were: marking the "hard" spots and syllabification failed to prove helpful as a knowledge of word meaning; systematic methods of learning to spell are more important than any single method.[72]

The last two decades have witnessed a considerable falling off of methodological interest in spelling research.[73] One reason may be the greater emphasis on "creative writing," a reaction against formal teaching which included a reaction against spelling. Correct spelling is not acquired incidentally from reading and writing but must be acquired as a combination of factors: visual attention (sight); writing (kinesthetic); and auditory (sound) discrimination.[74]

The teaching of spelling involves the same pedagogic questions encountered in the teaching of any subject: *what* relates to the question of content; *how* relates to the issue of methodology. From the standpoint of utility, it is natural that spelling should emphasize the words most commonly used in children's writing. The 1945 Rinsland list,[75] based on an analysis of one hundred thousand scripts written by children, was graded by Hildredth in 1953. According to Hildreth, one thousand words acounted for 89 percent of children's word usage. An increase of the list of words to two thousand only increased word use frequency by 6 percent.[76] This suggests that the child should learn to spell the most commonly used words. But, since there is no way of knowing what the spelling needs of any individual will be, it could be assumed that the basis of a comprehensive

67. F. J. Schonell, *Backwardness in Basic Subjects* (London: Oliver and Boyd, 1942); G. M. Fernald, *Remedial Techniques in Basic School Subjects* (New York: McGraw-Hill Book Co., 1943).

68. J. M. Rice, "Futility of the Spelling Grind," *Forum* 23 (1897): 163-72.

69. Ernest J. Ashbaugh, *The Iowa Spelling Scales: Their Derivation, Uses, and Limitations* (Bloomington, Ind: Public School Publishing Company, 1922).

70. B. R. Buckingham and E. W. Dolch, *A Combined Word List* (Boston: Ginn and Company, 1936).

71. Arthur I. Gates, *A List of Spelling Difficulties in 3876 Words Showing the "Hard Spots," Common Misspellings, Average Spelling Grade Placement, and Comprehension Grade-Ratings of Each Word* (New York: Bureau of Publications, Teachers College, Columbia University, 1937).

72. Thomas George Foran, *The Psychology and Teaching of Spelling* (Washington: Catholic Education Press, 1934), pp. 76-95.

73. Horn, "Handwriting and Spelling," p. 168.

74. Margaret L. Peters, *Spelling: Caught or Taught* (London: Routledge and Kega Paul, 1967), pp. 1-2, 16-17.

75. H. D. Rinsland, *A Basic Vocabulary of Elementary School Children* (New York: Macmillan Company, 1945).

76. Gertrude Hildredth, *Teaching Spelling* (New York: Henry Holt and Company, 1955).

spelling program must lie in one which systematically teaches phoneme-grapheme correspondence.

In teaching spelling, it has been common to use a special list of words in a speller. Spellers generally allege a utility based on word frequency. There is very little concurrence. Betts's 1940 study indicated agreement on 543 words in 17 spellers containing 8,645 different words. His 1949 study showed a concurrence of only 483 words in 8 spellers containing 8,652 different words. When the same words do occur, there is little grade placement concurrence.[77] There is no reason for any school to go to the expense of buying "spellers." The material of instruction provides the necessary words. In the primary grades, spelling may be most fruitfully taught as an adjunct to reading; in the middle grades, as a part of all subject matter instruction. Children in the United States typically perform less well on comparative measures of spelling than do children in other English-speaking countries.[78] This results from the fact that less attention is given to spelling. And because less attention is given to spelling, writing productivity is low. Writing necessarily involves spelling.

There is little experimental evidence regarding the efficacy of spelling rules, but Foran recommends that they be kept to a minimum.[79] In the phonic approach, the rule is made explicit; in the linguistic approach, the rule is inferred. In either case, however, words must be grouped together on the basis of spelling pattern regularity to permit either rule practice, inference, or generalization. Linguistic and phonic readers thus are organized in such a way that they can function as spellers.

In creative writing, teachers frequently write needed words in a child's personal dictionary. But where attention is not directed consciously to phoneme-grapheme correspondence, mere copying of the word is insufficient as a means for learning to spell it. Drill is prerequisite to correct spelling, even when the words are taken from the context of the child's own writing. Because of forgetting in learning, a good deal of review is necessary.[80]

In teaching spelling, it is important to emphasize the perception of the correct visual image, to not rely upon copying blindly. Much copy work in spelling— "Write each word five times"—is futile because the child is not attending; the act is purely mechanical. Children frequently copy words and even spell orally with no attention to their visual or aural discrimination. Without attention to such detail even short monosyllables, especially homophones, e.g., *fur* and *fir,* will present difficulties. Here is a ten-step synthesis of effective procedures for teaching spelling:[81]

1. Emphasize spelling patterns; do not overemphasize verbal rules.
2. Teach in a systematic, sequential, rule-engendering manner, using phonic and

---

77. E. A. Betts, *Spelling Vocabulary Study; Grade Placement in Seventeen Spellers* (New York: American Book Company, 1940); idem, *Second Vocabulary Study: Grade Placement of Words in Eight Recent Spellers* (New York: American Book Co., 1949).

78. Irving H. Anderson, *Comparisons of the Reading and Spelling Achievement, and Quality of Handwriting of Groups of English, Scottish, and American Children,* U.S.O.E. Cooperative Research Project no. 1903 (Ann Arbor: University of Michigan, 1963); Carl Personke, "Spelling Achievement of Scottish and American Children," *Elementary School Journal* 66 (March 1966): 337-43.

79. Foran, *Psychology and Teaching.*

80. Peters, *Spelling,* pp. 50-51; Hildreth, *Teaching Spelling,* p. 36.

81. Peters, *Spelling,* pp. 78-82.

3. Use multisensory approaches.
4. Emphasize retention of the visual image.
5. Keep practice sessions short and intensive.
6. For more advanced pupils, test before teaching.
7. Have a child work only on words difficult for him.
8. Do not introduce words which are not understood.
9. Provide for review.
10. Have each pupil keep a chart of his progress.

Handwriting

The term "handwriting" is used in this section to emphasize the acquisition and extension of the psychomotor skills used in writing. It is a skill prerequisite to encoding thought in written form, and, even in this age of technology, continues to be second only to speech in importance as a means of personal communication. It is possible, however, to write with a good hand and have nothing of significance to say, so that it is necessary to distinguish between the psychomotor ability of writing and the intellectuality of thought and expression in written composition, the subject of another section.

Writing is a psychomotor skill which has a high motor content, particularly relating to finger dexterity, and a high perceptual content.[82] This results from the fact that learning to write involves the use of models, and the capacity to visualize and reproduce the visual signs which make up the alphabet. As with other psychomotor abilities, writing is improved with practice, although in recent years there has been a deemphasis on linguistic arrangements of regular words.

practice.[83] Writing gradients, such as those of Ames and Ilg,[84] represent performance after instruction. The fact that such gradients begin with manuscript characteristics simply reflects the fact that since the introduction of print script, or manuscript writing, from England in the early 1920s, this type of writing is the one children are taught, with a transition to cursive writing in the latter part of the second or third grade.[85] The many alleged advantages of manuscript as the introductory form[86] are based on practice and common sense rather than research, and a minority of schools still teach only cursive.[87] Today the major emphasis in handwriting is on legibility rather than calligraphy, writing as an art form, and there is conflicting evidence as to whether there is systematic attention given to handwriting skill development in school programs.[88] As a research area, however, handwriting receives little attention,[89] and most of the interest in handwriting

82. Herbert J. Klausmeier and William Goodwin, *Learning and Human Abilities,* 2d ed. (New York: Harper & Row, Publishers, 1966), pp. 303, 305, 313, 323.
83. Ruth G. Strickland, *The Language Arts in the Elementary School* 3d ed. (Lexington, Mass.: D. C. Heath and Company, 1969), pp. 380-81.
84. Louise B. Ames and Francis L. Ilg, "Developmental Trends in Writing Behavior," *Journal of Genetic Psychology* 79 (1951): 29-46; Gertrude Hildreth, "Developmental Sequences in Name Writing," *Child Development* 7 (1936): 291-303.
85. Paul S. Anderson, *Language Skills,* p. 96.
86. Pose Lamb, "Teaching and Improving Handwriting in Elementary Schools," *Guiding Children's Language Learning,* ed. Pose Lamb (Dubuque, Iowa: Wm. C. Brown Company Publishers, 1967), pp. 182-83.
87. Virgil Herrick, ed., *New Horizons for Research in Handwriting* (Madison, Wis.: University of Wisconsin Press, 1963), p. 19-20.
88. Ibid.; Walter Petty, "Handwriting and Spelling: Their Current Status," *Elementary English* 41 (December 1964): 839-44.
89. Horn, "Handwriting and Spelling," p. 168.

improvement comes from the publishers of the commercial programs, of which there are several.[90]

Manuscript writing is characteristically introduced with learning the letters of the alphabet in reading programs,[91] and progressively expands to include the writing of words in study books and later simple sentences. The introduction of writing concurrently with reading is important for a number of reasons: it facilitates visual discrimination, thus reinforcing reading instruction, and it provides another means for checking comprehension by eliciting individual responses which are not contaminated by other pupils. Concise directions for teaching manuscript writing are given in Anderson and in Lamb. The teaching of the circle, vertical, horizontal, and diagonal lines, which make up the four elements of manuscript writing, is often introduced by blackboard work. Since work at the blackboard involves a vertical plane and arm movements while writing at the desk involves a horizontal plane and finger dexterity, it is equally expedient to begin work with children at their desks.

The use of models with arrows and dotted outlines to copy, available commercially or prepared by the teacher, is an excellent means of controlling initial writing efforts. Since many children come to the first grade able to write, it is desirable that the teacher distinguish as soon as possible the range of writing ability. In this way, pupils who already know how to write some or all of the letters can be given advanced copy while the teacher works more intensively with those who have not yet learned how to write.

The usual lined writing paper for initial manuscript writing, product of the "big muscle" stage of thinking and use of awkward, oversize crayons, forces little hands to make unnaturally large letters. The use of standard pencils or ball point pens, which young children use at home, and paper with narrower lines permits children to make smaller letters which are more natural. Some children will write smaller and some larger; the object is not a uniformity of size but the attainment of a legible size which is comfortable for each child. Some will need to be encouraged to write larger, and some to write smaller. A slanted manuscript, attained by holding the paper at the angle used for cursive, is somewhat more comfortable to write than vertical manuscript, and facilitates the subsequent transfer to cursive. Boys are less concerned with neatness than girls, and overemphasis on neatness and uniformity rather than legibility can create a negative reaction toward writing.

It is not necessary that cursive be introduced to replace manuscript—it is neither faster nor more legible.[92] Since the cultural expectancy is for adults to write in cursive rather than in manuscript, schools generally start a shift in the second or third year. Some children, in emulation of their older brothers or sisters, will attempt to write in cursive in the first grade. There is no reason

---

90. Seven programs are listed in Lamb, "Teaching and Improving Handwriting," p. 206; fourteen in Paul S. Anderson, *Language Skills*, p. 127; Nineteen programs are analyzed in Virgil Herrick, et al., *Comparison of Practices in Handwriting* (Madison, Wis.: University of Wisconsin Press, 1960).

91. For example, see: *Manual, Level 1, Scott Foresman Reading Systems* (Glenview, Ill.: Scott, Foresman and Company, 1971), p. 128 . . . ; *Workbook A, Lippincott's Basic Reading* (Philadelphia: J. B. Lippincott Company, 1969).

92. Lamb, "Teaching and Improving Handwriting," p. 195.

why they should not be helped to make the transition early when they wish.

The type of cursive writing taught in the school is largely determined by the commercial system selected, although some of the larger school systems have developed their own programs.[93] The advantage in using any sequenced programs, commercial or system constructed, is that they provide uniform models for pupil emulation and, based on experience, provide adequate emphasis on the more difficult problems of letter formation.

In evaluating pupil progress, however, it is always useful to bear in mind that the progress of a pupil in a particular grade should largely be measured against other pupils in that grade, not against the adult model. Standards can be informally developed, by collecting and evaluating samples of work at different grade levels, or some of the writing scales may be utilized. Among the most common of these are the Ayres, West, and Freeman scales.[94] The Ayres scale involves the writing of the first few lines of the Gettysburg address. This is done on the assumption that the purpose of writing is to communicate, and thus one of the primary considerations is legibility.[95]

There is no uniformity of opinion as to the desirability of special practice periods for handwriting. Some practice is desirable, probably some sixty minutes a week divided into three twenty-minute sessions. Only one program should be followed in improving handwriting; the minor differences in various programs are enough to interfere with sequential development. After a child has attained an approximation of handwriting deemed satisfactory for that level, however, it does not seem desirable to continue drills which are likely to bring about little improvement. The time of the teacher can be utilized more effectively in working with the few children who experience more difficulty in learning to write and need additional help and encouragement.[96] Speed of handwriting gradually increases from about 30 letters per minute in the second grade to 80 letters per minute in the eighth.[97]

Attention needs to be given handwriting improvement throughout the primary and intermediate grades. The fact that American children seem to write less legibly than do children in the United Kingdom appears to be in part a function of the amount of time spent in learning.[98] In the general language arts program, there is an increasing tendency to overlook handwriting practice. It is therefore desirable to assign some regular time every week to the development of a skill which still remains important in business and personal communication.

It is sometimes suggested that in this age of technology, the typewriter, and typing, elementary children should be taught typewriting. Children in grades four and five can be efficiently taught to use the typewriter. However, the acquisition of this skill at an earlier age would not eliminate the need for the development of legible handwriting.[99]

93. Paul S. Anderson, *Language Skills,* pp. 11?, 117.
94. Leonard P. Ayres, *Ayres Handwriting Scale,* rev. (Princeton, N.J.: Educational Testing Service, 1917); F. N. Freeman, "A New Handwriting Scale," *Elementary School Journal* 59 (January 1959): 219; Paul V. West, *American Handwriting Scale* (New York: A. N. Palmer Co., 1957).
95. Lamb, "Teaching and Improving Handwriting," p. 203.
96. Paul S. Anderson, *Language Skills,* p. 113.
97. Frank N. Freeman, "Teaching Handwriting *What Research Says to the Teacher* (Washington, National Education Association, 1954).
98. Irving H. Anderson, *Comparisons of the Reading and Spelling.*
99. Lamb, "Teaching and Improving Handwriting," pp. 202-3.

Grammar

One of the most persistent and troublesome aspects of the language arts program is the teaching of grammar. What is grammar? In one sense, it is scientific description. According to Noam Chomsky, "A grammar of a language aims to present in a precise and explicit form just those facts about the language that its speakers know intuitively."[100] Since the publication of Chomsky's *Syntactic Structures* in 1957,[101] the emphasis has shifted in college cloisters from structural grammar, as exemplified by the work of Fries,[102] to transformational generative grammar.[103] Structural grammar emphasizes the basic contrastive arrangements that identify the separate grammatical units which, in turn, signal the structural meanings of a language.[104] Transformational generative grammar constitutes a set of symbols and rules which permits a native speaker to determine the grammaticality of any novel sentence.[105] Traditional grammar, which prevailed until about 1960, was based upon the assumption that the structure of language was based on canons of logic and hence constituted a prescriptive system for determining usage.[106]

In the last few years, English textbooks reflecting the "new" grammar have been developed for the elementary and middle grades, such as that of Roberts[107] and the revised Macmillan English Series.[108] In addition, new English curriculum guides have been produced incorporating principles of transformational generative grammar.[109] The new grammars are as sterile as the traditional grammars, and their persistence in the schools is a continuing witness of the bankruptcy of English teaching. If elementary teachers knew how to help children to increase their production of oral and written language, there would be no need to depend on mechanical instruction in parts of speech and sentence structure.

One of the most vocal critics of the new grammar teaching, as well as of the old, is James Moffett.[110] According to Moffett, what students need to improve their oral and their written language is not rules, but awareness. While many teachers would not accept a nongrammar approach to language in secondary school and college, Moffett's techniques for stimulating discourse deserve the sympathetic study by elementary and middle grade teachers.[111] These methods include the provision for intensifying personal experiences; movement, pantomime, and dramatics; speaking out in a variety of situations—individual, small group, and class dis-

100. Paul Roberts, *English Syntax* (New York: Harcourt, Brace, Jovanovich, Inc., 1964), p. ix.

101. Noam Chomsky, *Syntactic Structures* ('s-Gravenhage, The Hague: Mouton & Cie, 1957).

102. Charles C. Fries, *The Structure of English* (New York: Harcourt, Brace & World, 1952).

103. Emmon Bach, *An Introducton to Transformational Grammars* (New York: Holt, Rinehart and Winston, Inc., 1964).

104. Charles C. Fries, "Advances in Linguistics," in *Readings in Applied Linguistics,* ed. Harold B. Allen, 2d ed. (New York: Appleton-Century-Crofts, 1964).

105. Owen Thomas, *Transformational Grammar and the Teacher of English* (New York: Holt, Rinehart and Winston, Inc., 1965), pp.7-8.

106. Leonard Bloomfield, *Language* (New York: Holt, Rinehart and Winston, Inc., 1933), p. 6.

107. Paul Roberts, *The Roberts English Series: A Linguistic Program* (New York: Harcourt, Brace & World, Inc., 1966).

108. Thomas Clark Pollock, Florence B. Bowden, and Robert J. Geist, *The Macmillan English Series* (New York: Macmillan Company, 1969).

109. Georgia Department of Education, *A Design for an English Curriculum* (Atlanta, Ga.: State Department of Education, 1968).

110. James Moffett, *Teaching the Universe of Discourse* (Boston: Houghton Mifflin Company, 1968), p. 202.

111. James Moffett, *A Student-Centered Language Arts Curriculum, Grades K-13: A Handbook for Teachers* (Boston: Houghton Mifflin Company, 1968).

cussions and reports; reading widely; and writing from dictation and written composition.[112]

Criticism of mechanical grammar teaching in the elementary school is not new. Ever since the Report of the Committee of Ten of the National Education Association in 1894 there has been a recognition that formal grammar study and sentence analysis has little place in the elementary curriculum.[113] The idea that correct usage could be taught by grammatical rules has nevertheless persisted, as if knowing the parts of speech somehow extended their use. One of the most disappointing developments of the so-called linguistic revolution in English grammar is the perpetuation of the grammar routine in the guise of new names and labels. Pooley has been one of the most outspoken critics of teaching grammar in the elementary grades. According to him, too much grammar is taught too early and so poorly that it makes language hateful to children.[114] The time utilized in grammar studies should be devoted to using language, not talking about language which is a function of grammar.[115]

While most textbooks on language arts generally agree that formal grammar is not a proper subject of the elementary curriculum, they nevertheless then proceed to outline the sequences of grammar instruction and give specific instructions for teaching grammar. The reason that the ghosts of Dionysius Thrax[116] and Lindley Murray[117] linger in the elementary classroom is that collegians like Tiedt are not bold enough to abandon the teaching of grammar.[118] Scrambled sentences and the jargon of sentence patterning may be an alternative to traditional grammar, but the main reason such types of exercise persist is that they give the teacher the illusion of teaching without the creative art which requires the development of experiences, word power, and the stimulation of language usage. As indicated by Chomsky's definition of grammar, this should be based upon the children's intuitive knowledge of the structure of language which they have already acquired, and not on descriptions of language. If this alternative is not pursued, the new grammar will likely become just as formalized in the elementary curriculum as traditional grammar.[119] For this reason, no sequence of grammar development is proposed. However, by the upper middle grades, about the seventh or eighth, some consideration may be given to grammar as a descriptive language system.

Even more than a description of language, the term grammar has connoted correct

112. See Paul S. Anderson, *Language Skills* Lamb, *Guiding Children's Language Learning.*
113. Wallace W. Douglas, "The History of Language Instruction in the Schools," *Linguistics in School Programs,* in Sixty-ninth Yearbook of the National Society for the Study of Education, Part II, ed. Albert H. Marckwardt (Chicago: University of Chicago Press, 1970), p. 164.
114. Robert C. Pooley, "What About Grammar," in *Readings on Contemporary English in the Elementary School,* ed. Iris M. Tiedt and Sidney W. Tiedt (Englewood Cliffs, N.J.: Prentice-Hall Inc., 1967), pp. 79-84.
115. Robert C. Pooley, *Teaching English Grammar* (New York: Appleton-Century-Crofts, Inc 1957), pp. 126-28.
116. Hellenistic grammarian from Alexandria whose *Techne Grammatike* of the second century B.C. became the model for subsequent grammar
117. American author of grammar texts; his *English Grammar,* first published in 1795, went through many editions and was very influential in helping to set the pattern of grammar instruction
118. Iris M. Tiedt and Sidney W. Tiedt, eds *Contemporary English in the Elementary School* (Englewood Cliffs, N. J.: Prentice-Hall, Inc 1967), especially pages 9-10, 31-37.
119. See Walter T. Petty, ed., *Issues and Problems in the Elementary Language Arts* (Boston: Allyn and Bacon, Inc., 1968), pp. 104-20.

usage. This inevitably implies some arbitrary standard of perfection, of which the schoolmaster was all too often the custodian. Both the *Webster's New International Dictionary*, 2d ed.,[120] and *Webster's Third New International Dictionary*[121] indicate that the lexicographer is not a dictator of good usage, but records the shifts in usage which come from the diverse influences of changes in time, occupation, and regional variation. Ever since 1935, the National Council of Teachers of English have recommended that the teacher, like the lexicographer, find correct usage in the living language of the day, not on the basis of an arbitrary standard imposed by the erroneous and archaic application to English of Latin grammar forms.[122]

In terms of usage, the six-level analysis of Pooley is still one of the most descriptive.[123] These are: illiterate, homely, informal standard, formal standard, technical, and literary. Examples of the first four are:[124]

> I seen him.
> It don't matter a bit.
> I will try and do it.
> Neither of those men was injured.

At the present time, there is no agreement to the extent to which correct usage should be taught. On the one extreme is the position of Moffett, who holds that it is ineffectual to try to teach correct usage and it is more humane not to do so; the motivated high school student may seek to correct his usage by deliberate intent.[125] On the other hand, as indicated in the section on speaking, if severe deviation from usage is not changed, at least as concerns some classroom behavior, the student will have difficulty not merely with grammar, but the whole process of expression and reception.

Consequently, a sequential program of teaching correct usage in the model of English as a second language is desirable. When this is done systematically and sequentially, without the constant admonitions of wrong that go with correcting usage, there is some indication of benefit of correct language learning without rules of grammar. It may be inhumane not to teach the child correct oral usage, because society still places some value on acceptable usage; it does not value language which connotes illiteracy, either in spoken or written form. Over fifty years of life as an adult follow the years of the child in school.[126]

In schools where an informal standard English prevails, this level is appropriate for the elementary school. The distinctions between informal and homely are often a matter of degree, and have regional variations. The development of formal usage may

120. *Webster's New International Dictionary*, 2d ed. (Springfield, Mass.: G. & C. Merriam Company, Publishers, 1934), p. xir.
121. *Webster's Third New International Dictionary* (Springfield, Mass.: G. & C. Merriam Company, Publishers, 1961), p. 6a.
122. National Council of Teachers of English, Curriculum Commission, *An Experience Curriculum in English* (New York: D. Appleton-Century Company, Inc., 1935).
123. Robert C. Pooley, "The Levels of Language," *Educational Method* 16 (March 1937): 290; idem, "What is Correct English Usage?" *NEA Journal* 49 (December 1960), pp. 12-19.
124. Paul S. Anderson, *Language Skills in Elementary Education* (New York: The Macmillan Company, 1964), pp. 372-73. Reprinted with permission of the Macmillan Company, © copyright by Paul S. Anderson, 1964.
125. Moffett, *Student-Centered Language Arts*, pp. 280-81.
126. At a meeting March 18, 1971, the Language Arts Committee of Primary Teachers of the Hancock County School District, Sparta, Georgia, was unanimous in affirming that one of the objectives of the language arts program was to teach "correct usage." Hancock County is a school system in which over 90 percent of the children and teachers are Negro.

be postponed to high school. In any case, development of correct usage should first occur orally before the application of writing or of rules.

Composition: Oral and Written

The energy and efforts dissipated in elementary formal grammar training may be more wisely used to help pupils develop facility in oral expression and in written composition. In the American preoccupation with teaching reading, there has been a concomitant neglect of the art of expression. In criticizing the neglect of writing, Riemer has observed that a nation is not known for its readers, but for its writers. While written language is based on the oral language, it involves a higher level of intellectuality. "The written sentence is the awesome sacrament of cognition . . ."[127] Writing is the medium which transcends space and time, so that the present communicates with the past and projects itself into the future.[128]

Just as there are different levels of oral communication, there are different levels and types of written composition. There are the folksy, idiomatic letter of friendly communication and the formal business letter; there are accurate expository writing and imaginative writing to create a mood or sentiment. Children in the elementary and middle schools require frequent exposure to various types of writing, so that a blank sheet of paper and pen serves as a stimulus rather than a barrier to written communication. Initially, the habitual oral usage level will be expressed in the written form. In the elementary school, this level of usage should be accepted in writing.[129] Efforts to improve the level of usage should be a part of speech improvement, not the writing program.

Oral Expression. To have an idea to write, one must first have words to express thoughts, and thus the development of writing begins in the cultivation and extension of the use of oral language. All too often the elementary teacher restricts oral expression to the ubiquitous first grade period of show and tell, while children require a variety of opportunities to express themselves as they progress in the grades. In the primary grades, many situations can be created in which children are encouraged to talk. These include such activities as rhythm, pantomime, dialogues, monologues, conversation, discussion, storytelling, learning with puppets, reading poetry and prose aloud, creative dramatics, and a variety of adjunct curricular activities, such as club meetings and assemblies for special days.[130] Moffett expresses the essence of the cultivation of oral expression in the two concepts "acting out" and "speaking up."[131]

These activities continue through the elementary and middle grades. The enactment of ready-made stories of kindergarten and the primary grades gives way in the middle school to more formal drama and the writing of scripts; small group discussions led by the teacher are eventually replaced with panel discussions initiated by students with

127. George Riemer, *How They Murdered the Second "R"* (New York: W. W. Norton and Company, Inc., 1969). Note: This book is now available from Creative Writing Service, 149 Clinton Street, Brooklyn Heights, N.Y.

128. See Donald R. Ferris, "Teaching Children to Write," in *Guiding Children's Language Learning,* ed. Pose Lamb (Dubuque, Iowa: Wm. C. Brown Company Publishers, 1967), pp. 137-38, 141.

129. Carrie Rasmussen, *Speech Methods in the Elementary School* (New York: Ronald Press Company, 1949).

130. Ibid.

131. Moffett, *Student-Centered Language Arts*

audience feedback. These are not discrete, but continuous experiences, developing and expanding with the increased logical and aesthetic sensitivities of the speaker.

There is an overlap in the techniques of developing visual and language aesthetic sensitivity, as indicated in chapter 17. These overlapping techniques include the oral verbalization of experience, observation, and recall, and the use of written language to stimulate expression. In visual art, the expression takes the form of an artifact created in some art medium; in the language arts, the aesthetic creation is expressed in words.

Oral expression, like written expression, is molded by function and audience. While much emphasis in oral language is on the imaginative use of poetic and prose forms, oral communication most frequently requires clarity rather than imagery, simplicity rather than complexity, and directness rather than allusion. The subject matter courses, such as the social and the natural sciences, are ideally suited to the use of scientific language, and the development of oral expression in such courses is just as appropriate as the development of more imaginative expression in English classes. Experience with receiving and giving simple traffic directions is a constant reminder that the most ordinary situation involves facility in oral language. Facility in language does not mean loquacity, but rather an appropriateness of words and sentences to the occasion. But students who learn to use language and acquire the vocabulary to match the occasion are more likely to translate such sentiments into the written form, whether with the terseness of military command, the formality of business communication, the languor of a sonnet, or the terror of a science fiction thriller.

Written Composition. Writing is one of the most difficult areas of the language arts, because it requires efficiency in so many skills concurrently—penmanship, choice of words, sentence structure, usage with respect to grammar, and the thinking processes of selection and discrimination.[132] Under the aegis of Project English, a number of curriculum projects specifically dealt with the improvement of writing in the elementary grades,[133] including "A Curriculum in English Composition" at the University of Georgia.[134] The results of the research at Georgia,[135] like other research in written composition, is equivocal as to the most desirable treatment effects. This is due in part to the lack of reliable criterion measures,[136] and lends credence to the opinion that the development of facility in writing is not a matter of discrete treatment, but a combination of many interacting variables of language and experience, in which the teacher is a crucial variable. But first he must provide time for his charges to write, and give encouragement to writing.

Some research at the high school level indicates that frequency of writing is no

132. Lou Labrant, "Writing—The Most Difficult of the Language Arts," in *Readings on Contemporary English in the Elementary School,* ed. Iris M. Tiedt and Sidney W. Tiedt (Englewood Cliffs, N.J.: Prentice-Hall, Inc., 1967), p. 138.

133. *English Curriculum Development Projects* (Champaign, Ill.: National Council of Teachers of English, 1968).

134. Rachel S. Sutton and Mary J. Tingle, *Written Composition, Grades K-6, Final Report,* English Curriculum Study Center (Athens, Ga.: University of Georgia, 1968). Publications of this Center are available through ERIC.

135. *Research in Cognate Aspects of Written Composition,* English Curriculum Study Center (Athens, Ga.: University of Georgia, 1968).

136. William W. West, "Written Composition," *Review of Educational Research* 37 (April 1967): 160.

guarantee to improvement, nor is correction more efficient than mere praise of writing in the elementary school.[137] These conclusions are not consistent with the common assumptions that one learns to write by the practice of writing, and that improvement comes not by mere repetition but through enlightened attempts at correction. Over fifty years ago Brown described the rigorous and systematic processes by which the French developed their acknowledged facility in writing, and his book, reissued in 1963 by the National Council of the Teachers of English, is still pregnant with suggestions for today.[138] Of particular value is the emphasis on the cumulative nature of writing experience, the interrelationship of all the language arts with developing the capacity to write, and the advantages of prevision as opposed to the American emphasis upon correction and criticism of the composition.

The expression of written thought requires writing in sentences, and nothing is more inimical to writing than the short cut monosyllabic response, whether in reply to the too numerous questions of the reading primer or workbook exercises in English and content areas. Easy to correct, they give the child little experience in translating ideas into sentences of his own generation, which become the building blocks of composition. So infrequently is the elementary child given written work that such an assignment is often traumatic.

The first grade is not too early to begin writing, first by the pupil dictating sentences to the teacher or to an older child, and then by the writing of short sentences within his own writing skill. Nor should writing be restricted, as it is all too often, to an "English" period. No subject is taught without language, and all subjects should involve writing. In this way the child naturally begins to acquire the type of writing appropriate to the subject matter. A return to the keeping of orderly notebooks might help facilitate an awareness of writing and provide a measure of the child's own progress. The bits and pieces of paper which so often characterize the elementary classroom are not conducive to tidiness of any kind—physical or mental.

The previous section on oral expression has emphasized the important relation of oral language and other types of experiences to writing. The subject matter of reading, whether realistic or inventive, supplies not only vocabulary for development but patterns of expression which can be utilized in writing. One advantage of using literary selections for the subject of reading instruction is that the reading supplies not only a standard for aesthetic criticism and appreciation but also a stimulus to imaginative writing.

The concept of prevision also emphasizes the importance of the preparatory experiences which preceeds writing. All too often, the elementary child is merely told to write on something, and there is hardly any preparation which helps him organize his experiences, develop his thoughts, extend his vocabulary, clarify his ideas, or consider appropriate usage. The resulting product is frequently low in quantity and quality because he has not been sufficiently prevised.

Many of the new approaches to writing, such as those outlined by Moffett, Sutton and Tingle, Anderson, and Tiedt, emphasize the importance of similar prescriptions in the teaching of writing. While certain forms

137. Ibid., pp. 161-62, 164.
138. Rollo Walter Brown, *How the French Boy Learns to Write* (Champaign, Ill.: National Council of Teachers of English, 1963).

of writing are highly affective and appeal primarily to the emotions, all writing is not imaginative. The fetish made of creative writing obscures the fact that all writing is a creative act, whether a corporation report or a novel. Only some writing, however, acquires literary merit, and persists over generations. The naiveté of juvenile writing is often confused with creativity.[139] Such writing should be recognized for what it is— the first efforts at imaginative writing. But such writing is not art.

Among the most neglected aspects of elementary composition is the expository mode which develops in an extended form a point of view. Deficiencies in much of school writing result from an overemphasis on personal experiences, imaginative writing, and letters.[140] However, the dramatic personal experiences of the disadvantaged appear to be one of the best means of stimulating writing in children from disadvantaged backgrounds.[141] In any form, writing for most individuals is hard work; the results do not come easily. For this reason, much emphasis is placed upon the creation of motivational situations in which the writing involved appears a natural extension of pupil interest.[142]

The major problem today in teaching writing in the schools is not lack of knowledge about how to stimulate pupil writing, but the failure to provide time for writing. Reading is a significant part of the elementary language arts program, but it is all too often pursued with such restricted vision that inadequate time is given to develop the equally important skill of writing. Writing should be a daily experience and include all subjects. Frequent experience in writing is more important than the occasional long exercise, all too frequently carelessly written— then ignored by pupil and teacher alike.

Literature: Poems and Stories

The literary strand of the language arts program is concerned with the development of appreciation of written language as an art form. The content consists primarily of two types of material: classics, or material which continues to be judged of literary merit long after it is written; and material of a contemporary nature, adjudged of superior merit, frequently represented by winners of the Caldecott and Newberry Medals.[143] There is no dearth of advice as to suitable reading material for children. In addition to standard anthologies and reviews of children's literature, there are numerous book selection aids.[144] Most books are purchased by school libraries from such lists, and it is desirable that the teacher work with the school librarian to obtain the most desirable books to promote good reading.

The promotion of good reading includes not only literature, but books which emphasize material of a factual nature, whether

139. Reed Wittemore, "A Caveat on Creativity," *Creativity in English,* Dartmouth College Seminar on the Teaching of English (Champaign, Ill.: National Council for the Teachers of English, 1966), pp. 45-47.
140. Sutton and Tingle, *Written Composition,* p. 5.
141. Don M. Wolfe, "A Realistic Writing Program for Culturally Diverse Youth," *Improving English Skills of Culturally Different Youth,* Office of Education Bulletin 1964, no. 5 (Washington, D.C.: Government Printing Office, 1964), pp. 83-90.
142. Richard Corbin, *The Teaching of Writing in Our Schools* (New York: Macmillan Company, 1966), p. 14.
143. May Hill Arbuthnot, *Children and Books* 3d ed. (Chicago: Scott, Foresman and Company, 1964), pp. 45-51.
144. Among these are the *Booklist and Subscription Books Bulletin, Bulletin of the Center for Children's Books, Elementary English, Hornbook, School Library Journal, and Children's Catalog.* See: Paul C. Burns and Alberta L. Lowe, *The Language Arts in Childhood Education* (Chicago: Rand McNally and Company, 1966), p. 116.

dealing with animals or travel, biology or rockets. In the middle grades in particular, reading interest expands, as a result of instruction, to include more nonfiction and scientific material.[145] The development of such personal reading appropriately belongs to the development of subject matter interests and the acquisition of factual knowledge. The emphasis on literature, however, has another function. It is designed to show the relationship of writing to the expression of human emotion, sentiment, and ideals, and to develop a discrimination with respect to style and individuality of expression.

The cultivation of an interest in literature begins with oral reading and storytelling, an emphasis which must be continued in the primary grades because the reading abilities of children must be first developed before they can read effectively, either orally or silently. This results from the fact that children have the capacity to hear, enjoy and discuss selections read by the teacher long before they have the capacity to read them independently.[146] Such reading develops their feeling for literary style, and stimulates a later return to read independently and resavor the excitement, drama, or poignancy of a familiar story or poem.

Appreciative oral reading should concentrate on material of acknowledged literary merit. Children have ample time to read later the series in which they often take much pleasure, whether it is the *Hardy Boys* or *Hitchcock* mysteries. In selecting material for reading, the first prerequisite is that the teacher himself enjoy and savor the narrative or poem. Irrespective of how highly recommended is a piece of reading, if the teacher does not like it he can scarcely read it to convey a sense of appreciation. Some expressiveness is required, both in narration and dialogue, so that change of pace and intonation help convey the mood of the story or poem. When longer selections are read which extend beyond one reading, it is well to note in advance a suitable stopping point, so that the limitation of time will not spoil the effect. Much of the connotative impact in the material for very young children is conveyed by the pictures. Time must be provided for young children to see the pictures and incorporate their meaning with the sense conveyed by words.

The selections in many reading series include pieces of literary merit. These provide the basis for a common reading experience. All too often, however, these pieces are talked to death by the innumerable questions the teacher asks to probe reading comprehension. Such detailed questions are more appropriate for selections read to communicate knowledge, rather than selections chosen to express facets of mood, characterization, setting, and climax. The totality of the piece has to be grasped by the children, not the minutia of detail. It is more desirable in literary questioning to pose general issues of interpretation and discussion, so that eventually the student is led to develop an appreciation of the whole and their constituent parts rather than a factual knowledge of discrete elements without a sense of the context.

Such questions, of course, have to be related to the knowledge and experience of the child. But the process is developmental not one ignored in the primary grades and

145. Margaret Hayes, "The Status of Personal Reading," in *Developing Permanent Interest in Reading*, ed. Helen M. Robinson (Chicago University of Chicago Press, 1956), p. 44; Arthur E. Traxler, "Recent Findings and Trends in Research on Reading," *The Reading Teacher* 1 (December 1959): 90.
146. Strickland, *Language Arts*, p. 423.

suddenly introduced in the middle grades. As students mature in age and instruction, the comparative technique may be introduced, in which the different works of the same author are compared, as well as the works of different writers. By the end of the middle grades, more formal types of literary analysis may be introduced, but this development is not alien when based on the earlier foundations of cumulative critical appreciation.

Poetry has a special, if often neglected place, in the elementary literature program. Poetry conveys more than prose the rhythmic qualities of language, and in its figurative presentation appeals more to the imagination than narrative description. Consequently, the union of prosody and impression impart a more abstract image, permitting the reader to bring to the enjoyment of poetry highly personal interpretations from his own experience and sentiment. For this reason poetry should be recited and read for the heroic, the fantastic, the whimsical, or the lyrical qualities it suggests, rather than as some mundane adjunct to science or social studies, as is sometimes suggested.[147]

Long before many children have entered school, they have been introduced to the nursery rhyme and jingle. But poetry is more than rhyming words, and even very young children acquire an ear for more sophisticated forms when given the background for deriving meaning. Thus preschoolers have responded with pleasure to Sandburg's *Fog* after they have felt the dawn mists damp against their faces, and asked repeatedly for *Hiawatha's Childhood* after they have stalked deer in an imaginary forest glade. One advantage of general anthologies, in comparison to selections for a particular age, is that the teacher is encouraged to experiment—to read maturer forms to younger students. The teacher is often pleasantly surprised to encounter the favorable reaction such selections generate.[148]

Much research has been devoted to the reading interests of children.[149] Since the early reading of children is guided by adult tastes of what is appropriate for children, such studies overlook the fact that reading interests are often induced by cultural preferences as much as by individual choice. Any literary program, however, deliberately seeks to guide children's independent reading interests. The best guarantee to independent reading of high quality is to have a carefully selected and extensive school library collection of varied types of children's books—biography, historical fiction, poetry, fairy tales, folk stories, myths, legends, fantasy, travel, and adventure as well as informational and reference books.[150] In addition to regular library periods permitting free choice reading, reading clubs and similar interest groups are often utilized to encourage independent reading. Discussion and reports of independent reading are important means of recognizing achievement in individual reading and in stimulating additional effort. Some children eventually learn that discriminating reading sometimes provides more pleasure and satisfaction than the hypnotic repetition of many TV programs.

147. See for example, Paul S. Anderson, *Language Skills*, p. 305.
148. Among the useful general anthologies of prose and poetry is: Edna Johnson, Evelyn R. Sickels, and Frances Clarke Sayers, *Anthology of Children's Literature* 4th ed. (Boston: Houghton Mifflin Company, 1970). It offers a bibliography of poetry on pages 996-1000.
149. Burns and Lowe, *Language Arts*, pp. 111-14.
150. Arbuthnot, *Children and Books*, p. 26.

Teachers should not, of course, expect that children will be always engrossed in reading. After all, in the process of growing up they have many other things to do. But habits begun in childhood are more likely to reassert themselves at a later date, and thus the foundations of adult literary appreciation are laid in the formative years. The language arts program, although commanding a dominant part of the elementary years, seldom provides sufficient time for the concurrent pursuit of literary work in connection with the reading program and in an English program. Reading and English often provide a double allocation of literature pursued under different labels. In the middle grades in particular, adequate time must be found for the content subjects. Economy of time therefore requires that much of the literary program be pursued in connection with reading, rather than as an independent entity.

Vocabulary Development

In the classroom, language and thought appear as inseparable facets of the same behavior. While competence in language may be a biological endowment, the fact nevertheless remains that performance in a language depends upon one's cultural environment.[151] The size and complexity of vocabulary is used as a general index to intellectual ability in school, and specific mastery of the language of a particular subject matter ranks highly in correlating with school performance.[152] From a linguistic point of view, schooling does nothing to teach the structure of language. Schooling nevertheless extends the nuances of thought which are expressed in words and encourages a more elaborate sentence usage. Symbolic manipulation of the environment through language becomes increasingly important as the child grows.

For the past few years, the restricted vocabulary in disadvantaged children has been recognized as a deterrent to success in school. As a result, there has been a tremendous emphasis on providing concrete experiences for children (see chapter 23). A concrete experience unless accompanied by the use of language adds nothing, however, to one's capacity to symbolize experience. Personal instances can be multiplied endlessly of the child or adult on a field trip or vacation who finds no communicable meaning in the experience because of the failure to acquire the necessary word labels to accompany the experience.

Thus while in itself experience does not develop language, language has the power of constituting a vicarious experience. Irrespective of the ambiguities with which psychologists and linguists surround the expansion of language, practical school men have for years attempted to expand the power of the child's mind through vocabulary. Perception itself, the capacity to discriminate visually, is frequently much more dependent upon the labels through which to see than the science of optics and the psysiology of perception.

The development of vocabulary is not the peculiar province of the language arts teacher. Each subject area has its own

---

151. For a brief discussion of the distinction between competence and performance in linguistic theory, see: Richard W. Dettering, "Language and Thinking," *Linguistics in School Programs,* in Sixty-ninth Yearbook of the National Society for the Study of Education, part II, ed. Albert H. Marckwardt (Chicago: University of Chicago Press, 1970), pp. 281-86.

152. Herbert J. Klausmeier and William Goodwin, *Learning and Human Abilities* 2d ed. (New York: Harper & Row, Publishers, 1966), p. 245.

specialized language, and all elementary teachers in any subject should always be conscious of vocabulary development. Meaning is derived not only from context, but from the specific word.[153] There are two approaches to teaching vocabulary. The inductive method emphasizes deriving meaning from content. In this approach, children are encouraged to look for words in reading or oral language which they do not know, and attempt to infer the meaning from the context. The deductive approach uses new vocabulary as one type of advance organizer. In introducing the new lesson, the teacher calls attention to the new words which will be encountered in the lesson. If not listed in a text study guide, these may be written on the board, pronounced, used in sentences, explained, and then written by the children. This approach emphasizes the acquisition of knowledge of the appropriate word as a key to deriving meaning from the context.[154] The direct teaching approach is based on the assumption that it is wasteful of time and energy of children to rely exclusively on contextual clues for reading comprehension, and that their study time may be used most effectively when they know the meaning of what they are studying.

Irrespective of whether inductive or deductive methods of vocabulary development are used, the use of "word power" notebooks are helpful. The pupil is encouraged to write in this notebook new words, to define their meaning, and to use them in appropriate sentences. If organized by subject matter, such word books become useful means of review. In particular, children should be encouraged to find new words and their meaning in independent reading. If not, the child may fail to expand his vocabulary—and his willingness to read books with more difficult content—simply because of his failure to expand vocabulary.

From the earliest days in school, children enjoy word games which may be used to increase their vocabulary. These include such games as word treasure hunts, letter substitutions, and spoonerisms.[155] As children advance in the grades, more formal methods may be used, such as those described in connection with the word power notebook. In particular, older children enjoy study of recently coined words and noting the shift in meanings of old words.[156] The development of simple aids to study, such as the pictionary as an early introduction to the dictionary, helps a teacher to develop word awareness and specificity in children at an early age.

There will be a tremendous expansion in language development in the school, even where teachers are not conscious about word usage. This results from the fact that much subject writing is quasi-definitional in nature—meanings of words are explained, illustrated, and clarified in the context of the exposition. Some children are more curious about words than are other children, and find various devices to expand their own vocabulary. The abler students generally imitate adult usage—looking up words in a dictionary and searching for meaning in the context.

153. Ethel R. Oyan, "Words: Their Power and Their Glory," in *Readings on Contemporary English in the Elementary School,* ed. Iris M. Tiedt and Sidney W. Tiedt (Englewood Cliffs, N. J.: Prentice-Hall, Inc., 1967), pp. 170-80.

154. See Georgelle Thomas, *Pronunciation Guide to a Programmed Text in Archeological Methods* (Athens, Ga.: Anthropology Curriculum Project, University of Georgia, 1967).

155. Tiedt and Tiedt, *Contemporary English,* p. 280.

156. Strickland, *Language Arts,* p. 250.

All children, however, do not have this curiosity, and can pass over a new and unknown word without showing the slightest remorse for the nonrecognition. It is a function of teaching to make children aware of word power and to assist them in its development. The language arts teacher of literature will assist children in appreciating the imagery and robustness of expression which comes through word use. In teaching composition, the teacher will assist children to find words to more appropriately express their thoughts and to prevent the dull repetition which comes from the use of overworked words. Subject matter teachers will attempt to help children acquire and use the special vocabularies of their subjects.

Only through the use of words can the attainment of concepts be measured and expressed. If a child says "I know it but I can't say it," it is more likely that he can't say it because he doesn't know it, and he doesn't know it because he lacks the appropriate language. The development of vocabulary therefore is not mere pedantry, but is a way of assisting students develop their powers of thought and expression. The arbitrary nature of the vocal signs and their referents indicate the need for systematic rather than casual vocabulary development. The ability of children in the elementary grades to extend their cognitive perceptions through vocabulary development is one of the most neglected aspects of elementary instruction. Mastery of new vocabulary is a prerequisite to new subject instruction, whether the method is oral, by reading, or as it generally is, a combination of methods.

Creative Dramatics and Drama

Creative dramatics is the imaginative interpretation of a story, poem, or incident without the use of a fixed script for dialogue and play directions. It is extensively used in the elementary school for two major purposes—to impart realism and assist in the conceptualization of language and in self-expression. The first purpose is to help give meaning to instruction; the second purpose is to help a child depict his feelings and sentiments. Thus, creative dramatics serve both utilitarian and expressive purposes in the school curriculum.[157] While creative dramatics is generally thought of primarily as part of the language arts program, it is frequently used as an adjunct to social studies, either as a form of role playing or of historical reconstruction.

Drama, no less than creative dramatics, involves the use of imagination and interpretation. In drama, however, the emphasis shifts from free imagination to the discipline of an actor attempting to create and project the mood, the character, the sentiment as perceived by the dramatist. The requirements of craftsmanship and line memorization make drama in the elementary school less important than creative dramatics, but the study of selected parts of plays is a useful way of clarifying intent and purpose in creative dramatics.

In the primary grades, the emphasis in creative dramatics is largely on story interpretation. With a few props from the dress-up box and supplementary art work, children can learn to interpret and present a great variety of stories, so that creative dramatics functions as a complementary strand to the literary program. In fact, these are often interpreted merely as different facets although naturally all that can be read aloud

---

157. H. Beresford Menagh, "Creative Dramatics," in *Guiding Children's Language Learning*, ed Pose Lamb (Dubuque, Iowa: Wm. C. Brown Company Publishers, 1967), pp. 63-91.

to children cannot be interpreted in dramatic form.

In the middle grades, however, children are less interested in simple story interpretation. Because of greater familiarity with TV than the stage, the writing and production of TV scripts can serve as a useful motivational device.[158] Since dialogue eventually becomes a key element in drama, some initial practice may begin in the transcription of dialogue.[159]

It is the upper middle grades, the early years of adolescence, that are better suited for the systematic creation of drama. When drama is conceived of as a language activity rather than entertainment, the emphasis shifts from presenting a play to the creation of dramatic forms in writing, whether in the form of dialogue or monologue. While one act plays are suitable for presentation at this age level, it is more important that students engage in the total act of dramatic creation, not merely in the memorization and interpretation of scripts. It is more important to continue to create than to work up showcase productions. Where a script is developed and produced, the appropriate audience is not a group of adults but of classmates who are engaged in similar activities. Presentation for adult audiences, even in the middle grades, too frequently subverts the purpose of dramatic experience and converts it into entertainment for adults. This may be satisfying to the few performers who are on stage, but it hardly helps large numbers grow in dramatic awareness and appreciation (as, for example, the very professionalization of the athletic program has already debauched that program). This should not occur with dramatics, even in those systems in which a drama specialist is available to aid teachers.

Middle grade teachers often find that students will come to regard creative dramatics as "kid stuff." When this happens, it is usually because the work is not taken seriously. Thus many students can develop facility in dramatic reading without devoting the time necessary to stage a production, but the work must be taken seriously by the teacher. The reason that dramatic work in the middle school often deteriorates is because of the absence of workmanlike habits associated with practice and writing. A good discussion of procedures for the middle school years, particularly grades seven and eight, are given in Moffett.[160]

Foreign Languages

The teaching of foreign languages in the elementary school (FLES) is not new, but received new emphasis in 1952 when Earl J. McGrath was U.S. Commissioner of Education.[161] The extension of foreign language teaching has grown slowly, however, due to the lack of properly trained and certificated teachers. Few general elementary teachers have had even introductory courses in a foreign language as part of their general education. Certification requirements interfere with the use of native speakers of Spanish, of which there is a large population.

Young children can be taught a second language easily. Because young children are less self-conscious, the direct aural-oral method is even more effective with them

---

158. Paul S. Anderson, *Language Skills,* pp. 70-71.
159. Moffett, *Student-Centered Language Arts.*
160. Moffett, *Student-Centered Language Arts,* see especially chaps. 19 and 20.
161. Marguerite Eriksson, Ilse Forrest, and Ruth Mullauser, *Foreign Languages in the Elementary School* (Englewood Cliffs, N. J.: Prentice-Hall, Inc., 1964.)

than with older students.[162] The major problem with early instruction in a foreign language is the lack of continuity. Unless a child follows a sequential curriculum with sufficient continuity to maintain foreign language learning, the early learning is quickly forgotten.

Foreign language instruction in the 1960s shifted radically from the word grammar approach to the spoken language approach with pattern drills.[163] To facilitate instruction by nonnative speakers, the language laboratory was also introduced.

Students who participate in FLES programs generally indicate a favorable attitude toward foreign language study. Most FLES students are serious-minded in their desire to acquire language competency, not merely exposure or familiarization. After two years of verbal instruction, it has been found that interest lags if reading and writing are not introduced. FLES experiences stimulate an interest in the culture of the language being studied and a desire to continue the same language in high school. In high school, FLES trained classes are more animated and participant-oriented than are high school classes in which foreign language study is first initiated. FLES trained high school classes also show a greater diversity of interests and background, while those who begin a foreign language in high school are almost exclusively college bound. Not all FLES instruction is beneficial. Where it has suffered too much from the "fun and games approach," secondary instruction is likewise adversely affected.[164]

Carefully supported and articulated FLES programs contribute in a meaningful way to the education of elementary pupils. A study utilizing 25 percent of all foreign language majors in the United States in 1964 indicated that students who started a foreign language in the elementary school performed substantially better than those who started in high school or college. It is Carroll's thesis that a high degree of competence in a subject is more closely related to time spent in learning than age in learning. The chief advantage in starting a language early is that it allows more time for learning.[165]

Television teaching of FLES is effective for both Spanish[166] and French,[167] but it is desirable to have television instruction supplemented by class work under the direction of the classroom teacher. The theory of reinforcing play and games has been extensively used in connection with foreign language instruction, but long term language gains seem to be inversely related to the play-like approach. The evidence for using games, music, dancing, and other devices popular in elementary foreign language pedagogy does not substantiate the use of

162. Harold B. Dunkel, *Second-Language Learning* (Boston: Ginn & Company, 1949), p. 72.

163. Mildred R. Donoghue, ed., *Foreign Languages and the Schools* (Dubuque, Iowa: Wm. C. Brown Company Publishers, 1967).

164. Edward H. Bourgue, ed., *The FLES Student, A Report of the 1967 FLES Committee of the American Association of Teachers of French* (Philadelphia: Chilton Company, 1968).

165. John B. Carroll, "Psychological and Educational Research," in *Languages and the Young School Child,* ed. H. H. Stein, for International Meeting of Representatives of Institutions and Experimental Schools Concerned with Second Language Teaching in Primary Education—Research and Development, Hamburg, 1966 (London: Oxford University Press, 1969), p. 63.

166. J. L. Hayman, Jr., and J. T. Johnson, *Audio-Lingual Results in the Second Year of Research,* 1961-62 (Stanford, Calif.: Institute for Communication and Research, Stanford University, 1963).

167. R. Garry, and E. Mauriello, *Summary of Research on 'Parlons Francais,' Year Two* (Boston: Massachusetts Council for Public Schools, Inc., 1961).

such approaches, except as occasional diversions.[168] More important is the feedback to the student which conveys information about meaningful content and grammatical structure.[169] These conclusions are consistent with the self-reports of FLES students concerning their perceptions of elementary foreign language instruction. Elementary students who elect FLES approach it from the standpoint of acquiring competency, not as a diversion.[170]

If a community is interested in serious foreign language instruction, it is preferable that the language chosen be one which is spoken in the community. This has the advantage of providing a source for a native speaker of the language, as well as an opportunity for children to hear the language as a living means of communication. FLES teaching typically utilizes the spoken approach, in which patterns are introduced and practiced until they become automatic. Intonation and rhythm of the models should always be that of an educated native speaker. While English should be used sparingly in a FLES class, it is always appropriate to use it to clarify vocabulary meaning. When vocabulary meaning is not clear, children acquire facility in exercises which have no meaning. But in the early stages of language teaching, rules of grammar have little place; once patterns have been established, as with tenses, rules may be generalized from inflections and the context of the sentence.

Teachers and parents interested in elementary foreign language learning will find it desirable to contact the Modern Language Association of America[171] for assistance. The major prerequisites in a foreign language program are good methods of instruction and continuity. If continuity cannot be maintained, it is wasteful of time and money to teach a foreign language in the elementary school.

Cumulative Nature of the Language Arts

The language arts deals with the many different facets of written and oral language. In some ways, it has a distinctive subject matter, as in the appreciation of literature or poetry. Most of the time, however, the language arts does not function as a distinctive subject area but as a tool to assist in the communication skills. These communication skills range from the informality of a thank you note or telephone invitation to the formality of an expository essay or prepared address, depending on the age of the learner and the variance in purpose. Since language is used in all subjects—on the playground and gym as well as in science and English classes—teachers of all subjects in the elementary school need to be concerned about the use of language. Using language more efficiently and effectively for communication is an important aid to increasing knowledge.

Occasionally, attempts are made to identify a structure for the language arts, as with subject matter areas. When this is done, the results are not fortunate. The "structure" usually is merely an outline of English grammar or a description of the kinds of reading materials and writing activities a student is expected to engage in. An alternative is the listing of learning experiences in which students engage, as shown in Figure 11.1.

168. For example, see Margit W. MacRae, *Teaching Spanish in the Grades* (Boston: Houghton Mifflin Company, 1957).
169. Carroll, "Psychological and Educational Research."
170. Bourgue, *The FLES Student*.
171. The address is: 4 Washington Place, New York, N.Y. 10001.

Oral Language

	K	1	2	3	4	5	6
Auditory discrimination	*	*					
Appreciative or recreational listening	*	*	*	*	*	*	*
Informational listening							
To develop correct speech	*	*	*	*	*	*	*
To follow directions	*	*	*	*	*	*	*
To find out "why"	*	*	*	*	*	*	*
To answer specific questions	*	*	*	*			
To find new interests, information							
Critical listening		*	*	*	*	*	*
To determine accuracy					*	*	*
To determine authenticity				*	*	*	*
To detect bias					*	*	*
Conducting interviews					*	*	*
Use of voice, articulation, pronunciation	*	*	*	*	*	*	*
Language usage	*	*	*	*	*	*	*
Conversation	*	*	*	*	*	*	*
Discussion		*	*	*	*	*	*
Relaying messages, announcements			*	*	*	*	*
Giving directions and explanations			*	*	*	*	*
Social courtesies	*	*	*	*	*	*	*
Telephoning	*	*	*	*	*	*	*
News reporting				*	*	*	*
Other reporting			*	*	*	*	*
Storytelling			*	*	*	*	*
Choral speaking	*	*	*	*	*	*	*
Dramatic play	*						
Creative dramatics		*	*	*	*	*	*
Formal dramatization				*	*	*	*
Appraising oral expression			*	*	*	*	*

Written Language

	K	1	2	3	4	5	6
Alphabet and alphabetizing skills	*	*	*	*	*	*	*
Dictionary use		*	*	*	*	*	*
Spelling		*	*	*	*	*	*
Capitalization and punctuation			*	*	*	*	*
Use of abbreviations					*	*	*
Syllabication	*		*	*	*	*	*
Learning parts of speech		*	*	*	*	*	*
Proofreading, using correction symbols					*	*	*
Writing names, labels	*						
Recognizing and writing sentences		*	*	*	*	*	*
Writing paragraphs				*	*	*	*
Dictating creative expression to teacher	*	*					
Writing composite (cooperative) stories		*	*	*	*	*	*
Informal and creative writing		*	*	*	*	*	*
Letter writing		*	*	*	*	*	*
Recording information					*	*	*
Other functional writing					*	*	*
Outlining					*	*	*
Reference activities, note-taking					*	*	*
Handwriting							
Manuscript printing		*	*	*	*		
Cursive writing				*	*	*	*

Fig. 11.1. Sequence of Learning Experiences in Oral Language and in Written Language. From: John U. Michaelis, Ruth H. Grossman, and Lloyd F. Scott, **New Designs in the Elementary School Curriculum** (New York: McGraw-Hill Book Company, 1967), pp. 74-75.

An examination of Figure 11.1 indicates that the language arts curriculum does not consist of certain topics which are studied only at a particular grade level, but that most language arts experiences begin in the primary grades and continue throughout the elementary school. The particular grade placements are merely illustrative. Thus some children may profitably learn to listen critically to detect bias or to syllabify before the grade indicated. Certainly most students do not need to wait until the third grade to write in paragraphs. Figure 11.1 is a useful summary, however, of many of the oral and written components of the language arts program.

An Appraisal of Language Arts Instruction

The language arts is a broad and demanding curriculum area. It is so broad that elementary teachers frequently overlook the need to plan for specific learning experiences in various aspects of the language arts, a tendency sometimes reinforced by broad field rather than subjects-in-isolation curriculum patterns (see chapter 4). Thus in planning language arts experiences, it is desirable that the lesson plan include allocations of time and specific experiences in the diverse facets of the language arts, such as listening, speaking, spelling, writing, reading, interpreting, and creative dramatics. If a foreign language is offered, specific additional time allocations are required. Teaching of a foreign language cannot merely be absorbed into the regular time allocated to language arts in the English language.

The training of most elementary teachers in the language arts is general rather than specific, and few teachers are trained to have the performance skills needed for such diverse fields as dialect training, dramatization, and teaching a foreign language. Consequently, one of the first demands of a language arts teacher is to assess the needs of the children he is teaching and his particular skills at being able to meet those needs. Few of us can do all things well, and it is more desirable to arrange with fellow teachers, when possible, some division of labor to permit attention to the more pressing priorities, such as teaching English as a second language in schools where there are large numbers of non-English speaking children. In some circumstances, creative dramatics might be used as a tool to elicit language growth and expression. If a teacher has no flair for dramatics but is nevertheless an excellent teacher with TESL, it is desirable that he concentrate his efforts on those aspects of language arts in which he can produce results. It is better to do a few things well than it is to try to do everything—some of it poorly.

Language arts offers to teachers opportunities for continuous personal and intellectual growth, owing to the fact that in this area teachers can make so many choices which help them to meet their own needs while helping children to learn and grow intellectually. Whereas in science, mathematics and social studies, teachers tend to expect the gradual development of a sequence of skills and knowledge, there is less subject matter emphasis in the language arts. We wish to help children appreciate poetry and literature, but what a rich fare, almost without end, awaits the teacher. Here the teacher does not have to read and reread the same selections, but can choose from the many alternatives which abound in literature. Teachers can make a point of working in a cycle of readings; in this way they can bring a freshness to their own interpretations. Literary selections too often repeated by a teacher tend to become stereotyped—the teacher only perceiving and becoming immersed in his own interpretation, rather than the many views which children bring with their different backgrounds of experience.

The same is true of writing. Certainly, there are certain kinds of writing needed for utilitarian ends and the art of clear explanation is always prized, whether it is how to sew on a button or make a model airplane. Teachers will find that writing is never dull, if they have the wit to devise many new situations and experiences which stimulate thought. The reason that writing is often neglected is not only because of the chore of reading and grading, but because teachers themselves do not enjoy writing. Now it is rather useless to assume that a teacher who finds writing a dull job will stimulate enthusiasm in his class. Under such conditions the time might be more profitably spent in something children and teacher mutually enjoy.

Many teachers assume that the only way to correct writing is by the laborious task of individual review. Papers may be critiqued in class, and often the criticism of classmates, especially in the higher grades, can be more relentless than that of the teacher. Even elements of usage can be corrected, and sometimes the tyranny of peers is more effective in approaching standards than the admonitions of the teacher. Such a situation, however, demands a standard clearly in the majority. In most cases, imitation tends to follow corrupt rather than correct models, unless a class itself can articulate a sense of correctness.

Where an elementary teacher is in a self-contained classroom, it is possible to allocate language arts activities to other subject areas. Thus in a hypothetical day students might write an account of their observations in a science class; make verbal reports in a social studies class; and use committee discussions to plan art projects. Each of these situations lend themselves to different language emphasis, but they all contribute to language growth.

Use and development of language as a tool always requires more care and planning than the use of language as a subject, as outlined in an "English" course. The danger of such an approach to language arts is that the emphasis might be transferred to a subject, and the opportunities for language arts teaching throughout the day in many different aspects is neglected. Moreover, the typical English curriculum begins formal grammar instruction too early. Let us teach children how to speak and write words. There is time for parts of speech later.

Selected References

Anderson, Paul S. *Language Skills in Elementary Education.* New York: Macmillan Company, 1964.

Allen, Harold B., ed. *Readings in Applied English Linguistics.* Second edition; New York: Appleton-Century-Crofts, 1964.

Burns, Paul C., and Lowe, Alberta L. *The Language Arts in Childhood Education.* Chicago: Rand McNally & Company, 1966.

Lamb, Pose, ed. *Guiding Children's Language Learning.* Dubuque, Iowa: Wm. C. Brown Company Publishers, 1967.

MOFFETT, JAMES. *A Student-Centered Language Arts Curriculum, Grades K-13: A Handbook for Teachers.* Boston: Houghton Mifflin Company, 1968.

National Society for the Study of Education. *Linguistics in School Programs,* Sixty-ninth Yearbook, part II, edited by Albert H. Marckwardt. Chicago: University of Chicago Press, 1970.

PETTY, WALTER T., ed. *Issues and Problems in the Elementary Language Arts.* Boston: Allyn and Bacon, Inc., 1968.

STRICKLAND, RUTH G. *The Language Arts in the Elementary School.* 3d ed. Lexington, Mass.: D. C. Heath and Company, 1969.

THOMAS, OWEN. *Transformational Grammar and the Teacher of English.* New York: Holt, Rinehart and Winston, Inc., 1965.

TIEDT, IRIS M., and TIEDT, SIDNEY W. *Contemporary English in the Elementary School.* Englewood Cliffs, N.J.: Prentice-Hall, Inc., 1967.

TIEDT, IRIS M., and TIEDT, SIDNEY W., eds. *Readings on Contemporary English in the Elementary School.* Englewood Cliffs, N.J.: Prentice-Hall, Inc., 1967.

12 teaching mathematics

Prior to 1957, the arithmetic program in the first six grades of the elementary school consisted largely of teaching the fundamental operations of addition, subtraction, multiplication, and division, with integers and rational numbers. This teaching attempted to give children a rudimentary skill in the basic fundamentals of arithmetic. Since 1957, there has been a concerted effort to prepare children mathematically for the conditions which they confront in living in the highly technological Space Age.[1]

As a result, the curriculum has changed. In addition to fundamental operations, elementary mathematics now includes such topics as sets, nondecimal numeration systems, exponents, algebra, and geometry. This infusion of new content is intended to promote better pupil understanding. Consequently, it is no longer proper to view mathematics in the elementary school as merely arithmetic. Beginning algebra and geometry, formerly restricted to high school mathematics, are presently being taught to some extent in the new elementary mathematics.[2]

There are many new mathematics curricula which have been and are being developed as departures from the traditional arithmetic program of the first half of the century.

New Mathematics Curricula

Four of the nationally known mathematics curricula developed since 1957 are the School Mathematics Study Group (SMSG), Greater Cleveland Mathematics Program, the Stanford Project, and the Educational Services Arithmetic Project. A brief discussion of these new curriculum materials follows.[3]

SMSG Program Materials. In all probability, the SMSG materials have influenced

---

1. David Rappaport, *Understanding and Teaching Elementary School Mathematics* (New York: John Wiley & Sons, Inc., 1966), pp. 2-3.
2. Ibid.
3. See: M. Vere De Vault, "New Mathematics in Elementary Schools," in *New Directions in Mathematics* (Washington, D.C.: Association for Childhood Education International, 1965), pp. 12-14; Edwina Deans, *Elementary School Mathematics: New Directions* (Washington, D.C.: U.S. Office of Education, 1963). *New Mathematics* (Washington, D.C.: National Council of Teachers of Mathematics, 1963).

the new elementary mathematics curriculum more than any other. The SMSG effort was supported by a grant from the National Science Foundation. The SMSG writing teams consist of teachers, supervisors of mathematics, mathematicians, and mathematics educators and work primarily under the leadership of Stanford University's Professor E. G. Begle. Beginning in 1959, these writing teams developed new mathematics materials for grades K-6.

Some of the topics included in the SMSG kindergarten and primary grade materials include: sets, geometric shapes, fundamental operations, linear measurements, length and area, and sets of points. Sets, numeration systems, geometry, measurement, ratio, exponents, factors and prime numbers, and the fundamental operations are included in the SMSG materials for the fourth, fifth, and sixth grades.[4]

Greater Cleveland Mathematics Program. Through the Greater Cleveland Educational Research Council, public school educators in Cleveland have cooperated with local business and industries to develop mathematics materials for grades 1-6. Major topics included in the materials of the Cleveland project are: exploration and discovery, systems of numbers and numerals, sets, mathematical sentences, measurement, functions, geometry, statistics, and logic.[5]

Stanford Project. Professor Patrick Suppes at Stanford University has developed three elementary mathematics programs. *Sets and Numbers* for grades K-6 includes units on sets, set operations, and numbers.

Geometry for Primary Grades teaches geometry through the medium of geometric constructions. Use of protractors, compasses, and rulers are stressed to construct angles, equilateral triangles, and other geometric shapes.

Mathematical Logic for the upper elementary grades introduces students to principles of logical relations.[6]

Educational Services Arithmetic Project. Materials covering such topics as whole numbers, fractions, integers, exponents, equations, functions and the commutative, associative, and distributive laws have been developed under the leadership of Professor David Page who formerly was associated with the University of Illinois. The materials are not designated for any grade level. Teachers may select appropriate materials from the project for classroom use in terms of the abilities and instructional needs of their pupils. The major thrust of these materials is to present content which will increase student interest in and understanding of mathematics through discovery and intuition.

This project has greatly influenced the use of *frames*, e.g. $\Box + 2 = 5$, in the development of the newer mathematics curriculum materials. Max Beberman's work at the University of Illinois was largely instrumental in this movement. In the fore-

---

4. *School Mathematics Study Group* (Stanford, California: Stanford University, School of Education—E. G. Begle, Director).

5. *Greater Cleveland Mathematics Program* (Educational Research Council of Greater Cleveland—George Cunningham, Director).

6. *Experimental Teaching of Mathematics in the Elementary School* (Stanford, California: Institute for Mathematical Studies in the Social Sciences, Stanford University—Patrick Suppes, Director).

See also Patrick Suppes and Shirley Hill, *First Course in Mathematical Logic* (New York: Blaisdell Publishing Company, 1964); Newton Hawley and Patrick Suppes, *Geometry for Primary Grades* (San Francisco: Halden-Day, Inc., 1961).

going illustration, ☐ is the placeholder for the numeral 3.[7]

Scope and Sequence of Mathematics

The scope and sequence in the more recent mathematics programs for the elementary school can be seen in Figure 12.1 as outlined by Michaelis and others. A perusal of it will provide a basic understanding of what the curriculum in mathematics is for the elementary school.

[7]. *Arithmetic Project* (Watertown, Massachusetts, Educational Services Incorporated—David Page, Director). Note: This project was formerly known as the University of Illinois Arithmetic Project.

	K	1	2	3	4	5	6
Set and set operations							
Equal sets, subsets, empty sets, union, separation	. x x	x x x	x x x	— — —	— — —	— — —	— — —
Notation, symbols, terminology	.	. x x	x x —	— — —	— — —	— — —	— — —
Finite and infinite sets			. . .	x x x	x x x	— — —
Number and numeration							
Cardinal numbers as properties of sets	. . x	x x x	x — —	— — —	— — —	— — —	— — —
Ordinal numbers	. .	. . x	x x x	x — —	— — —	— — —	— — —
Recognition and reproduction of collections	. . x	x x x	x x x	x — —	— — —	— — —	— — —
Frames, numerals	. . .	. x x	x x x	x x x	x x	x x x	x x x
Use of number line		. . x	x x x	x x x	x x x	x x x	x x x
Concept of 10 and 100	.	. . x	x x x	— — —	— — —	— — —
Uses of zero	.	. . x	x x x	x x —	— — —	— — —	— — —
Understanding millions				. . x	x x x	x x x	x x x
Roman numerals				. . x	x x x	x x x	x x x
Place value		. . x	x x x	x x x	x x x	x x x	x — —
Nondecimal bases						. . x	x x x
Positive and negative integers					. . .	. x x	x x x
Approximate numbers					. . .	. x x	x x x
Exponential notation						. .	. x x
Fractions: 1/2	. . x	x x x	x x —	— — —	— — —	— — —	— — —
1/3, 1/4	. .	. x x	x x x	x x x	— — —	— — —	— — —
1/5, 1/6, 1/8		. .	. . .	x x x	x x x	— — —	— — —
Decimal fractions notation				. .	. . x	x x x	x x x
Operations							
One-to-one correspondence	. . x	x x x	x x x	— — —	— — —	— — —	— — —
Rote and rational counting	. . x	x x x	— — —	— — —	— — —	— — —	— — —
Counting by 2s, 5s, 10s, etc.		. x x	. x x	x x x	— — —	— — —	— — —
Addition	. . .	. x x	x x x	x x x	x x x	x x x	x — —
Subtraction	. . .	. x x	x x x	x x x	x x x	x x x	x — —
Multiplication	.	. . .	. x x	x x x	x x x	x x x	x x x

Note: Dots indicate periods of readiness.
Cross marks indicate instruction and development.
Dashes indicate levels of reinforcement or mastery.

Fig. 12.1. Scope and Sequence of Topics in Elementary School Mathematics. From John U. Michaelis, Ruth H. Grossman, and Lloyd F. Scott, **New Designs for the Elementary School Curriculum** (New York: McGraw-Hill Book Company, Inc., 1967), pp. 176-77.

teaching mathematics 237

	K	1	2	3	4	5	6
Division	.	. . .	. x x	x x x	x x x	x x x	x x x
Generalization of properties of operations	.	. . .	x x x	x x x	x x x	x x x	x x x
Number sentences		. . x	x x x	x x x	x x x	x x x	x x x
Operations upon rational numbers					. . x	x x x	x x x

Relations

	K	1	2	3	4	5	6
Comparison vocabulary and symbols	. . .	. x x	x x x	x x x	x x x	x x x	x x x
Use of graphs		. . x	x x x	x x x	x x x	x x x	x x x
Use of scale drawings				.	. . .	x x x	x x x
Ratio					. . .	. x x	x x x
Per cent						. . .	x x x

Measurement

	K	1	2	3	4	5	6
Time of day, use of calendar	. . x	x x x	x x x	x x x	x x x	- - -	- - -
Measurement: temperature, weight, volume, linear	. . x	x x x	x x x	x x x	x x x	x x x	x x x
Standard units	.	. . x	x x x	x x x	x x x	x x x	x - -
Monetary units		. x x	x x x	x x x	x - -	- - -	- - -
Surface and volume measurement				.	. . x	x x x	x x x
Estimation, error interval					. . .	x x x	x x x

Geometry

	K	1	2	3	4	5	6
Recognition of two-dimensional shapes	. . x	x x x	x x x	x x x	x x x	x x x	x x x
Understanding points, lines, planes	. .	. . .	. x x	x x x	x x x	x x x	x x x
Recognition of solid figures	.	. . .	. x x	x x x	x x x	x x x	x x x
Rays, angles, properties of circles		.	. . .	. x x	x x x	x x x	x x x
Perimeter, area, volume				. . .	. x x	x x x	x x x

Proof or Verification:

	K	1	2	3	4	5	6
Using experience, concrete materials	. . .	. x x	x x x	x - -	- - -	- - -	- - -
Using counting, number line		. x x	x x x	x x x	- - -	- - -	- - -
Using inverse operations		. .	. x x	x x x	x x x	x x x	x - -
Using estimation		. . .	. . .	. x x	x x x	x x x	x x -
Using alternative procedures			. .	. . x	x x x	x x x	x x x
Using logical reasoning				. . .	. . .	x x x	x x x

Fig. 12.1. (Cont'd)

Purposes of Mathematics Instruction

There have been many objectives advanced for instruction in traditional elementary school arithmetic. Basically, they can be reduced to three in number. They include teaching children: (1) the meanings of number facts and processes, (2) the number facts and processes, and (3) how to apply the number facts and processes to life or lifelike situations.[8]

One can find several helpful lists of purposes for the newer elementary school math-

8. Wilbur H. Dutton, and L. J. Adams, *Arithmetic for Teachers* (Englewood Cliffs, N.J.: Prentice-Hall, Inc., 1961), p. 6.

ematics program.[9] It appears that there are about four major objectives for mathematics instruction in elementary school: (1) to develop mathematical concepts, (2) to master mathematical knowledge, (3) to develop mathematical skills, and (4) to develop an appreciation for mathematics. A brief discussion of these objectives follows.

To Develop Mathematical Concepts. It is extremely important in the teaching of elementary school mathematics to develop clear concepts about such topics as sets, number, operation and the like. For example, children can see the need for learning about the set of rational numbers if they clearly understand the concept of closure. In closure, the sets of numbers are closed under certain operations. To illustrate, the set of whole numbers is *closed* under addition and multiplication. Take addition with whole numbers as a case in point: when any two whole numbers are added, the sum is a whole number. An illustration of how the closure concept could be presented is as follows:

The foregoing illustration shows that if one wishes to make any desired division (excluding division by zero) he must have the set of rational numbers, which includes the whole numbers and integers as proper subsets, since the set of rational numbers is closed under the four fundamental operations. A clear understanding of the concept of closure therefore helps the child comprehend the relationships which exist between the sets of whole numbers, integers, and rational numbers and the fundamental operations that are always possible within each set. Such understandings contribute towards his comprehension of the basic structure of mathematics.

9. See: E. Glenadine Gibb, "Basic Objectives of the Program," in *New Directions in Mathematics* (Washington, D.C.: Association for Childhood Educational International, 1965), pp. 17-21; Esther J. Swenson, *Teaching Arithmetic to Children* (New York: Macmillan Company, 1964), pp. 14-18; John L. Marks et al., *Teaching Elementary School Mathematics for Understanding* 2d ed. (New York: McGraw-Hill Book Co., 1965), pp. 33-37; Frances Flournoy, *Elementary School Mathematics* (New York: The Center for Applied Research in Education, Inc., 1964), chap. 1.

Set of Numbers	Concept of Closure Closed under:	Illustration of Concept
WHOLE NUMBERS $\{0, 1, 2, 3 \ldots\}$	Addition Multiplication	$4 + 5 = 9$ $4 \times 5 = 20$
INTEGERS $\{\ldots\ ^-3,\ ^-2,\ ^-1,$ $0,\ ^+1,\ ^+2,\ ^+3 \ldots\}$	Addition Multiplication Subtraction	$4 + 5 = 9$ $4 \times 5 = 20$ $4 - 5 = {^-1}$
RATIONAL $\{\ldots\ ^-1/1,\ ^-3/4,$ $^-1/2,\ ^-1/4,\ 0/1,\ ^+1/4,$ $^+1/2,\ ^+3/4,\ ^+1/1 \ldots\}$	Addition Multiplication Subtraction Division	$4 + 5 = 9$ $4 \times 5 = 20$ $4 - 5 = {^-1}$ $4 \div 5 = .80$

To Master Mathematical Knowledge. Modern mathematics in the elementary school still emphasizes the mastery of certain mathematical facts. The mastery of such knowledge is preceded by building readiness, clearly presenting and explaining the concept or concepts involved, and checking on comprehension. Once these crucial aspects have been expressed concretely, selected facts, such as the multiplication tables through 9, can be mastered and internalized.

To Develop Mathematical Skills. Another objective of mathematics instruction in elementary school is the development of mathematical skills, such as logical reasoning, computation, checking computations for accuracy, and measuring and constructing. A viable instructional program in mathematics provides opportunities for the child to apply his skills to the solution of problems.

Becoming a good problem solver implies more than knowing which operation to perform or being skillful in making computations. It involves gathering and interpreting data, recognizing the relevance or irrelevance of data, and being able to use tables and graphs.[10] Much of the newer mathematics materials for the elementary school has been designed to develop problem solving skills.

Extremely important among the skills objectives is the development of the child's ability to engage in intuitive and analytical thinking. Optimal opportunities need to be provided in which children are encouraged to discover, to verify, and to generalize. In illustrating this point, recall the example given earlier in this chapter about the concept of closure. If a child were to discover that there are some algorisms calling for the operation of division which cannot be computed in the sets of whole numbers and integers because they are not closed under division, he should verify his discovery. Once verified, he could generalize that any division algorism (excluding division by zero) can be worked within the set of rational numbers.

There are some deterents to intuitive and analytical thinking in mathematics about which the mathematics teacher should be knowledgeable. Some of these deterents include excessive drill, repetition, memorizing, and learning by rote.

To Develop an Appreciation for Mathematics. One of the major purposes of mathematics instruction is to help the child learn how mathematics can be used to solve his own daily problems. He must be able to use quantitative language. Such elementary terms as *bigger* and *smaller,* and *half-past ten* are quantitative terms necessary in communicating with others.

Counting members on a ball team, making change, and using a recipe are three simple examples of how mathematics serves a child in his every day living. More sophisticated applications can be made to bookkeeping, computer technology, and engineering. The many scientific discoveries of the modern age, including such technological breakthroughs as space flight, would be impossible without mathematics. Many preliterate cultures remained simple cultures not only because of the lack of writing, but because of the lack of mathematical concepts more sophisticated than rudimentary counting. Mathematics is the handmaiden of science.

10. J. Houston Banks, *Learning and Teaching Arithmetic* 2d ed. (Boston: Allyn and Bacon, Inc., 1964), p. 15.

Approaches in Teaching Mathematics

The approaches employed in teaching elementary school mathematics have gone through at least three distinct stages in the twentieth century.[11] The first of these, during the 1900s preceding 1925, was the *drill* emphasis or "mental discipline" period. The theory underlying such teaching was to make the problems difficult and the processes complex in order to "train the minds of the pupils and teach them how to think." Shipp and Adams have given the following characteristic problem out of one of the old mental discipline arithmetic books: "Change .821437437 . . . to a common fraction."[12] The answer is 102577/124875. Typically, drill was emphasized in the arithmetic class and little explanation was offered concerning the meaning of number facts and processes. Children learned by rote in which they identified the individual elements of an operation and mastered it through the medium of drill. It is little wonder that many children as well as adults of the time were not mathematically literate.

Prompted by the Progressive Education Movement in the 1920s and 1930s, the social aspects of arithmetic began to be emphasized. This second approach was known as the *incidental* or activity approach in which children in modern child-centered schools learned arithmetic incidentally through unit teaching in the activity programs. This unsystematic and unstructured teaching of arithmetic rapidly waned. By 1935 the third approach—the *meaning* approach—was initiated. The meaning approach predominates in modern elementary school mathematics.

Research since the initiation of the meaning approach has shown that teaching the meaning of number facts and processes leads to pupil retention for a longer period of time. Also, it has shown that such teaching results in greater transfer potential and ability to solve problems independently.[13]

Let us illustrate the utility of the meaning approach in teaching elementary school mathematics with an algorism ($\frac{1}{2} \div \frac{1}{8}$) involving the division of common fractions.[14] For years, many elementary school children have not clearly understood division of common fractions. The reason for this was that they were simply given a rule: "In dividing common fractions, invert the terms of the divisor and proceed as in multiplication." The question was: "Why?" Why invert the terms of the divisor and multiply? Children could see the "how" when taught by the drill method but few of them were able to understand the "why."

Presently, this operation (the division of common fractions) is taught in a meaningful way by using, for example, the idea of *reciprocal*. A reciprocal of a given number is a number by which the given number must be multiplied to yield a product of 1. For example, the reciprocal of $\frac{1}{2}$ is $\frac{2}{1}$ because $\frac{1}{2} \times \frac{2}{1} = 1$.

To give the "why" of the rule mentioned above in working the algorism $\frac{1}{2} \div \frac{1}{8}$, two principles must be reviewed with the children. First, that when both the numerator and denominator of a fraction are multiplied by the same number, the value of the fraction is unchanged, to wit: $\frac{1}{2} \times \frac{2}{2} = \frac{2}{4} = \frac{1}{2}$. Second, 1 is the identity element of division, e.g., $2 \div 1 = 2$.

11. Dutton and Adams, *Arithmetic for Teachers,* pp. 4-5.
12. Joseph Ray, *New Higher Arithmetic* (New York: American Book Co.), p. 119.
13. Dutton and Adams, *Arithmetic for Teachers,* p. 5.
14. Charles F. Howard and Enoch Dumas, *Basic Procedures in Teaching Arithmetic* (Boston: D. C. Heath and Company, 1963), pp. 256-57.

Having reviewed these two principles which the children will have previously learned, the teacher can use the chalkboard to show that it may be written as a compound fraction:

$$\tfrac{1}{2} \div \tfrac{1}{8} = \frac{\tfrac{1}{2}}{\tfrac{1}{8}}$$

He can then show how to change the denominator of the compound fraction to 1 by multiplying it by its reciprocal. However, he must remind the children of the compensation principal reviewed earlier: "When both the numerator and denominator of a fraction are multiplied by the same number, the value of the fraction is unchanged." Therefore, the numerator must also be multiplied by the denominator's reciprocal as follows:

$$\tfrac{1}{2} \div \tfrac{1}{8} = \frac{\tfrac{8}{1} \times \tfrac{1}{2}}{\tfrac{8}{1} \times \tfrac{1}{8}}$$

The teacher can then demonstrate to the children that the denominator of the compound fraction now equals 1 as follows:

$$\tfrac{1}{2} \div \tfrac{1}{8} = \frac{\tfrac{8}{1} \times \tfrac{1}{2}}{\tfrac{8}{1} \times \tfrac{1}{8}} = \frac{\tfrac{8}{1} \times \tfrac{1}{2}}{1}$$

The next step for the teacher is to invoke the second principle reviewed prior to working the algorism (1 is the identity element of division and, hence, when a number is divided by 1 its value remains unchanged) and then work the next step in the algorism thusly:

$$\tfrac{1}{2} \div \tfrac{1}{8} = \frac{\tfrac{8}{1} \times \tfrac{1}{2}}{\tfrac{8}{1} \times \tfrac{1}{8}}$$
$$= \frac{\tfrac{8}{1} \times \tfrac{1}{2}}{1}$$
$$= \tfrac{8}{1} \times \tfrac{1}{2}$$

The teacher could point out to the children that in the last computation above that $\tfrac{1}{2} \div \tfrac{1}{8} = \tfrac{8}{1} \times \tfrac{1}{2}$ and, by the commutative law of multiplication (the product of two numbers is not affected when their order is reversed), $\tfrac{8}{1} \times \tfrac{1}{2} = \tfrac{1}{2} \times \tfrac{8}{1}$. Thus, in this algorism, to divide a fraction ($\tfrac{1}{2}$) by the given fraction $\tfrac{1}{8}$ is the same as multiplying $\tfrac{1}{2}$ by $\tfrac{8}{1}$, the reciprocal of the fraction $\tfrac{1}{8}$.

When the children understand that $\tfrac{1}{2} \div \tfrac{1}{8} = \tfrac{8}{1} \times \tfrac{1}{2}$, as shown above, and when they apply the commutative order principle to the algorism; that is, $\tfrac{8}{1} \times \tfrac{1}{2} = \tfrac{1}{2} \times \tfrac{8}{1}$, they can then understand the "why" of the "invert and multiply" rule. At this point, they are, in fact, ready for the "invert and multiply" rule since it provides them a "short cut" in computation, i.e., $\tfrac{1}{2} \div \tfrac{1}{8} = \tfrac{1}{2} \times \tfrac{8}{1} = \tfrac{8}{2} = 4$. One major shortcoming of the *drill* approach during the first quarter of the twentieth century was that it provided children with too many "short cuts," thereby circumventing meaning.

In reality, a combination of all three approaches is considered to be the best, rather than any one individually.[15] That is, children certainly need to understand the meaning (the *why*) of the number facts and processes initially. So equipped, they are ready to do necessary drill (*the how*) for mastery. Finally, such quantitative learnings are reinforced through incidental classroom and social usage.

Presently, there are two methods being widely used in *meaningful* mathematics teaching in the elementary school. They include inductive and deductive discovery methods. Let us briefly examine how each of these contributes to the meaning approach to mathematics instruction which has been in vogue since it was initiated around 1935.

Inductive Discovery. Teaching the meaning of mathematics by inductive discovery is

---

15. Dutton and Adams, *Arithmetic for Teachers,* p. 5.

that strategy whereby the child is encouraged to use different bits of related factual information to formulate a generalization. One can illustrate inductive discovery easily by returning to the concept of closure alluded to earlier in this chapter. Let us say that the child has five related factual bits of information in algorism form according to the following.

SET OF NUMBERS	ALGORISM
Whole Numbers $\{0, 1, 2, 3 \ldots\}$	1. 4 $+5$ $\overline{9}$
Integers $\{\ldots -3, -2, -1, 0, +1, +2, +3 \ldots\}$	2. $+4$ $+ +5$ $\overline{+9}$
	3. $+4$ $+ -5$ $\overline{-1}$
Rational Numbers $\{\ldots -\frac{1}{1}, -\frac{3}{4}, -\frac{1}{2}$ $\%_1, +\frac{1}{4}, +\frac{1}{2}, +\frac{3}{4},$ $+\frac{1}{1} \ldots\}$	4. $+4$ $+ +5$ $\overline{+9}$
	5. $+4$ $+ -5$ $\overline{-1}$

From the above factual information, the child can generalize about the law of closure (perhaps on his own or with teacher guidance) that for every pair of numbers $(a + b)$ within each set of numbers, i.e., whole, integers, and rational, there exists a unique number $(a + b)$ which is called the sum of a and b.

In short, inductive discovery is going from the specific to the general. The teacher who is adept in utilizing inductive teaching perceives his role as that of a guider of learning.

Deductive Discovery. The inverse of inductive discovery is deductive discovery; that is, moving from the general to the specific. When this teaching strategy is applied to teaching mathematics meaningfully, the teacher presents a rule or law. An example of a rule was suggested in the preceding section on *inductive discovery,* to wit: "for every pair of numbers $(a + b)$ within each set of numbers, i.e., whole, integers, and rational, there exists a unique number $(a + b)$ which is called the sum of a and b." The child would then take this rule and discover its applications, as in the five algorisms outlined in the preceding section of this chapter.

Deductive discovery teaching, therefore, is more closed or tightly structured than is the inductive strategy. A number of factors will impinge upon which strategy to use in the classroom, such as which method the teacher personally feels more comfortable with and which one serves to meet the pupil needs better. For example, it will be suggested in chapter 23 that culturally disadvantaged children normally achieve more in highly structured or closed learning situations.

Obviously, the teacher will want to use both the inductive and deductive strategies in teaching from time to time. His judgment will dictate when each strategy is called for in meaningful teaching. The main thing he should be cautious of in selecting appropriate teaching strategies is to avoid an overuse of the *telling* technique. This is not to suggest that there are not times when he will *tell* his pupils certain information which is arbitrary but unchanging such as the names of the elements of the various sets of numbers.

Planning Effectual Mathematics Lessons

There are some common sense procedures that the elementary school teacher of mathematics can use in planning his lessons. Broadly, the lessons should begin with the meaning phase, proceed to drill for mastery, and then provide opportunities for applying what has been learned to life and life-like situations. Marks, Purdy, and Kinney have suggested an exemplary five point guide for planning lessons, as can be seen in figure 12.2, which cares for the three points mentioned above: (1) meaning, (2) drill,

STEP	PURPOSE	ACTIVITIES	MATERIALS
1 Preparation	To provide readiness, both subject-matter —including prerequisite skills, vocabulary, and concepts —and interest.	A checkup—formal or informal—on prerequisite skills and vocbulary.	Tests, if necessary, teacher-made or commercial. Models, real objects, and other learning aids as necessary.
2 Exploration and discovery	To lead the pupil to develop the concept (or operation) as a solution to a problem situation.	Presenting a stimulating problem situation requiring improvisation of the process, concept, or operation as a means of solution.	Learning aids as needed to provide the setting. Materials as required for manipulation in exploratory activities.
3 Abstraction and organization	To develop an understanding of the nature of the operation (or concept) and its interrelationship with other operations.	Development of generalizations about the operation (or concept) and its interrelationships to others.	Textbooks and semi-symbolic manipulative materials.
4 Fixing skills	To make manipulation of the operation automatic, and to provide overlearning to assure retention.	Memorization of facts, organization and memorization of tables, repetitive practice with the operation.	Textbooks, practice materials, tests.
5 Application	To promote transfer of training by developing ability to recognize the typical situations calling for use of the operation (or concept).	Experience in application to a variety of situations, with emphasis on identifying the appropriate situations.	Life and simulated problem situations; models, visual aids, textbooks, bulletin boards.

Fig. 12.2. Flow Chart of the Learning Sequence. From: John L. Marks, C. Richard Purdy, and Lucien B. Kinney, **Teaching Elementary School Mathematics for Understanding**, 2d ed. (New York: McGraw-Hill Book Company, 1965), p. 59.

and (3) application. Steps 1, 2, and 3 of their suggested guide adequately cover the meaning phase while step 4 provides the necessary drill and step 5 cares for the application of what has been learned in social usage situations.

In administering the lesson proper, there are four steps, i.e.: (1) social experience, (2) concrete manipulative, (3) visualization or semi-concrete, and (4) abstract, outlined by Dutton and Adams for the teacher to use when appropriate.[16] Let us briefly examine each of these in teaching an addition algorism (3 + 2) at the first grade level.

The Social Experience Step. Normally, teaching is more effectual in mathematics if it proceeds from the simple to the complex. In teaching the 3 + 2 algorism at first grade level, the teacher might appropriately begin with a problem growing out of the social experiences of the children. For example, he might say to the class: "Suppose Bill had three softballs and Tom had two. How many would they have between them?" Thus, the social experience step which provides a period for readiness, as suggested in the Marks, Purdy, and Kinney model, has been established.

The Concrete Manipulative Step. If possible, the teacher might use five softballs from the playground equipment stock of the upper grades to let the children manipulate them and learn the concept of "threeness" and "twoness." From discussions in the concrete manipulative step the teacher could develop the number ideas of "three" and "two" and introduce the symbols or numerals "3" and "2" which represent or stand for the number ideas. This concrete manipulative step is basically equivalent to the exploration and discovery phase outlined by Marks, Purdy, and Kinney in figure 12.2.

Visualization or Semiconcrete Step. During this transitional step the teacher might let circles represent the baseballs and relate them to the numerals which express the number ideas on the chalkboard as shown in the example below.

This visualization or semiconcrete step can be equated with the abstraction and organization step depicted in figure 12.2.

The Abstract Step. In this step of administering the lesson, the teacher formally and abstractly structures the algorism (3 + 2) and has the children compute it. If necessary, the teacher can revert

16. Ibid., p. 8.

(Semiconcrete Step)

	Bill's Softballs:	Tom's Softballs:
Visualization of Semiconcrete Referent	◯◯◯	◯◯
Visualization of Numerals Representing Number Ideas	3	2

back to any preceding step in order to clarify meaning and move the children along to abstraction. This abstract step coincides with steps 4 and 5 suggested by Marks et al., as presented in figure 12.2.

Of course, all of the topics in elementary school, particularly many of those in the middle grades, do not yield themselves quite as well to the Dutton and Adams model just discussed as did the primary addition illustration. Wherever possible, however, mathematics teaching is likely to be more effectual if one works from the social experience step on one end of the continuum to the abstract step on the other.

Principles of Mathematics Instruction

There are a few fundamental principles of mathematics instruction that the teacher should keep in mind in his teaching. A brief discussion of five of the more important principles follows.

1. The teacher of mathematics is confronted with a wide range of individual differences extant among his pupils. Among sixth-graders, for example, it has been found that the range of pupil arithmetic achievement differences varies six or more years.[17] In meeting the diverse instructional needs in arithmetic, it is good pedagogical practice to form intraclass groups when necessary to further understanding, develop skills, master facts and the like. Generally, such groups should be created on a temporary basis in terms of the observed common instructional needs of certain children. In working on common needs among children, the teacher likely will be more effectual if he uses manipulative aids in conjunction with the printed mathematics materials.

2. In presenting mathematics concepts to children, three sequential steps are normally followed: (a) meaning, (b) drill, and (c) application. Children are more adept in learning mathematics if they first understand the "why" or meaning of a given concept or operation. Once the "why" is understood, they can then learn or internalize the "how" of a given operation through appropriate drill exercises. Finally, learning situations should be provided for children in which they apply the "why" and "how" to life or simulated life-like problem situations.

3. Generally, mathematics lessons are more effectual when they proceed from the simple to the complex. That is, the lesson begins with the presentation of a concept growing out of the social experiences of the children. The teacher, in moving to the abstract phase, then depicts the concept concretely and semiconcretely with some manipulative visual aids whenever possible. Of course, the most complex step, abstraction, is covered last in presenting the lesson.

4. Student learning in mathematics is facilitated when the teacher varies his teaching strategies appropriately. The three most common teaching strategies that the teacher will use includes explanation, induction, and deduction. There is a place for each strategy in the teaching of mathematics. For example, there are times when the teacher will use the explanation technique and provide the children with certain mathematical information to economize on time, such as the fact that we have a decimal or base of ten number system. Explanation should, however, be balanced with teacher use of the inductive and deductive techniques. A

---

17. Oscar T. Jarvis, "An Analysis of Individual Differences in Arithmetic," *The Arithmetic Teacher* 11, no. 7 (November 1964): 471-73.

perceptive teacher will know when each is called for in the day-to-day teaching task.

5. *Mathematics learning should be active for the pupils; not passive.* The use of inductive and deductive teaching and learning strategies in the mathematics classroom will insure the fact that students are active participants in the teaching-learning situation. An over-reliance by the teacher on explanation will automatically place the student in a more passive role. Generally, it is thought that active participation by the students in the mathematics teaching-learning situation promotes more effective learning.

An Appraisal of Teaching Mathematics

Teaching elementary school mathematics is a great challenge; it always has been—it always will be. This is particularly true with the infusion of the new math into the mathematics curriculum. Let us examine some of the reasons why the teaching of mathematics is presently a challenging task.

We live in a quantitative world and a highly technological culture. One cannot cope successfully with that world and culture if he is not mathematically literate. The beginning of mathematics literacy obviously begins in the home and in the child's subculture. But the elementary school mathematics program initiates the formal training designed to establish and extend mathematics literacy; thus the challenge to the elementary school teacher of mathematics. Not only is he teaching children to acquire a basic facility in mathematics upon which extended learning in high school, college, and graduate mathematics can be achieved, but he is also teaching them to become mathematically literate so they can become active and effectual participants or adults in the quantitative world of their technological culture.

As a teacher of mathematics, you are privileged to profit from the mistakes which teachers of mathematics made in former years. This point can be illustrated in a number of ways. First, we know that the best approach to use in teaching mathematics now is the meaning approach. This has been proven through trial and error with two approaches which preceded the meaning approach; the drill and incidental approaches. Second, we know that pupil learning in mathematics is facilitated if the learners are active participants in the teaching-learning situations. Teaching strategies which insure active student involvement include inductive and deductive discovery methods. Actually, these two methods are integral aspects of the in-vogue "meaning" approach to teaching mathematics which has been practiced since about 1935. Third we know that the presentation of a lesson is made more effectual when the teacher proceeds from *simple to complex* or from *concrete to abstract* on a teaching continuum.

As a mathematics teacher you will discover that much of the "old math" has been included in the "new math" material and curriculum. That is as it should be. In teaching the new math, don't go overboard on the inductive discovery approach as some authorities would advise you. Certainly, there is a place for inductive discovery. But there is also a place for deductive discovery for all children—particularly the culturally disadvantaged which are discussed in chapter 23. And there is a place for explanation or telling as well in your repertoire of teaching strategies. Once you have gained a knowledge of the sub stantive content of mathematics and have experimented with the different teaching strategies in the elementary school classroom, you will most likely be able to know when to use alternative teaching strategies.

Selected References

Banks, J. Houston. *Learning and Teaching Arithmetic.* 2d ed. Boston: Allyn and Bacon, Inc., 1964.

Dutton, Wilbur H., and Adams, L. J. *Arithmetic for Teachers.* Englewood Cliffs, N.J.: Prentice-Hall, Inc., 1961.

Flourney, Frances. *Elementary School Mathematics.* New York: The Center for Applied Research in Education, Inc., 1964.

Fujii, John N. *Numbers and Arithmetic.* New York: Blaisdell Publishing Company, 1965.

Garstens, Helen L. and Jackson, Stanley B. *Mathematics for Elementary School Teachers.* New York: Macmillan Company, 1967.

Gundlach, Bernard H. *The Laidlaw Glossary of Arithmetical-Mathematical Terms.* River Forest, Illinois: Laidlaw Brothers, Publishers, 1961.

Howard, Charles F. and Dumas, Enoch. *Basic Procedures in Teaching Arithmetic.* Boston: D. C. Heath and Company, 1963.

Marks, John L.; Purdy, C. Richard; and Kinney, Lucien B. *Teaching Elementary School Mathematics for Understanding.* 2d ed. New York: McGraw-Hill Book Company, 1965.

Michaelis, John U.; Grossman, Ruth H.; and Scott, Lloyd F. *New Designs for the Elementary School Curriculum.* New York: McGraw-Hill Book Company, Inc., 1967.

Rappaport, David. *Understanding and Teaching Elementary School Mathematics.* New York: John Wiley & Sons, Inc., 1966.

Shipp, Donald E., and Adams, Sam. *Developing Arithmetic Concepts and Skills.* Englewood Cliffs, N.J.: Prentice-Hall, Inc., 1964.

Spitzer, Herbert F. *Teaching Elementary School Mathematics.* Boston: Houghton Mifflin Company, 1967.

Swain, Robert L. *Understanding Arithmetic.* New York: Rinehart & Company, Inc., 1957.

Swenson, Esther J. *Teaching Arithmetic to Children.* New York: Macmillan Company, 1964.

Weber, Evelyn, and Weber, Sylvia. eds. *New Direction in Mathematics.* Washington, D.C.: Association for Childhood Education International, 1965.

Wirtz, Robert W.; Botel, Morton; and Nunley, B. G. *Discovery in Elementary School Mathematics.* New York: Encyclopaedia Britannica Press, 1963.

PART FOUR

teaching the unit study subjects

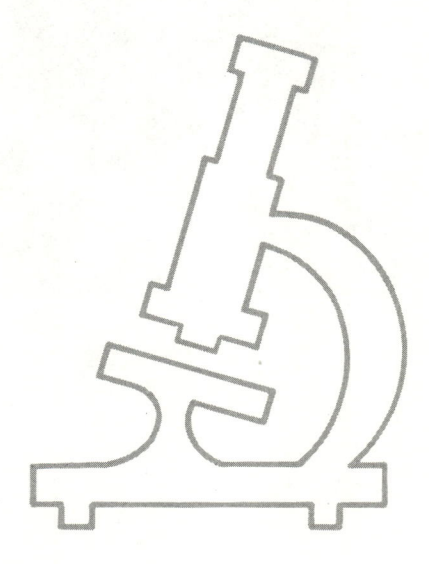

Photo: Courtesy of El Paso (Texas) Independent School District.
Photography: Seth J. Edwards, Jr.

teaching science

13

The teaching of elementary school science in this century has changed from a "nature study" orientation to that of an "activity" approach. Formerly, much emphasis was placed on appreciation of the natural environment, its beauty and wonder. In this approach, the study of science was deferred until the pupil had a proper appreciation of nature and was of "sufficient mental maturity" to engage in a sophisticated study of science. When children were taught science, the teachers were careful to see that they learned a given body of factual information; they taught the results of extant scientific investigations and scientific principles. Teachers checked on pupil progress mainly by ascertaining how much knowledge each child had acquired during each reporting period and globally over the term or year's study.[1]

In recent years, particularly within the Space Age, teachers of elementary school science have been more concerned with teaching the science processes, i.e., the methods and skills of investigation that scientists use in experimenting, discovering, expanding and ordering knowledge. Modern teaching of science in elementary school then involves two important areas: (1) the teaching of the basic processes of science, and (2) the teaching of science products, i.e., generalizations, concepts, principles.[2]

In summarizing the changed orientation of science teaching from a "nature study" to a "basic processes" approach, it is now considered that the mere teaching of science content and principles in which pupils are deprived of the opportunity to make their own investigations is unwise. Modern science teachers believe that simply teaching factual information, principles, generalizations, or concepts of science apart from teaching the processes of science in which "discovery" is emphasized is not really teaching science in an effectual manner.[3]

There have been several curriculum development projects in elementary school science in recent years which are in the process of developing science materials em-

---

1. Peter C. Gega, *Science in Elementary Education* 2d ed. (New York: John Wiley & Sons, Inc., 1966), pp. 5-6. By permission of John Wiley & Sons, Inc.
2. Ibid.
3. Paul E. Blackwood, "Science," in *New Curriculum Developments*, ed. Glenys G. Unruh (Washington, D.C.: Association for Supervision and Curriculum Development, NEA, 1965), p. 59.

phasizing the processes approach.[4] A number of these have been financed by the National Science Foundation. One of the better known ones is the NSF funded *Science—A Process Approach*,[5] in which the Commission on Science Education of the American Association for the Advancement of Science, under the leadership of codirectors John R. Mayor and Arthur H. Livermore, developed pupil materials treating the basic process skills of science. In these preprimary and primary grade materials exercises have been planned for certain levels, e.g., Part A can be used in the kindergarten or grade 1, Part B is used in grade 1 or 2, et cetera, in which the science process skills or those skills which are part of a scientific method are maximized. The basic processes included in the kindergarten and primary materials include: (1) observing, (2) using numbers, (3) measuring, (4) using space/time relationships, (5) classifying, (6) communicating, (7) inferring, and (8) predicting. The content introduced in teaching these primary grade basic process skills in science is drawn from the physical, social, biological, and behavioral sciences.

The lessons and exercises in the intermediate grade materials of *Science—A Process Approach* are designed to promote the retention and refinement of the basic process skills taught in the primary grades. At the intermediate levels the sequence of the materials becomes more complex, comprehensive, and more akin to the activities a scientist engages in when solving a problem. The intermediate materials emphasize a scientific approach in covering the integrated process of: (1) formulating hypotheses, (2) controlling variables, (3) interpreting data, (4) defining operationally, and (5) experimenting.[6] The content of the intermediate grade materials is drawn from the same basic sciences as in the primary materials.

Now that we have investigated the basic reorientation of the science program in the elementary school, let us turn our attention to the matter of objectives. As we shall see, the objectives are changing in order to be consonant with the newer emphasis on the basic processes approach.

Elementary Science Objectives

There are many objectives which can be found in the materials of the nation's various elementary school science projects and in public school science programs. There is a great deal of commonality in all of them; however, it appears that the following are representatives of the stated objectives appearing in the project and programs.

1. MASTERY OF THE PROCESS SKILLS. By the time the child has completed his work in the elementary school, he should have acquired the basic processes that the scientist uses in his scientific approach to solving problems. These processes, as alluded to earlier, include the following.[7]

Kindergarten and Primary Grade Basic Processes: K-3

1. Observing
2. Using space/time relationships

---

4. For a discussion of some of these, see: Maxine Dunfee, *Elementary School Science: A Guide to Current Research*, (Washington, D.C.: Association for Supervision and Curriculum Development, NEA, 1967), pp. 9-16.
5. *Science—A Process Approach: Part B*, (New York: American Association for the Advancement of Science/Xerox Corporation, 1967).
6. *Science—A Process Approach: Part E* (New York: American Association for the Advancement of Science/Xerox Corporation, 1968).
7. *Science—A Process Approach*.

3. Using numbers
4. Measuring
5. Classifying
6. Communicating
7. Predicting
8. Inferring

Intermediate Grade Integrated Processes: 4-6
1. Formulating hypotheses
2. Controlling variables
3. Interpreting data
4. Defining operationally
5. Experimenting

Quite obviously, the mastery of all these skills entails the demonstrable ability of the student to perform many tasks, such as critical thinking, problem solving, and evaluating and applying knowledge.

2. ACQUISITION OF BASIC SCIENTIFIC KNOWLEDGE: THE PRODUCTS OF SCIENCE. Formerly, the teaching of the science products was the major objective in science instruction. It is most important that children learn scientific knowledge but the acquisition of such knowledge is basically a by-product of instruction which maximizes process mastery. It is through highly structured activities and manipulative exercises that the child develops and perfects the process skills. In so doing, he learns scientific knowledge but in the context of a basic structure designed primarily to help him master the investigative processes the scientist uses.

3. APPRECIATION OF HOW SCIENCE CAN SERVE MANKIND. It is highly important that science instruction deals with the affective dimensions of education. Man, equipped with a knowledge of science and possessing expertise in the processes of science, has created much technology which has made his life more meaningful. Yet, man has abused nature in many instances as we are painfully aware in the 1970s. Ecologists are reminding us on every hand that misuse of natural resources, pollution, and the like must be rectified if life, as we know it, is to continue to exist on earth. It is only logical to conclude, therefore, that elementary school children should learn to distinguish between the beneficial and the detrimental uses to which scientific knowledge and processes may be put. Affectively, they should develop an appreciation for the former and eschew the latter.

Instruction in the affective dimension of science can help children learn to live with change—one of the inevitable consequences of living in a highly technological culture. Although children can become better enculturated or integrated into a mass technological culture through appropriate science instruction, this is not to suggest that they must be completely accepting of life as they find it. One of the important affective goals of science instruction is that children develop an attitude that man, unlike other animals, can adapt or control many aspects of his own environment. Herein lies a major challenge in teaching science; helping children to see how science and technology can be harnessed better to serve mankind.

In our scientific and technological culture, there are many issues involving science and technology that must be resolved in the immediate future. How can we adequately protect and properly use our natural resources such as land, minerals, and forests, for example, so that present and subsequent generations can benefit from them? Appropriate instruction in science can help children acquire requisite, cognitive and affective understandings of science and technology which they may use to cope with such problems.

4. SCIENTIFIC INFORMATION FOR PROPER PHYSICAL HEALTH AND GROWTH. Scientific information which enables children to take care of their bodies, for example, includes facts about communicable diseases, immunization, and the inherent dangers of cigarette smoking and drugs. Teaching children to select a balanced diet, keep their bodies clean, care for minor injuries, and have regularly scheduled check-ups with their dentist, ophthalmologist, and medical doctor is important information which contributes towards their improved physical health and growth.

5. DEVELOPMENT OF A SCIENTIFIC ATTITUDE. Just as the factual information can be taught and skills can be perfected in the teaching and learning situation, so too can a scientific attitude on the part of the children be developed in the science classroom. Some of the important attributes or characteristics of one who possesses a scientific attitude involve his ability to: (1) be objective or open-minded, (2) formulate conclusions only after extensive investigation, (3) secure appropriate evidence from reliable sources, (4) establish cause and effect relationships, and (5) plan and conduct investigations carefully and make accurate observations.[8] These are the abilities which teachers should strive to help children acquire behaviorally in developing a scientific attitude.

Organizing for Science Instruction

Basically, there are two dimensions to the elementary school science program—the planned and the incidental dimensions.[9] Let us examine these two dimensions separately.

The Science Program's Planned Dimension. The planned dimension of the science program largely represents *scope* and *sequence;* that is, what is taught and when. In the conventional science program, broad areas of content normally are included and each area is taught in greater depth each year. In this instance, the concepts or generalizations inherent in the content are developmental in nature. In other words, pupils are assured exposure to the major areas of science and their learning is cumulative since these major areas are studied in more detail each year. This is known as a spiral curriculum.

An outline of the scope and sequence of the elementary school science course of study as prepared by the Science Manpower Project is shown in figure 13.1. It is an illustration of the conventional spiral curriculum. A perusal of this figure will clearly show how the broad science areas are retaught in grades K through 6 by including new units of work each year for each broad science area.

When content or subject matter is the basis for determining scope and sequence, as it is in a conventional science program, teaching the process skills of science must be integrated into that structure. Of course, it is possible as in the *Science—A Process Approach* materials alluded to earlier in this chapter, to use the process skills as

---

8. Glenn O. Blough and Julius Schwartz, *Elementary School Science and How To Teach It,* 4th ed (New York: Holt, Rinehart and Winston, 1969) p. 16.

9. See: Willard J. Jacobson and Harold E. Tannenbaum, *Modern Elementary School Science* (New York: Teachers College, Bureau of Publications, Columbia University, 1961), pp. 32-42.

Broad Areas	Kindergarten	Grade I	Grade II	Grade III	Grade IV	Grade V	Grade VI
The Earth on Which We Live	A variety of science experiences from all broad areas of science	Study of Rocks	Study of Soil	Weather and Climate	The Earth's Changing Surface	History of the Earth	The Earth's Resources
Healthful Living Through Science		Foods We Should Eat	Preventing the Spread of Disease	Our Ears and Hearing	Our Eyes and Sight	Good Nutrition	Community Sanitation and Health
The Earth in Space		The Earth and the Sun	Air and the Atmosphere	The Sun and the Planets	Oceans and the Hydrosphere	Space Exploration	The Milky Way and Beyond
Machines, Materials, and Energy		Simple Machines	Heat and Temperature	Energy and Energy Sources	Water and Water Supply	Simple Electronics	Flight in Air and in Space
The Physical Environment		Study of Magnets	Fire and Fire Protection	Sound and Music	Light and Photography	Electricity	The Materials of Our Environment
The Biological Environment		Animal Life	Plant Life	Living Things and Their Environment	Organization of Living Things	Adaptations of Living Things	Man's Use of Living Things

Fig. 13.1 The Planned Dimension of the Elementary School Science Program. Reprinted by permission of the publisher from: Willard J. Jacobson and Harold E. Tannenbaum, **Modern Elementary School Science** (New York: Teachers College Press, 1961; Copyright 1961 by Teachers College, Columbia University), p. 43.

255

the scope and sequence. When this structure is used, content or subject matter is chosen from the selected scientific disciplines as it facilitates process development.

An outline of the scope and sequence of the *Science—A Process Approach: Part B* materials which can be used at first or second grade levels is shown in figure 13.2. In studying this figure, one can see that the processes become the basis for determining what is taught and when in the planned dimension of the science program. Also, it can be seen how the spiral curriculum works when predicated on processes. For example, the process of "measuring" is first covered in Exercise D and then it is retaught in a spiraling manner in Exercises J, L, N, U and Z. Likewise, "measuring" is retaught in subsequent years up through *Part E** designed for fourth or fifth grades where two exercises, N and S, are included.

FIRST OR SECOND GRADE EXERCISES

Processes	Exercises
Observing	E,G,M,O,V
Classifying	A,I
Communicating	H,P,W,X,Y
Using Space/Time Relationships	B,C,Q,S,T
Using Numbers	F,K,R
Measuring	D,J,L,N,U,Z

Fig. 13.2. Part B Exercises. From: **Science—A Process Approach** (New York: American Association for the Advancement of Science/Xerox Corporation, 1967).

*Note: Part E is the last level completed at the time of this writing.

The Science Program's Incidental Dimension. A corollary to the science program's planned dimension is the incidental dimension. That is, the planned dimension structures the program in terms of what processes or broad areas are to be taught. The incidental dimension is an outgrowth of the science program's planned scope and sequence in that it allows children to raise, discuss, investigate, and study questions and problems which interest them as a result of their study in the prescribed or planned program.[10] The planned program, therefore, is normally highly structured while the incidental dimension of the program is open-ended or unstructured.

It has frequently been said that we educate children in the elementary school in terms of where they are as opposed to where we wish they were in content or skills mastery. The questions they ask indicate where they are in their development. The incidental dimension of the science program permits the teacher to deviate from the structured, planned dimension to meet the individual needs of children when they are evidenced. Where possible the incidental aspect of the program can be administered on a one to one pupil-teacher ratio, but usually it is provided on a teacher and group basis by forming intraclass groupings of children based upon the commonality of their expressed needs and interests as determined by the questions they ask. As teachers treat the questions children ask in the incidental dimension of the science program, they have ample opportunity to demonstrate the use of the science process skills in the scientific approach to problem solving. In fact, "teachable moments" characterize the flexible dimension of the science program and the teacher should be alert to these opportunities.[11]

10. Ibid., pp. 32-33.
11. Ibid., p. 33.

Effective Science Program's Characteristics. There are several identifying characteristics of an effective science program. Some of the more important characteristics are briefly discussed in the following:

First, the planned dimension of the science program is clearly laid out in the course of study so that teachers know the nature or structure of the program. Second, teachers adequately provide for the incidental dimension of the science program in which the questions that children raise are attended to in the teaching and learning situations by referring to activities already conducted or by conducting relevant activities. Third, teachers give appropriate attention to teaching the processes and products of science. Fourth, teachers receive help from a science consultant or consultants within the school system. Fifth, a planned in-service training program in science is conducted periodically in the school system so that teachers can stay abreast of developments in science education for the elementary school. Sixth, teachers and students are provided with appropriate and adequate materials and equipment for the science program. Finally, much emphasis is placed on the affective dimensions of science instruction. Children must learn to appreciate science for its benefit to mankind.

Planning for Teaching Science

Most science teaching in the elementary school is accomplished through the unit approach. It is within the unit of work that the teacher attends to the objectives of science, e.g., teaching the processes and products of science, and providing for the planned and incidental dimensions of the program. Primarily, a unit is thought of as a planned sequence of related content (or processes) with supporting activities which are organized around a central theme or topic. Let us examine some of the integral aspects of unit teaching in science.

Steps in Unit Teaching. There are several steps or phases which customarily are followed in teaching a science unit. The title of the unit delimits the topic to be considered, e.g., "Telling Time." The eight steps which many teachers use are as follows.

STEP 1: SETTING OBJECTIVES FOR THE UNIT OF WORK. The teacher must decide which objectives he will attempt to achieve in his teaching of the science unit. If his major goal is to maximize mastery of the basic processes in unit instruction, he should set his objectives in behavioral terms. That is, after instruction has been administered, the pupils should be able to do what he has taught. For example, in the second or third grade unit on "Telling Time," the behavioral outcomes might be the following:[12]

The children can:
1. State the time orally to the nearest five minutes, given the position of the hour and minute hands on a clock.
2. State the time orally to the nearest five minutes, given the time as written numerals such as 8:25.
3. Write, given the clock face, the time using numerals.
4. Write, given the time orally, the time using numerals.
5. State the names in order for every fifth counting number beginning with five and ending at sixty.
6. State the number of days before or after a particular event and locate the particular day on a calendar, such as: It is eight days after Valentine's day, or it is five days before the class goes to the zoo.

12. *Science—A Process Approach* (Washington, D.C.: American Association for the Advancement of Science, 1965), p. 35.

7. State the number of hours before and after a particular time and identify the time on a clock face such as: three hours ago it was nine o'clock, or six hours from now it will be four o'clock.

Or, if the teacher wished to stress the products of science as teaching objectives, he should set his unit objectives accordingly. As an example, Gega has suggested that a primary unit on "Machines and Force" might contain certain generalizations as products.[13] Stated as product objectives, they might be as follows:

To understand that:
  I. Force needed to use an inclined plane changes as its tilt is changed; a wedge is like an inclined plane.
  II. Force needed to use a screw changes as its pitch is changed.
  III. Force needed to use a lever changes as length of the effort arm is changed; equal lever arms or loads, or combinations, permit objects to balance.
  IV. Force needed to use a wheel and axle (windlass) changes with wheel size; the speed and direction of rotation of linked wheels can be changed.
  V. Force needed to use a pulley changes as the number of ropes supporting the load is changed.

STEP 2: SELECTING CONTENT FOR THE UNIT. The content for a unit in science may come from the school system's curriculum guides, from the packaged materials originating with foundations or publishers such as *Science—A Process Approach* materials, textbooks, or local events and interests of children. The important thing to remember, as a teacher, in selecting content is to choose that set of objectives, content and activities that facilitate learnings which appear to be the most relevant for the instructional needs of the students in terms of available time for unit study.

STEP 3: INITIATING THE UNIT. There are many ways that the teacher might initiate the unit. He might show a film or a filmstrip, unveil a new bulletin board display of pictures, display relevant science objects, or have a resource person speak and give a demonstration about the new unit to be studied. Or, he might use some combination of these activities. The alternatives in initiating the unit are open-ended.

Essentially the initiation aspect of the unit is designed to create pupil interest in the unit of work. It may have other salutary advantages as well, such as providing the teacher with some measure of what the pupils already know about the unit. Too, the class members may learn the broad perimeters of the study which will be helpful in orienting them to the unit's activities and exercises.

STEP 4: SELECTING APPROPRIATE ACTIVITIES AND EXERCISES. The activities and exercises that are carried on within the unit where children become active participants in the learning process facilitate the accomplishment of the teaching objectives. The unit ideally should include a variety of activities which will help the teacher better provide for the individual instructional needs extant among the pupils. In attempting to teach the five generalizations for the primary unit on "Machines and Force" mentioned earlier, the teacher and pupils might plan activities involving the use of inclined planes, wedges, screws, levers, wheels and axles, and pulleys.[14]

Part of selecting the activities and exercises that are to be done involves making adequate time allocations for unit work. A three week time allocation for schedule

---

13. Gega, *Science in Elementary Education,* 305.
14. Ibid., pp. 304-25.

the unit "Machines and Force" is shown in figure 13.3. A perusal of it shows that allocations have been made for fifteen instructional days with forty-five minute daily instructional periods. Also, the generalizations are laid out in terms of the activities which promote student understanding of each.

	April 6-10	April 13-17	April 20-24
MONDAY	1. *Inclined plane; force changes with its tilt.* Introduce with pictures. Do experiments 1, 2, 3.	3. *Lever; force changes with force-arm length.* Do experiments 1, 2.	4. *Windlass; force changes with size of wheel.* Do experiments 1, 2. Remind class for extending activity.
TUESDAY	Do experiments 3, 4, 5. Remind class for extending activity.	Do experiments 3, 4, 5.	Do experiment 4. Do extending activity.
WEDNESDAY	Do experiments 6, 7. Do extending activity 1. Make bulletin board.	Do extending activity 2.	5. *Pulley; force changes with number of supporting lines.* Do experiments 1, 2, 3.
THURSDAY	2. *Screw; force changes with pitch.* Do experiments 1, 2. Remind class for extending activity.	Do extending activity 2. Remind class for extending activity 1.	Do experiments 4, 5, 6.
FRIDAY	Do experiment 3, and extending activity. Order film 370.15 for April 24.	Do extending activity.	Show film 370.15 "How Simple Machines Help Us" (20 min.). Discuss and evaluate whole unit.

Fig. 13.3. A Block Plan for a Primary Unit on Simple Machines, Scheduled Forty-Five Minutes Daily for Fifteen Days. From Peter C. Gega, **Science in Elementary Education** 2d ed. (New York: John Wiley & Sons, Inc., 1970), p. 131. By permission of John Wiley & Sons, Inc.

STEP 5: UTILIZING RESOURCES IN UNIT WORK. In conducting the unit of work, the teacher and children may use any or all of the science resources available. For example, they may utilize human resources such as chemists, nurses, medical doctors, ecologists, and anthropologists when they are available and when their particular expertise will benefit their studies. They may use natural resources within the community, such as an inland lake, a forest, or a hydroelectric plant. Obviously, they will use all of the equipment and materials that are available within the school, such as those provided by the media center.

STEP 6: STUDY AND RESEARCH PERIOD. During this phase of unit work, the children engage in study and research which was mapped out in step 4 when the activities and exercises of the unit were planned. The study and research period is flexible enough so that it cares for both the planned and incidental dimensions of the science program. In such a structure, the questions and problems which arise incidentally in unit development may be attended to in this period.

Periodically, during the study and research phase of unit work, the children report such activities as group projects which prove a scientific principle, give demonstrations which undergird a generalization, report results of individual and group experiments that have supplied answers for problems, or demonstrate to the class proper processes in conducting a scientific investigation. Sharing of study and research work can come at the end of the separate segments of the total unit (see figure 13.3), at the conclusion of the entire unit of work, or at any time the sharing of information contributes to the successful completion of the unit.

STEP 7: THE CULMINATING ACTIVITY. Usually, the unit of work will end with some relevent culminating activity. For example, it might simply be the sharing of information for the total unit as suggested in step 6. Or, it could be the construction of a panorama in which, for example, each of the five generalizations for the "Machines and Force" unit, alluded to earlier in step 1, could be stated and pictorial demonstrations of scientific products which support each generalization could be portrayed.

It is not necessary to culminate each unit with a test. Surely this procedure has been abused in the past and frequently has had the effect of creating an imbalance among students between the mastery of the products of science on the one hand and their acquisition of the process skills of science on the other. If the children know that each unit concludes with a test, they can hardly be blamed for studying and internalizing those things which are likely to appear on the test. Frequently, such tests are characteristically product orientated. When this occurs notwithstanding how much the teacher attempts to teach for other objectives, such as appreciation of science and processes in science, many children will maximize their unit study activities in terms of the habitual nature of the teacher's test.

STEP 8: EVALUATING LEARNING OUTCOMES. It is through the process of evaluation that the teacher makes judgments about how effective unit teaching has been, and how well the children have learned. Obviously, the teacher should attempt to judge children's growth and development in terms of the objectives for the unit as outlined in step 1.

Observation and *testing* are the two major techniques in evaluation that the teacher c science uses. It is through the day to day process of observation and verbally interacting with children that the teacher makes judgments about what adjustments should be made in the planned dimension of the science unit.

In all likelihood, observation is the teacher's most useful method of evaluation in the science program. Through observation he gives children immediate corrective feedback about such matters as content, process, or affective learnings. Direct and immediate corrective feedback and reinforcement is invaluable in instruction and is made possible through perceptive observation.

Through this medium of evaluation, the teacher can check to see if the child has internalized some learning. For example, in the unit mentioned earlier on "Telling Time," can the child orally state the time to the nearest five minutes when he is given the hour and minute hand positions on a clock? In other words, he must be able to demonstrate to the teacher that he has mastered the learning. If he can, the teacher may reinforce the learning in some manner, such as orally stating a time, e.g., 8:15, and then asking the child to set the hour and minute hands on a clock to represent the orally stated time. Or, if the child cannot state the time to the nearest five minutes when he is given the hour and minute hand positions on a clock, the teacher can give immediate corrective feedback to him and assign necessary drill for mastery.

The administration of a teacher-made test to a classroom of children for purposes of evaluation in science is a frequent practice in the elementary school. For a teacher who is truly skillful in the observation technique of evaluation, the test most likely will tell him little that he does not already know from observation. A periodic test may be useful, however, as a check against the teacher's observations. For example, he may find that some children who verbalize very little actually learn a great deal and demonstate their learning quite well but fail to perform well on tests. The point is that one does not have to use the teacher-made test very often to establish the types of performance which are readily observable in a classroom of children. When the test is used, however, it should be so constructed that it fairly tests for the attainment of the objectives the teacher had in mind in teaching the science unit.

A caveat about testing appears to be in order. It is better for the teacher to utilize the test in science evaluation minimally, and concentrate on developing his skill in observation. It is through the process of daily observation that the teacher develops a relevant and viable instructional program in science.

An Appraisal of Teaching Science

Teaching elementary school science is changing to the use of a "processes" approach as the major emphasis. The desired result is that by the sixth grade, the children will have learned the basic and integrated processes to the extent that behaviorally they can:[15]

1. Observe
2. Construct questions to be investigated
3. Construct hypotheses
4. Identify the variables
5. Construct operational definitions
6. Test hypotheses
7. Collect and display data
8. Interpret data
9. Modify hypotheses as needed
10. Repeat part or all of the cycle as needed.

15. Ibid., p. 557.

These are the integral behaviors that the scientist uses in his work. These are the behaviors towards which much of the teaching in modern elementary school science classrooms is directed. Content is selected from the physical, biological, social, and behavioral sciences which can be used in teaching the basic and integrated processes.

When the processes to be taught are the major thrust of the science program, they constitute its scope and sequence. When this occurs, the processes represent the planned dimension of the science program. The science program has a second dimension we call the incidental dimension. It is in this dimension of science teaching that the teacher deviates from the highly structured, planned dimension to attend to the questions and interests of the children. An example of an incidental interest of children which can be allowed for in the science program is a televised space shot to the moon.

Much of the present instruction in elementary school science is concerned with the affective dimensions of learning. That is, children need to develop appreciations of how science benefits mankind. Likewise, they should develop attitudes about the wisest uses to which science and technology can be put in serving man. Science instruction provides an additional and much needed learning affectively, to wit: it can prepare the child for learning how to adjust to rapidly changing circumstances in a highly developed technological culture such as ours.

As an aspiring teacher of elementary school science, you may feel that your undergraduate program in college or university has not adequately prepared you to be an effectual teacher from the standpoint of either substantive knowledge or teaching procedure. This should not cause you undue alarm for a number of reasons. First, most children like science; pupil interest in a subject makes teaching easier. Second, your pupils will not expect you to know all the answers. In fact, when you are teaching the processes, for example, this provides an excellent opportunity for you to demonstrate the process skills involved in helping children find answers to the questions they ask. Third, you can learn science as you teach but you must stay ahead of the children. Fourth, you are not entirely on your own in teaching science. Ask your experienced colleagues for assistance occasionally. Too, many of the school systems have science consultants who offer invaluable assistance. And, fifth, many of the newer science materials such as *Science—A Process Approach* are so tightly structured that you will be effectual in your teaching if you follow the program closely.[16]

SELECTED REFERENCES

BLOUGH, GLENN O. and SCHWARTZ, JULIUS. *Elementary School Science and How to Teach It.* 4th ed. New York: Holt, Rinehart and Winston, 1969.

Commission on Science Education. *Science—A Process Approach.* Washington, D.C.: American Association for the Advancement of Science, 1965.

Curriculum Department. *Guide to Teaching Science; Kindergarten-Grade Six.* Madison Wisconsin: The Madison Public Schools 1960.

Dunfee, Maxine. *Elementary School Science A Guide to Current Research.* Washington D.C.: Association for Supervision and Curriculum Development, NEA, 1967.

16. For a thorough discussion of these points see: Blough and Schwartz, *Elementary School Science*, pp. 2-5.

ERICKSON, JAY WILLIAM. *The Earth in Space.* New York: Teachers College Press, Teachers College, Columbia University, 1965.

GEGA, PETER C. *Science in Elementary Education*, 2d ed. New York: John Wiley & Sons, Inc., 1970.

KARPLUS, ROBERT, and THIER, HERBERT D. *A New Look at Elementary School Science.* Chicago: Rand McNally & Company, 1967.

KUSLAN, LOUIS I., and STONE, A. HARRIS. *Readings on Teaching Children Science.* Belmont, California: Wadsworth Publishing Company, Inc., 1969.

LANGLEY, RITA. *Teaching Elementary Science.* West Nyack, N.Y.: Parker Publishing Company, Inc., 1968.

NAVARRA, JOHN GABRIEL, and ZAFFORONI, JOSEPH. *Science Today for the Elementary School Teacher.* New York: Harper & Row, Publishers, 1963.

LEWIS, JUNE E., and POTTER, IRENE C. *The Teaching of Science in the Elementary School.* Englewood Cliffs, N.J.: Prentice-Hall Inc., 1961.

PILTZ, ALBERT, and SUND, ROBERT. *Creative Teaching of Science in the Elementary School.* Boston: Allyn and Bacon, Inc., 1968.

ROMEY, WILLIAM D. *Inquiry Techniques for Teaching Science.* Englewood Cliffs, N.J.: Prentice-Hall, Inc., 1968.

San Diego County Schools. *Science Grades One through Eight.* San Diego, California: Department of Education, San Diego County, 1960.

SUND, ROBERT B.; TROWBRIDGE, LESLIE; TILLERY, BILL W.; and OLSON, KENNETH V. *Elementary Science Teaching Activities: A Discovery Approach.* Columbus, Ohio: Charles E. Merrill Books, Inc., 1967.

THIER, HERBERT D. *Teaching Elementary School Science: A Laboratory Approach.* Lexington, Mass.: D. C. Heath and Company, 1970.

GLENYS G. UNRUH, ed. *New Curriculum Developments.* Washington, D.C.: Association for Supervision and Curriculum Development, 1965.

VICTOR, EDWARD, and LERNER, MARJORIE S. *Readings in Science Education for the Elementary School.* New York: Macmillan Company, 1967.

social studies, democracy, and citizenship

14

The social studies is a broad curriculum area, analogous to the language arts or science. Thus in one class students may be studying differences in family structure, nuclear and extended. In another, students are reading letters of two Revolutionary War youths, one who became a patriot with Washington at Trenton and the other a tory with Howe in New York. In the first class, students are attempting to ascertain relationships between family structure to personality development and patterns of social cooperation; in the latter, the basic value systems of two boyhood friends that led them to choose different loyalties.

Other vignettes of classroom study would merely emphasize the diversity of content and practices included in the social studies. Running through the emphasis on knowledge and scientific methodology is the common theme that in a democracy the schools should contribute to democratic behavior and responsible citizenship, a task which falls particularly within the province of the social studies.

In a chapter of a general text, only superficial treatment can be given to a curriculum strand that embraces material from over eight academic disciplines and many more applied fields. In this overview consideration will be given to such issues as definition, objectives, sequences, content, teaching method, and "new" social studies projects.

What's In a Name?

From the first official introduction of the term social studies in 1916 much effort has been spent on definition. When first used the term was used in three different ways: as a synonym for established subjects, such as history, geography, and civics; as a new label for problem oriented, multi-disciplinary courses; and as a convenient, short title to refer to the several social sciences, including history, or as a synonym for an eclectic social science.[1]

1. "Statement of Chairman of the Committee on Social Studies," in *Preliminary Statements by Chairmen of Committees of the Commission of the National Education Association on the Reorganization of Secondary Education,* U.S. Bureau of Education Bulletin no. 41 (Washington, D.C.: Government Printing Office, 1913), pp. 16-28; *The Social Studies in Secondary Education,* Report of the Committee on Social Studies of the Commission of the National Education Association on the Reorganization of Secondary Education. U.S. Bureau of Education Bulletin no. 28 (Washington, D.C.: Government Printing Office 1916).

Over the years, advocates of a particular persuasion argued their case. Social studies as problem solving with a multidisciplinary emphasis was most persuasively argued by Harold Rugg,[2] a view which was certainly consistent with the emphasis on community civics and problems of democracy.[3] This approach was also one of the best researched curriculum efforts ever undertaken in the United States, which makes social studies curriculum development of the 1960s pallid in comparison.[4] The unitary movement had limited success at the high school level, except in the twelfth grade Problems of Democracy course, and was successful in the elementary school more as correlation than as fusion. An examination of the course sequences in figure 14.2 will indicate that in the intermediate school courses predominantly historical or geographical in emphasis tended to predominate in 1926 as well as in 1970.

Opposed to the view which held that the social studies implied a unified organization was that of Wesley, dean of social studies educators, who asserted in his classic definition that "The *social studies* are the *social sciences* simplified for pedagogical purposes."[5] Wesley contended that in the schools the social studies were merely adaptations of the social sciences, either separately or in combination, and did not imply any particular organization as to subject matter. This immediately raises the question of the utility of a separate name, for it is common practice to simplify any material for elementary instruction, without changing the name. In one of those curious paradoxes of semantics, as nature study was being converted into science, the social sciences had been renamed for school instruction.

The third point of view emphasized the utility of general social science. This tradition is older than the separate disciplines in the social sciences. Comte in France with his *Positive Philosophy,* Spencer in England with his *Social Statics,* and H. C. Carey in the United States with his *Principles of Social Science*[6] had all attempted to make a synthesis of social philosophy. The American Social Science Association was formed in 1865, nineteen years before the American Historical Association was formed in 1884 and almost half a century before sociology, geography, and political science organized professionally. The movement toward synthesis soon faltered, as the disciplines bifurcated, but never died. Social science survey courses at the college level were popular in lower divisions before World War II, and influenced designs for school instruction.[7]

Not only did the terms social studies and social sciences lead to ambiguity, but the

2. The Rugg Social Studies Series, a comprehensive curriculum K-14, published by Ginn and Company, 1929-33.

3. J. Lynn Barnard et al., *The Teaching of Community Civics,* U.S. Bureau of Education Bulletin no. 23 (Washington, D.C.: Government Printing Office, 1915).

4. A partial list of monographs are given in Harold Rugg, *American Life and the School Curriculum* (Boston: Ginn and Company, 1936), pp. 194-95, footnote 4. Also, see the preface to Harold Rugg, *Changing Government and Changing Civilization* (Boston: Ginn and Company, 1933).

5. Edgar Bruce Wesley, *Teaching the Social Studies* (New York: D. C. Heath and Company, 1937), p. 4. Reprinted by permission of the publisher.

6. H. C. Carey, *Principles of Social Science* (Philadelphia: Carey and Hart, 1860).

7. Leon C. Marshall and Charles H. Judd, "An Introduction to the Social Studies," in National Society for the Study of Education, *The Social Studies in the Elementary and Secondary School,* the Twenty-second Yearbook, Part II (Bloomington, Ill.: Public School Publishing Company, 1923), pp. 76-98.

tendency to substitute new terminology led to more confusion. The title of the official organ of the National Council for Social Studies is *Social Education,* a term sometimes used as a synonym for social studies.[8] Eventually, such terms as social living, social learning, social competency, and civic competency were added, so that the social studies became a veritable hash in the elementary schools without clearly defined subject matter. Its liaison with language arts in a core program also had the unfortunate result of giving a literary rather than scientific approach to social studies, with little attention to the methodology of the social sciences and their organizing ideas.

After a decade of curriculum reform, the identity of the social studies with the parent social sciences is firmly established. Notwithstanding differences in content and emphasis, there was general consensus that irrespective of the pattern of organization, the social studies should reflect the structure of the discipline, not only with respect to knowledge but with respect to methodology.

There are those, including the authors, who think that the use of a name does make a difference. The label social sciences affirms without equivocation the relationship of school instruction to the parent disciplines; the label social studies invites deviation, according to any new crisis that arises. However, the term social studies is in general vogue, and may be used to indicate two things; a subject matter relating "directly to the organization and development of human society, and to men as a member of social groups;"[9] and a structure based on the social sciences.

The next section will briefly review the distinctive subject matter focus of the several disciplines.

Social Science Foundations

The disciplines of the social sciences provide the basic content for the social studies. Two have inherent structural characteristics which relate to the way knowledge may be organized: *history* and *geography.* All social phenomena occur in *time,* and consequently history is a *universal* methodology. All social phenomena occur in *space,* and hence geography is a universal methodology. When material is organized to reflect growth or change in time, the method is historical; when the material is organized to reflect areal relationship, the method is geographical.

The other social sciences are based on the logical structure or relationship of ideas developed through categorization, differentiation, analysis, and synthesis. In recent years it has been popular to emphasize the behavioral sciences—anthropology, psychology, and sociology—and to deemphasize the importance of history and geography. While political and military history has diminished and physical geography has largely been absorbed by the earth sciences, history and geography persist because they are not logical but universal categories of description, explanation, and interpretation.[10]

Anthropology is the study of man in culture. The major organizing concept of cul-

8. Richard E. Gross and Glen F. Ovard, "A Review of Aims and Objectives in Social Education," *The Social Studies* 51 (October 1960) 170-74.

9. *Social Studies in Secondary Education,* p. 1

10. Two discussions of the social sciences, prepared especially for teachers, are: American Council of Learned Societies and the National Council for the Social Studies, *The Social Studies and the Social Sciences* (New York: Harcourt, Brace & World, Inc., 1962); Erling M. Hunt et al *High School Social Studies Perspectives* (Boston Houghton Mifflin Company, 1962).

tural anthropology is the concept of culture, a word which emphasizes that the major adjustment of man to his environment is through learned behavior, not biological adaptation. Behavior is transmitted by groups of people who are the bearers of a culture. Anthropology has traditionally focused on the study of preliterate peoples, and the basic data of anthropology consists of systematic descriptions of the total way of life of a particular group of people, reported as *ethnographies*. The data of ethnography are used for cross-cultural comparison, a way of looking at the variation in traits to identify similarities and differences.

In addition to ethnography, a large part of cultural anthropology is concerned with archeology, the history of extinct people reconstructed from their artifacts. Physical anthropology is concerned with the origins of man, and is closely allied to paleontology. Anthropology, like psychology, is concerned with the biology of man in relation to human behavior. While the psychologist is concerned primarily with such biological facets as the nervous and endocrine system, the anthropologist is interested in all biological facets as they relate to culture. Man is an animal, and many cultural characteristics are biocultural in function. Anthropology has made its greatest impact on area studies, giving a greater cultural depth to the older geographic regional studies. Neglect of biocultural behavior, however, has tended to limit the behavioral impact of anthropology in the social studies.

Anthropological concepts have been emphasized in the new curriculum projects. As separate disciplines, anthropology has been emphasized in two projects: *Man: A Course of Study*, a middle school project of the Educational Development Center which provides a year course of study;[11] and *A Sequential Curriculum in Anthropology* of the University of Georgia, which provides units in anthropology for K-8.[12]

Economics is concerned with the universal problem of the scarcity of resources to meet unlimited wants. Men everywhere have wants which can be satisfied only through the allocation of resources. Since the wants of man are unlimited and resources limited, all societies are faced with the problem of scarcity.

In studying this central issue, economics follows two traditions: macroeconomics and microeconomics. Macroeconomics is concerned with the grand design of economic systems in relation to economic development, such as market economies in the U.S., command economies in Russia, mixed economies in England, and exchange economies in tribal Africa. The economic system develops from the institutions which are used to allocate and consume resources.

Microeconomics is concerned with the consumption and production of particular products and services. Economics thus considers such factors as labor, technology and transportation, human capital, the structure of the market in relation to the supply of money, the demands for goods and services, and systems of banking and finance. Economics also requires a consideration of the values of the total culture, which is evident in such matters as the money supply, employment level, economic growth rate, and welfare programs.

11. Educational Development Center, *Man: A Course of Study* (Cambridge, Mass.: Educational Development Center, 1965-70).

12. Anthropology Curriculum Project, *A Sequential Curriculum in Anthropology, K-8;* (Athens, Ga.: University of Georgia, 1965-70).

There have been three curriculum projects in economics at the elementary level. The most comprehensive is the Developmental Economic Education Program (DEEP) which provides materials for kindergarten through grade 8.[13] The Purdue Experiment in Economic Education[14] has developed material from grades 1-3 while the Elementary School Economics Program has developed material for grades 4-6.[15]

Geography once performed the functions of a universal science, and was the first of the present social sciences to achieve wide elementary acceptance. Today the subject matter which geography formerly taught is the subject of other disciplines, and the distinctive contribution of geography now lies in the explanation of the areal distribution of phenomena. Persistence of environmental determinism in school geography after it was abandoned in scholarly geography tended to discredit geographic instruction. But today the concept of culture, so important in anthropology, is just as important to the geographer as it is to the anthropologist. Man is not perceived as living in two distinct environments—natural and cultural—but in one environment which has interacting natural and cultural aspects.

Geography includes two major traditions for organizing study material—systematic and regional. Systematic geography is arranged according to the subject of investigation, e.g., population geography, urban geography. Regional geography is concerned with regions or areas of the world and has been the typical method for the presentation of school geography.

Separate curriculum development in elementary geography has not been emphasized. An exception is the Geography Curriculum Project at the University of Georgia which has developed systematic grade level units to be used in connection with regular social studies instruction. The purpose is to provide for more explicit teaching of geographic concepts.[16] The Providence, Rhode Island Social Studies Project used geography as the core discipline in the elementary grades.[17]

History has two characteristics which, in addition to chronology, set it apart from the other social studies. It has a cast of characters, a dramatis personae, and it has a national story. While man may aspire to a wider world of understanding, the citizen of a particular country also wish to assert their identify so that they have a sense of destiny on the universal stage. The drama is that of national history, and is to a literate people what tradition was to the preliterate tribesman attempting to explain his origin and destiny.

The assertion of a national consciousness is essential to an integrated nation. Events which merely have cognitive significance in general history have affective import in the history of a people. Contrast the significance of July 4 and Bastille Day, both of which symbolize the transfer of loyalty and change in the locus of sovereignty. To an American

---

13. The Joint Council on Economic Education has many different publications. A list of publications may be obtained from the Joint Council, 1212 Avenue of the Americas, New York 10036.

14. The publications of the Purdue Experiment authored by Lawrence Senesch, are published by Science Research Associates, Inc., Chicago.

15. Materials of the University of Chicago Elementary School Economics Program are available from The Allied Education Council, P. O. Box 78, Galien, Michigan 49113.

16. Systematic units in geography may be obtained from the Geography Curriculum Project, University of Georgia, Athens, Georgia 30601.

17. Materials are available from the Rhode land College Bookstore, 600 Mount Pleasant Avenue, Providence, Rhode Island 02908.

July 4th evokes a train of precious memory; it is his birthday. And so is Bastile Day dear to a Frenchman.

National history is not like the anonymous face of ethnography or archeology. It has its heroes and its villains, and it is inconceivable to think of the American story without Alexander Hamilton and Aaron Burr as it is to recount the story of France without Robespierre or Bonaparte. Most of the virtues claimed for history, such as predicting the future or profiting from the past, are denied by the idiosyncratic nature of history. Like other disciplines, history attempts to collect more reliable evidence and make more careful interpretations, and is just as much a science within the restrictions of its field as other disciplines which flaunt the term. But the dual characteristics of event and person impart to history the characteristics of literature, and it is unfortunate that the texts in school, constrained by limited content and vocabulary, so rarely capture the excitement and the drama which is a part of history.

History, however, is not static, and historians are forever reinterpreting the past. Thus in recent years the Spaniard has been exonerated, the Puritan acclaimed, and Reconstruction reinterpreted. The historian retells the story to accord with the needs of new times; the past is reinterpreted, but never recaptured.

Historical scholarship affords the schools so much new and relevant material dealing with industry, economics, urban problems, minority groups, and other relevant material that the problem of an overemphasis on political and military history no longer exists. The problem of school history is one of selection of points of emphasis.

There have been no separate curriculum projects devoted to history at the elementary grades. History is prominent in all the multidisciplinary projects, especially in the middle years of the Greater Cleveland Social Studies Program.[18]

Political Science is concerned with the structure of government, the formulation of public policy, and the behavior of individuals and groups in relation to government. In the United States, the major concern of political science is with the national government, but attention is also given to the study of state and local governments and political parties. Additional special areas of interest are concerned with public administration, comparative government, international relations, and political theory and philosophy.

For many years, political science was closely identified with philosophical, historical, and legal approaches to the study of political institutions. Since World War II, political science has borrowed heavily from social psychology and sociology, and attempted to substitute an alternate behavioral approach as the core of political science. The key word in political science is government. Irrespective of the approach used—and it is easy to identify a minimum of eight—the matter falls within the domain of political science if governmental institutions are involved.

Civics was for many years part of the elementary curriculum, but the study of government was transferred to the middle grades beginning in the 1920s. Community studies without a political emphasis were introduced in the primary grades. One of the most neglected areas of the social sciences in the elementary social studies curriculum

---

18. A revised, commerical edition of the GCSSP is published by Allyn and Bacon. Information may also be obtained from the Educational Research Council of America, Rockefeller Building, Cleveland, Ohio 44113.

today is politics and government. Regrettably, no particular curriculum development has been undertaken in political science at the elementary level. Most information about government is introduced historically in connection with the Constitutional Convention. The school depictions of the national government at work are a travesty on human intelligence, and depict a mechanical structure of checks and balances.

Psychology is the study of individual behavior; social psychology is the study of group behavior. Since individual behavior reflects the behavior of the culture in which a person is reared, the areas of personal and social psychology overlap. Psychology is concerned with such questions as the biological basis of behavior, the relationship of sensation and language to knowing about the world, the effect of learning on how people change, the nature of intelligence, the nature of individual differences, the basis of adjustment and maladjustment, the relationship of the individual to the group, and the basis of belief. Psychologists use methods common to the social sciences, but place most emphasis on experimental methodology, a procedure which provides statistical methods for testing the validity of answers to questions which have been formulated. Experimental methodology is heavily emphasized in educational research.

There has been little incorporation of psychology into elementary social studies. The Michigan Elementary Social Science Education Program combined psychology and sociology in middle grade material commercially available as *Social Science Laboratory Units for the Elementary Grades*.[19] Psychology was long considered a college subject, but the ideas of psychology have now become a part of the general culture.

Psychological concepts are useful even for elementary students because they help provide a scientific foundation for understanding aspects of behavior and adjustment.

Sociology is the study of the social life of human beings in groups, primarily groups of modern rather than traditional societies. Sociology is concerned with the interrelationships of culture, biology, and geography to social organization; facets of behavior relating to group organization, role and status, social control and conformity, and crowds and publics; the development of personality from the standpoint of the interactions of the group, culture, and socialization; human ecology; social institutions; and the process of social change. In recent years, one of the major emphases of sociology has been the changing nature of western institutions under the forces of urbanization and industrialization. While public policy and expenditures are often devoted to trying to maintain the status quo, e.g., the family farm in a technological system, sociologists frequently emphasize the importance of making policy decisions in terms of the future, not in terms of the past. Thus, while much effort of city planners and urban renewal is directed toward an attempt to preserve the central business district of the city, urban sociologists tend to emphasize planning in terms of suburban changes rather than preservation which is inconsistent with new habits of social behavior.

Sociology has exerted great influence in interpretations of history emphasizing industrial and urban trends. Sociological concepts are therefore prominent in all of the comprehensive social studies, although no curriculum projects specifically based on

19. These materials are commercially available from Science Research Associates, Inc.

sociology have emerged at the elementary level, except jointly with psychology in the Michigan program previously mentioned.

Philosophy embraces three divisions which are increasingly identified with the social studies: *ethics,* which deals with the principles of right conduct; *axiology,* which is concerned with the problem of value; and *logic,* which deals with the consistency and validity of statements.

The ethical-value content of the social studies is indicated by many concepts, among which are citizen, country, democracy, dignity of the individual, duty, equality, freedom, general welfare, government of the people, justice, liberty, loyalty, patriotism, power, pursuit of happiness, reason, right, and science. While the discipline of logic relates to all school instruction, it is unusually pertinent to the social studies. This results from the fact that belief and opinion in the social studies is so frequently interpreted as fact. Teaching and learning in the social studies is often pursued with a complete disregard for logical fallacies and a lack of appreciation of the fundamental characteristics of scientific method.

At the elementary level, concerns stemming from philosophy have had little influence on specific material. One reason is that it is rare for elementary teachers, or even high school teachers for that matter, to have any training in philosophy. However, value considerations affect the overall rationale of curriculum design, as seen in the next section dealing with goals and objectives.

Goals and Objectives in the Social Studies

No area of instruction is surrounded with so many and such grandoise goals and objectives as the teaching of social studies.[20] This results not only from the fact that the social studies reflect many different approaches, but also transmit the national morality. The social sciences have never been value free,[21] and school men, as noted in the Prologue, have never entertained the illusion of scientific neutralism. From the very beginning, history, geography, and government were not merely designed to transmit useful knowledge but also to inculcate national virtues.

It is therefore useful to make a distinction between goals and objectives.[22] A functional distinction is made on the matter of attainability. Goals are great beacon ideas which light man's striving, but may never be obtained. They reflect what man and society might become if the individual and collective acts of man reflected his highest aspirations. Goals are not measurable within the life of the child in school, much less in a single course of study. An objective, on the other hand, implies a task which can be accomplished, whether it is the acquisition of a particular quantum of knowledge or exer-

---

20. For a discussion of objectives in social studies education, see: Richard E. Gross and Glen F. Ovard, "A Review of Aims and Objectives in Social Education," *The Social Studies* 51 (October 1960): 170-74; A. John Fiorino, "Why Social Studies," *The Elementary School Journal* 67 (February 1966): 229-33.

21. For the relationship of values to social science, see the essay by Peter Odegard, et. al., "The Social Sciences in the Twentieth Century," in *The Social Studies: Curriculum Proposals for the Fuure,* (Papers presented at the 1963 Cubberley Conference, School of Education, Stanford University, ed. G. Wesley Sowards (Chicago: Scott, Foresman and Company, 1963), pp. 33-40.

22. For a distinction between the generality of goals and the specificity of objectives, see: Roy A. Price, "Goals for the Social Studies," in *Social Studies Curriculum Development: Prospects and Problems,* 39th Yearbook of the National Council for the Social Studies, ed. Dorothy M. Fraser (Washington, D.C.: NCSS, 1968), pp. 33-64.

cise of a particular skill. Objectives are the immediate learning tasks through which a course of study is implemented, and vary with the particular emphasis of teaching. The goals, however, remain constant despite the shift in objectives. Four major goals are democracy and citizenship, knowledge and skills, critical thinking and problem solving, and sensitivity to cultural change.

Democracy and Citizenship. The basic secular ethic of the United States is democracy, and the goals of civic education can be achieved only in terms of democracy. The democratic ethic is not confined to the rhetoric of July 4; it reflects the community fabric which gives the whole social structure stability and purpose.

The fact that there is sometimes hesitation and uncertainty in the interpretation of the democratic ethic is an expression of the frailty of human execution rather than a lack of vitality in democratic ideas. The democratic ethic is not something received, but is something which man creates as he tries to give practical meaning to the values of liberty, justice, and equality. It is from this pursuit that the body politic grows in strength and vigor. Recent interpretations of the democratic ethic are additional safeguards to the accused, an expansion of procedural rights, and extension of due process of law to give added protection to minority groups, an expansion of substantive rights.

Measured by concern for individual welfare, the democracy of the 1970s is a more humane society than that of the 1870s; measured by ability to participate in the blessings of liberty, a greater percentage of people are able to participate in the 1970s than were in the 1870s. In recent years, extremist groups of various persuasions have belittled the democratic ethic, alleging that it is merely a mask for special privileges. While inequities have existed and will no doubt continue to exist, the very fact that such groups can express their dissidence is but one indication that the democratic ethic supports an open society.

But a body politic requires agreement as to its goals and its values, and one function of the social studies is to involve young learners in the reconstruction of the democratic ethic to meet changing needs and conditions. The United States is a democratic country with a democratic heritage. Democracy is a keystone in the social studies which requires no defense or apology.[23]

Knowledge and Skills. It has long been a justification of public education that an informed citizen is a better citizen, and that the intelligent participation of citizens in democratic government requires knowledge. In the age of the specialist, general knowledge does not permit technical decisions. A citizen may not pass on judgment on architectural specifications, but he can weigh evidence to decide if tax resources should be spent for vocational education or college preparation.

In a democracy, the citizen becomes even more remote from government as it grows in size. The sovereign will is often no more than the exercise of the franchise. But this alternative is a key in a democracy—the electorate has a choice, and is not confined to a single slate of candidates approved by the governing party. If candidates for office do not address themselves to issues, it is because the electorate does not demand

---

23. Helen McCracken Carpenter, "Skills for Democratic Citizenship in the 1960's," in *Skill Development in Social Studies,* Thirty-Third Yearbook of the National Council for the Social Studies, ed. Helen McCracken Carpenter (Washington, D.C.: NCSS, 1963), pp. 1-16.

consideration of policy alternatives. Knowledge and skills acquired in the social studies provide no easy political recipes for future decision making. But knowledge and dispositions formed in the social studies help lay the foundations for a continuing concern in public issues.

Critical Thinking and Problem Solving. The goal of critical thinking and problem solving involve all of schooling, not merely the social studies. But the phenomena of social issues and public policy present alternatives of value as well as of fact. The ability to appraise issues, collect evidence, make inferences, and simulate applications before making a decision are highly desirable attributes. Knowledge has limited utility if it cannot be applied.[24]

In addition to the simulation of decision making, much attention is given to practicing the processes of investigation used by social scientists.[25] Writing history from simple materials, utilizing the observer technique, and developing instruments for data collection are processes which further the development of thinking skills. Learning to learn is not, however, all process. It also requires a substantive amount of knowledge. Critical thinking and knowledge acquisition are not exclusive, but complementary facets of learning.

Sensitivity to Social Change.[26] Accelerating changes from technology have wrought vast transformations in the twentieth century world, and yet there is no end in sight to the remaking of culture and the shaping of new behavior within the context of a changed culture. For over half a century, the social studies have been attempting to sensitize children to the fact that they will live in a world yet to be created, not in the past of their fathers. Thus while the social studies is concerned with the transmission of the cultural heritage, it is also prospective in its emphasis.

The social change emphasis in social studies is not merely descriptive, but is also based on the premise that man is a rational animal who can make decisions which control his destiny. It reinforces the democratic ethic which postulates the ability to devise new courses of democratic action consistent with changed conditions.

The concept of change does not mean that history and geography are less important in the social studies. Change involves both

24. Shirley H. Engle, "Decision Making: The Heart of Social Studies Instruction," *Social Education* 24 (November 1960): 301-4, 306.

25. The emphasis on "learning how to learn" is an important strand in social studies education theory. See Irving Morrissett, ed. *Concepts and Structure in the New Social Science Curricula* (New York: Holt, Rinehart and Winston, Inc., 1967) and Norris Sanders, "Changing Strategies of Instruction: Three Case Examples," in Fraser, *Social Studies Curriculum Development,* pp. 139-73.

26. The thesis of social change and social trends are widely used in curriculum development not only in the social studies but in other fields. See B. Othaniel Smith, William O. Stanley, and J. Harlan Shores, *Fundamentals of Curriculum Development* (New York: Harcourt, Brace & World, Inc., 1957); Gail M. Inlow, *The Emergent in Curriculum,* rev. ed. (New York: John Wiley & Sons, Inc., 1966). One of the most comprehensive statements of the theory of a social science curriculum structured on the concept of social change is given in Harold Rugg, "The Study of Man and His Changing Society," in *American Life and the School Curriculum* (Boston: Ginn and Company, 1936), pp. 394-417. The social trend thesis is emphasized in such recent social studies publications as: Stanley Dimond, "Current Social Trends and Their Implications for the Social Studies Program," in *Social Studies in the Elementary School,* The Fifty-sixth Yearbook of the National Society for the Study of Education, Part II (Chicago: University of Chicago Press, 1957), pp. 48-75; Raymond Muessig, ed., *Social Studies Curriculum Improvement,* Bulletin 36 (Washington, D.C.: National Council for the Social Studies, 1965).

Anthropology	Economics	Geography	Political Science	Psychology	Sociology
acculturation	allocation	area	apportionment	abnormal behavior	accommodation
age group	banking	association	authoritarian	adjustment	assimilation
animism	business cycle	atmosphere	authority	anxiety	association
archaic culture	capital	biosphere	behavior	attention	business cycle
archeology	competition	climate	Bill of Rights	attitude	caste
association	consumer	cultural resource	city	behavior	class
behavior	consumption	culture	civil liberty	competition	community
breeding population	credit	diffusion	constitution	concept	compromise
bride price	distribution	direction	county	conflict	conflict
carbon dating	division of labor	distribution	decision making	connectionism	cooperation
ceremony	economic system	earth complex	democratic	cooperation	culture
change	exchange	earth-sun relationships	due process of law	creativity	custom
consanguinity	command	economic development	electoral	culture	division of labor
contract	market	environment	executive	development	environment
cult	mixed	industrialization	federal system	differential	family
cultural dynamics	traditional	interaction	freedom	drives	nuclear
forces	factors of production	landform	government	emotion	extended
institutions	free trade	landscape	parliamentary	environment	folkways
culture	G.N.P.	lithosphere	presidential	experimental	group integration
folk	goods	location	judiciary	feedback	groups
industrial	growth	map	justice	forgetting	innovation
material	market	morphology	legislate	frustration	institutions
nonmaterial	money	natural resource	legislative	heredity	integration
preindustrial	monopoly	occupant	local government	intelligence	invention
diffusion	prices	sequence	nation	learning	leadership
domestication	production		nationalism	maturation	learning
	resource			motivation	marriage

Fig. 14.1. Concepts from Six Social Science Disciplines, Alphabetically Arranged as Discrete Concepts.

social studies, democracy, and citizenship

the structural categories of time and space, and provides a means of focusing attention on broad cultural processes and their consequences. A study of the processes of cultural change is not merely cognitive. It is also designed to create an attitude which accepts the reality of change and to use it in the service of mankind. A healthy nostalgia for old things helps cherish the contributions of the past, but should not impede social adjustments to the changing world. One of the great goals of social studies is to help close the gap between man's technological and his social inventiveness.

Concepts and Concept Clusters

Each social science deals with social phenomena, but abstracts certain aspects for particular emphasis. This leads to different perceptions and explanations of reality.

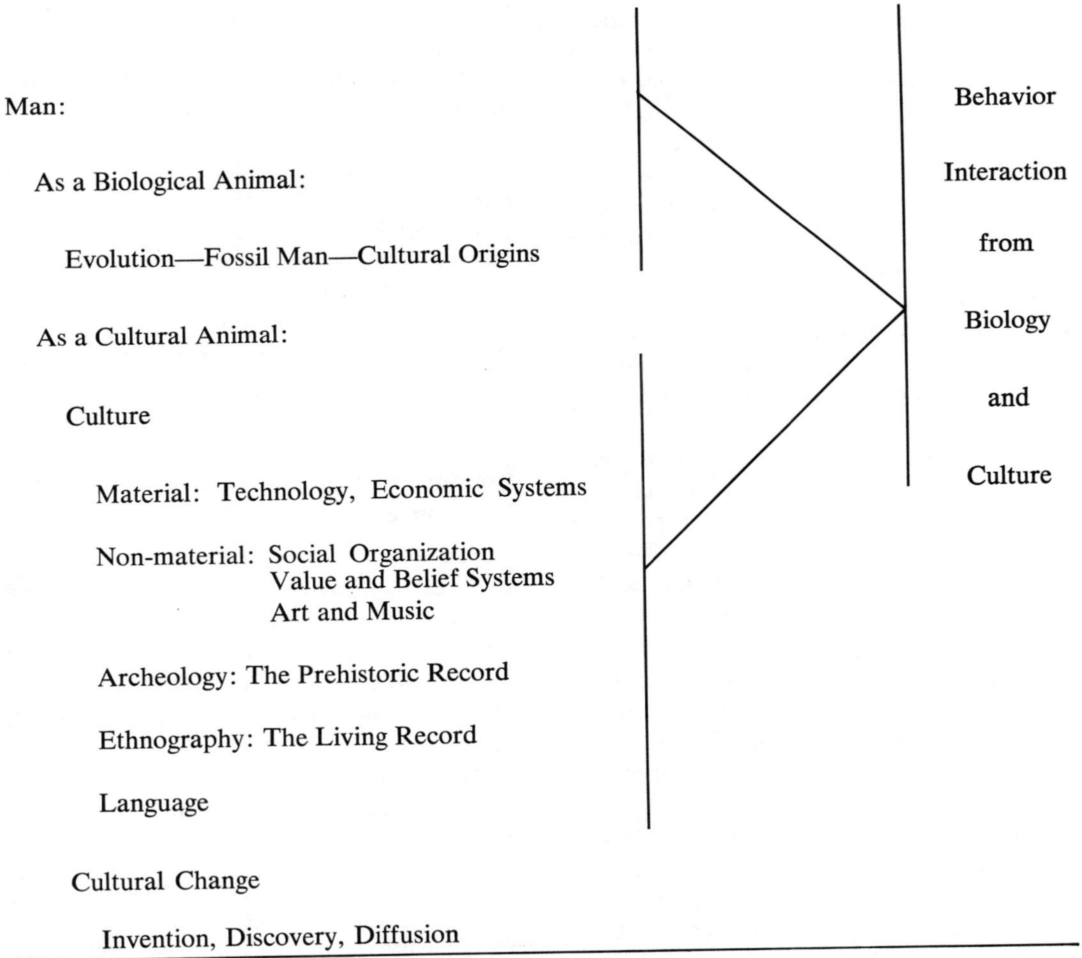

Man:

   As a Biological Animal:

      Evolution—Fossil Man—Cultural Origins

   As a Cultural Animal:

      Culture

         Material: Technology, Economic Systems

         Non-material: Social Organization
                        Value and Belief Systems
                        Art and Music

      Archeology: The Prehistoric Record

      Ethnography: The Living Record

      Language

   Cultural Change

      Invention, Discovery, Diffusion

Behavior Interaction from Biology and Culture

Fig. 14.2. Anthropology as a Discipline. Schematic Representation of Conceptual Structures in Anthropology.

Reality is mediated through language, and language consists of words in a syntactical arrangement. A concept is a *word*, a symbol of reality. Concept teaching thus begins with *vocabulary development* in its best form: definition, illustration, and application in deductive teaching; illustration, definition, and application in inductive teaching. An alphabetical list of concepts of six social science disciplines is given in figure 14.1.

Reality is not apprehended through discrete concepts, but through a conceptual structure. A *conceptual structure* consists of the organization of related concepts which develop a major concept systematically. A discipline, such as anthropology, consists of the several conceptual structures used for organizing concepts. Figure 14.2 is a schematic presentation of conceptual structures within anthropology.[27]

The typical arrangement of conceptual structures is by concept cluster, a logical arrangement by key concept. This device is followed in figure 14.2. Conceptual structures, however, do not depend only on organization by major concept. For example, the Anthropology Curriculum Project, University of Georgia organized units specifically dealing with the "Concept of Culture." The high school Anthropology Curriculum Study Project,[28] however, chose to use a thematic organization, such as "Early Man" and "The Great Transformation," and utilized the concept of culture throughout the development of these themes.

Conceptual structures in disciplines may be utilized in different arrangements, according to the nature of the learning task and focus. Thus in the Georgia Anthropology Project, ethnographic, comparative, and historical arrangements were used. In ethnographic presentation, as in "Three Cultures," the focus was on a description of the culture of a people, and the material was organized by concepts to emphasize the way of life of the particular group. In the fourth grade material, the concepts were organized historically around the theme "Development of Man and His Culture."

There is no one optimum arrangement of concepts; the arrangement depends upon the focus and the learning tasks. The arrangement must result in a conceptual structure, however, if it is to facilitate learning. One of the major contributions of the last decade of curriculum reform has been to assert the importance of concepts in social studies learning.

It will be remarked that figure 14.1 does not include concepts from history. Almost any concept in figure 14.1 may be treated historically. Themes of both a chronological and subject nature are used to provide conceptual structure to history. Examples from American history are: chronological, "The Age of Jackson;" topical, "The Urbanization of America."

Considerations in Curriculum Development

The abundance of social science content requires selectivity for inclusion in the social studies. Criteria for content selection and arrangement are not fixed, but involve such considerations as rationale, social trends, psychological maturity of the learner, and statutory requirements.

The term *rationale* is used to describe the premises which guide content selection and arrangement. A rationale primarily reflects

---

27. A useful visual presentation of the interrelation of concepts and structure are given in Morrissett, ed., *Concepts and Structure*.
28. Commercial versions of these materials are now available from Macmillan Company.

a system of *values,* since there is little scientific evidence to justify a particular selection or arrangement of content. Diversity in content and organization schemes permit different preferences to be expressed. Curriculum preferences, however, are all too often justified as a curriculum fact, such as the emphasis on the behavioral sciences instead of history or a multidisciplinary organization instead of some other arrangement. Statement of curriculum rationale are helpful to teachers in the selection of material for teaching, even when they are not engaged in direct development.

Social trends refers to the attempt to relate content selection to social changes. The alleged advantage of the social trends emphasis is the matter of relevancy, such as the emphasis on Black Studies in the latter part of the 1960s or the current concern with ecology. Contradictory as it may seem, the social trend emphasis often ends up with a retrospective rather than a prospective emphasis. This is because trends which are urgent today frequently loom less importantly tomorrow. An excellent example is the Cold War concern with the evils of communism. In a period of detente fifteen years later, the relevancy of yesterday may become an intellectual trap. Social trends are frequently used in the selection of social studies material to provide a contemporary emphasis.

Psychology of the learner is a way of expressing the fact that children of different age, achievement, experience, and maturity require different material. Frequently, some curriculum ideas are justified on psychological grounds when there is little supporting evidence, such as the long popular expanding environment schema.[29] As a result of research dealing with the different interests and capacities of children, there is a recognition of the ability of elementary children to handle social science concepts.[30] Children in the middle grades have better reading skills and the benefit of more experience. Consequently, a spiral curriculum development is frequently used to permit a more complex and sophisticated development of concepts introduced earlier, an approach well illustrated in the teaching of American history. To avoid the duplication that repetitive spiraling implies, the technique of content concentration, popularly called postholing, is frequently utilized to give a different chronological, geographical, or problem emphasis. Thus, in American history, the lower elementary grades typically emphasize the colonial period; the upper middle grades, the nineteenth century; and the eleventh grade, the twentieth century. Such a shift in content focus can also mean a shift in long-term learning outcomes.

Legal requirements refer to state requirements for subject matter coverage, usually restricted to American history and government and state history and government. Few go as far as Pennsylvania, which prescribes not only the teaching of intergroup education and racial and ethnic group history, but prescribes an interdisciplinary curriculum organization.[31] Emphasis on state and local history is usually provincial and adulatory. In teaching implementation, the

29. Ronald O. Smith and Charles F. Cardinell, "Challenging the Expanding Environment Theory," *Social Education* 28 (March 1964): 141-43.
30. Marion J. Rice, "Educational Stimulation in the Social Studies: Analysis and Interpretation of Research," in *Readings on Elementary Social Studies,* ed. Jonathon C. McLendon (Boston: Allyn and Bacon, Inc., 1970), pp. 526-32.
31. Pennsylvania Department of Education, Bureau of General and Academic Education, *Social Studies Today* (Harrisburg, Pa.: Pennsylvania Department of Education, 1970), pp. 60-62.

Denver, 1926		Traditional, 1970
K		Local Topics: Home, Family, Fire Station, etc.
1	A Home Life B Home Life	Family, Home, School
2	A Community Life B Community Life	Community, Neighborhood, Community Helpers
3	A Indian Life B Child Life in Foreign Lands	City, Town—Community Types, Transportation, Shelter
4	A Colonial Life B Westward Movement	Peoples Around the World, Our State, U. S. Areas
5	Interdependence: Agriculture and Extractive Industries	United States or Western Hemisphere The United States and its Neighbors
6	Interdependence: Manufacturing and Industry	Old World, Other Nations, Eastern Hemisphere
7	*1 U.S. Commercial Development 2 Interdependence of Modern Industrial Nations 3 Changing Agricultural Nations	U. S. Geography, World Geography, State Geography, State History
8	4 Westward Movement 5 Industrial History of American People 6 Growth of American Democracy	Civics, Geography, U.S. History, State History

*Unit Topics

Fig. 14.3. Social Sciences in the Elementary Grades, 1926 and 1970, from: Rolla M. Tryon, **The Social Science as School Subjects**, Report of the Commission on the Social Studies, American Historical Association, Part XI (New York: Charles Scribner's Sons, 1935); pp. 467-69; Fraser, **Social Studies Curriculum Development**, p. 72.

New York

K Local Environment Studies
    Family and school

1 Geography
   Patriotism

2 Community Studies
   Social, ethnic, religious groups
   Politics and economics of local community

3 Geographic studies of communities
   Patriotism

4 American People and Leaders
   Contributions of ethnic groups
   Leaders in government, industry, civil rights, art, science

5 Major Culture Regions
   Western Hemisphere: Interdisciplinary study of Canada and Latin America

6 Middle East and Europe: Interdisciplinary

7 Our Cultural Heritage
   Pre-Columbian and Colonial Periods
   State history and government

8 United States History—1800 to Present
   Also Federal government and civil rights

Fig. 14.4. New York State Social Studies Sequence, New York State Department of Education, Flow Charts for Elementary and Secondary Social Studies Programs (Albany, N.Y.: State Department, 1965).

device of teaching state and local history and government as a part of national history and government is often utilized. Whatever the merits or demerits of legal curriculum requirements, they cannot be overlooked in social studies curriculum development or in teaching.

The recommendations or requirements of state education departments also are factors which influence content at the local level, as shown in figure 14.4.

Sequences in Social Studies, 1926-70

Sequence is a curriculum term used to refer to the vertical or graded organization of learning experiences. Planned sequences are designed to provide adequate coverage, eliminate duplication, and adjust learning tasks to ability levels.

As a result of curriculum reform in the 1920s, multidisciplinary, problem oriented curricula became popular. One of the best known sequences of the 1920s was that of the Denver Public Schools, which is presented in figure 14.3, in comparison with the established curriculum pattern at the beginning of the 1970s.

A comparison of the two curriculum sequences indicates considerable similarity. While there are minor variations, the sequence of 1970 is little different from the major emphasis of forty years ago. If anything, the traditional curriculum of the 1970s is more conventional than the Denver curriculum in 1926, which was heavily influenced by the work of Harold Rugg. A comparison of the Denver curriculum with the Greater Cleveland Sequence in figure 14.5 indicates some striking parallels.

A contemporary state sequence, that of New York, is shown in figure 14.4. It is typical of many state sequences. A more radical topical organization proposed for California, emphasizing concepts and inquiry, was not approved by the California State Department of Education.

Curriculum Projects of the 1960s

The ego shattering advent of Sputnik in 1957 added to the urgency of calls for curriculum revision, not only in the natural sciences but also in the social sciences and other curriculum areas. By the middle of the 1960s several curriculum projects were well under way, and by the end of the decade had developed a series of alternatives.

Space will permit little more than mention of several projects, some of which Sanders and Tanck classified in 1970 as follows:[32]

Comprehensive

>Greater Cleveland Social Science Program, K-8
>Minnesota Project Social Studies, K-8[33]
>Providence Social Studies Curriculum Project, K-8
>Taba (Contra Costa) Curriculum Development Project, 1-8[34]

Discipline Oriented

Anthropology

>Educational Development Center, Man: A Course of Study, 5
>Georgia Anthropology Curriculum Project, K-8

---

32. A critique of these projects is given in Norris M. Sanders and Marlin L. Tanck, "A Critical Appraisal of Twenty-six National Social Studies Projects," *Social Education* 34 (April 1970). For an extended discussion, see R. Murray Thomas and Dale L. Brubaker, *Curriculum Patterns in Elementary Social Studies* (Belmont, California: Wadsworth Publishing Company, Inc., 1971).

33. Materials may be obtained from the Green Printing Company, 631 Eighth Avenue North, Minneapolis, Minnesota 55411.

34. Commercially published by Addison-Wesley Publishing Company.

Economics
    Developmental Economic Education Program (DEEP), K-8
    Elementary School Economics Program, Univ. of Chicago, 5-7
    Experiment in Economic Education, Purdue, 1-3

Psychology-Sociology
    Michigan Elementary Social Sc. Ed. Program, 4, 5 or 6

Special Purpose Projects
    Law in American Society, 5[35]
    Intergroup Relations Curriculum, Lincoln-Filene Center for Citizenship, 1-6[36]

Some particular characteristics of these projects are: Minnesota and the Providence material is primarily in the form of resource units; the Greater Cleveland material provides a complete set of teacher background and pupil text material for each grade level; geography is the core discipline in the Providence material; the Taba project is primarily a cognitive learning rather than a material development project; the Lincoln Filene material is a resource guide for teaching intergroup relations; the Georgia Anthropology Curriculum material provides units for use at the various grade levels, complete with teacher background material, pupil text, guide, and tests; *Man: A Course of Study* provides the greatest amount of media offerings.

Figure 14.5 gives a comparison of the Minnesota and Greater Cleveland sequences with a traditional sequence. Figure 14.6 indicates differences in multidisciplinary and single discipline sequences as represented by the Providence Project and projects at the University of Georgia.

Some common elements of these new projects are:[37]

1. More emphasis on the behavioral sciences and economics
2. Interdisciplinary emphasis; even single discipline projects incorporate materials form other social sciences
3. Concern for structure of knowledge; structure variously designed as logical arrangement of concepts or as methodology
4. Emphasis on discovery or inquiry methods, but no agreement as to definition or methods
5. Training in various social science methodologies
6. A concern for values, generally implicit but sometimes explicit
7. More social realism
8. More open-ended questions
9. Common use of cross-cultural studies
10. Added emphasis on the non-western world
11. In-depth study of selected topics
12. Abandonment of traditional expanding environment schema
13. Variety of materials in lieu of single text
14. Package of instructional materials to minimize need for library or community resources
15. Emphasis on teacher preparation and guidance
16. Use of social scientists to provide most recent knowledge
17. Field testing of materials

An exception to the emphasis on discovery and inquiry methods is found in the procedures of the Anthropology Curriculum Project, University of Georgia, which explicitly follows a deductive approach.[38]

35. Materials are available from The Law in American Society Foundation, 29 South LaSalle Street, Chicago, Illinois.
36. Materials are available from the Lincoln-Filene Center, Tufts University, Medford, Massachusetts.
37. This précis is adapted from Sanders and Tanck, "Critical Appraisal," pp. 385-86.
38. Marion J. Rice and Wilfrid C. Bailey, "A Sequential Curriculum in Anthropology for Grades 1-7," *Social Education* 29 (April 1965): 211-12.

Grade	Traditional	Minnesota Project Social Studies	Greater Cleveland
K	Local Topics Store, Home, etc.	Earth as Home of Man	The Child Begins to Know His World
1	Family and School	Families Around the World	Learning About Our Country
2	Neighborhood Studies	Families Around the World	Communities at Home and Abroad
3	Community Studies	Communities Around the World	Making of Anglo-America and The Metropolitan Community
4	Area Studies: state, regional in U.S. or world	Communities Around the World	Story of Agriculture India-Society in Transition
5	Early America (U.S. History)	Regional Studies	Ancient, Classical, Medieval Civilization Area Study of Middle East
6	Western or Eastern Hemisphere	Formation of American Society	Rise of Modern Civilization—(Formative Period) Later Modern Civilization Area Study of Latin America
7	Eastern or Western Hemisphere	Man and Culture	Contemporary Civilization Principles of Geography Area Study of Sub-Saharan Africa
8	U.S. History	Our Political System	American Generations: Civil War to early 20th Century Area Study of North America and Caribbean

Fig. 14.5. Sequence for Traditional and Minnesota and Greater Cleveland Comprehensive Projects.

MULTIDISCIPLINARY	SINGLE DISCIPLINE	
Providence Social Studies	*Anthropology* (Univ. of Georgia)	*Geography* (Univ. of Georgia)
Integrating Discipline: Geography, K-7 Neighbors K-3		
K Family	Concept of Culture and How We Study People	Earth as the Home of Man
1 Man's Basic Needs	Concept of Culture Three Ethnographies	Place and Environment
2 Neighborhood Patterns	Development of Man and his Culture: New World Prehistory	Resource and Production
3 Community Regions 4-7	Changing Culture: Changes in Culture	Regions and Regionalization
4 A Type Study of Regions: Physical, Cultural, Extractive	Concept of Culture: Comparative Cultures	The Urban Landscape
5 One Culture Region Anglo-America	Development of Man and His Culture: Old World Prehistory	The Rural Landscape
6 Comparison of Two Culture Regions: Africa and Latin America	Changing Culture: How Culture Changes	Population
7 Studies of Three Culture Regions: Southeast Asia, Western Europe, and Soviet	Life Cycle	
Integrating Discipline, History Civilizations, 8-12		
8 Contemporary Civilizations East Asian Muslim (Optional—Classical Greece)	Political Anthropology	

Fig. 14.6. Scope and Sequence in Multidisciplinary and Single Discipline Social Studies.

Appraisal of Social Studies Projects

Since the 1960 curriculum projects have epitomized the "new" social studies, it is appropriate to consider some of their distinctive characteristics at some length. Four salient characterists are: emphasis on structure of the discipline, behavioral sciences and economics, the nonwestern world, and inquiry-discovery approaches.

Structure of Discipline. In historical perspective, the most noteworthy characteristic of the curriculum projects was an emphasis on the relationship of the social studies to the social sciences expressed as "structure."[39] One of the most influential exponents of structure was Schwab, who looked at structure from two perspectives: a conceptual facet which emphasizes the system and organization of concepts on which the structure of knowledge is built; and a syntactical facet which emphasizes the procedures by which knowledge is acquired.[40] These distinctions are roughly comparable to anatomy and physiology, of organization to function. The concern for structure has raised the cognitive level in the projects, because structure has emphasized a greater use of abstractions. And abstractions are invariably connotative rather than denotative.

Since the social studies are usually subject to shifts in utilitarian emphasis, the future of "structure" is uncertain. Less than a decade spans the 1961 meeting of the National Council for the Social Studies with its emphasis on the disciplines[41] and the 1970 meeting with its theme "The Human Condition: What Must Be Done."[42] The special purpose projects also reflect a shift in emphasis from an academic to a problem approach.

As a practical matter, the projects have suffered a serious lack of diffusion. Some have been taken up by major publishing houses; many are still available only in trial form. Most schools of education do not even attempt to purchase the materials for their curriculum laboratories, but request complimentary copies.[43] Many teacher training institutions have given little attention to the implications of the new content for the training of elementary teachers in social studies. A few survey courses at the lower divisional level scarcely equip the elementary teacher with the prerequisites to handle conceptual and structural teaching.

Behavioral Sciences and the Non-Western World. A cursory examination indicates that the social science curriculum projects have consistently emphasized the non-Western world. This is a consummation of a trend begun half a century ago, and is not a new departure. In view of the disparity in consumption and productive capacity between the Western and non-Western worlds, this emphasis is a shift from technological-industrial to traditional economies, and on the world scene is the equivalent of empha-

---

39. Phi Delta Kappa, *Education and the Structure of Knowledge,* Fifth Annual Phi Delta Kappa Symposium on Educational Research (Chicago: Rand McNally & Company, 1964).

40. Joseph J. Schwab, "The Concept of the Structure of a Discipline," *Educational Record* 43, no. 3 (July 1962): 197-205.

41. The featured speeches at this meeting resulted in the joint publication by the American Council of Learned Societies and the National Council for the Social Studies, *The Social Studies and the Social Sciences* (New York: Harcourt, Brace & World, 1962).

42. The phrase "The Human Condition" was used by Dorothy McClure Fraser in her article "The Changing Scene in Social Studies," in *Social Studies Curriculum Development: Prospects and Problems,* 39th Yearbook, ed. Dorothy McClure Fraser (Washington, D.C.: National Council for the Social Studies, 1969), p. 11.

43. Files, Anthropology Curriculum Project, University of Georgia.

sizing rural cultures to the neglect of the urban world. This shift reflects a value judgment, and there is no way of determining its pedagogical desirability.

While economics is well represented in the new curricula, a behavioral approach has not really materialized except in *Man: A Course of Study* and the *Social Science Laboratory Units for the Elementary Grades*. A behavioral emphasis is difficult to achieve unless the content is drawn from the behavioral sciences—anthropology, psychology, and sociology—or uses behavioral concepts as content organizers.

Inquiry-Discovery Teaching Strategies. With few exceptions, inquiry has played the dominant role among the 1960 projects, with practically no consideration given to research on instruction which raises questions about the alleged efficacy of inquiry methods.[44] Sanders has been almost alone among social studies educators to raise a caveat about the fervor for inquiry-discovery methods. While there are various interpretations of inquiry, the most reasoned expositions, such as that of Fenton, follow the Schwab model, previously described under "Structure." Structure as syntactical inquiry is not a panacea, but is related to the knowledge system of the discipline.

The deficiency of social science as knowledge in the training of elementary teachers has already been noted. It is difficult to see how teachers who lack a knowledge base can teach effectively using inquiry methods. Space does not permit a critique of the inquiry-discovery technique. Inductive methods certainly have a place in school instruction, and are needed for a change in pace for both teacher and pupil even when learning products cannot be measured. Neglect of the basic social studies skills[45] and the ability to read for meaning[46] may convert inquiry methods in the hands of the poorly trained teacher into procedures just as sterile as the frequently criticized assign-study-recite-test method. In fact, where documents are the basis for inquiry questions, there is frequently little difference in the two procedures, despite differences in rationale. Just as the abuse of the problem-solving methods discredited social studies teaching, inept inquiry methods may have a similar result. Thus far teachers are admonished to use inquiry methods, but procedures for training in this skill appear sadly deficient.

Appraisal of Social Studies Education

A major defect in social studies education is found in all areas of the elementary curriculum from art to social studies. This defect is the lack of subject matter knowledge which comes from specialization. While increased knowledge as measured by number of courses is not always related to pupil performance, subject background is related to favorable perceptions of innovative curricula. In turn, these favorable perceptions are related to pupil performance.[47] The halting acceptance of social studies innovations

44. See the articles by M. C. Wittrock, "The Learning by Discovery Hypothesis" and Lee J. Cronback, "The Logic of Experiments on Discovery" in *Learning by Discovery: A Critical Appraisal*. eds. Lee S. Schulman and Evan R. Keislar (Chicago: Rand McNally and Co., 1968).
45. Carpenter, ed., *Skill Development in Social Studies*.
46. Ernest Horn, *Methods of Instruction in the Social Studies*, Report of the Commission on Social Studies of the American Historical Association, Part 15 (New York: Charles Scribner's Sons, 1937), pp. 151-205.
47. William A. Imperatore, *Evaluation of a Conceptual Geography Unit for Kindergarten* (Athens, Ga.: Geography Curriculum Project, University of Georgia, 1970).

may be directly attributed to the lack of social science background of elementary teachers.

Most social studies projects emphasize the importance of inservice education. In view of the lack of project acceptance and heavy teacher turnover, this approach seems less promising than changes in basic teacher preparation programs. It is not likely that the problem of adequate subject matter preparation can ever be solved as long as the division of labor horizontally in elementary teaching remains to be the self-contained classroom. Under extant circumstances, it seems desirable for prospective elementary teachers to select a proposed area of concentration and attempt to develop additional competency in that area.

As a new teacher in a school, you will find an established social studies sequence and selected materials. Materials available will most frequently reflect traditional rather than innovative curricula. The new teacher should nevertheless keep in mind that traditional materials frequently provide more knowledge and skills than is ever taught in the course of the year. Wise use of the traditional materials will be a more efficient use of time than a decision to create your own social studies program. Generally, traditional materials are superior in execution and design to the average teacher-made unit.

The emphasis of a teacher should be on thorough preparation so that he can thoroughly master the conceptual organization of the material. Projects and activities may then be used to supplement class discourse to make conceptual learning more concrete. A useful way for teachers to study is to prepare an alternate form of organization. If material is arranged topically, try a historical organization; if it is arranged historically or geographically, try a topical organization. One reason the text is seldom used as a research source is the tendency to think of the text as a static organization which can only be used beginning with page one. The use of alternate conceptual schemes are particularly useful in reviews. A topical review after regional geographic studies is an excellent device for bringing out new insights and relationships.

A continuing problem in social studies instruction is the lack of facilities which characterize the usual self-contained classroom. If some type of departmentalization is possible, it is recommended that the school budget for maps, charts, globes, magazines, pictures, and other related social studies materials be used to equip rooms designed as social science laboratories. Careful use needs to be made of the media center to supplement the resources of the social science laboratory.

The colored filmstrip and movie provide the modern social studies teacher with the means to make concept teaching vivid through living illustrations. It is important to understand that pictures and artifacts are conceptually meaningful only to the extent to which they are used with language. If multimedia are primarily used on the assumption that it makes learning easier and more palatable, the teacher is soon disappointed. After the novelty disappears, multimedia are regarded with almost the same indifference as language learning. Much misconception still persists in instructional television today by making the false analogy with an entertainment model.

The social studies as a curriculum area frequently receives low scores for achievement. This is, in part, due to its overstatement of goals and objectives and the failure to distinguish between the ultimate ends of education, measurable only in the life of an individual, and the immediate objectives of social studies instruction. Immediate objectives can be expressed for affective as well as cognitive outcomes when they relate to instruction. As more attention is given to value analysis in social studies instruction, however, it is important that the pupils and teachers both know when the focus is on moral judgment rather than on knowledge. Otherwise the social studies, already identified with a low cognitive output, will become even more identified with a "preachy" outlook which commands little respect in a scientific age. This does not mean that social studies teachers are not involved in valuing. Curriculum construction and teaching are inextricably intertwined with a teacher's values. But in the teaching process, students are quick to note when opinions are expressed as facts, and values as knowledge. The tendency of the former to prevail may be one reason why the social studies frequently fare so poorly in the esteem of students.

Selected References

American Council of Learned Societies and the National Council for the Social Studies, *The Social Studies and the Social Sciences.* New York: Harcourt, Brace & World, Inc., 1962.

Carpenter, Helen McCracken, ed. *Skill Development in Social Studies.* Thirty-third Yearbook of the National Council for the Social Studies. Washington, D.C.: NCSS, 1962.

Fenton, Edwin, ed. *Teaching the New Social Studies in Secondary Schools; An Inductive Approach.* New York: Holt, Rinehart and Winston, Inc., 1966.

Fraser, Dorothy McClure, ed. *Social Studies Curriculum Development: Prospects and Problems*, 39th Yearbook of the National Council for the Social Studies. Washington, D.C.: NCSS, 1969.

Gross, Richard E.; McPhie, Walter E.; and Fraenkel, Jack R., eds. *Teaching the Social Studies: What, Why, and How*, Scranton, Pa.: International Textbook Company, 1969.

Horn, Ernest. *Methods of Instruction in the Social Studies.* Report of the Commission on the Social Studies of the American Historical Association, Part 15. New York: Charles Scribner's Sons, 1937.

Krug, Mark M. *History and the Social Sciences.* Waltham, Mass.: Blaisdell Publishing Company, 1967.

McLendon, Jonathon C.; Joyce, William W.; and Lee, John R. *Readings on Elementary Social Studies: Emerging Changes.* 2d ed. Boston: Allyn and Bacon, Inc., 1970.

Michaelis, John U., ed. *Social Studies in Elementary Schools.* Thirty-second Yearbook of the National Council for the Social Studies. Washington, D.C.: NCSS, 1962.

National Society for the Study of Education, *Social Studies in the Elementary School.* The Fifty-sixth Yearbook of the National Society for the Study of Education, Part II. Chicago: University of Chicago Press, 1957.

Sanders, Norris M., and Tanck, Marlin L. "A Critical Appraisal of Twenty-six National Social Studies Projects," *Social Education* 34, no. 4 (April 1970): 383-449.

Tryon, Rolla M. *The Social Sciences as School Subjects.* Report of the Commission on the Social Studies of the American Historical Association, Part 11. New York: Charles Scribner's Sons, 1935.

health and safety in the school

15

Man is an animal, a creature of bones, tissue, nerves and muscle. He needs food for energy and sleep to recuperate. A highly developed mammalian invertebrate, he is peculiarly subject to organic disorders. Many of these result from the chemical imbalances which occur in the functioning organism, some of which are either genetic or congenital in origin. Other diseases and ailments come from the external attack of hostile bacteria and viruses. Man is also peculiarly subject to injury. His skin continually renews itself, but his complex neurological and physiological structure contains no powers of regeneration, as in the coelenterata. Once an eye or leg is lost, the function of that member is lost. Man needs to be concerned about his safety, for many are the hazards that cut life short, even on the school playground.

But the health of man is not purely physical. Man is a cultured animal; he adjusts to his environment not merely with his body but with his culture. Man's developed brain consists primarily of the cerebrum, which has to do with learned behavior. Not only do the complex psychological phenomena of consciousness, intelligence, and memory depend on the cerebrum, but also the interpretation of sensations and the application of meanings. Man thus surrounds himself with an attitudinal and emotional world. Health is also a thing of the mind and of the personality.

Man once tried to protect his health by magic and incantation. Tied to the mystery of birth and of death, the *shaman* or medicine man often vied with the war or hunting chief in power and prestige. Today science and medicine have been substituted for prayer and incantation. But our application of knowledge still lags behind its development. Longevity and infant mortality in the United States compare unfavorably with some other countries, largely because access to health services is related to social class. Poor people have poor health care. A large part of the population have problems of malnutrition. Malnutrition not only affects the overall health and energy level of the body, but in pregnancy and early infancy it is especially related to neurological development on which intelligence depends.

Health and safety are therefore important school considerations, not merely for the child as a student but for mankind.

This chapter is divided into four parts— the healthful school environment, common health problems, health services, and health instruction. The first briefly indicates characteristics of physical plant, school organization, and teacher-pupil relations which characterize a healthy school environment. The second summarizes common health problems with which teachers should be familiar in order to make proper use of school and other health services. The third discusses appraisal, preventive, and corrective aspects of a school health program. Finally, health instruction is concerned with the principles of healthful living, and the integration of these principles into school and home living. Physical education, one of the most important aspects of a comprehensive program in health education, is the subject of chapter 18.

The Healthful School Environment

The healthful school environment may be examined from three aspects—the physical plant and housekeeping, school organization and routine, and teacher-pupil relationships.

The Physical Plant. Modern school plants are built to architectual specifications which conform to minimum health, safety, and sanitation standards. Plant deficiencies, resulting from building economies, are therefore rarely found today in the plant that is provided, except by what is later discovered to have been omitted.

One of the major deficiencies is in the psychological environment. There is a lack of aesthetic appeal which comes from a blend of architectural, landscape, and interior design. School buildings are likely to be physically healthful, but aesthetically bleak.

Another major deficiency is usually found in the lack of provision for specialized space. Except in wealthy school districts, children are most likely to spend their day in a healthful box. There are no specialized indoor and outdoor activity areas. While it is well known that growing children are active, few elementary schools provide areas for vigorous indoor play and games. In regions of clay topsoil, heavy winter rains, and mild climate, children are often roombound for days because there are no large outdoor surfaced play areas (see "Physical Education").

Architectural specifications do not assure that a building will be maintained in a healthful fashion. Rooms may be underheated or overheated, toilets may be allowed to clog up, and drinking fountains of the approved jet type may be collecting bacteria. The odors which come from many toilet rooms are offensive and reflect poor cleanliness, even when no direct health threat exists. The most rigid equipment and personnel standards may be enforced in the lunchroom, but economies in soap and towels, which discourage hand cleanliness, may result in outbreaks of infectious hepatitis.[1] And a school layout, carefully designed to enhance safety, may prove ineffective from a safety standpoint if practices are permitted which contribute to accidents. Teachers in a school have little to do with the design of physical environment in which they teach, but they are responsible for the practices which take place within that environment.

School Organization and Routine. Most school systems have a regular building maintenance schedule administered from a physical plant office. If forms are not available

---

1. Oliver E. Byrd, *School Health Administration* (Philadelphia: W. B. Saunders Company, 1964), p. 380.

for teacher reporting interim maintenance requirements, such as fixing a loose tread, handrail, or piece of tile, they should be developed.

The schedule of the elementary school day normally provides for a balance of sitting and moving activities, interspersed with lunch. Provisions are sometimes made for younger children to rest or be very quiet, but provisions of sleep are rarely found except in day-care nurseries. Inadequate lunchroom space, with its attendant scheduling problems, often creates overly long or short mornings, in which case an afternoon or morning snack is desirable, especially for primary children. To provide for clean hands before lunch, it is helpful to have children line up and take turns washing and drying hands.

The school safety patrol is often a valuable adjunct to the school routine. Patrolmen caution pupils about street crossing, direct bicycle traffic and parking, open and close car doors from the parking dock to speed traffic flow, assist with fire drills, and perform other duties related to traffic flow and safety. The school fire marshals not only make children conscious of better housekeeping in school, but help children to be aware of fire hazards at home. Where the functions of the school safety patrol and fire marshals are established as a part of the school routine, their prestige is enhanced and the program of school safety becomes part of the socialization function of the school.

Since many accidents occur in connection with transportation, routines need to be established for the flow of pedestrian, bicycle, car, and bus traffic. Procedures for orderly traffic flow are just as important as emergency drills, whether it is walking in the hall or getting on the school bus. Since accidents are the third leading cause of death in the nation for all age groups, particular attention needs to be given to safety in coming to and leaving school, in the building, and on the playground. It is recommended that the Standard Student Accident Report Form of the National Safety Council be submitted on accident cases involving a doctor's care or absence from school.[2]

One of the routines established in most schools is the collection of an "Emergency Information" sheet on each child. The amount of detail varies with the school system, but most require address and telephone information on such individuals as father, mother, relative or friend, and family physician. This permits the school to contact an appropriate adult during the school day, when many mothers cannot be reached at home.

It is generally the function of administrators to make periodic checks of the school environment from the standpoint of health and safety.[3] Inclusion of children as well as teachers in this activity makes it not merely an administrative function but a part of the learning experiences in the school health program.

Teacher-Pupil Relations. Relations between teachers and pupils are a significant part of the school environment, as well as procedures relating to the kind of promotion policies and type of pupil reporting (see

---

2. Alma Nemir, *The School Health Program*, 2e ed. (Philadelphia: W. B. Saunders Company 1964), p. 263. A copy of the form is given in Appendix B, p. 365.

3. See Cyrus Mayshark, Donald D. Shaw, and Wallace H. Best, *Administration of School Health Programs* (St. Louis, Mo.: C. V. Mosby Company 1967), pp. 293-99.

chapter 20). The importance of the teacher in creating a positive emotional environment for learning is discussed in detail in the chapter relating to classroom management and teaching (see chapter 21). It is sufficient to emphasize that the school environment is not merely made up of the plant and procedures—it is above all made up of an environment which grows out of the interaction between teachers and pupils. Pupil discipline, homework, school pressures, and helpful teachers all contribute to the total atmosphere which is thought of as a school environment. It therefore happens that some schools in dilapidated buildings located in crowded areas have an environment favorable to healthful school living while other schools in beautiful buildings do not. People as well as things are part of a healthful school environment. And people have problems. The next section examines some of the more common health problems with which teachers need to be familiar.

Common School Health Problems

Common school health problems include those which have to do with physical defects and illnesses, emotional maladjustments, and accidents. It is not expected that teachers will have the skills to treat school health problems. Teachers should be sensitive to some of the more common problems, in order that they may cooperate more effectively with school health and psychological services.

Physical Health Problems. There are many physical health problems about which the elementary school teacher should be knowledgeable. A discussion of some of the more important ones follows.

NUTRITION. One of the most common school health problems relates to nutrition and the common method of treatment is the school lunch program. The objective of most school lunch programs is to provide each child with the minimum of one well-balanced and nourishing meal a day, so that over a period of time any dietary deficiencies at home, especially in terms of vitamins and proteins, might be met. Many schools are now serving breakfast in addition to lunch, particularly in schools which primarily serve economically disadvantaged areas.

Dietary habits are culturally formed, and children's perceptions of desirable foods often differ from those of the school lunch director; the refuse of any school lunch garbage can bears this out. Having good food is no guarantee that it will be eaten, even by children who need milk or vegetables. And a child can know the proper recommended food to answer a test in nutrition, and still not choose the right foods to eat. It is probable that too much emphasis in the past has been devoted to caloric intake, and schools have inadvertently pushed foods rich in cholesterol which may be in the long run harmful to health, particularly from the standpoint of arterial disease. Evidences of malnutrition are often indirect—restlessness, retarded school progress, inattention and difficulty in mastering content or perfecting skills. While malnutrition can result from improper eating habits in affluent homes, it is more likely to be associated with poverty. While all poor children are not malnourished, they may be poorly nourished. Because school energy and productivity are related to food intake, many schools provide breakfast for children of low income families in addition to lunches.

EYES. Some common eye defects include myopia (nearsightedness), hyperopia (farsightedness), astigmatism, and strabismus (cross or squint eyes). They usually may be corrected by wearing glasses. The earlier cross eyes are detected and treatment begun in infancy, the more favorable are chances of successful correction—80 percent for children up to two years of age compared to 40 percent for children four to seven.[4] Epidemic conjunctivitis, popularly known as pink eye, spreads rapidly by indirect contact. Children should be sent home who have pus discharging from the eyes. Because the eye is very sensitive—blindness has occurred from a flip of a rubber band or a paper-clip bullet from a rubber band—eye safety must be continually enforced. Chemical eye burns must be *immediately* treated with running water. Color blindness is the result of a sex-linked hereditary trait, and about 4 percent of males are color blind compared to 0.4 percent in women. Children who are color blind have gaps in learning where color discrimination is important, such as with maps, charts, pictures, and traffic signals. Once some bizarre clothing combinations could be attributed to color blindness. While this phenomena now may be primarily cultural, it is important for the teacher to know when children have color discrimination problems. The Isihara and Stilling charts provide an easy and convenient way to ascertain defective color discrimination.

TEETH. The teeth are not only useful to chewing; they are also an adjunct to good speech. Infected teeth can also affect the whole body. The elementary years are the years in which permanent teeth replace the primary or baby teeth. By the time most children are twelve, the second molar has emerged. Because of the tendency of some parents to neglect the care of the baby teeth, many children have failed to establish dental hygiene habits by the time the permanent teeth begin to emerge. The emphasis of brushing the teeth in the school—"Here's the way we brush our teeth"—is not a misplaced objective. Practically all children suffer from dental caries. Systematic home care and regular visits to the dentist are required. Gingivitis (pink toothbrush) is an inflammation of the gums resulting from improper oral hygiene.

Malocclusion of teeth interferes with good oral hygiene, speech and, in severe cases, causes deterioration of the self-concept. What child wants to smile when his protruding overbite has earned him the sobriquet of Ronald Rabbit or Minnie Mouse? The alignment of teeth requires orthodontic treatment, an expense which many poorer families can ill afford. Because tooth injuries often occur in contact sports, tooth guards should be worn in any supervised and planned competition, such as football. An injured tooth should be immediately treated by a doctor. If a tooth is knocked out completely, try to find it. If found, wash the tooth with water only and take the patient to the dentist. Often such a tooth can be successfully implanted.[5]

EAR, NOSE, AND THROAT. In the anatomy of the body, the ear, nose, and throat are linked together. As a result, common respiratory infections, so prevalent in childhood, frequently affect all three. Naso-

4. Nemir, *School Health Program*, p. 65.
5. Ibid., p. 116.

pharyngal infections pass quickly through the eustachian tube to the middle ear, and are the most frequent causes of infections. Because the middle ear is encased in bone, middle ear infections are usually very painful. Outer ear infections not only can cause a good deal of pain, but are often related to conduction hearing loss, a hearing impairment resulting from the failure of sounds to pass from the auricle to the acoustic nerve. A second type of hearing loss involves auditory nerve fibers, and may result in nerve deafness. This distinction is primarily important to the kind of treatment which is given.

A teacher, however, should understand the distinction between a deaf child, one who has no serviceable hearing, and a hard-of-hearing child, one who can still hear but with reduced efficiency. Hearing loss not only impairs message reception, but it also impairs speech production. Children with hearing of 30 to 50 percent in the better ear require special auditory and speech training, including lipreading, and should use a hearing aid. Those with hearing of between 50 and 70 percent require special training, but do not require continuous use of a hearing aid. Children born with no hearing or whose hearing became impaired before natural speech and language developed may be placed in special classes or schools for training.

Tests for hearing loss are easily administered and, where there is a regular program of school health appraisal, hearing tests are regularly administered. Early detection is important in order to provide the child with appropriate corrective treatment.

COMMUNICABLE DISEASES. Fortunately, the development of vaccines and other public health measures have substantially reduced such communicable diseases as poliomyelitis. However, some children are not immunized against such infections as diphtheria, a dangerous disease of which there are over one thousand cases a year. Some diseases, such as rubella and chicken pox, may be relatively mild if given proper treatment. Teachers should be sufficiently familiar with symptoms such as persistent coughs, itching, complaints of headaches and sore throats, unusual quietness or excessive irritability, nausea, red eyes, and fever so that the child may be referred to the school health nurse or referred to the parents for further diagnosis by the family physician.

Other types of communicable disease or infections with which the teacher needs to be familiar are those resulting from gastrointestinal infections, fungi, and lice.

ALLERGIES. About 7 percent of school children suffer from some type of allergy. The two main types are nasal and skin allergies. Although some allergies may prove fatal, as from wasps or bees, most allergies result in discomfort. Asthma is one of the severest of the allergies, and is often accompanied by emotional and behavioral problems. The health information obtained from parents should include information about allergies. Teachers may use this information to exclude from their room flowers, pets, perfume, or other things to which their pupils might be allergic.

SKIN. The most common skin problems in the elementary school are impetigo, scalp ringworm, and lice infestation. Impetigo is a contagious bacterial disease which frequently appears on the lower part of the face and can initially be confused with a cold sore. Impetigo is transmitted quickly by indirect contact. The infected child should be required to remain home until he has a note from a physician indicating that the impetigo has been arrested.

Scalp ringworm is endemic in certain parts of the United States and is transmitted by pets, direct contact with other children, and indirectly. If discovered in one child, it is likely to be found in others. Children may continue in school, but skull caps should be worn to prevent infected hairs from falling where they can spread infection. Several weeks of treatment are necessary to cure the infection, and close cooperation with the home is essential.

Head lice, body lice, and crab lice are three types of louse infections. In some parts of the country, practically all children at school and all members of the family are infected. Treatment usually requires less than thirty hours, but unless the source of infestation in the home and the community is removed, reinfestation quickly occurs.

Other types of common skin infections are scabies, athlete's foot, and acne. Acne is one of the most frustrating complaints of adolescence, and frequently makes its appearance in the upper grades of the intermediate school. Students need to understand the physiology of acne, which is related to the imbalance in androgen (male) and estrogen (female) hormones. Both sexes possess both hormones. The androgen content is stable, whereas the estrogen content fluctuates. A decrease in estrogen content is associated with an increase in oil production of the sebaceous glands.

The basic cause of acne is hormonal; the immediate cause is excessive fat gland activity. In some form, mild to severe, it is endured by practically every adolescent. Treatment includes diet control in which all types of fatty foods are avoided. If elementary children do not become dependent on such foods as popcorn, nuts, fried foods, and other fatty foods, diet control is easier in adolescence. Careful washing of the skin, morning and night, reduces bacteria and excessive oils. Blackheads are produced by plugged pores, and the reaction of the surrounding skin produces a pimple. The pimple attracts bacteria and stimulates the development of a pustule. Cleanliness is therefore essential in the control of acne.

ABDOMEN. "Upset stomach" is frequently encountered in school. It may be related to anything from improper eating to an emotional upset concerning school work; it may be the symptom of an allergy, the onset of gastroenteritis, or an early indication of appendicitis. Since digestive maladjustments are internal rather than external in their manifestations, when children complain of abdominal pains the rule is clear—attempt no treatment and get him to his parents.

Sometimes food poisoning occurs in school or on a school outing. Preventive measures include prompt refrigeration of foods and exclusion of personnel with skin infections from food handling. On field trips, foods which are most susceptible to bacterial growth when not refrigerated properly, such as meat, salads, custards, and puddings, should be eliminated.

HEART. Another health problem in otherwise normal children is associated with the heart. Many heart difficulties are congenital, originating in embryonic developmental anomalies. Many of these are now corrected by surgery. Common childhood diseases usually leave no heart impairment, but one form of rheumatic fever can result in permanent and extensive damage. This is known as carditis.

Rheumatic fever occurs most frequently between the ages of five and eighteen. It tends to occur most frequently in lower income groups where crowded and unsanitary homes are associated with poor nutrition, poor health, and weakened resistance. Diagnosis is often difficult, ranging from the acute manifestations of loss of muscular coordination in chorea to the insidious generalized symptoms associated with fatigue, sore throat, and so-called growing pains.

Teachers should understand the fact that many children have innocent or functional heart murmurs. The distinction between an innocent or organic murmur must be made by a physician. Where children have an innocent murmur, there is no need for coddling and overprotection. Where blood circulation is impaired, however, the overt signs of decompensation are readily observable—breathlessness, flushed cheeks and bluish lips. When children appear breathless after short exertion or they restrict their physical activities, the observant teacher may suggest additional investigation by a physician. Today many cardiologists recommend some physical activity for children who have organic heart disorders in order to maintain good muscle tone. Many adapted programs can be developed which permit an affected child to associate with his friends and, at the same time, protect the school. As with other aspects of the health program, information on heart defects needs to be kept up-to-date. A handicap in the third grade may have been corrected or "outgrown" in a later grade.

DIABETES. There is no cure for diabetes mellitus. It is a disease associated with insulin deficiency which interferes with the production of energy, resulting from the oxidation of glucose into carbon dioxide and water. Urine tests in school sometimes reveal a diabetic. Where a child follows the regimen of diet and insulin supplement prescribed by a physician, there is no need to limit or make concessions to him. But a teacher needs to know if he has a diabetic in his class. Symptoms of drowsiness might indicate the onset of a coma. An untreated coma may result in death.

HYPERACTIVITY. In recent years, more attention has been given to the hyperactive child in the classroom. Physiological causes account for almost half of hyperactivity, with neuroses, mental retardation, organic brain damage, and childhood schizophrenia among the causes. Symptoms of hyperactivity include excessive activity, continuous motion, disregard of disciplinary activities, lack of attention, and sudden physical aggression. If not corrected, the hyperactive child eventually develops retroactive emotional adjustments. Medication, psychiatric treatment, and special educational efforts are needed with the hyperactive child.

EPILEPSY. The word epilepsy means "seizure." It is not a disease as the word is usually meant, but is a manifestation of chemical disturbance in the brain which results in loss of consciousness and muscular control. Electroencephalograms (EEG) of epileptics show an 85 percent deviation from normal wave patterns compared to 15 percent of normal persons who show minor irregularities. Epilepsy is thus a neurological disturbance. The incidence is about one in two hundred.

There are several types of epilepsy—petit mal, grand mal, and focal are the most common. Psychomotor and minor motor attacks are also classified as epileptic.

Petit mal, more prevalent in infancy and early childhood, is accompanied by temporary lapses from reality. There is no muscular jerking, but there are sometimes slight manifestations, such as twitching of eyelids, generalized trembling, rolling eyes, and staring. These symptoms usually last no longer than thirty seconds, and are often classified as spells or blackouts. They can result in inattention.

Grand mal is characterized by generalized motor seizures, but the pattern varies with individuals. The commonly described attack has three characteristics: abrupt unconsciousness, rigidity, and jerking of muscles. Focal epilepsy, limited to one part or side of the body, is also characterized by rigidity and jerking.

Improved medication has substantially altered the picture for epileptics. They attend regular classes, and require no change in curriculum or discipline. They should be expected to fill the same expectations as other class members. Teacher, parent, and child need to cooperate in maintaining treatment. In the event of a grand mal seizure in class, the epileptic needs to be moved to a safe place where he cannot hurt himself. He should be laid down and his head turned to the side to permit saliva to come from the mouth. No objects should be inserted in the mouth to try to prevent tongue-biting, since this often causes more harm than good. After the attack, the person needs to be allowed time to rest and regain his orientation before returning to school tasks. Where there is no complete loss of consciousness, sometimes this is only a matter of minutes. An epileptic's classmates who understand the symptoms can provide supportive help. The epileptic child should be accepted as a normal person who occasionally has some neurological manifestation over which he has no control. The attitude of the teacher and classmates is very important in establishing a supportive emotional tone in the classroom.[6]

HEADACHES. Headaches are more common at school than fainting. A headache is a symptom, frequently indicative of emotional disturbances. Repeated and recurrent headaches should have a follow-up by a physician. Ordinarily the student who faints should be allowed merely to lie quietly until he wishes to move.

The preceding section on physical health problems is not intended to imply that the teacher either diagnose or treat health problems. Early prognosis, however, is one of the best means of reducing the seriousness of school health problems. It is the classroom teacher who comes into the most sustained contact with pupils of all the school personnel. An alertness to health problems is thus important for him in order that he can provide the necessary link between pupil and parent or pupil and school health services. Since many school health problems are associated with problems of emotional disturbances, relating to self-concept as well as school tasks, a knowledgeable and sympathetic teacher may be very helpful to student and family.

Emotional Problems. It is estimated that one out of every twenty persons will eventually have some kind of temporary or permanent psychological disorder which will require psychiatric or hospital treatment.

---

6. Additional information on epilepsy may be obtained from publications of the Epilepsy Information Center, Inc., 73 Tremont Street, Boston, Massachusetts.

Mental disorders are not restricted to adults. In the first six grades alone, it is estimated that 12 percent of the children are sufficiently maladjusted to need mental health assistance.[7] As indicated in the chapter dealing with exceptional children (see chapter 8), treatment may range from being placed in a regular class with a sympathetic and understanding teacher to psychiatric hospitalization for the severely disturbed.

An observant teacher may frequently help in the identification of children with emotional problems. Outward behavior—changes in appearance, attitude, hyperactivity, withdrawal, infantile behavior, exhibitionism, and escape mechanisms, to name a few, are sometimes symptoms of emotional disturbance. The teacher in the regular classroom who is understanding, patient and free from intolerance can often provide an atmosphere which combines support with guidance toward independence. In cases of severe disturbance, the teacher provides a useful link between psychological services and the pupil.

Accidents. Pupil medical emergencies occur throughout the school day on school grounds. Most of these emergencies result from accidents, primarily falls. Boys are involved in three times as many accidents as are girls. There are no sex differences, however, in other types of emergencies. Of those not involving accidents, convulsions and fainting occur most often.

Most teachers accept responsibilities for giving assistance to pupils in medical emergencies. When overly concerned, often because of lack of training, they transmit their anxieties to pupils.

There are only three emergencies which may result in death in minutes if care is not given. These are severe loss of blood, cessation of breathing, and stopping of heart beat. The most direct method of stopping bleeding is by use of a compress. Mouth-to-mouth resuscitation is the preferred technique to revive a person who has stopped breathing, but the arm lift, back pressure method may be used as an alternative. The use of external cardiac massage should be attempted only by a trained adult.

The organizational procedure to give first aid along with concomitant teacher responsibility are subsequently discussed.

School Health Services

The provision of school health services is primarily an administrative, not a teaching function. It consists of the direct procedures used by health personnel to protect and promote the health of students. The dominant view in the United States is that the primary responsibility for student health rests with the parent or guardian.[8] Supplementary, rather than comprehensive services are provided, and the responsibility for providing needed health services for low income families is usually the responsibility of the local public health department. As a result, many children never receive the needed health care. Some 10 percent of the cases of chronic illness each year never receive medical attention and over half of school children have never been to a dentist.[9] Spiraling medical costs and doctor shortages indicate that the adequacy of health services may de-

7. Delbert Oberteuffer and Mary K. Beyrer, *School Health Education,* 4th ed. (New York: Harper & Row, Publishers, 1966), p. 19.

8. Mayshark, Shaw, and Best, *Administration of School Health Programs,* p. 162.

9. Oberteuffer and Beyrer, *School Health Education,* pp. 337-38.

cline in proportion to population increase over the next few years.

The school is an ideal place to provide comprehensive medical services to children of school age. The children can be easily reached, because they come together in school, and there can be a planned follow-up from examination through treatment. While it is generally recognized that the United States leads in the development of advanced medical technology and practices, its record of preventive medicine compares unfavorably with some other countries. One reason is the political unacceptability of "socialized" medicine, although quite acceptable for military employees and veterans. Another reason is that where extensive public health services are available, the services are rarely tied to the schools in an efficient organization. As a result, many children do not receive the benefits of early diagnosis and treatment.

The previous review of common health problems indicates that the ordinary approach to school health services—some examination and little treatment—is totally inadequate to give satisfactory protection to the school population. The common types of school examination—sight and hearing—merely serve to emphasize the inadequacy of most school health services. Few school systems provide as extensive services as Philadelphia.[10] There will, however, be little improvement in the general kinds of school services until more funds are made available. And this will require a change in attitude toward public health. The following section describes briefly some of the common types of services available where school health services exist.

Health Appraisal. The term "appraisal" is now generally used to refer to the process of accumulating information on the physical and emotional health of pupils. It includes the process of accumulating health histories; teacher referrals; screening tests for vision, ear, and dental care; and physical examinations. The amount of detailed appraisal depends on the resources available. The general view is that examinations conducted by school physicians are general and tentative, and are no substitute for the thorough detailed examinations that should be obtained from a private physician.[11] Another view, tied to a concept of functional health organization, would place more responsibility on school health services.[12]

Follow-Through. Identification of medical, dental, or psychological deficiencies is merely a first, though important, step in health care. Actual improvement of health depends on the remedial and corrective action taken in the follow-through stage. Generally, the procedure is to inform the parents of the deficiency, and place on them the responsibility of follow-up through private channels. As noted previously, with children of low income families this frequently means no follow-through, particularly where there is a lack of coordination of school with community health services.

Protective services provided by some schools include vaccinations, innoculations, control of contagion through medical and nonmedical treatment, and other preventive measures, including safety precautions.

Emergency or first aid assistance is provided in case of injury or illness, even where

10. Ibid., p. 339.
11. Nemir, *School Health Program,* p. 281; Oberteuffer and Beyrer, *School Health Education,* p. 341.
12. Mayshark and Shaw, *Administration of School Health Programs,* p. 193.

schools do not have a school nurse. School personnel are legally liable for providing appropriate immediate care.[13]

Some minimum essentials of a first aid program include having trained first-aiders, as recognized by the American Red Cross, in the school, and clearly established policies relating to extent of first aid, parent notification, and removal from school for treatment.[14] If a teacher is entrusted with maintenance of the first aid kit, he should document any failure of school administrators to provide the necessary supplies. There would be a strong implication of negligence if administration of proper first aid to a child were to be impaired by deficient first aid supplies.

The School Nurse is a key person in most school health programs. If her time is devoted to record keeping which might be entrusted to a clerk or in becoming merely an administrator of first aid to insignificant injuries, she will have little time to serve in her professional role as counselor to pupils; provide liaison with parents; serve as an assistant to the school physician or family physician in referrals; and serve as a resource person to teachers in the school health program.[15] School nurses do not consider it among their duties to do secretarial-type work, check attendance, taxi sick children, do formal health teaching in classes, plan lunchroom menus, or visit many schools on the same day. On the matter of health appraisal, if the time of school nurses is entirely consumed with weighing, measuring, hearing, and vision tests, they have little time for follow-up work which is the most important part of a school health program.[16]

This section has said very little about *treatment* as part of the school health program. As presently constituted, little treatment is provided by school health services. Under the stimulus of Title I funds, many school systems now provide contractual services in the form of the purchase of glasses, hearing aids, and other devices for the handicapped children as well as direct medical, dental, and psychological care for them.

One of the objectives of the school health services, in conjunction with the total health program, is to reduce school absences resulting from illness. There is a high correlation between illness and poor scholastic achievement. However, emphasis on perfect attendance when usually healthy children have a fever or other symptoms of physical impairment are often detrimental to good school health practices.[17]

The final section of this chapter is concerned with teaching about health to children.

Health Instruction

The total health program of the school contributes to knowledge and attitudes about health. The environment and school health services are particularly concerned with immediate health outcomes for the pupil. Health instruction, however, has both immediate and long term ends. It is designed to help develop beneficial health practices through habit. This is especially important for the primary child. In the long run, health instruction is designed to develop appro-

---

13. Byrd, *School Health Administration*, p. 221; Mayshark, Shaw, and Best, *Administration of School Health Programs*, p. 208.
14. Mayshark, Shaw, and Best, *Administration of School Health Programs*, pp. 221-40.
15. Ibid., p. 169.
16. Ibid., p. 192.
17. Carl E. Willgoose, *Health Education in the Elementary School* 3d ed. (Philadelphia: W. B. Saunders Company, 1969), p. 55.

priate health attitudes. Attitudes are important because they are related to the disposition to act in a particular manner. Health knowledge, based on factual information and experience, provides the scientific basis for healthful living and reinforces proper attitudes.

Scope of Health Subject Matter. Health education is an eclectic subject, drawing on such diverse fields as medicine, biology, nutrition, public health, sociology, psychology, and psychiatry. Kilander identifies eleven health areas, with some adjustments to the maturity of the learner. These areas are: personal health, community and environmental health, consumer health, mental and emotional health, stimulants and depressants, family life and sex education, first aid, home nursing, driver and traffic safety education.[18] Since health education does not reflect a tight body of subject matter, it is peculiarly subject to repetition. There is no one pattern, and it is therefore incumbent upon a school system to follow a planned sequence to provide for both adequate coverage and study in depth.[19]

General Topics in the Primary Grades. In the kindergarten, health education is quite informal, but is a time in which training in attitudes and habits can be effectively begun. Emphasis should be on personal health and minimum safety education. Large health charts, now available from many publishers, are adapted to either kindergarten or first grade use. These health charts are means of verbalizing health and safety attitudes with which children can identify.

In grades one, two, and three, health education is largely of an informal nature and continues, as in the kindergarten, to focus on immediate health practices rather than health knowledge. A comparative list of health topics recommended for the primary grades is given below:

After Anderson[20]	*After Turner, Sellery, Smith*[21]
Personal and school cleanliness	Cleanliness
Rest and sleep	Sleep
Eating practices	Food habits
	Table manners
Posture	
Play practices	Play and exercise
Dental health	Teeth
Lighting	
Common cold	
	Communicable disease control
Safety to and from school schoolroom playground home	Safety
Body growth	Growth and health
	Sanitation
	Harmful substances
Mental health	Mental and emotional health

Duplication with other subjects should be avoided. For example, Anderson lists many topics in primary health which are frequently included in primary social studies, e.g., sharing, working together, kindness, being friendly, orderliness, depending on oneself, attaining goals, and home life.

18. H. Frederick Kilander, *School Health Education,* 2d ed. (New York: Macmillan Company, 1968).
19. Oberteuffer and Beyrer, *School Health Education,* p. 154.
20. C. L. Anderson, *School Health Practice,* 4th ed. (St. Louis, Mo.: C. V. Mosby Company, 1968), p. 312, The C. V. Mosby Company.
21. C. E. Turner, C. Morely Sellery, and Sarah L. Smith, *School Health and Health Education* 5th ed. (St. Louis, Mo.: C. V. Mosby Company, 1966), pp. 299-301.

	1	2	3	4	5	6
Nutrition and growth	x	x	R	x	R	x
Personal cleanliness and appearance	x	R	x	R	x	R
Dental health	x	x	R	x	R	x
Accidents and safety	x	x	x	x	R	x
Mental health	x	R	x	R	x	R
Sex and family living education	x	R	x	R	x	R
Body structure and function	x	x	x	x	x	x
Disease control	x	R	x	R	x	R
Community health	x	x	R	x	R	x
Physical activity, sleep, rest, relaxation	x	x	x	x	R	x
Tobacco, alcohol, and drugs					x	x
Consumer health		x	R	x	R	

Fig. 15.1. Summary of Major Health Areas by Grade, Showing New Emphasis (x) and Brief Treatment by Review (R). From Carl E. Willgoose, **Health Education in the Elementary School** 3d ed. (Philadelphia: W. B. Saunders Company, 1969), p. 149.

Sources of water and milk, sunshine and health might be considered in science. It is largely immaterial in which course of study some of these topics are studied. From the standpoint of intellectual development, it is more important how they are studied. However, efficient use of limited school time and avoidance of boredom and repetition require the elimination of duplicate topics from courses of study.

General Topics in the Intermediate Grades. There is more formal emphasis on knowledge acquisition and concept development in the intermediate grades. By the time pupils are in the fifth grade, there should be special instruction regarding the effects of alcohol and tobacco.[22] It is probable that instruction should begin earlier, as Kilander suggests,[23] because attitudes are sometimes developed before overt acts, such as smoking. Most of the areas introduced in the primary grades are repeated in the intermediate grades, with a more technical emphasis. Careful attention to topic selection is most important for developing new knowledge and concepts.

Suggested Curriculum Sequences. Major health topics receive different emphasis at different grade levels, and the recommendations of suitable topics reflect the preferences of health education specialists. There is general agreement, however, as a comparison of figures 15.1 and 15.2 indicate.

It is necessary to distinguish between the recommendations of health educators and actual practice in health instruction, which frequently departs markedly from recom-

22. Willgoose, *Health Education*, p. 145.
23. Kilander, *School Health Education*, p. 278.

Health Areas	Grades and Levels					
	Pre-school level	Grade 1	Grades 2-3	Grades 4-6	Grades 7-9	Grades 10-12
1. Personal health	xx	xx	xx	xx	xxx	xx
2. Nutrition	xx	xx	xx	xx	xxx	xxx
3. Community and environmental health	x	x	x	xx	xxx	xx
4. Consumer health			x	x	xx	xxx
5. Mental health	x	x	x	xx	xx	xxx
6. Stimulants and depressants			x	x	xxx	xxx
7. Family life education	x	x	xx	xx	xxx	xxx
8. Safety education	x	xx	xx	xx	xxx	xx
9. First aid		x	x	xx	xxx	xxx
10. Home nursing			x	x	xx	xxx
11. Driver education				x	xx	xxx

Note: xxx—Major emphasis on this area at this grade level
xx—Moderate emphasis on this area at this level
x—Some attention, particularly to attitudes and practices rather than to knowledge
Blank—No attention to this area at this grade level

Fig. 15.2. Recommended Major Health Areas by Grade Level. From H. Frederick Kilander, **School Health Education** 2d ed. (New York: Macmillan Company, 1968), p. 278. Reprinted with permission of the Macmillan Company. Copyright © by H. Frederick Kilander, 1968.

mendations in both time and content. The smaller the school system, the less emphasis there is on a planned health sequence. A direct comparison of actual practices (figure 15.3) with recommended practices (figures 15.1 and 15.2) is not possible because of differences in the taxonomy. In general, however, the survey indicated that emphasis in health teaching in K-3 was on the establishment and practice of healthful habits for daily living and development of good attitudes toward health. This is compatible with the growth characteristics of primary children. But whether such teaching results in the development of healthful habits was not revealed by the School Health Education Study.

In the intermediate grades, the emphasis is continued but there is added emphasis on giving the reasons for desired health behavior. Knowledge is emphasized more and more in relationship to health practices. In the last years of the intermediate grades, the emphasis shifts to making decisions about health.

The compatibility between recommended health education and actual health education emphasis largely results from the fact that the health education series published by major publishers[24] and used as the basic in-

health and safety in the school

Health Content Areas	K	1	2	3	4	5	6	7-8
Accident Prevention	●○x	●○x	●○x	●○x	●○x	●○x	●○x	x
Alcohol						○	x	
Boy-Girl Relationships								x
Cleanliness and Grooming	●○x	●○x	●○x	●○x	●○x	●○x	●○x	x
Communicable Diseases	○	●○	●○x	●○x	●○x	●○x	●○x	x
Community Health Programs					●○	●○	●○	
Community Helpers	●○x	●○x	●○x	●○	●○	●	●	
Consumer Education								
Dental Health	●○x	●○x	●○x	●○x	●○x	●○x	●○x	x
Drugs and Narcotics							x	x
Environmental Hazards						○x	○x	x
Exercise and Relaxation	●○x	●○x	●○x	●○x	●○x	●○x	●○x	x
Family Life	●○	○	○	○	○	○	○	x
First Aid	○	○	○	○	○x	○x	○x	x
Foot Care								
Food and Nutrition	●○x	●○x	●○x	●○x	●○x	●○x	●○x	x
Health Careers								
Health Examination and Appraisals	●○	●	●	●	●○	●○	●○	
Health Heroes						●		
International Health Activities								
Mental Health and Personal Adjustment					●○	●○	●○	x
Non-Communicable Diseases								
Personality Development	○	○	○	●○	●○	●○x	●○x	x
Physical Changes During Growth and Development	○					x	●○x	x
Posture and Body Mechanics	●○	●○x	●○x	●○x	●○x	●○x	●○x	x
Rest and Sleep	○x	●○x	●○x	●○x	●○x	●○x	●○x	x
Sex Education								
Skin Care					●	● x	● x	x
Smoking							● x	x
Structure and Function of the Human Body					○	● x	●○x	x
Venereal Disease								
Vision and Hearing	○	●○	●○	●○x	●○x	●○x	●○x	x

● Large System ○ Medium System x Small System

Fig. 15.3. Health content areas emphasized in grades K to 8 by 50 percent or more of sample public school systems, 1961-62, School Health Education Study. From Elena M. Sliepcevich, **Summary Report of a Nationwide Study of Health Instruction in the Public Schools, 1961-63** (Washington, D.C.: School Health Education Study, 1964), p. 34.

structional tools[25] are written by health educators. Any lack of adequate health education, notwithstanding omission of some areas, does not reflect lack of adequate content so much as failure to allot sequential time for instruction. This, in turn, reflects inadequate support given to health education in many schools.

Any broad taxonomy of health instruction, whether represented by topics, areas, or concepts (see "Curriculum Development in Health Education"), merely outline the general structure of a health curriculum. As in other subject areas, it is necessary to plan for specific sequential objectives, and to reduce as much overlap as possible.

Omissions in Health Education: Family Living and Mental Health. Many courses of study omit important items. For example, lack of preparation, controversy, or careless planning may result in the neglect of some aspect of health education. Principal areas of controversy in health education usually relate to sex education, healing, administration of medical care, alcohol and tobacco, and local problems, such as fluoridation of public water.[26] The general principles of teaching controversial issues apply to these matters, if included in the curriculum. However, two areas, because of their importance, need additional comment. These are family life and sex education, and mental health. The two areas are interrelated, and the lack of success in the area of mental health teaching is directly related to the many taboos normally associated with family life and sex education.

It is unfortunate that the terminology "sex education" was ever introduced into questions of public school curricula, because the term not only confuses the issue but arouses a good deal of needless emotion.

Three characteristic approaches to sex education involve: analogy to plant and animal reproduction; human anatomy and physiology; and an idealized family life approach. Plant and animal reproduction may be interesting biologically and show the continuity of reproductive systems with that of man, but have no relationship to the elaborate cultural patterns with which man surrounds sex.

The second approach is akin to that of the first. It provides more useful information relating to man, but still equates sex with reproduction. Certainly, students need more accurate information about their bodies, but human anatomy and physiology can be taught in a less emotional context within biology than it can under "sex education." Earlier puberty associated with better nutrition and health indicates the need of upper elementary students for more information on growth and development relating to puberty.[27] Increased knowledge of human anatomy and physiology, however, does not necessarily bring about an increased ability to control emotions.

Many topics taught under the rubric of sex education do not require this flag-waving

---

24. American Book Company, *A.B.C. Health Series;* Benefic Press, *Health Action Series;* Bobbs Merrill Company, *Health for Young Americans;* Ginn and Company, *Health for Better Living Series;* D. C. Heath and Co., *Health Science Series;* Laidlaw Brothers, *New Road to Health Series* and *Laidlaw Health Series;* Lyans and Carnahan, *My Health Book Series* and *ABdimensions in Health Series;* The Macmillan Science Series; Scott, Foresman and Company, *Curriculum Foundation Series* and *Health for All Series.*

25. Larger school systems place more emphasis on locally prepared guides than do intermediate and smaller school systems, which depend more on state guides, if any guide is used.

26. Oberteuffer and Beyrer, *School Health Education,* pp. 157-61.

27. Nemir, *School Health Program,* p. 311.

handle for inclusion in the curriculum. Some of the topics included relate to the general process of socialization and enculturation. Listed below are several concepts from the curriculum recommended by the Committee on Health Guidance in Sex Education of the American School Health Association.[28] (These selections from two grades indicate that many "sex" concepts are simply concerned with approved behaviors accepted in the culture or are statements related to principles of group integration.)

Kindergarten and Grade One.
4. Every person needs to have a feeling of belonging.
5. Each member of a family is an important member. Children and parents working and playing together help make a home a happy place to live. There are many ways in which children can help to make their homes happy ones.
6. Each member of a family is interested in the well-being of every other member.
7. Using good manners lets other people know that we like and respect them. Thoughtful boys and girls are courteous to each other, to their mothers and fathers, their brothers and sisters, and to everyone else.

Grade Four
11. Having a hobby is one way a person can use his leisure time constructively. Hobbies add enjoyment to living. Sometimes the members of a family enjoy sharing the same hobby.
12. A friend is someone who likes you and whom you like. A person can have many different kinds of friends among people of all ages.
13. One of the best ways to make new friends is to be friendly to other people. Being friendly lets others know that we would like to have them as our friends.

The intent of the family life or human situation approach is to develop both a cognitive and attitudinal approach to sex role identity and division of labor based on sex. At a time when TV, movies, pornography, and the new cult of male-female libertarianism is blatantly phallic, health educators are striving to develop a concept of sexuality. This approach might be briefly described as an appreciation of male-female interdependency and division of labor by sex, characteristic of all cultures, which permits men and women to fulfill the appropriate sex roles ascribed to the culture. In such a time of behavioral flux, it is difficult to find appropriate curriculum means because of disagreements in the culture with regard to value postulates. Health educators in the United States thus far have overlooked the cross cultural comparative technique. Experiments with this approach might reveal some promising alternatives in sex education.[29]

Because of the many taboos associated with the label "sex" and because of the fact that little if any of the subject matter of "sex education" has anything to do with the subject, many health educators prefer to use the term "family living." The curriculum in this area should be carefully planned. Irrespective of the quality of the materials and the preparation of a teacher, it would probably be unwise for a teacher to initiate individually such teaching if not specifically included in the school curriculum. If not

---

28. "Growth Patterns and Sex Education: A Suggested Program K-12, *Journal of School Health* 37, no. 5a, supplement (May 1967): 1-136. This entire issue is devoted to sex education.
29. An anthropological publication which looks at behavior in different cultures on the continuum of biological change is: Pauline Persing, Wilfrid C. Bailey, and Milton Kleg, *Life Cycle* (Athens, Ga.: Anthropology Curriculum Project, University of Georgia, 1968).

included in the curriculum, it is thought that teachers should not be unduly concerned.

The reason is this. Sex education is primarily related to attitudes and values, not cognitive knowledge. The schools in our culture are not organized on the principles of Pavlovian conditioned response training as in *Brave New World*. The method available to the schools for teaching values consists primarily of verbal instruction. School-transmitted values are often more orthodox than patterns reflected in the community; and verbal instruction in values bears little weight in relating to community standards. Sex education may, therefore, embroil the schools in unnecessary controversy in an area in which it may be completely ineffective anyway.

In contrast, the efforts might be directed toward improved mental health. In contrast to sex education, the concept of mental health carries a positive image. Furthermore, many of the objectives of a better adjusted personality, found in sex education curricula, are also found in mental health curricula. Mental health in the school begins, as previously noted, in a healthy school environment and in teacher-pupil relations which promote individual personality and group integration.

One of the most comprehensive reports dealing with the mental health curriculum is contained in the report of the Committee on Mental Health in the Classroom of the American School Health Association.[30] The Committee emphasizes that many areas of mental health are not taught in the conventional verbal sense, but must be developed out of the relationship of teachers and pupils. Example is an important teacher in mental health, as in other aspects of health education.

The Committee did not attempt to define mental health, but merely indicated certain attributes of the mentally healthful person, e.g., emotional adjustment so that a person would live with reasonable comfort and function acceptably in his community. The Committee sharply differed from the World Health Organization's definition as "complete . . . mental well-being" and emphasized that mental and emotional adjustment is never complete, but is a result of satisfaction in goal achieving. Not surprising, therefore, is the Committee's recommendation that instruction related to mental health should never be undertaken in isolation, but as a part of the total health program.

The concepts, learning experiences, and materials recommended by the Committee for grades two and four are reproduced in figures 15.4 and 15.5. A comparison of these concepts with selected concepts from the report of the Committee on Health Guidance in Sex Education of the American School Health Association indicates the overlap in these two areas.

There is no conclusive evidence regarding either the content or methods of a mental health strand of a health curriculum. The whole spectrum of human behavior is related to mental health, but it is related specifically to problems of emotional and intellectual adjustment. These include feelings of acceptance and rejection, prejudice and selfishness, alibi and projection, jealousy and rage, security and worry, and success and frustration. Boys and girls, no less than adults, meet these same problems. Perhaps one of the most valuable contributions of a mental health program consists in permitting

30. "Mental Health in the Classroom," *Journal of School Health* 33, no. 7a supplement (September 1963): 1-36; also reprinted as Appendix D in Nemir, *School Health Program,* pp. 386-410.

youngsters to verbalize and project these sentiments. Discussions within the context of mental health provide the elementary student with a nontechnical vocabulary to both verbalize emotions and rationalize alternate courses of behavior. The pupil thus learns that even though he is frequently not able to change his condition or the situation, he is able to change his perception of either, or both. But his perceptual growth is not automatic; it must be learned.

Time Allotment for Health Instruction. Notwithstanding some emphasis that the same amount of time per day should be given to health instruction as to other major subject areas in the curriculum,[31] actual recommendations of health education specialists are more modest. Optimum time allotments recommended by Oberteuffer and Beyrer are one period a day in the primary grades, twenty minutes daily in lower intermediate grades, and one period a day for the year in upper intermediate grades.[32] Kilander indicates that if there is correlated health instruction, as in biology, minimum time for basic instruction would be a period of thirty minutes twice a week in primary grades and three periods a week for intermediate grades. The Oberteuffer-Beyrer and Kilander recommendations are just the opposite in time emphasis by grade level, the latter providing more time for health in the intermediate grades.

Since it is likely that only minimum time will be available for health instruction, the physical and emotional aspects of health need to be emphasized. Otherwise, a great deal of time may be consumed which contributes to little practical knowledge of health. Many examples of this may be found in suggested health curricula, such as "Ancient civilizations and cleanliness," "The meaning and wise use of leisure time," and "Survival in the Nuclear Age."[33]

Curriculum Development in Health Education

Paralleling the interest in the separate subject approach to the organization for instruction has been an emphasis on the identification of concepts and generalizations which are related to the structure of knowledge.[34] Following the lead of nationally known projects in mathematics (chapter 12) and science (chapter 13), health educators have attempted to apply the structural approach to health. The results have not always been as felicitous as they have been in the other two subject areas, primarily because health education is preeminently a *practical* subject rather than a *logical* subject. Emphasis on oral hygiene, specifically brushing of teeth, is introduced in kindergarten and the first grade for a practical end. The permanent teeth are about to erupt, and oral hygiene is necessary to reduce cavities. In a *logical* organization, the structure and functions of the teeth are considered as a subsumption of the mouth cavity as part of the digestive system.[35]

Curriculum developers who are concerned with both practical and logical aspects of subject matter have more difficulty in sequencing material than do those who are

31. National Committee on School Health Policies, *Suggested School Health Policies* (Chicago: American Medical Assoc., 1964).
32. Oberteuffer and Beyrer, *School Health Education,* p. 161.
33. Willgoose, *Health Education,* Appendix A.
34. Phil Delta Kappa, *Education and the Structure of Knowledge,* Fifth Annual Phi Delta Kappa Symposium on Educational Research (Chicago: Rand McNally & Company, 1964).
35. Claude A. Villee, *Biology* 3d ed. (Philadelphia: W. B. Saunders Company, 1957), Chapter 19.

CONCEPTS	LEARNING EXPERIENCES	MATERIALS
I. Personality structure and development		
Satisfaction in creative activities Importance of cultivating sense of humor and pleasant voice Progress in caring for self and possessions Satisfactions from new experiences	Discuss and develop standards for care of belongings Provide opportunities for pupils to have responsibilities	Kaune, Merriman: *My Own Little House* Thurstone, Thelma and Katharine Byrne: *Mental Abilities of Children*
II. Interaction of an individual with others, including influences of cultural patterns		
Harmonious relations with brothers and sisters Contributions to family teamwork; taking turns Development of friendships Control of hands and feet Use of "please" and "thank you" Courtesy and kindness to others Participation in solving individual and group problems Respect for rights of others Understanding of various cultural patterns	Provide opportunities for pupils to take turns, wait for teacher's help, etc. Encourage pupils to tell about people, objects, and events in other countries Read stories about people in other countries Teach pupils some words in another language	Sound Motion Pictures *Patty Garman, Little Helper, The Hare and the Tortoise* Books about other cultures, holidays, national heroes Gramatky, Hardie: *Loopy* Barr, Jene: *Good Morning, Teacher* Osborne, Ernest: *How To Teach Your Child About Work*
III. Socioeconomic status and its influence on mental health		
Consideration for children of different backgrounds	Read stories about children from various homes Dramatize selected stories	Pictures of children and families of various places Bauer, W. W.: *Just Like Me Being Six*
IV. Emotional climate in home and classroom		
Development of a constructive emotional climate (rapport) through pupil-teacher planning Understanding what is expected how to work, how to wait, how to play with others Willingness to get help when needed	Read to pupils, then ask them to act out the story Make experience charts dictated by pupils Plan with pupils to make a gift for their parents Develop the respect of the group by asking pupils what *they* think Use indirect remarks such as "We're waiting for someone," in order to regain group control	Transcription *Timid Timothy* Ridenour, Nina: *Building Self-Confidence in Children*

Fig. 15.4. Grade One. Teaching Mental Health in the Classroom. From Committee on Mental Health in the Classroom, American School Health Association, **Journal of School Health** 33, no. 7a, supplement (September 1963): 11.

CONCEPTS	LEARNING EXPERIENCES	MATERIALS
I. Personality structure and development		
Standards for acceptable behavior including self-control Cause and effect relationships Importance of evaluating and accepting criticism Relaxation through creative experiences, hobbies, clubs, interests Growth in self-direction Responsibility for own actions, clothing, appearance	Plan a "Hobby Show" Discuss appropriate remarks when one is corrected Develop standards for acceptable behavior Prepare a check list on appearance and grooming	Bauer, W. W.: *Going on Ten* Hunt, Mabel: *Double Birthday Present*
II. Interaction of an individual with others including influence of cultural patterns		
Appreciation of qualities and responsibilities of leadership and followership Use of humor: differences between teasing and practical jokes Appreciation of relationship of home, school, and community to pupil success in learning and adjustment	List the qualities pupils like in people. Discuss ways these qualities may be developed Ask pupils to read about the contributions of individuals of the United States and other countries Identify qualities necessary for a leader; a follower Discuss the meaning of "friend"	Filmstrip *Making Friends — Two to Make Friends* Ullmann, Frances: *Life with Brothers and Sisters* Wagoner, Jean: *Jane Addams, Little Lame Girl*
III. Socioeconomic status and its influence on mental health		
Adjustment to facing difficulties squarely Maintenance of self-respect regardless of socioeconomic status	Help pupils to face their problems and select an appropriate solution Give opportunities to pupils to have specific responsibilities	Friedman, Frieda: *Dot for Short* McGinley, Phyllis: *Plain Princess*
IV. Emotional climate in home and classroom		
Participation in evaluation and solution of problems Establishment of effective study habits Appreciation of the rights and actions of others	Help pupils make group decisions and abide by the decisions Plan small group activities Give guidance in the understanding of tolerance	Cleary, Beverly: *Otis Spofford*

Fig. 15.5. Grade Four. Teaching Mental Health in the Classroom. From Committee on Mental Health in the Classroom, American School Health Association, **Journal of School Health** 33, no. 7a, supplement (September 1963): 16.

primarily concerned with the logical structure of knowledge. This is due to the fact that there are practical needs, as in health, which demand immediate attention rather than delayed sequencing. Thus the first grader may not be expected to practice first aid with respect to others, but he may need to know some rudiments so that he may not get panicky about himself, or that he may be able to observe and report coherently about a playmate.

Health educators have not followed, at least in a clear and definite fashion, the recommendations of the National Education Association Project on Instruction relating to distinctions in logical and applied knowledge. One suggestion of Professor Joseph J. Schwab was the differentiation of curricula into two parts—nuclear and cortical. The nuclear curriculum would be an applied curriculum, taught in the framework of subject matter where possible, but otherwise taught in a context which would emphasize principles designed for use. On the other hand, the cortical part would be representative of the major disciplines, with development designed to emphasize conceptual framework, methods of discovery and verification, and variety of problems to which a discipline addresses itself.[36] This distinction is implicit in the distinction in health curricula between health practices, which receive continuous emphasis, and health facts which may be cycled in a spiral curriculum.[37] These distinctions, however, have not been made a functional part of recent curriculum developments in health education.

The School Health Education Study (SHES) curriculum[38] is an outgrowth of the NEA-AMA Joint Committee on Health Problems in Education, which in 1960 recommended a survey to determine the status of health education in the schools. In 1961 a survey was begun, and a summary report was issued in 1964 which indicated that health instruction practices were of poor quality throughout the country.[39] Following the example of other curriculum projects, a conceptual approach was used to develop some pilot materials involving the complementary skills of health educators, supervisors, and teachers. The materials were tested in 1964-65. Since 1966, SHES has been supported by the 3M Company to continue curriculum development in health education.

SHES uses concept as a synonym for generalization and theme, and thus the theoretical frame of reference lacks the tightness of conceptual approaches in other disciplines. The materials nevertheless provide the newest approach in school health education, with an attempt made to make the knowledge component of health education behaviorally functional.

The ten major curriculum concepts developed by the project indicate the emphasis in SHES materials:

36. National Education Association, Project on Instruction, *The Scholars Look at the Schools* (Washington, D.C.: NEA, 1962), pp. 51-52.

37. Kilander, *School Health Education,* p. 279; Oberteuffer and Beyrer, *School Health Education,* p. 164.

38. School Health Education Study, *Health Education: A Conceptual Approach to Curriculum Design, Grades K-12* (St. Paul, Minn.: Visual Products, 3M Company, 1967-71); reprinted by permission of the publisher, Minnesota Mining and Manufacturing Company; copyright by School Health Education Study, Inc. Basic unit documents, together with teacher learning guides and printed originals for making overhead projection transparencies, are now available. It is not necessary to use the visuals, however, to implement the curriculum.

39. Elena M. Sliepcevich, *School Health Education Study: A Summary Report* (Washington, D.C.: School Health Education Study, 1964).

1. Growth and development influences and is influenced by the structure and functioning of the individual.
2. Growing and developing follows a predictable sequence, yet is unique for each individual.
3. Protection and promotion of health is an individual, community, and international responsibility.
4. The potential for hazards and accidents exists, whatever the environment.
5. There are reciprocal relationships involving man, disease, and environment.
6. The family serves to perpetuate man and to fulfill certain health needs.
7. Personal health practices are affected by a complexity of forces, often conflicting.
8. Utilization of health information, products, and services is guided by values and perceptions.
9. Use of substances that modify mood and behavior arises from a variety of motivations.
10. Food selection and eating patterns are determined by physical, social, mental, economic, and cultural factors.

While on the surface these ten statements have the vagueness which mark most generalizations, in comparison with previous health generalizations they indicate a subtle but important difference. The statements are less dogmatic and try to lay a foundation for a behavioral emphasis toward attitude change on the part of the student. This grew out of the fact that the SHES survey indicated that notwithstanding the low level of knowledge possessed by students, health knowledge still exceeded health applications.[40] Consequently, the new subject matter is designed to influence attitudes as much as to impart knowledge.

The question is frequently raised about the responsibility of teachers for planning health curricula. One point of view places heavy emphasis on local curriculum development.[41] It is suggested in chapter 21, however, that the classroom teacher might more usefully spend his time in lesson study and preparation. This is particularly true of the health teacher. Most health teachers are general classroom teachers, who have had little training in health education, usually a course at the undergraduate level. They also have many other demands on their teaching and planning time.

It would therefore seem more desirable for teachers to have available a good health curriculum guide or health series, and devote their attention to special unit development rather than the shotgun approach of general development. This permits teachers to utilize their limited time to develop health units particularly relative to the local community, e.g., air pollution, and to concentrate on aspects of health education which are sometimes poorly developed, e.g., mental health.

Social and cultural changes frequently cause any curriculum to become outdated. In the 1970s it is expected that more emphasis in health education at the elementary level will be given to environmental health, drug abuse and control, and community health services. The new emphasis on ecology has given man a new appreciation of the dependence of the health of man as a physical being on the health of his natural and cultural environment. Drug use is no longer confined to crime areas of a few big cities, but has even invaded the elementary schools. And there is not only a

40. Sliepcevich, *School Health Education Study*, p. 7.
41. Jack Smolensky and L. Richard Bonvechio, *Principles of School Health* (Boston: D. C. Heath and Company, 1966), chap. 19.

lack of articulation between school and community health services, but there is a shortage in health services for an expanding population. Local curriculum development can usefully fill in such curriculum gaps, until such time as national materials are made available. But it seems a waste of teacher resources to repeat curriculum development which is already available.

Methods in Health Instruction. The typical health curriculum, like other elementary subjects, is organized by units of study. There is the usual emphasis on the child-centered approach, activities, and problem solving. There are no distinct methods required, merely adaptations to the subject matter of health.[42] A particular hazard in health instruction requiring teacher ingenuity is how to avoid monotony and boredom from content repetition (e.g., "Safety Curriculum").

The teacher of health, however, has a tremendous resource to make vivid and concrete the teaching of health and health practices. This resource is the students, who bring to the classroom the very substance of what health education is all about—their own bodies and emotions. The subject matter of health is not remote and far away—it can always be applied or related to the individual. Good posture need not be just talked about; it can be practiced throughout the day. Students do not brush their teeth after lunch, but they can rinse their mouths out with water. The right kind of foods can be talked about, shown on a bulletin board, but even more important, eaten. The control of jealousy and of anger, the making of friends, and respect for the other sex can be practiced in the classroom, in the lunchroom, in the library, and on the playground. And health education can be applied at home. Unlike learning of history or chemistry, which for a youngster have little meaningful application except in the school, healthful living is a part of home living. Does the child brush his teeth at home? Does he eat the right kind of foods at home? Does he make friends in his neighborhood? Does he control jealousy within the family? And these same things apply in the community in which he lives.

One of the most critical links in health instruction is the parent. While in many schools and school systems there is a basic lack of health education in the curriculum, even where there are strong programs in the schools there is frequently a lack of parental support. This lack of support manifests itself in several ways: failure to support the health instruction program, failure to reinforce at home principles taught at school, and failure to follow up on health services where deficiencies have been noted. It is for this reason that health education is looked at in terms of three facets—school, home, and community. While these are frequently emphasized in all school programs, school-home-community cooperation is vital to the long-run objectives of health education.

The Teacher and Health Education. The School Health Education Study Survey indicated that some of the major deficiencies in health education relate to teacher lack of preparation and teacher disinterest.[43] As noted previously, elementary teachers are

---

42. Because of the large number of industries and commercial organizations associated with health, many types of free or inexpensive material may be obtained. Some of these materials need to be used with caution, because they are frequently disguised marketing media. An extensive list of teaching materials in health is given in Willgoose, *Health Education,* chap. 11.

43. Sliepcevich, *School Health Education Study,* p. 11.

likely to have little formal training in health education, and over half of the content of the usual health education books have nothing to do with health education per se, but address themselves generally to curriculum, philosophy, and methods of elementary education.

What can the general classroom teacher do to improve health instruction? The first thing is to study thoroughly the *content* and *related* procedures for the course of study used in the school. This helps to establish firmly the cognitive and attitudinal outcomes expected of the pupils. The second is to obtain supplementary reference materials for adults, and study material *related* to the particular unit. This will permit the teacher to enlarge upon the information provided students, and help answer questions that students raise.

This procedure may appear somewhat piecemeal, but concurrently with health education, the teacher of the self-contained classroom will have other preparations to make. Consequently, it is better to prepare a particular unit or lesson well than to try to study the whole field of health education. This type of sequential study will gradually permit a teacher to obtain mastery of the health essentials in the curriculum sequence for a particular grade level.

A part of health instruction concerns school safety. In the final section, consideration is given to the school safety program.

The School Safety Program

The school safety program is part of the broader field of health education, but it has an immediate practical end in view. That end is to prevent accidents to school children.

Accident Prevention. Pupils can be effectively involved in various phases of accident prevention. Not only can they serve on the school safety patrol or fire patrol, but they can help plan the school safety program, carry out safety inspections, search for safety hazards, report accidents, analyze accidents, help correct hazards, promote safeguards, promote safe attitudes, and develop safe practice lists.[44]

Much accident prevention emphasis in the elementary school has to do with traffic safety, but on the basis of accident frequency, the playground and gymnasium are the scenes of most accidents. These two places were found to account for 64 percent of all accidents. The most serious accidents, as measured by number of days absent from school, occurred at the bicycle rack area, stairway, athletic field, doorway, and school sidewalk.[45]

The importance of controlling traffic flow of students as a means of improving school safety has already been emphasized.

In many schools, a teacher serves as coordinator of the school safety program. This person works directly with the boys and girls in the safety and fire patrols, provides relevant safety information to the teachers, and serves as a liaison person with community safety agencies, such as the police and fire departments.

Fire Prevention. A specialized part of the accident prevention program is the fire prevention program. The school safety program must include periodic fire drills, and teachers and pupils must know the orderly sequence of leaving the building. Annual observance of National Fire Prevention Week in the schools

---

44. School Health Bureau, *Accident Prevention Can Be Learned* (New York: Metropolitan Life Insurance Company, 1962), pp. 25-30.

45. Gerald J. Case, "Nature and Frequency of Accidents Among Elementary School Children in New York State," *Journal of School Health* 28 (December 1958): 343-49.

also serves as a periodic means of making children conscious of fire prevention at home.

Safety Curriculum. The safety curriculum is part of the general health curriculum. A safety unit is generally included at each grade level. The third grade unit "Staying Safe" involved: skates on stairs; short circuit in electric cord; fire starting in paint, rags, and trash; not playing with matches; putting a fire out; putting out fire in someone's clothes; other home safety; first aid for a burn or cut; safety on the street; bicycle safety; pedestrian safety; play safety; swimming safety; playground safety; police department number; and fire department number.[46]

A similar broad approach is also seen in the eighth grade unit "Safe Living," although there is more material in depth. At the primary level the tone is admonitory; at the intermediate level, explanatory and factual. It is important for upper grade teachers to recognize that the factual base is one way of differentiating the content of upper grade from primary programs. If this element is not emphasized, upper grade safety education is likely to sound to children like so much "preaching."

Coordination of the safety curriculum with the school safety program is one of the best ways of making safety instruction concrete and meaningful to the students. It is one way to get students involved in a school project.

Appraisal of Health and Safety Education

The elementary program has many demands made on it. In giving priority to skill development and the acquisition of information, the elementary program all too frequently gives only lip-service to health and safety education. At the same time, the state of pupil health and the pupil accident rate indicates that health and safety education are matters which should not be left to chance.

The school alone cannot provide the resources for all of health and safety education; it has already been noted that the lack of parental support is a major deficiency in school health programs. However, the school cannot afford to exclude health and safety education from its curriculum if it is to make any pretense of caring for the needs of the child, not merely as a student but as a person.

There are many ways of improving health education which lie within the province of school action. These include the following:

1. Provision of definite time in curriculum for health instruction,
2. Planning or adoption of a sequential health curriculum,
3. Making certain that the health objectives are met as planned for each grade level,
4. Making use of the best instructional methods, as in other school subjects,
5. Making use of community services for health and safety.

Health education is an area in which there is frequently much duplication and many omissions, because of lack of agreement on content. Since most elementary instruction has been on the basis of one teacher in a self-contained classroom, there is absolutely no excuse for such neglect or duplication. Where textbooks tend to constitute the course of study, it is relatively easy to identify the overlapping units or parts of sub-

46. *The New Road to Health Series* (River Forest, Ill.: Laidlaw Brothers Publishers, 1960).

units, and decide, according to the conceptual context, whether some material appears to fit better with a health, science, or social studies emphasis. Even where some departmentalization is practiced, the teachers involved can decide who shall be responsible for particular subject matter.

Even a guide is no guarantee of eliminating omission or overlap. Frequently guides are designed, as are textbooks, to meet broad rather than narrow use, and it is necessary for the guides to be examined carefully to decide where duplicate effort exists. The fact that duplication may exist in materials prepared for instruction is no excuse for duplication in practice.

For the past ten years, health instruction has tried to do more than teach nutrition and care of the teeth. Courses of study at each grade level contain units which apply, more or less, to family living and mental health. Because of the limited experience and age of children, the textual material written for pupils often appears superficial. A teacher will need to draw upon insights gained from courses in sociology, psychology, and general education to help make these pupil texts more meaningful and interesting to children. The authors suggest the comparative anthropological approach as providing a more interesting and stimulating factual base to certain aspects of mental health and family life education.

School health services are primarily an administrative matter. Teachers concerned with the health of school children, however, should be concerned that the schools make effective use of community health where there is no school health program. Attitudes about adequate health care formed in early childhood have important implications for the adult future.

SELECTED REFERENCES

American Medical Association, National Committee on School Health Policies, *Suggested School Health Policies.* Chicago: American Medical Association, 1964.

American School Health Association, Committee on Health Guidance in Sex Education. "Growth Patterns and Sex Education." *Journal of School Health* 37, no. 5a, supplement (May 1967): 1-136.

———, Committee on Mental Health in the Classroom. "Mental Health in the Classroom." *Journal of School Health* 33, no. 7a, supplement (September 1963): 1-36.

ANDERSON, C. L. *School Health Practice.* 3d ed. St. Louis, Mo.: C. V. Mosby Company, 1966.

BYRD, OLIVER E. *School Health Administration.* Philadelphia: W. B. Saunders Company, 1964.

KILANDER, H. FREDERICK. *School Health Education.* 2d ed. New York: Macmillan Company, 1968.

MAYSHARK, CYRUS; SHAW, DONALD D.; and BEST, WALLACE H. *Administration of School Health Programs.* St. Louis: C. V. Mosby Company, 1967.

NEMIR, ALMA. *The School Health Program.* 2d ed. Philadelphia: W. B. Saunders Company, 1965.

OBERTEUFFER, DELBERT, and BEYRER, MARY K. *School Health Education.* 4th ed. New York: Harper & Row, Publishers, 1966.

SLIEPCEVICH, ELENA M. *Summary Report of a Nationwide Study of Health Instruction in the Public Schools,* 1961-63. Washington, D.C.: School Health Education Study, 1964.

SMOLENSKY, JACK, and BONVECHIO, L. RICHARD. *Principles of School Health.* Boston: D. C. Heath and Company, 1966.

TURNER, C. E.; SELLERY, C. MORELY; and SMITH, SARAH L. *School Health and Health Education.* 5th ed. St. Louis, Mo.: C. V. Mosby Company, 1966.

WILLGOOSE, CARL E. *Health Education in the Elementary School.* 3d ed. Philadelphia: W. B. Saunders Company, 1969.

PART FIVE

teaching the fine arts and recreation

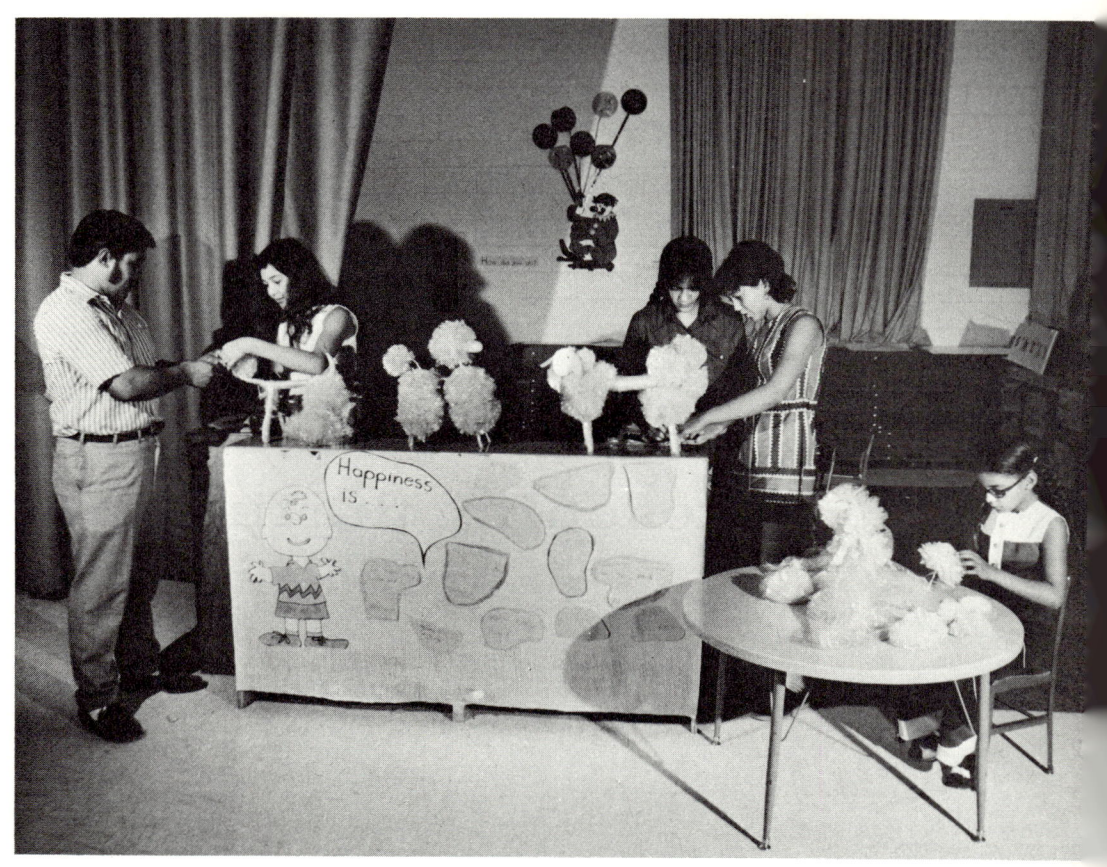

Photo: Courtesy of El Paso (Texas) Independent School District
Photography: Seth J. Edwards, Jr.

teaching music through singing and listening

16

For over a hundred years, music has been part of the recognized elementary school curriculum.[1] But the history of music education is as old as education. This stems from the fact that music is a cultural universal. No people, however primitive by technological standards, have been found without music. To express triumph in battle, success in the chase, lament for the dead, affection for the beloved, thanksgiving to the gods, or happiness for life, men make music by voice and instrument. Even the measured beat of a handclap or a stamping foot can create rhythms which excite the spirit or calm the soul. No wonder, then, that in the archaic Greek curriculum music held an honored place,[2] or that over the centuries, as in the cathedral schools of medieval Europe or the Renaissance schools of a later day,[3] music was a serious object of study.

More often excluded in practice than included, music is nevertheless recognized as a significant subject for aesthetic development and creative expression in the elementary grades. Most frequently this responsibility is entrusted to the general classroom teacher, who has little or no technical training in the teaching of music. This chapter, therefore, is written primarily to be of help to the generalist and to show that, with some care in planning and study, music can be made a part of the elementary curriculum.

Importance of Music in the Curriculum

Every text on the teaching of music in the elementary grades includes numerous objectives which allegedly are met by the teaching of music.[4] Only three reasons for teaching music are discussed here: increasing aesthetic appreciation, personal pleasure, and practical contribution to other school learning. More emphasis will be given to the third reason, on the assumption that

---

1. Edward Bailey Birge, *History of Public School Music in the United States* (Boston: Oliver Ditson Company, Inc., 1928), p. 47.

2. Kenneth J. Freeman, *Schools of Hellas* (London: Macmillan & Company, Ltd., 1907).

3. William Boyd, *The History of Western Education,* 6th ed. (London: Adam and Charles Black, 1952).

4. Robert L. Garretson, *Music in Childhood Education* (New York: Appleton-Century-Crofts, 1966), pp. 2-8; Parks Grant, *Music for Elementary Teachers* 2d ed. (New York: Appleton-Century-Crofts, Inc., 1960), pp. 12-21.

if the regular classroom teacher sees general pedagogical utility in the teaching of music he may give more attention to this subject area.

Aesthetic Appreciation. The refinement of taste and the discrimination between noble and vulgar music is a result of learning. The capacity to differentiate the nuances of a symphonic presentation from the hard beat of a rock 'n' roll guitar; the mood empathy which inspires a listener to be depressed or elated; or the development of a sense of beauty and grandeur in music which transcends the futile and drab, are only acquired after long exposure to music as an art form. Music as an art form is the creation of professional musicians and composers, and is the result of the inevitable complexity in music which is made possible by a division of labor. Few individuals will have the talent or the perseverance to pursue music as a profession, but all have the capacity to become appreciative consumers. But this consumptive capacity, as in literature or other forms of knowledge, scientific or humanistic, is not innate within the individual, but must be acquired. The school assists the child to acquire this musical sensitivity by having him participate in and attend to music making, both graduated to his abilities.

There is a school of thought which depreciates the attempt to develop musical sensitivity and discrimination. This approach may be found in art, literature, grammar, and even spelling, which suggests that there are no comparative standards, but merely certain practices preferred by individuals of different perceptions. Certainly, the distribution of radio and television time to noble music and to popular music indicates a dominance of the latter, just as there are more readers of the funnies than there are of Shakespeare.

As societies become more complex, there frequently develop two parallel traditions in art, the popular and the intellectual. The popular tradition tends to be more direct in form, with clear and appealing rhythm and melody. The more obvious pieces are catchy, and frequently destined to have a short if profitable life. But popular music, as all music, has structure.

The boogie-woogie is an excellent example of structure in a special piano style of jazz, which originated as early as 1919 but peaked in popularity in the late 30s. Boogie-woogie has a definite structure, with a repeated bass figure and treble variations. The basso ostinato or walking bass provides a sustained rhythm, accentuated by cross rhythms in the treble following the style of the classic 12-bar blues. This gives a driving, exciting effect with cross rhythms, particularly accentuated when the top and front of an upright piano is removed.[5]

And so it is with more recent music, such as the Latin rock of Carlos Santana. The second recording of his group, *Abraxas,* was described as "less propulsive than the first. . . . What it offers instead is a rare poetic delicacy. Rhythms move in parallel layers, interrupting, overlaying, penetrating one another, multiplying into mathematical complexity, finally merging into one overwhelming musical thrust."[6]

Popular music today has instant audience appeal and rejection through radio and television transmission. For a time, in the life

---

[5]. *Discovering Music Together,* Teacher's Edition, Book 8 (Chicago: Follett Publishing Company, 1967), p. 189a.
[6]. *Time,* September 21, 1970, p. 68, (Reprinted by permission from *Time,* The Weekly Newsmagazine; © Time, Inc., 1970); *Abraxas,* Columbia Records.

of a generation, the popular form is transmitted like any other popular element in the culture—through enculturation. But popular forms of music change, and the hard electronic rock of the late 60s eventually will join our musical heritage of blues and Dixieland jazz. Perhaps the Nashville sound will prove to be the most enduring popular tradition in the United States, outliving such periodic forms as jazz and rock. Because such music does enter into and become part of the musical heritage, popular forms of music deserve consideration along with the lieder of Schumann, the music dramas of Wagner, or the classical restraint of a Haydn quartet. There is need to learn to listen with discrimination to such productions as the Beatles' *Abbey Road* or a Louis Cottrell rendition of *Just A Closer Walk With Thee*. Much of this discrimination begins in the learning of a traditional Mother Goose tune, such as *Little Boy Blue,* or an American folk whimsey, such as *Blue-Tail Fly*. Beginnings in music, as in other types of learning, are relatively simple.

The intellectual tradition in music, as in other art forms, stands in marked contrast to the popular tradition. First, the intellectual tradition requires professionals to compose and craftsmen to perform, with knowledge and skills acquired only after long practice. While the productivity of a J. S. Bach or a Handel staggers the imagination, the intellectual tradition in music is associated with the unifying concept of all disciplines, science, or planned behavior based on knowledge. The intellectual conceptualization of a symphony on the part of a composer, and the translation of this concept into sound by a symphonic orchestra are not the accidents of a happy group playing together.

Second, the intellectual tradition requires an educated taste for enjoyment, developed through listening and acquisition of knowledge about music. Generally, one can only discriminate, and thus form judgments, about a nocturne or a madrigal, a czardas or a sonata, on the basis of experience and knowledge.

Much of the intellectual tradition in music has to do with a composer and his style. Music in the intellectual tradition is inevitably associated with the discriminating mind which conceived the work, rather than with the performer. The intellectual tradition is thus associated with the permanence of a product and not a particular performer or rendition. The masterpiece of Puccini's mature genius was *Turandot,* premiered by one of the greatest conductors of modern times—Toscanini. But the production of the composer transcends the performance of his great interpreter. In contrast, how permanent will be the songs of a Bob Dylan or a Johnny Cash?

The intellectual tradition in music is highly cognitive, and not something to be directly and completely embraced by the emotions, as with a popular song. One of the oldest art forms in music is the mass, and one of the greatest examples is J. S. Bach's *Mass in B minor*. The vastness and richness of this terrain in musical complexity might be compared to the visual complexity of a baroque cathedral with the austere simplicity of a whitewashed mission church. The latter has a rugged beauty in its simplicity, but the impact is direct, immediate. There are unending surprises of composition and vista in the baroque church. And so it is with the *Mass in B minor* and other music in the intellectual tradition. A first listening is a mere introduction, and the richness of the music is only grasped after many exposures and the intellectual attending to the composer's intent and its rendition.

The school is a link in the perpetuation of the intellectual tradition of culture. It is therefore not merely an appropriate place to teach music, but it has a responsibility to teach. The emphasis on music in the intellectual tradition is not to denigrate the importance of popular music. It is to emphasize the kind of musical experiences which are not immediately available in the contemporary idiom, and to lay a basis for discrimination in music. However, all music forms have their proper place in the school repertory.

Music for Personal Pleasure. There are many kinds of music in which people find personal pleasure, and it ranges from the ordinary to the great. Music listened to for its aesthetic character can certainly bring tremendous personal pleasure. But what is intended under this rubric is to suggest that many listeners, even after instruction, will not listen to noble music, just as all students of literature in school more often than not forget their lessons. Many a listener who twisted to Frank Loesser's *Baby, It's Cold Outside* would writhe to hear Lehar's *Merry Widow* and despise to hear Mahler's *Das Lied von der Erde.* And many an enthusiastic congregational singer of *A Mighty Fortress* would not dare a Handel oratorio.

For the child, music is preeminently a form for self-expression and communication. If he acquires these skills in a natural manner with his physical and mental growth in the elementary school, when he is less demanding in performance standards, he is more likely to use music in later years for continued self-expression and communication. The age at which a song or tune is learned is less important than its capacity to endure. For in life, as Shakespeare noted, man plays many roles, and *Little Red Caboose,* learned in first grade or kindergarten, may appear later in his repertory as older sibling, parent, or grandparent. See how many old favorites loom from the shadows of long ago: *Polly Wolly Doodle,* Grade 3; *Bluebells of Scotland,* Grade 4; *Prayer of Thanksgiving* (Netherlands Tune), Grade 6; or *Shenandoah,* Grade 8.

But all music for personal pleasure is not sung, and old favorites learned long ago provide a nostalgic quality and basis for discrimination. How sweet to meet such old and distinguished friends in later years, such as Debussy's *En Bateau,* Grade 1; Purcell's *Trumpet Tune,* Grade 3; Tschaikovsky's *Swan Lake,* Grade 5; or Bizet's *L'Arlesienne,* Grade 7.[7] A sustained program of music instruction not only meets the expanding interests of the growing child, but provides the basis for much pleasure in later life. One has only to listen to songs around a campfire or at church to sense the camaraderie and sense of unity which group singing imparts. Or attend a concert, light or serious, and perceive the mood and concentration evoked by the sound of instruments or voice. Knowledge of basic concepts of melody, rhythm, harmony, and form acquired through various types of songs and orchestral music serve the double purpose of permitting the youth of today and the

---

7. References to grade level in the preceding sections are: Grade 1, Holt, Rinehart and Winston, *Exploring Music,* 1966; other grades, Follett, *Discovering Music Together,* 1967. It should be remembered, however, that such grade placement is designed to form a particular series, and does not constitute a sequential difficulty hierarchy, as in mathematics.

aged of tomorrow to derive pleasure from music. And once engaged in the use and study of music, little of it appears serious and forbidding; in music learning can be fun.[8]

Pedagogical Applications of Teaching Music. In addition to teaching music for its inherent qualities, the teaching of music also has some practical advantages for the teaching of language arts and classroom management. Singing improves the fundamental language skills of listening and speaking, and is an asset in developing a group orientation for learning.

It has been increasingly recognized that many learning difficulties in school originate in deficit language, and that the improvement of instruction must begin with the improvement of language (see chapter 11). The fundamental language skill is *listening,* for the ability to emit language is dependent upon the ability to receive language. Many children come to school with little or no ability to listen. In this age of sound bombardment, many children have practiced tuning out as a matter of survival. Much listening discrimination is today emphasized as a part of language arts training. Frequently, this discrimination begins with sounds and then moves to the words of songs. Thus when a child is asked to "listen to the sound of the ocean" on a recording, he is not only increasing his attention span, but developing his acuity in sound discrimination with respect to tone, timbre, figure, and ground. Successful experiences with phoneme-grapheme teaching, as has been previously noted (see chapter 10), requires good sound discrimination.

Singing facilitates the development of clearer speech because it requires careful articulation and enunciation. In teaching reading, the teacher is often reluctant to ask a child to exaggerate his mouth movements to emit clearer speech; in fact, speech exaggeration is sometimes required to elicit any speech at all. But in singing, the teacher is less hesitant to ask a class to "sing so that I can hear the words." Certain words or phrases may be repeated again and again to insure correct pronunciation or to avoid elision. The latter requires particular care when a word ends in a consonant and is followed by a word which begins with a vowel. In oral reading many sentences become a meaningless jumble if the child says, as he so often sings, ". . . the dawn surly light. . . ." The emphasis on careful articulation in singing serves to sharpen the child's awareness of word endings and to carry over into his speech without the self-consciousness that so often characterizes choral speaking or verse choirs. Stress on the careful articulation of words in songs meets a parallel need in reading to have more stress on hearing and speaking of the sounds in words.

Learning words to songs in music is still another adjunct to reading improvement. Vocabulary expansion is aided by the introduction and learning of new words in songs. Since the verses of songs are frequently written more as poetry than as prose, singing acquaints the child with a certain amount of imagery. He becomes familiar with other ways of saying everyday expressions, and of the different meanings which some words convey.

The memorization of lines of verse also contribute to the development of sight vo-

8. The distinction between aesthetic cultivation and music for pleasure is sometimes difficult to express verbally. Grant, *Music for Elementary Teachers,* p. 19, attempts to distinguish between music as a fine art and amusement, of "enjoyment" and a "slap-bang 'good time'." Probably the music program should include more of the "good time" music than now admitted.

cabulary. This requires, of course, that the children have before them the written words, either in a song book or on a piece of paper. Repetitive song singing is not nearly as tiresome as repetitive re-reading, and often serves a similar end, provided a transfer opportunity is given. The skillful teacher cannot only use "Jack and Jill" or "Oh, beautiful for spacious skies" to teach a song, but also to increase sight vocabulary. Singing may thus be regarded as an important asset to a language arts program.

Music also helps the teacher develop a good emotional climate for learning. Different types of singing provide different types of energy control, and may be effectively utilized to create a disposition toward silence, as with a quiet "campfire" song, or to let off steam, as with a lung-stretching patriotic tune on a rainy day.

Notwithstanding the fact that elementary children are active, the morning block of time from nine to twelve is frequently allocated for "getting most of the work done." A five minute song break every hour can do much to prevent a build-up of fatigue and ennui. Especially good are activity songs which get the children out of their desks and permit them to stretch muscles as well as vocal chords. Such gesture songs as "O Chester, 'ave you 'eard about Harry?" and "Under the spreading chestnut tree" are ideal for this purpose.

One way of making the transition from physical exertion to quiescence, without the irritation of such verbal commands as "Keep quiet!" and "Be still!" is through the use of music. Children may be asked to sing a quiet song, seated at their desks or cross legged in a story circle, and then listen to a carefully selected recording with proper introductory remarks by the teacher. After the period of listening, questions asked by the teacher and responses by the children make an effective bridge to the verbal instruction which generally accompanies most school subjects.

Music not only provides an opportunity for tension control, but it also can be used as a part of the motivation management system, called by Homme "contingency management."[9] According to Homme, pupil behavior in school may be viewed from the perspective of highly desired as opposed to low priority behavior. Highly desired behaviors are frequently those which involve individual performance, and may be used as a carrot to lead the donkey through low priority tasks. Music provides a number of high priority tasks. Tapping out a new tune on the xylophone, passing out the rhythm band instruments, choosing and leading a favorite song, and starting and stopping the record player are examples of high priority jobs. Assigning high priority behavior to the successful completion of low priority tasks can be used meaningfully to reward learning.

The music program also contributes to a better learning climate by extending the range of opportunities in which children have an opportunity to achieve. Most of the elementary program focuses on symbolic, verbal learning. The lack of success which some children experience in these studies contributes to a lack of exertion and boredom with school, so that the learning deficit becomes cumulative. A good music program, which includes singing, listening to music, rhythmic movements, and playing on instruments, can provide alternative success routes, as do complementary programs in art, industrial arts, and physical education.

9. Discussed in chapter 21, Classroom Management.

Success in any area predisposes children to view the school environment more favorably and hence contributes to a more favorable disposition to learn.[10]

Music is an essential part of our western cultural tradition, and some appreciation of music is an essential aspect of the educated man. Music therefore requires no secondary justification for its inclusion in the elementary program. However, elementary teachers today are frequently overwhelmed with the mere challenges of teaching basic subject mastery. Teachers who strive to use music effectively in their program find that it contributes to, rather than interferes with, basic language learning and facilitates classroom management. Carefully sequenced programs for the disadvantaged sometimes specifically include music as an adjunct to language development.[11] Such music programs, however, are usually conducted by the classroom teacher, not by the music specialists. The next section looks at alternate ways of organizing the music program.

Organization for Teaching Music

There are three ways in which music is taught in the elementary school: by the general classroom teacher, by the classroom teacher with occasional supervision from a music specialist, and by a music teacher.

Most music teaching is entrusted to the classroom teacher. The alleged advantage of this arrangement is that the teacher knows his pupils, and is able to adapt the program to their interests and instructional needs. The major disadvantage is that the general classroom teacher rarely has any training in music. Unless he exerts an unusual effort to develop musical competency, the chances are that his students will have little or no music of the type that leads to sequential skill development. And even when one teacher may try, the fact that there is no sequential music development before or after his grade level often discourages additional pupil effort.

A compromise, using the classroom teacher and a music teacher, is the music supervisor program. In this organization, there is usually some attempt to carry out a sequential curriculum, with the music supervisor making periodic visits to classes or consulting with groups of teachers in a school. Responsibility for teaching is still the regular classroom teacher's, but he may use the supervisor as a resource person. The major disadvantage of this plan is that the number of elementary supervisors is generally too inadequate to be of substantial assistance to the classroom teacher, and the plan, while giving the illusion of a program, is without real substance.

In the music teacher plan, actual instruction is entrusted to a certificated music teacher who teaches in the regular room, or the class may be held in a specially designed music room. The advantage of this plan is that responsibility for music instruction is placed in the hands of a person who is presumably interested in and specifically trained in music. The major advantage, however, is the fact that the development of music skills can be sequenced. Instruction by a music teacher does not preclude the classroom teacher from using music for classroom

---

10. John Jarolimek, *Social Studies in the Elementary School* 3d ed. (New York: Macmillan Company, 1967), p. 60.

11. Carl Bereiter and Siegfried Engelmann, *Teaching Disadvantaged Children in the Preschool* (Englewood Cliffs, N.J.: Prentice-Hall, Inc., 1966), chap. 9. This chapter is equally useful for the primary grades. Specific songs and the ways they may be used most effectively, are suggested.

management or language instruction, as described in the preceding section. Nor does it preclude any relevant cooperation between the regular classroom teacher and the music teacher in songs or music for parallel learnings and special occasions.

But instruction by a trained music teacher does place the responsibility for the development of musical competency where it belongs—with someone who is trained in music. It is indeed remarkable that in this age of specialization, when we would think twice before recommending the teaching of mathematics to a music teacher, there is **no** hesitancy in recommending the teaching of music to a teacher who perceives himself as a reading-mathematics teacher. Once, many years ago, musical proficiency was regarded as part of the repertory of educated young ladies, and it was common place for ladies in the genteel tradition to bring to school teaching some rudiments of music, including playing the piano and singing. Musical training no longer has this emphasis in the education of women, and the brief contact which many students have with "Music for the Elementary School" in college classes merely reassures them of their lack of competency in this area. Thus music taught by the general classroom teacher has a historical basis, and also conforms to the de facto situation of low priority for aesthetic education. If there is no teacher of music, it is only natural for music enthusiasts to recommend that the general classroom teacher teach music. And if the child does not learn music in school, the public is not unduly concerned.

But it is the conviction of the authors of this text that music is an important part of school learning. The teaching of music not only contributes to development in music, but also enriches other aspects of learning.

Even where there are no district or system allotted music teachers, many schools have teachers who have been trained as music teachers, or who have some technical competencies in music. If they have the interest and desire to teach music, it would seem that the building principal could work out the desired schedule. But without this informal division of labor it is still possible for the classroom teacher to provide an adequate if not complete music program for his students. This is made possible by the development of musical recordings, and the sequencing of experiences which do not make technical training, although desirable, a prerequisite. Note reading, once so fashionable in teaching singing, is now largely ignored, and playing instruments to produce music is not a prerequisite to listening to music. A music program has different facets, and a teacher can emphasize those aspects of the music program in which he has some ability, competency or special interest.

Different Facets of Music Education

The five categories of musical experience discussed in this chapter are adapted from Ellison.[12] These are singing, listening, moving, playing, and creating. Similar classifications are used by other authors, such as expressive bodily movement, listening, singing, making music with instruments, and creative activities.[13] Less emphasis will be given to playing and creating music because these are the areas in which musical knowledge is definitely required, whereas the general classroom teacher can provide experiences

---

12. Alfred Ellison, *Music With Children* (New York: McGraw-Hill Book Company, 1959), p. 18.
13. James L. Mursell, *Music and the Classroom Teacher* (New York: Silver Burdett Company, 1951).

in the other three areas by using a recorded series.

Deciding to Have a Music Program. The greatest barrier to a music program by the classroom teacher is the will of the teacher. All too often he is so beset by his feeling of technical inadequacy that he rationalizes not having a music program. Certainly, if he does not play a musical instrument he cannot teach children about playing an instrument. And if he has not studied the elements of musical composition, he would be at a loss in composing. But these are only two aspects of a music program, and there are many others.

If a school system does not provide music teachers, and if there is no informal division of labor, the only way the children will have music is to be taught by the classroom teacher. So the first prerequisite is for the teacher to determine that his pupils will have music. This eliminates all the doubts and hesitations, and he can proceed in a forthright manner to see that those experiences occur.

Now the ideal objective, according to music educators, is to provide all children at each grade level with experience in the five facets of musical development. Even where there are music teachers, this ideal seldom materializes. So the classroom teacher needs to decide what he can do. Since no music program springs fullblown from the head of Zeus, the teacher can choose and build on one of the regular musical series which are available. Once he has decided to have music, he can play the records and study the directions which accompany them. He can thus *learn with his pupils.*

Time Allocation for Music. There may be different times during the day when music can be introduced to meet some particular need, but the music under such circumstances, however important, tends to be incidental. Examples of the incidental use of music are: the playing of recordings during the time when children are coming to class in the morning or at cleanup time in the afternoon, and the use of songs for opening and closing class or for a class break. Such incidental use of music can substantially increase the amount of time children use music in the school program.

It is nevertheless important to allocate some time on a regular basis for teaching music. Where the class schedule allows, a listening period after recess and a singing period before school dismissal provide good times for planned music activities. However, this planning autonomy is only available in the self-contained classroom. Where there is some departmentalization, the scheduling of music will have to adjust to the departmentalized schedule. There is no optimum time for teaching music; the important thing is to provide the time. At least two hours a week should be scheduled. In some departmentalized schedules, music alternates with art twice a week in hour blocks of time. Unless instruments are involved, music does not require the large blocks of time needed for experiences in art, and a half hour daily is preferable to two weekly periods of an hour each. However, in the primary grades the total amount of time allocated to singing, rhythm and movement, and listening and speaking skills associated with music will amount to almost an hour a day.

Making Music by Singing

A large part of the music program will be devoted to singing. Many teachers regard themselves as nonsingers, and feel very reluctant to help children sing. Any sense of embarrassment, however, is unnecessary. The classroom teacher of music is not a singing teacher, and needs no fine, clear, operatic voice to encourage children to sing. What he requires most of all is an enthusiasm for singing and a willingness to help children sing. If he is too uncertain of pitch and melody to trust his own voice, he can use what many music teachers successfully use in their own teaching—song records.

After eliminating any psychological blocks he has to encourage children to sing, some consideration needs to be given to what he will try to do with his children. Singing follows a development cycle, subject to improvement with instruction, so that at any age there are three categories of singing ability in children: those who sing spontaneously and model pitch and melody; those who merely sing portions spontaneously, and who have not yet developed the ability to imitate; and a small group, varying in number with age, who neither sing spontaneously or reproduce the songs of others.[14] The latter two groups formerly were characterized as nonsingers, and excluded from singing. While particular efforts may be made to assist these children, such as involving them in songs of less difficulty,[15] there is general agreement that the best remedy is to involve all children. And it is desirable to let children sing in their regular classroom seats or however they group themselves naturally in a singing circle, rather than to assign music seats.[16] No matter how careful the teacher is with musical seat assignment, children will decide that there is some voice standard used in assignment. Eventually, children use the ever-present excuse that they can't sing, so they don't have to sing, and thus deny themselves the many pleasures that singing can bring.

The classroom teacher of singing need not concern himself with teaching musical notation. If he becomes interested in this aspect of music, musical notation may be taught more effectively in connection with the playing of musical instruments than in connection with singing (see "Playing Instruments"). The tremendous emphasis on note reading, characteristic of older methods, did little to improve the quality of singing but taught children to hate music.[17] When notation is introduced with singing, it may fittingly be postponed until at least the fourth grade.[18]

Many of the books on music education have much to say about the appropriate pitch level for school singing. What is desired is a comfortable pitch level which will encourage children to sing, rather than some theoretically desired level. While some of the older books and records had songs pitched somewhat high, the teacher can err in the opposite direction, find a comfortable pitch for himself, and pitch the song too low. A pitch too low can contribute to monotone singing, because of the lack of range demanded.

If the teacher has a piano, or some other musical instrument, and can play it, it is appropriate to set the appropriate pitch by playing chords. Also, if the teacher can accompany the children, he should do so; there is no reason to require the children to sing without accompaniment. The autoharp

14. Ellison, *Music With Children,* pp. 35-41.
15. Bessie R. Swanson, *Music in the Education of Children* 2d ed. (Belmont, Calif.: Wadsworth Publishing Company, Inc., 1964), pp. 166-73.
16. Mursell, *Music and Classroom Teacher* pp. 200-202.
17. As an example of this emphasis, see E. W. Newton, *Music in the Public Schools* (Boston: Ginn and Company, 1909).
18. Ellison, *Music With Children,* p. 41.

makes it relatively easy to play strummed chords.

But if the teacher relies on the record to teach, let the record teach. This does not mean that the teacher should not learn the song and sing with the children, but if he must depend on the record, let the record set the pitch and let the children follow the melody and words from the record. There will be plenty of time, after the children have learned the words and melody, to try to improve the quality of the singing. There is no point in killing initial interest in a song by talking too much about it or by criticizing every phrase before it is learned.

It is assumed that the classroom teacher of music will wish to make use of one of the excellent matched record songbook series, now available from commercial sources.[19] These series provide teacher guides, pupil books, and recordings for each level. Because the songs have been carefully selected, use of an established sequence provides a variety and balance in the song repertory and limits duplication.

In initiating singing experiences with a class, a good way for a new teacher to begin is to ask children to select songs they already know. This permits singing to start on a note of confidence, and each child might be encouraged to lead his selection. Initial singing experiences should, above all, be happy experiences and e-v-ery-body s-i-n-n-g-g! At this time, it is best to forget every conception about head voices or angelic sounding, soft sweet voices. Any recollection of the loud voices children use at play should dispel any misplaced feeling about children ruining their voices if they sing loudly and lustily.

Once the children know the words and the melody, they can be asked to match the mood to the words. If the song has a dreamy mood, ask the children to try to identify the mood. It is surprising how quickly they can identify a happy or sad, light or heavy feeling, and match the singing to their own perception of the appropriate standard. This keeps the teacher from being always negatively saying "No, it's like this." The children can most frequently point the way. And by the time children reach the intermediate ages, there will be frequently one or two in the class who can, on their merit, help with the leadership of class singing.

In learning new songs, consideration should be given to selecting those recordings which are direct, simple, and imaginative. Pupils will often have preferences in learning new songs, and these should be considered when possible. But to provide variety, balance, and songs for special occasions, the teacher will frequently have to select a new song. There can be some explanation of the context of the song, but it should not be discussed to death, as is sometimes suggested in language arts classes. The song is to sing, not talk about. The song should be played through several times, with the children singing as much as they can with the song. If songbooks are available, they should be distributed to the pupils and the

19. Allyn and Bacon, Inc., *This is Music Series,* K-8, 1965-68; American Book-Van Nostrand Company, *Music for Young Americans,* 2d ed., K-6, 1966; Follett Educational Corporation, *Discovering Music Together,* K-8, 1964, 1966; Ginn and Company, *This Singing World Series,* K-8, 1959-61. *The Magic of Music,* K-6, 1965-68; Holt, Rinehart and Winston, Inc., *Exploring Music Series,* K-8, 1966-68; Prentice-Hall, Inc., *Growing With Music Series,* 1-8, 1966; Silver Burdett Company, *Making Music Your Own,* 1-8, 1964-68 and *Music for Living,* 1-8, 1959-62; and Summy-Birchard Company, *Birchard Music Series,* K-8, 1959-62.

lyrics read with the song. As the melody is learned, the volume on the record player should be reduced.

Even in the first grade, if the lyrics are not actually read, the songbooks can be used to help children extend their sight vocabulary. With young children, some initial drill in finding the numbers of pages quickly will save much time and reduce confusion. For this reason, some primary teachers prefer that children learn songs orally, without the use of songbooks, but eventually the need to memorize all the verses of songs limits the singing repertory. It also contributes to a lack of unenthusiastic singing, because children cannot sing full and joyfully when they are hesitant of the words. Much low singing and closed mouthing of young children has nothing to do with their voices, but is one way of concealing the lack of knowledge of the words of the song.

After the words of the song and melody are familiar to the children they can attempt to improve the standard of the new song by the directed self-criticism previously mentioned. Also, even though high and low, loud and soft, fierce and gentle are terms without precise technical application, the use of such verbal cues help the teacher and pupils set standards by which they improve their singing. In learning a new song from a record, they also have advantage of a model.

Many music books contain directions for teaching songs from records, in addition to the specific directions given in the series being used.[20] The older explanations—lack of good voice, don't know how to play piano, monotone singer—these and others like them are today inadequate alibis for a classroom teacher who fails to provide adequate singing experiences. One thing he should insist on, however, is a good quality record player. Many players in use in classrooms are of poor fidelity and produce an inadequate model for singing. And for himself, the teacher must insist that he learn and know the words of the song. He cannot help children sing if he is unsure of the words.

Responding to Music With Movement

Expressive movement of the body is not an aspect of experience peculiar to music; it overlaps with creative dancing, creative dramatics, and physical education. Theoretically, the use of music is paramount to body movement and dancing and incidental to creative dramatics and physical education. The objectives are also different: in physical education, development of physical grace and poise; in creative dramatics, expression of an inner sentiment; and in body movement to music, hearing and interpretation of musical ideas. In all three, music assists in making movement rhythmic and serves a complementary rather than exclusive function.

The main advantage to considering body movement and dancing as a facet of music for the classroom teacher is this: it is a way of getting children to listen to and find meaning in music, especially in kindergarten and the primary grades. In the intermediate grades, the factors of teacher and pupil self-consciousness tend to formalize body movement to more conventionalized forms, as in the dance. By this time, except where a classroom teacher is particularly interested in original and creative dance forms, it is likely that the teacher will prefer to con-

---

20. Ellison, *Music With Children*, p. 82; Mursell, *Music and Classroom Teacher*, p. 184; Swanson, *Music in Education*, pp. 159-62.

centrate on the listening aspects of music, discussed in the next section.

There is no need to depreciate the importance of body movement and musical enjoyment, and think of movement to music as primarily "kindergarten stuff." The enjoyment of music does not merely involve hearing; it involves the whole body. One way to lay a basis for the enjoyment of music is to bring children into contact with music bodily, and give them a chance to express musical feeling rhythmically and kinesthetically.[21]

In the kindergarten and first grade, it is relatively easy to encourage children to express musical feeling in body movement. An easy way to introduce the idea is to play "Let's pretend," a cue which serves to stimulate the mundane as well as the imaginative and fantastical. At first such movement can begin without music, with the gaits of animals particularly suggestive—gallop like a pony, waddle like a duck, leap like a gazelle, jump like a frog. Frequently, the enthusiastic participation of the teacher serves to stimulate movement. But there will be a great variation in how children participate, depending on their imagination and aptitude for movement.

Titles alone suggest certain activities. Who can refrain from stepping high to Anderson's *High Stepping Horses;* marching rigidly to Tschaikovsky's *March of the Tin Soldiers;* and gallop over the face of a redoubt to von Suppe's *Light Cavalry Overture.*

An easy transition to movement to music is made with the use of recorded songs, in which the words as well as the music suggest action. Most of these early rhythmic exercises are based on the basic movements of walking, running, skipping, galloping, swaying, and reaching. Suggestions for different types of movement are found in the various music series. The first three albums in *Rhythmic Activities* of the RCA Victor Record Library for Elementary Schools, RCA Adventures in Music for Grades 1, 2, and 3, and the Bowmar Orchestral Library of Marches and Dances provide a variety of music for excellence in listening as well as richness in tone and rhythmic quality to evoke creative movements.

Initially, the more obvious movements are made to the dominant beat, but in time the subtler elements are heard and interpreted by students. Here the teacher may use voice cues to help children recognize changes in the music from loud to soft, from slow to fast, from staccato to flowing, and to adjust their movements accordingly. Here the emphasis of the teacher is on listening to the music and doing what the music suggests, not what the teacher says.

It is not necessary that every child participate in every movement activity, or have all of the class engaged simultaneously. Space is often a limiting factor, and mood another. The waltz from Tschaikovsky's *Romeo and Juliet* may appeal more to the girl's perception of themselves as ballerinas. The boys can sit this one out, and then have exclusive rights to Schuman's *Wild Horseman.*

By the time children reach the third grade, they can be introduced to simple folk dances. Folk dancing provides variety and richness to the music program, and should be emphasized throughout the intermediate years. Folk dancing not only requires patterned movement, but careful listening for the musical cues to change movement. In American square dancing, in con-

---

21. Mursell, *Music and the Classroom Teacher,* p. 108.

trast, there is usually little variation in the music, with the change in patterns called.

To maintain interest in creative movement in the intermediate years, the music must be more subtle and appeal to older taste. Ballads and dialogue songs that suggest or tell a dramatic story are frequently more useful than orchestral music, which is more appropriate to creative dancing.

In the upper intermediate years, even more emphasis may be placed on dancing. In addition to folk dances from different lands, other dances may be learned, such as the polka, schottische, waltz, tango, habanera, samba, and even more contemporary steps.

While music educators rarely suggest the use of contemporary music for body movement and dancing, it seems desirable to give both primary and intermediate children an opportunity to interpret and dance to current song favorites in the prevailing idiom, whether it is "Pop Corn" or "Around the World." One reason why music in the school seems so sterile and artificial is that the children are not permitted to see the continuity in the music tradition.

The real folk music of a people is the contemporary idiom, not the so-called folk music selections which live primarily as museum pieces of our musical heritage. Admittedly, contemporary popular music is raucous, loud, and deafening, but even the waltz was regarded as a scandalous innovation at the time it was introduced. If the program of school music, whether for singing, movement, dancing, or listening, only includes music which music professionals consider "great" music, the program eventually dies under the weight of its own pretentiousness. There is a great variety of music, with enjoyment suited to the mood and occasion. The use of contemporary music can be an important link in the music program, and should be included in music programs.[22]

The study of jazz, America's original art form, frequently serves as a basis for enlarging the appreciation of music. The use of contemporary music also serves to extend the possibilities of enjoyment and, what is often overlooked, of providing additional outlets for success in school.

Listening

There are no technical obstacles which stand in the way of the classroom teacher's providing listening opportunities. Much of the previous section, relating to body movement, is concerned with listening to music and reacting to music with the body. But a teacher who feels awkward or self-conscious about body movement and music does not have this excuse with providing listening opportunities. There are outstanding collections of music for school use, selected to provide a variety of folk, traditional, and classical music. If these do not include jazz and rock, students are usually more than willing to supplement the school collection by bringing records from home. In the regular series of recordings, there are explanations of how to introduce and use the music. And rare is the class which does not have a record player. All that is required of the classroom teacher, then, is to provide the time for pupils to listen.

This does not mean that a teacher who both loves and knows music does not have an advantage in providing listening experiences for children. From his sensitivity to music and discrimination he is better able

22. E.g., comparisons of the improvised polyphony of Dixieland jazz with the composed polyphony of Bach; boogie-woogie with a Bach passacaglia; the use of jazz in Copland's *Lincoln Portrait* and in Bernstein's *West Side Story*.

to help students see the beauty in music. But there is nothing to stand in the way of the classroom teacher's giving his children adequate music listening opportunities. There is no substance in the popular notion that for a teacher to follow a prepared lesson is inferior teaching. Furthermore, if the classroom teacher does not know music, he is forced to follow a planned program or not have music. A classroom teacher should therefore have no hesitancy in following a prepared program of listening.

Some precautionary comments, however, may be helpful. Music listening, as used here, is not the equivalent of the usual stereotype of concert-silent music appreciation. This is only one way of showing appreciation for music. Singing and dancing are alternate ways of showing enjoyment, as are whistling, stamping out the beat, or musical composition. Listening is merely one way in which music may be enjoyed, and the object in learning how to listen to music is to give the student another dimension to musical enjoyment.

Listening to music for enjoyment has two dimensions—the affective and the cognitive. The affective dimension is evoked by the sound of the instruments, a dimension which may range from the kinesthetic to the spiritual. The cognitive dimension is evoked by the knowledge which one can bring to hearing a particular composition—knowledge of the composer and his style, the structural components and distinctive characteristics of the piece, the place of the composer and the work in the history of music, the influence of the composer on other musicians, and the discriminating characteristics of the various ways in which a particular composition can be played, to name a few.

The affective and cognitive, however, are not isolated but interacting dimensions, so that a favorable affective reaction to a piece of music may stimulate a pupil to seek cognitive information to better understand the composer and his work. At the same time, more knowledge about a composer and his work may lead to a desire to have more affective experience, i.e., hear more of the composer's works or work of a similar style, or it may lead to a rejection of that composer and his style. Affection and cognition thus form the basis of the much abused word "appreciation."

But appreciation is not synonymous with liking a piece of music or any other art form. Appreciation is discrimination based on experience and judgment, both of which are obtained through cultivation. The point in helping students to listen to music is for them to identify the kinds of music they enjoy. As their appreciation of music increases —and appreciation requires knowledge and experience with music—their preferences also frequently change.

Listening to music for enjoyment is an important part of Western culture. Much of the technically complex music in the Western tradition was designed to be enjoyed by listening. Only a small number of musical professionals, either in song, instrumentation, or dance, ever acquire the skills of a musical craftsman, although many derive pleasure as amateurs. Enjoyment in listening, as pleasure in so much of life, often depends on familiarity. As with other habits, it is desirable for children to begin to acquire a listening repertory early so that familiarity adds enjoyment to listening.

In addition to the regular opportunities for listening provided in the class, the teacher must strive to relate listening to out-of-school experience as much as possible. Otherwise, music listening will seem a schoolish exercise. Good radio and TV programs should be posted, called to the class' attention, and followed up with class discussion. Where live concerts are available, children should be encouraged to attend, especially concerts designed expressly for children. Students may be encouraged to bring their own records, share them with the class, and talk about them. Listening to music may be tied to books about music and composers, through which children can explore their interests in depth. In addition to the listening periods in the classroom, the library should have a collection of music with earphone players so that children can pursue their own listening interests.

Many different varieties of music may be used for listening enjoyment. Selections may vary from popular jazz to symphonic and operatic selections. There are different kinds of music to listen to for enjoyment, and no music is unsuitable for school listening, except the ribald and vulgar song.

The reason for emphasizing classical music in programs of listening rests on the fact that the enjoyment of such music depends on familiarity and knowledge. Since many children have few opportunities to hear this kind of music in the home, it is only natural that the school, in its function of cultural transmitter, should strive to bring these types of experiences to children. By doing so, it opens up, if to but a few, new avenues to musical enjoyment. But this should not be done in such a pompous manner, criticizing all other music, that children are offended. After all, they do listen to and enjoy contemporary music. And intense concentration in music listening is not restricted to the opera house or concert hall. In groups where young people gather to listen to contemporary artists or in meetings of jazz lovers, the intensity of emotional concentration and enjoyment equal that of the white-tied concert goer. Pupils need to listen to different types of music.

In listening to music, it is expected that children learn something about the composer, the distinctive characteristics of a piece, something about the composer's style, and something about the cultural milieu in which the composer lived and worked. The recording envelope frequently contains more of this type of information than pupils need to know. The point is to help them listen to music to learn to enjoy the music, not kill enjoyment with a stereotyped appreciation presentation. Older children will desire more of the latter kind of information.

Depending on his skill and knowledge, the classroom teacher may assist children to listen to and discriminate in mood and structural elements. In the primary grades, no emphasis needs to be given to technical musical terms, but these can be introduced gradually. In the intermediate grades, acquisition of a technical musical vocabulary facilitates musical discrimination and the verbalization of musical experience.

But there is a caution which the classroom teacher should be aware of: background music is not music for listening. In some schools, music is played in the library, in the cafeteria, and during study halls. It is the school equivalent of Muzak, and frequently has a quieting effect. But who is attending? The listening experiences suggested in this section are intended to be learning experiences to help children grow in their musical knowledge and enjoyment. They are not background experiences for other activities; listening *is* the activity.

Each graded series has various selections for listening as well as for singing. Unlike skills in mathematics, there is no prerequisite to musical enjoyment by age level. However, it is common to suggest that selections such as Tschaikovsky's *Sleeping Beauty* and Humperdinck's *Hansel and Gretel* be used with primary children and selections such as Copland's *Billy the Kid* and Moussorgsky's *Night on Bald Mountain* be used with intermediate age children. And don't expect even intermediate age children to listen to a full length symphony. There is time for that later. Selected portions should be used from longer works.

Making Music with Instruments

There are two ways of making music: by singing and by playing an instrument. This chapter has emphasized making music by singing, for the simple reason that each child carries his own voice box with him and songs can be learned without the skill of note reading. A child can thus produce his own music suitable to the occasion, whether in camp or church.

Making music by playing instruments requires two kinds of skill—ability to use the instrument and to read musical notation, both acquired by training and practice. Thus making music with instruments is ordinarily found only in schools where there is someone who knows how to play and teach an instrument. Sometimes schools which do not have a comprehensive music program for all students provide instrument lessons once or twice a week, a practice condemned by some musical educators as less desirable than that of having all students experience the playing of simple instruments.[23] They recommend the use of rhythm activities and simple instruments, most of which presume teaching competencies not attained by the regular classroom teacher.[24] Instructions about the use of xylophone, glockenspiel, autoharp, harmonic bells, recorders, and simple flutes, as well as directions for rhythmic orchestration, often tend to intimidate the classroom teacher.

There is an alternative, however, which permits children to make music without requiring instruction in music playing by the teacher. That is the use of a great variety of child-made rhythm instruments to accompany recorded music, singing, and moving to music. The playing of rhythm instruments facilitates sound discrimination and strengthens listening skills, particularly with respect to such elements of rhythm as metric beat, melody, rhythm, accent, and afterbeat.[25] While teacher-made and conventional rhythm band instruments will be mainly used in the primary grades, there is an additional bonus in the intermediate grades— the pleasure derived from making instruments.

In the primary years, the use of rhythm instruments may be directed primarily to sound discrimination and matching. Songs and music which have strong sound elements should be used. Some of the initial sound discrimination provided by the instruments of the rhythm band include: the booming of the drum; the tinkling of the triangle; the low tone of the drum and the high tone of the triangle; the difference in resonances of triangles, cymbals, drums, rhythm sticks; and different ways of playing to give different effects. Later children will learn distinctions with respect to the short, dry sounds produced by such different in-

23. Ellison, *Music With Children,* p. 160.

24. Grant, *Music for Elementary Teachers,* pp. 284-307; Swanson, *Music in Education,* pp. 101-39; Garretson, *Music in Childhood Education,* pp. 114-28; Ellison, *Music With Children,* pp. 122-66.

25. Swanson, *Music in Education,* pp. 80-92.

struments as sand blocks, coconut shells, and castanets; sustained, dry sounds produced by maracas and guiro; sustained tones with greater resonance produced by shaken tambourine and large skin-head drums; and the differences in the types of tinkling and ringing sounds.[26] The great variety of rhythm instruments used with Latin-American songs—cowbell, tambourine, conga drum, bongo drums, guiro (scraper), maracas, claves, and tubos (shaker)—and the unusual sounds they produce, are particularly appealing to intermediate students.[27]

Detailed instructions are available for making musical instruments.[28] The following simple suggestions indicate how easy it is to contrive rhythm instruments from such things as cans, salt and oatmeal boxes, typewriter ribbon cans, and even old light bulbs.

Shakers and maracas may be made from dried gourds filled with seeds. If gourds are not available, juice cans can be covered with construction paper or painted with a thick mixture of tempera and liquid soap. After a handful of seeds or pebbles have been put inside, the end can be covered with a circle of cardboard secured with masking tape. For an Indian rattle, a 12 inch dowel may be inserted in one end and feathers added for decoration.

Older children will enjoy making maracas by applying papier-mâché to an old electric light bulb. When the glue is dry, rap the covered bulb sharply on a table edge to break the glass inside.

Superior sand blocks can be made from fine sheets of emery cloth, fastened to pieces of 3 by 9 inch scrap lumber with tacks and a spool handle attached with screws. The emery cloth lasts longer than sandpaper. The cloth can be attached by gluing, but a better sound is obtained from tacking the cloth.

Rhythm sticks of contrasting sounds may be made from different size doweling, such as 1⅝ or ¼ inch. These can be cut in 12 inch lengths, ends sanded by children, and finished with a wipe-on stain wax.

A guiro or scratcher can be made by a series of saw cuts in a gourd or wood block. A smooth stick or wire is rubbed over these cuts to produce the scraping sound.

Oatmeal and salt box drums are old standbys in primary grades. Little is needed besides decoration and a drumstick, made by securing a ball of cotton or wrapping a strip of cloth around the end of a small stick. Another type of drum can be made from a flowerpot, with heavy brown wet paper, stretched over the head, and taped. This kind of drum can be struck lightly with the heel of the hand or fingertips. A more durable drum can be made from a wooden barrell or keg, and covered with hide or gum rubber tacked around the opening.

Coconut shells are fine for making galloping and trotting sounds. Shells for this purpose can be produced by cutting a coconut in half with a hack saw and scraping out the meat. Later the shells may be scraped and polished.

In addition to the rhythmic instruments, melodic instruments can be made by tuning

26. Ibid., p. 78.

27. Garretson, *Music in Childhood Education*, pp. 112-13.

28. Muriel Mandell and Robert E. Wood, *Make Your Own Musical Instruments* (New York: Sterling Publishing Company, Inc., 1957); Bernard S. Mason, *Drums, Tomtoms, Rattles* (New York: A. S. Barnes and Company, Inc., 1938). See also Humbert Morales, *Latin American Rhythm Instruments* (New York: H. Adler Publisher's Corp., 1954).

water glasses and bottles.[29] A variety of different kinds of metal shapes can also be used to provide appropriate accompaniment. A bass fiddle sound can be made by stretching a taut string over a broom stick held in a metal wash tub.

While the making of various types of musical instruments is a rewarding activity for older students, it must be recognized that there is nothing musical in the making of a drum or a scraper. The musical value of the instrument only comes into existence when the children play the instruments and listen to the sounds. The improvisation of musical instruments, however, often gives added zest to their use. It also permits children to see that the developed and standardized musical instrument has often evolved from very simple beginnings.

In using simple instruments, the purpose is not to try to create, as is so often done, a toy orchestra or a rhythm band. This soon palls, even for primary children. The purpose is to provide an opportunity to participate with music and to listen to music more attentively. It also provides an excellent basis for the study of music in preliterate cultures, where the music is often produced by a simple array of instruments playing rhythmic patterns. Special collections provide rich and varied offerings of the music of preliterate cultures.[30] The study of comparative music, as with comparative art, is often a neglected aspect in cross-cultural study.

Creative Activities in Music

The final aspect of music in a comprehensive program is usually denominated "creative," a term which has the advantage of encompassing such diverse activities as: making up additional verses to a song, making up a song, making up new verses to an old tune, trying to make up the music for a verse, arranging instruments in different rhythmic patterns, and composing. Choral speaking and creative dancing are sometimes classified as creative musical activities, but, if this is the case, the making of a musical instrument might as well be so listed.

While the tape recorder now offers possibilities of recording songs without the need for musical notation, the transferability of musical composition depends upon the ability to encode in musical notation. Unless a classroom teacher develops unusual talents or finds himself with an unusually talented class, it is not likely that he will deliberately seek to introduce musical composition.

Limited interest has been shown in the United States in the approach made by one of Germany's leading composers to teaching children to improvise. This is the method of Carl Orff, who has designed a complete set of instruments and a sequence for teaching composition.[31] The composition approach to music education also has been successfully piloted in the elementary grades, under the leadership of Edwin Gerschefski.[32] However, the composition approach to music education requires instruction by a person knowledgeable in music, particularly one who has been trained in music theory and

---

29. Ellison, *Music With Children*, pp. 186-91.
30. See, for example, Folkways Records, and the *Columbia World Library of Folk and Primitive Music*.
31. A brief discussion, with references, is given in Garretson, *Music in Childhood Education*, pp. 148-53.
32. Edwin Gerschefski, *Anyone Can Compose*, Mimeographed (Athens, Ga.: Music Department, University of Georgia, 1966).

composition, and is not recommended to the general classroom teacher.

Music and the Social Studies

It is common place to find music books suggesting the correlation of music and the social studies.[33] Some of the special collections available to the teacher include music and nationality,[34] incidents and stories about American people,[35] and the relationship of music and literature during various periods of United States history.[36]

Undoubtedly, music has much to contribute to an understanding of history and culture, but the usual method of having one or two popular songs accompany a unit on Mexico or Canada is probably poor social studies as well as bad music. From the standpoint of social understanding, the *Mexican Hat Dance* is only one vignette of Mexico, and probably contributes more to Mexican stereotypes than to international understanding. From the standpoint of music, the hop-skip of a little music of this and that country seldom contributes to any musical understanding, for with it there exists no study of music in depth.

There are many occasions in which there can be some correlation of social studies and music, but to tie all music to the social studies or the language arts is to substitute a mechanical correlation for achieving some understanding about music. The fundamental purpose is often forgotten by music educators when they recommend the correlation of music with the social studies. Music is a particular dimension for enjoyment and intellectual development, and does not require bootlegging into the curriculum in connection with other subjects. While music is a part of culture, and can best be understood in the context of a total culture, the cultural approach to the study of history is so rarely used in the social studies that there is little opportunity to present the arts in the context in which they originated. But while this is important cognitively, it is not necessary for the affective enjoyment of music.

A Sequential Music Curriculum

In the ordinary music program, children don't get enough music, they miss music quantitatively. Even more important, however, there is the absence of sequence; children miss music qualitatively.[37]

The qualitative aspects of music result when children participate, year after year, in a sequential music program, one which reflects learning abilities and previous learning experiences. There are a number of ways of listing musical experiences. One of the most complete ways is to indicate program objectives, instructional objectives, and learning experiences for each year, as shown by the revised sequence of the Georgia State Department of Education, now under development.[38] Another way is to provide a scope and sequence chart of music elements

33. Garretson, *Music in Childhood Education*, pp. 229-33; Swanson, *Music in Education*, chap. 9.
34. Raymond Elliott, *Teaching Music* (Columbus, Ohio: Charles E. Merrill Books, Inc., 1960), pp. 195-312.
35. Hazel Gertrude Kinscella, *History Sings* (Lincoln, Nebr.: University Publishing Company, 1948).
36. Ruth Tooze and Beatrice Krone, *Literature and Music as Resources for Social Studies* (Englewood Cliffs, N.J.: Prentice-Hall, Inc., 1955).
37. Aleta Runkle and Mary LeBow Eriksen, *Music for Today's Boys and Girls: Sequential Learning Through the Grades* (Boston: Allyn and Bacon, Inc., 1966).
38. Georgia State Department of Education, *Music for Early Childhood: A Music Curriculum for Georgia's Elementary Schools 1970-71*, Mimeographed (Atlanta, Ga.: State Department of Education, 1970).

by grade level. The one of the Los Angeles City Schools, included as a foldout in Nye and Nye, is divided into four constituent elements—melody, rhythm, harmony, and form; three expressive elements—tempo, dynamics, tone color; and teaching suggestions.[39] This scheme is then carried out for each grade level, providing a complex interrelation of musical learnings.

In addition to concept clusters, musical sequences are also arranged by objectives, performance (including instrumental), activities, and appreciation of form and style. These various parts are organized into a structure of music education.[40]

Because the listing of musical experiences by grade level would unduly lengthen this chapter—and still differ from the particular series you might select or which might be available in your school—the alternative will be followed of describing what is available to you as a teacher from two series at two different grades. In most series there is more than the average teacher and class can possibly use in the course of the year. This permits some pupil and teacher selectivity within the framework of a planned program.

Grade 3, *Exploring Music*.[41] There are 160 songs, which are classified as follows: twenty American folk songs and spirituals, e.g., *Home on the Range, Michael, Row the Boat Ashore;* eighteen animal songs, e.g., *Alouette;* eight boats and sailing songs, e.g., *Blow Ye Winds;* three cowboy songs, e.g., *Home on the Range;* eight dances and singing games, e.g., *Brother, Come and Dance With Me;* forty-two songs from nineteen countries, e.g., France, *Bring a Torch, Jeannette, Isabella;* seventeen songs for seven holidays and special days, e.g., Thanksgiving, *This is My Father's World;* four Indian songs, e.g., *Navaho Happy Song;* three lullabies, e.g., *The Little Sandman;* fifteen nature songs, e.g., *Winter Weather;* three patriotic songs, e.g., *Star Spangled Banner,* and ten songs of inspiration, e.g., *For the Beauty of the Earth.*

There are seventeen listening lessons, involving such composers and selections as Smetana, "Dance of the Comedians" from *The Bartered Bride;* Chavez, *Toccata for Percussion* (Third Movement), Chopin, *Waltz in C Sharp minor;* and Haydn, *Symphony No. 94,* "Surprise" (Third Movement).

The classified index of musical skills provide for dance improvisation, elements of music, experimentation and composition, expression, and instrumental skills. Twenty-two different instruments are featured in song recordings. There is a variety of supplementary material, such as The Brass Family, Latin-American Instruments, and New Sounds in Music.

The sequence for grade 3 is divided into seven sections, each of which introduces a new basic musical concept. Thus the book, as other planned music series, should be used from beginning to end. If time does not permit the inclusion of all songs, some selections should be omitted from each section in order to permit the sequential development. It is indeed a sad commentary on our musical literacy to realize that many a college student does not have the knowl-

39. Robert Evans Nye and Vernice Trousdale Nye, *Music in the Elementary School* 3d ed. (Englewood Cliffs, N.J.: Prentice-Hall, 1970).

40. John U. Michaelis, Ruth H. Grossman, and Lloyd F. Scott, *New Designs for the Elementary School Curriculum* (New York: McGraw-Hill, Inc., 1967), pp. 367-71.

41. This series is published by Holt, Rinehart and Winston.

edge of music in the intellectual tradition reflected in this sequence designed for third grade music experiences.

Grade 8, *Discovering Music Together*.[42] This collection provides a variety of music characteristic of the other series shown for grade 3, although the categories are somewhat different. There are folk songs of the U.S.A., e.g., *Tell Me Why;* folk songs of other countries, e.g., Nigerian (chant), *Kum Ba Yah;* religious vocal works, e.g., Latin, *Dona Nobis Pacem;* instrumental parts, e.g., guitar, *Buffalo Gals;* music for special occasions, e.g., *Lo, How A Rose;* opera and oratorio, e.g., *Elijah;* patriotic songs, e.g., *Hail, Columbia;* rounds and canons, e.g., *Summer is A-Coming In;* songs by well-known composers, e.g., Beethoven, *I Love You.* There are nineteen listening selections, such as Bach, *Little Fugue in G minor;* Copland, *Lincoln Portrait;* Mozart, *Symphony No. 40 in G minor* (First Movement), and R. Strauss, *Waltzes from "Der Rosenkavalier."*

The selections are designed to reinforce the basic elements of music, i.e., melody, form, rhythm, harmony, dynamics, and mood. The concepts are presented in a more complex manner at this level. Thus harmony at this grade includes a consideration of polyphonic and homophonic styles, whereas in the earlier level the emphasis was on the type of instrument or song. The growing technical complexity of the musical discourse is shown by the musical glossary.

The table of contents of this book indicates an interesting organization of thematic emphasis. The first deals with songs and music in general; the second shows the utilitarian use of music for dance, work, and recreation; the third expresses sentiments about various aspects of man's surroundings—home and family, nature, freedom, and country; and the fourth section is an historical overview of the western musical heritage from the middle ages to the origins and development of jazz.

The preceding descriptions, representative of two series, each at a different grade level, indicate to the prospective classroom teacher the rich type of musical experiences that await children in pursuing a sequential curriculum in music.

An Appraisal of Teaching Music in the School

This chapter has taken the position that music is an important part of the elementary curriculum. It has also asserted that the way to make sure children in school do have a sequential music program is to provide the trained manpower to teach music at a scheduled time. In this way, experiences with music can be cumulative, and different standards of musical understanding and enjoyment expected at various grade levels because of instruction.

In many parts of the country there are few trained music teachers in the schools. There are exceptions, as in the Dekalb and Atlanta school systems in Georgia, but the presence of music teachers in urban areas only serves to highlight the deficit in rural areas, where they are frequently nonexistent. To provide two periods of music a week for elementary students requires a teacher for every 300 students, exclusive of special teachers of orchestra, chorus, and band. At this ratio, many sections of the country have only one-sixth of the music teachers needed to teach music.

---

42. This series is published by Follett Publishing Company.

In the absence of a music teacher, however, the authors have taken the position in this chapter that the classroom teacher can make significant musical experiences available to children. This is not to discount the overwhelming importance of the trained teacher, but the recorded series provides any school with the opportunity to have a sequenced program. This permits children to grow musically. In the absence of a plan, teachers tend to repeat primary songs in the intermediate grades, and contribute to a stifling of musical interest with selections which are too juvenile. Children need to grow in music as well as in mathematics or science.

Even when a school does not use a sequenced program, the teacher can break the psychological barrier and decide to provide music himself. If children have not had music in their school at the previous level, except incidentally, the teacher can experiment with some of the selections for earlier grades, until he finds what he considers a more appropriate match in skill and interest. In the Holt, Rinehart and Winston series, the opera *Hansel and Gretel* is selected for level three listening and study, but younger children as well as adults enjoy the story and the music. Thus the teacher may not be unduly concerned about grade appropriateness, if he or the children express interest in music which does not bear some grade level approval. While in music there is a difficulty sequence, there is some flexibility with respect to listening so that deviations can be made.

There are different facets to handling music—singing, moving, listening, playing, and creating. It is likely that the regular classroom teacher, because of lack of technical expertise, will concentrate on the first three, whereas a trained music teacher might use creating as the approach to music education. In the experiences designed to increase musical interest and understanding, the major focus is on the music, although a number of related activities may be used as adjuncts to the music program.

In the final analysis, the object of the public school music program is not the development of musicians, although it may develop an interest in musicianship. The object of the music program is to let children experience music in an enjoyable and knowledgeable manner so that they may make this rich heritage a part of their experience for continued aesthetic and personal growth.

Most of you who read this chapter will be preparing to teach as general classroom teachers and not teachers of music. It is hoped that this chapter will challenge you to venture further into the area of music, and encourage you to invite your students, when you enter teaching, to share in that experience with you. The mutual experiences will be rewarding to all of you. The first time may seem difficult, but after making music a part of your school life and that of each of your children for a year or so you will wonder how it is possible to teach without teaching music. And you and your children will be all the richer for your teaching.

Selected References

Ellison, Alfred. *Music With Children.* New York: McGraw-Hill Book Company, 1959.

Garretson, Robert L. *Music in Childhood Education.* New York: Appleton-Century-Crofts, Inc., 1966.

Grant, Parks. *Music for Elementary Teachers.* 2d ed. New York: Appleton-Century-Crofts, Inc., 1960.

MARVEL, LORENE M. *Music Resource Guide for Primary Grades.* Minneapolis: Schmitt, Hall and McCreary Company, 1961.

MURSELL, JAMES L. *Music and the Classroom Teacher.* New York: Silver Burdett Company, 1951.

NYE, ROBERT EVANS, and NYE, VERNICE TROUSDALE. *Music in the Elementary School.* 3d ed. Englewood Cliffs, N. J.: Prentice-Hall, Inc., 1970.

PEARMAN, MARTHA; MILLER, RALPH G.; and BONNEY, EILEEN. *The Understanding of Music: A Guide for Teachers.* Rev. ed. Dubuque, Iowa: Kendall/Hunt, 1967.

RUNKLE, ALETA, and ERIKSEN, MARY LEBOW. *Music for Today's Boys and Girls: Sequential Learning Through the Grades.* Boston: Allyn and Bacon, Inc., 1966.

SWANSON, BESSIE R. *Music in the Education of Children.* 2d ed. Belmont, California: Wadsworth Publishing Company, Inc., 1964.

TIMMERMAN, MAURINE. *Let's Teach Music in the Elementary School.* Evanston, Ill.: Summy-Birchard Company, 1958.

teaching art through self-expression

17

Hallow'een cats in sterile black meowled;
Now psychedelic color cats loudly howl.

The windows of an abandoned school sometimes show the art of yesterday—cats in October, turkeys in November, Santas in December, and tulips in Spring. These cut-outs and paste-ups probably did little for the enhancement of art or the expression of sentiment, but they did develop an ambience which was unmistakably that of the elementary school.

Art had a tenuous development in the 1800s. The growth of public school art is contemporary with the progressive education movement. It was not until 1927 that school art was officially recognized by the National Education Association.[1] The little art education that existed had already gone through the formal periods of academic drawing and composition. Art education therefore enthusiastically embraced the notions of Dewey, child development, and the progressive movement. For the past forty years art education has attempted to translate into the school curriculum the notions of such pioneers as Whitford and Cizek. Experience and free expression are concepts which still dominate art education today, although creativity has become a more popular alternate to free expression. The early advocates of new approaches to art, however, were not as nondirective or as permissive as they were subsequently interpreted. According to De Francesco, Cizek was always stimulating, asking questions, encouraging, and even critical; his purpose was to encourage creativity in art through teaching. This attitude toward the teaching of art dominates this chapter.

This chapter, however, does not presume to be on the teaching of art or the history of art education.[2] It is designed to present a point of view relating to the significance of the arts in the program of elementary education, and applies only to the visual arts. Other chapters discuss the performing arts.

Objectives in Elementary Art Education

There is an inevitable tendency for each discipline in the school curriculum to over-

1. Itala L. De Francesco, *Art Education* (New York: Harper & Brothers, 1958), p. 85.
2. A brief but stimulating account in terms of international movements is given in Michael Steveni, *Art & Education* (New York: Atherton Press, 1968), chaps. 1 and 2. An account which emphasizes developments in the United States is given in De Francesco, *Art Education,* chap. 2.

generalize its objectives. Art education makes similar overclaims. Everything from the development of a wholesome personality to democratic citizenship is equated with experience in the arts.

But for over twenty years, the leitmotif of art education has been creativity.[3] Creativity is a term so generally discussed and vaguely defined that it tends to be often no more than a synonym for divergence of production.[4] Certainly, the practitioners of other disciplines would challenge the claim that art, narrowly or broadly conceived, has a monopoly on creativity. Chemists and comics are creative in their own way, as are doctors and divers.

If creativity is originality, there is a limit to the amount of originality any culture can stand. Instead, a premium is placed upon craftsmanship. The reason the fine arts press endless claims of creativity is the absence of a utilitarian test. The applied arts impose certain limits on originality because of structural prerequisites. We may in fantasy conceive a dome without support, as we can paint a three legged chair. Such originality, however, does not bear the test of function, however much it delights the mind's eye. Mere craftsmanship is not art, so we have no illusions that the plumber is an artist. However, the modern term of art derives from an earlier concept of *arte* or craftsmanship. It is therefore appropriate to consider for a moment the nature of art.

Art As a Planned Form. All the world is full of visual delight. The perceptive analysis of a garbage dump may be more visually stimulating than snow on jagged mountain peaks, if less beautiful. Yet, even though nature provides a stimulus for art as do the works of man, we do not call these works art except poetically. The spatial configurations of a petrochemical plant are often more visually exciting than the spires of a cathedral. The former is a mere factory; the other a work of art. Philosophically, the distinction becomes blurred, and even Henry Adams was constrained to compare the Virgin and the dynamo as he reflected on different sources of energy.

But the petrochemical plant is an objective visual object. The configuration of pipes, valves, tanks and cracking towers presents a surrealistic interpretation of space. But there was no plan to make such a representation. The plan drawn by the engineer was for the efficient use of equipment to produce a given product at a minimum cost. There was no intent to produce a given form visually. The imposition of any aesthetic evaluation on the petrochemical plant is in the visual perception and emotions of an observer. For this reason, art is not a synonym for nature.

In contrast, art is neither fortuitous, nor found, but is planned. The production conforms to some original intent of the producer; the outcome, even though changed in the course of development, conforms to the purpose of the artist. Art is the conscious and deliberate creation of form.

Nor is art mere emotion. Emotion is inevitably expressed in the form, but the artist and his creation are distinct from the product, as is the actor from the role he consciously creates. Art may begin in expe-

---

3. Ralph M. Pearson, *The New Art Education* (New York: Harper & Brothers, 1941), p. 14; Harold Gregg, *Art for the Schools of America* (Scranton, Pa.: International Textbook Co., 1941); Manuel Barkan, *Through Art to Creativity* (Boston, Allyn and Bacon, Inc., 1960); Blanche Jefferson, *Teaching Art to Children*, 2d ed. (Boston: Allyn and Bacon, Inc., 1963).

4. See Earl W. Linderman and Donald W. Herberholz, *Developing Artistic and Perceptual Awareness: Art Practice in the Elementary Classroom*, 2d ed. (Dubuque, Iowa: Wm. C. Brown Company Publishers, 1969), chap. 2.

rience, but experience is not art until it is expressed in an objective form.

Thus the first objective of art education may be conceived as the progressive transformation of perception and experience into form.

Art as a Skill. To translate experience into the form that we evaluate as art requires the application of skill to media. Skill is a result of learning and of experience. No culture is without art, but the art forms of a particular culture are a result of previous learning and invention. Culturally transmitted, they become institutionalized so that the experience and emotions expressed in art of an individual reflect the learnings of a culture. The forms are not infinite.

Interest in any field which leads to skill is acquired by familiarity and experience. Today the public school represents the institutionalization of resources for cultural transmission, and exercises many of the training functions formerly held by apprentice systems. In former years, artists as well as doctors and lawyers were trained as apprentices. Today they are trained in colleges and professional schools, as are dancers and musicians. But the language of art, although communicable in verbal terms, is nonverbal in expression. Art depends on sight as music depends on sound. The early cultivation of interest in art, which may subsequently lead to professional careers in art, are thus related to the curriculum of the early school. There is consequently equivalent justification for experience in art as there is for experience in letters and numbers.

Elementary children are thus exposed to art as a means whereby society continues to inspire and develop young talent. A few will become the artists of tomorrow. The fact that artistic talent is rare is no justification for not teaching art to all children. Society does not abjure the requirement of mathematics for all children because few become practicing mathematicians. The talent for art and mathematics can only be identified through learning and interest.

A second objective of art in the elementary school is the development of interests in art which may subsequently be cultivated and refined in the professional artist.

Art as a Value. Pragmatic definition of a value is simply a cultural preference, measured by the allocation of resources. From this perspective, distinctions of instrumental and intrinsic worth are immaterial. The fact that art is a value is demonstrated by the very fact that art exists.

Values in a culture are not evenly distributed, as shown by the fact that resources are not evenly allocated. Therefore, the proponents of certain values, as with the arts, must constantly claim a share of resources if the value they support is to be enhanced. The realm of sports and cinema reflect mass values and mass patronage. The rise to stardom of a Joe Namath or a Pete Maravich does not merely reflect the intrinsic skill of the sportsman, but the values which a Little League culture transmit to the very young. Preoccupation with the creativity and self-expression of the child obscures the fact that the school itself gives so little reinforcement to the teaching of art. The school mirrors the values of the larger culture. Values in a culture are cultivated and transmitted through the allocation of resources. The very young years are critical ones in forming the values of another generation. The early years are not only critical for cognitive and emotional development, but also in the formation of attitudes and values through the process of socialization.

If art is a mass and not merely capitalistic value based on commodity scarcity, cultivation through school resources is a demonstration of the democratic value of art. A third objective of teaching art in the elementary school is to make art an actual and not theoretical mass value.

Art as Self-Expression. The media of art afford to the young learner tangible and safe avenues to self-expression. From mud pies to space craft, man is a creator, imposing upon natural phenomena the force of his emotion and his intellect. The creative —and imitative—urge of the young child is limited not so much by his lack of perception and his imagination as by his lack of dexterity. The tools of adult creativity, such as in cookery or carpentry, are denied the child because of their danger and because the tools are beyond his ability.

But the media of the artist afford to even the very young safe tools suitable to his conceptual level and manual ability. Paint, clay, and collage afford no hazard to life or limb and yet give the child the opportunity to produce—to translate an idea into a form. The product is the result of his own efforts. Art is self-satisfying because it is self-doing; it is producing something tangible. Art is fun because it is productive. Eventually the skill of doing increases. The child gains mastery over technique, and production exhibits more predetermined conception. Thus self-expression through art media is gradually transformed into art through purpose and control. But even without this level of mastery, self-expression requires no other justification. For the time it provides an avenue for translating experience into reality.

A fourth objective for teaching art in the elementary school is thus simply to provide another medium for doing. And out of the doing, the spontaneity and originality that we associate with children's art may be encouraged and nurtured.

Art as Appreciation. Art is a fact, fine and applied. It is a part of man's history and his cross-cultural appreciation. It is not only a part of his experience; it is a part of his knowledge. Art history and aesthetics are rarely taught in the elementary school; the emphasis is almost exclusively on studio art. Art is as much a part of our intellectual baggage as political history, literature, or philosophy, and the subject matter is no more esoteric than other subjects of the elementary curriculum. In the long run, the vast majority of a population, even in a democracy, will be consumers rather than practitioners of art. Yet art history is seldom broached until the adolescent years, when the interest in art production has already declined for the majority of students. Psychologically, it would seem that the natural time to teach some rudiments of art history and criticism would be in conjunction with art production in the elementary years.

A fifth objective for teaching art in the elementary school, then, is to introduce children to our art heritage.[5] If extended beyond

---

5. The teaching of art appreciation is usually roundly censured. See, for example, Manfred L. Keiler, *The Art in Teaching Art* (Lincoln, Neb.: University of Nebraska Press, 1961), p. 65. In contrast, Linderman and Herberholz include art for study and appreciation as a fourth component in a beginning art program, *Developing Artistic and Perceptual Awareness,* pp. 121 ff. In view of the lack of experimentation with art appreciation in the elementary school, there is little evidence concerning the most appropriate content and organization. It is possible that teaching of art history might be related to art projects which students have completed, rather than formal units in art history unrelated to the child's experience. Robert B. Kent at the University of Georgia is experimenting with a discovery approach to art appreciation.

painting and sculpture to architecture and landscape design, there might be a new appreciation of the total environment of man in nature.

Art as Communication. Some individuals are fluent verbally; others less so. One thinks in verbal imagery, and communicates in poetry, drama, or prose. Other individuals may have equally vivid sentiments, which they are unable to translate into words. They should have the opportunity to communicate visually and to express their feelings in concrete media.

A sixth objective for teaching art in the elementary school is to provide an alternate visual form of expression and communication. Hence, there is a unity rather than a divergence in the teaching of art as a skill.

Stages in Artistic Self-Expression

Art educators have been strongly influenced by the developmental movement in child psychology. Extensive studies have been made of the sequence in which children express themselves artistically, especially in crayons and paints. With age and experience, the child displays more control of the media, conceptualization of form, enrichment of detail, complexity of design, awareness of color, and more realistic portrayal. Linderman and Herberholz[6] describe a three-stage sequence of scribbling, ages 2-4; symbolism, 4-8; and beginning realism, 9-12. Lowenfeld and Brittain,[7] who have extensively studied the relationship of various stages of expression to the child's personality, use a five-stage sequence. These five stages are scribbling, ages 2-4; preschematic, 4-7; schematic, 7-9; dawning realism, 9-11; and pseudonaturalism, 11-13.

The extent to which these authorities regard these stages as maturational or the product of experience in learning art, interacting with motor and psychological growth, is not always clear. However, it should be emphasized that the stages are descriptive and not fixed sequences. Some very young children draw realistically, just as older children sometimes adhere to simpler and earlier forms of expression. Furthermore, the stages should not be interpreted restrictively as to the experience appropriate for an individual child. A child talented in art at age seven who performs similar to a child several years older should be encouraged to develop his abilities, not discouraged because of some alleged descrepancy between age and sequence.

Scribbling, Ages 2-4. Melzi[8] has pointedly observed that scribbling is to drawing as babbling is to speech. Before the age of two a child is more interested in putting a crayon in his mouth than using it to draw. At times, around the age of two, the child will use a pencil or crayon to scribble. At first the scribbles are disorganized and aimless. This disorganized stage continues for several months. Then the scribbles become more organized, repeating a pattern of spiral, vertical, or horizontal strokes. The greater degree of organization reflects a greater degree of motor coordination, which is found in other activities. Later comes the naming stage, which is an indication of the relationships of visual shapes to verbal symbols. An adult or older sibling is often more amused than impressed by the solemn as-

6. Linderman and Herberholz, *Developing Artistic and Perceptual Awareness,* pp. 43, 49, 50.
7. Viktor Lowenfeld and W. Lambert Brittain, *Creative and Mental Growth,* 4th ed. (New York: Macmillan Company, 1964), *passim.*
8. Kay Melzi, *Art in the Primary School* (Oxford: Basil Blackwell, 1967), p. 4.

sertion that this scribble is "Me" or that scribble is "Daddy." The scribbling stage is one of variable interest, often short, with much paper apparently wasted for a few lines. Gradually, there is a transition to the preschematic stage, but scribbling is prolonged with painting, especially if the paper is on an easel and the paints thin rather than of creamy consistency.

Preschematic Stage, Ages 4-7. The kinesthetic emphasis of scribbling gradually gives way to a more conscious realization of what the child wants to present. The pursuit of form and visual reality permits the artist to will the destruction of form for his own subjective expression.

Most children begin kindergarten or first grade in the stage of this inchoate pursuit of form. Figures are transitional from scribbles, with the head characteristically distorted and limbs mere stick appendages. Space is merely an arrangement and is not representational. A variety of color is used for its own sake, not to express any concrete relationships. Because the representation of form in this stage is symbolic rather than real, the stage is sometimes called the symbolic. However, in common usage a symbol has a repetitive and conventional usage, while the symbols of this artistic stage change with the experiences and interests of the child.

Schematic Stage, Ages 7-9. The schematic stage has a number of characteristics which indicate the growing self-awareness of the child. The first of these refers to the permanence of the symbol, whether it is a tree, a man, or a house. While these vary with the individual, the stereotyping of representation facilitates economy in expression and is indicative of the emerging sensitivity of that individual. A second phenomenon, as universal as that of scribbling, is the introduction of the base line to represent the child's perception of space. Flowers, houses, people, and other objects are placed perpendicular to the base line. There is a sense of perspective, but not representational technique. Three dimensional space is often presented with inversions, such as double skies involving two base lines, a vertical representation of a flat surface, or simultaneous portrayal of interior and exterior views. There is also a conscious use of color to represent objects, often conventionalized, as are other aspects of this schematic stage. Boys in particular become more conscious of mechanical features, and attempt to impart more formal substance through graphic details.

Dawning Realism, Ages 9-11. In the stage of prerealism the child becomes more visually perceptive of his experiences and the environment in which he moves. Many details continue to be treated schematically, but the drawing becomes more representational. Figures are presented more proportionately, with less exaggeration. Emphasis by distortion is replaced with emphasis by detail. More importance is given to the overall design, and there is a more conscious perception of depth through overlapping. The child moves from vertical representation from a base line to representation on the plane, although the significance of the horizon in landscapes is just emerging. Cutaway drawing to represent concurrent interior and exterior scenes and inversions are abandoned as being unnatural. There is a greater awareness of color tones, such as intensity and appropriateness of different shades of blue and green. Sex differences are emphasized in pictures.

Pseudonaturalism, Ages 11-13. The preadolescent stage overlaps the upper elementary and junior high years. This stage is one which continues the urge to more realistic representation of the human figure relative to space. The visual perception of diminution of distant objects is reflected in three-dimensional representation of space, and there is a more refined use of color. But this is also a period in which children, if they have not already lost a spontaneity in artistic expression, frequently lose all interest in visual expression, irrespective of the media.

Much of this loss of interest in art reflects the tendency of children, as they become older, to become more specialized in their interests. It is not necessarily, as the books on art education emphasize so much, a loss of desire for self-expression. What happens is that the child no longer finds experience with art media satisfying and seeks other avenues of expression, as boys do in sports.

Another reason may be the failure of art teachers to teach technique. For example, advocates of the extreme discovery approach to art for children, such as Lowenfeld and Brittain, make the teaching of perspective contingent on the requests of visually-minded children.[9] They classify some children at this stage as nonvisual. It can be hypothesized that the child loses his feeling for artistic expression in the realistic and naturalistic stages because he is not helped to acquire the techniques to make his representations conform to reality. His awareness of the gap between his technical ability and perception of the real world makes him lose interest from lack of success.

The preceding discussion of stages in art development has concentrated on the sequence of drawing and painting, since this form of expression is the earliest and is continuous. The section on art materials, however, will indicate the variety of media which can be appropriately used at different ages.

Motivation For Self-Expression

An artistic experience is personal and subjective even when it represents reality. Many children, however, are deficient in self-awareness and in perception of the environment. The availability of art media is often no more encouraging than the availability of pencil and paper to the putative writer. Self-expression through art therefore often begins in the stimulation of the sensory experiences of the child. In fact, this aspect of experience is emphasized so much that, with the exception of an occasional reference to art materials, the reader of some art education books might think he was reading an introduction to language arts. Language, however, is as indispensable to art as it is to other subject matter. It is through language that the vividity of individual or collective experiences are made explicit, that discriminations are made in visual perception, and that communication of techniques and aesthetic judgments are expressed. Language is the vehicle through which subjective experiences visually expressed are made communicable.

Awareness Through Recall. Every child has personal experiences which are meaningful to him. The ability to recall these experiences and use them as effective stimuli for an art creation often depends upon the evocative capacity of the teacher's use of language. Natural phenomena, home life, and play are experiences within the life of

---

9. Lowenfeld and Brittain, *Creative and Mental Growth*, p. 233.

all children. But merely to suggest a subject, such as "Rain," or "Friends" is rarely sufficient stimulus to focus on a composition which results in an art product. "How do you feel when it rains?" "What does rain look like?" "Where does it rain?" "Why does it rain?" All are questions which assist the child to evoke the imagery of an event to which he can impart his own distinctive impression.

Awareness Through Direct Experience. Although experience is always individual, a heightened sense of collective awareness is sometimes gained through class experiences. This provides the opportunity for an individual to acquire a heightened sensitivity by contrasting his experiences with others. Direct experience shared by class and teacher also permits the teacher to use language cues to extend the scope of the child's awareness. Field trips which expose children to a variety of contexts can assist them become more visually perceptive of the world in which they live and sense such experiences in terms of design, composition, and pattern. A trip through a wooded park can be more than a stroll. It can become a feast of the senses. The sight of the variegated tapestry of greens and the differing textures of bark, the interplay of light and shadow fusing with the muted silence, and the feel of freshness of the air on skin—combine to make an ordinary experience an aesthetic and emotional one. Such direct, sensational experiences help children break the barriers to awareness of the commonplace.

Awareness Through Visual Perception. The affective experience which culminates in a visual representation often involves more senses than that of sight. But the production and enjoyment of a visual representation can only be expressed visually, although the visual representation may cue other associations. The world is infinitely rich in detail, if the time is taken to perceive. A rotted piece of wood, behind its monochrome decay, provides a rich variety of pattern and texture just as a newly plowed field often shows a strong pattern of rhythm and change in earth hues. Such subtle details become more appealing too as a child matures. But even for the younger one, stimulation can result from the sharp contrasts which are produced by the juxtaposition of a drape and a jug, or from the tremendous richness of shape and color to be observed in a butterfly wing.

In many art classes there is such a fear of representational efforts that the stimulus for art work is too often limited to imaginative recall. But the art class itself provides the opportunities for deliberately stimulating visual awareness. The provision of objects diverse in shape, dramatic in color, and arranged in forceful combinations permit the child to become more visually alert to the possibilities of design and pattern. Drawing or modeling directly from real objects has the added advantage of three-dimensional space. Principles of foreshortening and perspective, as well as evaluation relating to color, design, texture, and composition may be acquired more readily from the direct use of real objects which the child can see, as they relate to his art production.

Awareness Through the Teaching of Art. The most neglected aspect of art motivation is the successful teaching of art itself. No matter how much experience a child has had and no matter how much that experience is discussed, the production of an art product depends upon the use of a particular medium. While older children are often given an option as to the media used, proper management of art experiences requires instruction by the teacher of the class as a group when a new medium is introduced. The "express yourself" school of elementary art provides little or no instruction to the child, whereas good art teaching requires that the same care be given art instruction as instruction in any other subject.

Let us assume that a proper motivational set has been developed through experience and discussion. It is time to initiate the project. It is useful at the outset to discuss with the class objectives relating to color, texture, and other points of emphasis. This permits the establishment of standards against which evaluation comments may be subsequently made. In clarifying the learning goals, the students are able to gain a better perception of their own possibilities. If a new technique or medium is involved, this should be demonstrated. The teacher may wish to show slides, an appropriate film strip, or flat pictures. There may be some trial of the various media as well as discussion of their possibilities and limitations. During the project, the teacher will encourage and evaluate pupil work, especially stimulating students to achieve higher standards of excellence in their own work. In this way, the teaching of art is in itself motivational. Motivation is not merely a beginning with an isolated step called awareness but continues through the finished art production. Success in the creation of visually and emotionally satisfying art productions in turn motivates the child to additional expression.

Art Materials

Materials and facilities do not in themselves guarantee a good art program, just as an air-conditioned and carpeted school does not automatically provide a good learning environment. However, art materials are an indispensable prerequisite for artistic self-expression. An adequate and suitable supply is necessary if experiences of self-awareness are to be converted into any form of representation. And, as Steveni points out, materials not only modify an artistic conception but also may originate it.[10]

The following suggested materials are not meant to imply that there is no overlap of age in material use. It will be noted that all of the various stages show an age overlap, i.e., 2-4, 4-7. This is one way of emphasizing that the use of art materials should be individually adjusted to the child's developing self-expression and learning ability, and not to some arbitrary idea of what is generally suitable to all children. Since art expression does depend upon manual dexterity, attempts to introduce certain media prematurely may be an uneconomic use of time.

Ages 2-4. The material at this scribbling stage should facilitate the control of kinesthetic motion. The most suitable materials consist of unwrapped crayons and tempera paint of a creamy consistency. Light colored paper, such as 8½-by-11-inch mimeographed paper, is suitable for crayon work. Larger sheets of absorbent paper should be used with tempera. An assortment of medium-size brushes may be used. Different colored papers and paste may be used for making collages. Children enjoy the feel and consistency of clay, which may be stored in plastic bags. The clay should be of a firm consistency so that it is easy to work with and does not stick to the fingers. Finger painting does not provide the required kinesthetic

---

10. Steveni, *Art & Education,* p. 212.

control, and is not necessarily desirable at this stage. The cutouts and paste-ups typical of holidays and special occasions may not necessarily provide creative experiences for the child, but are often worthwhile as parent-relation activities.

Ages 4-7. Basic material of this stage includes crayons, tempera, and clay, as described for the scribbling stage. In addition, colored papers and collage materials, papier-mâché, salt ceramic, felt tipped pins, colored chalk, glue, scissors, and paste are used. A smock made from an old shirt keeps paint off school clothes and mothers happy. In the first and second grades, social studies often emphasizes the birthdays of famous men or some special events from history such as the landing of the Pilgrims. Mass produced scissor cut outs do not enhance creativity, but they develop manipulative dexterity. However, there is a risk that this stereotyped and repetitive type of public school decoration may be regarded as a substitute for art.

Ages 7-9. The schematic stage does not require the introduction of new materials. Increase in manual dexterity, however, permits the use of materials for some construction and some printmaking. Construction materials include wood, weaving and stitchery yarns, cloth, string, toothpicks, and natural materials which lend themselves to imaginative construction. A variety of printmaking devices may be introduced, including linoleum and silk screen. A frame or table loom may be used for weaving. In painting, hair brushes can be added to the bristle collection, and larger sheets of paper used.

Clay in particular takes on added significance. The plastic nature of clay is particularly suitable to the development of three-dimensional perception. Children model in two different fashions—taking small pieces and adding them together to make a figure, and taking the whole ball of clay and spreading it out to make a form.

Ages 9-11. Beginning realism requires no radical change in the kinds of materials available. Because of greater brush facility, thinner poster paints may be used. Smaller brushes are desirable due to increasing attention to detail. Collage work can be made bolder and more forceful, and craft work can be given increasing attention because of greater manipulative facility. The gimmicky productions which sometimes pass for art at this stage, such as decorating bottles for lamps, are seldom aesthetically pleasing, much less creative.

Ages 11-13. Additional art materials introduced at this time include water colors,[11] charcoal drawing, and India ink. There is primarily a shift in the emphasis on material use. This is particularly noticeable in the use of clay, which is now applied to creation of pottery.

The former spontaneity in the use of paints and crayons has declined, and manipulative art becomes more important in self-expression. At this time, the interests of boys show a substantial decline, and the art program is increasingly feminized. Decorated masks from papier-mâché, sculpture from wire and plaster, three-dimensional collages, and wood sculpture are different means of expression used to sustain art

11. Material placement by age is not scientific, but follows certain conceptions of development and teaching. Thus Wachowiak does not share the oft-repeated admonition against the early use of water color, which he uses in the primary grades. See Frank Wachowiak and Theodore Ramsay, *Emphasis: Art—A Qualitative Program for the Elementary School.* (Scranton, Pa.: International Book Co., 1965).

interest. The more serious student begins to identify himself professionally with the use of certain materials.

It appears contradictory that with an increase in age there is a shift in emphasis from visual to concrete representation, from the category of imagery to object. The extensive use of crafts which is required in the upper elementary schools is seldom matched by the separate space required for art development and expression. Tempera and clay may be used in the regular classroom in the primary grades; the craft projects of the upper elementary grades require space for preservation as well as production. All too frequently, the needed art facilities, critical for the upper elementary student, are not available.

Productions in Art

The preceding list of materials suggests certain content and technique. Tempera is used to paint with, not to make a construction, whereas the construction of a mobile may involve the use of tempera for embellishment. The artistic abilities of children are frequently underestimated. Because they are left to their own devices and not taught, it is useful to suggest certain types of content and techniques which appear to be suitable at various grade levels. Again, it should be forcefully emphasized that children's ability in art is not fixed by any grade level. In the selection of the same subject and the same media, however, differences in ability, according to maturity and learning, permit substantial variations in end result.[12]

Grade 1. The principal activities will include painting with tempera, drawing with crayon, modeling, constructing, and collage work. Substantial differences in product, however, are obtained by the application of crayon on colored rather than white construction paper. Although not generally recommended for this level, the crayon-watercolor resist on white drawing paper provides an exciting alternative to typical first grade work, and has the advantage of imparting a sense of control over media. The painting of murals on roll paper as class projects provide for collective participation. Collage work largely involves cutting and pasting, but may also involve found articles. Cardboard mobiles may also be constructed. Clay modeling of various subjects is useful for individual projects.

Grade 2. Printmaking is added to the content areas, using potato or other vegetable prints. The object is to create overall designs. Crayon technique is expanded with the introduction of the multi-crayon engraving on oak tag. Crayon is a more versatile medium for the primary grades than usually credited, but it requires the specific teaching of new techniques. The child will not discover them without assistance. In addition to the use of tempera on oak tag, bogus, or manila paper, tempera painting on colored construction paper or Multex is added.

Grade 3. In the area of drawing and painting, use of the felt nib marker and pencil are added to the technique. Modeling with clay is enlarged to include making ceramic pots by slab and coil methods. Stuffed mobiles may be constructed, and a variety of abstract stabiles created. Collage work may become more sophisticated with the forming of colored tissue shapes on white drawing paper. Application of tempera

---

12. This section follows the sequence suggested by Wachowiak and Ramsay, *Emphasis: Art,* pp. 41-50.

and India ink batik to printmaking on colored construction paper adds to the repertory of skills and the development of overall design.

Grade 4. The content and media of the primary years are continued. Charcoal stick and ink are added to the repertory, and a new drawing content is introduced—drawing the figure from memory and posed models. Modeling adds clay reliefs and clay jewelry, fired and glazed. Construction, formerly dominated by paper, adds wire and paris craft. The printmaking repertory expands with the addition of the plaster relief, cardboard, and linoleum prints.

Two new content areas are also introduced. One is carved sculpture. A recommended material for this initial effort is plaster of paris-vermiculite block molded in milk cartons. A second new content is mixed media. This may include the use of plaster reliefs from clay negatives, or three-dimensional collages combining found and relief material.

Grade 5. Drawing and painting continues the more sophisticated development of media previously introduced. Self-portraits are added to the content repertory with the use of monoprints. In modeling, clay relief designs are incised or made with found objects. Masks are constructed of plaster of paris gauze over bowl forms, and a variety of other mosaics may be created from vinyl plastic chips mounted on plywood. In print making, the linoleum block print is introduced, as is the lighter leaf stencil. Carving is extended to plaster of paris.

Grade 6. More formal attention is given to outdoor sketches, figure drawing from posed models, and figure compositions. Additional drawing tools are the Conté crayon, Sketcho, Craypas, bamboo pen, and pen and ink. The use of clay for modeling is now transformed into ceramics, and pot making by the clay or slab method emphasized. Many different objects are used for constructing, and celluloid engraving is an added technique for printmaking. Carving uses former materials, as well as such new media as driftwood, firebrick, sculpturing wax, and Featherrock. Manual dexterity and craftsmanship is emphasized in the new miscellanea of metal casting, metal enameling, etched aluminum jewelry, and repoussé reliefs in aluminum or copper.

The suggested sequencing follows a logical plan, but it is noteworthy that it makes no provision for weaving and for applications of design to fabrics, which are repeatedly emphasized in Melzi. The problem is one of time. Everything cannot be taught all children in the elementary school, and teachers will naturally encourage children in content and media in which they feel most interest and expertise. It is important, however, that the sequence of activities include a variety of experiences, so that children who are not successful in one medium of expression can have an opportunity to produce successfully in another. Some children, for example, enjoy the repetitive element in weaving, while others abhor it. The teaching of art requires sufficient experience with new media so that different levels of experience are available without forcing the child into avenues which he regards as stultifying. The fortunate plasticity in human learning, however, permits the teacher to plan new learning experiences for pupils.

Sequence in the Art Program

The previous descriptions of materials and products in the art program indicate the possibilities of providing a sequence so that while children enjoy the experience of self-expression, they do it with progressively more complex subjects and media.

Perhaps one of the greatest defects of art programs conducted by the general elementary teacher is the lack of sequence. Sometimes it is hard, even in an intermediate class, to distinguish material and purpose from that of the lower grades. This may be avoided even in schools without art teachers, if there is an art syllabus which sets forth the general scheme of work by grade level, content, and media, with suggested time allocations.

Wachowiak and Ramsay[13] suggest not only media and content by grade level, but types of subject matter which experience has indicated suitable for young children. A review of the preceding section will show, however, that about half the time of the elementary art program is devoted to drawing and painting. Melzi[14] offers a suggested schema for primary and intermediate grades on the basis of experience with twelve different media by quarters. Such schema may be consulted for suggested ideas. However, there is individuality in teacher interest and ability and it is preferable that the individual teacher plan specifically within a general framework. This planning not only applies to the media, but the subject matter of projected experiences. Only in this way can the development of awareness (see "Motivation for Self-Expression") lead logically to the final art production.

In planning art experiences, it is important that sufficient time be allowed for an activity. If four hours a week are devoted to art, it is preferable to have two 2-hour periods, rather than an hour period daily. This permits more time for the child to become completely involved in the activity and renew the feeling of identity which is severed when production is interrupted. It also allows time needed to give encouragement and stimulation to children who often become easily frustrated at their inability to project an idea into a form immediately. Patience, persistence, and perseverance are desirable by-products of art in the classroom.

Evaluating the Art Program

The problem of evaluation in the art program is complicated because of the emphasis on the one hand of the child's own subjective expression and the desire to encourage him to higher standards of excellence. The latter phrase inevitably suggests that there are norms in art outside of the child which a teacher uses to stimulate additional performance. Evaluation is an essential part of teaching, for if the teacher is to suggest he must also criticize, even if the criticism is always covert and suggestion is in the form of encouragement to do better. There is no set pattern for evaluation, and there are subjective differences in the art evaluator. It is nevertheless possible for the teacher to establish specific performance objectives, and make these objectives known to the class. This helps the teacher as well as the pupils clarify the expected product. A clear conception of what is expected also helps the teacher plan the entire art program (see "Sequence"). Based on the careful prescription of desired outcomes, a teacher can plan for more comprehensive evaluation. This requires a much more specific statement of art behaviors than is found in the typical art education book.

13. Wachowiak and Ramsay, *Emphasis: Art*.
14. Melzi, *Art in Primary School*.

Some general "Check Points" for evaluating art growth are listed by Linderman and Herberholz.[15] It is the authors' point of view as expressed in this chapter, however, that the teacher should plan the experiences of the children to bring about the desired learning. Evaluation then becomes an aid to teaching and to art motivation, and is thus not merely a description of art expression by maturational level.

Pedagogy of Art

The teaching of art, like other subjects in the elementary school, today suffers from a non-teaching approach. Teachers no longer teach—they guide children, they help children to discover, they establish experiences for children. Overwhelmed by the admonitions that teaching stifles creativity, the art teacher frequently becomes merely a passive custodian of the art period or the multi-purpose art room, handing out materials and keeping order. The result is that all too often most children reach a developmental plateau. When given the opportunity, they escape from the dilemma of their self-demanding performance expectancies and lack of skill by rejecting "that kindergarten stuff." And even when the art teacher teaches explicitly, he often does so with an apologetic countenance.

The point of view expressed here is that the teaching of art, like the transmittal of other areas of competency, is facilitated by direct teaching.[16] Although art may be an intensely personal form of self-expression, as with poetry or music, the development of art takes place within the context of a particular culture. Over the centuries, a culture develops an approach to art which is the mature expression of craft and sentiment. The art of a child is creative primarily because of its spontaneity, but the naiveté of children's art soon becomes stultifying when it does not develop in subtlety and complexity. A few rare individuals are artistically gifted, and through their heightened visual sensitivity and manual dexterity seem able to make artistic breakthroughs with little or no assistance.

But the art program in the elementary school is not merely for the artistically talented. It is designed to develop visual awareness and enhance the emotional satisfaction which comes from the achievement of an art production. An art production requires craftsmanship as well as sensitivity, and the teacher must strive to develop both.

Central to the success of a good art program is the ability of the art teacher not only to develop emotional and visual sensitivity but to encourage the student to perceive his work in ever increasing standards of performance. This does not mean that the teacher imposes adult standards or sets copy which the student dutifully repeats. But it does mean that the teacher must have some aesthetic conceptions of design and balance, texture and color, form and rhythm, pattern and harmony which reflect progressive conceptions of artistic enrichment. By encourag-

---

15. Linderman and Herberholz, *Developing Artistic and Perceptual Awareness.*

16. There is no adequate definition for what is meant by direct teaching, and the semantic problem of what is meant by stimulation and encouragement and teaching is perhaps not solvable by definition but only by observation. Thus Montgomery includes what might be regarded as many teaching suggestions under the rubrics of "Permitting, Inviting, Focusing, and Supporting." However, the tone is less teaching oriented than Wachowiak and Ramsay in *Emphasis: Art.* Chandler Montgomery, *Art for Teachers of Children: Foundations of Aesthetic Experience* (Columbus, Ohio: Charles E. Merrill Publishing Company, 1968), pp. 163-71.

ing the student to perceive these relationships with his own eyes, the teacher enables the student to grow artistically. He does not impose his standards, but he makes students more aware of the challenges and opportunities of artistic expression.

Wachowiak is one of the most vigorous exponents of the explicit teaching of art. He uses the example of four different approaches to children in the second grade drawing a live cat and kittens with crayon or chalk.[17] In one, the teacher merely suggests to students that they record their impressions after looking at the cat and kittens. The second teacher leads a motivational discussion period before drawing begins. A third adds to the former experiences discussion of design and compositional factors. A fourth teacher uses the preceding steps, but goes to the stage of more direct teaching. He moves about the classroom, asking questions of children about design and composition, and helping them evaluate their efforts as they proceed. The result is production more pleasing to the child because of the richness of design, variation in texture, variety and brilliance in use of color. These productions are not forced, but result because the child has been taught to evaluate his work more critically.

Direct teaching in the use of media is also essential.[18] This requires that the teacher have the skill to demonstrate the use of the media and supervise the trial application of new media. Art is expressed through certain materials, and techniques, and the students should have an opportunity to know what certain media can do before beginning a composition. This does not mean that the children should be discouraged from experimenting with media in different ways. But there are certain limitations inherent in the media and the techniques, mastery of which are reassuring and satisfying to the child. The production of a wax engraving or a tempera batik follows certain procedural steps. Even simple procedural steps should not be taken for granted. The limited amount of time available for art requires that the time be used for artistic self-expression through a product. Engaging in a process which leads to failure because of rudimentary skills not having been transmitted is a waste of children's time in the name of creativity. It also establishes retroactive inhibitions to artistic execution.

Appraisal of Art Education

Art education in the United States does not have a long history. Measured by performance criteria, it is often non-existent, notwithstanding the fact that rare is the elementary school which does not have elaborate objectives in the arts, as in other areas of aesthetics. Art is supposed to be a part of the child's school experiences, and this is assumed to occur if there is an occasional scratching of crayons and daubing of paint. There is no sequential development of expression, technique, or skill because

17. Wachowiak and Ramsay, *Emphasis: Art,* pp. 19-20.

18. Steveni offers two interesting examples of structured and non-structured approaches to working with clay. Since research in the structured and non-structured approaches to teaching for creativity is still in the primitive stage, there is no objective evidence upon which to base a judgment. Since Steveni has value-defined the end of art education as divergence from established norms, the criterion measure by its very nature precludes more traditional approaches—Steveni, *Art & Education,* pp. 207-10. The lack of longitudinal studies in child creativity and adult creativity factually preclude any conclusions about the relative contributions of unstructured and structured approaches in art education to long term creativity.

there is no planned curriculum. There will be no improvement in the teaching of art as long as teachers, principals, and administrators claim that art is a regular part of the curriculum. One can hardly expect the public to make an effort to support what is allegedly already being taught. As long as schools are dishonest about performance claims, it is not expected that much improvement can take place.

It has been suggested that the only way to have good art instruction is to have good art teachers. The frequently cited alternative, popular in the period of subject integration, was to have every elementary teacher a teacher of art. The bankruptcy of this approach was usually nonart and mere illustration of some other activity children might be engaged in. This approach was the denial of art as a form. Occasionally there was the rare teacher who had the capacity to make every activity an art experience. Parents, however, wondered what was happening to arithmetic, science, and other verbal school subjects. After Sputnik, there was an inevitable reaction to the activity approach in which art was such an important adjunct. As a result, there was a decline in an emphasis on art.

Faced with the recognition of other problems of schooling, such as reading and skills in other operations, it is difficult within schools to obtain resource allocations for art. The money wasted on teacher aides in many school settings would, however, provide the needed resources for a quality art program. It is pathetic to see teacher aides cutting out and pasting, and contrast this with what a stimulating art teacher can do with disadvantaged youngsters as he helps them find that they, too, have an imagination and something to say visually. Language used in connection with visual productions often opens up new avenues of verbal communication.

The usual solution to the problem of manpower and art education in school systems of any size is to have an art coordinator. This gives the illusion of manpower for art without substance, for there is no art manpower in the classroom to coordinate. There is, of course, the elementary teacher, who lingers in our culture as the last encyclopedist. However, the usual training of the elementary teacher in art leaves much to be desired. It is unfortunate that the many art-certificated teachers, who must work as general elementary teachers, cannot be utilized as art teachers. The existing division of labor in the elementary school in itself mitigates against a more rational use of personnel which would seem to be available by planning of principals and teachers within a school.

Take the example of a large city school system, which some years ago eliminated its itinerant art program and now has the equivalent of 2.5 coordinators of elementary art for thirty thousand pupils and some one thousand teachers. It would seem that honesty would require that the school system say: "We do not have a sequential curriculum in art." Instead, a considerable amount of energy is wasted in convincing the public that art does exist.

Perhaps one reason that art does not receive increased attention is due to the predominance of the nonteaching approach to art. In the kindergarten and first grade, parents are delighted to make approving responses to any scribbles or daubs that the child brings home. After a year or two of this, neither the child nor the parent pays much attention to these alleged works of creativity. There is rarely any variety of media and no different experimentation with technique. There is no exposure to any kind of skill acquisition.

To raise such questions about the teaching of art most frequently results in polemics rather than goal clarification. If art is merely subjective emotion, however, it is not reasonable to expect enthusiastic support for what is merely the public display of private emotion. There is nothing incompatible with self-expression and communication. Communication depends, however, upon a code. Art which communicates does so because it shares in the aesthetic code which is not merely a product of the artist but of the culture. There is thus no contradiction between encouraging children to express themselves artistically, and to teaching them procedures and techniques in which they can do this more effectively.

Art as history and appreciation is generally discouraged in the elementary art program. The very emphasis on child creativity as production mitigates against this approach because any study and reflection about art is intellectual and abstract and does not result in a tangible product. A major difficulty lies in the traditional separation of fine arts and applied arts. The training of artists and art teachers rarely includes work in architecture or landscape design, even when the two departments exist on the same campus. The Savannah Arts Council (Savannah, Georgia) in collaboration with Historic Savannah, has proposed as part of a comprehensive sequential curriculum in the arts for the elementary school the fusion of art history with a study of the urban landscape and land utilization. Since art education places such a premium on prospective thinking, urban environmental art education might present a unique challenge to functional creativity.

Let us assume that, as a general classroom teacher, you will be responsible for art education. You can nevertheless provide art experiences in your general classroom by careful planning and organization. Art under such circumstances is not just a happening, but requires you to use your management techniques to bring medium and children together in an effective working relatioinship. And there is time. Most elementary school days now run from six to seven hours. Many regular subject matter classes are overlong, and contribute to slow-motion teaching. Planning for art may force you to budget your time more carefully, and indirectly contribute to better teaching in other subjects. The art lessons may not only brighten the children's day, but your day as well.

Suppose you don't get turned on by art and the usual one semester art course in your professional preparation program leaves you even colder about art in the elementary school. Even in small schools there is some general teacher, perhaps a trained teacher in art, who would enjoy spending more time in working with children in art media. If you like math, you might arrange a division of labor—you teach math; he teaches art. Perhaps in this way you will help everybody out—yourself and your colleague as well as the children.

But there are so many varieties of art and crafts that there is no reason why you cannot find something exciting to do, and in doing it, transmit this feeling of interest to your youngsters. Ever since the cave man at Altamira and Lascau took ochre in hand to conjure up the gods, man has been intrigued with visual representation. But there are other forms of art. Working with clay can be really a fun thing, as some adults discover later in life. And the creation of a rug in a riot of color or symmetrical design is likewise rewarding.

But suppose you do not care for traditional art media. Cinema, television, advertising, and photography offer interesting subject possibilities to further study qualities of visual representation. And the simple box camera, which children can make, provides a tool for creativity which is visually intriguing. And finally, we all have eyes with which to see; we are sensate creatures. A teacher who evokes a feeling for art by word and percept may, after all, be a teacher of art.

Selected References

Art Education

Barkan, Manuel. *Through Art to Creativity.* Boston: Allyn and Bacon, Inc., 1960.

D'Amico, Victor. *Creative Teaching in Art.* Rev. ed. Scranton, Pa.: International Textbook Company, 1953.

De Francesco, Italo L. *Art Education: Its Means and Ends.* New York: Harper & Brothers, 1958.

Erdt, Margaret Hamilton. *Teaching Art in the Elementary School: Child Growth Through Art Experiences.* Rev. ed. New York: Holt, Rinehart and Winston, Inc., 1962.

Jefferson, Blanche. *Teaching Art to Children: The Values of Creative Expression.* Boston: Allyn and Bacon, Inc., 1963.

Keiler, Manfred L. *The Art in Teaching Art.* Lincoln, Neb.: University of Nebraska Press, 1961.

Linderman, Earl W., and Herberholz, Donald W. *Developing Artistic and Perceptual Awareness: Art Practice in the Elementary Classroom.* 2d ed. Dubuque, Iowa: Wm. C. Brown Company Publishers, 1969.

Lowenfeld, Viktor, and Brittain, W. Lambert. *Creative and Mental Growth.* 4th ed. New York: Macmillan Company, 1964.

Melzi, Kay. *Art in the Primary School.* Oxford: Basil Blackwell, 1967.

Montgomery, Chandler. *Art for Teachers of Children: Foundations of Aesthetic Experience.* Columbus, Ohio: Charles E. Merrill Publishing Company, 1968.

Pearson, Ralph M. *The New Art Education.* New York: Harper & Brothers, 1941.

Steveni, Michael. *Art and Education.* New York: Atherton Press, 1968.

Wachowiak, Frank, and Ramsay, Theodore. *Emphasis: Art—A Qualitative Program for the Elementary School.* Scranton, Pa.: International Textbook Company, 1965; 2d ed., 1971.

―――, and Hodge, David. *Art in Depth—A Qualitative Program for the Young Adolescent.* Scranton, Pa.: International Textbook Company, 1970.

Art Philosophy and History

Dewey, John. *Art as Experience.* New York: Minton, Balch & Company, 1934.

Malraux, Andre. *The Metamorphosis of the Gods.* Garden City, New York: Doubleday & Company, Inc., 1960.

Ocvik, Otto G. et al. *Art Fundamentals: Theory and Practice.* 2d ed. Dubuque, Iowa: Wm. C. Brown Company Publishers, 1968.

Art Techniques

Each media has specialized works describing in detail the appropriate sequence of technical procedures. The interested reader may consult classified lists in Linderman and Herberholz, sup., pp. 112-15 and in Wachowiak and Ramsay, sup., pp. 158-59.

physical development through movement and exercise

18

Man is an animal, a creature of bone, sinew, and muscle built for action. His vertical posture, two legs, and two arms with hands, equip him for a great variety of motion. He can walk, run, kick, hop, skip, and jump. He can dodge, pivot, twist, turn, and bend. He can shove, push, pull, and lift. He can grasp, strike, catch, and throw.

By the coordination of legs, torso, and arms with sight, the basic motions can be combined into an infinite variety of utilitarian, athletic, and art movements. He can push a lawn mower, pack a hundred pounds, scale a wall, bat a ball, throw a lateral pass, thread a needle, or execute a *grand jeté*.

The remains of early man are often found with the weapons and bones of the chase. It is therefore somewhat common to read that man's evolutionary nature suits him best for the life of a hunter. But man never accepted such a limitation where he could develop or borrow the skills to live otherwise. He has always sought to surround himself with the comforts of culture. Man is both a physical and a cultured animal, and from this dual nature arises both his longevity and his disinclination to move except for pleasure.

For millennia, the occupations of man forced him to exercise. Great bursts of energy and speed were required in the hunt; miles and miles were walked after the plough; long hours were spent in the saddle; and washing clothes and cooking were endless tasks of hard work. Today man's occupations tend to be more sedentary; the chores of housekeeping have been automated. Even the sustained need for walking has been largely eliminated. In a technological society, why include physical education in the school curriculum?

The Values of Physical Education

One of the most obvious and common emphases is that man's physical nature requires him to exercise for optimum health. But health is a relative concept, and if longevity is a measure of health, a comparison of longevity will indicate a superiority in countries with sedentary occupations—they have more productive economies which provide better medical services, housing, and diet.

Another emphasis is that men need to be physically fit. According to this point of view, children have gone soft and they need to be toughened up. The physical fitness emphasis led to the establishment by President Eisenhower of the President's Council on Youth Fitness, received added stimulation from President Kennedy's dedication to a vigorous life, and is now institutionalized with an agency in the Department of Health, Education, and Welfare. There is serious question, even among physical educators, as to the relevance of the physical fitness tests.[1]

The most popular point of view, however, is that of child development. The child is perceived as an organism needing certain kinds of activities, which physical education provides. An analysis of this approach, however, indicates the confusion of cultural perceptions with "needs." For example, a second and third grade child "Likes physical contact and belligerent games" and hence needs "Dodgeball games and other active games."[2] A more accurate explanation would be that in our culture we have taught second and third graders dodgeball and similar active games, and therefore we perceive children of that age as having a certain physical need characteristic.

The needs of children do not lie in the organism nearly as much as they do in the culture, and children grow into men. And the pretentious claims that physical education develop morals, leadership, and democratic living[3] are frequently belied by the corruption of organized sports.[4] The major values of physical education in the school are educational and social, and should be approached in that manner.

Educational Values in Physical Education. The foundation of intelligent behavior is the neurological structure of the body, which develops through the stimulation received by the senses. Motor stimulation is inevitably associated with verbal cuing, and contributes to the development of symbolic-perceptual systems which facilitate school achievement (see chapter 10). Studies of deprivation suggest that more careful attention needs to be given to physical stimulation, especially in the early years, a point of view consistent with the Piagetian conceptualization of the sensorimotor stage and Hebb's emphasis on neurological development (see chapter 2). From this point of view, there has been too little emphasis on physical education. These aspects are of utmost interest to the general classroom teacher, but are largely neglected by physical educators.

It should always be remembered that the motor learning process is, in part, cognitive, and constitutes what the psychologists refer to as psychomotor learning. The Guilford schema, showing the interrelationship of certain abilities to body parts,[5] has been little used in comparison with the physical educator's conceptualization of basic movements. This conceptualization of psychomotor abilities is important to the school curriculum, emphasizing, as it does, that motor skill development is related to both the opportunity to learn and the satisfaction derived from successful previous learning.

1. John E. Nixon and Ann E. Jewett, *An Introduction to Physical Education,* 7th ed. (W. B. Saunders Company, 1969), pp. 196-215.
2. Victor P. Dauer, *Dynamic Physical Education for Elementary School Children,* 3d ed. (Minneapolis: Burgess Publishing Company, 1968), p. 27. For more extensive treatments of this need analysis, see Leonard A. Larson and Lucille F. Hill, *Physical Education in the Elementary School* (New York: Henry Holt and Company, 1957), pp. 31-47.
3. Larson and Hill, *Physical Education,* pp. 5-9.
4. Martin M. Mackenzie, *Toward a New Curriculum in Physical Education* (New York: McGraw-Hill Book Company, 1969), pp. 110-11.
5. J. P. Guilford, "A System of the Psychomotor Abilities," *American Journal of Psychology* 71 (March 1958): 165-74.

While there are many studies which indicate the inefficiency of early training because of inadequate maturation, there are other studies which indicate the tremendous significance of instruction and practice in improving performance.[6] Many children are inept and awkward in physical movement, even when not handicapped by an overly skinny or fat build (see chapter 2), because they were never taught, and hence never learned, the appropriate movement sequences. Perceptual motor skill deficiencies appear to be related to symbolic-perceptual deficiencies,[7] indicating the desirability of more careful attention to perceptual motor development in relation to such abilities as balance, manual dexterity, finger dexterity, and aiming.[8] The slow learner, in particular, appears to profit from participation in psychomotor skills,[9] probably because it provides additional opportunities for success in school.

Social and Emotional Aspects of Physical Education. Whether a teacher cares a whit about the physical aspects of movement, he cannot be oblivious to the social and emotional aspects without endangering his success as a teacher. This derives from the fact that most movement and play situations within the elementary school are social situations—they involve a group. The first act of a child as a socialized being is often the occasion when he ceases individual play and joins a group of children. Cross-cultural studies of the participation of children in games and play indicate the importance of these psychomotor activities in enculturation.

Games, play, sports, and other outlets for movement become a part of the culture, and success in these activities contributes to social acceptance and the development of a favorable self-concept. Athleticism is not restricted in school to adolescents.[10] Because excellence in sports is a highly desired behavior, social acceptance and peer status in the elementary grades are highly related to psychomotor success and ability.[11] When children enter school, there is already a great variation in psychomotor performance. In part, this relates to more favorable body build (see chapter 2) as well as opportunity to learn. Because of class retention and differences in physiological development, there may be as many as five different age levels within a given class. Children who are initially successful in school games and play tend to dominate playground activities, so that the motor skill setting based on class grade may become an extremely frustrating one for many students. If the school does

6. A. Carpenters, "Tests of Motor Educability for the First Three Grades," *Child Development* 11, no. 4 (December 1940): 293-99; Lois Dusenberry, "A Study of the Effects of Training in Ball Throwing by Children Ages Three to Seven," *Research Quarterly* 23, no. 1 (March 1952): 8-14; Dorothy R. Davies, "The Effect of Tuition upon the Process of Learning a Complex Motor Skill," *Journal of Educational Psychology* 36 (1945): 352-65.

7. Barbara S. Godfrey, "Motor Therapy and School Achievement," *Journal of Health, Physical Education and Recreation* 35 (May 1964): 64-65, D. H. Radler with Newell C. Kephart, *Success through Play* (New York: Harper & Row, Publishers, 1960), p. 29.

8. These are some of the categories used in E. A. Fleishman, *The Structure and Measurement of Physical Fitness* (Englewood Cliffs, N.J.: Prentice-Hall, 1964).

9. Newell C. Kephart, *The Slow Learner in the Classroom* (Columbus, Ohio: Charles E. Merrill Publishing Company, 1960).

10. James S. Coleman, *The Adolescent Society* (New York: Free Press of Glencoe, 1961).

11. Martha Hardy, "Social Recognition at the Elementary School Age," *Journal of School Psychology* 8 (May 1937): 365; Lawrence Rarick and Robert McKee, "A Study of Twenty Third Grade Children Exhibiting Extreme Levels of Achievement on Tests of Motor Proficiency," *Research Quarterly* 20 (May 1949): 143.

not teach motor development, the free game and play activities frequently institutionalize differences in psychomotor abilities. The school provides little opportunity to learn. As a result, the school contributes to negative attitudes and negative image building, especially among boys.

The failure to develop socially desired movement skills in childhood, however, is not limited in impact to the elementary years. After all, the years of the child are few compared to the long years of the adult. Since the demands of the occupational culture make fewer demands for movement and exercise, these tend to occur more frequently in the context of formal recreational situations rather than work. Sports already are a part of the social life of many people, and increasing attention is given to the importance of sport socialization in childhood. This includes an introduction to a variety of sports and development of skill and competence in some sport on the basis of interest and satisfaction. This implies that much more attention needs to be given to the types of sports suitable to adults—tennis, golf, swimming, skating, hiking, biking—and less emphasis on high energy group sports—basketball, football, baseball.[12] The development of psychomotor abilities requires early learning. If the skills for recreational performance are not acquired in childhood, there is less chance of their later acquisition. Since sports and recreational activity are a part of the culture, the socialization of movement in early childhood may be appropriately regarded as a part of liberal education.

One of the great values in movement training is the socialization of utilitarian movement. Much gang work in field and forest was once done in the United States to the sound of song and in rhythmic sequence, much as age-sets in Africa today work together.[13] Such occasions are not merely productive of useful work—they are also social occasions, in which the common participation of the group serves a social purpose. Because such occasions are task-oriented rather than competition-oriented, cooperative work groups often provide excellent opportunities for group integration as well as opportunities for exercise. Such groups have been utilized among children and youth more effectively in Europe than in the United States. However, even the newer emphasis on kinesiology overlooks both the group work and the exercise opportunities which could be developed through group work approached from the standpoint of kinesics.[14]

In the next section physical education teaching sequences will be discussed. The first will describe the traditional elementary curriculum; the second, the emerging curriculum in kinesiology.

Traditional Elementary Physical Education Curriculum

The prevailing physical education curriculum attempts to adjust instructional activities to physiological development of the child, taking into consideration related characteristics of emotional, mental, and social growth. Sequential statements of this rationale are

---

12. MacKenzie, *Toward a New Curriculum,* pp. 52-56.

13. Paul Bohannan, *Africa and Africans* (Garden City, New York: Natural History Press, 1964), pp. 182-84.

14. MacKenzie, *Toward a New Curriculum.* A more descriptive title of his work would be *Kinesiology: An Alternate Curriculum for Physical Education,* in lieu of the actual title, *Toward a New Curriculum in Physical Education.*

found in most physical education textbooks. Figure 18.1 gives characteristics and program implications for primary children, and should be studied carefully, for it shows how the recommended activities by grade level are derived.

In the primary grades, there is very little differentiation in activity based on sex. This is also a period in which there is a continuing emphasis on individual and repetitive activities in which all children can experience success.

Characteristics	Implications to Physical Education Program

PHYSICAL AND MOTOR CHARACTERISTICS

1. Height and weight gains moderate and steady.

	Height	Weight
Boys 5 years	41.9-45.9"	37.7-48.7 lbs.
Girls 5 years	41.6-45.6"	36.1-47.9 lbs.
Boys 6 years	44 -48.2"	41.3-53.9 lbs.
Girls 6 years	43.7-47.9"	39.6-53.2 lbs.
Boys 7 years	46 -50.4"	45.4-59.6 lbs.
Girls 7 years	45.7-50.1"	43.7-58.7 lbs.
Boys 8 years	48.1-52.7"	49.5-66.9 lbs.
Girls 8 years	47.7-52.3"	47.5-66.3 lbs.

Average gain in height = 2"
Average gain in weight = 6 lbs.

1. Continuous provision for gross motor activities such as running, jumping, and climbing, same type of activities for boys and girls. General concern for postural development, need for early detection of structural anomalies. Children of this age have relatively small bodies, hence consideration should be given in relative size of supplies and equipment.

2. Proportional gains in weight are primarily attributable to growth in bone and muscular tissue and a reduced rate of increase in fatty tissue.

2. Continuous vigorous exercise throughout age range with special attention to developing strength and endurance.

3. Heart and lungs are not fully developed. Pulse and breathing rates show a gradual decline. By age 9, pulse rate is rarely above 90 beats per minute. Respiration rate is approximately 20. Easily fatigued and rapid recovery is a particular characteristic of this age range.

3. Vigorous activity, particularly running, climbing, and swimming, with provision for frequent rest intervals. Long periods of inactivity should be discouraged. Recess and periodic breaks throughout the school day should be encouraged and be characterized by vigorous and total body movement.

4. Eye-hand coordination not fully developed. Lack precise focus (tendency to farsightedness) and spatial judgment.

4. Provision for manipulation (catching, throwing, kicking, etc.) of various size balls. Initial instruction should include relatively slow speeds of throwing, etc., with short distances. Gradually increase speed, use of small objects, and increase distance as skill develops.

5. Reaction time slow but shows a persistent increase throughout this age range.

5. Participation in numerous activities involving a quick change of speed and direction. Games and stunts involving speed, dodging, and changing direction should be provided for all children throughout this age range.

Fig. 18.1. Characteristics and Implications to Program Development of Primary School Children (5-8 years). From Glenn Kirchner, **Physical Education for Elementary School Children**, 2d ed. (Dubuque, Iowa: Wm. C. Brown Company Publishers, 1970), pp. 19-22.

MENTAL AND EMOTIONAL CHARACTERISTICS

1. Gradual and sustained increase in attention span. Periods of restlessness in early grades and present throughout age range.

1. Provide large variety of activities within any instructional period. Games should be simple in purpose, rules, and directions.

2. Extremely creative.

2. Provide method and content that fosters creative interests and movements (creative dance and educational gymnastics).

3. Enjoys rhythm and music.

3. Provide various forms of dance experiences, including singing games, folk and creative dance. Musical accompaniment to self-testing activities is also strongly suggested (e.g., with rope skipping and other types of activities).

4. Keen desire to repeat activities they know and perform quite well.

4. Allow children to choose activities, such as playing one game "over-and-over" each recess period. In dance and self-testing activities, chronic interest in one activity is a characteristic. With patience, children will soon "run the course" and move on to other challenges. The challenge to teachers is to provide activities which are more interesting and more challenging.

5. Individualistic as well as showing a need for peer and adult approval.

5. In one respect, children are basically individualistic. Hence, provision should be made for numerous individual activities in which immediate success is possible for all children regardless of ability. Children of this age level are also in need of peer acceptance as well as adult approval. There should be planned experience which involves sharing, team play, and group cooperation.

6. General lack of fear and an extremely high spirit of adventure.

6. The spirit of adventure (climbing, testing one's own ability with other children), should obviously be encouraged. At the same time teachers must develop within each child the concern for personal safety as well as the general awareness and concern for the safety of others. Extensive use of Educational Gymnastic approach with self-testing activities.

SOCIAL CHARACTERISTICS

1. Little concern for opposite sex during early grades with gradual trend toward "mutual" antagonism.

1. Throughout the primary grades both sexes have no difficulty in playing together. In the third grade some provision should be made to allow boys and girls to choose their own games. Boys will normally show a higher skill level in team games and a keener interest in "team spirit" and competition. Some provision should therefore be made for this difference in the sexes.

Fig. 18.1. (Cont'd)

2. Indifferent to discrimination whether on the basis of race, or color, or religion.	2. Although teachers show no preference with respect to these factors, care should be taken in the methods and techniques used to choose teams, leaders, and various social groupings. The essential teaching characteristic should be fairness to all children.
3. Will accept just punishment for self and total group.	3. With respect to administering punishment, a whole group should not be punished for the "wrong doings" of one child. Children recognize inconsistencies in "degrees" of punishment; hence, teachers should be consistent and fair with the type and amount of discipline and punishment. Because of the "social awareness" and inherent fairness of children, stress should be on group control through self-discipline.

Fig. 18.1. (Cont'd)

The intermediate school years are the preadolescent years, and there is a tremendous range in physiological development. As a result, girls become more concerned with activities which emphasize femininity, while boys become more interested in vigorous competitive sports. Because of variations in growth patterns, more attention needs to be given to suitable program adaptations.

In planning the curriculum, consideration should be given to the five major activities, which include basic movement skills (sometimes classified with gymnastics), gymnastics, low organization games, team games, sports, and aquatics. Few elementary schools, however, are equipped to provide aquatics training. An examination of figure 18.2 indicates that the major difference in the content, not the skill level, between primary and intermediate grades is the introduction of team sports in the intermediate grades. While touch football is included, regular tackle football is not recommended as part of the elementary program. As a result of the intermediate emphasis on team sports, the proportion of time devoted to basic movement and gymnastics, which dominate in the primary years, are reduced to less than one-third of the program by the time children reach the eighth grade.[15]

15. Evelyn L. Schurr, *Movement Experiences for Children* (New York: Appleton-Century-Crofts, 1967), pp. 53-54.

Activity	Chapter	Page	K	1	2	3	4	5	6
GAME ACTIVITIES									
Games of Low Organization	8	117							
Simple Team Games	8	118	x	x	x	x	x	x	x
Relays	8	142	x	x	x	x	x	x	x
Tag Games	8/9	153	x	x	x	x	x	x	x
Active and Quiet Classroom Games	8	164	x	x	x	x	x	x	x
Individual and Dual Activities	8/9	178	x	x	x	x	x	x	x
Individual and Team Games	9	189							
Basketball	9	190					x	x	x
Soccer	9	215					x	x	x
Softball	9	238					x	x	x
Volleyball	9	256					x	x	x
Touch Football	9	273						x	x	x
Track and Field	9	288						x	x	x
Rounders	10	317					x	x	x	x
Goodminton	10	326							x	x
SELF-TESTING ACTIVITIES									
General Information	11	336	x	x	x	x	x	x	x
Introductory Activities	12	351	x	x	x	x	x	x	x
General Warm-up Activities	12	357	x	x	x	x	x	x	x
Rubber-band Activities	12	359	x	x	x	x	x	x	x
Mimetics	12	358	x	x	x	x	x	x	x
"Who can" . . .	12	358	x	x	x	x	x		
Circuit Training	12	363						x	x
Rope Skipping	12	366	x	x	x	x	x	x	x
Tag Games	12	367	x	x	x	x	x	x	x
Floor and Small Apparatus Activities									
Stunts and Tumbling	13	371	x	x	x	x	x	x	x
Partner Activities	13	380	x	x	x	x	x	x	x
Hoops	13	384	x	x	x	x	x	x	x
Beanbags, Braids and Indian Clubs	13	387	x	x	x	x	x	x	x
Blocks, Chairs, and Wands	13	389	x	x	x	x	x	x	x
Rope Activities	13	394	x	x	x	x	x	x	x
Large Apparatus Activities	14	415	x	x	x	x	x	x	x
Balance Beam and Benches	14	416	x	x	x	x	x	x	x
Springboards, Mini-tramp, Vaulting Box	14	423	x	x	x	x	x	x	x
Horizontal Bar, Ladder and Stall Bars	14	428	x	x	x	x	x	x	x
Climbing Ropes	14	436	x	x	x	x	x	x	x
Boxes, Sawhorse, Planks	14	438	x	x	x	x	x	x	x
Agility Apparatus	14	439	x	x	x	x	x	x	x
DANCE ACTIVITIES									
Fundamental Rhythm Skills	16	525	x	x	x	x			
Traditional and Contemporary Dances	17	549							
Singing Games	17	550	x	x	x				
Folk Dances	17	562		x	x	x	x	x	x
Square Dances	17	572				x	x	x	x
Creative Rhythms	18	581	x	x	x	x	x	x	x

Fig. 18.2. Suggested Activities by Grade Level. From Glenn Kirchner, **Physical Education for Elementary School Children** 2d ed. (Dubuque, Iowa: Wm. C. Brown Company Publishers, 1970), pp. 56-57.

One of the best ways to provide for experiences in the four major activity areas during the year is to provide for seasonal activity units. This permits children to engage in a variety of activities and, in the seventh and eighth grades, to concentrate in areas in which they have an interest and aptitude. Figure 18.3 indicates a possible way of organizing seasonal activity units.

FALL

Grade 3
Basic Movement Skills
Low Organized Games
Soccer Skills and Lead-Up Games

Grade 4
Basic Movement Skills
Low Organized Games
Soccer Skills and Lead-Up Games
Developmental Exercises

WINTER

Grade 3
Large Apparatus
Ball Skills and Games
Low Organized Games
Net Games
Dance
    Creative
    Folk
Stunts and Tumbling
Small Equipment

Grade 4
Apparatus
Basketball Skills and Lead-Up Games
Low Organized Games
Dance
    Creative
    Folk
Stunts and Tumbling
Volleyball Skills and Lead-Up Games

SPRING

Grade 3
Basic Skills of Track and Field
Ball Skills and Games
Low Organized Games

Grade 4
Low Organized Games
Softball Skills and Lead-Up Games
Track and Field

FALL

Grade 5
Soccer Skills Lead-Up Games
Developmental Skills
Individual and Dual Games

Grade 6
Soccer Skills and Lead-Up Games
Individual and Dual Games
Developmental Exercises

WINTER

Grade 5
Apparatus
    Parallel Bars, Horizontal Bar, Climbing Ropes, Balance Beam (36 in.), Vaulting Box
Basketball Skills and Lead-Up Games
Low Organized Games
    Co-recreational Games
Dance
    Creative
    Folk
Stunts and Tumbling
Volleyball Lead-Up Games

Grade 6
Apparatus
    Parallel Bars, Horizontal Bar, Climbing Ropes, Balance Beam (36 in.), Vaulting Box
Basketball Skills and Lead-Up Games
Dance
    Creative
    Folk
    Recreational
Modified Volleyball (6 ft. 6 in. net)
Stunts and Tumbling

Fig. 18.3. Seasonal Activity Units, Grades 3-8. From Evelyn L. Schurr, **Movement Experiences for Children** (New York: Appleton-Century-Crofts, © 1967), pp. 55-57. Reprinted by permission of Appleton-Century-Crofts, Educational Division, Meredith Corporation.

SPRING

Grade 5
Softball Skills and Lead-Up Games
Track and Field
Developmental Exercises

Grade 6
Softball
Track and Field
Wall Paddle Tennis

FALL

Grade 7
Modified Soccer
Track and Field
Individual and Dual Games
Flag Football (Boys)

Grade 8
Flag Football (Boys)
Regulation Soccer
Individual and Dual Games
Developmental Exercises

WINTER

Grade 7
Apparatus
  Parallel Bars, Balance Beam (40 in.),
  Horizontal Bars, Vaulting Box
Dance
  Creative
  Folk
  Round, Square, Social
Regulation Basketball
Regulation Volleyball
Tumbling
Paddle Badminton

Grade 8
Apparatus
  Climbing Ropes, Vaulting, Parallel Bars,
  Horizontal Bar, Balance Beam (48 in.)
Dance
  Folk
  Round, Square, Social
Regulation Basketball
Stunts
Paddle Badminton

SPRING

Grade 7
Modified Softball
Track, Field
Paddle Tennis

Grade 8
Paddle Tennis
Softball
Track, Field

Fig. 18.3. (Cont'd)

The dominant characteristic of the traditional elementary physical education program is the emphasis on the organized activity, whether it is a game, dance, or basic rhythm.[16] While the term "movement" has been popular for a number of years, in the traditional program it is identified almost exclusively with the primary rhythms. Even where basic movements are identified as part of more complex activities, e.g., bend, swing, strike, and turn in batting, there is little attention given to development of the basic skills, but the attention is focused on the game in which used.[17]

More recent traditional programs, however, attempt to incorporate the new emphasis on movement education. Schurr gives an analysis of the fundamental body actions which should be developed in the first three grades.[18] And Kirchner has attempted to assimilate the fundamentals of movement education to the traditional program under the concept of educational gymnastics.[19] How does movement education differ from traditional physical education?

16. Victor P. Dauer, *Fitness for Elementary School Children Through Physical Education* (Minneapolis: Burgess Publishing Company, 1962).
17. Gladys Andrews, Jeannette Saurborn, and Elsa Schneider, *Physical Education for Today's Boys and Girls* (Boston: Allyn and Bacon, Inc., 1960), pp. 5-11.
18. Schurr, *Movement Experiences*, chap. 9.
19. Kirchner, *Physical Education*, chap. 15.

The New Emphasis on Movement Education

Movement education takes its theoretical rationale and organization from the movement analysis of Rudolph Laban of England. His *Modern Educational Dance*[20] made a profound impact on physical education in England, and has subsequently spread to the continent and the United States. Since the exercises in movement education cannot be understood independent of the theory, it is important to discuss somewhat briefly his four-factor movement analysis, presented schematically in figure 18.4.

20. Rudolf Laban, *Modern Educational Dance* (London: Macdonald & Evans, 1948).

How the Body Moves	Time	Quick / Slow	
	Force	Strong / Light	
	Space	Direct / Flexible	
	Flow	Bound / Free	
What the Body Does	Body Awareness	Parts of the body	Body supports / Body leads
		Whole body	Curl-stretch / Twist-turn
	Skills	Locomotor	Walk, run, leap, jump / hop, skip, slide / gallop, run
		Non-locomotor	Stretch-curl / Push-pull / Swing-sway / Twist-turn
		Manipulative	Throw / Catch / Strike: kick, punch, bat
Where the Body Moves	Space	General / Personal	
	Direction	Forward-backward / Upward-downward / Sideward	
	Level	High / Medium / Low	
	Pathway	Straight / Curved	
With What Relationships	Parts of the body to each other	Near-far / Meeting-parting- surrounding	
	Individuals and groups to each other	Above-beneath alongside, in front- behind	
	Individuals and groups to objects	Leading-following / Unison-contrast	

Fig. 18.4. Movement Analysis. From Bette J. Logsdon and Kate R. Barrett, *Teacher's Manual for Ready? Set . . . Go!* **Level One** (Bloomington, Ind.: National Instructional Television, 1969), p. 6.

What the body does refers to learning body actions, such as stationary, independent and coordinated, and locomotor. Body weight transfer and receiving the weight of other objects are among the fundamental body actions. To gain control and precision of movement it is necessary to learn what the body can do.

Where the body moves refers to the fact that all movement takes place in space. The use of space can differ by direction, level, and type of pathway. Space awareness facilitates judgment of an individual's relationship to objects and other individuals.

How the body moves refers to the quality of movement in space, and involves four aspects: time, the speed of the movement; space, the pattern of the body in space; force, the amount of strength required; and flow, the sequenced rhythm. The effective combination of these four qualities result in skilled movement.

Relationships emphasizes the interrelationship of an individual with others or objects in most game, dance, and apparatus activities.

As a result of this conceptualization, the emphasis in the primary grades is on the development of basic movement skills which are prerequisite to use in later activities.

In the traditional program, there is a conglomeration of activities which do not result in any sequential development. One suggested program for grade one is divided into three categories: singing games, e.g., *Farmer-in-the-Dell;* rhythms, e.g., *High-Stepping Horses;* and stunts and mat work, e.g., ankle hope, ankle walk, duck walk, dog walk, jack knife, and rabbit hop.[21]

In contrast, the movement education in *Ready? Set . . . Go!* for grade one is carefully sequenced in thirty lessons. This reflects the adaptation to physical education of the emphasis on objectives and sequence in the decade of curriculum reform (see chapter 3). In this television series, the lesson is telecast once a week, with the classroom teacher providing the required follow-up activities.

The mere list of lesson plans, however, does not give the flavor of one of the movement lessons, which is best understood by studying the lesson plan and seeing the televised lesson. However, a study of figure 18.5, replicating Lesson 1, indicates how the children explore with a variety of movements and how the teacher is instructed to guide the children in the activity.

21. Leonard A. Larson and Lucille F. Hill, *Physical Education in the Elementary School* (New York: Henry Holt and Company, 1957), pp. 225-36.

Major Focus

Traveling on different body parts while emphasizing the use of general space.

Lesson Objectives

The child should be able to

1. Move freely about the total space on a variety of body parts.

2. Control his movements so he can start and stop activity in response to an outside signal.

3. Demonstrate an awareness of different body parts.

4. Perceive his surroundings and constantly remain well spaced by seeking and moving into less crowded areas.

Fig. 18.5. Lesosn 1. Traveling on different body parts while emphasizing the use of general space, **Ready? Set . . . Go!** From Bette J. Logsdon and Kate R. Barrett, **Teacher's Manual for Ready? Set . . . Go!, Level One** (Bloomington, Ind.: National Instructional Television, 1969), pp. 14-15.

physical development through movement and exercise

5. Respond continuously throughout the problem. Find new solutions.
6. Listen while he moves and remain attentive to the teacher.
7. Accept responsibility for avoiding collisions.
8. Be familiar with the following movement terms and phrases: body parts, traveling using own space and traveling using all space.

Necessary Equipment
One beanbag for each child

- beanbag

Place beanbags in several places at the outer edges of the activity area.

Note
You might choose now to begin a chart of movement words—space, travel, freeze . . .

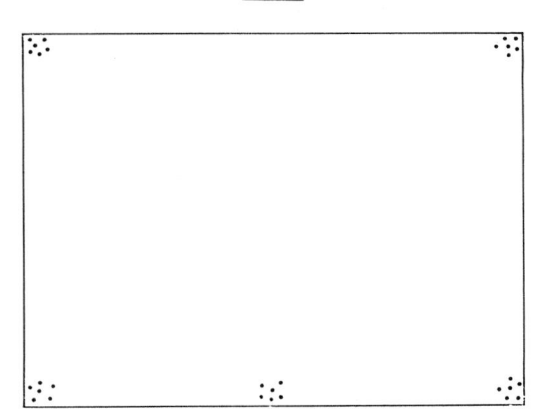

Learning Experiences	Ideas for Reinforcement	Notes
For the most part, this column presents movement problems as they are presented in the television lesson. It is not a verbatim record of the television lesson. It is the basis of the television teacher's work and consequently of your work. Sometimes problems not presented in the television lesson are included in this column because of their importance. These sections are clearly marked with an asterisk. Sometimes your children must give full attention to the television presentation. The mark + will warn you when the children are to give their attention to the television set.	This column is designed to help you assess the response of the children and prepare you for your role as a teacher of movement in the follow-up lessons. Your attention is drawn to crucial content concepts and desirable teaching emphases.	

+ Brief introduction in television lesson.

When you hear the signal, see how you can move about the space not touching anyone or anything except the floor. Listen as you move. When you hear the signal to stop, stop quickly right where you are and hold your position.	• Encourage 1. Listening while they move. 2. Moving to open spaces and away from others. 3. Continuous movement by every child. 4. Stopping quickly without falling down when they hear the signal. To develop proper response to the signal children should be stopped and started frequently. 5. Being able to return to the task quickly.	

Fig. 18.5. (Cont'd)

374 physical development through movement and exercise

Learning Experiences	Ideas for Reinforcement	Notes
Move about the space traveling on many different body parts. Try to see how many places you can go. Remember to move without touching anyone. When you hear the signal to stop, stop right where you are and hold your position: freeze. Be sure you are going everywhere in the room.	• Observe 1. How many different body parts are the children using? 2. Can they keep away from others and space themselves evenly? 3. Do they stop immediately on the signal? 4. Can they hold their stopped positions? 5. Are they working within the limitations of the problem? 6. Are they moving continuously?	
Try moving on different body parts. Use a different body part each time.	• When children stop, notice and comment on 1. Relation of the need to stop suddenly and move without touching anyone to daily life tasks. 2. How well they stopped. Did they stop quickly on the signal and were they able to hold their positions without falling? Reinforce signal to freeze if necessary. 3. How well they are spaced. Point out the space that is used well (children are less crowded) and the space that is not used well (children are too close together).	

+ Discussion of freeze in television lesson.

This time as you travel remember to watch for the empty spaces and move into them. Keep changing the body parts on which you are traveling again and again. Be careful! Do not touch anyone.	• Continue to encourage 1. Moving without touching anyone. 2. Frequent change of body parts by each child. 3. Moving into the empty spaces. • On the signal check to see if the children are holding their positions.	
Take a beanbag. Put it on a part of your body and then see how you can travel on other body parts. Be sure you are moving through all the empty spaces.	• Watch to see if they do change their modes of traveling. Encourage them to do so. • Continue to help them see the empty spaces and move into them.	

Fig. 18.5. (Cont'd)

One disadvantage of *Ready? Set . . . Go!* is the need to have a large inside play room or gymnasium to carry on the activities. This is true of any program which is conceived of with educational gymnastics as an organizing framework.[22] In attempting to adjust his work to the limitations of the normal school situation, Gober, at the University of Georgia, devised many movement exercises which can be used outside.[23]

One of the distinctive characteristics of movement education is movement exploration. Exploration in movement education is the equivalent of discovery in other subjects. Demonstration, the usual procedure in physical education, is not given in exploration. A movement situation is devised, but the child is free to explore and ascertain appropriate solutions. However, the technique is not one of laissez faire, as Lesson 1 in figure 18.5 indicates. While the teacher initially accepts any movement as appropriate, the teacher uses verbal cues and the performance of other students to guide and stimulate exploratory behavior. Thus the exploratory movement technique is not unlike the verbal cuing technique for art development (see chapter 17). The lessons of Gober are very explicit in suggesting verbal cues for teacher use. The approach can be used with the basic skills from grade to grade, with the quality and complexity of the movements increasing with practice in exploration. However, the need to make available further instructions to the regular classroom teacher has prompted the development of more carefully structured lessons, at least with respect to teacher cuing to elicit desired behaviors. The second level of *Ready? Set . . . Go!* was released for telecasting in 1970-71.

Intramurals in Elementary School

Most programs in elementary physical education provide for voluntary intramural competition. Intramurals are desirable because success in sports competition is a way of rewarding efforts to improve performance. No interschool competition on a varsity pattern is to be encouraged, and any kind of high pressure tactic—playing outside of school hours, encouragement of partisan spectators, championship leagues, grooming of selected players, long seasons—is to be avoided.[24]

Appraisal of Elementary Physical Education

Nowhere in the elementary curriculum does one find more robust rhetoric and flaccid execution than in physical education. As in much of education, guilt is multiple rather than individual, and the condition may be attributed to cultural emphases and social priorities as well as to physical educators.

The physical educators are at fault in attempting to embrace under one umbrella such diverse fields as health and safety, recreation, and physical education.[25] But physical education alone still includes such diverse forms as gymnastics, sports and

22. Kirchner, *Physical Education*.
23. Billy Gober *et al.*, *Primary School Physical Education Through Movement Exploration,* Practical Paper no. 26, Research and Development Center in Educational Stimulation (Athens, Georgia: University of Georgia, 1969). Practical Paper no. 25 by Gober *et al.*, is devoted to the pre-primary level.
24. Joint Committee. *Desirable Athletic Competition for Children* (Washington, D.C.: American Association for Health, Physical Education, and Recreation, 1952).
25. Mackenzie, *Toward a New Curriculum*, p. 7.

competitive athletics, rhythms and children's games, and dancing. The barnacle ship of physical education developed over the years as a result of certain enthusiasms, and there has been no clear subject matter identification. Considering the cultural emphasis on competitive athletics, the absence of a clear subject matter has made physical education peculiarly subject to subversion by athleticism. Athleticism may be simply defined as training to produce winners, and is the antithesis of the fundamental assumption basic to physical education—that the physical education program is designed to reach all children, not merely the athletically élite.

The cultural emphasis in American athletics is competition for winning rather than individual performance. This emphasis is so strong that even in communities where there is no school program of physical education there is the ubiquitous Little League baseball, staffed by adult enthusiasts and supported by eager parents who vicariously participate in sports through their offspring. The little league concept is being extended to other sports, such as football and basketball. Perhaps the major disadvantage in these programs is the creation of an attitude that physical education is the equivalent of competitive team sports, the very kind of activity which is least adaptable for adult living.

And finally, it must be recognized that physical education, as with art and music, is a low school priority in terms of facilities and manpower. The typical elementary school has no gymnasium or facilities for outdoor play.[26] Many an urban school yard looks more like a jail compound than a place for children, where they can move and exercise. And many a school which has ample space is sadly lacking in facilities. One or two basketball standards, a set of swings, a climbing cube, a horizontal ladder, and a rusty slide are frequently all that is found. There are no surfaced play areas, and a dust bowl takes the place of a playing turf. Supplies are also noticeably lacking. For example, how many classrooms of thirty pupils enjoy the recommended five to six soccer balls and volleyballs or the dozen softballs and softball bats?[27] The usual class is lucky to have one or two of each, thus forcing games with a low level of participation and presenting little opportunity for individuals to practice skill development.

Even more disastrous is the lack of teachers of physical education. In a 1965 survey by Caskey, 82 percent of physical education was allegedly taught by the regular classroom teacher.[28] It is common in school systems to have an elementary physical education coordinator who attempts to provide classroom teachers with a guide and to give demonstration lessons.[29] Observation indicates there is little follow-through by classroom teachers. But why should they try? They are not provided with equipment or facilities, and probably had only one general course in physical education, just enough to emphasize how little they know. Furthermore, there is a difference in role compati-

26. See Athletic Institute, *Planning Areas and Facilities for Health, Physical Education, and Recreation* (Washington, D.C.: American Association for Health, Physical Education, and Recreation, 1965); also National Council on Schoolhouse Construction, *Guide for Planning School Plants* (East Lansing, Mich.: The Council, Michigan State University, 1964).

27. Kirchner, *Physical Education,* p. 77.

28. Schurr, *Movement Experiences,* p. 18.

29. See, for example, *Curriculum Guide for Health, Physical Education, and Safety, Grades One Six* (Athens, Georgia: Clarke County Elementary Schools, 1967).

bility with the general elementary education teacher and the teaching of physical education.

The regular elementary classroom teacher is typically a woman, forty years of age, and married. She is expected to be poised and cool throughout the school day. How is she expected to be comfortable in the classroom after a hot and dusty period on the playground when there is no provision for showering and dressing? The general classroom teacher adjusts herself to unrealistic physical education expectations by being merely a reluctant playground supervisor.

Even where there are staffed physical education programs with gymnasiums, it is probable that the programs are productive of antisocial attitudes and as harmful to children as they are helpful. This is a result of the previously noted general cultural emphasis on athleticism. The awkward, handicapped, or just normal children spend most of their time waiting and watching while physical educators, turned coaches, lavish their time and efforts on the winner. But, after all, it is the competitive sports tradition which provides the recruiting ground for physical education. A physical educator never receives a "thank you" for a well-conceived and comprehensive program for all children; a winning coach basks in the adulation of patrons and players.[30]

As a counterweight to the athletic emphasis, Mackenzie[31] proposes that the allocation of resources to physical education be completely reversed. Instead of a required program in the high school and college years, he recommends an elective program whereas he would have a required foundation program in the elementary school. The learning focus in the primary stage would consist of exploration of movement concepts and fundamentals and in the intermediate stage, exploration of cultural sports and dances and their meanings. His required foundational program in kinesiology would consist of five areas: basic instruction, thirty activities; advanced instruction, two or three activities; dance or sport club participation, one season; intramural sports participation, one season; and general study of kinesics, two semesters.

It is nevertheless too early to evaluate the impact of kinesiology and movement exploration on American physical education; it is still a hope and a promise.[32] By once again making movement an aesthetic and not merely a mechanical concept, it may have the advantage of humanizing the concept of movement and giving additional outlets to expression. However, it is important to understand that the theory comes from the dance, a creative and dramatic art form which has little relationship to sports except that the body is the medium of expression. It remains to be seen whether the movement concept can successfully be translated to physical education. Thus far, it would seem that it is primarily a new vocabulary most compatible to the primary grades where there was a preexistent rhythmic emphasis. The physical education of the intermediate grades still appears to be largely a matter of games and sports.

Another aspect of movement education needs to be considered, and that is the tremendous emphasis on exploration. While

---

30. Jack Harrison Pollack, "Physical 'Education': Are Our Children Being Cheated?" *Family Health* 11, no. 9 (September 1970): 15-18.
31. Mackenzie, *Toward a New Curriculum,* chap. 4, especially pp. 76 and 84.
32. American Association for Health, Physical Education, and Recreation, *Promising Practices in Elementary School Physical Education* (Washington, D.C.: The Association, 1969), pp. 58-64.

all art forms can become inured in tradition, revolutions are not always successful because they neglect the development of the basic skills which underly the expression of art. Thus, while the ideas of Isadora Duncan influenced the dance, her approach became a cult. Diaghilev, on the other hand, with his emphasis on the mastery of form and technique, was able to apply the spirit of the art nouveau to the creation of daring new ballet styles which gave vitality to the dance.[33] It is therefore likely that in the long run some combination of traditional form training as well as movement exploration will be a happier synthesis. The present enthusiasm for movement exploration is not unlike the enthusiasm for free play which followed the gymnastic emphasis, but free play did not develop the skills which were assumed to exist "naturally" in the human organism.

Now where do these appraisals of a philosophic bent leave the regular classroom teacher with a program of physical education? In accordance with suggestions in the chapters dealing with art and music, a division of labor based on training competency should be attempted first. And these energies should appropriately be utilized in the primary grades. A second effort of the classroom teacher, it appears, should be concerned with the acquisition of better facilities. The negative attitude of the staff to physical education often precludes obtaining support from parent and civic groups who are interested in physical education. The values of psychomotor development require that the teacher give support to an effective physical education program, even if it is merely a means to obtain his own ends.

But what should the general classroom teacher do personally? Notwithstanding the fact that skill development requires supervised training, there are certain areas in which a teacher without training can be helpful to students. These primarily involve, in the absence of facilities, low organization games and creative rhythms and dancing. Excellent directions, given in many books for physical education teachers, can be applied by the general classroom teacher.

One of the most useful of the newer books is that of Kirchner, referred to many times in this chapter. In addition to the suggested activities by grade level, reproduced in figure 18.2, he provides a series of tables which outline the activities categorically by suggested grade levels, cross referenced to pages describing the activities. This permits a teacher to organize a series of units to provide for a variety of activities during the year. The many illustrations make the book particularly useful to a novice.

Another new book, which attempts to incorporate the new movement emphasis with traditional games, is the Schurr book, previously referred to. Gober has the advantage of providing lesson sequences which a teacher can follow throughout the year. This reduces the demands made on the classroom teacher for independent planning.

One of the best solutions, it would seem, would be for the regular classroom teacher to have access to the physical education sequence of National Instructional Television. Not only is the teacher provided with a sequential manual, but both the teacher and students have the opportunity to see a lesson in operation. This sets the stage for follow-up experiences by the teacher. At the present time, however, the NIT sequence is limited to grades one and two.

33. K. V. Burian, *The Story of World Ballet* (London: Allan Wingate, 1963), pp. 76-89.

If teachers find some of the newer materials more difficult to handle, it is still possible to use as a guide some of the older texts. For example, the Larson and Hill text gives suggested activities for six grade levels, divided in three categories. If a teacher does not have a music series (see chapter 16) which provides the records for rhythms, singing games, and dances, particular records are suggested with prescribed activities.

It is therefore possible for a teacher with little preparation in physical education to give some of these experiences to children.[34] The two prerequisites, as with other educational experiences, are planning and scheduling. Physical education will not happen unless there is time allotted, and the time will not be used effectively unless the teacher has a plan.

Selected References

American Association for Health, Physical Education, and Recreation. *Promising Practices in Elementary School Physical Education.* Washington, D.C.: The Association, 1969.

Andrews, Gladys; Saurborn, Jeannette; and Schneider, Elsa. *Physical Education for Today's Boys and Girls.* Boston: Allyn and Bacon, Inc., 1960.

Dauer, Victor P. *Dynamic Physical Education for Elementary School Children.* Minneapolis: Burgess Publishing Company, 1968.

———. *Fitness for Elementary School Children Through Physical Education.* Minneapolis: Burgess Publishing Company, 1962.

Gober, Billy et al. *Primary School Psysical Education Through Movement Exploration.* Practical Paper No. 26, Research and Development Center in Educational Stimulation. Athens, Ga.: University of Georgia, 1969.

Joint Committee on Athletic Competition for Children of Elementary and Junior High School Age. *Desirable Athletic Competition for Children.* Washington, D.C.: American Association for Health, Physical Education, and Recreation, 1952.

Kirchner, Glenn. *Physical Education for Elementary School Children.* 2d ed. Dubuque, Iowa: Wm. C. Brown Company Publishers, 1970.

———; Cunningham, J.; and Warrell, E. *Introduction to Movement Education.* Dubuque, Iowa: Wm. C. Brown Company Publishers, 1970.

Logsdon, Bette J., and Barrett, Kate R. *Teacher's Manual for Ready? Set . . . Go! Level One.* Bloomington, Ind.: National Instructional Television Center, 1969. This course was developed and produced in consultation with the American Association for Health, Physical Eduction, and Recreation.

Larson, Leonard A., and Hill, Lucille F. *Physical Education in the Elementary School.* New York: Henry Holt and Company, 1957.

Mackenzie, Marlin M. *Toward a New Curriculum in Physical Education.* New York: McGraw-Hill Book Company, 1969.

Nixon, John E., and Jewett, Ann E. *An Introduction to Physical Education.* 7th ed. Philadelphia: W. B. Saunders Company, 1969.

Schurr, Evelyn L. *Movement Experiences for Children: Curriculum and Methods for Elementary School Physical Education.* New York: Appleton-Century-Crofts, 1967.

---

34. Kirchner, *Physical Education,* p. 70; Schurr, *Movement Experience,* p. 18.

PART SIX

organizing for instruction

Photo: Courtesy of El Paso (Texas) Independent School District.
Photography: Seth J. Edwards, Jr.

vertical and horizontal organizational patterns

19

The vertical and horizontal organizational arrangements employed in the elementary school provide the framework in which curriculum development and teaching take place. The overall organizational framework must be congruent with the school's objectives, philosophy and curriculum if it is to be facilitating and effectual. Actually, the organizational framework serves this purpose only, i.e., it enables the school and its faculty to implement their philosophy and accomplish their objectives by providing the types of learning experiences that they deem advisable for their students. With this in mind, let us examine the elementary school organizational framework—its facets and alternatives.

Vertical Organizational Patterns

When children come to elementary school and are initially classified, i.e., assigned to a given instructional level such as grade 2, multigrade primary unit 1-3 or level 4 nongraded unit, they are then placed into a given vertical organizational pattern in which they move upward from the point of admission until they have acceptably completed the courses of learning to a point of departure and enter into another phase of schooling such as the middle school, junior high or senior high school.[1] The vertical organizational patterns into which children may be assigned for instruction include: (1) graded, (2) multigraded and (3) nongraded plans. A discussion of these plans follows.

The Graded Plan. Initially, America's first schools were ungraded. That is, they were, more often than not, rural one-teacher-per-building schools in which the teacher attended to the instructional needs of an inter-age group of children. Instruction was offered from a scanty array of textbooks in the ungraded setting of the "little red schoolhouse" by the teacher who attempted to teach each child according to the child's individual achievement level and general aptitude for learning.

In the early 1800s, however, a more manageable organizational scheme whereby instruction could be administered was man-

---

1. For a thorough discussion of the distinction between vertical and horizontal organizational patterns in the elementary school, see John I. Goodlad and Kenneth Rehage. "Unscrambling the Vocabulary of School Organization," *NEA Journal* 51, no. 8 (November 1962): 34-36.

dated largely by a rapidly increasing school-age population in conjunction with the compulsory school attendance laws of the various states and the dedication of this nation to the concept of free public education. This condition prompted Horace Mann, Henry Barnard and other educators to travel to Prussia to observe its system of graded schools. These educators were greatly impressed with the simplicity and effectiveness of the graded plan. They extolled its virtues upon their return to the states. After additional visits abroad by leading educators of the time to observe the graded school, much discussion and planning with public school people in America ensued about the feasibility of implementing the graded plan in the United States. As a result of these visits and subsequent planning sessions, the first graded elementary school in America was established in 1848 by J. D. Philbrick at Quincy Grammar School in Boston.[2] The school at Quincy was basically a prototype of the Prussian schools visited by Mann and his counterparts.

Essentially, the graded school, as first established, was a school in which students were classified according to their individual scholarly attainment as it related to a prescribed curriculum which had been arbitrarily divided into grades. Students who possessed similar degrees of educational proficiency were assigned to the same class for instruction.[3]

The graded elementary school did not appear overnight universally in the United States once it was introduced by Philbrick in 1848. There were several evolutionary steps which covered a minimum of twelve years before it was fully implemented in a majority of the nation's larger schools. These evolutionary and sequential steps included:

(1) the elementary education period divided horizontally into separate schools having two or more different grades, e.g., primary and grammer school; (2) two or more of these separate schools or broad grade units housed in one building; (3) pupils subsequently classified for one of the broad grade units and later, when gradedness became absolute, classified into single grade units; (4) building construction changed to implement the gradedness scheme.[4]

There were many advantages to commend the earliest graded elementary schools. According to Kiddle and Schem, the initial advantages of graded schools were:[5]

1. They economize the labor of instruction.
2. They reduce the cost of instruction, since a smaller number of teachers are required for effective work in a classified or graded school.
3. They make the instruction more effective, inasmuch as the teachers can more readily hear the lessons of an entire class than of the pupils separately, and thus there will be better opportunity for actual teaching, explanation, drill, etc.
4. They facilitate good government and discipline, because all the pupils are kept constantly under the direct control and instruction of the teacher, and, besides, are kept constantly busy.
5. They afford a better means of inciting pupils to industry, by promoting their

2. Ellwood P. Cubberley, *Public Education in the United States* (Boston: Houghton Mifflin Company, 1934), pp. 300-315.

3. Henry Kiddle and Alexander J. Schem, eds., "Graded Schools," *The Cyclopaedia of Education: A Dictionary of Information for the Use of Teachers, School Officers, Parents, and Others* (New York: E. Steiger, 1877), p. 375.

4. Henry J. Otto, *Elementary School Organization and Administration,* 3d ed. (New York: Appleton-Century-Crofts, Inc., 1954) pp. 11-12.

5. Kiddle and Schem, "Graded Schools," p. 376.

ambition to excel, inasmuch as there is a constant competition among the pupils of a class, which cannot exist when the pupils are instructed separately.

Early graded schools were not without their disadvantages, however. Shearer, writing in 1899, pointed out numerous disadvantages of graded schools such as: (1) they did not provide adequately for existing individual differences among pupils, (2) they kept children in intellectual lock step year after year and grade after grade thereby grinding out the individuality of each child, (3) some schools graded the work for the bright thereby requiring average and slow children to attend to learnings they were not capable of mastering while other schools graded the work for the slow and consequently failed to adequately provide for the educational needs of the average and bright pupils, (4) too many children failed to do acceptable grade level work and frequently dropped out of school.[6]

To cope with the shortcomings of the graded elementary school such as those enumerated by Shearer, educators began an attempt to modify it around the turn of the century. These earliest attempts to remedy the disadvantages of the graded school included providing:[7]

1. A shorter class interval to determine promotion or retention.
2. Abandonment of the promotion test.
3. An ungraded room in each building for those students who fell behind in their work.
4. Additional teachers and reducing the pupil teacher ratios.
5. Enrichment for brighter students.
6. Double-track course of study so that some could complete the graded program in four years while others would take six years. Children could switch from a higher to a lower track when their performance justified.
7. A return to a nongraded plan of organization.

Since 1900, many improvements have been made in the graded plan: teachers are better educated, individual differences among pupils are better provided for, higher percentages of children remain in school, more sophisticated materials and equipment are available for teaching and the like. Significantly, pupil failures have decreased. Larson found in studying the incidence of retention in Iowa's graded elementary schools, for example, that retention had decreased from 50 percent in 1900 to 10 percent in 1954.[8]

The monetary costs of retention in the graded schools of this nation are staggering. Di Pasquale has commented:[9]

> Finanical costs of grade failure can be gauged fairly accurately. From numerous studies, we can estimate that in 1963-64 at least one million children were required to repeat a grade in order to "catch up." The average cost of educating each child for the same year was $455. The failure therefore cost the nation approximately 455 million dollars, or an amount greater by 155 million dollars than the cost of operating Chicago's public schools for the same year.
>
> This sum spent on failure might have financed the following five-point program:
>
> 1. The establishment and support of 50,000 nursery school units.

6. William J. Shearer, *The Grading of Schools* 3d ed. (New York: The H. P. Smith Publishing Company, 1899), pp. 21-23.

7. Ibid., pp. 48-56.

8. Robert E. Larson, "Age-Grade Status of Iowa Elementary Schools Pupils" (doc. diss., State University of Iowa, 1955).

9. Vincent C. Di Pasquale, "Dropouts and the Graded School," *Phi Delta Kappan* 46, no. 3 (November 1964): 130.

2. The employment of 10,000 additional classroom teachers to help decrease class size.
3. The addition of 7,000 teacher aids in order to release teachers for exclusively professional services.
4. The addition of 4,000 specialists to increase medical, dental, psychological, and psychiatric services.
5. The establishment of free lunch programs for all children.

Since many of the disadvantages of the graded plan have persisted, recent experimentation with other vertical organizational alternatives has been conducted in an effort to find a more viable plan. The two plans most often experimented with include the multigraded and nongraded plans. Now let us examine them.

The Multigraded Plan. Multigrading in the elementary school is an attempt to force teachers, through the medium of the organizational pattern, to differentiate instruction among the children they teach. One of the chief complaints of the graded plan has been that teachers administer more or less uniform instruction to their charges and expect relatively uniform performance from them. Multigrading then attempts to force teachers into new patterns of behavior by widening the range of individual differences to such an extent that they can no longer give lip service to the matter of providing differentiated instruction.

Multigrading may be defined as a vertical organizational plan in which children are sectioned into classes that are comprised of pupils from two or more grade levels. The schematic representation in figure 19.1, which has been suggested by James, lucidly shows what the multigaded plan is and how it is distinguishable from the graded plan.[10]

GRADED PLAN

	Mrs. Smith	Mrs. Brown	Mrs. Jones
4th graders	30	....	....
5th graders	....	30	....
6th graders	....	....	30

MULTIGRADED PLAN

	Mrs. Smith	Mrs. Brown	Mrs. Jones
4th graders	10	10	10
5th graders	10	10	10
6th graders	10	10	10

Fig. 19.1. Placement of 90 students: 30 fourth graders, 30 fifth graders and 30 sixth graders, in a graded and multigraded plan. Adapted from: Butler James, "Multigrading in Elementary Schools," **Vertical Organizational Patterns in the Elementary School**, ed. Oscar T. Jarvis (Athens, Georgia: GDESP and College of Education, University of Georgia, 1969), p. 72.

In a multigraded classroom section which may be a grade 1-3 or grade 4-6 arrangement, for example, the child will enter the section as one of ten of the youngest children. The second year he will be in next to the oldest group of children and the third year he will be in the oldest student group. As the top third of the class moves up to a higher multigraded unit at the end of each year, a new group comes in as the youngest to replace the previous youngest promoting up.

During the three year period of time spent in a multigraded unit, the individual student can progress as rapidly as his ability will allow him under a differentiated pro-

10. Butler James, "Multigrading in Elementary Schools," in *Vertical Organizational Patterns in the Elementary School,* ed. Oscar T. Jarvis, Georgia Department of Elementary School Principals, GEA and The Bureau of Educational Studies and Field Services, (Athens, Georgia: College of Education, University of Georgia, 1969), pp. 69-79.

gram of instruction. For example, take the hypothetical mutigraded section of fourth, fifth and sixth graders shown in figure 19.2. Note Bill's placement in the various subject areas. Although he is ten years old and most likely would be placed in the fifth grade in a regular graded school, it is easy to see that Bill is grouped into an appropriate intraclass group in the various subject areas commensurate with his achievement level.

In some multigraded schools, students may stay with the same teacher in a multigraded unit for three years. This enables the teacher to know more about the needs of his children and to plan longitudinal programs for them.

Some of the reports to date indicate that multigraded pupils experienced: (1) improved academic achievement, (2) better personal and social adjustment, (3) increased social maturity and (4) evidenced better attitudes toward school than did their counterparts in the traditional single-graded classrooms.[11] The evidence comparing graded and multigraded schools is too meager to draw any widespread generalizations presently. However, many more schools appear to be experimenting with multigrading—particularly schools in the far western states.

The Nongraded Plan. As has been pointed out in a prior section of this chapter, the graded elementary school was instituted in this nation as a simple and efficient way to administer mass instruction for a burgeoning population in the United States in the mid-1850s. Since that time, there has been increasing criticism of it on the grounds that it is anachronistic in terms of what we now know about differences between children, how they learn, and how to managerially organize a school and its curriculum to insure continuous pupil progress. It is understandable then that the evolutionary process of vertical organizational patterns in the elementary school has witnessed the emergence of the nongraded plan. This plan was first devised in Western Springs, Ill. in 1934 but became widely known as a result of its being implemented in Milwaukee in 1942. According to an NEA survey report in 1965, 32 percent of the elementary schools in a national sample indicated that they either had or planned to initiate nongraded units in their schools.[12]

The nongraded plan has many advantages which helps to explain the rapidity with which it is being instituted in the nation's schools. Among its advantages are the following.[13]

11. Warren Hamilton and Walter Rehwoldt, "By Their Differences They Learn," *The National Elementary Principal,* 37, no. 2 (December 1957): 27-29.

12. *Nongraded Schools, Research Memo 1965-12* Washington, D.C.: National Education Association, Research Division (May, 1965) p. 2.

13. For a thorough discussion of nongraded advantages, see Ibid., pp. 6-7.

| | | | SUBJECTS | | |
Grade	Math	Reading	Science	English	Social Science
4		Bill			
5				Bill	
6	Bill		Bill		Bill

Fig. 19.2. Bill's achievement level and placement in various subject areas within a multigraded class. Adapted from: Butler James, "Multigrading in Elementary Schools," **Vertical Organizational Patterns in the Elementary School**, ed. Oscar T. Jarvis, (Athens, Georgia: GDESP and College of Education University of Georgia, 1969), p. 73.

It provides a viable plan whereby children:

1. Can experience continuous educational progress inasmuch as they do not repeat any work already mastered
2. Will not be stigmatized by failure since work successfully completed is not repeated
3. Will learn from appropriate materials through the medium of differentiated instruction according to their individual time requirements for mastery; hence, time varies—not quality of work
4. Are under less emotional strain since the fear of failure is removed and also because they are competing more with their own records rather than vying against their peers

Vertically, most nongraded programs are designed on a level basis. A graphic portrayal of the nongraded levels program as compared with the graded program for the primary years can be seen in figure 19.3. By studying this figure, one sees that a child can be placed rather easily at a nongraded level at the beginning of each school year at a point congruent with the work he has successfully completed.

Graded Plan	Nongraded Plan
	Level 9
	Level 8
Grade 3	Level 7
	Level 6
	Level 5
Grade 2	Level 4
	Level 3
	Level 2
Grade 1	Level 1

Fig. 19.3. Schema Comparing Graded and Nongraded Plans.

Conversely, under the graded plan, if he did not complete the work of a given grade level and was not socially promoted, he would not only repeat the grade, but also that portion of the work which he had previously mastered if the teacher failed to place him with an appropriate intraclass group.

There might be twenty-one or more levels in a nongraded program through the first six years of schools. In the first three years of the primary program, for example, some of the brighter students might complete the first nine levels in two and one-half years while others might require four years to successfully finish the work. The essential point, however, is that all children experience continuous progress and no children are retained in the nongraded program.

The subject matter for the various subject areas can be arranged to fit the various instruction levels.[14] For example, the Robert S. Gallaher School in Newark, Del., has developed its reading program into levels as follows:[15]

Level 1. Readiness
2. Preprimer
3. Primer
4. First Reader
5. Second Reader, I
6. Second Reader, II
7. Third Reader, I
8. Third Reader, II
9. Extended Reading or Enrichment

As yet, there is no conclusive proof to indicate that nongrading is superior to the

---

14. See: John L. Tewksbury, *Nongrading in the Elementary School* (Columbus, Ohio: Charles E. Merrill Books, Inc., 1967), pp. 41-52; Michael L. Hawkins, "Procedural Guide for Nongrading the Primary Schools," *Vertical Organizational Patterns in the Elementary School,* ed. Oscar T. Jarvis (Athens, Georgia: GDESP and College of Education, University of Georgia) pp. 47-68.
15. *Nongraded Schools,* p. 5.

graded plan of vertical organization although many of the reported studies are favorable.[16] Conclusive results will not be forthcoming until further experimentation is made.

Horizontal Organizational Patterns

The manner in which students and teachers are brought together in the classroom so that instruction can be administered is the horizontal organizational plan. There are therefore two aspects of horizontal organization; namely, the deployment of teachers and the deployment of children. Let us examine these two aspects or segments of horizontal organization.

Teacher Deployment. There are three primary plans whereby teachers are deployed horizontally in the elementary school. They include: (1) self-contained classroom, (2) departmentalization and (3) team teaching. A discussion of these three plans follows.

SELF-CONTAINED CLASSROOM. Beyond question, the self-contained classroom has been utilized more in America's elementary schools over the last one hundred years than has any other horizontal plan.[17] The reason for this is quite simple; the self-contained classroom plan is a flexible arrangement which will accommodate any curriculum pattern, sectioning practice, time allotment requirements, vertical organizational arrangement, and the like.

The self-contained classroom is a plan whereby twenty-five to thirty-five children are assigned to one teacher for all classwork for an academic year. The plan has many inherent strengths such as the following:[18]

1. It is possible for the teacher to acquaint himself thoroughly with the needs and interest of his charges since he works with the children for the entire day throughout the academic year.
2. It is possible for the teacher to integrate the learnings of the various subject areas in working with children since he teaches all subjects in the self-contained classroom plan.
3. The teacher and pupils can plan their own time requirements daily for the various curriculum experiences which transpire under the self-contained plan since each classroom is a relatively autonomous unit.
4. The teacher can see the progress each child is making in the various course offerings since he teaches all subjects to his charges.
5. Children can gain many valuable lessons about democracy and group participation as they work, play and study together in the self-contained classroom.

There are some weaknesses of the self-contained classroom that its critics are quick to point out. Some of its disadvantages frequently alluded to include the following:

1. Under the self-contained classroom plan, the teacher cannot be expected to be fully competent in all areas of the curriculum; hence, he tends to stress those areas in which he is best prepared to teach.
2. The child who is assigned to a poor teacher under the self-contained classroom plan must suffer the brunt of

16. Ibid., p. 6.
17. See: Stuart D. Dean, *Elementary School Administration and Organization* (Washington, D.C.: U.S. Department of Health, Education and Welfare, 1960), p. 31.
18. For a discussion of the strengths and weaknesses of the self contained classroom plan, see Oscar T. Jarvis and Haskin R. Pounds, *Organizing, Supervising and Administering the Elementary School* (West Nyack, N.Y.: Parker Publishing Company, 1969), pp. 64-65.

inferior instruction for the school year; hence, does not receive an equal educational opportunity.
3. It is possible occasionally for serious child-child or teacher-child conflicts to arise in the self-contained classroom as a result of the prolonged association which results during the school year.
4. There is little and, more often than not, no time for the teacher to have an unassigned period in which he can plan lessons, keep records, score tests and the like.
5. It is difficult for the school to obtain or evaluate its overall objectives since, in the final analysis, each classroom teacher determines what he will teach from the vast array of subject areas that are to be included in the curriculum.

Presently, it is easy to find a modified self-contained classroom plan being utilized in the nation's schools. Under the modified plan, one can find teaching specialists in such areas as music, art or physical education who may teach these specialized areas at regularly scheduled periods during the week. When this occurs, the teacher of the self-contained classroom may assist with such instruction in some schools or, as practiced in others, have an unassigned period to make and score tests, prepare lessons and the like. Presently, however, there appears to be a movement towards the deployment of teachers into arrangements in which they can provide more specialized instruction in either team teaching or departmentalized settings.

DEPARTMENTALIZATION. One may define departmentalization as a horizontal organizational pattern in which the major subject areas of the curriculum, i.e., arithmetic, science, social studies, language arts, music, art and physical education, are taught separately by teachers who specialize in a given subject area. For example, an arithmetic teacher likely would teach only arithmetic daily to approximately five sections of children or a total of about 150 pupils. Depending on the deployment of the arithmetic teacher, he might teach five sections of fifth graders or he might teach two sections of fourth, two sections of fifth and one section of sixth grade arithmetic. Such factors as school size and pupil teacher ratios would be variables which affect how the teachers are deployed in departmentalized arrangements.

There has been a rapid increase in the incidence of departmental organization in the nation's schools during the Space Age. This has been true at all levels—particularly in the intermediate grades.[19] It appears that the curriculum reform movement of the Space Age in education has witnessed a return to departmentalization where a more subject-centered orientation to curriculum development and teaching can be implemented and where the pupil is viewed more *as student,* a proposition set forth in chapter 1.

Many advantages and disadvantages are frequently mentioned in connection with departmentalized organization.[20] On the positive side of the ledger, departmentalization provides an organizational arrangement in which: (1) children can study under a subject matter specialist who "knows" (has expertise in) his speciality, (2) teacher specialists can sequentially develop the curriculum in their individual subject areas,

19. See: *The Principals Look at the Schools* (Washington, D.C.: National Education Association, 1962), pp. 13-14.
20. See: Jarvis and Pounds, *Organizing, Supervising and Administering,* pp. 66-67.

(3) educational opportunity for all children is equalized since children have several teachers daily, (4) gifted children can study in depth with subject matter specialists and (5) specialists can effectively employ the teaching aids peculiar to their individual speciality areas. Conversely, departmentalization has frequently been criticized because it: (1) freezes the time schedule for all teachers within the building, (2) is difficult for teachers to familiarize themselves with the individual instructional needs of the approximately 150 pupils each teaches daily, (3) lessens the correlation and integration of learnings among the various subject areas, (4) makes differentiated instruction difficult to administer, and (5) frequently results in students being overloaded with homework assignments since each student will have approximately six teachers daily, and more often than not there is no systematic school plan for coordinating assigned student homework.

TEAM TEACHING. Team teaching was initially introduced to the elementary school as a horizontal organizational plan in the mid-1950s. It began to receive more attention and use with the coming of the space era and the press for teaching excellence in the curriculum reform movement of the 1960s.[21]

Operationally, team teaching may be defined as a horizontal organizational arrangement in which two or more teachers are deployed as a team with a group of students on a ratio of about twenty-five to thirty pupils per professional teacher. In an hypothetical and ideally organized functioning team, as depicted in figure 19.4, the organizational arrangement would be hierarchical in nature.[22]

At the base of the pyramid supporting and facilitating the work of the professionals in the superstructure would be teacher aides and a clerk who would be permanent members of the team and in the employ of the school. Also, the baseline of the hierarchical pyramid would be supported by the services of student teachers who might work in the team unit for a quarter or a semester during their senior year at the college or university, and resource consultants such as medical doctors, lawyers, chemists, fireman and the like who might volunteer their services periodically to assist with the program of instruction.

Immediately above the baseline group of team teaching personnel would be the cadre of young and beginning teachers who are, for the most part, new in the profession although a professional teacher may serve at this rung of the hierarchy for many years should he not choose or be chosen to move up within the hierarchical pyramid. These teachers may be generalists or specialists in nature but, when they are employed, they are chosen to contribute a particular expertise that will provide balance among team members within the pyramidal structure of the teaching team.

One rung above these teachers, yet one rung below the pinnacle position in the hierarchical pyramid, are found the "master teachers." These teachers are chosen to fulfill the master teacher role because of their proven excellence in teaching.[23] Usual-

21. See: "Team Teaching," *NEA Research Bulletin*, 45, no. 4 (December 1967): 114-15.
22. See: Robert H. Anderson, *Teaching in a World of Change* (New York: Harcourt, Brace & World, Inc., 1966), pp. 85-87; David R. Fink, Jr., "The Selection and Training of Teachers for Teams," *National Elementary Principal*, 44, no. 3 (January 1965): 54-59.
23. For a thorough discussion of the roles and qualifications of the professionals included in the teaching team, see: Fink, "Selection and Training," pp. 54-59.

ly, they are specialists in one of the subject areas of the curriculum.

At the top of the pyramid is the supervising teacher or team leader. He is chosen primarily for his leadership ability and may or may not be a master teacher. His most important functions include coordinating the work of the team and supervising curriculum development in the sense that he provides the leadership in planning what is done and seeing to it that balance in program is effected.

The basic rationale behind team teaching is that a great deal of instruction can be administered more effectively to 90 to 150 students at one time by given teachers in the instructional team who are best qualified to provide such instruction than will obtain when children are parceled out in groups of 30, with several teachers providing the same instruction simultaneously in separate classes. Also, instruction is enhanced by team teaching when the children are deployed periodically into small groups of 5, 15 or 30 pupils in terms of their special needs where teachers can work with them on a differentiated instructional basis.[24]

As one would suspect, there are advantages and disadvantages to team teaching.[25] Some of its advantages follow:

1. It provides a hierarchical arrangement whereby teachers can promote up to more prestigious positions within the hierarchy.
2. It provides an on-the-spot and continuous supervisory leadership from the supervising teacher or team leader not possible to the same degree when the elementary principal tries to provide the same supervision for an entire faculty of twenty-five or thirty teachers under the traditional self-contained classroom plan.
3. It becomes possible to give each teacher unassigned periods within the

24. For a discussion of alternate team teaching models, see: John A. Brownwell and Harris A. Taylor, "Theoretical Perspectives for Teaching Teams," *Phi Delta Kappan,* 43, no. 4 (January 1962): 150-57.
25. See: Henry J. Otto and David C. Sanders, *Elementary School Organization and Administration* 4th ed. New York: Appleton-Century-Crofts, 1964), pp. 80-81.

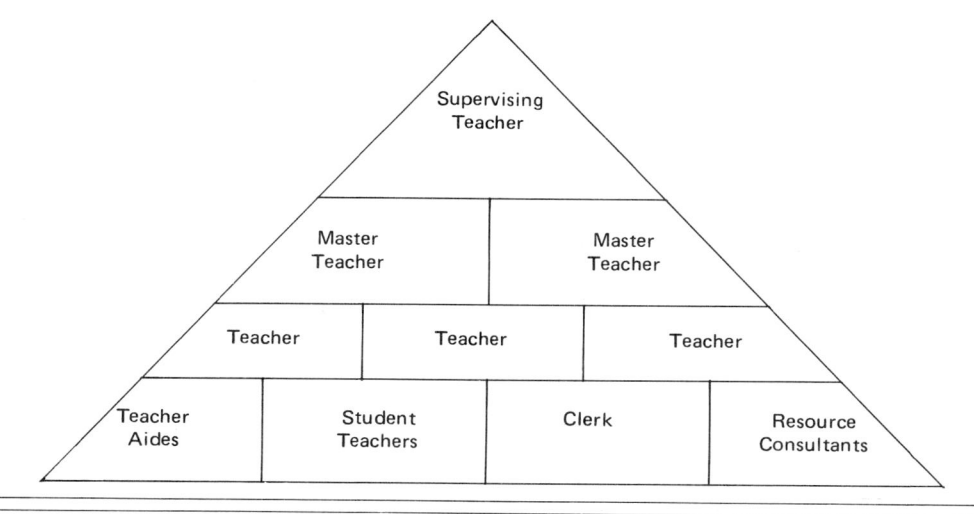

Fig. 19.4. Schema of Hierarchically Arranged Teaching Team.

day during which he can perform such necessary tasks as make or grade tests, prepare lessons, hold parent conferences, work on curriculum committees and the like.
4. It provides a great deal of flexibility with respect to time allotment, pupil and teacher deployment, et cetera.
5. It maximizes the individual expertise of the staff within the teaching team.
6. It provides an equal educational opportunity for all children within the team since they are taught by all team members.
7. It provides an in-service arrangement in the course of which the younger teachers can learn from the master teachers.

Of course, team teaching is not without some basic disadvantages. Those most often mentioned include:

1. Some teachers lack personality of the kind which will assure the necessary close interaction and cooperative work essential for successful team teaching.
2. Many school building facilities are not designed to effectually incorporate team teaching at an optimum level.
3. It is possible that team members do not get to know each student individually as well as is reputedly possible in the traditional self-contained classroom.
4. Some children may experience difficulty in adjusting to several teachers and numerous peers which results in team teaching.
5. The deployment of teachers into teaching teams may fragment the total faculty and divide it.

When compared with the traditional method of organizing the elementary school horizontally, team teaching has not demonstrated conclusively its superiority.[26] It appears, however, to be a viable plan of organizing instruction which is congruent with the curriculum reform emphasis of the times.

Student Deployment. Another aspect of horizontal organization in addition to teacher deployment previously discussed is the matter of student deployment. Basically, student deployment may be accomplished in the elementary school in some form of homogeneous or heterogeneous sectioning of children into classrooms. Let us briefly examine the methods whereby students are deployed for instruction in elementary schools.

Homogeneous Sectioning. There are many ways which children could be sectioned homogeneously into classrooms for instruction in the elementary school.[27] Three of those frequently mentioned include: (1) ability, (2) achievement and (3) interclass.[28]

Ability sectioning is a plan whereby the intelligence scores of children at every instruction level are rank ordered and then the pupils are placed into sections based upon IQ range bands. For example, a fifth-grade instructional level might contain 120 children at the beginning of a year who are to be sectioned into self-contained classrooms. The intelligence scores of the 120 children are rank ordered from highest to lowest. If there are four classrooms into

26. See: Glen Heathers, "Research on Implementing and Evaluating Cooperative Teaching," *National Elementary Principal* 44, no. 3 (January 1965): 27-33.

27. For a comprehensive discussion of sectioning in the elementary school, see Willard S. Elsbree, Harold J. McNally and Richard Wynn, *Elementary School Administration and Supervision* 3d ed. (New York: American Book Company, 1967), pp. 202-25.

28. Jarvis and Pounds, *Organizing, Supervising and Administering*, pp. 76-80.

which the children will be deployed, the rank ordered pupils will be divided into four quartiles with each quartile constituting a separate section. The Detroit Public School System was one of the first systems to experiment with this student deployment plan.[29] This plan has been used infrequently in recent years.

Achievement sectioning is a method of placing children possessing similar academic accomplishments in previous school experiences together into classrooms for instruction. Measures of prior academic accomplishments are derived from many sources such as reading achievement scores, student marks, teacher opinion and the like.

A plan whereby children are initially assigned to a home room for attendance accounting and counseling but are subsequently reassigned during the day, depending upon their achievement levels in such subjects as reading and arithmetic, is known as *interclass* (or cross-class) *sectioning*. For example, if there were three sections of third-grade reading, all third-grade teachers would teach reading simultaneously and the children would be sectioned into high, average and low achieving sections. This practice would then be repeated for other subjects to be taught on an interclass sectioning basis, such as arithmetic, where the children would be resectioned based upon similar achievement levels.

Heterogeneous Sectioning. There are many plans which have been used in the nation's schools to section children for instruction heterogeneously. Three frequently employed include the (1) randomized, (2) quasi-controlled, and (3) interage plans.[30]

Randomized sectioning is a plan whereby children at each instructional level are sectioned into classrooms without regard to their achievement or intelligence profiles. In other words, students are randomly assigned by sorting the enrollment cards at the various instructional levels into roughly equivalent numbers of children for each section to be created. The only control which is customarily invoked when this plan is used is to see that relatively the same number of boys and girls are included in each section.

The *quasi-controlled* heterogeneous sectioning plan is one in which designated numbers of high, average and low achievers are placed together into classrooms for instruction. For example, ten high, ten average and ten low achievers might be sectioned together for work in a self-contained classroom. Theoretically, the practice replicates life outside of the school and also facilitates the ease with which the classroom teacher can establish intraclass or within class groupings for subjects like reading or arithmetic.

Interage sectioning permits the placement of children together who have diverse backgrounds. It is a practice which is congruent with the multigraded vertical organizational pattern. The rationale behind interage sectioning is that diversity among students contributes more to teaching and learning than does similarity of pupil background experiences.[31] Under the plan, children who

---

29. J. Wayne Wrightstone, *Class Organization for Instruction: What Research Says to the Teacher*, no. 13 (Washington, D.C.: Association of Classroom Teachers. A Department of the National Education Association, 1957), p. 13.

30. Jarvis and Pounds, *Organizing, Supervising and Administering*, pp. 80-83.

31. See: Marian Pope Franklin, "Multigrading in Elementary Education," *Childhood Education* 43, no. 9 (May 1967): 513-15; Bernice J. Wolfson, "The Promise of Multiage Grouping for Individualizing Instruction," *Elementary School Journal*, 67, no. 7 (April 1967): 354-63.

are six, seven and eight years old might be sectioned together into an interage section for instruction in a vertical multigraded 1-3 unit, for example.

Intraclass Grouping. There is a third aspect to deploying children for instruction in the elementary school. It is intraclass grouping and, although it could be discussed here, it will be discussed in detail in chapter 21 where matters involving classroom management will be examined.

Regulating Student Progress

Under the multigraded and nongraded vertical organizational plan discussed in the first section of this chapter, the regulating of student progress up through the instructional levels is controlled internally. That is, these two vertical plans are congruent with and facilitate continuous pupil progress. Somewhat antithetical to the concept of continuous pupil progress, as has already been pointed out in this chapter, is the graded plan. When this plan is practiced, logically some children must pass while others must fail. For those failing, continuous pupil progress is virtually impossible.

Much research has been done in this century to investigate the effects of failure or grade retention on children.[32] Generally, it has been found that higher standards of achievement results in graded schools when the practice of 100 percent or universal promotion is employed and that children are better adjusted socially and emotionally. It has been found, for example, that only about 20 percent of the children retained will do better work the ensuing year when they repeat a grade, 40 percent of the repeating children will do about the same inferior work and 40 percent of the repeaters will actually do poorer work during the repeat year. Although there may be unique circumstances when a child should be retained in the graded school, generally it is better to promote all children and make a greater effort to meet their instructional needs at a higher grade level through differentiated instruction.

An Appraisal of Vertical and Horizontal Organizational Patterns

The purpose of any plan to organize pupils and teachers for instruction, as the preface indicates, is to facilitate instruction and learning. This broad concept, however, is seldom operationally defined. The product of the organization might, for example, be defined as an increase of pupil performance in proportion to teacher and pupil time devoted to the learning tasks.

The original concept of grading in Quincy school was grading based on performance level. However, in the development of the graded schools, the various grades through the years became more associated with the chronological ages of children rather than with performance level. In view of the fact that children of the same chronological age perform at different achievement levels, the solution to these

---

32. See: Charles H. Keyes, *Progress Through the Grades of City Schools, Teachers College Contributions to Education,* no. 42 (New York: Bureau of Publications, Teachers College, Columbia University 1911); Otto and Sanders, *Elementary School Organization,* pp. 134-45; Walter W. Cook, "Some Effects of the Maintenance of High Standards of Promotion," *Elementary School Journal* 41 (February 1941): 430-37; William H. Coffield and Paul Blommers, "Effects of Non-Promotion on Educational Achievement in the Elementary School," *Journal of Educational Psychology* 47, no. 4, (April 1956): 235-50; John I. Goodlad, "Some Effects of Promotion and Non-promotion upon the Social and Personal Adjustment of Children," *Journal of Experimental Education* 22 (June 1954): 311-28; Norman M. Chansky, "Progress of Promoted and Repeating Grade I Failures," *Journal of Experimental Education* 32 (Spring 1964): 225-37.

pupil differences has been social promotion after years of unsuccessful emphasis on retention.

Organizational solutions, vertically emphasizing multigradedness or nongradedness, have not yet shown conclusively the expected promise of acceleration of low achievement. Theoretically, the multigraded plan permits children of different chronological ages to be grouped by performance level (see figure 19.2) but it is entirely possible that some children will achieve above or below the performance levels contained in a multigraded unit.

The nongraded plan is, in reality, a graded plan in which the performance levels are subdivided. A variation of this plan is actually practiced in many graded primary schools, at least in reading and arithmetic, by the expedient of social promotion and teaching in the next grade at whatever performance level groups of children have attained.

Team teaching horizontally has been frequently used with the vertical multigraded, nongraded, and graded plans. In this manner, a team of teachers provides the division of labor necessary to handle pupils of different performance levels by subject area, irrespective of the system of vertical organization used. Where team teaching is not organized on some sequential division of labor, it is often abandoned after an exploratory period. This is because the amount of planning time required by the teachers is greater than the planning time required for individual efforts. While the hierarchy of a teaching team organized into supervising, master, regular teacher and teaching aide is sometimes tried, especially in schools which have a pod facility arrangement which permits the organization of a school within a school, this organization may not be popularly viewed by teachers who typically expect remuneration based upon level of certificate and years of teaching experience.

Departmentalization is not new to the elementary school. Although it has not been used to the extent of the self-contained classroom in recent years, it has been employed in the intermediate grades when there was a subject matter emphasis. It appears to have been abandoned primarily as a result of the upward movement of the "whole child" approach from the primary to the intermediate grades during the progressive education era. Its revival reflects a renewed emphasis on subject matter mastery in the curriculum reform movement of the Space Age and, in some schools, an organizational response to racially integrated teaching staffs.

From the point of view of academic achievement alone, the problem of reduction in teacher-pupil learning performance level might be approached from the organization of the curriculum into mini-segments, which would permit students to progress from one level to another according to their level of ability. This approach would seem to be consistent with the large elementary schools. Even in this system, however, there would be a certain number of children who would take so long at their tasks that some type of automatic promotion would have to be utilized, to reduce the age span among children and permit older children to work within their peer groups. It appears inconsistent, however, to consolidate schools and then return within these large populations to variations of the Little Red School House, unless it is assumed that there is an inherent virtue in having older children work with younger children. This might be the case. The rigid age-grade groups which characterize our culture today are, in part, a product of our age-graded schools. Before school consolidation in rural areas, it was not unusual to have several grades in a class under one teacher. Children associated more on the basis of their mutual interests and abilities, rather than on age-set alone.

You will undoubtedly find within whatever school system you teach different plans of vertical and horizontal organization. You will find no agreement among your colleagues as to the optimum method of organization. Their contradictory opinions about the relative merits of the various organizational patterns not only will reflect differing value perspectives, but also reflect the difficulty we have in controlling the numerous variables associated with the complex symbolic learning which is a major objective in school instruction. With this possibility, it would seem that the best approach for a novice teacher to take is one of flexibility. You will have to adapt yourself to the organization of the school system in which you work. Your pupils will learn under any system of vertical or horizontal organization. Your challenge is to always keep in mind the growth of your pupils. Perhaps some day you will be given a choice as to the type of organizational pattern in which you work. On the basis of theory and experience, you can then select the pattern which conforms to your ideal. But in selecting it, remember that this is one alternate which fits you and your teaching style; it is not the only alternative and not necessarily the best solution for a colleague and his pupils. Also, remember that the vertical and horizontal organizational arrangements need to be consonant with the curriculum pattern you employ in your classroom (refer to chapter 4).

SELECTED REFERENCES

ALEXANDER, WILLIAM M., et al. *The Emergent Middle School.* New York: Holt, Rinehart and Winston, Inc., 1968.

ANDERSON, ROBERT H. *Teaching in a World of Change.* New York: Harcourt, Brace & World, Inc., 1966.

BURR, JAMES B., et al. *Elementary School Administration.* Boston: Allyn and Bacon, Inc., 1963.

ELSBREE, WILLARD S., et al. *Elementary School Administration and Supervision.* 3d ed. New York: American Book Company, 1967.

FRANKLIN, MARIAN POPE, ed. *School Organization: Theory and Practice.* Chicago: Rand McNally & Company, 1967.

GROOMS, M. ANN. *Perspectives on the Middle School.* Columbus, Ohio: Charles E. Merrill Books, Inc., 1967.

HEATHERS, GLEN. *The Dual Progress Plan.* Danville, Illinois: Interstate Printers & Publishers, Inc., 1967.

HALPIN, ANDREW W. *Theory and Research in Administration.* New York: Macmillan Company, 1966.

HILLSON, MAURIE, ed. *Change and Innovation in Elementary School Organization.* New York: Holt, Rinehart and Winston, 1965.

JARVIS, OSCAR T., ed. *Elementary School Administration: Readings.* Dubuque, Iowa: Wm. C. Brown Company Publishers, 1969.

―――, and POUNDS, HASKIN R. *Organizing, Supervising and Administering the Elementary School.* West Nyack, N.Y.: Parker Publishing Company, 1969.

KIMBROUGH, RALPH B. *Administering Elementary Schools: Concepts and Practices.* New York: Macmillan Company, 1968.

MINSER, PAUL J., et al. *Elementary School Administration.* Columbus, Ohio: Charles E. Merrill Books, Inc., 1963.

Otto, Henry J., and Sanders, David C. *Elementary School Organization and Administration.* 4th ed. New York: Appleton-Century-Crofts, 1964.

Polos, Nicholas C. *The Dynamics of Team Teaching.* Dubuque, Iowa: Wm. C. Brown Company Publishers, 1965.

Rollins, Sidney P. *Developing Nongraded Schools.* Itasca, Illinois: F. E. Peacock Publishers, Inc., 1968.

Shaplin, Judson T., and Olds, Henry F., Jr., eds. *Team Teaching.* New York: Harper & Row, Publishers, 1964.

Tewksbury, John L. *Nongrading in the Elementary School.* Columbus, Ohio: Charles E. Merrill Books, Inc., 1967.

evaluating and reporting pupil growth

20

It is important that the elementary school teacher have a thorough understanding of the processes and techniques of evaluating and reporting pupil growth or progress. If he does not possess this knowledge, his teaching effectiveness and relations with pupils and parents may be jeopardized. Some of the more important information about evaluating and reporting pupil progress that the elementary teacher should know is discussed in the following sections of this chapter.

Evaluating Pupil Growth

It is necessary to understand what evaluation is before one attempts to understand the purposes, principles, and techniques of evaluation. Accordingly, evaluation may be defined as a process by which pupil data such as intelligence, achievement, and social adjustment information are continuously acquired and analyzed for each child by the teacher through formal and informal procedures to determine the changes that should be made in the individual child's instructional program so that his unique educational needs may be more adequately met.[1]

Through an effectual program of evaluation, the teacher can make instruction more meaningful for each of his charges. That is, evaluation helps the teacher understand the appropriateness of the instruction he provides and what modifications should be made in the teaching-learning situations to more nearly meet the idiosyncratic needs of each child in his classroom.

Understanding Purposes for Evaluation

If evaluation is to be meaningful, the teacher must understand some commonly accepted purposes for it. Some of the more important purposes therefore, are the following.[2]

1. *The teacher, through systematic and continuous evaluation, can meet the differing educational needs of his pupils.* For example, through the process of evaluation,

---

1. Oscar T. Jarvis and Haskin R. Pounds, *Organizing, Supervising and Administering the Elementary School* (West Nyack, N.Y.: Parker Publishing Company, 1969), p. 90.

2. For other statements of purposes of evaluation, see: William B. Ragan, *Teaching America's Children* (New York: Holt, Rinehart and Winston, 1961), pp. 317-19; Jarvis and Pounds, *Organizing, Supervising and Administering*, pp. 91-92.

399

the teacher can determine what his pupils know, when they evidence readiness for new learnings, when to reinforce concepts already learned, when enrichment work is necessary, what differentiation of instruction should be made, and so on.

2. *Through appropriate evaluation, the teacher can ascertain how effective his teaching techniques have been.* If the teacher has been teaching the social studies inductively to disadvantaged learners, for example, evaluation will help him judge how effective that teaching strategy is for that type of student. Perhaps he will find induction effective or perhaps he will find that other strategies such as deduction will be more beneficial to use with disadvantaged children.

3. *Evaluation enables the teacher to determine how effective the materials are he is using with his students.* That is, as he makes his evaluation, the teacher can determine whether the materials he is using are well suited to the educational needs of the children.

4. *The process of evaluation provides pupil data that can be used in the elementary school's program of guidance.* The administration of different types of teacher-made and standardized tests, i.e., achievement, intelligence and aptitude, provides a bank of pupil data which can be used in helping pupils benefit from their school experiences at an optimal level.

5. *Pupils gain valuable information about their own progress at school through the medium of evaluation.* As the teacher's systematic and continuous program of evaluation proceeds, the pupils can acquire data which help them to assess their own status about such important factors as peer acceptance, general achievement, and skills mastery. Under proper teacher guidance, this information can assist the children in developing realistic educational goals and expectations for themselves.

6. *Evaluation supplies necessary pupil data to be used in reporting pupil progress to parents.* It is through the medium of evaluation that teachers organize pupil progress information for reporting to parents in terms of the values, principles, and purposes of education subscribed to in the school.

Of course, there are other and more global purposes which the process of evaluation helps to accomplish, such as providing a data base for curriculum revision and public relations. Let us turn our attention, however, to an investigation of principles of evaluation.

Principles to Guide Evaluation

There is a set of principles which the teacher should keep in mind when he conducts the process of evaluation in his classroom. The more important principles of evaluation appear to be the following.[3]

First, evaluation should be continuously and systematically employed by the teacher in an attempt to determine the intellectual development, status of academic achievement, physical growth and social adjustment of the children. Second, the teacher's evaluation program should be comprehensive. It is more than merely gathering information from informal and formal testing instruments. It involves planned teacher observation, sociograms, pupil opinionnaires, and the like. Third, all of the separate measures about each pupil which are ob-

---

3. See also Ragan, *Teaching America's Children,* pp. 320-21.

tained in the teacher's total program of evaluation should be assembled into a composite picture of the child as a functioning individual. Fourth, evaluation should be individualized for each child in an effort to determine if he is progressing acceptably in terms of his own unique capabilities. A fifth principle is that evaluation is an integral component of the teaching-learning process. That is, as the teaching-learning act transpires, the teacher and his pupils should jointly evaluate the outcomes which accrue. Sixth, the teacher should help each child develop skill in self-evaluation.

Obviously, the principles of evaluation mentioned here do not constitute a complete set. Rather, those mentioned here are illustrative of a much larger and perhaps open set of evaluation principles. Now, let us turn our attention to the techniques that a teacher may use in performing the evaluation function.

Techniques of Evaluation

The teacher needs to understand certain techniques of evaluation once he understands the purposes and principles of evaluation. A discussion of teacher evaluation techniques is given in the following paragraphs.

Teacher Observation. Through observation the teacher can learn many things about children that informal or formal test results will not tell him. He can learn through observation, for example, how well a given child interacts with his peers, accepts responsibility, meets difficult situations, exerts leadership, and the like. In short, the teacher can, through the medium of systematic and careful observation, make judgments about what adjustments in program should be made for his charges as a group and as individuals.

There are a number of caveats which should be heeded by the teacher in making evaluative observations. Some of the more important ones follow.

The teacher should:

1. Be careful not to form hasty judgments about pupil behavior.
2. Avoid stereotyping a group of children or an individual and then interpreting all future behavior in terms of his prior experiences with the group or individual.
3. Be cognizant that his own actions or behavior may contribute to or affect the children's behavior, i.e., the self-fulfilling prophecy which he may establish for his charges.[4]
4. Avoid the pitfall of viewing overconforming children too favorably and nonconforming pupils unfavorably.
5. Be aware that it is impossible to learn all of the facts about any child which affect his behavior.

Anecdotal Records. Occasionally, the teacher will record in the student's cumulative record folder anecdotal comments about individual pupil behavior gained from observation. These anecdotal comments, along with other information such as achievement and intelligence test results, health history, and the like, can be used by the teachers and guidance counselors in helping children achieve at an optimal level.

Anecdotal records have a basic and inherent weakness which involves objectivity. To overcome this pitfall, the teacher should be careful to record only facts and not opinion. He should guard against recording anecdotal remarks about a student only

---

4. Robert Rosenthal and Lenore Jacobson, *Pygmalion in the Classroom* (New York: Holt, Rinehart and Winston, Inc., 1968).

after experiencing some negative aspect of that student's behavior. When he enters negative anecdotal comments in the cumulative record folder, he should try to maintain balance by also including some positive anecdotal remarks. The reason for this is obvious: other teachers will teach his pupils in subsequent years and they need factual, unbiased information about students for purposes of evaluation and program development. A teacher ought not overgeneralize, however, on prior anecdotal records since they are vulnerable with respect to subjectivity.

Pupil Work Samples. Many teachers in the elementary schools make a practice of maintaining pupil work sample folders for each child in the classroom. The purpose of this practice is to provide samples of pupil work which the teacher can use to evaluate pupil progress. That is, by comparing present work with representative samples of former work, the teacher can get some idea of how well the individual pupil is progressing academically. When the teacher maintains pupil work sample folders, he should be careful to update the file periodically by selecting representative specimens of each child's work in the various subject areas for inclusion in the folders, and by discarding specimens included in the files which are no longer relevant.

Informal Teacher-Made Tests. Teachers can administer a number of informal tests in the elementary school for purposes of gathering pupil data for evaluation. The two most commonly administered teacher-made tests include the essay and objective tests.[5] The teacher's purpose for gathering data for evaluation determines which test should be administered. If he is checking on his pupil's ability to express their ideas through the medium of written composition, for example, the essay tests should be administered. The chief advantage of the teacher-made test, therefore, lies in the fact that it permits the teacher to test specifically what has been taught merely by constructing his test accordingly.[6] Some authorities have suggested that this may give it greater validity than more formal commercially prepared types of tests. Of course, the validity of the teacher-made test depends on the accuracy with which it measures learning objectives and the actual content of pupil learning experiences.[7]

Essay Test. The *essay* test has many inherent weaknesses that the teacher will want to keep in mind when he uses it. Some of these weaknesses include the following.[8]

1. The teacher can include only a limited number of questions on the essay test because of time limitations. Test items should be selected with care, therefore, to make sure that they give representative coverage to the materials taught.
2. Pupils may misinterpret essay questions. If this occurs, the resulting test

---

5. For a thorough discussion of teacher-made test construction and usage, see: Walter N. Durost and George A. Prescott, *Essentials of Measurement for Teachers* (New York: Harcourt, Brace & World, Inc., 1962), pp. 37-51; John E. Horrocks and Thelma I. Schoonover, *Measurement for Teachers* (Columbus, Ohio: Charles E. Merrill Publishing Company, 1968), pp. 509-55.

6. Jarvis and Pounds, *Organizing, Supervising and Administering,* pp. 93-94.

7. Willard S. Elsbree, Harold J. McNally and Richard Wynn, *Elementary School Administration and Supervision,* 3d ed. (New York: American Book Company, 1967), p. 245.

8. For a more comprehensive discussion of weaknesses in the teacher-made essay test, see Marie A. Mehl et al., *Teaching in Elementary School* 3d ed. (New York: Ronald Press Company 1965), pp. 351-63.

score may not be a true indicator of what has been learned because of the limited number of items which can be included on an essay examination.

3. All children do not express themselves equally well in writing, do not budget their time wisely among the various test items, nor do they write concisely. Marks on essay tests, therefore, may be related more to these variables than to what the children have actually learned.

Objective Test. The objective test may be constructed in a number of ways: true-false, multiple-choice, matching, or completion type questions. It is not uncommon for teachers to include all types of questions on an objective examination in the elementary school.

There are at least two major advantages of the objective test. First, it is easy to score. Second, it can be scored objectively in that there is only one correct answer for each test item.

Objective tests appear to have two major shortcomings. First, pupils may answer correctly on occasion by simply guessing. Or, second, they may get the right answer through the process of eliminating items which they know are incorrect.

Whether the teacher uses the essay or objective test to gather pupil data for purposes of evaluation, he should construct his tests in terms of a set of criteria which will help to insure their reliability and validity. The criteria might include test items on the examination, as follow:[9]

1. Represent a comprehensive sampling of what has been taught.
2. Range on a continuum from easy to difficult-to-answer questions which will enable all children to answer some correctly and at the same time provide a challenge for the more able students.
3. Items designed in a manner which make their scoring easy.
4. Items can be scored objectively.
5. Items requiring intuitive and associate thinking on the part of the students and not merely recall.

Sociogram. Another technique of evaluation that the teacher may use is the sociogram. Technically, a sociogram is a schematic diagram of the social relationships that exist among a group or classroom of children. When properly used, it can be of much assistance to the teacher in his evaluation procedures.[10]

Pupil data for constructing the sociogram are obtained quite easily by asking the pupils to answer one question such as: "If you were to volunteer to work on a classroom project, with whom would you most like to work?" The children would answer the question by indicating their first, second, and third peer choices on a sheet of paper and turning their choices in to the teacher. Teachers of very young children may elect to have them respond orally in an individual conference.

The children's individual choices subsequently are tabulated by the teacher in a form such as that shown in figure 20.1. The children's choices would be weighted in tabulating the total points for each child as follows:

First choice: 3 points
Second choice: 2 points
Third choice: 1 point

9. See: Ragan, *Teaching America's Children,* p. 323.
10. Oscar T. Jarvis and Lutian R. Wootton, *The Transitional Elementary School and Its Curriculum* (Dubuque, Iowa: Wm. C. Brown Company Publishers, 1966), p. 210.

404 evaluating and reporting pupil growth

When the tabulations are completed, as in figure 20.1, the sociogram can be made by using different geometric shapes to distinguish between boys and girls. Squares were used to designate boys in figure 20.2 and circles to identify girls, in constructing the sociogram. Also, in figure 20.2 numerals are used to indicate the children's rank-ordered preferences, arrows signify the direction of their choices, and joined arrow heads in the center of lines denote the pupil's mutual choices.[11]

The sociogram, once completed, indicates to the teacher who the leaders are within the classroom. It also tells him who the isolates are. If the teacher constructs a new sociogram each quarter or semester, he can learn much valuable information about the social relationships in the classroom which may have changed and make some judgment about how he can intervene to accomplish worthwhile objects, e.g., help isolates gain acceptance.

The teacher should know, in using the sociogram, that it is not uncommon for boys to choose boys and girls to choose girls in the intermediate grades. In grades one and two, however, sex does not appear to be a factor in making choices.[12]

11. James B. Burr, et al., *Student Teaching in the Elementary School,* 2d ed. (New York: Appleton-Century-Crofts, Inc., 1958), p. 292.

12. Ibid., p. 292.

CHOSEN → CHOOSERS ↓	Abbott, Samuel	Bishop, Annie	Cobb, Robert	Davis, Betty	Elam, James	Framm, Connie	Goldberg, Israel	Heil, Frank	Irvin, Deborah	Jackson, Edgar	Knight, Elsie	Lang, Charles	Macklin, Fannie	North, Sterl	Ochs, Grace	Pilcher, Homer	Number of 1st Choices	Number of 2nd Choices	Number of 3rd Choices	Total Points (1st-3)	Total times chosen	
	1	2	3	4	5	6	7	8	9	10	11	12	13	14	15	16	1	2	3	4	5	
1. Abbott, Samuel	×		3	1		2											0	0	0	0	0	Isolate
2. Bishop, Annie		×		1		2					3						0	1	2	4	3	
3. Cobb, Robert	3	×		1						2							1	0	1	4	2	
4. Davis, Betty	2		×	3		1											3	1	1	12	5	Leader
5. Elam, James				×		1			2					3			2	0	1	7	3	
6. Framm, Connie		3		×			2	1									1	3	0	9	4	
7. Goldberg, Israel	3	1	2		×												3	0	1	10	4	Leader
8. Heil, Frank		1		2	×	3											1	0	1	4	2	
9. Irvin, Deborah					3	×	1		2								0	3	2	8	5	
10. Jackson, Edgar				1			×		2					3			0	0	0	0	0	Isolate
11. Knight, Elsie			1			2	×	3									3	3	0	15	6	Leader
12. Lang, Charles				1			×	2		3							2	1	0	7	3	
13. Macklin, Fannie				1		3	2	×									0	1	3	5	4	
14. North, Sterl					3			1	×	2							0	1	1	3	2	
15. Ochs, Grace					2	1	3	×									0	1	0	2	1	
16. Pilcher, Homer								1	3	2	×						0	1	3	5		

Fig. 20.1. Sociogram Data Tabulation Form. From James B. Burr, Lowry W. Harding, and Leland B. Jacobs, **Student Teaching in the Elementary School,** 2d ed. (New York: Appleton-Century-Crofts, © 1958), p. 295. Reprinted by permission of Appleton-Century-Crofts, Educational Division, Meredith Corporation.

evaluating and reporting pupil growth

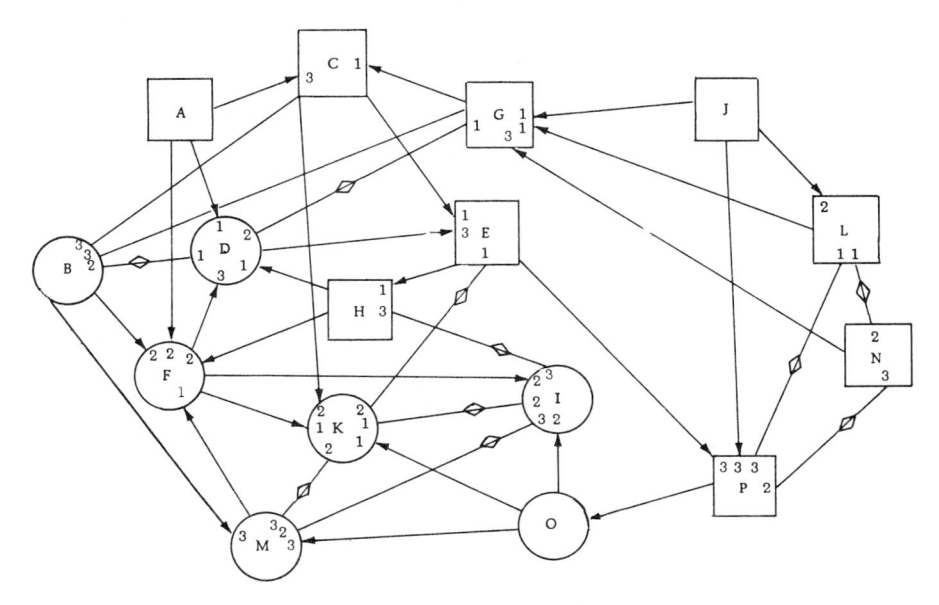

Fig. 20.2. Sociogram. From James B. Burr, Lowry W. Harding, and Leland B. Jacobs, **Student Teaching in the Elementary School,** 2d ed. (New York: Appleton-Century-Crofts, © 1958), p. 294. Reprinted by permission of Appleton-Century-Crofts, Educational Division, Meredith Corporation.

Standardized Tests. Several different types of standardized or formal tests can be used to gather pupil data for evaluation purposes in the elementary school. The teacher should know the nature of these tests and the purposes they serve. Some of the standardized tests which are administered in the elementary school are outlined in figure 20.3 with respect to types of test and specific uses.[13] Only the guidance counselor or psychologist should administer the personality tests.

The elementary teacher needs to understand the standardized testing program that his school follows in order to make the best use of pupil data in performing his evaluation function. It is not practical here to suggest an ideal standardized testing program for the elementary school. This is a matter to be determined locally. A hypothetical testing program, however, is depicted in figure 20.4 which will give the teacher some idea of the nature of tests administered at the kindergarten through grade 6 levels.

In studying figure 20.4, one can see that the scheduled time for administering the tests annually is early in the school year. One of the principal reasons for this is that it provides pupil data for teacher evaluation early in the year so that he may make the necessary adjustments for the children early in the school program.

Of course, the most commonly administered standardized elementary school tests are those for intelligence and achievement.

13. For an assessment of individual standardized tests, see: Oscar K. Burros, ed. *The Sixth Mental Measurements Yearbook* (Highland Park, N. J.: Gryphon Press, 1965).

TYPE OF TEST	SPECIFIC USES
Intelligence and mental ability	Individual type (Binet) and group type. (Otis). Attempts to measure verbal and nonverbal intelligence.
Achievement tests	Attempts to measure abilities, skills, concepts, content. May cover one subject, such as reading, or may test all elementary school subjects with a large battery of tests.
Aptitude tests	Used to measure tonal memory, rhythmical discrimination, manual dexterity, spatial relationships. Art, music, language, mechanical tests are available.
Attitude tests, scales or inventories	Attempts to measure feelings for or against a large variety of topics—minorities, church, civic beliefs, war, peace, or subjects like arithmetic.
Interest tests, scales, inventories, questionnaires	Used to collect data on pupil interests in vocations, reading, school activities, or recreational areas.
Personality tests, scales, inventories	Attempts to secure data on personal adjustment, ascendence-submission, or neurotic tendencies.

Fig. 20.3. Types and Uses of Standardized Objective Tests. From Wilbur H. Dutton and John A. Hockett, **The Modern Elementary School: Curriculum and Methods** (New York: Holt, Rinehart and Winston, Inc., 1959), p. 497.

Let us examine briefly some of the more important aspects of each about which the elementary teacher should be knowledgeable.

Intelligence Tests. The purpose of the intelligence tests is to obtain a measure of the child's performance on abstract reasoning tasks. Primarily there are two types of intelligence tests. They include the group tests and the individual tests. Generally, the classroom teacher administers the group intelligence tests and the guidance counselor or school psychologist administers the individual intelligence tests.

As a rule, it is impractical to administer an individual intelligence test to all children since a specially trained person must administer it and because its administration may take one to two hours. Only children who are tentatively identified as being exceptional, e.g., the mentally retarded or the gifted, or pupils who are experiencing unusual learning difficulties, are normally administered an individual intelligence test.

Pupil scores on intelligence tests predict academic potential reasonably well. In the past, however, some teachers have misused them by relying too heavily upon them as predictors of academic success and, in

Grade	Time of Administration	Use	Type of Test
Kindergarten	End of year	To aid in determining promotions	Gates Reading Readiness Test
First	First three months	To help set up reading groups	Gates Reading Readiness Test
Second	Second month	To check scholastic aptitude	California Test of Mental Maturity, Primary Level
Third	Second month	To determine reading difficulties	Durrell Analysis of Reading Difficulty
Fourth	First three months	To analyze the scholastic achievement of pupils	Stanford Achievement Test, Elementary, Form J
	Second month	To confirm scholastic aptitude	California Test of Mental Maturity, Elementary Level
Fifth	First three months	To reassess the scholastic achievement of pupils	Stanford Achievement Test, Intermediate, Form J
Sixth	First three months	To reassess the scholastic achievement of pupils	Stanford Achievement Test, Intermediate, Form K
	Second month	To determine pupil attitudes and concerns	Science Research Associates Junior Inventory, Form S

Fig. 20.4. Hypothetical Elementary School Testing Program. From Raymond N. Hatch and James W. Costar, **Guidance in the Elementary School** (Dubuque, Iowa: William C. Brown Company Publishers, 1961), p. 83.

Last Name	First Name	Middle Name	Name Called By	Sex	Race	Younger ____ Younger ____

Evidence of Birth:
Certificate Number ______________ Other (Specify) ______________
______________ Student I.D. No.

Date of Birth				Place of Birth				
Resident Yes | No	Date	Child's Address	Phone	Resident Yes | No	Date	Child's Address	Phone

	Father's Name			Mother's Name			Guardian			Step-Parents		
	First	Middle	Last	First	Maiden	Last	First	Middle	Last	First	Middle	Last
Address if Different from Child's												
Occupation												
Employed by												
If Deceased, Date												

Parents Divorced | Parents Separated

If Student Lives with Other than Parents, Explain:

Special Referral (Date) ______
Psych. ______ Couns. ______
Soc. Wkr. ______ Other ______

Medical Information

Indicate by a check mark (√) if pupil has had: Epilepsy ______, Asthma ______, Diabetes ______, Heart Condition ______,

Allergies (Specify) ______ Serious Physical Handicap ______, Serious Hearing Defect ______, Serious Vision Defect ______,

Serious Speech Defect ______, Other Serious Illness (Specify) ______

Give Date of Immunizations: Smallpox ______ D.P.T. ______ Booster ______ Other ______

Special Assignment

Specify ______
Date ______
Specify ______
Date ______
Specify ______
Date ______

Grade Record

Grade										
School										
Year										
Teacher										
Entered										
Withdrawn										
Re-Entered										
Promoted To										

Attendance Record

Quarter	1	2	3	4	1	2	3	4	1	2	3	4	1	2	3	4	1	2	3	4	1	2	3	4	1	2	3	4	1	2	3	4	1	2	3	4	1	2	3	4
Days Present																																								
Lawful Abs.																																								
Unlawful Abs.																																								
Times Tardy																																								

Fig. 20.5. Elementary Permanent Record Card of the Atlanta (Georgia) Public Schools.

STANDARDIZED TEST DATA

NAME OF TEST																								
FORM																								
DATE																								
GRADE																								
EXAMINER																								

DEVELOPMENTAL READING TEST

SERIES																								
DATE																								
LEVEL																								
POSSIBLE TOTAL SCORE																								
EARNED SCORE																								
% ILE OR RANK																								

ADDITIONAL TEST DATA

ELEMENTARY PERMANENT RECORD   ATLANTA PUBLIC SCHOOLS   ATLANTA, GEORGIA

Fig. 20.5. (Cont'd)

some cases, have been guilty of stereotyping children on the basis of intelligence test scores.

Volumes have been written in recent years cautioning teachers and adminstrators to be careful about the uses they make of intelligence test scores. The reasons for these cautions are legion. First, the intelligence test scores represent the verbal ability of children in terms of how well they manipulate the English language. The children with elaborated language codes, therefore, are at an advantage while the pupils with restricted language codes are at a disadvantage.[14] Second, the children from the ghetto or inner-city areas, whose parents were from Appalachia, or were poor southern Caucasians or Negroid and those children from bilingual family backgrounds such as the Mexican-Americans in the southwest and far west or the Puerto Rican immigrants in the large cities frequently make low scores on intelligence tests.[15] These low scores may reflect their underprivileged conditions and lack of meaningful experiences in terms of the middle class culture more than anything else. Third, intelligence tests are not designed to measure pupil motivation: occasionally a child's desire to achieve and his classroom performance excel what might be expected of him in terms of his intelligence score. As a result of these and other reasons which could be advanced, the intelligence test scores are frequently overemphasized in predicting academic success.[16]

Achievement Tests. There are two types of standardized achievement tests which are administered in the elementary school—the survey tests and diagnostic tests.

The survey achievement tests are usually in battery form and test such areas as reading, arithmetic, science, social studies, and the language arts. Raw scores obtained from the scoring of these achievement test batteries are converted into grade placement equivalents. For example, a child's grade placement equivalent of 3.6 in arithmetic fundamentals means that he is achieving at the sixth month of the third grade whether, in fact, he is in the third or some other grade.

The pupil data obtained from the survey achievement test can help the teacher as evaluator in a number of ways. First, he can acquire some idea of the level of work being done in the skill and content areas for each child and for the class collectively. Second, he can make some comparison about how each child and the class collectively compare with school and national norms.[17]

The diagnostic achievement test is administered to determine specific pupil weaknesses or difficulties encountered in learning such subjects as reading and arithmetic. They are partcularly beneficial in diagnosing the achievement problems of such children as those with learning disabilities who appear to fall within normal ranges on intelligence tests.[18]

---

14. See J. W. Getzels, "Pre-School Education," *Teacher's College Record* 68, no. 3 (December 1966): 219-28.

15. See Robert J. Havighurst, "Who Are the Disadvantaged?" *Education* 85, no. 8 (April 1965): 455-57.

16. G. Wesley Sowards and Mary-Margaret Scobey, *The Changing Curriculum and the Elementary Teacher* (Belmont, California: Wadsworth Publishing Company, Inc., 1961), p. 522.

17. Jarvis and Wootton, *Transitional Elementary School*, p. 209.

18. Willard S. Elsbree, Harold J. McNally and Richard Wynn, *Elementary School Administration and Supervision* 3d ed. (New York: American Book Company, 1967), p. 249.

GROWTH RECORD AND VISION

Date												
Grade												
Age												
Height												
Weight												
VISION Date												
Without Glasses R												
Without Glasses L												
Both Eyes												
With Glasses R												
With Glasses L												

*MEDICAL RECORD

Date						
Nutrition, Posture						
Bones, Joints, Gait						
Skin, Scalp						
Eyes						
Ear, Nose, Throat						
Lungs						
Heart						
Hernia						

HEARING

Date				
R				
L				

Code*

1—Normal

2—Needs attention

3—Urgently needs attention

(Circle number when under treatment)

* DENTAL RECORD

Date						
Dental Caries						
Prophylaxis						
Gingivitis						
Mal occlusion						

Code †

H.V.—Home Visit

T.-N.C.—Teacher-Nurse Conference

C.-N.C.—Counselor-Nurse Conference

Date	† HEALTH COUNSELING REMARKS	Worker

Fig. 20.6. Cumulative Health Record Card of the Houston (Texas) Public Schools.

Recording Pupil Growth Data

Elementary schools maintain some system of recording pupil growth or progress information for future referral so that teachers, administrators, counselors, psychologist, and others can use it. The normal practice is to record important information, such as standardized test results, health record, and anecdotal remarks, in the cumulative record folder. Cumulative records are important because they provide a permanent and uniform record of pupil information so that it can be continuously referred to by the school staff. Also, cumulative records enable children's subsequent teachers to know about the status of their growth intellectually, socially, emotionally, and physically. Selected cumulative record forms which are used in the Atlanta (Georgia) and Houston (Texas) Public Schools are shown in figures 20.5, 20.6, and 20.7. These forms are illustrative of the types of pupil information that are gathered and recorded in the elementary school cumulative record folder.

Reporting Pupil Growth to Parents

There are a number of ways whereby teachers in the elementary school report pupil progress information to parents. This may be done through one or a combination of the following methods: comparative marks on report cards, checklist, parent-teacher conferences, telephone, or letters to parents. Let us examine these individually.

Comparative Marks on Report Card. When schools have a more society- or discipline-oriented curriculum, they customarily have their teachers report pupil growth or progress in the form of comparative letter marks issued on the report card. In this instance, the comparative letter marks normally denote the following:

A - Excellent

B - Good

C - Fair

D - Poor

F - Failure

The use of comparative marks on report cards is usually held to be congruent with curriculum orientations and designs which are predicated upon a subjects foundation. That is, the children are subjected to a uniform curriculum and basically uniform materials. As a result, some excel in subject matter and skills mastery while others do work of a lesser quality.

The comparative marks, therefore, are held to be indexes of the degree of subject matter and skills mastery. When this practice is rigidly enforced, it logically follows that some children will pass and others will fail; some pupils will be promoted at the end of the academic year and others will be retained.

There are several weaknesses in the comparative marks method of reporting pupil progress information to parents. Some of the reasons most often mentioned include the following.[19] First, parents frequently do not understand the wide ranges of ability and achievement differences that exist among children in any classroom and, as a result, the letter marks may be misleading. For example, very bright students may earn high marks easily without putting forth their best academic efforts in some classrooms. Second, slow learning pupils may develop negative self-concepts when they repeatedly are issued

19. Jarvis and Pounds, *Organizing, Supervising and Administering,* pp. 101-2.

evaluating and reporting pupil growth

	BASAL READER*	PROGRESS**	SUPPLEMENTARY READERS
School _____ Teacher _____ Grade _____			
School _____ Teacher _____ Grade _____			
School _____ Teacher _____ Grade _____			
School _____ Teacher _____ Grade _____			

Name _____
Date of Birth _____

Houston Independent School District
READING PROGRESS RECORD -- Grades 1-6

*List basal readers in the order in which used.
**Indicate book completed or the page number reached.

• Keep up to date.
• Transfer from teacher to teacher.
• Send with record cards in case of transfer.

Fig. 20.7. Reading Progress Record, Grades 1-6, The Houston (Texas) Public Schools.

low marks. Third, teachers may let children's overt behavior influence the marks they issue on report cards, e.g., girls make better marks than boys as a general rule.[20]

Because of the disadvantages of comparative marks, many elementary schools use alternate forms of reporting, such as the pupil checklist or parent-teacher conference. Such reporting procedures, however, usually do not remove the fact that eventually the pupil will be marked in upper grades, either intermediate or secondary, on some comparative form by subject matter achievement. The discontinuity in the form of elementary evaluation and reporting and upper grade reporting may obscure lower level performance in the elementary school.

Some educators prefer a combination form of reporting pupil growth in which comparative marks are combined with pupil study traits, such as the one shown in figure 20.8. An "A" for a student who does not follow directions, does not complete work on time, or does not use time wisely may indicate that he needs to be put in a more challenging learning environment. On the other hand, a student who makes a low comparative mark of "C" when he manifests all the desirable study and behavioral traits associated with school success would seem to

20. See: Earl D. Hanson, "Do Boys Get a Square Deal in School?" *Education* 79, no. 9 (May 1959): 597-98; Bruce J. Kremer, "Is Coeducation Unfair to Boys?" *Catholic School Journal* 65 no. 8 (October 1965): 37-39.

414 evaluating and reporting pupil growth

PUPIL PROGRESS REPORT
GRADES 4 THROUGH 7

PUPIL'S NAME _____
                          Last   First
SCHOOL _____
TEACHER _____
PRINCIPAL _____
GRADE _____ SCHOLASTIC YEAR 19___-19___

EXPLANATION OF MARKS	CONFERENCE REQUESTED WITH PARENTS:
A—Excellent	Date: _____
B—Good	_____
C—Average	_____
D—Barely Passing	_____
F—Failing	_____

An "X" in one of the shaded squares indicates an area in which improvement is needed.
A check mark (√) in one of the shaded squares indicates satisfactory progress.

ATTENDANCE RECORD

Quarter	1	2	3	4
Days Present				
Days Absent				
Times Tardy				

REPORT PERIOD: 1 2 3 4

CONDUCT

HABITS AND ATTITUDES
- Meeting new situations
- Using self-control
- Showing consideration for others
- Accepting responsibilities
- Showing good sportsmanship
- Respecting school regulations
- Respecting property of others
- Following directions
- Using time wisely
- Working independently
- Evaluating own work
- Cooperating in group activities
- Participating thoughtfully in discussions
- Organizing materials
- Practicing good health habits
- Practicing traffic and safety rules
- Participating in physical activities
- Working with enthusiasm and interest

ART
- Working with a variety of materials
- Working creatively

MUSIC
- Participating in singing activities
- Participating in rhythm activities
- Working for skill in music reading

Instrumental
- Band instruments
- Orchestra instruments

REPORT PERIOD: 1 2 3 4

READING
- Reading with understanding
- Reading orally
- Using word recognition skills
- Reading for enjoyment

LANGUAGE
- Expressing ideas orally
- Expressing ideas in writing
- Using listening skills
- Using language skills in writing

SPELLING
- Learning spelling vocabulary
- Applying skills in written work

HANDWRITING (Cursive)
- Forming letters correctly
- Spacing letters and words correctly
- Writing neatly

ARITHMETIC
- Learning arithmetic facts
- Using fundamental processes correctly
- Understanding word problems

SOCIAL STUDIES
- Drawing conclusions based on facts
- Using suitable reference materials
- Interpreting charts, maps, globes, and graphs

SCIENCE
- Reading critically and drawing conclusions from facts and observations
- Participating in meaningful individual and group projects

LEVEL OF PERFORMANCE AND INSTRUCTION

	1st Quarter Grade Level	2nd Quarter Grade Level	3rd Quarter Grade Level	4th Quarter Grade Level
	Below | On | Above	Below | On | Above	Below | On | Above	Below | On | Above
Reading				
Language				
Spelling				
Arithmetic				

Fig. 20.8. Combination Comparative Marks and Checklist Reporting Form Used in Grades 4 through 7 of the Atlanta (Georgia) Public Schools.

evaluating and reporting pupil growth 415

indicate performance at his predicted output level.

The Checklist. Many teachers and school systems of more child-centered persuasions have changed the method of reporting pupil progress information to parents from the comparative letter marks to a checklist type of reporting. This change represents more than just changing the form of the report. It represents a changed philosophy, to wit: many contemporary teachers believe that the progress of pupils should be evaluated in terms of what they are capable of doing as individuals—not how they compare with other children. A checklist form for reporting pupil progress information that is in harmony with this philosophy can be seen in figure 20.9.

In studying figure 20.9, one can determine that the teacher marks expected pupil progress (not comparative progress) in one of three ways. First, the child *is making acceptable progress* in terms of what might be expected of him. Second, the child *needs improvement* in terms of his own expectancy. Third, the child *is making unsatisfactory progress* with respect to individual expectancy. Advocates of this technique claim that it overcomes the weaknesses of the comparative marks on report card method for reporting to parents alluded to in the prior section of this chapter.

An examination of figure 20.9, however, might raise some question about the practical utility of the checklist over comparative marking. In the important area of reading, the two reading skills of learning new words and understanding what is read are critical to success in school whereas the other two—reads good books and interesting oral reading style—may be desirable but largely irrelevant. Reading aloud in an interesting manner might be highly desirable for poetry, but not very germane to a science class. Furthermore, the three reporting standards of "making acceptable progress," "needs improvement," and is "making unsatisfactory progress" imply some comparative standard which is not reported to the parent. These observations are not designed to detract from the use of the checklist as a reporting system. They are designed to emphasize the limitations inherent in any reporting form, whatever it may be. When the number of items reported are increased, as on a checklist, it is possible that an increase in number of items reported increase overgeneralization on the part of the teacher from limited evidence.

Parent-Teacher Conference. For all intents and purposes, probably the best technique the teacher can use in reporting pupil progress information to parents is the parent-teacher conference. It is through this face-to-face interaction that the teacher can report factually to parents with less likelihood for misunderstanding of that which is reported.

There are a few commonly accepted guidelines which the teacher should keep in mind in conducting the parent-teacher conference. First, he should plan in advance the major points he wishes to cover in the conference. (The suggested parent-teacher conference reporting form shown in figure 20.10 may be used as a guide in this regard.) Second, he should conduct the conference on a professional basis, put the parents at ease by being friendly, and listening to them courteously when they speak. Third, he should avoid using professional jargon, if possible in reporting to parents, and whenever possible use synonyms they understand for technical terms. Fourth, he should speak

Name					Grade										
					\multicolumn{3}{c}{First 9 Weeks}	\multicolumn{3}{c}{Second 9 Weeks}	\multicolumn{3}{c}{Third 9 Weeks}	\multicolumn{3}{c}{Fourth 9 Weeks}
\multicolumn{5}{l}{ATTENDANCE RECORD}	Is making acceptable progress	Needs Improvement	Is making unsatisfactory progress	Is making acceptable progress	Needs Improvement	Is making unsatisfactory progress	Is making acceptable progress	Needs Improvement	Is making unsatisfactory progress	Is making acceptable progress	Needs Improvement	Is making unsatisfactory progress
GRADE PERIOD	1	2	3	4											
Days Present															
Days Absent															
Times Tardy															
PERSONAL GROWTH															
Takes pride in neat and accurate work															
Helps to keep room neat and clean															
Listens to and follows directions															
Works well alone															
Works well with others															
Is courteous															
Finishes work on time															
Makes good use of time															
Practices good conduct															
Practices safety															
Takes care of school property and materials															
Gives and receives criticism in a friendly way															
SOCIAL STUDIES															
Cooperates in activities															
Evaluates and organizes information															
Uses reference materials															
Shares ideas and information															
READING															
Reads and shows interest in good books															
Learns new words															
Understands what is read															
Reads aloud in an interesting manner															
ARITHMETIC															
Knows number facts															
Knows addition processes															
Knows subtraction processes															
Knows multiplication processes															

Fig. 20.9. Pupil Progress Reporting Checklist for the Intermediate Grades in the Port Arthur (Texas) Independent School District.

evaluating and reporting pupil growth

	First 9 Weeks			Second 9 Weeks			Third 9 Weeks			Fourth 9 Weeks		
Teacher _____ School Year _____	Is making acceptable progress	Needs Improvement	Is making unsatisfactory progress	Is making acceptable progress	Needs Improvement	Is making unsatisfactory progress	Is making acceptable progress	Needs Improvement	Is making unsatisfactory progress	Is making acceptable progress	Needs Improvement	Is making unsatisfactory progress
PROMOTION RECORD												
Grade _____												
Section _____												
Room _____												
Knows division processes												
Solves stated problems requiring reasoning												
Works accurately												
SPELLING												
Learns required list of words												
Spells correctly in all written work												
LANGUAGE												
Expresses ideas clearly												
Uses correct forms in speaking and writing												
WRITING												
Writes legibly												
Forms letters correctly												
ART												
Is learning to use materials												
Is learning to express own ideas												
MUSIC												
Responds to simple rhythms												
Participates in group singing												
Is learning music skills												
INSTRUMENTAL MUSIC												
HOMEMAKING AND SHOP												
Learns necessary facts												
Uses facts learned												
PHYSICAL EDUCATION												
Takes part in all activities												
Practices good sportsmanship												
Dresses neatly for gym work												
Takes part in swimming activities												

Fig. 20.9. (Cont'd)

positively and objectively and avoid negative statements which reflect unfavorably upon the parents' child. Finally, he should conclude the conference on a positive note and assure the parents that they can mutually arrange subsequent conferences when necessary.

The parent-teacher conference reporting form suggested in figure 20.10, once completed, outlines the child's general potential for learning, his academic achievement record, his performance profile by subject area in terms of expectancy and his study habits and attitudes. Also, it provides a space for the teacher to record his observations about the pupil's overall behavior, and a space for recording a course of action to improve the child's educational program, which the parents and teacher can plan.

As previously indicated, schools normally report pupil progress by the periodic issuance of letter marks on report cards or by issuance of a checklist. Utilization of the parent-teacher conference, coupled with one of these methods, would likely improve the reporting of pupil progress information to parents.

Telephone Report. The teacher can use the telephone to report pupil progress information to parents, but for a number of reasons it should be used sparingly for this purpose. Two of the more important reasons are the following. First, examples of the child's work cannot be visually examined by the parent in a telephone conversation. Secondly, parents may misinterpret the nature of the conversation which could most likely be clarified in a face-to-face parent-teacher conference.

Letters to Parents. Teachers in the elementary school occasionally use a personal letter to report pupil progress information to parents. Care should be exercised to see that it is written in an objective manner using language that communicates effectively to parents. Also, derogatory statements about the child should be scrupulously avoided in writing the letter. If a problem involves the overt behavior of the child, it is better to deal with it in a parent-teacher conference than through the medium of the letter.

An Appraisal of Evaluating and Reporting Pupil Growth

There has been a tendency in recent years to extend the scope of pupil evaluation. The gross measure of pupil deportment is frequently broken down into a number of behavioral traits, concern is expressed for social adjustment, and clinical types of evaluation have supplemented the traditional types of marks assigned on the basis of pupil test performance.

There is little evidence to suggest however, that there is any relationship in improvement of teacher instruction or pupil performance to increased emphasis on evaluation. In fact, this emphasis is somewhat contradictory to elementary teacher training. Most elementary teachers are certificated at the baccalaureate level. Few training programs for initial certification include systematic training in test construction and evaluation. Most frequently teachers in training read about evaluation in general courses or in educational psychology, just as you are reading in this text.

It is likely that you will be expected to participate in a type of evaluation system for which your formal training has not prepared you. You should seek out as much

evaluating and reporting pupil growth 419

Pupil _____ School _____ Grade _____ Date _____

GENERAL ACADEMIC APTITUDE POTENTIAL	
High	Pupil is capable of mastering academic school subjects readily
Average	Pupil is capable of accomplishing grade level work with appropriate dedication to his studies
Low	Pupil may encounter learning difficulties in some subjects
Test Dates:	

ACADEMIC ACHIEVEMENT RECORD

Subject Area \ Grade	1st	2nd	3rd	4th	5th	6th	7th or Above
Reading Vocabulary							
Reading Comprehension							
Arithmetic Reasoning							
Arithmetic Fundamentals							
Language Mechanics							
Spelling							
Test Dates:							

CLASSWORK PERFORMANCE PROFILE

Subject	Below Grade Level	At Grade Level	Above Grade Level	Is overall achievement consistent with the pupil's aptitude potential?	
				Yes	No
Reading					
Arithmetic					
Language					
Spelling					
Writing					
Social Studies					
Science					

PUPIL STUDY HABITS AND ATTITUDES

Criteria	Occasionally	Generally	Always
Assignments completed on time			
Takes pride in neat and accurate work			
Listens and follows directions well			
Works and plays well with others			
Accepts responsibility for own actions			
Uses leisure time wisely			
Shows initiative			
Demonstrates resourcefulness			

TYPES OF PUPIL DATA REVIEWED

Homework assignments
Classroom assignments
Teacher-made test results
Previous school marks
Previous achievement test results

Teacher observation comments:

Parent-teacher proposed plan of action:

Parent's Signature _____   Teacher's Signature _____

Fig. 20.10. Teacher-Parent Conference Reporting Forms. From Oscar T. Jarvis, "Why Not Report All Pupil Progress Facts to Parents?" **Georgia Education Journal** 57, no. 2 (October 1963): 17.

help as you can from whatever evaluation instruction and in-service assistance your school system affords. The main thing to remember is that whatever the nature of the evaluation system, you should plan your procedures to collect data to provide for the judgments that you will finally make, whether the reporting form is a traditional report card, checklist, parent interview, or some other procedure.

This chapter has not looked at evaluation of pupil progress as a means of evaluating a school system's effectiveness. The traditional approach to evaluation is that schools and teachers report on the performance of pupils to parents. In this tradition, it is the pupil that made an "F" or the pupil that "Needs to Improve."

This is a very one-sided approach to evaluation, however. Every measure of pupil growth is concurrently a measure of teacher and school effectiveness. The school takes the credit for teaching children successfully, but frequently blames the pupil, parent or the community for its failures. The parents and the community might just as well take the credit for the successes, since the child learned the critical skills of language use and group interaction before he ever entered school. Grades and standardized scores are so seldom used to improve instruction because teachers and schools frequently are unwilling to face up to the fact that pupil performance is a measure of teacher and school effectiveness. As noted in the chapter on objectives, the schools rush in with grandiose social objectives and yet are not willing in most cases to accept the responsibility for the fact that pupil failures in reading are quite possibly school and teacher failures in reading.

Your report to parents on the progress of children is also a report on how well you are doing as a teacher. Admittedly, there are many children that you will not be able to teach effectively. In some cases you may not be able to find the appropriate method or means of motivation. Even the most skilled surgeon loses some of his patients, and a teacher need not feel guilty because he is not always able to teach all of his pupils effectively. But evaluation is a two-edged sword—one for the pupil, the other for teacher. We could, of course, also say that it is an evaluation of the total society and all that has gone before a teacher has a particular pupil in class. If this route is taken, however, the teacher is in effect putting the entire onus back on the pupil. As the chapter on disadvantaged learners indicates, the problem cannot be successfully attacked until the schools accept their share of responsibility. Lip-service usually is given to the question of taking pupils where they are, but when the going gets tough—and it often does—the school reaction has been to place the responsibility for not learning on some low "potential" or "ability" of the pupil. A chapter on the evaluation of pupil progress is a convenient place to remind both new and old teachers that evaluation of pupil progress is also an evaluation of school-teacher effectiveness.

The literature on testing all too often gives the impression that standardized tests are superior to teacher-made tests for evaluating pupil performance. Recently, there has been a more critical evaluation of standardized tests, especially by the Center for the Study of Evaluation, University of California, Los Angeles. Skager has recently condemned the widespread use of standardized tests for evaluation and accountability studies on the grounds that they are virtually useless for program evaluation and educational accountability. He also contends that they are ineffective tools for management of instruction within the classroom.[21] Despite the technical defects of many teacher-made tests, such tests are superior to standardized tests in content validity, provided they are based on the objectives of instruction. While most teachers need to practice better test construction, the use of standardized tests is no substitute for carefully prepared teacher-made tests.

Selected References

AHMANN, J. STANLEY, *Testing Student Achievements and Aptitudes*. New York: Center for Applied Research in Education, Inc., 1962.

BURROS, OSCAR K., ed. *The Sixth Mental Measurements Yearbook*. Highland Park, N.J.: Gryphon Press, 1965.

CHADWICK, RUTH E., et al. "The Report Card in a Nongraded School," *National Elementary Principal* 45 no. 6 (May 1966): 22-28.

CHANSKY, NORMAN M. "Preferred Items on Pupils' Report Cards," *Education* 86, no. 3 (November 1965): 169-73.

DUROST, WALTER., and PRESCOTT, GEORGE A. *Essentials of Measurement for Teachers*. New York: Harcourt, Brace and World, Inc., 1962.

GLASSER, WILLIAM. *Schools Without Failure*. New York: Harper & Row, Publishers, 1969.

HATCH, RAYMOND N., and COSTAR, JAMES W. *Guidance Services in the Elementary School*. Dubuque, Iowa: Wm. C. Brown Company Publishers, 1961.

HOLT, JOHN. *How Children Fail*. New York: Pitman Publishing Corporation, 1964.

HORROCKS, JOHN E., and SCHOONOVER, THELMA I. *Measurement for Teachers*. Columbus, Ohio: Charles E. Merrill Publishing Company, 1968.

"How to Design a Report Card Parents Can Understand," *School Management* 8, no. 5 (May 1964): 72-74.

KINGSTON, ALBERT J., and WALSH, JAMES A. "Research on Reporting Systems," *National Elementary Principal* 45, no. 6 (May 1966): 36-40.

MELBY, ERNEST O. "It's Time for Schools to Abolish the Marking System," *The Nation's Schools* 77, no. 5 (May 1966): 104.

ROSENTHAL, ROBERT, and JACOBSON, LENORE. *Pygmalion in the Classroom*. New York: Holt, Rinehart and Winston, Inc., 1968.

ROTHNEY, JOHN W. M. "Improving Reports to Parents," *National Elementary Principal* 45, no. 6 (May 1966): 51-53.

---

21. Rodney Skager, "The System for Objectives-Based Evaluation—Reading," *Evaluation Comment* (Center for the Study of Evaluation), 3, no. 1 (September 1971): 6.

classroom management and teaching

21

The dichotomy in American education between administration and teaching frequently obscures the fact that the successful teacher must first be a successful administrator. Admittedly, teaching is his most important task. But the amount of time he has to teach often depends upon his success as a manager: efficiency of classroom routine, appropriateness of discipline, availability of supplies, empathy as a leader, and suitability of tasks. These management responsibilities are the province of the individual teacher, and often the difference in the performance of two adjacent classes has nothing to do with subject matter knowledge or level of teacher certification; the difference is in the management skills of the teacher.

The novice teacher usually underestimates the importance of classroom management. The concept of management evokes images of many "bad" associations: an authoritarian personality, neglect of pupil interests, lack of pupil freedom, repressive social control, rigid learning tasks. But even experienced teachers report their priority problems relate more to classroom management than to teaching. This results from the fact that a teacher's personal sense of job happiness and security is threatened by the failure to achieve a classroom climate which facilitates teaching.

As a result of the emphasis on democratic classroom organization, many teachers fail to develop a philosophical rationale for effective classroom management. The first section of this chapter uses the sociological constructions of group socialization and integration to underscore the importance of social control. Remaining sections address themselves to the practical questions of classroom management, such as physical environment, routines, discipline, and teaching strategies. Good teaching strategies have more than merely a learning end; they are also a means of social control.

Group Integration and Social Control

The first prerequisite of good management is for the teacher to recognize that he is responsible for teaching a section of children. Notwithstanding the emphasis in college pedagogy on clinical and individual approaches to teaching, the reality of teaching has little to do with the image of Mark Hopkins and a boy seated on a hollow log. Children in school, irrespective of the method of organization (see chapter 19), are assigned for instruction to a section or class. A class is simply the school name for a section of children established for instructional purposes. The leader of the class is an adult, who has some particular credentials. The roles of the members of the class (pupils) and that of the adult (teacher) are culturally ascribed. The management of the classroom for teaching is based on the differential ascribed roles assigned to teacher and pupils, and reflect different expectations based on age, ability, and authority.

The more students have an opportunity to learn and exercise their roles, the more they become socialized. But even the beginning student is not totally at a loss in school. He has already had previous experience with adult figures, which are automatically authority figures in the process of enculturation. Some of the behavioral expectancies a child brings with him to school include: being directed (have tasks prescribed), being corrected ("No" is one of the most positive words of socialization, notwithstanding its negative form); being encouraged (to try new tasks); being assisted (with difficult tasks); being approved (for attempts as well as successes); following rules; and being reprimanded. Depending upon the extent to which a child has learned to trust and distrust adults, based on his prior experiences, the child may be cooperative, apathetic, or hostile to the surrogate adult authority represented by the teacher. Irrespective of his initial reactions, the fact remains that the child is already familiar with the general direction of authority socialization in a group before he enters school.

In establishing social control for the class, the teacher is therefore not imposing a pattern alien to the child or the culture. Because of ethnic and class differences in child rearing practices, however, children will have had different experiences with social control. Some writers hypothesize that relatively free patterns of early childhood education work well with middle-class children because they are subject to rigid home control.[1] In contrast, the independent-oriented child rearing of low class groups makes such children less socialized for class behavior. These children cannot cope with the freedom, which is emphasized by their lack of school know-how. More rigid control may therefore be required with such groups of children as a result of the authority patterns prevailing in the parent culture.[2]

Children bring to any class a predisposition favorable to social control. Class social control is therefore an extension of previous social control. A class is a collection of individuals, however, to which each individual has been more or less arbitrarily assigned. Where children from the same neighborhood attend a school, it is possible to find a few friends or acquaintances in any class. But American neighborhoods today rarely lack the intimacy of association which can transform a class of pupils into an automatically functioning cohesive group.

A class of students is an association of individuals for a common purpose, bound together primarily from the interstimulation

1. Carl Bereiter and Siegfried Engelmann, *Teaching Disadvantaged Children in the Preschool* (Englewood Cliffs, N. J.: Prentice-Hall, Inc., 1966), p. 17.
2. Ruth Landes, *Culture in American Education* (New York: John Wiley and Sons, Inc., 1965), p. 113. Independent-oriented with respect to physical activity and aggression, but, in reality, dependent-oriented in terms of school tasks, because of lack of previous learning experience.

that comes from communication. The informal play groups of children are generally small, and provide little experience for communication within the larger school class. Pupils therefore look naturally to the teacher as the leader to bring about class cohesiveness, the feeling of working together for a common purpose. Another term for cohesiveness is group integration. A class which is highly integrated is one in which the members have close ties with one another. In American education, the degree of class integration decreases from elementary school to college, and practically disappears in graduate work. In the lower grades of public school the high degree of interaction often makes elementary classes the most integrated units the students will ever experience, and one of the few places that all children have an opportunity to learn cooperative behavior outside the family structure.

As the leader, the teacher may initiate many acts which foster or retard group integration. When a teacher asks children to assist in the development of classroom procedures and rules, the teacher is involving the pupils in normative integration. Normative integration refers to group behavior which comes from expectancies of how individuals are supposed to behave. It is true that children have more difficulty in observing rules than in making them. But they understand the importance of having rules for players, and that it is difficult to play a game without rules. When a teacher and the class agree on the classroom norms, a consensus is reached which will serve as a useful reference point for subsequently controlling classroom behavior. The norm of the class rather than the teacher is the source of control.

Another type of integration results from a division of labor. There are many types of classroom chores which children can share, depending on their ability: taking absences, collecting lunch money, distributing supplies, collecting papers, adjusting the windows, fixing the bulletin board, erasing the chalkboard, to name a few. Rotation of class housekeeping helps pupils develop a sense of personal achievement and responsibility. But from the standpoint of the class, the important point is that such a division of labor develops *interdependence*. Members of the class do not merely compete for individual recognition; they learn to depend on each other and they learn to help each other.

While division of labor is a *differentiated integration,* a third type of integration is *assimilative* integration. Both boys and girls like to do many of the same class chores or participate in the same kinds of activities, notwithstanding the convention of sex antagonism. The teacher can arrange to see that all children have an opportunity to participate in many different class activities. Where children from different minority groups and social classes are represented the teacher can also see that they are included in the integrating experiences. Some teachers, in a misguided application of children's democracy, permit children to assume the initiative in allocating class jobs. If care is not exercised, this assignment may result in the development of cliques from which certain children are deliberately excluded. In such cases, conflict rather than cooperation frequently comes to characterize the atmosphere of the classroom, inhibits learning, and sometimes leads to disruptive behavior.

One object of good classroom management is to facilitate learning; another is to encourage good behavior; and a third is to contribute to the total development of the child. An approach to classroom management from the perspective of group integration and social control encompasses all three objectives.

Physical Environment

The teacher and pupils that make up a class are allotted a definite space within the school to carry on their activities—the classroom. Notwithstanding various attempts to change the shape and size of the classroom, it is usually rectangular in size and rarely large enough to house the numerous activities which are recommended for the self-contained classroom. Furniture, equipment, and storage facilities are more likely to consist of the bare essentials—chalkboard, tackboard, pupil desks or table and chairs, teacher desk, open shelves, coat hooks, and perhaps a storage cabinet and filing drawers. Over a period of time, the departmentalized classroom offers the opportunity to procure the needed specialized equipment for instruction. But a teacher enters an on-going institution in which decisions for self-contained, team teaching, or departmentalized classrooms normally have already been made. And even as an experienced teacher with tenure, his voice in school decisions will be merely one of many. Seldom will he be able, if ever, to create the ideal physical environment.

Involvement of Children in Creation of the Environment. A teacher inevitably takes a proprietary interest in "his" room. With the class, a more desirable attitude is that it is "our" room. Subtle but important attitudinal shifts accompany this emphasis. As long as the teacher thinks of it as his particular environment, he is likely to assume all initiative with the room. The result is a tremendous loss of pupil-power. Pupils are seldom able to cut out, mount, and arrange pictures on a bulletin board as expertly as the teacher. But what is the important product—to have a pretty bulletin board or to have children gain in experience? Where the teacher requires a partciular teaching aid—whether it is a picture, a cartoon, a drawing or some other representation—there is always justification for discriminating teacher selection in terms of the learning objectives. But even here, pupils can be taught to discriminate. For example, one social studies class was studying "comparative rural landscapes."[3] The class organized itself into committees, each taking a country to report. Japan was the subject of the first committee reporting. The first pictorial report showed many different pictures of Japan, but not one showed a Japanese rural landscape. Pupil evaluation under teacher guidance helped to clarify the concept of landscape, and the pupils were able to successfully complete the project. The teacher could have prepared the bulletin board initially from her visual file (see chapter 9), but the objective was the total learning outcome, not merely the mounted pictures.

Teachers, as well as pupils, have different personalities, and there is no one best classroom environment. Some teachers find the environment of an activity-oriented classroom cluttered and confusing. Under such circumstances, it is difficult for them to work and prefer what appears to be a more

---

3. John E. Steinbrink, *Comparative Rural Landscapes: A Conceptual Model* (Athens, Ga.: Geography Curriculum Project, University of Georgia, 1970).

sterile environment. The appearance of physical sterility, however, should never be interpreted as intellectual sterility. It is not the color of the walls, the type of floor, or the arrangement of the furniture that is the most important environment for learning; it is the environment of language. Things in the classroom become meaningful and significant primarily through language, and things are useful in teaching because they make more concrete the association and discrimination of labels.

But if a teacher wants a rich classroom environment, there are many things he can do to obtain them even though necessary materials are not provided by the school. If the teacher were in need of a rocking chair for the reading corner, he could ask if anyone has a discarded one at home they could donate. Covering and refinishing the chair would, moreover, provide a useful manual activity. Or suppose the class needed a rug for a story or game circle. The children could make a hooked rug on a burlap backing from strips of cleaned clothing. The rug would be eminently durable, and many people could be involved in working on it. These are but two examples of how the classroom teacher could involve the children in creating an effective classroom environment in which they exercise the initiative in attending to their equipment needs.

In this world in which teachers are bombarded with teaching aids hawked by commercial houses, they sometimes forget that the physical environment for learning is the world in which children live. Most children are happy to bring the world into the classroom. Even the most improvished area is not devoid of things that children can bring to school and use in learning. But a teacher must always remember that the amount of housekeeping in a room increases in proportion to the things in a room.

Types of Classroom Environments. Applying the psychological principles of cue specificity and stimulus reduction, it is probable that children need different types of learning environments. One learning environment eliminates all distracting visual cues. It is a room with bare walls and is windowless. Visual and auditory attention is focused on the specific learning task, and no extraneous stimulus is permitted to intrude. This type of *receptive learning* environment would attempt to capture, for intensive moments of symbolic learning, the entire intellectual and sensory attention of the child.

The *personal interaction environment,* on the other hand, is one that fosters pupil discussion and interaction. This type of environment, essentially, predominates in most elementary schools, but generally with some compromise because of the need for receptive verbal learning. Other types of environments appropriate to specific types of learning are the *aesthetic productive* (specialized according to art, music, or dance forms); the *manipulative* (requiring coordination of hands and eyes as in woodworking, metal work, machinery repair, and other mechanical operations); and the *physical-recreative,* requiring planned indoor as well as outdoor areas. Each of these specialized areas carries with it a particular sign, functionally related to the desired behavior.

The enriched environment of the classroom characteristically contains contradictory signs, and thus in itself contains suggestions for behavior which increases the need for teacher-voice control. Children from lower income families typically come from spatially limited and behaviorally undifferentiated environments, which are alleged to have adverse reactions on the background for schooling. At the same time, most of the recommendations for classroom environments fall into the "enrichment" category.[4] One attempt to provide differentiated learning enviroments, according to the learning task, is the separation of receptive verbal learning activities in small rooms for small group instruction while retaining a large room for personal interaction activities.[5]

Arrangement of Furniture. Much has been written about the advantages of movable furniture in the classroom. Suffice it to say that the type of furniture is usually the result of a decision by the business manager on the basis of bids received in accordance with specifications. As with the room, the teacher has little say about the furniture in it, and today it is invariably of the movable type.

Movable furniture can be arranged in straight rows, just as fixed desks usually are. It can also be arranged in diverse patterns that defy pupil sight, increase hearing difficulties, and make classroom transit hazardous. The principle involved in the use of movable furniture, often overlooked, is not the arbitrary assignment of the furniture to fixed patterns, but the adjustment of the arrangement pattern to fit in with the instructional activities of the class. There are times when the teacher will be working with the class as a whole and the arrangement of furniture should facilitate seeing, hearing, and responding by the total class. The straight row arrangement is often the most desirable for total class work. A paired straight row arrangement, suggested by Sylvester, adapts itself readily to an arrangement for open class discussion and to small group interaction. This arrangement is perhaps best suited to the intermediate grades (see figure 21.1).

In the primary grades, it is often desirable to have the chairs or tables for instructional groups prearranged, with pupils moving to the furniture, rather than moving the furniture. The more time spent in moving furniture, the less time the teacher will have to teach. Not only is there wasted time moving furniture, but in settling down into the learning act after the furniture is moved.

Even in self-contained classrooms, children spend a great deal of time going in and out of the room to lunch, play, recess, and to the rest room. The pattern of traffic flow should be functional, rather than ingenious.

No arrangement of room furniture is ideal. Whatever arrangement is used, it should help pupils. When pupils cannot see the teacher's face when he is using language for group instruction, the arrangement of the furniture is not instructionally functional.

Planning the Daily Routine

The classroom routine does not encompass merely one day, but some 180 days annually, and the last day of school is not like the first. Any routines, therefore, must not only start by accommodating the schedule of the school, but be sufficiently flexible to accommodate the inevitable adjustments which come from day to day.

Non-Teaching Routines. Pupils spend much of their time at school in school living, not in book learning. This is, in part, due to the very nature of class instruction. From the

---

4. Dorothy G. Petersen, *The Elementary School Teacher* (New York: Appleton-Century-Crofts, 1964), pp. 197-260.

5. Bereiter and Engelmann, *Teaching Disadvantaged Children,* p. 71.

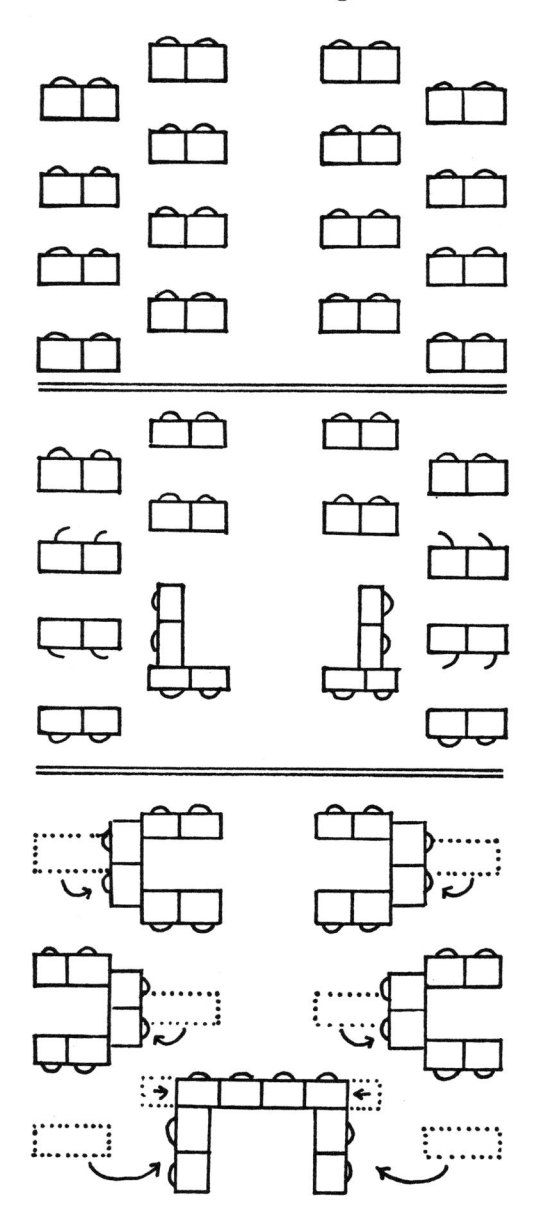

Fig. 21.1. Flexible Classroom Arrangement for Teacher Presentation, Group Discussion by Class, and Small Group Work. From Robert Sylwester, **Common Sense in Classroom Relations** (West Nyack, N.Y.: Parker Publishing Company, Inc., © 1966), pp. 62-64. Reprinted with permission.

outset, the teacher must accept the fact that teaching carries with it certain functions involving group living in a school. Effective non-teaching routines require considerations of such matters as checking absences, reporting absences to the principal's office, taking up lunch or milk money, giving out supplies and books, sharpening pencils, and collecting papers.

Most of these routines involve logistic problems of supply and traffic control. Routines which are effective should be made habitual. There is no point in the children and the class wasting a good portion of the day deciding, in the name of democracy, what to do and when to do it. Knowing what to do not only contributes to more efficient use of time, but it also contributes to a sense of security. Since there is always some uncertainty growing out of encounters with new subject matter, there is an advantage in having stability in nonteaching routines.

Many of these routines can be established in conjunction with pupil decision-making. For example, it can be agreed that the pencil sharpener will be used at specified times within the school day. This reduces the amount of noise and confusion that accompanies pencil sharpening, and encourages pupils to have an extra pencil or two sharpened and ready for use (see "normative integration"). Class committees can be organized, with teachers making adjustments which help group growth (see "assimilative integration"). Having a procedure for taking up papers, whether passing forward or a pupil collecting them, reduces the amount of time. Even the use of a single color for such things as pencils and notebooks is a time saver, because it eliminates the amount of pupil hesitation involved in choice. Where choice is unrelated to level of quality or performance, choice may be regarded as an idiosyncratic rather than significant variable. Practical suggestions for establishing routines are offered in many books on teaching, specifically those which deal with classroom procedures. Helpful suggestions are particularly found in Sylwester[6] and in McDonald and Nelson.[7]

Teachers should periodically review nonteaching routines. A stop watch can be used to see how long it takes to accomplish certain routines. Children frequently can help save much classroom time when improvement is stated in measureable terms against their own performance. A teacher needs to be conscious of time for the simple reason that this is one of the most important variables in learning. Many teachers are able to have time for many additional learning activities as a result of reducing time required in nonteaching activities.

The Teaching Schedule. There are two polar approaches to planning for teaching. One emphasizes subject matter; the other is expressed in terms of the interests and needs of the child. While new emphasis on subject matter occurred in the last decade, this emphasis was primarily associated with curriculum projects.[8]

A teaching schedule based upon subject matter premises is generally divided into definite blocks of time. The teacher must plan to achieve his instructional objectives within each block of time. The time allocation, therefore, becomes a constraint within which the teacher must plan and teach, and careful attention must be given to the instructional objectives and to pacing. The advantage of a closed time schedule lies in the stimulus to both teacher and pupil to attain predetermined instructional objectives by making more efficent use of time for instruction. Even in programmed instruction, the use of timed pacing contributes to more learning than when children make their own speed adjustments.[9]

Another advantage in the closed time schedule is that subject matter coverage is not left to chance, and judgments of pupil learning may not only be made in terms of some general curriculum suggestions but also in time spent in learning. Whenever a school utilizes specialized teachers for departmentalized teaching, it is mandatory that some blocks of time be rigidly scheduled. However, even where there is no departmentalized teaching, it is thought that the self-contained classroom teacher who follows a subject matter emphasis will be assisted in his work by closed time scheduling. Closed time scheduling in subjects is one way to assure that time is included for activities of a less verbal nature.

The open schedule, on the other hand, does not prescribe a set amount of time to be utilized at a given hour. Some general suggestions are made, such as 50 percent of the time to reading and the language arts in the primary grades,[10] but the individual teacher may vary the amount of time per day and the types of experiences. Certainly,

6. Robert Sylwester, *Common Sense in Classroom Relations* (West Nyack, N.Y.: Parker Publishing Company, Inc., 1966), pp. 62-64.
7. Blanche McDonald and Leslie Nelson, *Successful Classroom Control* (Dubuque, Iowa: Wm. C. Brown Company Publishers, 1955).
8. G. W. Bassett, *Innovation in Primary Education* (London: John Wiley and Sons, Ltd., 1970), p. 59.
9. W. R. Dunn and C. Holroyd, eds., *Aspects of Educational Technology,* vol. 2, Conference on Programmed Learning and Educational Technology, University of Glasgow, 1968 (London: Methuen & Co. Ltd., 1969), p. 251.
10. Petersen, *Elementary School Teacher,* pp. 266-67.

older schedules, which included every subject every day and had as many as twelve different areas,[11] could not provide any adequate time for study in depth or to help individual students. Closed schedules of the last three decades, however, have provided larger time blocks, frequently scheduling no more than five different areas a day.

The open schedule is based largely on the premise that teaching is built on teacher determination of interests and needs of children, rather than on subject matter attainment. To this older rationale, which undergirds much of the progressive movement, is the point of view that it is not the *product* of learning, but the *process* of learning, which is most important. This view dominates much of the current teaching emphasis in American education on inquiry and discovery, and serves as a rationale for the upward extension of infant school methods into the British junior school.[12]

From a comparative standpoint, however, one might note that the new British methods were anticipated by the progressive movement in American education. The first principle of the activity school was the self-learning of the child through pursuing his own interests, utilizing large blocks of time,[13] a principle which such early educators as Rousseau, Pestallozzi, and Froebel had enthusiastically endorsed. Neither is the concept of the "integrated day" a new one.

In the newer nongraded programs in America, it should be pointed out that time for mastery varies as a general rule. But quality of work does not.

In planning his schedule, the teacher must remember that there is no evidence, as measured by pupil learning, to substantiate or refute claims of advantages for either open or closed scheduling. Previous decisions made by the school system or the school may actually commit the teacher to one or the other, with little or no choice on his part. But varying with the circumstances, it is nevertheless possible for the teacher to plan a schedule which is most compatible with his image of himslef as a teacher. It is possible for a teacher to feel very comfortable with a schedule, and still be an inefficient teacher. Teacher choice is no guarantee of efficiency. However, the assumption is made that where teachers are personally committed to a particular teaching style as reflected in the schedule, the foundation is laid for more effective teaching as measured by pupil performance. This performance is not restricted to cognitive performance, but includes a variety of group living and personal skills which are now frequently included on reports to parents of pupil growth and achievement (see chapter 20). A teacher who prefers to follow an open time schedule should nevertheless remember that *parents* are still very much concerned with the *product* of education. It is perhaps a minority of parents who will accept the view that attitudes, ideals, and enthusiasms gained in school are more important than knowledge or the cognitive processes.

Establishing an Image. Irrespective of particular philosophies or approaches, there is general consensus that the teacher, if he is to achieve the role of leader, has a limited

---

11. Charles Myron Reinoehl and Fred Caleton Ayer, *Classroom Administration and Pupil Adjustment* (New York: D. Appleton Century Company, 1940), p. 83.

12. Vincent R. Rogers, ed. *Teaching in the British Primary School* (New York: Macmillan Company, 1970), pp. 16-17.

13. Gustav G. Schoenchen, *The Activity School* (New York: Longmans, Green and Company, 1940).

time in which to develop his right to exercise leadership. The mere fact of being an adult, of course, establishes the teacher's authority. But to exercise *moral leadership*, the teacher must demonstrate his ability and performance as a teacher working with the class. Moral leadership differs from authoritative leadership, and is perhaps a crucial factor in teaching. Moral leadership may be thought of as the empathy which a leader achieves as a result of his behavioral competences.

Students approve of teachers who are well organized, who know where they want the class to go, and who are successful in communicating a sense of direction and purpose to the class. The time to develop a purposive image begins on the first day of class, and includes two basic ingredients. The pupils must feel that their time is being used wisely, and that the teacher is helpful.

The week of preschool planning provides an opportunity for the teacher to study pupils records, make necessary classroom preparations, arrange supplies, and plan the first sequence of activities. The first day can be made to count in many ways, even if the books have not arrived and the school appears in chaos.

One of the first things is for pupil and teacher to learn the members of the class. In this day of tape recorders, a simulated "Today Show" featuring the new celebrities of the class can begin the year with a flair. A quick pace of self-introduction and get acquainted pointers helps break the ice. A number of name games can be played, so that by the end of the day the class does not consist of just another list of names, but names related to and descriptive of live boys and girls.

Preliminary committees can be pupil-selected on such matters as fire and safety, school policies, classroom housekeeping, and class rules. This gives the pupils a chance to interact, and the teacher to observe what pupils take the initiative and to whom the pupils defer as leaders. Often these patterns emerge the first week of school.

Quick oral review quizzes can be given in selected subjects, such as mathematics and spelling. Students can write short essays, which give the teacher concrete data on spelling, writing, syntax, and vocabulary. On the first day it is better to overplan rather than to underplan, and have alternate activities in mind if some do not go well. From a behavioral standpoint, the way to teach the students about yourself as a teacher is not to talk about the way you propose to teach, but to engage in the actual teaching behavior you will demonstrate throughout the school year.

Business-like planning on the first day does not imply rigidity. A teacher may wish to establish the fact that pupils are responsible for their own paper and pencils. On the first day have extra paper and pencils to supply the forgetful; there is time for making the point later when standards are being set. A business-like pace, perhaps somewhat more structured than would be normal, should be carried over into the first week.

By this time the teacher has had a chance to make his point: controlled behavior to achieve learning but there are times for fun and play. After this work-orientation has been established, there can be relaxation when desirable. Most experienced teachers advocate being strict at first, and then easing up, rather than starting out very leniently then trying to tighten up. Often nothing seems to fall in place, because the leadership of the class was assumed by others. And to recapture lost leadership is more difficult than to assert it initially.

The initial exertion of leadership, however, does not imply a dour countenance, a harsh voice, or a brusque manner. Even if the teacher is somewhat unsure of himself, he can try to smile, speak firmly but pleasantly, and strive to project an image of friendly helpfulness. And he can indicate that he has a sense of humor. But the humor and friendliness, if it is to be effective, is not that of a pal. Children do not expect teachers to be familiar, and a certain amount of reserve—the reserve of an interested and friendly adult—is appropriate for teacher-pupil relations.

Pupils are also observant of the way teachers dress and look. While dress need not be dowdy and old-fashioned, neither should it be the extreme in style. A moderation in dress as well as behavior is appreciated by children.

On the first days of school, teachers are constantly sizing up the children in the class. It is a two-way street. Pupils are also making judgments of the teacher, judgments which influence the whole pattern of behavior for the remainder of the year.

Behavior and Discipline

Discipline in a general sense refers to the organization and procedures a system uses to obtain its objectives. In school, however, discipline refers to the maintenance of pupil behavior. The importance of discipline cannot be underestimated. It is prerequisite to two types of success: pupil success in learning, and teacher success in teaching. Teachers unsuccessful with discipline either retreat from teaching or become stern and unsmiling class disciplinarians. The latter often create a situation in which repressive class control merely stimulates aggressive pupil behavior, with unfortunate consequences for school morale and personality development for teacher no less than pupil.

Ideally, the teacher as group leader should achieve such a high degree of class integration that task deviations and disruptive behavior are nonexistent. This happy state, highly desired by all teachers, overlooks two important considerations. The first is that a class never becomes a monolithic entity; it is always made up of individuals, even when they share a common purpose. Eventually, the very process of living and working together creates tensions which manifest themselves as behavior problems. Furthermore, elementary children, even under the best circumstances, are only partially socialized. Verbal rationalization as an alternative to overt behavior is only partially developed. The rub of living together in an established routine and a prescribed class occasionally becomes too much.

Behavioral accommodation by withdrawal is not available to the child in school. In neighborhood groups, the disgruntled or unhappy child has the option of leaving the group. When he becomes angry, frustrated, tired, or resentful, he can quit. When he becomes bored with a play task, he can change it. Thus Todd does not have to play with Bill and Al when he thinks they are unfair. He can play with Don. And when he gets tired of Don's hotwheels, he can ride his bike with Jay.

School for the child, however, is more like the world of adult work. School participation is based on the principle of constraint, no matter how many school adjustments are made to child needs. The school child is expected to attend regularly, unless he is really sick, whether he is out of sorts mentally or physically. Sleepy or bored, he must pretend to be interested and attentive. Even at home he is never so confined with his parents as he is with his teachers. And he can't withdraw for a moment's respite for self-adjustment. Manifestations of behavioral difficulties are rarely hostile acts directed toward the teacher, but a function of the group situation and the maturity of the learner. While it is easier said than done, the teacher must strive to exercise behavioral control from the standpoint of task performance and group integration, not from the perspective of personal authority challenge. The latter approach tends to become highly emotional and raise barriers between teacher and child which interfere with teaching effectiveness.

Setting of Norms. Every school district and school has established policies and procedures. These should be communicated to pupils in a matter-of-fact, straightforward way, without apology. In cases where the rules appear unreasonable or arbitrary to pupils, a teacher can help them explore alternatives and attempt to understand the reason for certain regulations. The teacher will also have certain rules he wishes to have observed. As noted previously under normative integration, children should be involved in some norm making—we don't run in the hall, we don't talk in a loud voice, we always walk to the right, we take turns, for example. Children frequently become so enthusiastic with norm making that the teacher has to firmly intervene and emphasize that most of the time good manners and the observance of the golden rule will be sufficient guide posts for class behavior. A complicated norm system quickly loses efficacy because of the numerous violations and exceptions which it encourages.

Even when children have shared in norm making, the teacher should anticipate that it will not be unusual for pupils to try to find methods to circumvent them. Congressmen demonstrate every year that participation in rule making is no guarantee of observance. But having shared in setting class standards, pupils are more likely to see observance of the rule as a part of social control rather than the arbitrary dictates of a teacher.

Some teachers find it useful to develop a room standards chart. This chart can be referred to periodically when group behavior deviates from the standards. It should not be used, above all, as a subtle way of nagging at individual pupils. In the intermediate school, a draft of standards for the class may be entrusted to a committee for subsequent class discussion, amendment, and ratification.[14]

Types of Behavior Adjustments. Behavior problems range from merely annoying and distracting behavior to deviant behavior that often requires clinical treatment. And some behavior problems are never solved, but merely repressed.

One of the most common types of behavior problems is inattentiveness and boredom—whispering, passing of notes, playing with small objects, and sheer woolgathering. Inattention in itself is fairly innocuous but is often the beginning of more serious problems. The inattentive pupil seldom is inattentive alone; he involves others and the teacher loses class control. Without pupil attention there can be no pupil learning.

14. An example of a brief list of "room standards" is given in McDonald and Nelson, *Successful Classroom Control,* p. 7.

A repeatedly listless and inattentive class should stimulate the teacher to ask questions about teacher effectiveness. Is the subject matter stale? Are the lessons paced to pupil ability? Are methods stimulating? Are pupils involved? Are adjustments made for both fast and slow learning pupils (see "Differentiating Instruction")?

Pupil behavior may react adversely on a class in the form of factions. Any group carries within it the germ of factionalism, and a classroom is not immune. If not controlled, factions often assume pro and con teacher characteristics, with unfortunate results for teacher leadership. Factions develop from many different situations: a referee's decision, an imagined snub, a student contest, or issues keenly felt. Factionalism over public issues may be anticipated and usefully diverted into social analysis. Other types of factionalism may be reduced by eliminating the source, such as an emphasis on over-competition, and arranging opportunities for persons of different alignments to work together.

While factionalism is a signal of group conflict, many behaviors are symptoms of individual maladjustment. An analysis of the situation, the pupil, and the particular behavior are required, and easy remedies are not prescribed. Since socialization is a type of learning, the patience that is required in teaching subjects is likewise required in teaching proper behavior. Reactions to misbehavior should be prompt—indecision stimulates anarchy. But reactions should be restrained, and moderate; simple reminders, although not always effective, are preferable to overreacting. If this technique does not generally work, it may be an indication of the lack of mutual teacher-pupil rapport and respect.

Nagging and scolding are common corrective practices of teachers as well as parents. After a few times, pupils do not hear; they literally turn their receivers off. Scolding often leads to threatening, a verbal device that separates teacher and pupil. Threatening backs the pupil into a corner, and the pupil often calculates the odds of escape by challenging the teacher, particularly if the threat is overstated. The pupils soon learn that the threat is an idle bark, and class respect is destroyed.

One of the great contradictions in dealing with behavior problems is that misbehavior gets attention from the teacher, while good behavior is largely ignored. A tantrum may end in a trip to the principal's office; crying, in excessive coddling; abuse of school property, in delinquent notoriety.

Praise and reward are helpful in shaping desired behavior, and more useful than punishment. Punishment is more useful than neglect, however, to obtain desired behavior. Praise and reward should not be used indiscriminately, however, because they soon loose their effect. In general, more praise and reward are used with younger children—tapering off with older children. However, even the more highly motivated and achieving child profits from occasional praise and reward, and some anxious or dependent children will require more sustaining praise than others.[15]

An attempt to convert the principles of positive reinforcement into more systematic behavioral control are utilized in such learning approaches as programmed learning and contingency management. Contingency management is simply a term which emphasizes

---

15. Herbert J. Klausmeir and William Goodwin, *Learning and Human Abilities,* 2d ed. (New York: Harper and Row, Publishers, 1966), pp. 454-56.

the appropriateness of positive rewards as a part of an instructional system, and reflects no new insight as much as it attempts to incorporate rewards systematically. Teachers interested in contingency management from both the standpoint of learning and classroom discipline will wish to follow the work of Lloyd Homme and his associates at the Westinghouse Learning Center in Albuquerque, New Mexico.[16]

Discipline Through Punishment. The preceding sections have emphasized discipline through *correction*. In the correction approach to discipline, the emphasis is on an alternate form of behavior. Punishment, however, emphasizes the use of a *penalty* which is not necessarily related to the correct behavior.[17] It is for this reason that penalties are less effective than correction.

The correction and penalty approaches can be illustrated by these examples:

John and James are good friends. They sit with different groups, but have so moved their chairs around that they sit back to back. Their constant talking interferes with the work of their respective groups. *Correction*: James is assigned to another work group on the other side of the room. *Penalty*: James is required to stay after school for "talking in class."

The class is engaged in craft projects. John is sawing a piece of wood with a nail in it. He discovers that by sawing against the nail, he can make a grating, scratching noise that runs shivers over the class and attracts much attention. *Correction*: *John is given a piece of wood without a nail and demonstrated the proper use of the saw. Penalty*: John is removed from participation in the project.

Notwithstanding the emphasis on positive behaviors through correction leading to self-discipline, punishment is sometimes necessary. The teacher need not feel guilty about resorting to punishment under circumstances where a penalty is necessary. Children are already familiar with penalties prior to the initiation of schooling, and the application of appropriate penalties does not have long term adverse emotional effects.[18]

The form of penalty should, if at all possible, be related to the offense: if property is defaced, repair it; if property is stolen, return or replace it; if a pupil is ill-mannered toward another, apologize. Such penalties, however, are closely related to the principle of correction.

The trouble with any system of penalties, whether in school or in civil society, is that it is extremely difficult to apply any Benthamite utilitarian theory. What is the appropriate penalty for creating a classroom disturbance? Doing extra work, staying after school, receiving demerits, forced apology to the class, or class suspension?

Because situations differ and individuals react to penalties in different ways, there is no ready-made recipe for using penalties. Here are some general negative admonitions found in the literature.

16. *Reading Newsreport* 3, No. 6 (April 1969): pp. 7-8. See especially, Lloyd Homme, "A Behavior Technology Exists—Here and Now," Unpublished paper, n.d. Westinghouse Learning Corporation, Albuquerque; also Roger M. Addison and Lloyd E. Homme, "The Reinforcing Event (RE) Menu," *NSPI Journal* 5, no. 1 (January 1966).

17. The correction approach corresponds to the more usual application of democratic versus authoritarian discipline. These constructs are useful in dichotomizing polar approaches to discipline, but are not functional in the context of the school, since few teachers display the characteristics of polar democratic and authoritarian control described in the literature. See David P. Ausubel, "A New Look at Classroom Discipline," *Phi Delta Kappan* 43 (October 1961): 28.

18. R. L. Solomon, "Punishment," *American Psychologist* 19, no. 4 (April 1964): 239-53.

1. The penalty should not be oversevere. Otherwise both the individual punished and the class tend to identify against the punisher, i.e., the teacher.
2. Mass punishment should be avoided where the individual offender cannot be identified. Veritable class slow-ups or strikes sometimes result.
3. Class or school suspension merely postpones resolution of the behavioral problem, and frequently intensifies it.
4. Penalties should never be associated with rejection of the offender. The teacher should strive to convey the attitude that the deed, not the child, is being punished.
5. Aspects of the school program, such as extra homework, staying in at recess, or after-school detention, should not be used as penalties.
6. Peer assignment of penalties are not appropriate; this is a teacher responsibility.
7. Where product performance is involved, failure to complete the product should be the penalty, e.g., costumes for a Christmas party, learning a part for a play.
8. Corporal punishment should be used only when authorized, used sparingly, and preferably in the presence of another adult.
9. Psychological isolation stifles communication and encourages resentment.
10. Penalties should be used sparingly; the more frequent the use of penalties, the less effective they become.[19]

At one time, the discipline literature reflected an absolute prohibition against the use of any type of corporal punishment[20] as well as a somewhat uncritical tendency to categorize all penalty control methods as authoritarian. Whether in reaction to the former emphasis on child permissiveness or a better understanding of the relationship of the child's culture to discipline, the early dogmatic point of view associated with mental hygiene is somewhat modified. Where corporal punishment is an anticipated method of control in the referent culture, it may be a prerequisite to the creation of authority acceptance favorable to social control. Furthermore, the studies of laissez-faire, democratic, and authoritarian social control practices are deficient because they leave out a very important category—benevolent autocracy.[21] In such a system, penalties can be used which are neither vindictive, harsh, or abusive. Because of differences in patterns of behavioral expectancy which children bring with them to school, it is likely that a wider range of disciplinary methods are actually exercised in the schools than the professional literature admits as being appropriate. Probably these result not so much from the teacher's inability to understand or implement the recommended democratic procedures, but as a result of teacher adaptation to the social control expectancies of the community. After all, teacher-pupil interaction is not a one-way street, and the very burden of numbers suggests that the teacher accommodates himself as much to the class as the class reacts to the teacher.

Special Problems and Discipline

From the standpoint of the teacher, all behavior may be viewed as a discipline

---

19. Dorothy Petersen, *Elementary School Teacher*, pp. 116-19; Klausmeier and Goodwin, *Learning and Human Abilities*, pp. 411-15; Sylvester, *Common Sense*, pp. 149-53.
20. See, for example, Fretz Redl and William W. Wattenberg, *Mental Hygiene in Teaching*, 2d ed. (New York: Harcourt, Brace & World, Inc., 1959), p. 375.
21. Boyd R. McCandless, *Children: Behavior and Development*, 2d ed. (New York: Holt, Rinehart and Winston, Inc., 1967), p. 563.

Rank	Serious to the Child	Troublesome to the Teacher
1	Stealing	Interrupting
2	Untruthfulness	Carelessness in work
3	Unreliableness	Inattention
4	Cruelty and bullying	Restlessness
5	Cheating	Silliness, smartness
6	Heterosexuality	Whispering and note taking
7	Impertinence	Tattling
8	Impudence	Thoughtlessness
9	Selfishness	Disorderliness
10	Laziness	Inquisitiveness

Fig. 21.2. Serious and Troublesome Pupil Traits as Rated by Teachers. From J. N. Sparks, "Teachers' Attitudes Toward the Behavior Problems of Children," *Journal of Educational Psychology* 43 (1952): 284-91.

problem. Most of the teacher's troublesome problems can be reduced if talking, carelessness, and inattention are eliminated. These appear to require more effective teaching rather than disciplinary treatment.[22]

A 1952 study of Sparks indicated that teachers are able to distinguish between problems which might be of most serious consequences to the child and those which are most annoying to the teacher. Figure 21.2 sets forth salient findings by Sparks.

Problems considered serious to the child are evaluated in terms of the values of the general culture, whereas those that are regarded as troublesome to the teacher primarily reflect the particular needs of the culture of the classroom. It should not be anticipated that there will be a complete overlap in the clinical point of view and the teaching point of view. They have different concerns; the former emphasizes the personality adjustment of the individual whereas the latter is concerned with intellectual as well as personal growth.

Since classroom management problems are related to problems of individual emotional adjustment, it is important for the teacher to be able to recognize signs which may indicate that the problem of adjustment

Physical signs

facial twitching
nervous spasms
stuttering
biting nails
scratching self
vomiting
enuresis
digestive disturbances

rocking feet
drumming with fingers
twisting hair
restlessness
fidgeting
rapid, nervous speech
crying easily

Behavior deviations

aggressiveness
negativism
night terrors
bullying
lying
voluntary mutinism
poor school work
oversensitiveness

retiring
easily embarrassed
sleep disturbances
walking in sleep
masturbation
stubborness
regression

Emotional manifestations

given to excessive worry
feelings of inferiority
abnormal fears
pouting

disposition to hate
resentful
temper tantrums
extreme timidity

Fig. 21.3. Symptoms of Personality Maladjustment. From Karl C. Garrison, Albert J. Kingston, and Arthur S. McDonald, **Educational Psychology**, 2d ed. (New York: Appleton-Century-Crofts, © 1964), p. 475. Reprinted by permission of Appleton-Century-Crofts, Educational Division, Meredith Corporation.

22. J. E. Greene, Sr., "Alleged 'Misbehaviors' Among Senior High School Students," *Journal of Social Psychology* 58, (December 1962): 371-82.

should be approached from the standpoint of clinical treatment rather than classroom discipline. Figure 21.3 of trait maladjustment has been compiled by Garrison, Kingston, and McDonald. Where teachers suspect inappropriate behavior related to personal maladjustment, the assistance of specialized personnel should be requested. The services of specialists dealing with the emotionally disturbed child are now available in many school communities (see chapter 8).

Management for Instruction

The previous sections have emphasized that the key to effective classroom discipline is good instruction which keeps children interested and occupied. Other chapters have discussed specific content and teaching in the subject areas. It is nevertheless appropriate at this point to emphasize aspects of classroom management which more properly relate to instruction.

Effective planning for instruction is an extension of curriculum development and the general selection of instructional objectives (see chapters 2 and 3). In theory the elementary curriculum includes three categories of pupil growth: cognitive, affective, and psychomotor development. Instruction, therefore, is not merely knowledge oriented, but includes a wider range of outcomes. But most curriculum guides and curriculum materials are rarely specific with respect to learning objectives, irrespective of the category. It is therefore the responsibility of the teacher to convert the general curriculum suggestions into specific teaching plans.

Planning for Instruction. There is no one best way to plan for instruction; the kind of planning depends upon the curriculum orientation—child-centered, subject-matter centered or some eclectic approach. A type of open-ended, tentative kind of planning characterizes the child-centered approach, due to the fact that if adjustments in experiences are made to accommodate the self-revealing interests of the child, any instructional plans must be flexible. A characteristic feature of the child-centered school are the *interest centers,* designed in such a way as to make it possible for children to use their own interests as a key to projects and experiences in which they engage. Interest centers are frequently found even in subject matter class rooms. There is an essential difference in the organization of the interest center. In the child-centered school, the interest center serves as a focal point for learning experiences; in the subject matter curriculum, it serves to *enrich* or *supplement* the existing curriculum.

A subject matter curriculum lends itself to highly structured or closed planning. This results from the fact that the learning objectives grow out of the subject matter, and can be broken down into concepts and facts which in turn can be divided into small lesson segments, sometimes referred to as modules of instruction or mini-lessons. Subject matter curriculum planning may therefore be thought of as a planned hierarchy, in which the mastery of parts of lessons contribute to total lesson mastery; daily lesson mastery contributes to unit lesson mastery; unit lesson mastery ultimately leads to the general course objectives. The subject matter curriculum permits differentiation according to pupil interest and ability.

Teachers whose teaching style is more compatible with such ideas as child-centered, creative, or integrative day are less likely to look with favor on structured lesson plans. Teachers who are interested in subject matter content, contingency management, task variables, and measureable performance outcomes are more likely to accept the principle, if not the practice, of structured lesson plans. Structured lesson planning by subject matter area is most developed in Teaching English as A Second Language (TESL), mathematics, and the sciences, with some development in reading. It is less developed in the language arts and in the social studies, probably because the subject matter is less sequential and because of the greater emphasis on attitudes and values.

At the present time, teachers obtain effective results who use either open or closed methods of planning. Other variables are more important than the plan itself in teaching success.

Unit Organization and Teaching. One of the most widely used terms in curriculum and instruction is "unit," a term still popular in the 1960s. In the high school, unit had a relatively limited meaning: the careful selection and organization of content and procedures to meet the instructional objectives. A unit of work therefore included aspects of curriculum, methodolgy, and evaluation.[23] This was a more limited approach to the unit than was originally intended by Morrison, who first used the term.

In elementary education, in contrast, unit tended to be identfied with every new emphasis in elementary pedagogy. As reviewed by Jarvis and Wootton in 1966,[24] aspects of unit planning and teaching included: problem solving, cooperative planning, multidisciplinary approach, integrated activities, flexible class schedule, large time blocks, content selection on basis of children's interests or development, group work, interest centers, and democratic procedures, to mention the most obvious. A review of these diverse elements indicates that the general concept of "unit" has no functional variables, and is so loosely conceived that none of the alleged claims for unit teaching have been experimentally verified. The educational literature on unit teaching, like much other educational literature, is merely subjective and persuasive, with no evidence to support the alleged merits.

It is possible to give a descriptive, rather than normative, definition of what units are as they appear in textbooks, courses of study, and curriculum guides. "A unit is a selection of content to meet specific learning outcomes, with suggestions as to teacher implementation and evaluation." In terms of length, the unit may be long or short; in subject matter organization, single discipline, correlated, fused, or integrated; in teaching material, project, activity, experience, multimedia, or textbook; in teaching methodology, expository, inquiry, discovery, structured and closed, or non-structured and open; in learning psychology, reception, association, conditioning, insightful, intuitive, or maturational; in learning outcomes, cognition and intellectual processes, habits and skills, values and attitudes, and tastes and interests. The particular points of view that underlie unit development are merely instructional and curriculum alternatives; they are not unit attributes.

The four specific characteristics of a unit are: learning objectives; content; methodology; and evaluation procedures. Specific learning objectives are important for a closed

---

23. C. R. Maxwell and W. C. Reusser, *Observation and Directed Teaching in Secondary Schools* (Englewood Cliffs, N. J.: Prentice-Hall, Inc., 1939), p. 224.

24. Oscar T. Jarvis and Lutian R. Wootton, *The Transitional Elementary School and Its Curriculum* (Dubuque, Iowa: Wm. C. Brown Company Publishers, 1966), chap. 9.

unit: they suggest content and the methodology and require the evaluation of specific learning outcomes. The content is training specific to the objectives, and may involve a field trip, the construction of an object, the study of a chapter, or research in the library. Content refers to what is to be learned. In selecting unit content, it is assumed that the learning objectives have already taken into consideration two important factors—the previous experience or knowledge of the learner and his psychological maturity.

There should be an optimum fit with methodology, which is the bridge between the learning objective and content. Thus exposition might be more appropriate to the introduction of new concepts, library research to the application of previously learned concepts, discovery to the elaboration of open questions, or use of a programmed text for differentiating instruction. Evaluation grows out of the objectives, rather than the development of the unit. Evidence of pupil growth and the success of the unit is based upon the a priori determined objectives, and not on subjective feelings of unit success. If this rigid principle of evaluation is not adhered to, it is quite possible that the children will have had profitable learning experiences and an enjoyable unit, but there will be no guarantee that the unit was pursued by the children in accordance with the objectives.

An *open* approach to unit planning may be used, in which objectives and evaluation are stated globally. It permits more latitude and flexibility, but it must always be remembered that this type of unit can only be reconstructed, with all the many hazards of recall and disregard of certain variables. The evaluation that occurs indicates where the class ended as a result of the unit, but it is no indication of how well they learned the content of the unit.

The unit definition given lends itself to either a *curriculum* construction emphasis or a *teaching* emphasis. If the curriculum approach is taken, the actual curriculum must be either written or assembled. It is not sufficient to merely have a *resource* unit which outlines content in terms of a selection to be read or a film to be viewed. Unless the material is available when required, these resource units give the illusion of planning but are inefficient pedagogy: they consume teacher time in preparation but do not control content or classroom experiences.

A unit which has a *teaching* emphasis, in contrast to the curriculum unit, assumes a previously existing curriculum and materials for instruction. Development of the teaching unit is a way the teacher *studies* the material and makes plans to *implement* the unit with his class. Development of the teaching unit by a teacher has this advantage. The teacher develops a teaching map or cognitive field, and is thoroughly cognizant of where he wants to go (objectives); why he wants to go there (content); and how he wants to get there (methodology). A thorough understanding of these three aspects also permits him to differentiate instruction, *within* the unit framework, to meet the expressed interests and needs of children.

Most publisher and project materials have teacher guides which include units of study. These unit guides can be of tremendous assistance to a teacher, provided the teacher thoroughly *internalizes* the guide. This means that the teacher does not merely glance or look at the guide, but becomes so familiar with the guide that he can recall, manipulate vicariously, and apply all the guide variables. In the process of internalization, the teacher can also make adaptations appropriate to his class and school resources. For example, a unit dealing with resource and production might suggest a field trip to a brick plant, cement plant, or other local manufacturing industry. In a dairy farming community, the teacher might substitute a field trip to a dairy farm.

No project or publisher-prepared unit can anticipate every local need or requirement. In fact, the general rule applicable to teaching and curriculum development is: the more emphasis on the local community, the more the local teachers will have to take the initiative in modifying or adapting units. While the quality of project- or publisher-prepared units is unequal, a comparison of the former types of units with teacher-prepared units indicates that the "canned" units are frequently more carefully developed than teacher prepared units. The general tone of the professional literature has nevertheless implied that the individual classroom teacher was also a curriculum developer.[25]

In view of the many superior units which have been developed by various projects and publishers for different subject areas and different grade levels, it is probably an uneconomic use of teacher time to develop new curriculum units. Although many superior units are developed by teachers, frequently these units result from the availability of released time to teachers, provision of clerical help, and availability of consultants.[26] In such cases, the resulting unit development is more like that of a project than that of a regular classroom teacher who must develop curriculum units coincidentally with his regular teaching duties. It is the point of view of the authors of this book that the use of teacher time to internalize and adapt prepared units coming from major projects and publishers (see the various subject matter chapters for some of the new curriculum developments) will probably be more effective in the improvement of classroom teaching than requiring the teacher to be his own curriculum unit developer. This viewpoint regards the adult leader in the classroom primarily as a teacher; his role is to teach children. A curriculum developer, on the other hand, is primarily concerned with the selection of experiences and content for learning. The developer may suggest methodology, but that is the particular province of the teacher. It is he who has developed a particular teaching style and who interacts with the children in his class. The competencies which are useful in curriculum development are not identical with the competencies in teaching. What are some of these desirable traits of good teaching? What are some of the differences in teaching methods? A discussion of these follows.

Traits in Good Teaching. Over the years two intriguing and interrelated questions relating to teachers and teaching have been "Who is a good teacher?" and "What is good teaching?" Today, studies which seek to answer these questions are usually classified

---

25. William B. Ragan, *Teaching America's Children* (New York: Holt, Rinehart and Winston, 1961), pp. 107-10; William H. Burton, *The Guidance of Learning Activities,* 3d ed. (New York: Appleton-Century-Crofts, Inc., 1962), chap. 14; Petersen, *Elementary School Teacher,* pp. 279-305.

26. *The Australian Aborigines* (West Newton, Mass.: Newton Public Schools, 1964); *Life in the Arctic* (West Newton, Mass.: Newton Public Schools, 1965). These resource units for Grade 3, developed by the Elementary Social Studies Project Team are excellent examples of teacher-developed curriculum materials when given the proper resources and support.

in the category of "teacher effectiveness." Most of the time these studies are correlations of characteristics which are related to a desirable teacher image.

A. S. Barr was one of the pioneers in the study of good and poor teachers. His classic 1929 study still has relevance for today.[27] His study indicated that there were no clearly identifiable factors which separated good teachers from poor teachers. Characteristics which appeared more often with the group classified as "good" teachers included:[28]

1. Ability to stimulate interest
2. Wealth of commentarial statements
3. Attention to pupil's recitation
4. Topical or problem-project organization of subject matter
5. Well-developed assignments
6. Frequent use of illustrative materials
7. A well-established examination procedure
8. Effective methods of appraising pupils' work
9. Freedom from disciplinary difficulties
10. Knowledge of subject matter
11. Conversational manner in teaching
12. Frequent use of pupils' experiences
13. An appreciative attitude (as evidenced by nods, comments, and smiles)
14. Skill in asking questions
15. Definite study helps
16. Socialized class procedures
17. Willingness to experiment

One of the most comprehensive studies of teacher characteristics was sponsored by the Commission on Teacher Education of the American Council of Education, popularly known as the "Ryans' Study." This study, like previous studies, indicated the variable qualities of good teachers, and the tendency of teaching traits to interact rather than appear as discrete qualities. The "good" characteristics of women teachers in the elementary grades are listed in figure 21.4.

The Barr and Ryans studies indicate the viewpoint of adult professionals. What are the viewpoints of students? Witty analyzed (1950) the letters of 14,000 pupils in the first to fourth grade who wrote about "The Teacher Who Helped Me Most." Responses were categorized into this list of trait frequencies which stated that students liked teachers who were:[29] (1) democratic and cooperative, (2) considerate of the individual student, (3) patient, (4) interested in many things, (5) pleasing in appearance and manner, (6) fair and impartial, (7) in possession of a good sense of humor, (8) consistent in behavior, (9) interested in pupils' problems, (10) objective and flexible, (11) prone to praise students, and (12) knowledgeable and effective in teaching subject-matter.

In an earlier study, Hart requested high school seniors to give their perceptions of teachers they liked and from whom they could learn best. Their ten most desirable teacher characteristics were:[30]

1. Is helpful in schoolwork
2. Is cheerful and good humored

27. A. S. Barr, *Characteristic Differences in the Teaching Performance of Good and Poor Teachers of the Social Studies* (Bloomington, Ill.: Public School Publishing Co., 1929).
28. William H. Burton, *The Guidance of Learning Activities* 3d ed. (New York: Appleton Century-Crofts, © 1962), pp. 260-61. Reprinted by permission of Appleton Century-Crofts, Educational Division, Meredith Corporation.
29. Paul A. Witty, "Some Characteristics of the Effective Teacher," *Educational Administration and Supervision* 36, no. 4 (April 1950): 193-208.
30. F. W. Hart, *Teachers and Teaching, by Ten Thousand High School Seniors* (New York: Macmillan Company, 1934).

3. Is companionable
4. Is interested in and understands pupils
5. Stimulates interest
6. Has control of the class
7. Is impartial
8. Avoids sarcasm and nagging
9. Is businesslike
10. Has a pleasing personality

A comparison of the items on the earlier (1929) Barr list with subsequent lists indicate a shift in emphasis from behavioral items related to teaching to behavioral characteristics related to personality. It is likely that this shift is as much an artifact of the interests and methodology of the researcher as it is of the respondent. From the standpoint of personality, the lists do not suggest that prospective teachers attempt any general reform of personality, if that were possible.

A. "High" group members more frequently (than "low"):
 1. Manifest extreme generosity in appraisals of the behavior and motives of other persons; express friendly feelings for others.
 2. Indicate strong interest in reading and in literary matters.
 3. Indicate interest in music, painting, and the arts in general.
 4. Report participation in high school and college social groups.
 5. Manifest prominent social service ideals.
 6. Indicate preferences for activities which involve contact with people.
 7. Indicate interest in science and scientific matters.
 8. Report liking for outdoor activities.
 9. Are young, or middle-aged.
 10. Are married.
 11. Report that parental homes provided above-average cultural advantages.

B. "High" group (compared with "low" group):
 1. Indicates greater enjoyment of pupil relationships (i.e., more favorable pupil opinions).
 2. Indicates greater preference for nondirective classroom procedures.
 3. Is superior in verbal intelligence ($I_.$ scores).
 4. Is more satisfactory with regard to emotional adjustment ($S_.$ scores).

A. "Low" group members more frequently (than "high"):
 1. Are from older age groups.
 2. Are restricted and critical in appraisals of the behavior and motives of other persons.
 3. Are unmarried.
 4. Indicate preferences for actvities which do *not* involve close contacts with people.

B. "Low" group (compared with "high" group):
 1. Is less favorable in expressed opinions of pupils.
 2. Is less high with regard to verbal intelligence ($I_.$ scores).
 3. Is less satisfactory with regard to emotional adjustment ($S_.$ scores).

Fig. 21.4. Personal Characteristics of Female Elementary School Teachers Classified "High" and "Low" with Respect to Overall Classroom Behavior. From David G. Ryans, **Characteristics of Teachers: A Research Study** (Washington, D.C.: American Council on Education, 1960), pp. 365-66. Used by permission.

A great variety of persons are successful in teaching, because there is no one teaching situation. A teacher successful with one group of pupils is not successful with another; successful in one school and not in another; successful with a large group but not with a small one; successful with younger but not with older children.

The various lists of personality and teacher traits which accompany good teaching suggest, however, that teachers should improve those desirable traits in which they are strongest, and attempt to reduce traits which are negative. Thus, if a teacher is inclined to be impatient (personality), he may strive to pay more attention to pupil participation and provide definite study helps (teaching traits). He may appear to become less impatient simply because he takes more time with certain definite teaching acts. If he shows little interest in pupil problems (personality), he might try to make more use of pupil experiences (teaching). It is thought that the best way to improve personality characteristics of teachers is for them to teach in a context in which the desired behavior is elicited. According to operant conditioning theory, the desired behavior will be reinforced. Thus admonitions to teachers about undesirable personality characteristics, as with negative statements to younger pupils, are not very effective. The teachers may intellectually apprehend the desired behavior, but they have not gained experience in the desired behavior. This defect has been, and will continue to be, one of the major defects in training teachers: desired behavior is talked about, but it is not elicited in the training situation and it does not become habitual before the prospective teacher begins teaching.

One of the problems in the improvement of teacher behavior is the difficulty in getting a teacher to observe his behavior. One of the major ways teachers interact with pupils in the classroom is with language. The language a teacher uses is one of the most important ways he influences his pupils. One device for making a teacher more conscious of his behavior in the classroom is the use of interaction analysis, such as that developed by Amidon and Flanders. This strategy emphasizes verbal behavior only, and is divided into the two major categories of "Teacher Talk" and "Pupil Talk." The summary of categories for interaction analysis is given in figure 21.5. A teacher may use a tape recorder to make a transcript of a lesson, and then analyze the lesson according to the manual. On the basis of his analysis, he may try to change his behavior to conform to the assumed desired behavior.

While the Flanders system has recently become very popular in classroom analysis, there is no experimental verification that the change in behavior really is related to teacher effectiveness. What, after all, is teacher effectiveness?

Measuring Teacher Effectiveness. There is no single answer to this question, and the diversity of judgments over how to measure teacher effectiveness is merely one of the many indications in the field of education of professional differences as to what education is all about. There are three principal ways of measuring teacher effectiveness: (1) by the amount of training, (2) by conformity to an ideal model in the classroom, (3) by the product.

Amount of training is the most common method of measuring teacher effectiveness. The teaching certificate, license to teach issued by a state agency, primarily reflects two elements: level of training and conformi-

Teacher-Initiated Talk	1.	Gives Information or Opinion: presents content or own ideas, explains, orients, asks rhetorical questions. May be short statements or extended lecture.
	2.	Gives Direction: tells pupil to take some specific action; gives orders; commands.
	3.	Asks Narrow Question: asks drill questions, questions requiring one or two word replies or yes-or-no answers; questions to which the specific nature of the response can be predicted.
	4.	Asks Broad Question: asks relatively open-ended questions which call for unpredictable responses; questions which are thought-provoking. Apt to elicit a longer response than 3.
Teacher Response	5.	Accepts: (5a) Ideas: reflects, clarifies, encourages or praises ideas of pupils. Summarizes, or comments without rejection. (5b) Behavior: responds in ways which commend or encourage pupil behavior. (5c) Feeling: responds in ways which reflect or encourage expression of pupil feeling.
	6.	Rejects: (6a) Ideas: criticizes, ignores or discourages pupil ideas. (6b) Behavior: discourages or criticizes pupil behavior. Designed to stop undesirable behavior. May be stated in question form, but differentiated from category 3 or 4, and from category 2, Gives Direction, by tone of voice and resultant effect on pupils. (6c) Feeling: ignores, discourages or rejects pupil expression of feeling.
Pupil Response	7.	Responds (7a) Predictably: relatively short replies, usually, which follow category 3. May also follow category 2, i.e., "David, you may read next." (7b) Unpredictably: replies which usually follow category 4.
	8.	Responds to Another Pupil: replies occurring to conversation between pupils.
Pupil-Initiated Talk	9.	Initiates Talk to Teacher: statements which pupils direct to teacher without solicitation from teacher.
	10.	Initiates Talk to Another Pupil: statements which pupils direct to another pupil which are not solicited.
Other	11.	Silence: pauses or short periods of silence during a time of classroom conversation.
	Z.	Confusion: considerable noise which disrupts planned activities. This category may accompany other categories or may totally preclude the use of other categories.

Fig. 21.5. Categories for Verbal Interaction Analysis of Teacher and Student Talk. From Edmund Amidon and Elizabeth Hunter, **Improving Teaching: The Analysis of Classroom Verbal Interaction** (New York: Holt, Rinehart and Winston © 1966). Reproduced by permission.

ty of training to an approved program. Salaries are typically based on the level of the degree and certificate (baccalaureate, master's, or specialist) plus the number of years of teaching experience.

Observing the performance of a teacher in the classroom, usually in accordance with some observational scale or checklist which includes instances of desired and undesired behavior, is the next most common way. The perceptions of the evaluator are frequently as important as the behavior of the teacher, and special training is required to reduce the appraiser's subjectivity. Principal ratings tend to emphasize control rather than teaching behaviors. It is sometimes hypothesized that the type of rating used within the public school eventually eliminates the most creative and non-conforming teachers. A good example of the strengths and weaknesses in the observation of student and pupil behavior is shown in figure 21.6 as compiled by Klausmeier and Goodwin. This kind of observation is important in terms of the relation of teacher behavior to the overt behavior of the pupil in the classroom climate, but it tells nothing about the *product* performance of teaching, as measured by pupil learning.

The least common method used in measuring teacher effectiveness is to check the behavior of the pupil. This is called product measurement, and is highly unpopular with both teachers and administrators. Both find it threatening.

The new attempts at performance contracting and efforts to provide for accountability are, however, based on product measurement. It is quite true that every conceivable variable affects learning, and that the school and the teacher are merely additional variables in the learning process.

Schooling, however, is the institutionalization of formal instruction. It therefore appears that school systems and teachers should be accountable for pupil learning.

If teachers were accountable for pupil learning, more care might be exercised in planning and directing pupil learning. However, the research studies as to the effectiveness of different methods of teaching are generally inadequate, because too few variables have been controlled. The most common error is to compare method A with method B when, in fact, no consideration is given to task and content variables, differences in pupils, and differences in teachers. While the literature abounds in admonishments to teachers, experimental efforts indicate that some methods are particularly suited to certain pupils when taught by some teachers under certain conditions. There is no one acceptable best method.

Teaching for Cognitive Outcomes

In teaching for cognitive outcomes, however, there are two distinctive approaches—didactic and heuristic, or inquiry. What are the characteristics of these two methods?

Deduction. A didactic method is essentially a deductive method, making use of systematic exposition and narration. It emphasizes telling. Jarvis in 1967 defined the deductive method as "the closely directed, explanatory process by which children are given generalizations along with supportive evidence and are helped by the teacher to draw valid conclusions."[31]

In its simplest form, the deductive mode is teaching by telling. It is the oldest and

---

31. Oscar T. Jarvis, "The Deductive Method of Teaching Anthropology," *Teaching Anthropology in the Elementary School* (Athens, Georgia: Anthropology Curriculum Project, 1967), p. 1.

classroom management and teaching

Teacher Behavior

Warmth

Sentimental Personal identification with students	Warm, understanding, self-controlling Listens attentively Accepts feelings Accepts students' ideas Observes students' reactions skillfully Asks questions Praises and encourages	Aloof, egocentric Fearful, anxious

Planning and Execution of Classroom Behavior

Unplanned, slipshod	Responsible, businesslike Systematic Flexible Integrative Orderly work-oriented Explains things clearly Rewards fairly Explains reasons for criticism	Dominative Prescribes arbitrarily Uses power and coercion indiscriminately Asks for more than students can do Uses nonconstructive criticism

Approach to Student Behavior and Subject Matter

Impulsive, turbulent, variable	Stimulating, imaginative, surgent	Dull, routine

Related Instructional Procedures

May handle one type reasonably well, perhaps independent study best	Effective with group discussion, lectures, recitation, and independent activities	May handle one type well, perhaps lecturing best

Student Behavior

Related Subject-Matter Achievement of Students

Inconsistent, varying with interest and ability of the students, insecure students do not learn well	High and consistent when procedures are selected in terms of objectives and student characteristics	May be high in outcomes emphasized by the teacher; rebellious students do not learn well

Related Emotional Security

Low for already unhappy children; might be high for a child who identifies with the teacher	High, when balance of direction and freedom is maintained in various activities	Low for most children

Fig. 21.6. "Comparison of Teacher Leadership Behavior and Learning Outcomes." From **Learning and Human Abilities**, 3d ed., by Herbert J. Klausmeier and Richard E. Ripple. Copyright © 1971 by Herbert J. Klausmeier and Richard E. Ripple. By permission of Harper & Row, Publishers, Inc.

most common form of teaching, notwithstanding the fact that in recent years it has been in such disrepute that very little attention has been given to the ways teachers can use language to tell more effectively. This neglect of the deductive method grows out of certain assumptions that school learning is better if active (listening is regarded as "passive"); and that activity is more real than language. In common with many approaches in elementary education, the means (activity) is equated with the end (learning).

There is, however, a new appreciation of the importance of language in learning emerging.[32] The teaching construct of tell includes a wide range of declarative language behavior, ranging from giving directions to making applications. Some of the different behaviors relating to telling include:

To illustrate, as in giving an appropriate example.
To direct, as in making an assignment.
To inform, as in supplying new information.
To narrate, as in relating in detail.
To enumerate, as in the listing of traits or qualities.
To explain, as in making plain or clearer.
To interpret, as in bringing out the meaning.
To elucidate, as in making clearer by additional explanation.
To define, as in giving the attributes of a concept.
To compare, as in the identification of similar qualities.
To contrast, as in the identification of different attributes.
To categorize, as in arranging taxonomically.
To infer (induce), as in making a conclusion based on data.
To deduce, as in the application of a principle to a case.
To generalize, as in extending a rule by analogy.

To analyze, as in separating a narration into components.
To synthesize, as in arranging discrete elements into a system.
To apply, as in the selective use of evidence.
To reason, as in the use of data to arrive at a decision.
To decide, as in the resolution of an issue rationally.

From the standpoint of formal method, telling is classified as exposition. While exposition is used by all teachers, the emphasis on exposition as method belongs to the turn of the century, but was still regarded as an appropriate method of teaching in the 1920s.[33] In the United States, the steps of Herbartian psychology were reinterpreted, first by McMurry[34] and later by Morrison[35] and were standard aspects of pedagogical teaching until all methodology—project, problem solving, differentiated instruction—lost their identity in the ubiquitous and amorphous unit method.[36] While the five stages of formal exposition—preparation, presentation, comparison, generalization, and application—do not embrace the range of learning experiences necessary for children's intellectual development, they might be profitably studied as a means whereby teachers could improve their use of classroom discourse. In the learning theory of Ausubel,

32. See, for example, Garrison, Kingston, and McDonald, *Educational Psychology*, chap. 5.
33. John Adams, *Exposition and Illustration in Teaching* (New York: Macmillan Company, 1926).
34. Charles A. McMurry, *The Elements of General Method: Based on the Principles of Herbart* (New York: Macmillan Company, 1904).
35. Henry C. Morrison, *The Practice of Teaching in the Secondary School* (Chicago, Ill.: University of Chicago Press, 1926).
36. Roy O. Billett, *Fundamentals of Secondary School Teaching with Emphasis on the Unit Method* (Boston: Houghton Mifflin Company, 1940), pp. 496-500.

the concepts of "advance organizer" and "meaningful reception" give new insights into the Herbartian stage of presentation and deductive learning.[37] And even Burton, who is no friend of formalism, points out that the use of Herbartian presentation would be a tremendous improvement over the way so many assignments are made by simply routine designation of so many pages or exercises without any consideration of objectives or the previous knowledge of the learner.[38]

While Ausubel has a rather complex theory of verbal reception learning, the approach is definitely deductive in tenor. The four elements are reception, meaningfulness, subsumption, and advance organizers. Reception is a term which emphasizes the fact that the pupil does not discover knowledge; he receives it through the meaningful structure of language. Verbal learning in the school is not rote, because the learning tasks are sequentially built upon the learner's cognitive structure. Subsumption is the process of incorporating new subject matter into relevant existing knowledge structures. An advance organizer is the most general and inclusive concept for the organization and explanation of the material it precedes. The advance organizer provides the "ideational scaffolding" for the meaningful and relevant incorporation and retention of the detailed information which follows.[39] Allen[40] and Steinbrink[41] have applied the concept of advance organizers to teaching social studies to elementary children. The results indicate that the reception, i.e., deductive verbal approach, can be effectively used with young learners, including disadvantaged learners.

The use of deduction, like any other teaching method, must always be adjusted to the age of the child. Length and language must always be adapted not only to the learning objectives, but the previous experiences and the psychological maturity of the learner. But to contend that telling is never appropriate for young children is to transform the liberating concepts of self-directed activity and learning to mere formalism. It also tends to reduce the effectiveness of inquiry when it is undiscriminatingly assumed that inquiry is the best and only way learning experiences should be organized.

Inquiry. The most popular approach to teaching in the 1960s, as evidenced by curriculum development projects as well as the pedagogic literature, was inquiry. Curriculum projects sympathetic to inquiry include mathematics, such as that of the School Mathematics Study Group (SMSG) (see chapter 12); science, such as the AAAS sponsored *Science—A Process Approach* (see chapter 13); and social studies (see chapter 14). Inquiry for the 1970s will likely be what problem solving was to the 1950s and the progressive era—an educational panacea.[42]

37. David P. Ausubel, *The Psychology of Meaningful Verbal Learning* (New York: Grune & Stratton, 1963).
38. Burton, *Guidance of Learning Activities*, p. 291.
39. Ausubel, *Psychology of Meaningful Verbal Learning.*
40. D. I. Allen, "Some Effects of Advance Organizers and Level of Retention of Written Social Studies Material" (doc. diss., University of California, Berkeley, 1969).
41. John E. Steinbrink, *The Effectiveness of Advance Organizers for Teaching Geography to Disadvantaged Rural Black Elementary Students* (Athens, Ga.: Geography Curriculum Project, University of Georgia, 1970).
42. For a discussion of problem solving and its applications to elementary teaching, see Jarvis and Wootton, *Transitional Elementary School,* chap. 8.

The tremendous vogue of inquiry is due, in part, to its affinity to problem solving. Inquiry, in fact, is frequently used as a synonym for problem solving. As the term problem solving became passé, it was easy for educators to substitute the label inquiry. For the scientists who came lately to curriculum development, the inquiry approach appealed to their humanitarian and idealistic perceptions of the way children ought to learn. Implicit in the advocacy of inquiry is the assumption of superiority to didactic learning. Notwithstanding the lack of empirical or laboratory evidence to support this assumption, inquiry is de rigueur in curriculum and college circles if not in the classroom.

Pedagogically, inquiry may be defined simply as a process by which the students are stimulated to ask questions and to find answers, and may be contrasted with the didactic mode in which the student receives the answers to questions posed by the teacher. This distinction is particularly apt when the textbook is compared with the case or documentary method in the teaching of a subject, such as history.[43] General explanations of inquiry, however, tend to be circular as well as tautologous. Thus Crabtree[44] uses such words as "problems," "inductive," "discovery," "creative thinking," "divergent thinking," as well as "highly integrative behaviors" to refer to inquiry. Highly integrative teacher behavior is characterized as supportive, accepting behavior, similar to that often considered attributes of the democratic teacher or the good teacher as described by Barr.

In the social studies, Fenton has been one of the most incisive advocates of inquiry, both from the standpoint of theory and application to curriculum and teaching. Following the lead of Joseph M. Schwab that the structure of a discipline consists of hypothesis formation and proof processes, Fenton identifies hypothesis formation with concepts, and proof processes with validation. Structure is therefore not an inert body of knowledge, but an analytical tool, a method of inquiry. Expressly recognizing the seminal influence of John Dewey, he outlines six steps of inquiry related to structure as systematic analysis. These six steps are:[45]

1. Recognizing a problem from data
2. Formulating hypotheses
   a. Asking analytical questions
   b. Stating hypotheses
   c. Remaining aware of the tentative nature of hypotheses
3. Recognizing the logical implications of hypotheses
4. Gathering data
   a. Deciding data
   b. Deciding what data will be needed
   c. Selecting or rejecting sources on the basis of a statement of the logical implications
5. Analyzing, evaluating and interpreting the data
   a. Selecting relevant data from the sources
   b. Evaluating the sources
      (1) Determining the frame of reference of the author of a source
      (2) Determining the accuracy of the statements of fact
   c. Interpreting the data
6. Evaluating the hypothesis in the light of the data
   a. Justifying the hypothesis

43. James A. Banks and Ermon O. Hogan, "Inquiry: A History Teaching Tool," *Illinois Schools Journal* 48 (Fall 1968): 176-80.

44. Charlotte Crabtree, "Inquiry Approaches: How New and How Valuable," *Social Education* 30 (November 1966): 523-25, 531.

45. Edwin Fenton, "Social Studies Curriculum Reform: An Appraisal," *California Social Science Review* 6 (June 1967): 23-33.

   b. Modifying the hypothesis
      (1) Rejecting a logical implication
      (2) Restating the hypothesis

A comparison of the six steps in Fenton's analytic inquiry system indicates a continuation of the various problem solving steps as developed by Dewey and elaborated by Thorndike, Kilpatrick, and Gray.[46] However, there is a definite superiority in the inquiry steps of Fenton compared with previous descriptions of problem solving steps. This results from the fact that Fenton places his analytic system within the subject matter of school teaching, and the process of hypothesis validation involves the conceptual structure of the discipline. In contrast, many of the previous problem solving approaches, such as Kilpatrick's illustration of the mother and the crying baby, were related to "real life" problems and did not elaborate a theory specifically related to gaining subject matter knowledge as well as process skills through inquiry. Fenton also recognizes that analytic inquiry does not provide for conceptual or chronological continuity, and combines textbook-type essays which link the discrete case material. Fenton's approach is therefore a moderate rather than extreme inquiry approach, and undoubtedly has contributed to the acceptance of his point of view as well as of his materials. His analytic approach, however, appears to lend itself more readily to intermediate and older students than to primary students, where more attention needs to be given to directed concrete experiences, as in the work of Charlotte Crabtree.

From the standpoint of methodological analysis, it appears that the distinctive element of inquiry (problem solving, learning by discovery and similar approaches), is induction.[47] The general theory of inquiry, however, does not provide any systematic explanation of how students acquire the previous knowledge of concepts and data which are prerequisite to the inquiry mode.

In his provocative monograph, *The Conditions of Learning,* Gagné identifies eight types of learning—signal (classical conditioning), stimulus response, chaining, verbal association, multiple discrimination, concept learning, principle learning, and problem solving. Each type of learning is a prerequisite to the subsequent, so that problem solving may be regarded as a more complex or higher type of learning. While sympathetic to problem solving, Gagné cautions that the emphasis on problem solving will not necessarily result in greater creativity or greater thinking skill, because knowing the process of thinking is merely a part of what is needed. Large amounts of structurally organized knowledge are required, and this knowledge consists primarily of content, not heuristic, principles.[48]

As the schools seek to improve instruction, they will make even more extensive use of inquiry. Teachers will need to make adaptations according to the nature of the subject matter and the particular nature of the learner. Much teacher effort to improve inquiry may be centered around the attempt to ask questions which require more complex responses, rather than simple recall questions.[49] Older students may be

46. See Jarvis and Wootton, *Transitional Elementary School,* pp. 242-45.
47. M. C. Wittrock, "The Learning by Discovery Hypothesis," in *Learning by Discovery: A Critical Appraisal* eds. Lee S. Shulman and Evan R. Keislar (Chicago: Rand McNally & Company, 1966), pp. 33-75.
48. Robert M. Gagné, *The Conditions of Learning* (New York: Holt, Rinehart & Winston, Inc., 1965).
49. Norris M. Sanders, *Classroom Questions: What Kinds* (New York: Harper and Row, Publishers, 1966).

encouraged to engage in less structured inquiry, whereas younger pupils will be taught primarily by guided discovery. In this method, the verbal cues provide the information for the next stage. Wherever sequential material is used, it is likely that students will be engaged in guided rather than pure discovery. More responsibility is generally given the older student to answer questions. Pure discovery methods, such as those advocated by Massialas and Zevin in social studies,[50] are likely to be used sparingly by teachers.

Teachers deliberately use inquiry methods, even when they lack a complete theory or methodology of inquiry. In the ordinary course of classroom work, teachers use both didactic and heuristic modes as seem most appropriate at the moment—they tell and they ask. They ask not merely to check a pupil's knowledge, but as a means of leading him to another step in new knowledge. Teachers ask problematic questions to stimulate discussions, and force students to weigh evidence and present different views. They also use inquiry as a change of pace, for the effect of novelty. Teachers cannot wait until the researchers specify the answers to the five variables specified by Cronbach.[51] At the same time, however, they should remember that inquiry is but one mode of teaching and that poor inquiry is just as inefficient for learning as poor deduction. Inquiry is an inefficient means with which to acquire the conceptual base necessary for asking questions. The most effective way to acquire a data base is through deductive methods. Once some fundamental data have been secured, inquiry can be used to structure matters of relationship. Even when teachers do not have so-called inquiry materials at hand,

it is possible to use the textbook in a more stimulating method by asking questions which challenge students to seek rather than repeat answers.

Inquiry methods have largely been tested with advanced students. Although advocated for slower learners, there is no evidence to indicate any superiority. It may be that the limitations of a restricted language code inhibits the slower learner, no matter the mode of instruction. In managing the instructional system, however, it is possible for teachers to adapt learning tasks and methods to the student. This is the focal area of the next section.

Differentiated Instruction

Pupils differ in aptitude, interests, and performance. They come to school having had differences in the opportunity to learn largely as a result of culture and social class. As a result of schooling, the range of differences becomes even more marked; the range of achievement differences of students at the end of elementary schooling are much more pronounced than at the end of the first grade. As a result, teachers are exhorted to "individualize instruction."

Individualized Instruction. The principle of individualized instructions is based on the premise that school instruction should be adapted to the special needs of the individual learner. It is consistent with a child-centered emphasis which puts the learner and not the subject matter at the center of curriculum and teaching.

---

50. Byron G. Massialas and Jack Zevin, "Teaching Social Studies through Discovery," *Social Education* 28, no. 7 (November 1964): 384-87.

51. Lee J. Cronbach, "The Logic of Experiments on Discovery," in Shulman and Keislar, *Learning by Discovery.*

It is easy to identify and describe individual differences; it is much more difficult to plan instruction to take care of these differences. Individualization is fundamentally a tutorial concept, a concept which in previous training and experience is largely alien to teachers. There is a vast difference in a teacher being individually helpful to members of a class as each experiences difficulty or needs encouragement, and actually providing individual instruction. The former are isolated acts within uniform instruction; individualization is a sequential plan for the individual. In its developed form, it depends upon careful diagnosis and takes the form of prescriptive teaching. Rare is the school which has the resources to carry out such efforts.

An illusion of individualization is given by projects and activities, adjusted to the two variables of pupil interest and aptitude. While adjusting a project to pupil ability, this method lacks the sequential development of basic skills which are essential to the slow learner.

The concept of individualization is basically a tutorial concept. However desirable and idealistic, individualization does not give sufficient recognition to the fact that the basic organization of the school for instruction is for classes of children. Any management system which provides the teacher the logistic support for meeting individual differences must take into account class organization. Otherwise, individualization is likely to remain a mere exhortation. For this reason, it is preferable to think of differentiated instruction, rather than individualized instruction, a more neutral if less exciting term. Teachers may be able to differentiate instruction, but it is unlikely that they can provide for individual differences. While there are many adaptations of differentiated instruction, there are actually only two major approaches: one is to vary the time to achieve a set task, and the second is to vary the task within a set time. Under any of these arrangements it is likely that the slower learning pupil will learn less. A third approach, increase in time for learning task, is little used, although it theoretically provides the variable needed—time—to permit slower achieving pupils to attain a level of basic skills.

Variation in Time of Learning Task. One of the oldest and best known systems of differentiated instruction is programmed learning. Today programmed learning is presented in the form of teaching machines, tutor texts, and computer-assisted instruction.[52] While the modern interest in programmed instruction has its psychological base in Skinner's operant conditioning, the historical antecedents of programming are found in the management efforts of Frederick L. Burk prior to World War I who sought to find an alternative to the "lock-step" of instruction. Burk's efforts influenced the development of subsequent systems, such as the Winnetka and Dalton plans.[53]

While the modern variations of programmed instruction have been worked out in more sequential detail than some of the earlier efforts, they all have common char-

---

52. Center for Curriculum Planning, State University of New York at Buffalo, *Computer-Based Resource Units in School Situations* (Buffalo, N.Y.: State University, April 1969).

53. Carleton W. Washburne, "Burk's Individual System as Developed at Winnetka," in *Twenty-fourth Yearbook, 1925*, Part II, National Society for the Study of Education (Bloomington, Illinois: Public School Publishing Company, 1925).

acteristics, as first outlined by Burk. These include:

1. Organization of the curriculum into a progressive sequence.
2. Breaking down of the curriculum into specified learning tasks.
3. Preparing simple and clear material to assist the learner, through his own efforts, to accomplish the learning tasks.
4. Providing tests which demonstrate mastery of the learning tasks.
5. Progression to the next "grade" on the basis of the completion of the work allotted. (Grades are not necessary, merely a series of learning levels would suffice. A grade is empirically determined by the number of tasks which the normally industrious pupil may complete in an academic year.)

Educational technology of the 1970s makes it possible for schools to provide for differentiated instruction in most subject areas. The failure to use this technology reflects a lack of school acceptance and financial investment.

Many teachers react negatively to variations of programmed instruction because they regard it as dehumanizing; they want to see children as active and involved learners. This represents a naive interpretation of involvement, for programmed instruction requires the direct commitment and attention of the learner. The pupil has some interaction with the delivery system, but the major interaction is with the program, the skills and intellectual ideas which have been sequenced to facilitate learning.

In American education, there is always a tendency to attempt "all out" solutions. It is not necessary to differentiate instruction in every subject to take advantage of educational technology. As in the Winnetka plan, it is quite possible to have some subjects differentiated and other subjects, such as the aesthetic, undifferentiated. It is also possible to use programmed instruction for a subject like mathematics and small group methods and projects for a subject like social studies.

Variation in time spent in task is particularly adaptable to a sequential nongraded plan (see chapter 19). In the absence of a systematic plan to differentiate instruction using time as a varaiable, it is likely that individualization will be sporadic and haphazard.

Variation in Amount of Learning Task. An alternate to the variation in time pattern is the adjustment of the learning task to the level of the learner. This is the prevalent approach where the emphasis is placed on groups of individuals rather than materials (see Grouping). Three achievement groups for high, average, and low achievers are usually formed. The learning task is adjusted downward for low achieving pupils and upward for high achieving pupils, even where a common text is used, as in history. For example, the high group might be asked to write a comparative essay; the average group a descriptive essay; and the lower group to list five items. Generally, however, it is assumed that because of difference in aptitude, there will be a difference in materials, especially in the intermediate grades where reading differences often amount to several grades. Thus in a seventh grade history class, a slow group might be using a book written for the fourth grade reading level whereas the advanced group might be using materials written for high school.

In general, differentiated learning which makes its adjustment in the learning task rather than in the time is more difficult from the standpoint of management. There is an absence of clearly defined mastery tests, which indicate functional achievement levels. The range of material is often lacking, and teachers find it difficult to obtain materials after groups are formed. There is also retroactive feedback—lower achieving pupils quickly identify differences in task expectancies based on the material and frequently develop negative attitudes. There have been inadequate longitudinal studies of the multiple variables affecting task and time variables in differentiated instruction to make any claims to experimental superiority of either system.

Grouping. There are various types of homogeneous and heterogeneous groupings within the classroom. The practice of homogeneous grouping attempts to cope with the problem of individual differences by reducing the range of pupil achievement differences.

Formerly the IQ score was extensively used to assign students to homogeneous sections of low, middle, and high ability classes. Since IQ and social class are positively correlated, low IQ sections tend to be disproportionately composed of children of lower income families. The school, therefore, institutionalizes social class differences when this practice is followed. Another disadvantage is that while IQ is related to performance, there is more variability in achievement by subject than can be predicted from the IQ. The IQ measure does not reflect such facts as interest, persistence, opportunity to learn, and other variables which influence performance.[54] Furthermore, the stigma of low IQ has always had a self-fulfilling effect. Children of low IQ are not taught as much, because they are regarded as lacking in capacity. They therefore have less opportunity to learn, and learn less. For the low ability student, homogeneous IQ sectioning or grouping tends to be a vicious cycle. It is little used today except when schools, as a matter of policy, choose it to discriminate in assigning pupils to sections or teachers use it in establishing instructional groups. Intraclass achievement groups are much more defensible. They reduce the range of variability that a teacher is confronted with at a given time, but do not lock a student into a rigid within-class grouping pattern. A child may belong to several different groups, on the basis of his actual performance.

Other Individualizing Techniques. In 1951 Berthold identified 160 items which indicated different ways in which school systems attempted to provide for individual differences.[55] Most of these items fall into the two main categories (previously given) —variation in time or variation in task. His extensive list reemphasizes the soundness of an earlier list which differentiated twenty-nine items, which also were basically a variation in task or variation in time.[56] Notwithstanding the fact that the variation in time approach was managerially more sound, in the 1930s as well as in the 1950s and 1960s,[57] there was more emphasis on variation in task. This may be one reason

54. Evelyn W. Cummins, "Grouping: homogeneous or heterogeneous," *Educational Administration and Supervision* 44, no. 1 (January 1958): 19-26.
55. Charles A. Berthold, *Administrative Concern for Individual Differences* (New York: Teachers College, Bureau of Publications, Columbia University, 1951).
56. Roy O. Billett, *Provisions for Individual Differences, Marking and Promotion*, Bulletin no. 17, U.S. Office of Education (Washington, D.C.: Government Printing Office, 1932).
57. Nelson B. Henry, ed., *Individualizing Instruction: The Sixty-first Yearbook of the National Society for the Study of Education*, Part I (Chicago: University of Chicago Press, 1962).

why so little actual progress is made with differentiated instruction.

Some other techniques of differentiation should be mentioned by name. *Acceleration* in simply a device in which a pupil of above average ability is permitted to work at a performance level more equal to his academic achievement by advancement to a higher grade (task variation). *Enrichment* is the attempt to provide students, according to their achievement, with projects or activities which also reflect their interest (task variation). *Guidance* is an external device to instruction, and may be used to try to assist students in selecting more realistic tasks—high for high achieving students and low for low achieving students.

Notwithstanding the fact that for over fifty years different approaches have been tried with individualizing instruction, most teachers still teach toward the mean of the group. The extremes at both ends, the exceptionally gifted and the very slow, are neglected. Since it is difficult to differentiate instruction within the traditional school framework, it would appear that more attention needs to be directed toward establishing management systems to help the teacher bring about the appropriate match between student differences and tasks to be performed.

Appraisal of Classroom Management and Teaching

The previous section has emphasized that the teacher has two major management roles—one relates to the general classroom environment and the other to instruction. But the interaction of pupil and teacher takes place within the class and the two roles are blended in one. The teacher is the adult leader.

One set of classroom tasks which confronts the teacher are nonteaching tasks. At one time there was much emphasis placed on the need to relieve the teacher of these nonprofessional tasks so that more time could be devoted to teaching. Experience with teacher aides, however, indicates that the teacher projects his image to students in nonteaching as well as in teaching tasks. Furthermore, the performance of nonteaching tasks are sometimes welcomed by the teacher because they provide a change of pace or a chance to get out of the classroom. We therefore frequently find the teacher in the mimeograph room or the media room, with the teacher aide left in the class. Noninstructional tasks are a part of teacher behavior, and should be managed effectively to provide more time for learning and for fun.

The cultural norms of child rearing have changed, and 1970 American school pupils tend to be more outspoken, more questioning, more egalitarian, and less accepting of authority than in former years. This is what they learn at home and what they will bring to school. Younger teachers are more likely to adjust to this greater spirit of independence on the part of pupils than older teachers, who may be more likely inclined to interpret an independent attitude as a challenge of authority. But at the same time, the school need not be afraid to assert its responsibility. A culture based on principles of independence and freedom does not preclude having some taboos. It is a mistake to assume that freedom means license, or that respect for the child means deferment to every wish.

Social control in the future classroom will probably be more of an issue than it has in the past. This results from the fact that while there is a general direction in the form of greater responsibility for students, there are many parents who want the school to solve the behavioral and value conflicts that arise from the wider culture. In many communities exaggerated problems of classroom management and discipline will manifest themselves as reflections of race prejudice and white-black student conflict. Such behavioral problems in the school cannot be solved by the school alone; they reflect the malaise and prejudices of the general community. In such matters, the school can do more than is being done, but the issue is a community moral responsibility, not that simply of the school.

The threat of the drug culture moving down into the elementary school will be a specter frightening both to parents and to teachers. Formerly, it was assumed that drug use was merely an idiosyncratic quirk or a sign that the person had bad associates. Today parents who have provided children with every opportunity and privilege see them throw away a life for trips on speed and acid. What does a teacher do? What can he do? What insights can he help bring to his pupils?

Teachers should also anticipate that the public will ask more and more about school system accountability and teacher accountability. The question "How well do you teach?" will also be asked more and more. Teachers are very likely to be caught in the middle of parental demands for cognitive outcomes and the traditional posture of the school that it is committed to teaching the whole child. Is a teacher responsible for the whole child? Are the parents and other community agencies responsible for some learnings which are incidental to the school? The issue of teacher accountability, therefore, not only engenders questions of methodology related to teaching, but is likely to influence a reexamination of the aims and purposes of education.

Should there be a commonality of aims and purposes, or should there be different schools with different purposes to accommodate different interests of parents (the child is a captive client)? Would this permit teachers to find schools which best suit their own teaching styles and personality? It might be that there should be many different types of schools in a community, reflecting many different approaches to education. All of these might be equally meaningful, in terms of the value systems of their patrons.

It is likely that teacher organizations will prevent any serious attempt to measure teacher effectiveness. As prospective teachers move out into the teaching profession, however, they must assume that not only the system, but the individual teacher, will be more critically appraised in future years. Hence, effectual management techniques within the classroom are essential.

Selected References

ADAMS, JOHN. *Exposition and Illustration in Teaching.* New York: Macmillan Company, 1926.

AUSUBEL, DAVID P. *The Psychology of Meaningful Verbal Learning.* New York: Grune & Stratton, 1963.

BIDDLE, BRUCE J. and ELLENA, WILLIAM J., eds. *Contemporary Research on Teacher Effectiveness.* New York: Holt, Rinehart & Winston, Inc., 1964.

BURTON, WILLIAM H. *The Guidance of Learning Activities.* 3d ed. New York: Appleton-Century-Crofts, Inc., 1962.

FENTON, EDWIN. *Teaching the New Social Studies in Secondary Schools: An Inductive Approach.* New York: Holt, Rinehart & Winston, Inc., 1966.

GAGNÉ, ROBERT M. *The Conditions of Learning.* New York: Holt, Rinehart & Winston, Inc., 1965.

GARRISON, KARL C.; KINGSTON, ALBERT J.; and MCDONALD, ARTHUR S. *Educational Psychology.* 2d ed. New York: Appleton-Century-Crofts, 1964.

HENRY, NELSON B., editor. *Individualizing Instruction: The Sixty-first Yearbook of the National Society for the Study of Education,* Part I. Chicago, Ill.: University of Chicago Press, 1962.

JARVIS, OSCAR T. and WOOTTON, LUTIAN R. *The Transitional Elementary School and its Curriculum.* Dubuque, Iowa: Wm. C. Brown Company Publishers, 1966.

KLAUSMEIER, HERBERT J., and GOODWIN, WILLIAM. *Learning and Human Abilities: Educational Psychology.* 2d ed. New York: Harper & Row, Publishers, 1966.

LANDES, RUTH. *Culture in American Education.* New York: John Wiley & Sons, Inc., 1965.

MCDONALD, BLANCHE, and NELSON, LESLIE. *Successful Classroom Control.* Dubuque, Iowa: Wm. C. Brown Company Publishers, 1955.

MCKOWN, HARRY C. *Activities in the Elementary School.* New York: McGraw-Hill Book Company, Inc., 1938.

MEHL, MARIE A., et al. *Teaching in Elementary School.* 3d ed. New York: Ronald Press Company, 1965.

PETERSEN, DOROTHY G. *The Elementary School Teacher.* New York: Appleton-Century-Crofts, 1964.

RAGAN, WILLIAM B. *Teaching America's Children.* New York: Holt, Rinehart & Winston, Inc., 1961.

RIEBE, H. A.; NELSON, M. J.; and KITTRELL, C. A. *The Classroom: Management, Administration, Organization.* New York: Cordon Company, 1938.

REINOEHL, CHARLES M., and AYER, FRED C. *Classroom Administration and Pupil Adjustment.* New York: D. Appleton-Century Company, 1940.

SYLWESTER, ROBERT. *Common Sense in Classroom Relations.* West Nyack, N.Y.: Parker Publishing Co., Inc., 1966.

SHULMAN, LEE S., and KEISLAR, EVAN R., eds. *Learning by Discovery: A Critical Appraisal.* Chicago: Rand McNally & Company, 1966.

PART SEVEN

the teacher confronts major issues

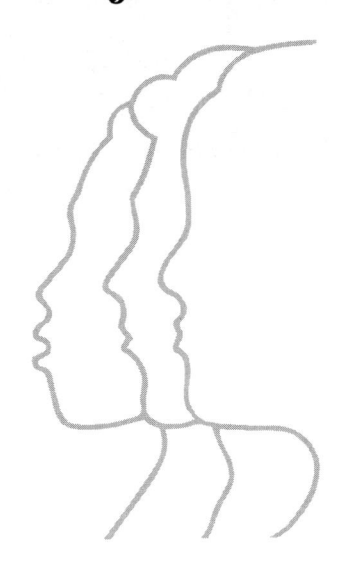

Photo: Courtesy of El Paso (Texas) Independent School District.
Photography: Seth J. Edwards, Jr.

integration: the challenge of democracy in race relations

22

At the beginning of the 1970s, school officials in the South are seeking to eliminate the operation of dual school systems, in compliance with court orders or pressure from the Department of Health, Education, and Welfare. On the streets, Negro students are demonstrating against the closing of Negro schools. In the South, the ratio of students attending all-black schools has decreased. Outside of the South, the number of Negro students attending predominantly black schools has increased. At the same time, Negro leaders are calling for an increase in Negro control over all-black schools and an increase in the number of Negro principals and teachers.

Almost two decades have passed since the historic *Brown* decision. During this time, the unconstitutionality of government enforced segregation has been changed to require operation of unitary school systems, characterized by teacher and pupil racial balance. There has been an increase in black awareness, and with this renewed self-esteem, an increase in the spirit of black separatism.

Is there to be a retreat from the principle of *Brown* affirming the importance of education on equal terms as fundamental to our democratic society? It is the thesis of this chapter that racial separatism is inimical to the long term interests of the United States. If the schools are concerned, as most educators and jurists assert, with more than academic achievement, teachers cannot close their eyes to the challenge of racial separatism. And teachers cannot cope with the challenge by responding with the easy clichés of bussing costs or the concept of the neighborhood school.

This chapter gives a brief overview of the legal basis of desegregation, research related to desegregation, and suggestions for teaching in integrated schools. Throughout the chapter, the point of view is taken that the legal as well as moral requirements of a democratic society require the elimination of segregated education, whether of the de jure or de facto type. This chapter focuses on the Negro minority. Even after *Brown,* however, discrimination against Americans of Indian or Spanish-speaking origin is widespread.[1] Elimination of dis-

1. Texas State Advisory Committee to the United States Commission on Civil Rights, *The Civil Rights Status of Spanish-Speaking Americans in Kleberg, Nueces, and San Patricio Counties, Texas* (Washington, D.C.: Government Printing Office, 1967); U.S. Commission on Civil Rights, *The Mexican American* (Washington, D.C.: Government Printing Office, n. d.).

crimination against all minority groups is therefore linked with the elimination of Negro discrimination.

Legal Basis of School Integration

In the last twenty years, the concept of the elimination of legal segregation has moved from desegregation to the establishment of unitary school systems.

In 1954 the Supreme Court held in the *Brown*[2] case that the legal segregation of public education was a denial of the equal protection of the laws, as provided by the Fourteenth Amendment, and that the "separate but equal" doctrine of the *Plessy*[3] case had no place in public education. In the following year, the companion *Brown* ruling established the doctrine of admission to public schools on a racially nondiscriminatory basis with "all deliberate speed."

No judicial decision, however, is self-implementing. Application of the *res judicata,* the substantive ruling of the case to analogous circumstances, depends upon the actions of individuals. While in the border states there was rapid voluntary compliance, in general, the reaction to the *Brown* ruling from politicians, school officials, and the public was extremely hostile. There was no commitment from the presidency for executive implementation, no parallel legislation by the Congress, and no moral national commitment. The burden of bringing about desegregation in each individual case was imposed on the Negro minority.

The history of school integration during the first decade is a story of snail-paced development. The most notable legal development during this period is the affirmation in the Little Rock case that the constitutional rights of children to attend desegregated schools cannot be sacrificed to violence induced by the governor or legislature of a state.[4] The old states' rights doctrines of nullification and interposition were legally dead, although they continued very much alive in the form of lack of positive action to desegregate schools, hostility to Negro plaintiffs, and continued dalliance which reduced the principle of "all deliberate speed" to no speed.

It was not until the Civil Rights Act of 1964, however, that legislation was enacted which provided for the termination of federal funds to school districts which excluded or discriminated against children on the basis of color, religion, or national origin.[5] The Civil Rights Act of 1964 heralded the period of the "guidelines," in which officials of the Office of Education set minimum conditions for the achievement of desegregation. These guidelines began with "freedom of choice" plans, which permitted any child to request attendance at the school of his choice. Freedom of choice did not work, because school officials took the cynical position that they could have a legally desegregated school system in which no Negro child exercised his freedom of choice to

---

2. Brown v. Board of Education, 347 U.S. 483 (1954).

3. Plessy v. Ferguson, 163 U.S. 537 (1896). Critics of the 1954 Brown case have frequently alleged that the ruling was based on social science theory and not on legal precedent. These critics have seldom noted that the *Plessy* precedent, which was overruled, was a blatant legal blessing of the racist assumption of white superiority which was characteristic of the late nineteenth century. Mr. Justice Harlan, in his dissenting opinion, expressed the famous *dicta* "our constitution is colorblind, and neither knows nor tolerates classes among citizens." He further stated the view that the *Plessy* doctrine "will, in time, prove to be quite as pernicious as the decision made by this tribunal in the Dred Scott Case . . ."

4. Cooper v. Aaron, 358 U.S. 1 (1958).

5. 42 U.S.C. § 2000d.

attend a white school; or, if he did so, he frequently had his petition denied with flimsy excuses such as inadequate facilities in the receiving building. As in judicial litigation, the burden of exercising "free choice" was placed on the Negro child, for it was tacitly assumed that no white child would request assignment from a white to a Negro school. The climate of community hostility, also reflected in students and teachers, was expected to cause Negroes to exercise their freedom of choice to continue attendance in Negro schools.

Freedom of choice proved to be a means of continuing the status quo. Notwithstanding the prohibitions in the Civil Rights Act of 1964[6] against assignment of pupils to overcome racial imbalance, both the Office of Education and the courts began to approve desegregation plans on the basis of racial quota assignment. Judicial approval of racial balance was indirectly stated in *Jefferson* in 1967.[7] In March 1968, the HEW guidelines set the school year 1969-70 as the latest for the establishment of integrated, unitary school systems in which there would be no Negro or other minority schools and no white schools.[8]

The school year 1969 not only saw the replacement of the concept of school desegregation by the concept of a unitary school system, but it also saw the abandonment of the Brown doctrine of "all deliberate speed." In reversing the Fifth Circuit Court, which had granted a delay in integration in Mississippi schools on intervention of the U.S. Attorney General, the Supreme Court ruled in *Holmes* that the continued operation of racially segregated schools under the standard of all deliberate speed was no longer constitutionally permissible. "School districts must immediately terminate dual school systems based on race and operate only unitary school systems."[9]

The 1969-70 school year also brought other significant developments. Not only did the decisions require the establishment of a unitary system, but the principle was established that teachers of both races should be assigned, as in Atlanta, on a pro rata basis to white and Negro students. It was now mandatory that white teachers be assigned to teach Negro students, and Negro teachers, white students, even in schools which were predominantly or entirely of the other race.[10]

Another trend was the initiation of action against state boards of education, rather than individual school districts as in *United States of America* v. *The State of Georgia*.[11] This action involved eighty-one school districts which had failed to meet criteria for

---

6. " 'Desegregation' means the assignment of students to public schools and within such schools without regard to their race, color, religion, or national origin, but 'desegregation' shall not mean the assignment of students to public schools in order to overcome racial imbalance." 42 U.S.C. § 2000c (b). Also, ". . . nothing herein shall empower any official or court of the United States to issue any order seeking to achieve a racial balance in any school by requiring the transportation of pupils from one school to another or one school district to another in order to achieve such racial balance . . . ." 42 U.S.C. § 2000c-6(a).

7. United States v. Jefferson County Board of Education, 380 F. 2d 385 (1967).

8. 33 F. Reg. 4956 (March 1968). "Compliance with the law requires integration of faculties, facilities, and activities, as well as students, so that there are no Negro or other minority group schools and no white schools—just schools."

9. Alexander v. Holmes County Board of Education, 396 U.S. 19, 20 (1969); Carter v. West Feliciana Parish, 396 U.S. 226 (1969). See also Griffin v. School Board, 377 U.S. 218, 234 (1964) and Green v. County School Board of New Kent County, 391 U.S. 438 (1968).

10. Singleton v. Jackson Municipal Separate School District, 419 F. 2d 1211 (1970).

11. 428 F. 2d 377; also Lee and United States v. Macon County Board of Education, 317 F. Supp. 95 (1970).

the establishment of unitary school systems. Another trend was the greater emphasis on judicial consolidation of cases involving many school districts in South Carolina, in contrast with individual judicial disposition of each case.[12]

Judicial action thus far has applied primarily to the Southern states, where there was de jure segregation. It is clear that a school district may not be gerrymandered to bring about the appearance of de facto segregation.[13] Legally unresolved, however, is the entire problem of de facto segregation, the segregation of education which results from segregated living patterns.[14] In his address concerning school integration, President Nixon affirmed his support of the elimination of every vestige of de jure dual school systems. He distinguished, however, between segregation arising from law and custom, saying: ". . . de jure segregation arises by law or by the deliberate act of school officials and is unconstitutional; de facto segregation results from residential housing patterns and does not violate the Constitution."

However, a California Superior Court Judge ruled in 1970 that Los Angeles had practiced de facto desegregation and should provide for complete pupil integration by September 1971.[15] Residential segregation is not merely found in one region; it is a national pattern. Efforts to reduce de facto segregation varies from school district to school district.[16]

Extent of De Facto School Desegregation

During the last twenty years, emphasis on school desegregation has focused on the southern states where dual school systems persisted into 1970. At the same time, efforts to bring about racial balance in southern school systems caused more attention to be given to the de facto segregation in northern states. The extent of northern de facto segregation is so great that it led Senator Ribicoff to charge his colleagues with "monumental hypocrisy" in dealing with the matter of southern school desegregation. In 1970, the State of Georgia filed an action in the District Court of Columbia alleging (a) unconstitutional imposition of racial quotas prohibited by the Civil Rights Act of 1964 or (b) uniform application of the principle of racial balance to all the states.[17]

A January 4, 1970 news release by the U.S. Department of Health, Education and Welfare shows that in Fall 1968 only 23.4 percent of Negro pupils enrolled in the Nation's public schools attended schools with a predominantly white enrollment. Sixty-one percent of the country's black pupils were enrolled in almost totally black schools, i.e., schools with 95 to 100 percent black enrollment. The trend toward the increase in attendance by Negroes in all black schools is not new. The 1967 report of the Commission on Civil Rights indicated

12. Whittenburg v. Greenville County [S.C.] School District, 298 F. Supp. 784 (1969); 424 F. 2d 195 (1970).
13. Taylor v. Board of Education 294 F. 2d 36 (2d Cir.), cert. denied 368 U.S. 940 (1961). Clemons v. Board of Education, 228 F. 2d 853 (6th Cir.), cert. denied, 350 U.S. 1006 (1956).
14. *Atlanta Constitution,* 25 March 1970, p. 12-A.
15. 1 *Race Rel. L. Survey* 258 (March 1970). It was declared that deprivation of any part of the people of equal educational opportunity is "a denial of their rights as human beings, the inalienable rights of life, liberty and pursuit of happiness as citizens of our state and country."
16. T. Bentley Edwards and Frederick M. Wirt, eds., *School Desegregation: The Challenge and the Experience* (San Francisco: Chandler Publishing Co., 1967).
17. The State of Georgia v. John N. Mitchell, Civil Action No. 265-70, United States District Court for the District of Columbia.

integration: the challenge of democracy in race relations

a substantial increase in racial polarization in the schools of the North, as table 22.1 shows.

Even in school districts where Negroes constitute a small minority—10 percent in Hamilton, Ohio; 18 percent in Peoria, Illinois; 6 percent in Penn Hills Township, Pennsylvania; and 9 percent in Fresno, California— most Negroes attend schools in which Negroes are a majority. Racial polarization in nonsouthern states is thus not merely a product of the urban ghetto.[18]

States outside of the South also discriminate against Negroes in the matter of teacher employment. There are fewer Negro teachers in northern school districts, whereas in the southern states the ratio of Negro teachers is equivalent to the pupil enrollment. The problem of racial imbalance among teachers in districts outside of the South is handled by the simple expedient of little employment of black teachers. This discriminatory action cannot be justified by de facto housing segregation. In New York City, with a black public school enrollment of 32 percent, only 24 of the 893 school principals are black.[19]

It is likely that the question of de facto school segregation will become increasingly critical in the 1970s. Certainly, there will be a great difference of opinion on this matter. It is likely that the question of the affirmative duty to integrate will be increasingly

18. HEW IBM data sheets for 1968-69 showing the extent of de facto segregation in certain states outside of the south were entered into the *Congressional Record* by Senator Stennis as follows: Ohio, 25 November 1969, S 14986; New Jersey, 2 December 1969, S 15378; Pennsylvania, 3 December 1969, S 15485; Illinois, 6 December 1969, S 15998; New York, with reply by Senator Javits, 9 December 1969, S 16179; and California, 11 December 1969, S 16492.

19. *Time*, 6 April 1970, p. 46.

Table 22.1. Change in number and proportion of Negro elementary enrollment in 90-100 percent Negro and majority-Negro schools in Northern school systems. From United States Commission on Civil Rights, *Racial Isolation in the Public Schools* (Washington, D.C.: Government Printing Office, 1967), table 3, p. 9.

City	Year	90-100% Negro Enrollment (Percentage)	Majority Negro Enrollment (Percentage)	Year	90-100% Negro Enrollment (Percentage)	Majority Negro Enrollment (Percentage)
Cincinnati	1950	43.7	70.7	1965	49.4	88.0
Milwaukee	1950	51.2	66.8	1965	72.4	86.8
Pasadena	1950	0.0	26.2	1965	0.0	71.4
Philadelphia	1950	63.2	84.8	1965	72.0	90.2
Pittsburgh	1950	30.4	51.0	1965	49.5	82.8
Indianapolis	1951	83.2	88.2	1965	70.5	84.2
Cleveland	1952	57.4	84.4	1962	82.3	94.6
Oakland	1959	7.7	71.1	1965	48.7	83.2
Detroit	1960	66.9	91.1	1965	72.3	91.5
Buffalo	1961	80.5	89.4	1965	77.0	88.7
San Francisco	1962	11.6	75.8	1965	21.1	72.3
Chester	1963	71.1	85.8	1965	77.9	89.1
Harrisburg	1963	58.1	82.7	1965	54.0	81.3
Springfield, Mass.	1963	0.0	58.8	1965	15.4	71.9
New Haven	1963	22.5	71.0	1965	36.8	73.4

tested in the courts where adherence to school attendance policies, such as residence patterns, inevitably though not intentionally result in segregation. Fiss has taken the position that de facto segregation is not a matter of private action. He contends that economic disabilities, coupled with a likely hostile reception in white neighborhoods, will continue racial discrimination in housing. Moreover, he believes that the familiar invasion-succession sequence deprives many black people the opportunity of moving out of the ghetto and this leads to the subsequent creation of other ghettos in areas where negroes are able to move.[20]

The effect of de facto segregation has the same practical consequences of de jure segregation. It deprives students of the intellectual stimulation that comes from the exchange of ideas in racially heterogeneous schools and the development of personal relationships in a socially heterogeneous context.[21] Wright has indicated that elimination of the restrictive conditions of "practical" and "feasible," both of which emphasize financial limitations, permit a great variety of solutions which will facilitate integration.[22]

In 1970, however, additional questions are being raised about the whole issue of using the schools to bring about greater black-white assimilation. One concern in the North is greater control by blacks over black schools, which reflects disillusionment with the pace and consequences of desegregation. Thus "While the courts and HEW are reassigning faculties in Atlanta to reflect the racial composition of the school and bring white teachers to black pupils and black teachers to white ones, Negro leaders in the North are asking for black principals and black teachers for black schools." Bickel advocates that rather than trying to do away with black schools, the energies and resources of the country should go into their improvement.[23]

The doctrine of school improvement is a disguised revival of the separate but equal doctrine, and is a convenient way of ignoring the entire array of practices which support de facto segregation. Among the most important of these practices, institutionalized in American society, are job discrimination and housing discrimination. A retreat from school integration may herald even further retreat from a commitment to equalize opportunities of all American citizens to share in the benefits of American society.

A frequently expressed fear of school integration is the detrimental impact of Negro performance levels on the achievement of white pupils. This fear stems from a combination of factors—racist assumptions of inferior Negro intelligence,[24] lower Negro achievement and intelligence test scores,[25] and the knowledge that a dual school system tolerated inferior schools for Negroes.[26]

20. Owen M. Fiss, *Racial Imbalance in the Public Schools: The Constitutional Concepts,* 78 HARVARD LAW REVIEW 564, 585 (1965).
21. Notes. *Racial Imbalance in the Public Schools: Constitutional Dimensions and Judicial Response* 18 VANDERBILT LAW REVIEW 1290, 1295-96 (1965).
22. J. S. Wright, *Public School Desegregation: Legal Remedies for De Facto Segregation,* 40 YALE UNIVERSITY LAW REVIEW 285 (1965).
23. Alexander M. Bickel, "Desegregation: Where Do We Go From Here?" *New Republic,* 7 February 1970, pp. 20, 22.
24. Audrey M. Shuey, *The Testing of Negro Intelligence,* 2d ed. New York: Social Science Press, 1966).
25. Wallace A. Kennedy, V. Van de Riet, and James C. White, *The Standardization of the 1960 Revising of the Stanford-Binet Intelligence Scale on Negro Elementary School Children in the Southeastern United States* (Talahassee: Human Development Clinic, Florida State University, 1961).
26. Aaron Brown, *An Evaluation of the Accredited Secondary Schools for Negroes in the South* (Chicago: University of Chicago, 1944).

The academic consequences of integration have not been as favorable to increments in Negro achievement as advocates might wish, but neither has integration had the disastrous effect on white achievement that critics imagined. Carefully conducted integration research has been limited. In a 1968 survey of fourteen studies conducted between 1958 and 1967, Weinberg concluded that integration benefits the achievement of Negro children, and that white children do not suffer any disadvantage.[27] While the Coleman report is somewhat ambiguous with respect to the effects of class and race, it shows that there is an achievement advantage for Negroes in integrated schools, where there is a majority of white students.[28] A second federal study, that of the U.S. Commission on Civil Rights, presents a similar conclusion.[29] The McPartland study indicates the favorable effect of integration on Negro achievement, but also demonstrates that no beneficial results occur when Negro children attend segregated classes in a desegregated school.[30]

Aspirations of Negro children are not enhanced by attendance at desegregated schools. Negro children in all black schools have equally high aspirations as Negro children in desegregated schools. This finding, which is contrary to the research of the 1940s which was incorporated into *Brown*,[31] reflects the Civil Rights revolution of the 1960s. During this period, however, Negro Americans developed a new sense of identity and self-awareness that substantially altered their aspirations.[32] These aspirations, as Coleman notes, may often be idealized and not related to behavior which is systematically organized to lead to goal achievement.[33] The fact nevertheless remains that Negro students now often reflect higher aspirations than white students, whether they attend integrated or segregated schools.[34] The high vocational aspirational level of Negro children is evidenced as early as the sixth grade.[35]

A review of the more recent research findings relating to Negro self-esteem continues to show both negative and favorable self-concepts. With respect to self-concept, Wein-

27. Meyer Weinberg, *Desegregation Research: An Appraisal* (Bloomington, Ind.: Phi Delta Kappa Commission on Education, Human Rights, and Responsibilities, 1968). pp. 52-53.

28. James S. Coleman and others, *Equality of Educational Opportunity* (Washington, D.C.: Government Printing Office, 1966), pp. 29, 307, 331.

29. U.S. Commission on Civil Rights, *Racial Isolation in the Public Schools*, I (Washington, D.C.: Government Printing Office, 1967), pp. 98-99.

30. James McPartland, *The Relative Influence of School Desegregation and of Classroom Desegregation on the Academic Achievement of Ninth Grade Negro Students.* Interim Report (Baltimore, Md.: Center for the Study of Social Organization of Schools, Johns Hopkins University, 1967), pp. 3-4.

31. The Brown case accepted the prevailing evidence that enforced segregation contributed to denigrative self-perception and aspiration, saying that to separate Negro children "from others of similar age and qualifications solely because of their race generates a feeling of inferiority as to their status in the community that may affect their hearts and minds in a way unlikely ever to be undone." Brown v. Board of Education, 347 U.S. 483, 494 (1953). See appellant's brief incorporating a statement by thirty-two social scientists of the harmful effects of segregation. *The Effects of Segregation and the Consequences of Desegregation* 37 MINNESOTA LAW REVIEW 427 (1953).

32. Thomas F. Pettigrew, *A Profile of the Negro American* (Princeton, N. J.: D. Van Nostrand, 1964), p. 184.

33. James S. Coleman, *Race Relations and Social Change* (Baltimore, Md.: Center for the Study of Social Organization of Schools, Johns Hopkins University, 1967), p. 31.

34. Meyer Weinberg, *Desegregation Research: An Appraisal* (Bloomington, Ind.: Phi Delta Kappa, 1968), pp. 65-82.

35. Robert G. Brown, "A Comparison of the Vocational Aspirations of Paired Sixth-Grade White and Negro Children Who Attend Segregated Schools," *Journal of Educational Research* 58, no. 9 (May-June, 1965): 402-4.

berg concludes that desegregation has tended to benefit Negro self-esteem and helped Negroes to accept color in a more consructtive manner.[36] Desegregation, however, has been a critical factor in developing Negro pride. The emphasis on negative Negro self-image, characteristics of the Ausubel's synthesis of 1963,[37] is no longer consistent with research or the changed social climate. Consequently, teachers who predicate instruction based on the older concepts of negative self-image may inadvertently develop a self-fulfilling prophecy. The need is for communities to raise the levels of aspirations for all low status students, not merely that of the Negro.

Psychological Aspects of Integration

It has been one of the great contradictions of American culture that it could tolerate a caste system alongside an ideology of a mobile society of equal opportunity. It is this kind of contradiction which led the Swedish economist Gunnar Myrdal to describe the issue of the Negro in American culture as *The American Dilemma*. Under conditions of slavery, bondage institutionalized the separation of white and Negro. After emancipation, the Negro was socially treated as an outcaste, although he was legally free. This pattern of behavior had an effect on the behavior of both white and Negro. Essentially, it might be described as one of mutual distrust. Behind the servility that permitted survival, the Negro acted as if there was little hope. He acted out the role of the self-fulfilling prophecy. And the institution of Jim Crow merely betrayed the paranoia in which the white lived.

Segregation was thus a double-edged sword. It kept the Negro in his place, but it also made the white captive to a host of fears. Political demagoguery, religious bigotry, and intellectual malnutrition were three products of prejudice and discrimination. Denial of jobs to the Negro, education, fair housing, and civil liberties also denied them access to association with the whites. The fact that the South has so long been a region of economic and educational underdevelopment merely reflects the fact that when one group seeks to limit the opportunities for another, the restrictive measures eventually work to the impoverishment of the oppressor; a paradox.

Integration of the races in all matters of public contact is therefore liberating not merely to the Negro, but to the white as well. It is liberating psychologically, because it removes the burden of guilt which segregation imposes on the white and permits the development of vast talent resources which have been untapped. It is liberating sociologically, because it permits the Negro to participate in any aspect of the culture he chooses, based on his ability and interests.

The last decade of rapid Negro development has nevertheless witnessed a sharp increase in black segregationist sentiment. Part of this is the result of relative deprivation. While the Negro is better off today in absolute terms, his progress has not matched his aspirations.[38] Consequently, there has developed a new concept of segregation which gives comfort to the older white segregationist thought—the black power ghetto. According to this thesis, reflected in such

36. Weinberg, *Desegregation Research*, pp. 100-101.

37. David P. Ausubel and Pearl Ausubel, "Ego Development Among Segregated Negro Children," in *Education in Depressed Areas*, ed. Harry A. Passow (New York: Teachers College, Columbia University, 1963), p. 118.

38. Thomas F. Pettigrew, *A Profile of the Negro American*, pp. 178-79.

measures as Black Studies for Negroes only, the Negro will move to a status of integration after he has developed a sense of pride and autonomy in himself.[39]

It is the thesis of this chapter that fully integrated institutions are the best means for both whites and Negroes to resolve the problem of living in a multi-ethnic society. Individuals of both races need to share common tasks and work together to achieve common purposes. The demographic distribution of the population may make it impossible to achieve fully integrated institutions for large numbers of Negroes. In these cases, special compensatory efforts in housing, education, jobs, health, and welfare will be required. But the long-term solution should be a concerted effort to make the institutions and opportunities of American culture available to all Negroes and other minority groups, as well as whites. While the schools and teachers of America cannot do the entire job alone, they can make a beginning. School integration, therefore, is not merely a matter of Negroes and whites going to school together. It is learning to behave in a micro-society which someday may be translated to the larger society. Whether conceived from the viewpoint of desegregation or more positively from the viewpoint of integration, the initial period frequently creates stress for parents of both races as well as teachers and pupils in the school.[40] A rational approach to the complex factors involved has indicated nevertheless that workable solutions can be found which enhance cooperative participation in a common democratic ideal.

A Curriculum to Promote Race Relations

Most schools have been forced to desegregate. As a result, there has often been inadequate preparation for the consequences of integration. Not only has there been a lack of staff preparation, but there has been a lack of student preparation. Long rooted prejudices among both whites and blacks do not suddenly disappear simply because they find themselves attending classes together. In fact, association in a similar school environment frequently serves to stimulate aggressive behavior on the part of both races. A curriculum to promote race relations therefore should be regarded as an essential part of the learning experiences of white, black, or other minority students. "Curriculum" as used in this sense applies not merely to the bookish aspects of learning about race and prejudice, but it includes those aspects of school behavior—from student council to playground and lunch room—where children have the opportunity to practice behavior which displays both good manners and respect for the dignity of each pupil.

Ethnic Studies; Black Studies

An examination of the content of many school books still used in the public schools indicate perjorative or stereotyped interpretations of minority groups. Or, even more, the role of Negroes, Spanish-speaking Americans, Indians, or others may be simply neglected. This has led to the charge that American history has deprived minority groups of any knowledge of their past. As a result, the last few years have seen a tremendous increase in the production of materials, often of poor quality, dealing with

---

39. Thomas F. Pettigrew, "Racially Separate or Together," *Journal of Social Issues* 25 (January 1969): 43-69.

40. Committee on Social Issues, *Emotional Aspects of School Desegregation* (New York: Group for the Advancement of Psychiatry, 1960).

minority groups, especially the Negro experience. While Black Studies have received more publicity at the college and high school level, most large urban systems now maintain Black Studies centers which provide materials for elementary as well as high school use. These Black Studies programs, however, are designed primarily for schools in which the population is entirely or primarily Negro.

In a period during which Negroes are asserting a new sense of identity, it is inevitable that special programs should be established and special emphasis given to the Negro experience. Where there has been a void, there will be an over-compensation, whether in teaching about the Negro past or in trying to secure jobs for Negroes on a quota basis, as in the Philadelphia Plan. But it should be recognized that such movements are ethnocentric and, in the long run, self-defeating. The Negro in America shares a common heritage with the culture of this country, and, just because he is black, is no closer to the music of some rhythmic tribal dance than he is to the music of Wagner. *White* children and *black* children need to share common educational experiences about the Negro past, and the emphasis on Black Studies which excludes the *white* learner is not educationally defensible. Certainly, the contribution of all groups to the development of this country should be recognized. And if a Pulaski is recognized as a Pole or Banneker is recognized as a Negro, the intent is not to laud a particular ethnic group, but for students to understand that men from diverse backgrounds have all contributed to this country's development. Such recognition is also designed to develop the idea that ethnic or racial origin has nothing to do with competency, but that where men have an opportunity to learn they have an opportunity to create.

Representative Pucinski, Illinois, proposed in 1969 the appropriation of federal funds for the establishment of Ethnic Study Centers.[41] At first sight, this proposal appears to be a legitimate one. Do we not have the Irish with St. Patrick's Day, the Chinese with their New Year, or the Jews with Purim? Such special occasions are often recognized in the public schools in communities which have such ethnic elements. The creation of ethnic study centers is predicated on the assumption that there are different ethnic contributions which need to be identified and to be preserved. The danger in such splinter approaches is that we forget the fact that the school is an institution for the education of a common citizenry, with a common devotion to the American democratic tradition. Persons of diverse ethnic backgrounds should be recognized, but the ethnic adulatory approach should be avoided.

The curriculum of all schools should be designed for Americans, irrespective of the composition of the student body in a school at a given time. In a community where there are no minority groups, the absence of class membership and community contact will naturally create a different context in which information about minority groups is transmitted. Lacking will be the opportunity for direct contact and the experience of going to school, playing, and working with boys and girls of another race. The curriculum, however, should include certain minimum elements. Some of these elements are suggested below.

Race and Prejudice. Elementary students should be specifically taught race as

---

41. H.R. 1490, 91st Cong., 1st sess., 1969.

a biological concept.[42] A social concept of race is a product of ignorance, false learning and prejudice. Physical differences do exist among different populations. Children need to be able to put these differences into scientific perspective, as a counteraction to the bigotry that is often associated with racist interpretations. Teachers also need to be more aware of prejudice as a phenomenon reflecting learned behavior.[43]

Race and Poverty. It is not sufficient to merely talk about race as a biological concept. Race in the United States has been accompanied by a long history of discrimination, leading to high incidences of minority poverty. As noted in the next chapter on "The Culturally Disadvantaged," poverty usually deprives children of the chances for a successful and happy life. Elementary pupils need to become aware of the fact that differences in income do not merely make for differences in the kind of neighborhood or fun children can have as children but income differences affect their futures as adults.[44] Children who are reared in suburbia in particular need educational content which is more socially realistic.[45] Some of the time now devoted to comparative cultures around the world might well be diverted to providing better factual information about cultural diversities in the United States reflecting race, caste, and prejudice.

Race and Intergroup Relations. Unlike systematic sciences, in which knowledge is organized into some logical framework, teaching to improve intergroup relations is not the function of a unit, or a course. It depends upon the entire climate of the school and the attitude of adults as they work with children in a fair and friendly manner. It is nevertheless possible to plan certain experiences which will require children of different backgrounds to empathize verbal interaction. This means that children may not only be introduced to factual information, but also asked to interpret that factual information in terms of their own value orientations and sense of fair play. It is one thing for children to learn factually that Negro high school graduates now can expect to earn $1,000 less than white high school graduates. It is another thing for them to be asked: "How would you like to make $1,000 less a year because the color of your skin is white?" It is one thing to talk about segregated housing. It is another thing to have to answer the question: "Why can't I live where I want to live?"

Attempts to provide suggestions for teaching intergroup relations in the schools have been developed, such as those by Gibson[46] and Kleg and Rice.[47] There is no evidence as to the effectiveness of these approaches in substantially changing beliefs and atti-

42. A suitable manual on which teachers may draw for resource material is Milton Kleg, Marion J. Rice, and Wilfrid C. Bailey, *Race, Caste, and Prejudice* (Athens, Ga.: Anthropology Curriculum Project, 1970).
43. Kenneth B. Clark, *Prejudice and Your Child*, 2d ed. (Boston: Beacon Press, 1955); Charles Y. Glock and Ellen Siegelman, eds., *Prejudice, U.S.A.* (New York: Frederick A. Praeger, 1969).
44. See the economic status essays in Kenneth B. Clark and Talcott Parsons, eds., *The Negro American* (Boston: Beacon Press, 1966) and "The Revolt Against Welfare Colonialism" in Charles E. Silberman, *Crisis in Black and White* (New York: Random House, 1964).
45. Alice Miel, *The Shortchanged Children of Suburbia,* American Jewish Committee, Pamphlet Series no. 8 (New York: Institute of Human Relations Press, 1967).
46. John S. Gibson, *The Intergroup Relations Curriculum: A Program for the Elementary School*, vol. 2 (Medford, Mass.: Lincoln Filene Center for Citizenship and Public Affairs, Tufts University, 1969).
47. Milton Kleg and Marion J. Rice, *Teacher and Pupil Manual for Race, Caste and Prejudice* (Athens, Ga.: University of Georgia, Anthropology Curriculum Project, 1970). The activities suggested may be adapted to elementary students.

tudes, but teacher feedback has been favorable. Most of the material, however, consists of manuals of teacher suggestions, rather than materials which can be placed in the hands of elementary pupils.[48]

Recognition of Minority Contributions. Because the history of minority groups has been ignored or distorted, teachers will have to make a special attempt to include consideration of minority groups in learning experiences. Perhaps there is no ideal way. Units which concentrate on particular groups in culturally mixed classes do not seem appropriate because the concentrated attention on one group is negatively interpreted by another. For example, in social studies, it would appear more appropriate to specifically recognize the contributions of Negro leaders, inventors, scientists, artists, and musicians in the appropriate context of instruction rather than to have separate units on Negroes. Where the text fails to include appropriate material, reading lists should include Negro biographies and related supplementary material. Class and individual projects, such as murals, plays, papers, and reports, should include options which permit recognition of Negroes as a part of American cultural development. The birthday of Martin Luther King, Jr. should be recognized not merely as a Negro leader in Negro schools, but in all schools as a great American who spoke to the moral conscience of mankind.

Similar procedures can be used in classes other than social studies. While most white children are aware of the eminence which Negroes have achieved in sports, few are aware that there are Negro artists, composers, and writers. While many of them are concerned with interpreting the Negro experience, many of them also address themselves to a universal audience. *White* children as well as *black* children need to be aware of the particular points of view of the Negro as he looks at himself within the context of American culture.

In many cases, American history has been grossly unfair to the Negro in the treatment given slavery as an economic and social institution, in the interpretation of the Reconstruction period, and in the understatement accorded the systematic denial of equal protection of the law since emancipation.[49] More historical accuracy is required, but the student also needs an understanding of the relationship of ethnohistory to the present status of the Negro. In particular, he needs to understand why extraordinary compensatory efforts are and will be required in education, housing, and job opportunities in order for him to achieve equality of opportunity.[50]

In some instances, the redress creates another kind of imbalance, in which the study of slavery, reconstruction, and the denial of civil liberties is used to stimulate hatred and distrust of American political institutions. This type of Maoist-inspired historical dis-

48. See, for example, North Central Association of Colleges and Secondary Schools, *Human Relations in the Classroom,* NCA Publciation no. D-14; Anti-Defamation League of B'nai B'rith, *Prejudice and Discrimination* (New York: B'nai B'rith, Inc., 1967).

49. An attempt to give a fairer account of this aspect of the American past is found in the following: Jeannette Moon and Ruby Crowe, *Changing Culture: Georgia History,* Book I (Atlanta, Ga.: Joint Curriculum Project, Atlanta and Fulton County School Systems, 1966), pp. 62, 78, 96; idem, *Changing Culture: Georgia Culture,* Book II (Atlanta, Ga.: Joint Curriculum Project, Atlanta and Fulton County School Systems, 1966), pp. 91, 139.

50. A resource book to assist teachers provide additional emphasis on American Negro history in their teaching is: William L. Katz, *Teachers' Guide to American Negro History* (Chicago: Quadrangle Books, 1968).

tortion is as indefensible in the public schools as are apologies for slavery and Reconstruction.

Reassessment of African Culture. The achievement of independence by African states in the last decade has had a tremendous impact on the sense of identity of Americans of African origin. At the same time, newer anthropological and historical research has led to a reassessment of African culture before European contact. There is newly kindled appreciation for the fact that the Africans had developed political institutions for the control of large territories, built large cities, and had achieved notable levels of artistic expression, especially in the Western area south of the Sahara and on the east coast—instead of a past devoid of accomplishments, as previously portrayed. In both cases, stimulus from culture contact, as with other peoples, appeared to be significant in their development.[51]

Certainly, the picture of Africa as a dark continent, devoid of any cultural developments, is an error which needs to be corrected—not only to understand Africa better, but to counteract the racist interpretations of spokesmen who depict the cultures of Africa as debased and primitive.

Recognition of the accomplishments of such states as Cush, Meroe, Aksum, Mali, Ghana, and Songhai serve to correct our interpretations of Africa's past. But, from the anthropological point of view, it would perhaps be better to develop an appreciation of concepts of isolation and diffusion in relation to cultural development, rather than spend so much time in trying to exhume a remote history.[52] The desiccation of the Sahara separated the peoples of Africa from the major cultural developments which diffused from East Asia. Rather than an emphasis merely on African developments, students might be given selections from Caesar's *De Bello Gallico* or Tacitus's *Germania* which show the peoples of France and Germany, before culture contact with the Mediterranean, living on the level of a folk culture, not unlike the way most Africans live today. An account of the Swedes in Russia in the ninth century by the Arab traveller Ibn Fadhlan shows, from his cultivated perspective, uncouth boors with a revolting repertory of customs, including human sacrifice.[53] While certain selections are not suitable for elementary children, it is more important to understand that European culture is not *sui generis,* but stands on the shoulders of past civilizations long since vanished. Isolated peoples of every culture and every race, cut off from the main stream of cultural development, frequently show little development. The heroic backwoodsman of American history was frequently depicted by European travellers as a degenerate type; and the theory of American degeneration was widely held by European scientists in the eighteenth century.[54]

51. Teachers may wish to familiarize themselves with such books as: R. Oliver and J. D. Fage, *A Short History of Africa* (Baltimore: Penguin Books, 1962); J. D. Fage, *An Introduction to the History of West Africa* (Cambridge: at the University Press, 1962); Henri Labouret, *Africa Before the White Man* (New York: Walker and Co., 1962); Basil Davidson, *The Lost Cities of Africa* (Boston: Atlantic Monthly Press, 1959); idem, *A History of West Africa* (Garden City, New York: Doubleday and Co., 1966); idem, *A History of East and Central Africa* (Garden City, New York: Doubleday and Co., 1969); Robert O. Collins, *Problems in African History* (Englewood Cliffs, N.J.: Prentice Hall, Inc., 1968).
52. C. Putnam, *Race and Reason: A Yankee View* (Washington, D.C.: Public Affairs Press, 1961).
53. Carleton S. Coon, *A Reader in General Anthropology* (New York: Henry Holt and Company, 1948), pp. 410-28.
54. D. Echeverria, *Mirage in the West* (Princeton, N.J.: Princeton University Press, 1957).

Geographic isolation persists in many parts of the world today. The whites of Appalachia are geographically isolated, for example. But isolation can also result from cultural causes, such as deliberate denial of the opportunity to participate in the larger culture. One of the most striking examples of this denial were the laws against teaching slaves to read and write, and the failure to provide education for Negroes for almost a hundred years after emancipation.

It is appropriate, therefore, to reassess the history of Africa, not only for the black student's sense of pride but, even more, for the sake of historical accuracy and the truth. At the same time, the reassessment might be more profitably accompanied by an examination of the factors of cross-cultural fertilization and diffusion in the development of peoples. Now that more learning opportunities are being made available to Negroes in the United States and in Africa, it can be projected that their contributions will increase because they will have had an opportunity to learn and grow.

Resource Materials for Intergroup Relations. In the past few years, schools with large Negro populations have added to their material resources dealing with Negro culture and history. However, *all* schools, including those which will continue to be all white as well as those which are to become integrated, should reassess their media and library holdings to provide adequate resources dealing with minority groups. Magazines such as *Ebony* should be available, in addition to *Look* and *Life*. Selections of pictures used for illustrations, posters, displays, and bulletin boards should include Negroes and other minorities as well as whites. Teachers should seek the assistance of the media specialist in the media center to develop class and school resource materials for teaching intergroup relations. In areas where there are large numbers of Spanish-speaking or Indian Americans, it is anticipated that more attention will be given to these reference groups than to Negroes. Minority groups, irrespective of their color, tend to suffer from discrimination. Teachers will also wish to systematically collect their own resource materials, an abundance of which is now found in contemporary magazines and newspapers.[55]

Teacher and Pupil Behavior in Race Relations

Teaching for better race relations is not merely a matter of word; it is preeminently a matter of deed. The curriculum and resources described in the previous two sections will help but they are not nearly so important as the climate of the school and teacher behavior. The question of teacher behavior and attitude is of utmost importance, because it is likely that teaching staffs will more and more be assigned to children of different ethnic groups on some kind of pro rata basis. This means that some Negro teachers will teach predominantly all white classes, and some white teachers will teach predominantly all Negro classes. Such assignments will test the professional quality of the teacher and his commitment to equality of educational opportunity for all children.

Discipline. In chapter 21 "Classroom Management," it was emphasized that the beginning of learning lies in school discipline.

55. See, for example, *Time* articles as: "The Grapes of Wrath, 1969: Mexican-Americans on the March," 4 July 1969; "The American Indian: Goodbye to Tonto," 9 February 1970; "Black v. Jew: A Tragic Confrontation," 31 January 1969; and "Black America 1970," 6 April 1970.

School discipline carries a double connotation—a system of rules and a system of training. Students appreciate a business-like approach to teaching and learning and they are equally sensitive to impartiality of treatment and fair play. A teacher is not merely an authority figure; he is a moral surrogate for the community in the socialization of the young. White children need to learn from and respect black teachers no less than black children need to learn from and respect white teachers. It is the moral authority of the socialized world that the teacher represents, and this world is neither black nor white. It is man.

Under this heading of discipline, nothing has been said of punishment. Punishment may be an adjunct of discipline, but it is not the essence of discipline. Practices relating to punishment of children sometimes vary from school to school within a system, because of different patterns of parental expectancy. It is expected that the teacher will conform to those practices, irrespective of his race or that of his pupils.

The establishment of discipline is important for any meaningful work in race relations, because it is the foundation on which both formal and other informal learning is based.

Seating and Other Assignments.[56] In the integrated class, it is desirable that children of the minority group be geographically distributed in class activities. Initially, this may be accomplished by alphabetical assignment, with subsequent adjustments as necessary to fit individual cases. Children numerically in the minority will tend to assume the minority role, and it is important that the teacher be alert to keep children working as members of the total group, not as cultural isolates. Thus whether in the lunchroom or in a class committee, the teacher will see that there is minority representation. Even where the classes are more equal in racial composition, the teacher will have to provide for inter-ethnic participation, until this behavior pattern becomes automatic.

Objections can be raised that group assignments should be made on the basis of merit and not on minority quotas. This condition may be the ideal. If, however, the school is to *practice* intergroup relations for developing more effective working relationships in and outside of school, the matter of intergroup participation cannot be left to chance.

Language in the Classroom. Both Negroes and whites have acquired stereotypic expressions about the other which are sometimes inadvertently used. The best rule, of course, is never to use disparaging language about any group. If it is not in the verbal repertory, it is less likely to be uttered. The teacher should not merely correct any tendencies toward name-calling, but should have the class discuss together why certain terms are objectionable to the other ethnic group. "Nigger," "whitey," "honky," and similar labels should never be tolerated.

It is inevitable that the teacher will use certain language which he may regard as a faux pas, such as saying to a Negro child of a poster: "Why do you use so much black. It makes the picture ugly." In the days when the slogan "Black is Beautiful" is increasingly heard, there will be times when teachers as well as pupils may use the color black in a sense that it can have

---

56. Helpful suggestions in the domain of teacher behavior with students in an integrated classroom are given in: Gertrude Noar, *The Teacher and Integration* (Washington, D.C.: Student National Education Association, 1966).

double meaning. If offense is given, whether to a child or to a colleague, an apology is frequently the easiest way of indicating that no offense was intended.

In calling names, a teacher sometimes fails to make the connection and substitutes the ubiquitous "You" or perhaps "Boy" or "Girl." If this occurs with a Negro child and it brings an angry response, it will be well for the teacher to recognize that on this point there is an extra element of sensitivity. For too long, especially in the South, it was customary not merely to deny Negroes courtesy titles, but sometimes even the use of their names.

There may be certain idioms which are unfamiliar to pupil or teacher. Sometimes the use of such expressions may interfere with effective communication. In formal class communication, standard English and not idiomatic or colloquial expressions should be encouraged. Use of colloquial expressions is appropriate in role playing, simulation, and dramatic play where there is a need to develop the sentiment of the group.

The next chapter includes specific suggestions about teaching the culturally disadvantaged child. School routines and procedures are similar despite the complexion of the pupils, and most pupils acquire the repertory of behaviors expected in their school by the end of the first grade. There are some differences, however, in the use of language and procedures which make careful use of language appropriate. "Double file" might be misinterpreted if children have been accustomed to forming "Two lines." Language and behavior are learned, and if there has been no previous exposure to language use, the necessary connections will not have been made. Specific and careful directions should be given by teachers until they are confident that students understand the behaviors and routines expected in the classroom.

Activities. Every activity of the school ought to be open to all children. In the elementary school, athletic events and social dances which frequently create tension at the high school level are absent. Most younger children do not object to physical contact in games, square dancing, and athletics. In the rare case where a child refuses to participate, there should be no attempt to coerce him. Even though he may not express it, he is undoubtedly trying to be behaviorally consistent with the learning sets acquired at home. In time, most children do participate.

Sometimes children desire to elect minority candidates to school offices where the nominee is not qualified. Noar suggests that the teacher should intervene to prevent a child from being placed in a position he cannot fulfill.[57] It would seem, however, that this is one of the things children need to learn. The nominee needs to learn that election and execution in office are not synonymous, and the class needs to learn that while color should be no bar to office, neither is it a qualification.

Sectioning in the Integrated School. Chapter 19 describes organizational patterns including sectioning or placement practices. After some schools have been integrated, large numbers of Negroes have been practically resegregated on the basis of achievement sectioning. Here the school faces a real dilemma. The achievement spread of students is sometimes so great that the individualization of instruction would mean

---

57. Noar, *Teacher and Integration*, p. 52.

tutorialization, while strict achievement sectioning would substantially segregate the student body. While the actual achievement performance will vary by schools, it is thought that in most elementary schools multi-level performance levels by class can permit the involvement of both Negro and white students. If a school is being integrated for the first time and there is Negro distrust that the purpose of sectioning is to resegregate and not improve instruction, it is preferable to provide for heterogeneous sections of classes. In this context, it is suggested that for the next few years the value of improved ethnic relations in the school might justify a decrease in cognitive learning emphasis. The evidence does not suggest this, as we have noted in the section on "Educational Achievement and Integration." However, in terms of a new commitment to human values, it may be necessary for the schools to give second rather than first priority to achievement sectioning.

Refraining From Contemptuous Acts. In recent years in integrated high schools the competing strains of "Dixie" and "We Shall Overcome" have frequently led to school disturbances, as has the display of the Confederate flag and the Black Power salute. Younger years minimize the chance for overt conflict in the elementary school, but the symbols nevertheless exist in the culture and are transmitted to children. It is appropriate to display the Confederate flag in connection with some related ceremony, such as the birthday of Jefferson Davis or Robert E. Lee. It is not appropriate to display the Confederate flag at football games or school events. It may be appropriate to play "Dixie" at a meeting of the Sons or Daughters of the Confederacy, but it is no longer appropriate to play "Dixie" at school events. It is appropriate for all students to sing "We Shall Overcome" in connection with the observance of Martin Luther King's birthday, but it is not appropriate for general school use. In both instances the reason is the same—in the last decade these symbols became symbols of racial strife. The Confederate symbols have been soiled by making them the property of the white supremacists; the symbols of Negro Civil Rights have been converted into symbols of black supremacy. When the use of a symbol contributes to negative racial reactions, the symbols should be discontinued and even young students ought to know why such symbols are no longer suitable for general use.

Black-White Teacher Relations. Teachers have been even less integrated than pupils, and both frequently enter dual staff assignments with a sense of foreboding. Despite the lack of previous contact, an integrated professional staff will find that they share a common educational tradition, hold common aspirations for their pupils, and are concerned with common educational problems. They will also learn to measure each other's competency and find that there are good and indifferent teachers of either race.

Negro teachers frequently approach integrated professional teaching with a feeling of job insecurity. Too often, staff integration has meant eventual replacement of Negro with white teachers or the downgrading of positions. In the dual school system, Negroes were responsible as department heads, principals, coaches, and counselors for their school. On the basis of past experience, the Negro is not always confident that he will retain his status on the integrated staff.

A school system and a school should be absolutely fair in their professional assignments. Teachers who honestly work together will find much to learn from the other—and will also learn that race has no monopoly on frustration. The courtesies of adult behavior should be scrupulously followed, until such time as a greater degree of acquaintanceship leads to less formal relations. White teachers should be equally zealous of protecting the privileges of their Negro colleagues as their own. The fact that teachers, after all, are human beings and share the prejudices of their culture has been reflected by the separate professional organizations for Negro and white teachers in the South. Under pressure from the National Education Association, it seems as if most of these separate state organizations will unite. Teachers have even more to learn than pupils. In many cases, they will have to unlearn patterns of behavior which were developed for teaching their own race in segregated schools.

An Appraisal of School Integration

By 1964, ten years after *Brown,* a mere 1 percent of the Negro children in the South were attending desegregated schools. By 1970, the figure had risen to 40 percent. It is likely that by the school year 1970-71, most Negro children in the South will have attended unitary school systems, in racial balance if not in spirit. In the rest of the country, de facto segregation will continue to be a matter of unfinished resolution. In the absence of a Supreme Court ruling to require affirmative action to eliminate de facto segregation, there is a lack of uniformity in court rulings. Thus in Pontiac, Michigan and in Pasadena, California, a U.S. District Court and a California Superior Court ordered an end to de facto segregation whereas in Cincinnati the Sixth Circuit Court of Appeals absolved the high school board from charges of racial discrimination resulting from residential patterns.[58]

Many factors have contributed to the slow pace of school desegregation. Among these are inappropriateness of the legal remedy, political interference, lack of enforcement machinery until recent years, the opposition of school superintendents and school boards, the apathy of professional organizations, and, above all, the lack of a moral commitment of Americans to end discrimination.

The Legal Remedy. The 1955 *Brown* decision[59] remanded to the federal district courts and to the local school authorities the responsibilities for implementing the principles of racial nondiscrimination enunciated in the 1954 decision. The principle of "all deliberate speed," however, was interpreted to mean "all deliberate slowness." Except in the Border states, there was little voluntary compliance. Responsibility for initiating actions against local school boards rested with the ones who could least afford to undertake the action. As Lusky points out, implementation of equitable principles through the very institutions responsible for segregation could only invite subterfuge and delay. Federal district courts, like other local institutions, are more subject to local pressures than are higher courts. This legal remedy encouraged the invention of artificial reasons for delay.[60] This delay convinced Negroes that white

---

58. 1 *Race Relations Legal Survey* 254-55, 257-58 (1970).

59. Brown v. Board of Education, 349 U.S. 294 (1955).

60. See Louis Lusky, *Racial Discrimination and the Federal Law: A Problem in Nullification,* 63. COLUMBIA LAW REVIEW 1163, 1172, n. 37 (1963).

educators would not act in good faith, despite the legal right that had been established.

There was also a misjoinder of parties. States were not made parties to the finding, notwithstanding the fact that it has long been established that education is a governmental function of the state, exercised in trust by local boards which are trustees of the State. As a result, decisions in individual cases were not generalized to other school systems. In each case, desegregation litigation began as if new principles had to be established.

Political Interference. There was a general tendency throughout the South for governors and legislators to interfere with the progress of desegregation, even where voluntary or initiated under court order. One of the most notable cases is that of Little Rock, where the school board had voluntarily desegregated. Unrest stimulated by the governor with the support of the legislature finally required President Eisenhower to send in federal troops to enforce the court decision. However, the spirit of recalcitrance has not died. In 1970 Governor Kirk of Florida personally intervened in Manatee School District, and only withdrew when he was ordered to desist or be held personally in contempt. George Wallace of Alabama made his 1970 gubernatorial bid for reelection primarily on the basis of preventing school integration. Racism is still a part of the political demagoguery of the country. Elections in all parts of the country, however, show that the South does not have a monopoly on this vice. It is found from Boston to San Francisco, and from Milwaukee to New Orleans.

Lack of Enforcement Machinery. Prior to the Civil Rights Act of 1964, there was no executive machinery available to implement desegregation. The burden was left on the Negroes in a particular school system to initiate court action, a costly as well as hazardous undertaking. The 1964 Civil Rights Act, however, defined desegregation, authorized the Commissioner of Education to provide technical assistance to school systems in the drafting of desegregation plans, empowered the Attorney General to bring suits to compel desegregation, and authorized the withholding of federal funds from school systems not found in compliance.[61]

Original attempts of the Office of Education to bring about compliance were under freedom of choice plans.[62] These plans, as with the former legal remedies, placed the responsibility of exercising choice on the Negro child. There was, therefore, a gradual shift to the concept of racial balance, notwithstanding the clear prohibition in the Act against any action by courts or individuals to bring about racial balance.[63] As a result, there has been a shift from the concept of desegregation and the elimination of dual school sytsems to that of integration and the establishment of unitary systems.

Again, it should be emphasized that this development has been brought about by federal enforcement. The original plaintiffs in the *Brown* case from Prince Edward County, Virginia and Clarendon County, South Carolina, never attended a desegregated school. Left to voluntary implementation, the public schools of the South would have remained as they had been before Brown-segregated systems.

61. 42 U.S.C.A. § 2000 c, d.
62. 31 Fed. Res. 5623 (1966).
63. Similar restrictions with respect to racial balance are written into the Demonstration Cities and Metropolitan Development Act of 1966, 80 Stat. 1255, § 103 (d).

Opposition of School Superintendents and School Boards. School superintendents and boards of education are part of the political structure of a state, and as such have been peculiarly subject to the pressures of custom and convention, all in favor of preserving rather than removing desegregation. They have, moreover, been almost entirely white.

Not only have many school superintendents and school boards failed to take the necessary steps to bring about desegregation, but many of them have often failed to act in a responsible educational manner for all the children.

A recent case from Candler County, Georgia is indicative of what has happened in too many places. In 1968, the county lost all federal monies because of failure to meet minimum desegregation standards. In January 1970, federal monies were restored in connection with the action brought by the United States against Georgia. The school board failed to apply for a 1970 Title I summer program. It was reported that the reason for the failure to apply was that the beneficiaries of the summer program would be Black. On May 1, 1970, U. S. District Judge Edenfield issued an order directing the superintendent and school board to show cause why they should not administer a summer remedial reading program, or show cause why they should not be suspended from their duties and a special master appointed to run the schools and apply for such a program.[64]

In 1970 it is indeed an obtuse public which will condone the denial of education to children because they are Black. Under Title I of the Elementary and Secondary Education Act of 1965 most federal money is earmarked for compensatory education for poor children. In many southern school systems, poverty and Negro are synonymous. If local control is tested by the responsibility which many superintendents and school boards have displayed in integration, the record demonstrates that local control has been invariably found wanting.

Professional Organizations. The records of many teachers, however, are no better than that of school officials. In systems where teachers have annual contracts without tenure, a characteristic of the South, teachers are especially sensitive to community mores. Teachers who take unpopular stands can be easily removed by the simple expedient of not having a contract offered for the next school year.

Not only were there dual school systems in the South, but there were dual professional organizations. Only until expulsion ultimata were issued by the National Education Association in the late 1960s did the dual professional organizations begin negotiations looking toward merger. The Negro organizations approached merger with considerable distrust, fearing that in an integrated professional organization they would lose the means to protect their personal interests. This fear is not an idle one. Integration has inevitably brought about the release of Negro teachers and the loss of Negro principalships.[65] Where Negro teachers have been released solely because of race, courts have reinstated the discharged teachers.[66] However, race is no bar to discharge when dis-

64. *Atlanta Constitution,* May 2, 1970, p. 5-A.
65. In Georgia, for example, such changes lead to Black demonstrations in Athens, Covington, LaGrange, and Perry. *Atlanta Constitution,* May 2; 1970, p. 5-A.
66. Rolfe et al. v. County Board of Education of Lincoln County, et al. 391 F. 2d 77 (1968); Hill v. County Board of Education, 390 F. 2d (1968); Braxton, et al. v. Board of Public Instruction, Duval County, 303 F. Supp. 958 (1969).

charge is made on the basis of lack of teaching competency after due process.[67] On the whole, the story of desegregation-integration indicates a high degree of racism among educators of the Nation.[68]

Lack of School and Community Preparation for Integration. One of the greatest deficiencies in the implementation of desegregation is the lack of staff and community planning. The last-ditch resistance posture often means that pupils and teachers are hastily thrown together at the beginning or even in the middle of the school year. White and black children both reflect the prejudices of their ethnic communities. It is a credit to both teachers and pupils that integration has not been as disruptive as it might otherwise have been.

Not only does integration require careful planning of instructional content, but it requires teachers to be alert to the climate of the school. Insensitivity to black feelings, such as clubs without Negro participants, monopoly of the school paper by whites, and changing the name of a former Negro school, contribute to racial tensions. The teacher is responsible not merely for knowledge, but the context in which learning takes place.

As a teacher, you may be called upon to teach in a variety of ethnic conditions. You may find yourself a minority teacher in a school where the pupils and other teachers are a majority from another race. In these circumstances, the important guides are two. First, you are an American, not a black American or a white American, but an American. Second, you are a teacher. Not a black teacher or a white teacher, but a teacher. As an American, you can apply the democratic creed in action. As a teacher, you can teach to develop not only the cognitive abilities of your charges, but their affective beliefs as well—values, attitudes, appreciations and interests.

Lack of a Moral Commitment by the American People. The slow pace of school desegregation, the continuation of de facto segregation, and the increase in black separatist sentiment reflect the moral bankruptcy of the nation on the racial issue. This indictment rests particularly heavy on school people, however, because it is they who, more than any other group, talk the rhetoric of the "full development of each individual's potentiality."

What the entire country has failed to realize is that discrimination is not merely a legal problem. Discrimination is, above all, a moral problem.[69] Law, after all, is the mere facade of morality. Law is no stronger than the values on which it rests. A strong law and weak values means weak law, because it is individuals with their value perceptions that translate law into reality; no law is self-implementing. The chief criticism of President Nixon's 1970 address on school desegregation is that while it was legally correct it was morally vapid. The country does not require merely a commitment to end de jure segregation in the South; it requires a commitment to end de

---

67. Walton and McGhee v. Nashville, Ark., Special Sch. Dist., et al., 401 F. 2d 137 (1968); Bonner v. Texas City Independent Sch. Dist., 305 F. Supp. 600 (1969).

68. Robert L. Greer, editor, *Racial Crisis in American Education* (Chicago: Follett Educational Corporation, 1969), pp. 149-66.

69. Erwin N. Griswold, Dean of the Harvard School of Law, wrote "Discrimination is basically a moral problem. We tend too often to forget that. Nevertheless, it is only on a moral basis that the questions will be finally resolved. To this end we need moral leadership, which has not always been strong and clear." Vern Countryman, ed., *Discrimination and the Law* (Chicago: University of Chicago Press, 1965), p. v.

facto racial separatism throughout the Nation.

Relation of Schooling to Cultural Values

From time immemorial, men have been aware that the school as an institution encompassed more than a system for transmitting knowledge. In *Brown,* the Supreme Court noted that education

> . . . is the very foundation of good citizenship. Today it is the principal instrument in awakening the child to cultural values, in preparing him for later professional training, and in helping him to adjust normally to his environment.

Even President Nixon was constrained to note that the school fulfills a similar purpose.

> It is a place not only of learning, but also of living—where a child's friendships center, where he learns to measure himself against others, to share, to compete, to cooperate . . .

Because the school is important in the rearing of the future citizen de facto segregation cannnot be ignored after de jure segregation is eliminated. Black and white Americans have been bound together in this country from the formative years of the colonial period. The black bore the badge of servility; the white, of freedom. Failure to include all our citizens within the principle of equality has led to a dangerous polarization of the races.[70]

A major problem of the 1970s will be the issue of de facto segregation in northern and western states which have not had a history of de jure segregation. In the long awaited bussing decision, the United States Supreme Court on April 20, 1971 upheld the practice of bussing to achieve a racially balanced unitary school system where there has been a history of de jure segregation.[71] On the following day, however, the Senate defeated an amendment to the Emergency School Aid and Quality Integrated Education Act of 1971, Bill S. 1557, introduced by Senator Ribicoff, which would have required schools in all metropolitan areas to enroll a fixed percentage of minority students within ten years or lose federal aid to education.[72] At the present time there is no uniform school desegregation policy for the nation, and no consistent plan to eliminate minority isolation in the schools.

School integration will not solve all of the problems of minority groups in a democratic society. But it is a beginning which can be made from the earliest years. You as a teacher can do something for the improvement of race relations and better citizenship training. You can begin with a child in your classroom. You can begin by helping your children meet the challenge of democracy in race relations. You can plan with all of your fellow teachers to include in your school experiences that will make all children proud of our diverse heritage. You can work with all of your colleagues to create a climate which makes the rhetoric of democracy a reality. As an individual and as a teacher, you can make a moral commitment to meet the challenge of democracy in race relations.

---

70. *Report of the National Advisory Commission on Civil Disorders,* (New York: Bantam Books, 1968), p. 407.
71. Swann et al. v. Charlotte-Mecklenburg Board of Education et al.,———U.S.———(1971); 39 *Law Week* 4437.
72. *Congressional Record,* 91st Cong., 2d sess. 21 April, 1971, pp. S5305-S5317.

Selected References

Clark, Kenneth B. *Prejudice and Your Child.* 2d. ed. Boston: Beacon Press, 1955.

———, and Parsons, Talcott, eds. *The Negro American.* Boston: Beacon Press, 1966.

Coleman, James S. *Race Relations and Social Change,* Baltimore, Md.: Center for the Study of Social Organization of Schools, Johns Hopkins University, July 1966.

Coleman, James S. et al. *Equality of Educational Opportunity.* Washington, D.C.: Government Printing Office, 1966.

Edwards, T. Bentley, and Wirt, Frederick M., eds. *School Desegregation: The Challenge and the Experience.* San Francisco: Chandler Publishing Co., 1967.

Gibson, John S. *The Intergroup Relations Curriculum: A Program for the Elementary School.* Medford, Mass.: Lincoln Filene Center for Citizenship and Public Affairs, Tufts University, 1969.

Glock, Charles Y. and Siegelman, Ellen, eds. *Prejudice, U.S.A.* New York: Frederick A. Praeger, 1969.

Greer, Robert L., ed. *Racial Crisis in American Education.* Chicago: Follett Educational Corporation, 1969.

Katz, William L. *Teachers' Guide to American Negro History.* Chicago: Quadrangle Books, 1968.

Kleg, Milton; Rice, Marion J.; and Bailey, Wilfrid C. *Race, Caste, and Prejudice.* Athens, Ga.: University of Georgia, Anthropology Curriculum Project, 1970.

Miel, Alice. *The Shortchanged Children of Suburbia.* American Jewish Committee, Pamphlet Series no. 8. New York: Institute of Human Relations Press, 1967.

Noar, Gertrude. *The Teacher and Integration.* Washington, D.C.: Student National Education Association, 1966.

Pettigrew, Thomas F. *A Profile of the Negro American.* Princeton, N.J.: D. Van Nostrand, 1964.

Report of the National Advisory Commission on Civil Disorders. New York: Bantam Books, 1968.

Silberman, Charles E. *Crisis in Black and White.* New York: Random House, 1964.

U. S. Commission on Civil Rights. *Racial Isolation in the Public Schools.* Washington, D.C.: Government Printing Office, 1967.

Weinberg, Meyer. *Desegregation Research: An Appraisal.* Blomington, Ind.: Phi Delta Kappa Commission on Education, Human Rights, and Responsibilities, 1968.

23 the culturally disadvantaged: challenge to performance teaching

In the mid-1960s the United States came face to face with a specter supposedly vanquished in the prosperity that came with World War II. It came face to face with poverty. In the midst of an affluent society, there were not just a few men, women, and children barely surviving; there were millions whose standard of living gave the lie to the economics of equality. They were all over the country—crowded in the decaying tenements of the cities and scattered over the countryside in rickety, weather-beaten houses. They came in all colors and were found in all regions, but they had many things that bound them together in a common, Dantian destiny. Along with little money went ignorance, malnutrition, poor health, short life, spawning from one generation to another the fateful cycle.

Not only did politicians and welfare workers rediscover the poor, so did the school teacher in whose class the children of the poor so often languished, if they weren't ignored altogether. Federal pump priming helped recall the public schools to a mison half-forgotten—they were established to educate the poor. But in the euphemisms that surround education the child of poverty was jargonized; he was metamorphosized into the culturally disadvantaged. Irrespective of the name, there is an old challenge to the teacher—to help the children of the poor to learn, not merely to pass the days until they become semi-illiterate dropouts. The challenge is even greater today, because three minority groups are more than ever aware that they have been short-changed by the American educational system as well as by the American economic and political system. These are the Chicanos, Indians, and Blacks. And even among the larger numbers of the white poor, there are stirrings indicating that they, too, feel that the largesse of America has somehow passed them by.

As the United States moved into the decade of the 70s, the War on Poverty had been reduced to a skirmish. Many of the educational-work programs of the Office of Economic Opportunity had been reduced or transferred to other agencies. Title I of the Elementary and Secondary Education Act of 1965, the major means for allocating funds to schools with a high incidence of low income families, had been cut back rather than expanded, but fiscal year 1970 brought an upward trend. There was nevertheless, the sobering realization that many compensatory education programs for the disadvantaged had not met the objective of increased school achievement. The decade of the 70s may therefore be one in which there are less ambitious aims of educational reconstruction and more emphasis on performance teaching.

Sociological Factors

The use of any term, from poor to disadvantaged, carries with it certain pejorative connotations. For this reason, many educators are loath to equate the culturally disadvantaged with the poor, and point out that many children from moderate and well-to-do homes may be culturally disadvantaged. Despite their affluence, they do not participate in those activities which stimulate intellectual, aesthetic, and social development. The fact nevertheless remains that "life chances" are highly related to income and social class.

Low Income and Life Chance. Life chance is a sociological concept which describes the relationship of income to the chance of enjoying not only a standard of living but of life itself. While social classes in the United States are not perfectly formed, it is common knowledge that social rewards are not evenly distributed. The life chances of children to enjoy leisure, freedom, security, and the other good things of life are closely related to the income of their parents.

Numerous studies have indicated that persons with low incomes have a higher degree of infant mortality, higher sickness rate, more severe psychiatric disorders, and shorter longevity. Children from low income homes drop out of school earlier, have less chance of getting a college education, and are more likely to become juvenile delinquents. They are less likely to develop helpful personalities, obtain justice in the courts, and survive in the armed forces. Income also affects the total life style and their self-perception. They underestimate their abilities in school and even depreciate their physical looks. Differential life chances for the poor begin from the moment of conception.

It is not surprising therefore to find that there is a relationship between social class and school achievement. The deficit of social class and school achievement is cumulative rather than uniform. The depressing effects of low socio-economic status become more pronounced the longer a child remains in school. The cumulative deficit has been demonstrated with a variety of groups and settings: with the native stock of Appalachia and of urban ghettoes; with poor blacks and whites; with Spanish-speaking Chicano children; and with American Indians. Many children are two to three years behind norm expectancy when they finish the middle school. Dropout and remedial programs for high school students merely confirm the old saw of too little too late.

Who Are the Disadvantaged? Disadvantaged children are poor children. Between 1960 and January 1969, the number of poor persons dropped from 40 million to 22 million. However, in 1965 there were 14.3 million poor children under eighteen, a figure which accounted for 20.5 percent of all children.

There were 8.7 million poor white children, which accounted for 14.5 percent of all white children. There were fewer nonwhite poor children—5.6 million compared to 8.7 million. But the incidence of poverty was over three times as great among non-whites.[1]

There are both regional and racial differences in income. In the South, the number of white families with incomes of less than $3,000 is 20.5 percent compared with 11.9 percent in the North and West. The difference, however, is even more marked for Negroes; 50.2 percent of Negro families in the South have incomes of less than $3,000 compared to 22.2 percent in the North and West.[2]

According to Robert J. Havighurst,[3] the 12.5 million poor children, based on the 1963 "economy budget," had the following geographic and ethnic distributions. (See chart below)

From the above data, the following summary may be made. The largest number of disadvantaged are urban, but the percentage of rural poor is higher. The largest number of poor by ethnic group are white, but the highest incidence of poverty is among the rural Negro, who is southern. The incidence of poverty among Indians equals that of Negroes, and is even higher for off-reservation Indians. While numerically a small group, the Spanish-speaking Americans of the five southwestern states constitute an ethnic group with distinctive poverty problems.

Sociological Characteristics of the Disadvantaged. There is a large body of literature which describes the many limiting

1. *Statistical Abstract of the United States, 1968,* table no. 482.
2. *Statistical Abstract of the United States, 1968,* table no. 476.
3. South Central Region Educational Laboratory, *Education for the Culturally Disadvantaged;* Proceedings of the National Conference on Educational Objectives for the Culturally Disadvantaged, 1967, p. 9.

Characteristic	Percent of Sample	Percent of All Poor Children	Millions
Urban-Rural			
Urban	20	60.0	7.5
Rural	28	40.0	5.0
Color-Rurality			
White	24	31.0	3.8
Negro	60	9.0	1.2
Regional-Rurality			
South	40	24.0	3.1
(62% of rural poor)			
Northeast, North			
Central, West	19	16.0	1.9
(38% of rural poor)			
Other Ethnic, Mainly Rural			
(Previously included in			
"white" above)			
Spanish Americans,			
Southwest	35	4.0	0.5
Indian Children			
On or near reservation	60	0.8	0.1
Not on or near reserv.	80	0.3	0.04

conditions for education imposed by poverty. Much of this literature uses social disorganization as a thematic construct. The result is a pathological portrayal of the disadvantaged in a stereotype that often merely reinforces the teacher's prejudiced attitudes toward the poor.

It is true that illiteracy of parents, low income, poor neighborhood, dilapidated housing, inadequate medical care, negative home attitudes and values, and a nonsupportive approach toward education present handicaps that the school alone is ill-equipped to overcome. Publication of the Coleman Report[4] has emphasized what reformers have known for a long time—that improvement of the condition of the poor requires a prolonged and many-faceted attack. Over a hundred and fifty years later we are still trying to cope with problems of educational and social amelioration that challenged Owen in the early nineteenth century.[5] Jensen has more recently indicated that expenditures for compensatory education might be futile in the face of dysgenic prenatal and child-rearing practices.[6]

The complex of sociological factors involving poverty and education inevitably suggests that the means of educational improvement are not through schooling as much as through the general improvement of all conditions in which the poor live—better paying jobs, decent housing, and improved medical care, to name a few.

More than anything else it suggests that the federal bureaucracy of the Department of Health, Education and Welfare coordinate programs for the disadvantaged. School teachers who have attempted to utilize available community agencies to help in the solution of educational problems know how frustrating it is to work with government departments which act more like warring feudatories than service agencies for the poor. The idea of coordinated action was implicit in the original OEO Community Action concept, but this thrust was soon blunted by underfinancing, community infighting, bureaucratic conflicts with established agencies, heavily publicized incidents of waste and abuse, and a distrust of giving responsibility to the poor. Title I has encouraged a package approach within the context of the school, and has provided funds for medical, health, welfare, and parent-home services as well as instructional assistance. Title I, however, is unable to provide assistance in the areas to which the child returns after school—the home and neighborhood. Since the home is the primary agency of socialization, sociologically oriented educators are inclined to be very pessimistic about compensatory education programs.

One of the persistent strands in the social-psychological literature relates to the lack of school support by parents of the disadvantaged. The research is inconclusive. Parents of poor children are frequently semi-illiterate and not very school wise. Though they lack self-identity with the school, poor parents generally want their children to stay in school; most of them expect their children to finish high school. If anything, one might conclude that the poor have an almost naive faith in the

4. James S. Coleman et al., *Equality of Educational Opportunity* (Washington, D.C.: Government Printing Office, 1966).
5. Robert Owen, *A New View of Society, or Essays on the Principle of the Formation of the Human Character* (1813; reprint ed., Glencoe, Ill.: Free Press, 1948).
6. Arthur R. Jensen and others, *Environment, Heredity, and Intelligence* (Harvard Educational Review, Reprint Series no. 2, 1969).

benefits of education and that each new generation starts off in the first grade or kindergarten with high hopes of success. But somehow the school fails the child. Psychological research is now concentrating more on the conditions which may affect learning in the context of school instruction.

Psychological Characteristics

Motivation and School Success. Educational and occupational aspiration are related to class level, when intelligence is controlled. Parental encouragement, internalized values, and a favorable self-image are related to high aspirations.

Most young children come to school with the desire to succeed. They have yet to learn the experience of continuous and successive failure. While the older emphasis was on extrinsic motivation, it is now recognized that success in school is one of the most potent forces to stimulate higher successive levels of aspiration. Hence, it is important to set school tasks which bring success to the young learner, rather than setting tasks in which he repeatedly experiences failure.[7]

Self Concept. One of the most popular forms of psychological research in the past has been the self-concept. These studies seemed to indicate that lower class children had an unfavorable self-image, which interfered with their social adjustment and success in school. This research seldom made it clear whether this unfavorable self-concept was a preexistent function of the subculture or resulted from school contacts and the lack of success in school. In contrast to older surveys, more recent surveys of Negro self-concept indicate a positive rather than negative self-image.[8]

A similar shift has taken place in appraisal of Mexican-American self-image. Instead of Spanish-speaking children seen as having an inferior self-perception, the emphasis has shifted to the negative interferences which come from cultural barriers.[9] These findings raise some question as to the rationale for ethnic studies programs which are frequently justified on the need to improve the self-image.

The structure, management, and organization of the school should not discriminate against children from poverty backgrounds. This means that teachers and administrators frequently need to balance the representation of poor children in activities from which they are often unconsciously excluded by their peers.

Language and Social Class. Forty years of research on language and social class has confirmed what has been known by simple observation and listening. Lower class children do not have the same language in terms of syntax and vocabulary as do middle and upper class children. The detrimental deficits of language become more pronounced the longer the student remains in school. This deficit is reflected in sentence maturity and complexity, sound discrimination, range of oral vocabulary,

7. Martin Deutsch, *Minority Group and Class Status as Related to Social and Personality Factors in Scholastic Achievement,* Society for Applied Anthropology, Monograph no. 2, 1960 (Ithaca, New York: Cornell University, 1960).

8. James E. Conyers and William J. Farmar, *Black Youth in a Southern Metropolis* (Atlanta, Ga.: Southern Regional Council, 1968); Anthony T. Soares and Louise M. Soares, "Self-Perception of Culturally Disadvantaged Children, *American Educational Research Journal* 6 (January 1969): 31-39.

9. T. P. Carter, "The Negative Self-Concept of Mexican-American Students," *School and Society* 96 (30 March 1968): 217-19.

and articulation, especially with final consonants. Minority group membership accentuates language social class differences among Indians, Spanish-speaking Americans, and Negroes. Differences in the morphological and phonological characteristics of oral language as spoken by blacks and whites are less pronounced in the South than in the North.

Language deficiency shows up markedly in the ability to label, discriminate, categorize, and generalize. This leads to a severe comprehension gap, in ability to follow directions, poor visual imagery, defective conceptualization, and poor transition to abstract thought. These general language deficiencies show up in such general measures as intelligence and aptitude.

The cumulative effects of a deprived language background show up in less total use of language in the school setting. This has given some investigators the impression that the disadvantaged child is a nonverbal child. The disadvantaged child in his play group is vocal, although syntax may be substandard, sentences short, and word usage unvaried.[10] What the disadvantaged child lacks is the complex language required for school use.

The description of the relationship of social class to language has not been very useful, however, in explaining the relationships of language to intellectual functioning in the context of school expectancy. The theoretical work of Vygotsky[11] and Luria[12] and the research of Deutsch[13] and Bernstein[14] have emphasized the generalizing intellectual functioning of language and the specific type of school performance imposed by deficient language.

According to Bernstein, there are two basic language codes for communication. One is public or restricted; the other is formal or elaborated. Public language is the language of ordinary face to face communication; the structure is simple grammatically; and the meaning is often assumed from the context in which communication takes place. The context of personal relationships does not require extensive verbalization. Formal language, on the other hand, is grammatically complex and involves an extensive vocabulary. Many nuances of thought may be expressed through use of a range of conjunctions and subordinate clauses, prepositions which indicate logical relationships, and qualification of propositions through the use of adjectives and verbs. As a result, public language is restricted whereas formal language is elaborated.

The middle-class child learns both public and formal language codes in the home. Strodtbeck[15] refers to the elaborate conversational structure of the middle-class home as "the hidden curriculum." The disadvantaged child comes to school with a restricted

10. Susan Houston, "Child Black English in Northern Florida: A Socio-Linguistic Examination," Communication Skills Development Project mimeographed (Hapeville, Ga.: Southeastern Education Laboratory, 1969).

11. L. S. Vygotsky, *Thought and Language* (Boston: M.I.T. Press, 1962).

12. A. R. Luria and F. Y. Yudovich, *Speech and the Development of Mental Processes in Children* (London: Staples, 1959).

13. Martin Deutsch, "The Role of Social Class in Language Development and Cognition," *American Journal of Orthopsychiatry* 35 (January 1965): 78-88.

14. Basil Bernstein, "Social Structure, Language, and Learning," *Educational Research* 3 (June 1961): 163-76.

15. Fred L. Strodtbeck, "The Hidden Curriculum of the Middle-Class Home," in *Urban Education and Cultural Deprivation,* ed. C. W. Hunnicutt (Syracuse: Syracuse University Press, 1964), pp. 15-31.

language ill-suited to the learning tasks of the school. In addition, this restricted language deficit is compounded by a dialectical handicap, which impedes public communication.

Except for the structured verbal stimulation programs of Bereiter and Engelmann,[16] few language programs attempt to remedy specifically the abstract language deficit. Most language programs for the disadvantaged tend to emphasize the increase in general vocabulary through sense-label association, as with the Peabody Language Development Kits[17] or the multi-sensory program of Francis.[18] A variation combining a multi-sensory approach with teaching English as a second language (TESL) is the Oral Language Program of the Southwestern Cooperative Educational Laboratory.[19]

Language and Cognitive Style. The relationship of social class and restricted language usage has led some observers to infer that lower class children have a difference in learning style. Reissman[20] has described the learning style of disadvantaged children as motoric. Disadvantaged children differ in both the rate of learning and the amount of learning as measured by achievement tests. To describe this difference as one in cognitive style may be a form of stereotyping which is not diagnostically helpful for the correction of specific language learning disabilities.

Culture Fair Testing. Repeated psychoeducational appraisals of children have shown that performance on standardized tests, whether achievement or of IQ measurement, are related to socioeconomic status. As a result, various attempts have been made to devise tests which are allegedly more fair to the disadvantaged student. One of the best known of the culture fair tests is the Davis-Eells Test of General Intelligence or Problem Solving Ability. Repeated uses of this test with different population groups shows that it does not eliminate social class bias. Lower mean scores have been obtained on this test with Mexican-American children than on conventional measures.[21]

The fact that disadvantaged children do not perform well on Stanford-Binet and Wechsler intelligence tests is no reason to abandon the use of these measures. These tests are useful because they accurately measure the limited range of abstract behavior which is pertinent to the school setting. Furthermore, Western society has evolved a complex, hierarchical job structure in which there is a correlation between job placement and the abstract intellectual skills which are developed with schooling. School tasks are not arbitrary tasks but have been defined over the years in response to the needs of society.

16. Carl Bereiter and Siegfried Engelmann, *Teaching Disadvantaged Children in the Pre-School* (Englewood Cliffs, N.J.: Prentice-Hall, Inc., 1966).
17. Lloyd M. Dunn et al., *Peabody Language Development Kits* (Circle Pines, Minn.: American Guidance Service, Inc., 1966).
18. Azalia Francis, *Multisensory Language Development Project,* Communication Skills Development Program, (Hapeville, Ga.: Southeastern Education Laboratory, 1969).
19. Robert T. Reeback et al., *Oral Language Program* (Albuquerque: Southwestern Cooperative Educational Laboratory, Inc., 1967).
20. Frank Riessman, *The Culturally Deprived Child* (New York: Harper and Row, Publishers, 1962).
21. John E. Stablein, Darrell S. Willey, and Calvin W. Thomson, "An Evaluation of the Davis-Eells (Culture Fair) Test Using Spanish and Anglo-American Children," *Journal of Educational Sociology* 35 (October 1961): 73-78.

The challenge is not to use different kinds of measures to give a more favorable picture of the achievement of the disadvantaged learner. Such an approach does not increase his performance level. The challenge is to devise more effective school instruction. IQ tests are primarily school oriented tests, and are not measures of innate capacity or even general intelligence. The high correlations between aptitude and IQ tests result primarily from the fact that they measure essentially the same abstract, verbalizing factors, whether denominated g or by some other name. IQ tests, however, are often abused when they are used to track students and to deprive them of the type of instruction which might be helpful to the disadvantaged learner.

Intelligence: Race, Heredity, and Culture. The problem of intelligence, heredity, and culture has long interested psychologists and sociologists as well as educators. The matter is of more than theoretical interest. If intelligence is primarily inherited, efforts to improve intelligence are largely fruitless; if intelligence, however, is a product of cultural experiences, one may be more optimistic about the effects of intervention.

Earlier studies tended to emphasize the influence of heredity. Where different populations were compared, the early studies tended to support a racist explanation of differences in intelligence. More recent studies have tended to emphasize the influence of environment, and have led to extravagant expectations of the possibilities of early intervention, as in Headstart programs.

The problems of race and culture and of heredity and environment are complicated because the factors are nested. Biologically, race may be viewed simply as a breeding population separated from other breeding populations by natural and social barriers. The same barriers to population hybridization are also barriers to acculturation and cultural diffusion. Thus, throughout the world there are certain culture worlds which roughly approximate the distribution of geographical populations. The rise and fall of empires and the course of civilization indicate that some underdeveloped countries today were at an apogee of culture development when the antecedents of the modern European were still savages.

In modern times, there has been a tremendous transfer of stocks, in particular that of Europeans and Africans to the New World. Racist explanations were developed in part to justify the institution of chattel slavery in the New World. As a slave, the Negro never participated in the total culture of the European. A hundred years after obtaining his freedom in the United States, he is still discriminated against in terms of education, housing, jobs, and social participation in the general culture. A genetic explanation of IQ differences, as revived by A. R. Jensen, simply does not take into account cultural history of the Negro in the United States.

Negroes are disproportionately represented in the lower income groups. It is inevitable that differences in intelligence and achievement may appear as racial differences when the differences are primarily class differences.

From a standpoint of educational policy, however, the genetic-racial controversy is fruitless. Educators are not eugenicists; they can not change the genetic make-up of individuals or control their breeding habits. All they can do is manipulate the environment in which children are trained. Jensen tacitly accepts this point of view when he emphasizes that the schools can do a lot to improve achievement even if they can do little to change intelligence per se.

The two other minority ethnic groups in the United States are the Indians and the Spanish-speaking Americans. In contrast to the Negro, they are separated from the "Anglo" world by differences in language as well as differences in culture. Their low income status merely confounds the other learning problems arising from differences in value orientation, child rearing and familial practices, and different status and role expectancies. Spanish-speaking Americans and Indians have long been stigmatized by such descriptions as "lazy" and "poor." The lower school performance of these groups, however, may be attributed to differences in life chances rather than to differences in genetic potential.[22] The extensive body of literature dealing with ethnic groups, like other literature on the disadvantaged, suggests few solutions. A variety of programs of different types are being tried, but most are too new to measure their effectiveness.

Approaches to Teaching the Disadvantaged

A review of the methods used or advocated to improve instruction for the disadvantaged does not present a very encouraging picture. In general, enthusiasts propose for the disadvantaged what has already been tried and found wanting. In a 1966 critique of compensatory education, Gordon and Wilkerson[23] concluded that most programs are based on sentiment rather than fact, that they increase traditional resource allocations without changing the nature of instruction, and are typically set up without any experimental controls with respect to the innovation bringing about increased school performance. Evaluative studies were few, and when conducted the outcomes were vague and amorphous.

Four years later the situation had not changed, at least in the area of the social studies. In the winter of 1970, the National Council for the Social Studies, in collaboration with the Georgia Council for the Social Sciences, sponsored a regional conference on "The Social Studies and the Disadvantaged."[24] Leading social studies educators from the west to the east coasts participated, and some of the "new" social studies projects were represented.

But not one major project had been specifically conceived with the learning problems of the disadvantaged in mind, and no project was able to present evidence as to increments in performance of the disadvantaged on previously specified criterion measures related to treatment. In contrast to the hundreds of studies describing the characteristics of the disadvantaged, there is little concrete evidence to show that programs for the disadvantaged make a difference in learning outcomes. "Promising practices" are all too often merely an exhortation to do something without any specific regard to ends and means.

22. A more extensive discussion may be found in M. J. Rice, "Social and Psychological Characteristics of the Disadvantaged," in *Social Studies and the Disadvantaged*, ed. J. C. McLendon (Athens, Ga.: University of Georgia, 1970), pp. 93-128.

23. Edmund W. Gordon and Doxey A. Wilkerson, *Compensatory Education for the Disadvantaged* (New York: College Entrance Examination Board, 1966).

24. Georgia Center for Continuing Education, University of Georgia, February 22-24, 1970.

In this section consideration will be given to various approaches used in working with the disadvantaged. These approaches may be conveniently described as compensatory. Although the term *compensatory* is sometimes criticized, it conveys the special focus of educational efforts for the disadvantaged—increments in experience and learning which offset the handicaps of a deprived background.

Early Intervention. The most popular and pervasive model for compensatory education is preprimary education. Animal and child studies of the effects of early environmental deprivation, a new appreciation of the interaction of genotype and phenotype, a shift in the predeterminism of fixed intelligence, studies showing the significance of early experience in the development of intellectual processes, and the increments in task performance from early stimulation have combined to give a theoretical rationale for environmental manipulation in the years from birth to traditional schooling. J. McV. Hunt has been one of the most articulate exponents of intervention, and in his writings has synthesized much of the research findings which support early intervention efforts.[25]

The tremendous expansion of preprimary education, described in chapter 5, has nevertheless been disappointing. It has not been harmful, but it has thus far failed to provide desired compensatory benefits.

THE TRADITIONAL PREPRIMARY SCHOOL. The traditional preprimary school in the United States is a maturation-play-developmental school, adjusted to the interpretation of needs of the middle-class child. While the United States borrowed heavily from such European educators as McMillan and Montessori who worked with slum children, the United States failed to develop management-instructional systems for the disadvantaged. The dominant curricula available for use in Head Start and similar programs were nonlanguage and nonschool oriented. Any culture always tends to meet new challenges by using repertoires of old behavior. It was therefore inevitable that traditional programs would be used for compensatory early intervention, with innovations of a mechanical type—reduction in teacher ratio and parent involvement.

Evaluation of the effects of traditional preprimary compensatory programs show that such early intervention is neither harmful nor helpful. While there appear to be some values in socialization, the traditional curricula fail as *compensatory* curricula because they do not concentrate sufficiently on aspects of intellectual development related to scholastic success—especially language development.[26] Those curricula which appear to be most effective as *compensatory* programs emphasize language development, number skills, and involve children scholastically. As the children succeed in the school-oriented tasks, they also seem to acquire not merely the requisite cognitive skills, but the related affective learnings—of attitudes and values—which are also related to success in the school situation.

25. See especially: J. McV. Hunt, *Intelligence and Experience* (New York: Ronald Press Company, 1961); idem, *The Challenge of Incompetence and Poverty* (Urbana: University of Illinois Press, 1969).

26. Hunt, *The Challenge,* p. 170; Roslyn A. O'Brien and P. Lopate, *Preschool Programs and the Intellectual Development of Disadvantaged Children* (ERIC Clearing House on Early Childhood Education, 1968); D. P. Weikart, "Preschool Programs: Preliminary Findings," *The Journal of Special Education* 1, no. 2 (1967).

As a result, a number of alternatives to the traditional preprimary program are being developed with more academic emphasis. Generally, these programs are not welcomed by the traditional wisdom, and have thus far made very little impact on preprimary schooling.

BEREITER-ENGELMANN ACADEMIC PREPRIMARY PROGRAM. One of the best known and least accepted alternatives to traditional preprimary schooling for the disadvantaged is the academic preprimary program developed by Bereiter and Engelmann at the University of Illinois.[27] They are among the severest critics of the traditional preprimary program as compensatory education for the young. They affirm that traditional nursery and kindergarten programs resemble a slum, not in the physical environment, but in the kinds of experiences provided.

Their rationale is very clear cut. The preprimary program should not try to deal with the whole child. There are opportunities for other experiences outside of school. Those experiences are not nearly as limiting as the usual developmental literature implies. Sensory experience occurs in a slum as well as a palace. What is lacking is the language development prerequisite to success in school.

The focus of a compensatory program should therefore be on the development of the formal language necessary to school success. Success in specific school tasks will eliminate the problems associated with the disadvantaged, such as emotional adjustment, peer relations, and other personal problems. By identifying specific tasks related to school success, a limited means-end curriculum objective specific may be developed. Fifteen preprimary learning tasks are identified in the Bereiter-Engelmann materials such as, ability to use affirmative and not statements, polar opposites, selected prepositions, if-then relations, positive and negative instances of classes, *not* and *or* in deductions, name basic colors, count to ten, name vowels and fifteen consonants, and rhyme.

On the basis of these specific objectives, one hour a day of intensive, direct verbal instruction is devoted to the three subject-matter areas of language, arithmetic, and reading. The periods are generally managed in 20 minute blocks, alternating between unstructured (play) or semi-structured (art) activities to highly structured and intensive direct verbal instruction. In contrast to the play routine of the traditional school, a work routine is emphasized; a child is not permitted to abandon an activity at his will. The context is task oriented, and behavior is shaped to perform the task. The teacher is not present merely to give support and warmth to the child's activities. He teaches directly to elicit, transmit, and increase language behavior. The sequence of experiences is carefully developed to economize time. Frequent use is made of questions to provide a pupil-response feedback cycle for evaluation and teaching. The pace is rapid. The pupil moves through a highly structured program, paced to achieve specific learning tasks and not paced to reflect interests of the learner. The object is to prepare the young learner for school by teaching him school-specific skills that the middle class child acquires in the normal process of rearing.

27. Descriptions of the theory and practice is given in: Bereiter and Engelmann, *Teaching Disadvantaged Children;* Siegfried Engelmann, *Preventing Failure in the Primary Grades* (Chicago: Science Research Associates, Inc., 1969).

THE NIMNICHT MATERIAL-CENTERED PROGRAM. At the other extreme of the Bereiter-Engelmann teacher centered program is a material centered program developed by Glenn Nimnicht at the New Nursery School in Greeley, Colorado. In this autotelic environment the children begin very much as they do in traditional schools, and much use is made of play, sandbox, and dress-up activities. The teachers do not teach directly, but respond to children's requests. As the year passes, children voluntarily decrease the amount of time in play-oriented activities and spend more and more time in activities using the language, reading, and number materials provided. A typewriter is used, but not the expensive talking typewriter of O. K. Moore fame.[28] This material-centered program attempts, as in the Montessori environment described in chapter 5, to capitalize upon children's interests and activities, and is not teacher centered.

THE GRAY AND KARNES PROGRAMS. The programs of Susan Gray at Peabody and Merle B. Karnes at Illinois, combine teacher centered and material centered activities.

The Early Training Project[29] at Peabody utilizes many different materials. There is a low student-teacher ratio of 1:5, and the teachers are actively involved in asking questions, talking, praising, and evoking talk in children. It is less structured, however, than in the Bereiter-Engelmann program.

The Karnes program has utilized a variety of materials and games, but it has also emphasized science and social studies goals, language arts and reading, and the development of useful number skills. In program scope, the Karnes program resembled the broad cognitive emphasis of the former Research and Development Center in Educational Stimulation, University of Georgia.

EVALUATION OF EFFECTIVENESS OF ACADEMIC-ORIENTED PREPRIMARY PROGRAMS. Evaluation of any preprimary program, as with intervention at later ages, will show that the intervention "works." Since there is rarely a comparison of one intervention with another on uniform measures, it is impossible to ascertain comparative effectiveness. Another difficulty in preprimary evaluations is the lack of longitudinal research. If compensatory education is to be effective, the results must be sustained in schooling, and not make a difference merely in the experimental population which has had training, and a control population which has had no preprimary training. If the results of preprimary intervention have disappeared by the end of the preprimary years, the case for preprimary intervention as *compensatory* education cannot be maintained. It may be desirable to have the children in a supervised environment, where they may play safely under adequate supervision, have good food, and receive adequate health care. These desirable outcomes, however, are in themselves not scholastically compensatory.

The most carefully controlled comparative research of preprimary program effectives has come from Merle B. Karnes and her associates. A 1968 study compared the effectiveness of a traditional program with the Karnes structured program for disadvantaged three year olds. On the three

28. Described in Hunt, *The Challenge*.
29. Susan W. Gray et al., *Before First Grade: The Early Training Project for Culturally Disadvantaged Children* (New York: Columbia University, Teachers College Press, 1966).

measures used—Stanford-Binet IQ, Illinois Test for Psycholinguistic Abilities,[30] and Frostig Visual Perception[31]—gains of students in the structured Karnes academic program exceeded gains of students in the traditional program.[32] In a follow-up study, Karnes compared the achievement of disadvantaged four year olds in four different programs—a traditional nursery program, a community-integrated program, a Montessori program which met the standards of the National Montessori Society, and the Karnes structured program. It was assumed that children would make the greatest gains in the structured programs—Montessori and Karnes—and would make the least gains in the nonstructured traditional and community-integrated programs. The children who participated in the Montessori program showed the smallest average gain and those in the Karnes program the greatest gain. Gain in the traditional program was modest but exceeded that in the community-integrated program. The Montessori program does not lack structure in sensorimotor activities, neither does not provide for a high level of teacher-child verbalization necessary to associate language with sensory perception and motor performance.[33] This would seem to indicate that children need experience with language more than they need sensorimotor experiences, one of the chief assumptions of traditional preprimary programs.

A third Karnes[34] study is a longitudinal study involving the relative performance of children at the end of the first grade who had been in traditional, ameliorative (Karnes), and direct verbal (Bereiter-Engelmann) programs. Both of the structured programs—ameliorative and direct verbal—showed gain superiority on level of Binet IQ retention, although there was a substantial drop. There was also superior performance on school achievement tasks, which was at the second grade level on reading, a superior performance for children who entered compensatory programs at IQ levels bordering on mental deficiency. The failure in the first grade of the public schools to maintain the IQ gains for the upper performing children in all three programs is merely another indication of the extent to which the public schools fail disadvantaged children. As noted in chapter 5, this results from a failure to accommodate primary programs to the initial gains made by preprimary children.

Follow Through Programs. As a result of the failure of traditional Head Start programs and the public schools to provide beneficial compensatory education for the disadvantaged, the United States Office of Education established "follow through" programs to provide continuity in public school programs with preprimary programs.[35] Mod-

30. S. A. Kirk and J. J. McCarthy, *Illinois Test of Psycholinguistic Abilities* (Urbana: University of Illinois Press, 1961); S. A. Kirk, J. J. McCarthy, and Winnifred Kirk, *The Illinois Test of Psycholinguistic Abilities,* rev. ed. (Urbana: University of Illinois Press, 1968.)
31. Marianne Frostig, *The Frostig Program for the Development of Visual Perception* (Chicago: Follett Publishing Co., 1964).
32. Merle B. Karnes, *Research and Development Program on Preschool Disadvantaged Children.* Final report, Project no. 5-1181, Contract no. OE-6-10-235 (Urbana: University of Illinois, Institute for Research on Exceptional Children, 1969), pp. 187-96.
33. Merle B. Karnes and Audrey Hodgins, "The Effects of a Highly Structured Preschool Program on the Measured Intelligence of Culturally Disadvantaged Four-Year-Old Children," *Psychology in the Schools* 6 (January 1969): 89-91.
34. Karnes, *Research and Development Program,* pp. 147-83.
35. U.S. Office of Education, Bureau of Elementary and Secondary Education, Division of Compensatory Education, "Preliminary Report of the Advisory Committee on Follow Through," July 1967.

el programs were selected in the spring of 1968 by school districts awarded Follow Through Grants, training institutes for teachers held in the summer, and programs initiated in the school year 1968-69 with a plan for national evaluation. Programs were continued in 1969-70. No evaluation of the effectiveness of Follow Through models, comparable to the Karnes studies, has been reported.

Parental Involvement and Child Care Centers. In addition to the preprimary programs, which focus upon compensatory efforts with children in an institutional setting, efforts have been made to involve parents as home educators. This type of approach contrasts with the usual welfare and child-rearing approach which counsels parents about child-rearing practices, but fails to provide them with the effective tools for home intervention. Gray,[36] Karnes,[37] and Gordon,[38] are early interventionists reporting successful efforts to teach mothers of disadvantaged children to teach their children in the home. The focus of these successful efforts is to provide the mother with the skills needed to work with the children—how to read a story, how to ask questions, how to talk—and not to change the whole spectrum of child-rearing practices and the home environment. In addition to the increments in child performance, techniques of home intervention also have a positive effect upon mothers with respect to motivation for further education, improved employment, better home care, and general improvement of the home condition.

This approach, which may involve home visits, parent participation in preprimary programs, or a combination of approaches, seems to be relatively efficient in terms of cost and benefits. It promises to be particularly effective with parents of children too young for institutionalized training. Parent intervention programs seem to have benefits of both vertical and horizontal diffusion. They affect not only the target child in the family, but spread to practices with other siblings. The practices also appear to be imitated by other parents in the neighborhood. Flint, Michigan initiated (1963) a home-school program beginning at the kindergarten level.[39] Children of parents involved in the program showed gains which were significant compared to control children of parents not in the program.

The success of planned use of parents as home educators has led to the proposal for Parent and Child Centers. These centers would provide not merely a range of professional services to the families served by the center, but would actively involve the families, including older siblings, in the conduct of the services of the Center. In 1967 the Office of Economic Opportunity was authorized to establish twenty-five experimental day care centers.[40]

Elementary Intervention Programs. While preprimary intervention has received

36. Gray, *Before First Grade,* pp. 102-9.
37. Karnes (1969) *Research and Development Program,* pp. 197-203.
38. Ira J. Gordon, ed., *Reaching the Child Through Parent Education* (Gainesville, Fla.: University of Florida, Institute for Development of Human Resources, 1969).
39. School and Home Program, Flint, Michigan (Elementary Program in Compensatory Education, Office of Education, OE-37023).
40. The following ERIC publications are available from ERIC Document Reproduction Service, P.O. Drawer O, Bethesda, Maryland 20014. ED 027 969, *Good References on Day Care* and ED 024 453, *Group Day Care as a Child-Rearing Environment* by Elizabeth Prescott. *Day Care and Child Development in Your Community* is a 32-page pamphlet available from the Day Care and Child Development Council of America, Inc., 1426 H Street, N.W., Washington, D.C. 20005.

the most publicity and attention, numerous attempts have been made to provide compensatory education at the elementary level.

Most of these have focused on reading[41] and other communication skills,[42] although some have involved diverse aspects as busing,[43] dramatics,[44] home contacts,[45] and a multi-purpose program with many specialists.[46] It is difficult to interpret the results of these programs as to comparative effectiveness and to long term effectiveness. In a multi-faceted program, such as the More Effective Schools Program of New York City, there are so many different experimental variables that it is difficult to ascertain what aspect of the program is compensatory. In 1966, Fox[47] gave a negative appraisal followed by a favorable appraisal in 1968 by Forlano and McClelland.[48] "Shot-gun" compensatory programs are difficult to evaluate, especially when there is no specification of the task increments and the specific means by which the task increments are to be achieved.

In general, programs for the disadvantaged repeat elements suggested in the Economic Opportunity Act of 1964 and Title I of the Elementary and Secondary Education Act of 1965. These include general cultural enrichment, field trips, tutoring, and remedial work, especially in the skill subjects. There is a dearth of research evidence, however, concerning the effectiveness of particular approaches for teaching the disadvantaged. Such collections as Cowles,[49] Frost and Hawkes,[50] and Passow[51] contain excellent articles on the social and psychological characteristics of the disadvantaged. These collections, however, contain little more than anecdotal accounts concerning the specific teaching of reading, writing, science, and social studies. A 1970 review of curriculum, methods, and media in the social studies and the disadvantaged[52] failed to differentiate any aspects uniquely pertinent to the disadvantaged. Research in the social studies tends to concentrate on naive methodologies which ignore specific learning theories related to the disadvantaged or any conceptualization of increased performance of the disadvantaged. Comparisons of different media and methods are so poorly controlled with respect to criterion learnings that the conclusions often amount to no more than special pleading in the guise of research.

One of the most common approaches to teaching the disadvantaged learner is task reduction. Many publishers purport to have

41. U.S. Office of Education, *Intensive Reading Instructional Teams,* Hartford, Connecticut OE-37038; *Elementary Reading Centers,* Milwaukee OE-37031; *Programmed Tutorial Reading Project,* Indianapolis OE-37029.
42. U.S. Office of Education, *Speech and Language Development Program,* Milwaukee OE-37028, *Communication Skills Center Project,* Detroit OE-37039.
43. U.S. Office of Education, *Project Concern,* Hartford, Connecticut OE-37030.
44. U.S. Office of Education, *Self-Directive Dramatization Project,* Joliet, Illinois OE-37037.
45. U.S. Office of Education, *Homework Helper Program,* New York City OE-27025.
46. U.S. Office of Education, *More Effective Schools,* New York City OE-37042.
47. D. J. Fox, *Expansion of the More Effective Schools Program* (New York: The Center for Urban Education, 1967).
48. G. Forlano and S. D. McClelland, *Measuring Pupil Growth in Reading in the More Effective Schools* (New York: Board of Education of the City of New York, 1968).
49. Milly Cowles, ed., *Perspectives in the Education of Disadvantaged Children* (Scranton, Pa.: International Textbook Company, 1969).
50. Joel L. Frost and Glenn R. Hawkes, eds., *The Disadvantaged Child* (Boston: Houghton Mifflin Company, 1966).
51. A. Harry Passow, Miriam Goldberg, and Abraham J. Tannenbaum, eds., *Education of the Disadvantaged* (New York: Holt, Rinehart & Winston, Inc., 1967).
52. McLendon, *Social Studies.*

programs especially conceived for the disadvantaged learner. The common element in all of these programs is the lowering of the task expectancy, as measured by the nuance of ideas and complexity of language usage, including sentence length and vocabulary. Reduction in task expectancy is an act of desperation, and is a measure of the bankruptcy of teaching. With tasks lowered, the school guarantees that the disadvantaged child will not be taught the skills to overcome his learning difficulties. It accepts the child where he is, but makes no compensatory effort to use methodologies which may be more appropriate.

Much of the reduction of task expectancy is justified in the name of individual differences or meeting the child at his level of development. According to the current vogue, each teacher is in some way supposed to individualize instruction to take care of the wide range of learner abilities. Since individualization is supposed to be "good," the educational pedagogy is full of talk about individualization, with little practical know-how transmitted. Many teachers admit that from a practical classroom management standpoint, they are incapable of taking care of the learning needs of pupils who fall in the extreme ranges. Little use is made of one tool that has been developed—programmed instruction. Given the fact that language is the common vehicle of school learning, even disadvantaged pupils are frequently able to benefit from instruction aimed at the middle group. In schools where the entire population is disadvantaged because of housing patterns and school attendance zones, the issue is frequently not nearly so much one of individualization as it is of finding a match of content and procedures which effectively increases the performance level of the entire school population.

Noncurricular Approaches to Education of the Disadvantaged. In the preceding sections, compensatory education has focused on the content of the experience brought to the child. In this section other approaches will be briefly examined.

ADDITIONAL STAFF SERVICES. Many compensatory programs provide additional personnel. These take a variety of forms—additional teachers to reduce the teacher-pupil ratio, teacher aides to relieve the teacher of routine tasks, subject specialists, and nonteaching specialists in guidance, psychological services, and school social work. The mere addition of personnel, without some specific curriculum in compensatory education, does not appear to justify the increased personnel expenditures. Reduction in class size, although generally popular with teachers, shows little relationship to increased pupil performance. All too often, the addition of additional personnel without a clearly determined performance objective merely adds to the already existing staff types of personnel in greater numbers who are already inefficient factors in compensatory education.

SCHOOL DROPOUT PROGRAMS. Dropout programs are typically high school programs. They are of concern to the prospective elementary teacher, however, because if a child does not succeed in elementary school there is a good possibility that he will become a school dropout, at the legal school leaving age, if not before. A variety of programs have been utilized—improving school performance in preventive programs, work orientation, counseling with vocational training, job experience, forced work experiences with pay, and expansion of more contemporary vocational training.

Middle grade dropout programs are rarely distinguishable in content from programs for the disadvantaged or slow learner. In recent years, emphasis at dropout prevention has shifted to compensatory education for the preprimary child. However, if instructional systems particularly suitable for the disadvantaged are not developed for the primary and intermediate years, the results of any favorable preprimary compensatory effort will be lost. An exclusive concern with preprimary dropout prevention will probably prove no more effective than the former exclusive high school concern with remedial dropout prevention.

TEACHER TRAINING. The Economic Opportunity Act of 1964 recognized the need for specific teacher training for the disadvantaged and authorized the establishment of VISTA (Volunteers in Service to America), a type of domestic Peace Corps. The program has been meagerly funded, and the impact has been negligible. From time to time various teacher training institutes have been granted special funds for the training of teachers of the disadvantaged. These have generally been ineffective, due to the fact that the institutions and individuals who conducted the institutes had no educational technology of demonstrated merit for the teaching of the disadvantaged. Most of the content of such institutes has relied heavily on teaching the sociological and psychological backgrounds of the disadvantaged. It has yet to be demonstrated that such information can be translated into more effective pedagogic procedures. Judging from the various books dealing with the disadvantaged, the answer appears to be negative.

Beginning in 1968, the Office of Education established the Triple-T (Training of Trainers of Teachers) Program at selected institutions. Originally, the purpose was to emphasize the reciprocal and joint responsibilities of liberal arts and education professors in the training of teachers. Just as a heavy parent emphasis was made in the guidelines for Follow Through, the guidelines were changed with Triple-T to emphasize a heavy community involvement. In the case of Triple-T, the "community" appeared in 1969-70 to largely reflect the desire of the Office of Education to give minority ethnic groups, especially Negroes, Indians, and Spanish-speaking Americans, a voice in the education of future teachers of the disadvantaged. The Triple-T programs are financed, as are many federal education programs, at a per-product cost considerably higher than that for comparable products in regular programs. These programs are still too new to permit an evaluation of their effectiveness in developing better teachers of the disadvantaged.

Most teacher training institutions have typically sought out ideal teaching situations for training their student teachers. These ideal situations in general have been in good, middle class schools. Here, children generally learn in spite of poor teaching. When new teachers are assigned to schools in disadvantaged areas, they frequently experience the equivalent of culture shock. They have no expertise in terms of method or ideology to cope with the special requirements for teaching. Until recently, few white student teachers have been assigned to predominantly Negro schools, especially in the South.

Some of the newer training programs for teachers of the disadvantaged emphasize early and sustained contact with disadvantaged learners and more emphasis on practical experience. Student teachers who have taught disadvantaged pupils are more likely to seek such employment later than students who have had no previous experience in such settings.

Much in-service effort is also being utilized to change teacher expectation of pupil performance. It has been demonstrated repeatedly that teachers often expect very little from disadvantaged children, who, as a result, become even more disadvantaged learners. One of the major problems appears to be in recasting a philosophy-of-teaching style. Most elementary teachers run a fairly loose, slow paced, activity-oriented school program. Apparently, this approach does not work with the disadvantaged, measured by their present performance. However, teachers frequently find it difficult to use more structured methods, not only because of their lack of experience, but also because their whole philosophic orientation is unsympathetic toward structured learning.

SUMMER SCHOOL. The term "summer school" inevitably conjures up the vision of imprisoned children sitting in fixed rows while outside their carefree peers romp and play. Teachers and adults as well as pupils project this stereotype. Summer school has been typically regarded as compensatory—it has provided children who did not succeed in the previous nine months the additional time necessary to catch up—or at least appear to.

Summer school has a number of theoretical advantages, however. In the first place, it is recognized that disadvantaged children have a slower learning rate. They need more time in which to accomplish a task. Summer school provides that additional time. In the second place, it is recognized that all children lose many of the skills over the prolonged summer vacation of three months. Skills laboriously achieved at the end of the spring are often forgotten over the summer vacation. Summer school provides the opportunity to continue to practice the skills already learned. And finally, the summer school can provide a much more useful environment to the disadvantaged child than he has in his own neighborhood. Failure to exploit the summer period for education reflects tradition and economy—not any educational fact. Perhaps no better investment could be made by our society than to increase its educational investment by one-sixth and operate the schools for two additional months.

UNDERSTANDING THE CULTURE OF THE CHILD. In the last decade the cultural approach to the disadvantaged learner has grown in popularity. It may be classified as a teacher training approach, since the objective of this approach is for the teacher to accord greater acceptance and increased support to the child through acquiring an appreciation of his cultural background.

There is nothing inherently wrong with this approach. If a knowledge of the background from which the child comes facilitates a more favorable teacher perception of his capabilities, the knowledge might assist the teacher to develop a more positive learning approach.

Unfortunately, this approach all too often leads to a patronizing attitude and a paralysis of teaching. It is not enough for a teacher to accept children, irrespective of their minority background. If the teacher accepts the cultural background of Spanish-speaking children, but is inept in teaching performance skills, the acceptance may be of little value toward the child's achievement. A teacher can be warm, understanding, and supportive, but so inept pedagogically that the child cannot achieve because he is not taught. The danger of the appreciative or cultural approach is that it attempts to substitute knowledge about the disadvantaged for performance skills in teaching the disadvantaged.

Structure and Teaching the Disadvantaged

Due to the diversity of theories about the nature of learning and the priorities of learning, it is possible that there will never be any consensus as to the most effective methods of teaching, much less teaching the disadvantaged. Programs which are designed to enhance creativity, and divergent thinking may have outcomes[53] which are completely different from receptive learning methods.[54] In the current vogue for discovery, expository and inductive methods are seldom mentioned as efficient methods, notwithstanding the fact that there is conflicting evidence to substantiate the claims made for discovery methods.[55]

It is nevertheless suggested that structured approaches to teaching the disadvantaged may be the more efficient methods, as measured by increase in pupil knowledge and performance, when contrasted with the more popular open-ended approaches. A structured approach is task-specific in four characteristics: the learning outcome, content, method, and evaluation measure.

"Structuring" is not absolute, of course, but a matter of degree. All schooling is structured. Conventional teaching methods in the elementary school which include activity, group work, problem solving, library research, and other open approaches to learning necessarily have some structure, usually imparted by the material or teacher directions. However, closed systems of instruction are highly or completely structured, and developed in such a way that they constitute an information feedback system to the learner. Examples of such closed systems are the programmed text, modular instruction, Moore's talking typewriter, computer-assisted instruction, and Montessori teaching devices. Pupil workbooks are often highly structured, and are frequently analogous to the teaching text, except that the purpose is not new learning, but the stabilization of learning through reinforcement by stimulus recall.

Theoretical psychologies related to structured learning are found in the work of Skinner, Ausubel, Jensen, Bereiter and Engelmann, and Scandura, to mention a few. While each uses a somewhat different approach, all imply that a structured approach is more conducive to teaching the slow learner than the prevalent open-ended approaches.

Skinner and Operant Conditioning. Operant conditioning, predominantly identified with Skinner, gave a tenuous revival to teaching machines and programmed texts in the 1950s. The movement, while having a tremendous impact on training programs in industry and the armed forces, has had little influence on school teaching. Programmed instruction, whether of the text or machine variety, has the common structured

---

53. See, for example, E. P. Torrance, *Education and the Creative Potential* (Minneapolis: University of Minnesota, 1963).
54. D. P. Ausubel, *The Psychology of Meaningful Verbal Learning* (New York: Grune and Stratton, 1963).
55. Lee Schulman and Evan Keislar, eds., *Learning by Discovery* (Chicago: Rand McNally & Company, 1966).

elements previously outlined: the learning outcome, content, method, and criterion measure are completely controlled. There is no ambiguity as to what is required or whether the program has been successful, in terms of required pupil behavior. In constructing a program, the burden is always on the program, not on the learner. In constructing programs, the learning frames are tried out repeatedly with learners of different ranges of abilities, and the teaching frames modified as necessary to eliminate ambiguity for the learner.

Research in the use of programmed texts with slow and fast learners brings mixed results. In some cases, slower students have benefited from programmed instruction. Research in the Anthropology Curriculum Project at the University of Georgia indicates that disadvantaged students are no more handicapped in using a teaching text than in conventional classroom instruction.[56] The lack of oral language may be a handicap for the disadvantaged learner if too much dependence is placed on the teaching text. Probably the greatest advantage in teaching texts lies in their being used by more able students while the teacher is enabled to spend the released time with students requiring supplementary instruction. But even when a teaching text is not used, a teacher may profitably study this technique for constructing and teaching micro-lessons to the disadvantaged learner.

Ausubel's Receptive Learning and Pre-organizers. Ausubel has been a consistent advocate of teaching methods based on receptive learning, in contrast to inquiry. Briefly, his learning model states simply that school instruction is concerned primarily with abstracts which are not discovered inductively, as with infant and preschool learning; they are received. In contrast to an hierarchy of learning, as presented by Gagné, Ausubel conceives of general and subsuming categories. Thus the principle in organizing material is to introduce the more abstract organizers, develop a cognitive set, and subsume lesser concepts and categories in the earlier cognitive set. In this model, rules and concepts are taught deductively; categories and other organizing material are taught explicitly; the student is not expected to infer rules, but to apply rules which have been learned in reference to a meaningful cognitive set. The development of a cognitive set, similar to the older Herbartian concept of apperceptive background, assures that the new verbal material is meaningful, i.e., related to a meaningful intellectual field, and not acquired simply by rote.

Jensen's Associative Learning. Modern associative learning is associated with M. R. Guthrie, but is as old as the psychology of Locke. Modern associational theory posits multi-directional cognitive growth involving three fundamental operations of comparing, contrasting, and grouping.

Typical instructional procedures in the schools assume the existence of previous cognitive structures. Associational theory makes no such assumption, and emphasizes learning on a factual level. Bloom's Taxonomy has probably been a disservice, as interpreted in the social sciences, because of the implied denigration of factual recall and the emphasis on "higher" intellectual processes. Emphasis on the latter, for which the disadvantaged learner is not prepared, may preclude his acquisition of the factual

---

56. Georgelle Thomas, "Programmed Instruction for Teaching Anthropology in the Fifth Grade," *The Journal of Experimental Education* 36 (Summer 1968): 88-92.

data base on which more abstract or conceptual learning must be erected. Jensen has yet to convert his theoretical model into an actual curriculum, but the approach is congruent with other approaches to teaching the disadvantaged learner.

Bereiter-Engelmann and Direct Verbal Learning. One of the most successful early childhood programs for disadvantaged learners is the direct verbal prototype developed by Bereiter and Engelmann at the University of Illinois, previously described.

Child developers invariably criticize the direct verbal learning approach as failing to develop "the whole child." The success of the program is undoubtedly due to its parsimony of objectives. Teaching children to acquire the formal language required in school instruction is consistent with Bernstein's elaborated language concept and Carroll's and Vygotsky's emphasis on school learning as verbal learning. Verbal learning implies direct verbal instruction by the teacher, not merely asking questions of children based on their reading ability. Verbal learning demands oral instruction in content. Work in the Anthropology Curriculum Project as well as the Geography Curriculum Project at the University of Georgia with slow learners indicates that disadvantaged learners can acquire sophisticated, abstract concepts when these concepts are taught explicitly.

Probably the greatest handicap that the disadvantaged learner faces today is the low verbal approach of the elementary school. Other elementary children continue to increase their verbal skills at home. The majority of disadvantaged learners do not have this opportunity, and school instruction does nothing to overcome this deficit. Consequently, there occurs a cumulative deficit as the disadvantaged learner progresses through school. Part of this deficit is due to the type of instruction received, not merely to the learning ability of the individual. As Jensen has noted, preoccupation with teaching all students on the basis of their having a high level of general intelligence frequently precludes use of methods appropriate to the disadvantaged learner. As long as learning as a process precludes emphasis on learning as a product, it will be difficult to examine the various alternatives which might be more efficient in increasing learning performance.

Classroom Practice and Methods for Teaching the Disadvantaged. The implications of learning theory and research for the disadvantaged do not require elaborate testing prior to the taking of remedial action. As a result of empirical classroom practice, some structured approaches have been identified which are helpful to the disadvantaged. Since these methods are also more efficient for the superior learner they facilitate his learning too. This suggests that the major difference between the disadvantaged and the superior learner is a time-quantity factor, and does not imply a different cognitive style.

Any teacher can program himself to provide more structured teaching for the disadvantaged. What is required is more careful lesson planning. The generalized, vague, and diffuse planning that accompanies activity unit development is not sufficiently specific. Many teachers do not make good teachers of the disadvantaged because their own planning and work habits are incompatible with the more rigid planning-teaching sequence required. The important thing for a teacher to understand is that individual differences are not met by talking about them. They must be planned for. The extension of the elementary school day to almost seven pupil hours is probably inimical to effective teacher planning, especially where a teacher has several preparations. Even where, say, a social studies teacher might only have three different social studies preparations, planning at three different levels would mean nine preparations. The requirements of planning time and the school expectancy load are incompatible with the admonitions of college colleagues who frequently have but one or two preparations.

TASK SPECIFICITY. The learning expectancy should always be made specific. You are a teacher; not the author of a "Who dunnit?" Do not merely make an assignment, "Read so many pages," "Write a composition on . . ." "Do some library research." In the pressure of time, we are all guilty of such ambiguity. The average and better learners get help at home or become so school-and teacher-wise that they can infer the learning task. The disadvantaged learner, however, is lost. Often times he does not work—we say he lacks motivation—simply because he does not grasp what is expected of him.

In assigning any task, whether to be executed in school or at home, the teacher of the disadvantaged learner should indicate by sub-tasks what is to be learned. This is the learning contract. You expect the student to learn A and not Z. When you evaluate, you measure for A and not Z. You do not improvise a learning outcome after the assignment of the learning task. Since college teachers often ask questions on footnotes, school teachers often do the equivalent with their pupils. Generally, students dismiss this as not being cricket. For the disadvantaged learner it is disastrous. Nothing is more frustrating than to study A, work hard to master it, and find that the teacher is looking for something else. Since the disadvantaged learner has a slower learning rate, what is expected of him must count. The teacher must order his learning priorities so that student effort will be worthwhile. Particular attention should be given to new vocabulary. New words should be correctly pronounced, written, and used in context. Possible learning difficulties, whether due to conceptual difficulty or text ambiguity, should be identified and pointed out. The disadvantaged learner does not approach the new task de novo; an apperceptive background, to use an old Herbartian term, has been developed for the reception of new information.

TASK LENGTH. The emphasis on microteaching has once again made respectable the corrollary of micro-learning. Long-term learning tasks, as exemplified in the unit approach, need to be broken down into short, day-to-day tasks which provide for prompt teacher feedback and correction. The overall unit tasks need to be approached in an additive and cumulative fashion, with frequent opportunity for review and integration of new learning with previous learning.

READING AND STUDY SKILLS: Intensive work is required to develop vocabulary and increase reading comprehension. Since most subjects use some kind of text or printed material, attention needs to be given to the use of the text for information gathering. New words need to be introduced, and recorded in a notebook. New words need to be studied before the reading lesson, in order that comprehension may be increased rather than hindered by the new vocabulary.

Specific questions should be used to guide information acquisition (see "Task Specificity") and the answers recorded in a notebook. The notebook should then be used as a tool for review.

Particular attention needs to be given to study skills. These include the survey, making questions, reading, reciting, and reviewing. Outlining and summarizing should begin early but on a small scale. Here the teacher needs to check and guide the student's organizing ability, and provide frequent opportunity for practice. While only one student may respond verbally, all students may respond in writing. Map, picture, and chart interpretation need to be systematically practiced, using the related vocabulary necessary for correct interpretation. At all times, the teacher must require use of the appropriate formal language, and not infer that the child understands the concept. When correct technical vocabulary is not used, the teacher should supply or elicit the appropriate response so that students acquire facility in speaking in the language of the subjects.

FIELD TRIPS. The learning contribution of a field trip is often negligible because of the lack of previous planning and preparation. Before a field trip, the students must acquire the verbal percepts through which they may internalize and communicate their experience. Exposure to a raw experience, without acquisition of the appropriate language to interpret and explain, often makes field trips meaningless. Field trips become meaningful proportionate to the extent they provide an opportunity for children to associate abstract labels with concrete data. After a field trip, the experience should be reviewed and interpreted using the new concepts associated with the field trip. A more complete discussion of planning meaningful field trips was given in chapter 5.

TASK CONSISTENCY. The disadvantaged learner has sufficient handicaps with content not to have to cope constantly with the effects of novelty. This does not mean that there should never be any variation in the teaching day. It does suggest, however, that some consistency in teaching method is advantageous. A bewildering variety of techniques—films, tapes, current events, role simulation, games, panel discussions, group activities—set up inhibitions to learning in two ways: The use of many different methodologies often makes it difficult to specify the learning task; and the effort expended in mastering the new techniques frequently precludes the acquisition of new concepts or skills. Where new techniques are introduced, care should be taken to orient the disadvantaged learner to the methodology as well as to the task.

TEACHER CLARITY AND TEACHING. Teaching disadvantaged learners places a premium on teacher clarity. This is not the equivalent of simplicity. The teacher must be clear about his own teaching expectancies in order to work precisely with pupils. Specific rather than diffuse planning is required.

Emphasis will necessarily be placed on *telling* and *showing*. Questions will also be extensively used, but primarily to stimulate language use and to provide feedback relating to concept formation. Exclusive use of the questioning technique—the practical form inductive and other open-ended instructional procedures taken in the classroom—is inappropriate for the disadvantaged learner. The verbal behavior of teaching requires an extensive repertory of language skills. The teacher is required to explain, define, illustrate, analyze, synthesize, infer, generalize, review, preview, summarize, categorize, compare, contrast, identify, and describe. He will also elicit these response behaviors in his pupils. Oral teaching in the elementary school is not a simple lecture, a verbal discourse equivalent to a narration. Many verbal skills enter into the classroom technique of telling. In turn, these become *models* for pupil-teacher interaction. The disadvantaged learner requires a teacher who regards his task as one of teaching. He does not require a Socratic questioner.

SUMMARY. This overview of structured approaches for teaching the slow learner has not revealed any magic way of increasing the achievement of disadvantaged learners. More than anything else, it has attempted to impart a point of view. This point of view may be summed up this way: the teacher must be jealous for the success of the disadvantaged learner. If he assumes, a priori, that the disadvantaged learner is incapable of abstract, conceptual thinking, one thing is certain: the student will continue to be a disadvantaged learner. If, on the other hand, he systematically helps the disadvantaged learner achieve an abstract repertory and orderly habits of work, the disadvantaged learner may become another instance of the "over achiever." The emphasis on open methods of teaching appear to be unsuitable for the disadvantaged learner; it places a premium on pupil learning rather than on teaching. It is suggested that more closed approaches to instruction, involving a great deal of structure predetermined by the teacher, may be more helpful. In practice, such procedures may appear to be old-fashioned, teacher-centered, authoritarian, and all the bad things associated with conventional teaching.

On the other hand, where structured materials and methods have been used with the disadvantaged, they appear to bring higher increments of performance than in open-ended approaches.

An Appraisal of Teaching the Culturally Disadvantaged

The United States, after a decade of experimenting with various approaches to teaching the culturally disadvantaged, has yet to develop an instructional technology demonstrably suitable to the learning difficulties of this segment of the population. The disadvantaged have the learning characteristics of the slow learner. While there is a rich body of literature on the characteristics of the disadvantaged, this information has not been translated into effective instructional systems which can be relied upon to produce higher learning levels.

In the past, compensatory efforts at the high school level in the form of dropout prevention came too late. The pendulum has now shifted to the preprimary years. However, the evidence thus far available indicates that most preprimary programs are not compensatory when success in school subjects is used as a criterion measure. This is caused not only by defects in the content of the preprimary programs, but also by the failure of the public schools to adjust school content to previous learnings.

The increase in school integration, discussed in chapter 22, will bring more and more teachers into contact with disadvantaged learners from minority groups. The disadvantaged population will no longer be as isolated from the main stream of American schooling. However desirable integration is from a culture-contact point of view, it is not in itself a sufficient compensatory mechanism; large segments of the white population are also disadvantaged.

As a prospective teacher, you will constantly hear the cry that more research is needed before sound education programs for the disadvantaged may be developed. The point of view adopted here is that there is no lack of research; what is lacking is the utilization of learning research to develop more efficent instructional systems for teaching the disadvantaged. It is likely that several suitable alternatives may be constructed according to internally consistent value premises and the evidence from learning research. The work of Bereiter and Engelmann has already demonstrated a structured approach to direct verbal learning for the preprimary years. This model has not proved very popular, however, because it runs counter to the conventional emphasis on activity methods in the schools. In our preoccupation with the way we think children *ought* to learn, we may neglect the clear cut evidence of the way they *do* learn.

Many prospective teachers approach the idea of teaching the disadvantaged with fear and trembling. Certainly, the disorganization which is frequently characteristic of the disadvantaged community is transferred to the school. At the elementary level, however, many teachers of the disadvantaged are pleasantly surprised to find that these disadvantaged children like school, are fond of their teachers, are well mannered and polite, and try to succeed. Parents may be less supportive in a direct way, but they want their children to behave and to succeed. There is extra satisfaction which comes from teaching the disadvantaged learner. In a middle-class school, the child, with his pre-existent knowledge and language level, has everything going for him, and for the teacher. With the disadvantaged learner, however, a premium is placed on your skill as a teacher. You teach and re-teach. And when your pupils learn, you know that they have gained new insights and understanding from your efforts. You have to give the disadvantaged learner more of your effort and plan more carefully. You have to compensate for what he did not get before he came to school and which he still does not get in his neighborhood. Every minute of your time and his time counts. The decade of the seventies is a challenge to performance teaching.

Selected References

Ausubel, D. P. *The Psychology of Meaningful Verbal Learning.* New York: Grune and Stratton, 1963.

Beck, John M., and Saxe, Richard W., eds., *Teaching the Culturally Disadvantaged Pupil.* Springfield, Ill.: Charles C. Thomas Publisher, 1965.

Bereiter, Carl, and Engelmann, Siegfried. *Teaching Disadvantaged Children in the Preschool.* Englewood Cliffs, N. J.: Prentice-Hall, Inc., 1966.

Bloom, Benjamin S.; Davis, Allison; and Hess, Robert. *Compensatory Education for Cultural Deprivation.* New York: Holt, Rinehart and Winston, Inc., 1965.

Coleman, James S. *Equality of Educational Opportunity.* Washington, D.C.: Government Printing Office, 1966.

Cowles, Milly, ed. *Perspectives in the Education of Disadvantaged Children.* Scranton, Pa.: International Textbook Company, 1969.

Engelmann, Siegfried. *Preventing Failure in the Primary Grades.* Chicago: Science Research Associates, 1969.

Frost, Joe L., and Hawkes, Glenn R., eds. *The Disadvantaged Child.* Boston: Houghton Mifflin Company, 1966.

GAGNÉ, ROBERT M., ed. *Learning and Individual Differences.* Columbus, Ohio: Charles E. Merrill Publishing Co., 1967.

———. *The Conditions of Learning.* New York: Holt, Rinehart and Winston, Inc., 1965.

GORDON, EDMUND W., and WILKERSON, DOXEY A. *Compensatory Education for the Disadvantaged.* New York: College Entrance Examination Board, 1966.

HEBB, D. O. *The Organization of Behavior.* New York: John Wiley & Sons, 1949.

HUNT, J. MCVICKER. *The Challenge of Incompetence and Poverty.* Urbana: University of Illinois Press, 1969.

———. *Intelligence and Experience.* New York: Ronald Press Company, 1961.

JENSEN, ARTHUR R., et al. *Environment, Heredity, and Intelligence.* Harvard Educational Review, Reprint Series no. 2, 1969.

KARNES, MERLE B. *Research and Development Program on Preschool Disadvantaged Children.* Institute for Research on Exceptional Children, Final report, Project no. 5-1181, Contract no. OE-6-10-235. Urbana: University of Illinois, 1969.

McLENDON, J. C., ed. *Social Studies and the Disadvantaged.* Athens, Ga.: University of Georgia, 1970.

PASSOW, A. HARRY; GOLDBERG, MIRIAM; and TANNENBAUM, ABRAHAM J., eds. *Education of the Disadvantaged.* New York: Holt, Rinehart and Winston, Inc., 1967.

RIESSMAN, FRANK. *The Culturally Deprived Child.* New York: Harper and Row, Publishers, 1962.

SARASON, SEYMOUR B. *Psychological Problems in Mental Deficiency.* 3d ed. New York: Harper and Brothers, 1959.

SKINNER, B. F. "The Science of Learning and the Art of Teaching." *Harvard Educational Review* 24 (1954): 86-97.

collective negotiations and activism

24

One of the most pervasive issues presently in education is the matter of collective negotiations. One cannot attend a professional conference, converse with colleagues or read an educational journal without being confronted with the negotiations issue.

Let us investigate why the matter of negotiations is such an important issue by examining: (1) what negotiations are in education, (2) why many teachers are activist, (3) how negotiations are conducted, (4) what is negotiable, (5) roles of professional groups in negotiations and (6) the future of negotiations.

Negotiations Defined

Negotiations in education are defined differently by various groups according to their orientation. The National Education Association prefers to refer to negotiations in education as *professional negotiations*. Professional negotiations has been defined as:[1]

> ... a set of procedures, written and officially adopted by the local staff organization and the school board, which provides an orderly method for the school board and staff organization to negotiate on matters of mutual concern, to reach agreement on these matters, and to establish educational channels for mediation and appeal in the event of an impasse.

The term *collective bargaining,* used in negotiations in industry by labor and management, is preferred by the American Federation of Teachers. Collective bargaining is:[2]

> The process by which teachers, through their designated representatives negotiate with the board of education, through its designated representative(s), with reference to salary, working conditions, and other matters of interest to the negotiating parties. Collective bargaining usually follows a labor-management format.

The term *collective negotiations* will be used in this volume in referring to negotiations in education since it describes professional negotiations sanctioned by NEA and collective bargaining used by AFT.

1. T. M. Stinnett, J. H. Kleinmann, and M. L. Ware, *Professional Negotiation in Public Education* (New York: Macmillan Company, 1966), p. 2. Reprinted with permission of the Macmillan Company. Copyright © the Macmillan Company, 1966.
2. George B. Redfern and Forrest E. Conner, eds., *The School Administrator and Negotiation* (Washington, D.C.: American Association of School Administrators, 1968), p. 77.

Accordingly, collective negotiations can be defined as:[3]

> ... a set of procedures by which teachers, acting through their designated representatives, and school boards co-determine the terms and conditions of employment for teachers.

With a working definition of collective negotiations in mind, let us examine why teachers have become activists in recent years. A discussion of some of the most salient reasons follows.

Why Many Teachers Are Activists

Teachers have frequently been accused of being militants in collective negotiations. However, the term militancy is a misnomer when ascribed to teacher behavior insofar as it relates to collective negotiations. Teachers are not combative or engaged in warfare against the profession or those individuals and institutions the profession serves, as the term *militancy* connotes. Rather, teachers are *activists* working for the improvement of the profession and for higher performance by their pupils. An activist, as the term is used here, can be defined as a person who identifies a reform needed by or within a governmental body and diligently works to effect the reform by exerting personal or political pressure upon the institution or agency involved.

The reasons why teachers have become activists are many. Some of the reasons most frequently mentioned are these:[4]

First, many teachers are no longer content with being without a voice in the establishment of policies and procedures which affect the conditions of their employment. They believe that administrators and school boards have unilaterally dictated the terms of their employment far too long. Therefore, they are actively engaged in forcing bilateral decision making through the medium of collective negotiations.

Second, many teachers are opposed to the paternalistic treatment they have received in the past from many administrators. This situation has been characterized by an attitude on some administrators' part that they know best and that if the teachers will stay in line and accept administrative dictums, they will be rewarded. This condescending attitude on the part of administrators of this type is anachronistic.

Third, teachers are no longer willing to sit docilely by, as they have done for so many years, while the citizenry in their communities espouse the need for quality education without raising the funds needed to promote an effectual education program. To make sure that the citizenry will adequately support improved education programs, teachers have, in recent years, resorted to strikes, professional holidays, walkouts and sanctions when necessary to achieve a more favorable bargaining position in collective negotiations. Of course, teachers can misuse this power. However, the instances in which teachers have misused their bargaining power have been few.

Fourth, teachers want to be paid salaries which are commensurate with their training and professional role in the community. Not

---

3. Stanley M. Elam, Myron Liberman, Michael H. Moskow, eds., *Readings on Collective Negotiations in Public Education* (Chicago: Rand McNally & Company, 1967), p. v.

4. See: Richard D. Batchelder, "Today's Militant Teachers," *NEA Journal* 54, no. 6 (September 1965): 18-19; William G. Carr, "The Changing World of the American Teacher," in *Professional Negotiation and the Principalship* (Washington, D.C.: Department of Elementary School Principals, NEA, 1969), pp. 31-40; Myron Lieberman, "Why Teachers Want to Negotiate," *Education Age* 5, no. 1 (September-October, 1968): 6-7.

only have teachers entered the teaching profession at decidedly smaller salaries than have many of their college classmates entering other professional fields, but the longer they remain in the teaching profession the wider that pay differential becomes. Teachers have helped create affluence in our society, but they have not fully participated in the monetary rewards which the society provides. Many teachers have been forced to moonlight to provide a respectable standard of living—particularly male teachers who have families to support.

Fifth, teachers have attained higher levels of academic preparation in the space age era than did their earlier counterparts and they are not content to teach under the inadequate or inappropriate conditions which may have met the educational demands of former times. Moreover, many teachers believe that they have been asked to teach too many children; to teach without adequate materials and equipment; to perform too many *nonteaching* chores such as playground supervision, bus duty and the like. They presently seek the conditions which are conducive to self-fulfillment in teaching and excellence in the educational program.

Sixth, there are more men entering public school teaching at both the elementary and secondary levels. Quite naturally, men who are breadwinners actively seek increased welfare and fringe benefits through collective negotiations for, if they don't and if they aren't successful in their efforts, most of them will have to resort to moonlighting—a practice which diminishes their enthusiasm and preparation time for teaching.

Seventh, the general tenor of the times in the nation is that of activism. This is the age of participatory decision-making among subordinates and superordinates in many different laboring groups. In education, the issue at stake is: who will set policies and procedures for school systems? Teachers are desirous of actively participating in establishing policies and procedures which affect their work, salaries, welfare benefits, and such. In short, collective negotiation has become the medium whereby many teachers have gained bilateral decision-making authority in educational matters in the 1960s.

Eighth, the competition between the National Education Association and the American Federation of Teachers to win improved contracts for teachers has contributed towards teacher activism. In 1961, a teachers union received bargaining rights in New York City to negotiate with the board of education. In 1962, the NEA passed its first resolution on professional negotiations —a resolution which has become substantially more favorable to teachers by requesting that boards of education negotiate written master contracts.[5] This NEA position may be accounted for in two ways. It enabled NEA to compete with the rival AFT for active membership (NEA has approximately 900,000 members while AFT has about 150,000 members) and it advanced a basic NEA belief, i.e., that teachers should participate in setting policies and procedures in school systems. At any rate, the improved working conditions which were won for teachers in the early 1960s by AFT have resulted in competition between NEA and AFT for membership, have heightened interest in collective negotiations, and have increased teacher activism.

Ninth, activism has flourished as a result of the urbanization of the nation and the

5. "NEA Resolutions, 1969" *Today's Education* 58, no. 7 (October 1969): 46, 72.

bureaucratization of its administrative processes. It is projected that two-thirds of the nation's population growth in the next generation will be concentrated in approximately fifty metropolitan areas.[6] As this process occurs, larger schools and school systems may develop. If they do, further anonymity of teachers and an increasing bureaucratic manner of dealing with them may result unless procedures for collective negotiations are developed to discourage such possibilities.

This list of reasons for teacher activism is not complete. It suffices to make the point, however, that many teachers will no longer play the passive employee role that they have assumed in earlier years when dealt with by paternalistic administrators and boards, bureaucrats in large bureaucratic systems, or both. Perhaps William Carr captured the spirit of the teacher activist movement best in stating:[7]

> . . . Teachers are determined to have a voice about the conditions in which they work. They expect a more equitable share in this affluent society which their services have significantly helped to create.
> Most American teachers have not become cynical, grasping clockwatchers, even though some of them may sometimes act in ways that create this unfavorable image in the public mind. I think, however, that teachers are militant; that is ready to fight for public recognition and respect. They are not willing to wait until retirement and then be overwhelmingly grateful for a farewell luncheon and an engraved silver tray, or misty-eyed for a set of matched luggage. They want action now, if not yesterday, and they are organized to get action.

Extent of Collective Negotiations

According to a 1967-68 NEA Research Division survey of school systems having an enrollment of one thousand or more students, 909,976 instructional staff members covered by terms of negotiation agreements were employed in 2,212 systems. These figures are in marked contrast to those of the preceding school year, 1966-67, in which only 1,531 school systems had negotiation agreements and 648,322 instructional personnel were covered by the terms of the agreements. Therefore, in just one year, the incidence of school systems with negotiation agreements increased by 44.5 percent and the number of instructional staff benefitting from the agreements rose approximately 40 percent.[8]

It presently seems safe to predict that by 1975 about 75 to 80 percent of the instructional staff members in the nation's schools will be employed under negotiated agreements. The school systems which likely will not have collective negotiation agreements will be the low-paying isolated and small rural systems.

How Negotiations Are Conducted

There are two major ways in which teachers and administrators and boards of education can bilaterally participate in decision making. These methods include *informal* and *formal* procedures.

Some school systems have used the informal decision making procedure for years.

---

6. Carr, "Changing World," p. 37.
7. From: James C. King, "New Directions for Collective Negotiation," *Professional Negotiation and the Principalship* (Washington, D.C.: Department of Elementary School Principals, NEA, 1969), pp. 135-43. Copyright 1969, National Association of Elementary School Principals, NEA. All rights reserved.
8. "Are Principals Represented in Bargaining Units?" *NEA Research Bulletin* 46, no. 3 (Washington, D.C.: National Education Association, Research Division, 1968): 84-85; Robert R. Asnard, "Directions in Negotiation," *The National Elementary Principal* 48, no. 1 (September 1968): 20.

Informal Decision Making
Cooperative Administration

[Figure: Schematic diagram showing Teacher Organization (columns of T's) on the left, Around the Table Consultation circle in the middle with T's, A's, and S's around it, and Superintendent and Board of Education boxes on the right.]

Ⓣ Teacher   Ⓐ Administrator   Ⓢ Supervisor

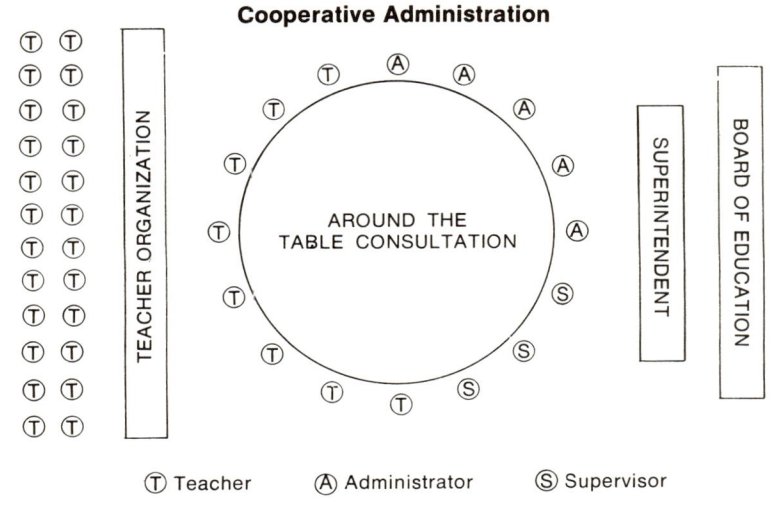

1. Identification of problems and issues
2. Presentation of evidence and arguments
3. Give-and-take discussion
4. Peer-level participation
5. Reaching consensus
6. Formulation of recommendations

Fig. 24.1. Schematic diagram of a model for informal decision making. From George B. Redfern and Forrest E. Conner, eds., **The School Administrator and Negotiation** (Washington, D.C.: American Association of School Administrators, 1968), p. 30.

It is a process whereby teacher representatives, on standing or ad hoc committees, sit together with administrators on an identity-of-interest basis in around the table consultation, as depicted in figure 24.1, and reach consensus on problems or issues confronting the school system. The discussions which transpire in these advisory consultation sessions are held on a peer-level basis. Decisions made through this informal method are subsequently channeled through the superintendent to the board of education for action.[9]

The major shortcoming of the informal decision making procedure, as vividly portrayed in figure 24.1, is that teachers have no guarantee that their recommendations will be accepted. This is not necessarily an indictment against administrators or boards of education. They frequently find that citizens in the community may resist or even defeat some of the teachers recommendations by various strategies, e.g., defeating bond issues, placing conservative members on the school board, and the like. Therefore, some teachers have come to recognize that the formal procedure by the medium of collective negotiations is a real way to insure the improvement of education and the profession since a new master contract must be agreed upon and ratified annually. Even in areas where the informal decision-

9. Redfern and Conner, *School Administrator,* pp. 11-13, 29-36.

collective negotiations and activism

making method has been utilized, it is not uncommon to find teachers changing to the formal negotiating process.

Instead of working on an indentity-of-interest basis as is the case when decisions are made in an informal manner, one customarily works on a conflict-of-interest basis when the formal procedure is invoked in decision-making. That is, the members of the various negotiating units within a school system, including the teacher unit, view themselves as subordinate to the superintendent of schools and the board of education whom they recognize as representatives of management. As such, members of the bargaining units enter into collective negotiations on an adversary basis where the shape of the table is square, as figure 24.2 shows, and attempt to negotiate for the best master contract obtainable.

During the decision making process or negotiation, for example, the teacher's organization will present its proposals through its bargaining team to a bargaining team representing the board of education. The administrative bargaining team of the board will study the proposals and set up a priority listing of those items in the list of proposals they choose to discuss. They may agree to some and make counterproposals on others. Generally, the administrative team will negotiate only one item at a time although the practice varies among school systems. There may be much heated discussion, presentation of evidence and concession-making before reaching consensus. Or, per-

Formal Decision Making
Negotiation

[Diagram: TEACHER ORGANIZATION | TEACHER TEAM | ACROSS THE TABLE NEGOTIATION | ADMINISTRATOR TEAM | BOARD OF EDUCATION]

1. Presentation of proposals (demands)
2. Submission of counter proposals
3. Pro-and-con arguments
4. Presentation of evidence and supportive data
5. Employment of tactics and strategies
6. Reaching consensus or impasse
7. Signing an agreement (contract) or resolving an impasse

Fig. 24.2. Schematic diagram of a model for formal decision making via collective negotiation. From George B. Redfern and Forrest E. Conner, eds., **The School Administrator and Negotiation** (Washington, D.C.: American Association of School Administrators, 1968), p. 30.

haps the negotiations will reach an impasse. If the latter occurs, both the teachers and administrative bargaining teams may have to agree to mediation, fact finding, arbitration or binding arbitration depending on the severity of the impasse. Once a contractual package is agreed upon by the teachers' and board of education's bargaining teams irrespective of whether the contract was by consensus or by some other means such as binding arbitration, the contract is then submitted to the teachers' organization and to the board of education for ratification.

In essence, formal collective negotiations is a process of power accommodation between the employees of the various bargaining units within the school system and the superintendent and board of education. In this power relationship the employee organizations are granted an increased measure of control in the decision-making process which formerly was considered the prerogative of management in the teaching profession.[10] The shape of the future with respect to making major educational decisions within a school system, appears to be that they will be made bilaterally through either informal or formal negotiation agreements. In fact, only four states in the union (Alabama, Georgia, Hawaii and Louisiana) have no negotiation agreements at this writing.[11]

What is Negotiable?

When collective negotiations first occurred in education, it was held that only certain matters were negotiable. More recently, however, it appears that every matter concerning education is negotiable.[12] The most frequently negotiated items include salaries, sick-leave policies, grievance procedures and other matters affecting the teachers' conditions of work, such as class size and teaching assignments. Less frequently negotiated items include such matters as in-service training, curriculum, instruction, and the health and safety of children.[13]

Roles of Professional Groups in Negotiations

The roles which the various professional groups assume in collective negotiations differ. A brief discussion of these divergent roles follows.

Teacher Role. The teachers assume the employee role commonly assumed by labor in industrial collective bargaining. Teachers must decide what organization will represent them at the bargaining table when negotiations are formal. In small school systems, this presents no problem since most systems of this size have teachers who are solely affiliated with NEA. Where this occurs, the organization representing teachers will be the local NEA affiliate and it will represent all teachers on an exclusive representation basis.

In larger school systems, particularly in metropolitan areas, some teachers may belong to AFT and others to NEA. Under this situation, the board of education may recognize both teacher organizations on a proportional basis for purposes of negotia-

10. Wesley A. Wildman and Charles R. Perry, "Group Conflict and School Organization," *Phi Delta Kappan* 47, no. 5 (January 1966): 245.
11. Asnard, "Directions in Negotiation," p. 21.
12. For a listing of items which appear on most negotiation lists, see: Redfern and Conner, *School Administrator,* p. 50.
13. Thomas P. Gilroy, et al., *Educator's Guide to Collective Negotiations* (Columbus, Ohio: Charles E. Merrill Publishing Company, 1969), p. 70.

tions. For example, if a school system had 10,000 teachers—8,000 of whom were NEA affiliated and 2,000 were members of AFT—a teacher bargaining team would be formulated based upon the proportion of professional employees represented by each organization. This bargaining team would negotiate for all teachers in the system irrespective of the allegiance of teachers individually. On the other hand, one organization, such as NEA in the above illustration, can exclusively represent all teachers if it can demonstrate majority support in the bargaining unit. Majority support is normally determined by teacher ballot.[14]

Whether teachers are represented by a bargaining team which is formulated on an exclusive or proportional basis, the team negotiates for all teachers in the school system (see figure 24.2). The team, in addition to its teacher representative members, would likely have in its membership consultants—a legal counsel, a team leader or chief spokesman, and representatives from state and national teacher organizations.[15] The teachers' bargaining team presents the teachers' initial master contract proposal to the bargaining team for the board of education and continues to function in a bargaining capacity until such time as a master contract has been agreed upon and ratified by the teacher organizations it represents and the board of education.

Administrator's Role. The role which administrators, e.g., building principals, assistant superintendents, instructional supervisors, personnel directors, and other central office staff assume in collective negotiations varies somewhat among school systems in the nation. In the 1967-68 NEA survey of 2,212 school systems who recognized only one teachers' organization for negotiation purposes, the professional bargaining unit in 62.1 percent of the cases represented only classroom teachers.[16] It was also determined in this study that 28.9 percent of the bargaining units were all-inclusive in nature representing teachers, building administrators and central-office personnel and 8.7 percent of the bargaining units represented teachers and building administrators. Only 0.3 percent of the bargaining units represented teachers and central-office personnel.[17] This study clearly showed that more often than not administrators are excluded from the ranks of the bargaining unit representing classroom teachers. In fact, AFT prohibits superintendents from affiliating with it.[18] Furthermore, in school systems which have AFT bargaining groups, principals are excluded from the teachers' bargaining units.[19]

The present role of building administrators and central-office personnel in negotiations seems to be one of two alternatives. First, they may have a representative from each group sit on the bargaining team representing the board of education (see figure 24.2) and align themselves with management. In this instance, they are at the mercy of the board of education with respect to salaries, welfare benefits, administrative assignments, and the like. Frequently, when they have assumed this role in negotiations,

14. For a discussion of exclusive and proportional representation in negotiations, see Gilroy, et al., *Educator's Guide,* pp. 16-17.
15. Redfern and Conner, *School Administrator,* pp. 33-38.
16. National Education Association, "Are Principals Represented in Bargaining Units?" pp. 84-85.
17. Ibid.
18. Gilroy, *Educator's Guide,* p. 60.
19. King, "New Directions," p. 139.

they have learned through bitter experience that the teachers' bargaining unit has won handsome salary increases and improved conditions of work which have resulted in diminished salaries and welfare benefits for all types of administrators and an eroding away of administrative prerogatives of principals. As a result, a new role is emerging in which building administrators and central-office personnel form their own bargaining unit and negotiate for the best written contract they can get. When this occurs, they may or may not have representatives sitting on the board of education's bargaining team.

Obviously, the superintendent as the chief school officer represents management in negotiations. During the early 1960s, he frequently assumed the role of chief negotiator with teachers representing the board of education. As a result, his rapport with the teachers was severely jeopardized. Presently, the superintendent tends to be assuming a liasion role between the administrative bargaining team and the board of education in which he serves as advisor to each. Under this model, the superintendent is less vulnerable to teacher ill will and is more effectual in helping to facilitate the negotiations process.

Future of Collective Negotiations

When negotiations first appeared in education, it seemed that a permanent cleavage between classroom teachers and administrators would develop. This was particularly true when collective negotiations were conducted on a formal, adversary basis. However, this fear is beginning to be dispelled. Although there is the ever-present danger of a disruptive and widespread cleavage, it has been found in many instances that collective negotiations has had a positive effect on the relationship existing between teachers and administrators in two major ways. First, teachers do have a right to participate in the setting of policies and procedures affecting their work. Their participation has had a democratizing effect on the school and has contributed to the harmonizing of the role expectations of the institution and the need dispositions of the teachers.[20] Hence, teachers are generally more effective and efficient in their professional endeavors. Second, many administrators have learned that involving teachers in the decision-making process does not lesson the importance of the administrative position; it simply changes the administrative function to bilaterally involve teachers in establishing policies and procedures and to the subsequent administering of the bilateral agreements.

Collective negotiations has been beneficial in other ways. It has: (1) increased the economic support for many school systems by achieving greater financial efforts from patrons in order to provide necessary funds for quality educational programs, (2) improved internal and external communications within school systems, (3) clarified the roles of professional employees within the establishment such as teachers, principals, supervisors and superintendents and (4) heightened the patrons' interest in and awareness of the program and problems of the school.

As negotiations in education come to be viewed as an accommodation process whereby policies and procedures are made bilaterally, and as a consequence many sub-

20. J. W. Getzels and E. G. Guba, "Social Behavior and the Administrative Process," *School Review* 65 (Winter 1957): 423-41.

sequent benefits accrue to the school system, it is safe to predict that the initial fear of seriously damaged rapport between teachers and administrators will abate. Emerging most likely will be a positive attitude towards collective negotiations in all quarters which recognizes the fact that negotiations can be used as a medium for improving every aspect of education in the public school.

An Appraisal of Collective Negotiations

On the face, the question of teacher negotiation with the board of education in a manner similar to blue collar labor bargaining seems to be in contradiction to the teachers' claims of professional status. Another anomaly occurs when teachers go out on strike against a governmental unit to enforce their demands. These contradictions largely result from the history of teacher employment practices in the United States which are no longer consistent with the size and importance of teaching.

It should always be remembered that the professional status of the public school teacher has primarily been more a matter of fiction than of fact. In terms of education, public school teachers have always qualified as members of a profession. The nineteenth century restrictions which were formerly placed on teachers are today often regarded as merely the puritanical whims of a stricter age. There is every reason to regard them as an indication that the teacher was regarded in the same light as domestic help, and therefore subject not only to poor pay but to the imposition of many demeaning personal restrictions. When teachers began to organize professionally, the pattern of management-employee relations had already come to characterize teacher employees. This was a natural outgrowth of the common law in the United States. The reward of the teacher was the ascription of "professional." Ego-satisfying, it neither increased take-home pay nor improved teaching conditions for teacher or pupil. Relief was sought in legislative activism. Most state educational associations, although the fact is never admitted, are a continuing lobby or pressure group to improve teacher salaries. This is particularly true in those states where over 50 percent of the support for education expended by local boards is received as part of a state minimum foundation program.

The teaching profession differs from all other professions in a very significant manner—it is almost an entirely socialized profession. Except for a small number of teachers in private schools, school teachers in the United States are public school teachers. Legally, they are civil servants, employees of governmental units.

One of the great problems in any governmental unit is to find a means by which governmental employees may negotiate to improve salaries and working conditions. In the United States civil service, the Postal Employee's Union, which includes the largest number of employees of the federal government in a single category, serves as the weather-bell for salary increases in the federal government. Failure of teachers in the past to accept their status as a professional and as a government employee has undoubtedly contributed to the failure to improve teacher working conditions and the total educational output of the country. The great challenge now confronting teachers is not so much the issue of collective negotiation, but how, as a profession, they can use collective negotiation not only to increase their salaries but to improve the total educational system. A similar challenge also confronts other public employees, such as firemen and policemen. There is a growing activism among many classes of civil servants.

As a teacher, you have an obligation to inform yourself of how collective negotiations can benefit the profession. It appears that it has at least two salutary effects. First, it is a medium for improving salary and other welfare benefits for all professional educators. Second, it is a medium for globally improving educational opportunities for children, e.g., it can assure adequate materials, facilities, personnel, and equipment to achieve the stated objectives of the school system.

Selected References

American Association of School Administrators. *School Administrators View Professional Negotiation.* Washington, D.C.: The American Association of School Administrators, 1966.

Bishop, Leslie J. *Collective Negotiation in Curriculum and Instruction: Questions and Concerns.* Washington, D.C.: Association for Supervision and Curriculum Development, NEA, 1967.

Department of Elementary School Principals. *Professional Negotiation and the Principalship.* Washington, D.C.: the Department, NEA, 1969.

Doherty, Robert E., and Oberer, Walter E. *Teachers, School Boards and Collective Bargaining: A Changing of the Guard.* Ithaca, N.Y.: New York State School of Industrial and Labor Relations, Cornell University, May 1967.

Elam, Stanley M., et al. *Readings on Collective Negotiations in Public Education.* Chicago: Rand McNally & Company, 1967.

Gilroy, Thomas P., et al. *Educator's Guide to Collective Negotiations.* Columbus, Ohio: Charles E. Merrill Publishing Company, 1969.

Law, Kenneth L., et al. *The Manual for Teacher Negotiations.* Windsor, Conn.: Educational Consultative Services, 1966.

Lieberman, Myron, and Moskow, Michael H. *Collective Negotiations for Teachers: An Approach to School Administration.* Chicago: Rand McNally & Company, 1966.

Lutz, Frank W. and Azzarelli, Joseph J. *Struggle for Power in Education.* New York: Center for Applied Research in Education, 1966.

Lutz, Frank W., et al. *Grievances and Their Resolution.* Danville, Illinois: Interstate Printers and Publishers, Inc., 1967.

Redfern, George B., and Conner, Forrest E., eds. *The School Administrator & Negotiation.* Washington, D.C.: The American Association of School Administrators, 1968.

Schmidt, Charles T., Jr., et al. *A Guide to Collective Negotiations in Education.* East Lansing: Social Science Research Bureau, Michigan State University, 1967.

Stinnett, T. M., et al. *Professional Negotiation in Public Education.* New York: Macmillan Company, 1966.

epilogue: change and the elemementary school

There are many ways in which the contemporary elementary school is changing. Space will not permit a discussion of all changes. The most profound ones, in the authors' view, will be discussed in this concluding epilogue. These changes involve social reform, curricula, organization, instructional media, and principal-teacher relationships. A discussion of each of these changes follows.

The School and Social Change

Prior to the 1960s, the elementary school had primarily mirrored the neighborhood in which it was set. That is, its curriculum and functions largely were geared to the expectations of the local clientele it served. And little thought was given to the school's role in resolving vexing social issues on the national scene; at least, it was seldom envisioned that the elementary school should or even could assume a change agent's role in social reform.[1]

However, two important federal movements intervened in the decade of the sixties to thrust a major role upon the elementary school in achieving social reform in the nation. These movements included: (1) meaningful integration of the schools as initiated by the Civil Rights Act of 1964, and (2) earlier intervention with schooling for disadvantaged children through the Office of Economic Opportunity's Head Start Program initiated in 1965. Brief discussions of the resulting effects of these movements on the changing role of the elementary school follow.

Integration. The elementary school was cast into the arena of social reform under the aegis of the Federal Civil Rights Act of 1964. This legislation spelled out "guidelines" under which segregated schools in the nation were to be desegregated. Later,

1. The advent of the depression of the 1930s had a profound impact on progressive thinking. From the highly individualistic emphasis of the 1920s, the emphasis shifted to a concern for the social purposes of education. Indications of these shifts were the challenge of George S. Counts, *Dare the Schools Build a New Social Order?;* the publication of *Social Frontier;* and the Rugg Social Studies Series which attempted to orient students more realistically to an urban, industrial, and technological culture. This has been one of the major curriculum thrusts in social studies for the past forty years. These philosophical shifts were, however, never accompanied by any change in the practices of the schools, which continued to reflect the mores of the general culture rather than the rhetoric of the school men.

in 1967, the *Jefferson* decision established a precedence for achieving racial balance in the public schools.[2] And the 1968 HEW "guidelines" for desegregation set 1969-70 as the latest year for establishing integrated or unitary school systems in which there would be no minority schools and no white schools.[3] Hence, the elementary school has become an agent of change to effect social reform with respect to integration of minority groups into the mainstream of American culture. There is little doubt that this role will continue to be fulfilled in the future as additional students, faculties, facilities, and activities are integrated. It might be added, notwithstanding the negative rhetoric voiced by opponents, that the elementary school has been successful in its social reform role of effecting racial integration.

Early Childhood Education. On the whole, the Head Start Program has been successful in the nation. Two major complaints, however, have been raised against it: (1) one summer's intervention before first grade is inadequate time to prepare children for formal schooling, and (2) the benefits which accrue from prefirst-grade intervention normally are lost during the first year or two of formal schooling. These objections have served as a basis for subsequent salutary changes within the elementary school: (1) the establishment of kindergartens, (2) revised curricula, and (3) a changed vertical organizational plan.

ESTABLISHMENT OF KINDERGARTEN. Since almost everyone connected with the Head Start movement agreed that it was of too short a period of time to be optimally effective as a preschool intervention measure, the success gained with Head Start has served as a springboard for a burgeoning movement towards kindergarten training within the public school. Many pilot kindergarten programs were established with Federal Elementary and Secondary Education Act (1965) funds. It now appears that many states are moving towards the establishment of kindergartens. Texas, for example, began phasing in kindergartens with State minimum Foundation Funds in 1970-71 for the most economically disadvantaged children and will complete the phasing in process by 1977 so that all five-year-old children can receive kindergarten instruction.

The reason for increased emphasis upon prefirst-grade training within the public school is evident. Children from disadvantaged homes, as a general rule, have a *restricted language code* and limited conceptualization skills. Early intervention helps provide them with the language tools and conceptualization skills necessary to be academically successful as they study in the elementary school where an *elaborated language code* is used by teachers in transmitting knowledge and where more advantaged children have already acquired and use an elaborated language code.[4] There is a second reason for prefirst-grade training; there seems to be no good reason for postponing the formal schooling of advantaged children until they are six years old.[5] For the most part, they represent the reservoir of human resources which is capable of making the

2. United States v. Jefferson County Board of Education, 380 F. 2d 385 (1967).

3. 33 F. Reg. 4956 (March 1968).

4. J. W. Getzels, "Pre-School Education," *Teacher's College Record* 68, no. 3 (December 1966): 219-28.

5. "Universal Opportunity for Early Childhood Education," Educational Policies Commission of the National Education Association and the American Association of School Administrators, (1966), pp. 3-12.

greatest contributions to their own and subsequent generations. Hence, early intervention enables them to begin formal training when they are extremely susceptible to learning.[6] In fact, the Educational Policies Commission has gone on record as favoring early intervention at age four (nursery school) for all children.[7] An NEA survey has shown that in the 1966-67 school year, 148 school systems in the nation of the 11,970 which enroll 300 or more pupils have established nursery school programs.[8]

REVISED CURRICULA. To avoid the washout or losses of achievement during the first year or two of school which have accrued during summer Head Start and year-long kindergarten training, many elementary schools have revised their curricula. That is, they now envision formal schooling as beginning whenever children start to school, e.g., nursery school, Head Start, or kindergarten. Viewed from this perspective, the learnings previously reserved for later grades have been brought down to the point at which formal instruction begins, as, for example, the kindergarten. By revising the traditional curricula so that appropriate learnings are incorporated into the child's learning experiences when he initially enters formal training at school, repetition of learning (the assumed major cause for the washout or attrition of achievement) is averted. As a result, each child more nearly experiences continuous progress.

A CHANGED VERTICAL ORGANIZATIONAL PLAN. As the learning experiences within the traditional elementary school have been revised and brought down into what was formerly thought of as the preschool, the vertical organization in many schools has undergone structural changes. This attempt has been made to effect continuous pupil progress, i.e., a plan whereby quality of work does not vary but time varies for all children.

One of the most noticeable changes that has been made vertically is the shift to the nongraded plan—a continuous progress plan (see chapter 19). In 1966, an NEA Research Bulletin showed that 36 percent of the nation's schools enrolling 25,000 or more pupils were using the nongraded plan in some manner.[9] One can predict that, as more school systems incorporate kindergarten and nursery school training into their instructional programs, the trend towards the nongraded plan will continue. A few schools have adopted a multigraded plan and some have made additional adjustments to the conventional graded plan in efforts to effect a vertical plan of continuous progress for children.

To summarize the role of the elementary school as a change agent in social reform, two things can be said. First, racial integration has brought and is continuing to bring minority groups into the *mainstream* of American life. And, second, a system of preschooling has been instituted in many schools, although still in the developmental stages, so that disadvantaged children can gain the requisite elaborated language code and conceptualization skills necessary to

6. Benjamin S. Bloom, *Stability and Change in Human Characteristics* (New York: John Wiley & Sons, Inc., 1964).

7. Educational Policies Commission, "Universal Opportunity"; Lendon K. Smith, "The (Medical) Doctor Looks at the Nursery School," *Education* 87, no. 8 (April 1967): 474-77.

8. "Nursery School Education," *NEA Research Bulletin* 46, no. 2 (May 1968): 54-56.

9. "Grade Organization and Nongrading Programs," *NEA Research Bulletin* 45, no. 4 (December 1967): 118-19.

gain access or achieve success in school which is a major precursor to a life of self-fulfillment.

Changing Curricula

There appear to be at least three major movements within the nation concerning changing curricula for the elementary school. They include: (1) performance-based instruction, (2) modular instruction, and (3) emphasis upon the processes of learning. A discussion of each of these follows.

Performance-Based Instruction. During the 1960s, a growing emphasis was placed upon performance-based instruction. That is, many teachers began stating their instructional objectives behaviorally in terms of *what they wanted their charges to be able to do once their influence over them had ended.*[10]

If behavioral objectives (see chapter 3) are to indicate what children are able to do once they have received instruction, they must, of necessity, be stated actively using action words or verbs, e.g., states, names, interprets, predicts, analyzes, lists. . . . A performance-based instructional objective in a second or third grade science unit, for example, is: "The child can orally *state* the correct time to the nearest five minutes when he is given the hour and minute hand positions on a clock."[11] In this example, the child must be able to *state* (an action word) as evidence that he has internalized the learning. The *conditions* under which he must demonstrate orally and correctly state (given the hour and minute hand positions on a clock) are clearly spelled out. All that remains in the finalizing of this performance-based instructional objective is to spell out the minimal *degree of performance*

excellence which is acceptable to indicate that the child has satisfactorily internalized the learning. Hence, the terminal behavior for the instructional objective might be stated as follows: "The child can orally *state* the correct time to the nearest five minutes when he is given the hour and minute hand positions on a clock for nine out of ten settings." The degree of excellence in this case is arbitrarily set at 90 percent accuracy (nine out of ten settings); it might be set at 70 or 80 percent accuracy depending upon the teacher's judgment.

It is clear that children learn more effectively when they know in advance what they are to learn, the conditions of their learning, and what the minimal acceptable performance will be. The use of performance-based behavioral objectives in the elementary school likely will be a major factor in the revamping of instruction for boys and girls in the seventies.

Modular Instruction. Another change in elementary school curricula that is occurring is the movement towards modular instruction, particularly in the science and social studies areas. That is, the traditional and large experience or subject matter units of work are increasingly being broken-up into small modules of instruction. A simplified and illustrative schematic diagram of a module is shown in figure E.1.

---

10. For helpful information in setting, teaching, and evaluating performance-based instructional objectives, see: Robert F. Mager, *Preparing Instructional Objectives* (Palo Alto, California: Fearon Publishers, 1962); Robert F. Mager, *Developing Attitude Toward Learning* (Palo Alto, California: Fearon Publishers, 1968); Robert F. Mager and Peter Pipe, *Analyzing Performance Problems* (Belmont, California: Fearon Publishers, 1970).

11. See *Science—A Process Approach* (Washington, D.C.: American Association for the Advancement of Science, 1965), p. 35.

epilogue: change and the elementary school

```
[Behavioral Objectives
(stated in performance
and terminal form)]
        │
        ▼
[Pre-Criterion Test] ──► [Instructional Activities] ──► [Post-Criterion Test] ──► Exit
                                ▲                              ▲
                                │                              │
                                └──── [Recycling (when necessary)] ────┘
```

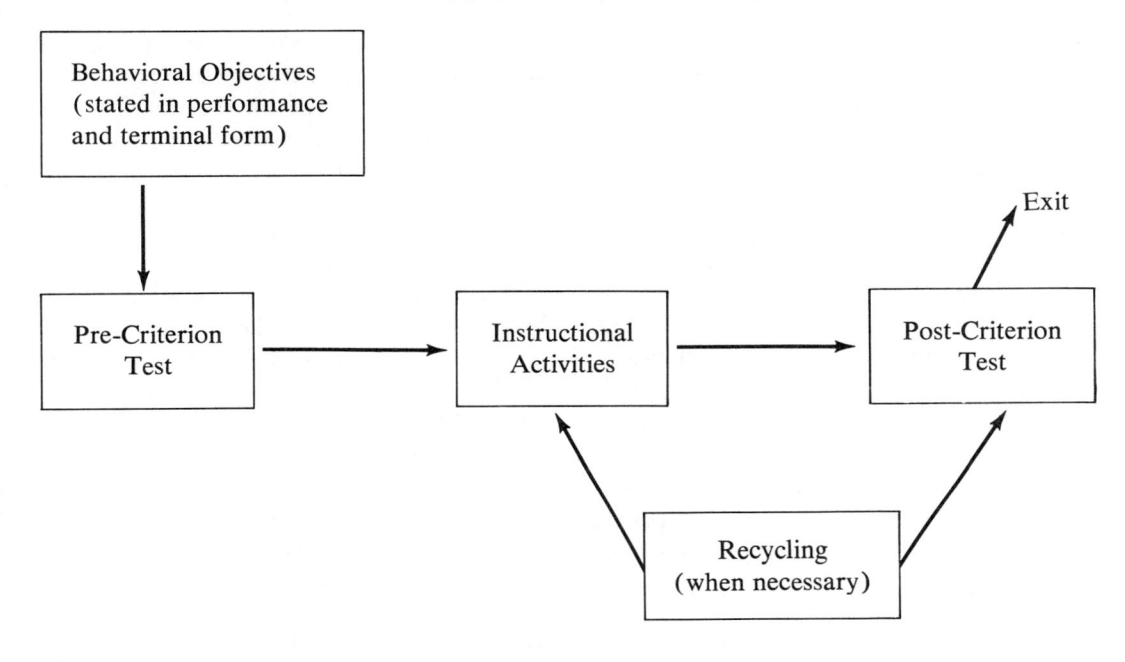

Fig. E.1. Schematic Diagram of an Instructional Module.

As figure E.1 shows, the performance-based behavioral objectives are specified for the individual module of instruction. A pre-criterion test is included within the module so that the teacher can ascertain for each child the behavioral objectives that have already been learned and those which remain to be acquired. Suggested instructional activities are included in each module of work specifically designed to achieve the desired behavioral or performance objectives. Each child need not complete those instructional activities designed for behaviors he has already acquired unless he, in consultation with his teacher, believes it necessary for either reinforcement or enrichment purposes.

Once each child has completed chosen instructional activities from the module of work, he takes the post-criterion test, the purpose of which is to determine whether the child has acceptably internalized all of the behavioral or performance objectives of the module. That is, can he demonstrate or perform under certain conditions a degree of mastery sufficient to indicate the successful acquisition of the initially specified behaviors for the module of work? If he cannot, he is recycled into additional instructional activities designed to fix the unmastered behaviors. Once the additional instructional activities are completed, the child may then take an alternate post-criterion test to check for behavior mastery. The routine is continued until the child successfully completes the module; hence, time varies but the quality of work remains constant. This is in sharp contrast to traditional unit work in which time remains constant but quality of work among children varies. The instructional module is but another step in individualizing instruction and effecting a plan of continuous progress for each pupil.

Modular instruction in the nation's elementary schools may prove to be the avant-garde practice in the seventies for individualizing instruction. Certainly, the performance-based dimension of modular instruction should have a profound effect upon the elementary school curriculum.

Emphasis Upon the Processes of Learning. During the 1960s a major curricula change, particularly in science and social studies, occurred in which a shift from emphasis upon teaching and materials geared for pupil mastery of knowledges and facts to that designed to promote pupil acquisition of the cognitive processes of learning was made. That is, it was deemed less essential to have students read about the work of the scientist or the social scientist and to learn certain factual information. What was deemed to be of more importance was to have the children learn the scientific processes or the modes of inquiry used by the scientists and social scientists. And rather than *studying about* science or social studies, the children were expected *to do* science and social studies—to use the scientific method in dealing with scientific or social phenomena: identifying problems, hypothesizing solutions, choosing and testing solutions, verifying data, making inferences, drawing conclusions and generalizations, experimenting. . . . That the change has been beneficial is seldom questioned by children, teachers, administrators, or parents.

The change to emphasizing the processes of learning is congruent with, has developed with, and is continuing to develop with performance-based instruction. This can be illustrated easily by recalling a previous segment of this chapter where behavioral or performance objectives were discussed. Emphasis was placed on the "verbs" in stating the behavioral objectives, e.g., the child predicts, infers, hypothesizes, classifies, observes, et cetera. In essence, these are some of the same processes that the scientist and social scientist use in their work.

One has only to look at certain new curricula in the sciences or social sciences that have been prepared for the elementary school to see that the processes of learning have been given preeminence and that the products of the content fields have been relegated to a position of secondary importance. The *Science—A Process Approach* materials are an excellent illustration of this curriculum change. In these science materials the following processes (performance based) are stressed.[12]

Kindergarten and Primary Materials:

1. Observing
2. Using numbers
3. Measuring
4. Using space/time relationships
5. Classifying
6. Communicating
7. Inferring
8. Predicting

Intermediate Materials:

1. Formulating hypotheses
2. Controlling variables
3. Interpreting data
4. Defining operationally
5. Experimenting

One can predict that increased emphasis will be placed upon students' mastering the processes of learning in the future. Likewise,

12. Ibid.

it appears that less emphasis will be placed upon pupil mastery of the products of the content fields although products continue to be of real importance.

Changing Patterns of Organization

Several changes in organization are presently going on within the elementary school. Some of the more important ones from the authors' viewpoint include: changing vertical and horizontal organizational patterns, diversified staffing practices, and the reorganization of instructional levels. Let us briefly examine each of these.

Change in Vertical Organization. As previously mentioned in this chapter, many schools are changing from the conventional graded plan of vertical organization to the nongraded plan. There are many reasons for this change but they all involve a desire to effect a plan whereby each child can experience continuous progress. Of course, the increased inclusion of preschool training and the increased capability of individualizing learning through modular instructional units have also affected the trend toward nongrading.

How then does the nongraded school provide for the continuous progress of, and hence, facilitate the individualization of instruction? This question can be answered, for example, by examining selected behavioral objectives for the P-1 and P-2 levels in reading and arithmetic devised by Hawkins for the Hancock County (Georgia) Public Schools as shown in figure E.2. Each child must, for example, master the seven major performance-based behaviors in reading at the P-1 Level before he can begin work on the six behaviors specified for the P-2 Level. Mastery of the P-2 Level behaviors is prerequisite to the P-3 Level behaviors and so on.

The illustrations for reading and arithmetic at the P-1 and P-2 Levels, as shown in figure E.2, are symbolic of how the curriculum can be made performance based and parceled out into the various instructional levels P-1 through P-21 (or however many levels are included in the elementary school) for all subject areas. Also, it is easy to see how modules could be developed by teachers for the performance behavior in each subject area and each instructional level. Or, it is easy to envision how teachers could adapt learning packages of modular materials to the subjects of the nongraded levels.[13]

The nongraded vertical organizational plan has the potentiality for expeditiously facilitating many of the new changes that presently are transpiring within the elementary school, such as formalized learning in what previously was thought of as the preschool program and performance-based curricula through modular instruction. In concert with these salutary changes, the nongraded school may prove to be the most viable vertical organizational plan yet devised for effecting a system of continuous pupil progress for the elementary school.

Change in Horizontal Organization. It appears that team teaching as an horizontal organizational pattern is becoming a more common practice in the nation's elementary schools. A 1967 NEA survey report showed that 50 percent of the large school systems (enrollments of 25,000 plus), 30 percent of the medium-sized systems (enrollments of 3,000 to 24,999), and 11 percent of the

---

13. For a discussion of learning packages, see the entire May 1970 issue of *Educational Leadership*.

528 epilogue: change and the elementary school

Reading Achievement Levels

Date Accomplished

Level 1 (P-1)

_____ Discriminates similarities and differences in pictures, forms, letters, and words

_____ Identifies the names of pictures that rhyme

_____ Uses picture clues to meaning

_____ Copies and reproduces geometric forms

_____ Handles book with ease

_____ Has acquired initial reading habits
-Left-to-right eye movement
-Reads from top of page to bottom
-Left page to right page

_____ Hears similarities and differences in words

Level 2 (P-2)

_____ Recognizes the first nineteen sight words

_____ Associates meaning with words

_____ Hears rhyming words

_____ Uses configuration of words to help in word memory

_____ Hears initial sounds of b, t, m, f, s

_____ Adds *s* to known words

Arithmetic Achievement Levels

Date Accomplished

Level 1 (P-1)

_____ Knows the sequence of number names

_____ Knows the one to one correspondence between objects and the counting names

_____ Recognizes two and three objects without counting

_____ Reads and writes numbers

_____ Knows age, address and telephone numbers

_____ Uses numbers to locate objects in a series through five

_____ Knows addition equations through five

Fig. E.2. Schema of Selected Behavior Objectives for the P-1 and P-2 Nongraded Levels in Reading and Arithmetic. From: Michael L. Hawkins, "Procedural Guide for Nongrading the Primary School," in **Vertical Organizational Patterns in the Elementary School**, ed. Oscar T. Jarvis (Athens, Georgia: Georgia Department of Elementary School Principals and College of Education, University of Georgia, 1969), pp. 51-57.

Level 2 (P-2)

_____ Knows subtraction equations through five
_____ Understands number sentences
_____ Uses measurements—time, foot, lines, calendar, money
_____ Identifies shapes—circles, triangles, squares, rectangles
_____ Is able to solve problems—composes number stories and solves simple oral work problems

Fig. E.2. (Cont'd)

small systems (enrollments of 300 to 2,999) were using team teaching horizontally.[14]

There appear to be two major reasons for the change to team teaching in the elementary school: (1) a desire to provide specialized instruction, and (2) a growing belief that many of the former reputed advantages of the self-contained horizontal plan (see chapter 19) are no longer valid. In assessing the change towards team teaching, Robert Anderson, one of the more instrumental educators identified with the movement, has observed:[15]

> ... The alleged advantages of the self-contained classroom are difficult to prove, however, and its disadvantages are becoming increasingly evident.
>
> As a matter of fact, a great deal of what we once thought we knew about the bases of pupil security, about the optimum teacher-pupil relationship, about children's emotional and personal needs, about the size and the composition of classes (and schools), about pupil grouping for this purpose and that, and about curriculum planning has been subjected to careful re-examination as a result of the iconoclastic development of team teaching. Some rather surprising discoveries have been made; and although the data are by no means complete, we can at least say that team teaching ... now stands confirmed as a legitimate and probably superior alternative to the self-contained arrangement that was once held sacred as the *sine qua non* of elementary education.

Diversified Staffing Practices. Developing concomitantly with team teaching in some schools has been the notion and practice of diversified staffing.[16] Whereas most teachers formerly have been paid on a single salary schedule which considers highest degree earned and number of years taught irrespective of the similarity or dissimilarity of service rendered, a trend is developing presently to pay teachers differently for different responsibilities. For example, in the hierarchical team teaching model outlined in chapter 19, some teachers would be paid for their responsibilities as supervising teachers, some as master teachers, and so on.

Differentiated staffing has a number of advantages. The primary ones, however, appear to be: (1) a system of promotion within the teaching ranks is provided as teachers can promote up the position and responsibility hierarchical continuum, (2) each promotion in rank affords higher salary increments, and (3) teachers are paid differently for different responsibilities.

The Open Classroom. This term is used in the beginning of the 70s to reflect an

---

14. "Team Teaching," *NEA Research Bulletin* 45, no. 4 (December 1967): 114-15.
15. Robert H. Anderson, *Teaching in a World of Change* (New York: Harcourt Brace Jovanovich, Inc., 1966), p. 82.
16. "Differentiated Staffing," *Nation's Schools* 85 (June 1970): 43-46.

eclectic procedure which results from combining both teaching procedures, such as the process approach, with administrative procedures, such as heterogeneous sectioning. Most of the procedures of the open classroom were pioneered by the Progressive Movement in American education, and are now being revived as a result of the impact of their application in the British "new" schools. Such "progressive" methods as guiding pupil learning and pupil activity have always characterized good elementary education, as noted in chapter 6, and were not abandoned with the eclipse of the Progressive Movement.

In Britain, the adoption of progressive methods has been carefully planned and studied, and is supported by a relevant pedagogy of teacher training. In the United States, however, the movement appears to be largely a fashion. The revival of progressive methods appeals to the humanistic notions of early childhood education. At the same time, however, it provides an escape alternative to the accountability implicit in modular, performance-based instruction. While the open classroom provides unusual opportunities for a master teacher to guide the growth of children, it likewise provides excellent opportunities for an inefficient teacher to conceal the lack of substantive pupil learning through pupil activity. This defect was the Achilles heel of progressivism.

Some teachers will find the concept of the open classroom very appealing; others will find its management demands beyond their capabilities. The open classroom is no panacea. If it is accepted as one, without the needed management skills to assure growth in pupil learning, the open classroom movement will merely repeat the earlier errors of the Progressive Movement of a half century ago.

Reorganization of Instructional Levels. Presently there is a realignment of instructional (grade) levels within the public schools. Expressed in the conventional grades, the organizational plans have included the 6-3-3, 8-4, 6-2-4, 7-5 and other grade groupings. With the increased emphasis upon nursery and kindergarten training in the nation's schools and with the emergence of the new middle school, it is likely that a N-4, 5-8, and 9-12, i.e., 6-4-4, organizational arrangement will evolve in the 1970s. And in many communities the junior college grades of 13 and 14 will be added at the top.

Should this evolving reorganization of instructional levels occur concurrently with the nongraded movement, which appears likely, the age groupings within the 6-4-4-2 plan would approximate ages 4-9 (pre- and primary school unit), ages 10-13 (middle school unit), ages 14-17 (high school unit), and ages 18-19 (junior college unit). Coupled with the idea of continuous pupil progress and performance-based curricula (in terms of modular instruction), children should be able to move up through the instructional levels during the 1970s as rapidly as they can master the prescribed terminal behaviors at each level. The age groupings by school unit stated above are therefore approximations.

A Changing Library Media Center

Clearly, the former elementary school library is becoming a multimedia center. As such, it serves two major purposes: (1) it serves as a learning resource center, and (2) it provides services to the classrooms. Let us briefly examine these functions of the changing library media center within the elementary school.

Learning Resource Center. The nature of the print, nonprint, and equipment collections of the centralized library media center were spelled out in chapter 9. These collections may include everything from books and programmed instructional materials, through 8-mm single concept film-loops, to dial-controlled random access systems. The facility in which the collections are housed has space allotted for all of the old library areas such as reading room, circulation and distribution area, stacks and so on. In addition, the new library media center includes new areas such as dark room, a media production laboratory, audiovisual equipment distribution and storage room, and it may even include a television studio, a computerized learning laboratory, and a storage and control center for remote access.[17]

All of these—print, nonprint, and equipment collections, in concert with the facility of the library media center and its personnel —constitute a viable and meaningful learning resource center. It is in this center that the individual child within the elementary school can acquire guidance and teaching as he develops skills for study and research in the media center. It is within this center that he can find the information he needs in his studies, prepare the visual aids he will need to make a report in class, listen to tapes or discs, do recreational reading, borrow collections of materials for use within his classroom or at home, or use countless other media center resources for a myriad of purposes.

Unfortunately, all elementary schools do not have a library media center like the one described above. It is, however, hard to find an elementary school faculty that does not accept the idea of the media center becoming a viable learning resource center, or a faculty that is not working to establish such a center. The change to the library media center as a learning resource center now is clearly established.

Service to Classrooms. In former times the library existed (in most instances) as an almost separate entity from the classrooms within the elementary school. The change to looking upon the library media center as a service agency to the classroom is now a foregone conclusion. Numerous examples can be cited to prove this point: the media technician in the media center makes or assists classroom teachers in making instructional materials such as transparencies or models for specialized classroom uses; the library media specialists offer instruction to children about how to use the library effectively, teachers and children can receive assistance in withdrawing collections of materials from the media center for classroom use, open scheduling, and the like.

The fact that elementary schools are almost all media-centered now is unquestioned. Where media centers do not exist, faculties normally are eagerly trying to establish them. The media center is truly the heart of the elementary school and its curriculum. Doubtlessly, it will become even more effective in the future as a learning resource center and as a service agency to classrooms.

Changing Principal-Teacher Relationships

The elementary school principalship historically evolved out of a situation in which the office itself was initially considered to

---

17. See: *Standards for School Media Programs* (Chicago: American Library Association; Washington, D.C.: National Education Association, 1969), pp. 39-50; see also, the entire April 1969 issue of *Library Trends*.

be a head teacher's office. That is, as the small elementary schools grew large enough, in terms of pupil enrollment and teachers, it became necessary to have someone in charge. Normally, the most outstanding teacher in each building was named the head teacher and had the responsibility of performing certain administrative and supervisory tasks in addition to his teaching responsibilities. As schools became larger, (normally twelve or more teachers) and justified a full time principal, the title was changed from "head teacher" to "principal teacher." Later, the term was shortened to "principal" and finally it became "supervising principal."[18]

Having evolved from the idea of "head teacher" or "principal teacher," holders of the principalship office were looked up to as master or expert teachers who in addition to their teaching and administrative responsibilities, could offer to their teaching counterparts and assumed less able teaching colleagues, advice and supervision in teaching. Frequently, in fact, more often than not, these principal teachers, plyed their administrative and supervisory skills unilaterally either as paternalists (the idea that "Daddy knows best") or as authoritarians (the practice whereby they established dictums and prescriptions for their staff members to follow). Even when the principalship became known as the office of the "supervising principal" in the last two decades, it has not been uncommon to find holders of the office behaving paternalistically and authoritatively.

This situation began to change drastically in the middle and late 1960s for a number of reasons. First, the new curricula, e.g., SMSG mathematics materials and AAAS *Science—A Process Approach* materials, were incorporated into the elementary school curriculum. These materials required a great deal of expertise in teaching that teachers acquired, and that few principals acquired. As a result, teachers grew increasingly hesitant to accept supervisory prescriptions from principals who knew less about teaching the new curricula than they did. Second, the liberal movement that ensued in the nation which gave impetus to increased respect for the rights of the individual had some influence on teachers wanting to have a voice in the establishment of policies and procedures affecting their work.

And, third, the collective negotiations movement in the nation provided teachers the instrumentation necessary to insure the fact that they had a voice in setting policies and procedures under which they would work.

The result of these events served to diminish the principals' prerogatives in terms of unilateral paternalistic or authoritarian actions. As a result, democratic administration, a principle advocated for years in the training of educational administrators, was ushered into practice for the fulfillment of the new role of the supervising principal. Teachers and the supervising principal began bilaterally formulating the policies and procedures to be used in the school. The principal assumed the role as administrator of the bilaterally formulated policies. Moreover, he assumed a collegial role in supervision in which he planned with the faculty the nature of in-service training and shared the leadership role with the staff in conducting such train-

18. *The Elementary School Principalship in 1968* (Washington, D.C.: Department of Elementary School Principals, NEA, 1968), p. 5.

ing. Furthermore, he assumed a coordinating supervisory role in which, for example, the special supervisors within the school system were used as consultants within the school to assist teachers with curriculum or teaching matters. In short, the contemporary elementary school principal has become a democratic leader, an administrator of bilaterally established policies and procedures, and a collegial supervisor in his professional relationships with teachers.

Of course, the above changes are not universally true. It is still possible to find principals making primarily unilateral decisions and behaving as paternalists or authoritarians. But one cannot deny the emergence of a large cadre of elementary school principals within the nation who are democratic in their leadership responsibilities. Certainly, this will be progressively the model that will be followed in the immediate future to accommodate the new principal-teacher relationships.

index

Abdomen, health problems related to, 294
Ability sectioning, 393-94
Acceleration, gifted children and, 133
Accidents
    health problems related to, 297
    prevention of, 313
Achievement sectioning, 394
Achievement tests, 410
Activism, political, 511-13
Activities, race relations and, 476
Adams, L. J., 245
Additional staff services, disadvantaged and, 499
Administrators, collective negotiations role of, 517-18
Adolescence (Hall), 118
Aesthetic appreciation, music and, 319-22
African culture, 473-74
Aid, federal, xiii-xiv
Alexander v. Holmes County Board of Education, 463
Allen, William, 97
Allergies, health problems related to, 293
American Dilemma (Myrdal), 468
American Federation of Teachers (AFT), 510, 512, 516, 517
American Historical Association, 265
American Social Science Association, 265
Ames, Louise B., 212
Anderson, C. L., 300
Anderson, Irving H., 181
Anderson, Robert, 529
Anecdotal records, evaluation and, 401-02
Anthropology, 266-67
Arbuthnot, May Hill, 81
Art
    as appreciation, 346-47
    as communication, 347
    pedagogy of, 356-57
    as planned form, 344-45
    as self-expression, 346
    as a skill, 345
    as a value, 345-46
Art education
    appraisal of, 357-60
    appraisal of, 357-60
    history of, 343
    materials in, 351-53
    motivation for self-expression and, 349-51
    objectives in, 343-47
    in the preprimary curriculum, 83-84
    in the primary curriculum, 105-06
    production in, 353-54
    sequence in, 354-55
    stages in self-expression, 347-49
Articulation, 197-200
Assignments, race relations and, 475
Assign-study-recite-test method, 61-62
Auding. *See* Listening
Aurally handicapped children, 137
Ausubel, D. P., 448
    receptive learning and preorganizers, 503-04
Awkwardness, 35-36
Ayers Handwriting Scale, 214

Bagley, William T., xviii, 7
Barker, Roger G., 34
Barnard, Henry, 384
Barr, A. S., 442, 443, 450
Barrett, Kate R., 373
Barzun, Jacques, 7
Beberman, Max, 235
Begle, E. G., 235
Behavior
    adjustment, types of, 433-35

discipline and (*see also* Discipline)
  classroom management, 432-36
  norms, setting, 433
  punishment, 435-36
  special problems, 436-38
  race relations and, 474-78
Beriter, Carl, 203, 490, 494
  Engelmann academic preprimary program, 494, 504
Bernstein, Basil, 81, 489
Betts, Emmett Albert, 181, 211
Beyrer, Mary K., 307
Bickel, Alexander M., 466
Binet, Alfred, 25, 26
Binet tests, 26
Biology, culture and, 15-20
"Black English," 201
Black studies, 469-74
Blair Bill (1881), xiii
Bloomfield, Leonard, 171
Body build, ideal type, temperament and, 30-31
Books, preprimary curriculum, 81-82. See also Literature; Reading
Brittain, W. Lambert, 347
Brown, Rollo Walter, 220
Brown v. Board of Education, xi, 462, 478, 482
Buchanan, James, 97, 98
Burk, Frederick L., 353, 354
Bussing, 482

California Psychological Inventory (CPI), 38
California Test of Mental Maturity, 26
Carey, Russell L., 88
Carr, William, 513
Chall, Jeanne, 180
  review of research (reading), 180-81
Character development, education and, xv-xvii
Checklists, 415
Chicago Primary Abilities Test, 25
Child-care centers, 497
Child-centered curriculum orientation, 57-59
Child development, understanding
  biology and culture, 15-20
  general, 14-15
  interests, 36-38
  motor development, 33-36
  physical appearance, 29-33
  prejudice, 23-24
  readiness and learning, 27-29
  socialization, values, and emotional growth, 20-23
Child development movement, 77-78
Child Speaks, The (Byrne), 198
Chomsky, Noam, 215
Citizenship, educational objectives and, 48
Civic responsibility, objectives (list), 46-47

Civics, 269-70
Civil Rights Act (1964), 462, 463, 479, 521
Clarity, disadvantaged and teacher's, 506-07
Classroom
  behavior and listening, 207
  language and race relations, 475-76
Classroom management, 9-10
  appraisal of, 456-57
  behavior and discipline in, 432-36
  group integration and social control in, 422-25
  importance of, 422
  physical environment and, 425-27
  planning daily routine in, 427-32
  special problems and discipline in, 436-38
Cognitive processes, education and, 8-9
Cognitive style, language and, 490
Coleman, James S., 467, 487
Collective negotiations
  appraisal of, 519-20
  conducting, 513-16
  definition of, 510-11
  extent of, 513
  future of, 518-19
  nature of, 516
  professional groups' role in, 516-18
Communicable diseases, health problems related to, 293
Compensatory reading approach, 175-76
Composition, 218
  oral, 218-19
  written, 219
Comprehension, listening and, 206-07
Compulsatory school age, xxix
Conditions of Learning, The (Gagné), 451
Conferences, reporting through, 415, 416
Continuing education, 49-50
Coordinating Center for First-Grade Reading Instruction, 178-80
Corrective reading, 176-77
Cowles, Milly, 498
Crabtree, Charlotte, 450, 451
Creative children, characteristics of, 135-36
Creative dramatics, 226-27
Creative teaching approach, 110
Criticism, education, 7-8
Cronbach, Lee J., 452
Culture
  biology and, 15-20
  disadvantaged and, 501-02
  education and, x-xii
  intelligence and, 24-27, 491-92
  reassessment of African, 473-74
  schooling and, 482
Culture-fair testing, 490-91
Curriculum (*see also specific type*)
  definition of, 55

index

development of
  health education, 307-13
  planning, 60
  social studies, 276-80
movements to change, 524-27
music in, 319-25
orientation of, 55-60
  child-centered, 57-59
  discipline-centered, 59-60
  society-oriented, 56-57
principles for organizing, 69, 71
promoting race relations through, 469-74
revision of, 523
setting objectives for, 43
Curriculum objectives (*see also* Objectives)
  appraisal of, 50-53
  list of, 46-47
Curriculum patterns
  appraisal of alternative, 71-73
  factors affecting, 55
  kinds of
    experience, 67-69, 70
    fused, 60-67, 70
    subject, 64-66, 70
    variant, 63, 70

Dacus, W. Pence, 120
Daily schedules, organizing, 69
  classroom management and, 427-32
Davis-Eells Test of General Intelligence, 490
Dearborn, Walter F., 181
Dechant, Emerald, 165
Decision-making (*see also* Collective negotiations)
  model for, 514-15
Deduction method, 447-49
Deductive discovery (mathematics), 242
De Francesco, Itala L., 343
Departmentalization, 390-91
Desegregation, de facto school, 464-68
Deutsch, Martin, 489
Developmental Articulation Test, 198
Dewey, John, xxvii, xxviii, 5
Diabetes, health problems related to, 295
Dialects. *See* Language; Substandard speech
Differentiated instruction, 452
  techniques
    amount of learning task varied, 454-55
    grouping, 455
    individualization, 452-53
    other, 455-56
    time of learning task varied, 453-54
Di Pasquale, Vincent C., 385
Disadvantaged children, culturally (*see also* Exceptional children)
  approaches to teaching, 492-93
    appraisal of, 507-08

elementary intervention, 497-99
follow-through programs, 496-97
noncurricular, 499-502
parental involvement and child-care centers, 497
preprimary intervention, 493-96
in general, 140
history of, 484-85
psychological characteristics of, 488-92
sociological factors and, 485-86
structure and teaching of, 502-07
Discipline (*see also* Behavior; Classroom management)
  punishment and, 435-36
  race relations and, 474-75
  special problems and, 436-38
Discipline-centered curriculum orientation, 59-60
Douglass, Harl R., 62
Drama, 226-27. *See also* Language arts
Dropout programs, 499-500
Dunlap, James M., 132
Durrell, Donald D., 165

Ear, nose, and throat, health problems related to, 292-93
Early childhood education, 522. *See also* Preprimary education
Early intervention, disadvantaged and, 493-96
Earning power, education and, xxix
Economic Opportunity Act, 498, 500
Economics, 267-68
Educable mentally retarded children, 133-34
Education
  and earning power, xxix
  history of, x
    character development, xv-xvii
    culture, x-xii
    criticism, 7-8
    federal aid, xiii-xiv
    hornbooks, texts, multi-media, xxi-xxiii
    individualization, monitorial, graded schools, xix
    philosophies and methods, xxiii-xxviii
    pluralism, xiv-xv
    social and individual purposes, xvii-xviii
    state and local control, xii-xiii
    teacher's changing role, 3-13
  objectives of, 44. *See also* Objectives
Educational Policies Commission, 523
Educational Services Arithmetic Project, 235-36
Education establishment
  compulsory school age, xxix
  enrollment, xxviii
  expenditures, xxix
  finances, xxxi-xxxii
  holding power, xxviii

need for elementary teachers, xxxii-xxxiii
salaries, xxx-xxxi
school systems, xxix-xxx
school years completed, xxviii-xxix
teachers, xxviii, xxx
transportation, xxx
Elementary intervention programs, 497-99
Elementary and Secondary Education Act (1965), xiii, xv, 6, 484, 498, 522
Eliot, Charles W., 117
Ellison, Alfred, 326
Emergency health assistance, 298-99
Emotional problems, 296-97
Emotionally handicapped children, 139-40
Engelmann, Siegfried, 175, 203, 490, 494
English as a second language
teaching, 204-05
teaching, 204-05
Enrichment method, gifted children and, 133
Enrollment, size of, xxviii
Epilepsy, health problems related to, 295-96
Erikson, E. H., 21
Essay tests, 402-03
Ethnic studies, 469-74
Evaluation
appraisal of, 418, 420-21
definition of, 399
principles to guide, 400-01
purposes for, 399-400
techniques of, 401-11
achievement tests, 410
anecdotal records, 401-02
essay test, 402-03
informal teacher-made tests, 402
intelligence tests, 406, 410
objective test, 403
pupil work samples, 402
sociogram, 403-05
standardized tests, 405-06
teacher observation, 401
Exceptional children
appraisal of instruction for, 141-43
classroom teacher and, 140-43
incidence of, 131
kinds of, 131
creative, 135-36
emotionally and socially handicapped, 139-40
intellectually exceptional, 131-35
physically exceptional, 131-39
Expenditures for education, xxix
Experience curricular patterns, 67-69
Eyes, health problems related to, 292

Family life, sex education and, 304-06
Farrell, Edmund J., 11
Fenton, Edwin, 450, 451

Field trips, 506
in preprimary curriculum, 87-88
Finances, educational establishment, xxxi-xxxii
Fire prevention, 313-14
First aid assistance, 298-99
Fisher, Dorothy Canfield, 75
Fiss, Owen M., 466
Follow-through programs, 490-97
Foreign languages, teaching, 227-29
Forlano, G., 498
Formalism, xxiii-xxv
Fox, D. J., 498
Francis, Azalia, 490
Free reading approach, 172, 174
Fries, Charles C., 171, 209, 215
Froebel, Fridrich, 75
self-development through play movement, 74-75
Frost, Joel, 498
Furniture arrangement, 427, 428
Fused curriculum patterns, 65, 70

Gagné, Robert M., 451
Garrison, Karl C., 438
Geography, 268
Gerschefski, Edwin, 337
Gibson, John S., 471
Gifted children
meeting the needs of, 132-33
negative characteristics of, 132
positive characteristics of, 132
Goals (*see also* Objectives)
in the social studies, 271-73, 275
Gober, Billy, 81, 375
Gordon, Edmund W., 492, 497
Graded plan of organization, 383-86
Graded schools, xix, xx-xxi
Grammar, 215-18
Gray, Susan, 451, 495, 497
and Kearnes programs, 495
Gray, William S., 169
Greater Cleveland mathematics program, 235
Grooms, M. Ann, 122
Grouping, 454, 455
Group integration, 422-25
Guidance, motor skills and, 33-36
Guilford, J. P., 25, 362
Guthrie, M. R., 503

Hall, G. Stanley, xxvi, 118
Handedness, 35
Handwriting, 212-14
Harper, William R., 118
Hart, F. W., 443
Havighurst, R. J., 29, 486
Hawkes, Glenn R., 498
Hawkins, Michael L., 527

Hay, Julie, 209
Headaches, health problems related to, 296
Head Start program, 496, 521, 522, 523
Health, safety and
 appraisal of, 298
 emotional problems, 296-97
 in general, 288-89
 physical problems, 291-96
 in the preprimary curriculum, 80, 90-91
Health instruction, 299-307
 appraisal of, 314-15
 controversial topics in, 304-07
 curriculum development, 307-13
 curriculum sequence, 301-04
 in the intermediate grades, 301
 methods in, 312
 in the primary curriculum, 105, 300-01
 scope of, 300
 teacher and, 312-13
 time allotment for, 307
Health record, forms for, 411
Health services, 297-99
 emergency assistance, 298-99
 follow through, 298
 health appraisal, 298
 protective services, 298
 school nurse, 299
Heart, health problems related to, 294-95
Herbartianism, xxv
Heredity, intelligence and, 491-92
Heterogeneous sectioning, 394-95
Hildreth, Gertrude, 210
History, 268-69
Hobson, J. R., 184
Holding power, teacher, xxviii
Homme, Lloyd E., 435
Homogeneous sectioning, 393-94
Hoppe, Ferdinand, 34
Hornbooks, xxi-xxiii
Human relationship, objectives of, 46
Hunter, Patricia, 131
Hunt, J. McV., 493
Hyperactivity, health problems related to, 295

Ideal type, body build, temperament and, 30-31
Ilg, Francis, 212
Image, establishing an, 430-32
Income, life chance and, 485
Individualized instruction, 107, 452-53
Inductive discovery method (mathematics), 241-42
Initial teaching alphabet, 172, 173, 208
Inquiry method, 449-52
Instruction, management for, 438-47
 measuring teacher effectiveness, 444-47
 planning for instruction, 438-39
 traits in good teaching, 441-44
 unit organization, 439-41
Instruments, musical, 335-37
Integration, curriculum, 108
Integration, school
 appraisal of, 478-82
 extent of, 464-68
 legal basis of, 462-64
 psychological aspects of, 468-69
 school role in, 521-22
 sectioning in, 476-77
Intellectually exceptional children, 131
 gifted, 132-33
 mentally retarded, 133-35
Intelligence
 culture and, 24-27, 491-92
 definitions of, 25-27
 race, heredity and, 491-92
Intelligence tests, 406, 410
Interage sectioning, 394-95
Interclass grouping, 395
Interests, child development and, 36-38
Intergroup relations
 race and, 471-72
 resource materials for, 474
Intermediate grades
 health instruction topics for, 301
 pupil progress checklist for, 416-17
Intermediate school (*see also* Junior high school; Middle school)
 appraisal of, 127-30
 evaluating, 125-27
 functions of, 122-25
 history of, 117-22
 program for, 122-24
Intervention programs
 early, 493-96
 elementary, 497-99
International phonetic alphabet, 164, 165
Intramural sports, 375

James, Butler, 386
James, William, xxviii
Jarvis, Oscar T., 447
Jensen, Arthur, 487, 491, 492
Johnson, Marietta, xxvi
Jones, Mary C., 120
Junior high school, 117-19. See also Intermediate school

Karnes, Merle, 495, 497
Keats, John, 7
Kiddle, Henry, 384
Kilander, H. Frederick, 300, 301, 307
Kilpatrick, William Heard, 5, 108, 109, 451
Kindergarten, 522-23. See also Preprimary
Kingston, Albert G., 438

Kinney, Lucien B., 243, 244, 245
Kirchner, Glenn, 378
Kleg, Milton, 24, 471
Kuhlman-Anderson Intelligence Tests, 26

Laban, Rudolph, 371
Language
   attributes of, 192-94
   cognitive style and, 490
   importance of, 188-90
   nature of, 190-92
   race relations and, 475-76
   social class and, 488-90
   structure of, 194-96
Language arts (*see also* specific type)
   appraisal of, 231-32
   cumulative nature of, 229-31
   in general, 188
   in the preprimary curriculum, 81
   in the primary curriculum, 102
Language-experience approach (reading), 172
Larson, Robert E., 385
Learning process
   emphasis on, 526-27
   readiness and, 27-29
   and teaching. *See* Teaching and learning
Lecture-listen method, 61
Lesson planning, 242-45. *See also* Unit teaching
Letters to parents, 418
Life chance, income and, 485
Linguistic approaches (reading), 171
Linguistics, 165-66
Listening, 205-06
   classroom behavior and, 207
   comprehension and, 206-07
   in the music program, 332-35
   speaking and, 206
Literature, 221-23 (*see also* Reading)
   in the preprimary program, 81-82
Livermore, Arthur H., 252
Logsdon, Bette J., 373
Lowenfeld, Viktor, 347
Luria, A. R., 489
Lusky, Louis, 478

McClelland, S. D., 490
McCullough, Constance M., 181
McDonald, Arthur S., 438
McDonald, Blanche, 429
McGrath, Earl J., 227
Mackie, Romaine, 131
Macmillan English Series, 215
McMillan, Margaret, 78
McMurray, Charles A., 108, 109, 448
McPartland, James, 467
Mann, Horace, 384

Marks, John L., 243
Massialas, Byron G., 452
Materials
   art education, 351-53
   intergroup relations resource, 474
Mathematics instruction
   appraisal of, 246-47
   approaches to, 240-42
   lesson planning, 242-45
   new curricula, 234-36
   in preprimary curriculum, 88-89
   in primary curriculum, 102-03
   principles of, 245-46
   purposes of, 237-39
   scope and sequence, 236-37
Mathews, Paul R., 83
Mayor, John R., 252
Mead, Margaret, 35
Media center
   appraisal of, 155-57
   changing role of, 530-31
   definition of, 145
   facilities for, 150, 151-53
   pupil and, 155
   purposes of, 145-46
   scheduling of, 150
   staff role and, 150, 154
   teacher and, 154-55
Media program
   organizing, 146
   scope of collection, 147, 148-49
   staffing, 147, 150
Mehl, Marie A., 62
Melvin, A. Gordon, 109
Melzi, Kay, 347, 354, 355
Merrill linguistic readers, 169
Mental health instruction, 306-07
Mentally retarded children
   educable, 133-34
   severely mentally deficient, 135
   trainable, 134-35
Methods. *See specific type*
Michaelis, John U., 236
Middle grades, reading in, 183-84
Middle school, 119-22. *See also* Intermediate school
Mills, Hubert H., 62
Mills, James, 98
Minnesota Multiphasic Personality Inventory (MMPI), 38
Minorities, 472-73. *See also* Disadvantaged children
Modern Educational Dance (Laban), 371
Modified alphabet approach (reading), 172
Modular instruction, 524-26
Moffett, James, 215, 217, 218

index

Monitorial schools, xix-xx
Montessori, Maria, 76
   self-development through work movement, 75-76
Morality, education and, xv-xvii. *See also* Objectives; Values
Morphemes, 194, 195-96
Morrison, Henry C., 448
Motivation
   disadvantaged and, 488
   for self-expression, 349-51
   in skill development, 34-36
Motor development, 33-36
Movement education. *See* Physical education
Movements for change, teacher role and, 8-9
Multiage sectioning, 107
Multigraded organization plan, 386-87
Multi-media, xxi-xxiii
Multisensory language development project, 203
Music
   aesthetic appreciation of, 320-22
   for personal pleasure, 322-23
   and the social studies, 338
Music education program
   appraisal of, 340-41
   categories of, 326-27
   creative activities in, 337-38
   decision-making for, 327
   expressive movement in, 330-32
   history of, 319
   importance of, 319-25
   instruments in, 335-37
   listening in, 332-35
   organizing, 325-26
   pedagogical applications of, 323-24
   in preprimary curriculum, 82-83
   in primary curriculum, 106
   sequential curriculum for, 338-40
   singing in, 327-30
   time allocation for, 327
Myrdal, Gunnar, 468

National Defense Education Act (1958), xiii, 6
National Education Association (NEA), 343, 387, 510, 512, 513, 516, 517, 523, 527
National purposes, education and, 8
National School Aid bill (1965), xviii
National Science Foundation, 252
Naturalism, xxiii, xxv-xxviii
Natural science, 103-04. *See also* Science
Naumberg, Margaret, xxvi
Neef, Joseph, xi, xxiv
Negotiations. *See* Collective negotiations
Nelson, Leslie, 429
Neuber, Margaret A., 131
Nimnicht, Glenn, 495
   material-centered program, 495

Nixon, Richard M., 482
Noncurricular approaches, disadvantaged and, 499-502
Nongraded school organization, 106-07, 387-89
Non-teaching routines, 427-29
Norms, setting, 433
Nutrition, health problems related to, 291-92
Nye, Robert Evans, 339
Nye, Vernice Trousdale, 339

Objectives
   appraisal of, 50-53
   classroom management, 424-25
   criteria to guide formation of, 50
   education, 45-47
   mathematics instruction, 237-39
   music instruction, 319-25
   science program, 252-54
   setting curriculum, 43-44
   social studies, 271-73, 275
   tomorrow's school, 47-49
Objective tests, 403
Observation and environmental studies approach, 110
Oliver, Albert I., 60
Open classroom, 529-30
Operant conditioning (Skinner), 502-03
Oral expression, 218-19
Organizational patterns
   appraisal of, 395-97
   horizontal, 389-95
      changes in, 527-29
      student deployment, 393-95
      teacher deployment, 389-93
   regulating student progress, 395
   vertical, 383-89
      changes in, 523-24, 527
      graded plan, 383-86
      multigraded plan, 386-87
      nongraded plan, 387-89
Orthopedically handicapped children, 138
Otis-Lennon Quick-Scoring Mental Abilities Tests, 26
Owen, Robert, 78, 96, 97, 487

Page, David, 235
Parents
   cooperating with, 91-92
   involvement of, 497
   reporting to, 418
Parent-teacher conferences, 415, 416
Parker, Francis, xxvi, 110
Passow, A. Harry, 498
Peabody, Elizabeth, 75, 95
   language development tests, 202, 490
Performance-based instruction, 524

542 index

Performance objectives approach, 107
Permanent record, form for, 408-09
Personality (*see also* Behavior)
  maladjustment symptoms, 437
  physique and, 32-33
Philbrick, J. D., 384
Philosophy, 271
Phoneme-grapheme sequences, 168-69
Phonemes, 194
  basic English, 166
Phonetics, 164
Phonic-linguistic basal readers, 171
Phonics, 164
Photo-articulation test, 198
Physical appearance, 29-31
Physical education
  appraisal of, 375-79
  intramurals, 375
  movement education, 371-75
  in the primary curriculum, 105
  social and emotional aspects of, 363-64
  traditional curriculum, 364-71
  values of, 361-64
Physical growth, advantage of early, 31-32
Physical health problems, 291-96
Physically exceptional children
  aurally handicapped, 137
  orthopedically handicapped, 138
  special health handicapped, 138-39
  speech handicapped, 137-38
  visually handicapped, 136-37
Physique, personality and, 32-33
Piaget, Jean, 88
Picture books, 81-82
Pierce, Charles S., xxviii
Platt, Caroline, xxvi
Play, 80-81
Plessy v. Ferguson (1896), 462
Pluralism in education, xiv-xv
Poetry, 223
Political science, 269-70
Pooley, Robert C., 216, 217
Poverty
  race and, 471
  early stimulation and, 78-79
Practice, motor skill development, 33-36
Prejudice, 23-24
  race and, 470-71
Preprimary education program
  appraisal of, 92-94
  cooperation with parents, 91-92
  curriculum, 74
    art, 83-84
    field trips, 87-88
    health and safety, 90-91
    language development, 81-82
    mathematics, 88-89
    music and songs, 82-83
    overview, 79-80
    play, 80-81
    reading, 81-82, 89
    science and social studies, 84-87
    socialization and, 89-90
  evaluation of, 495-96
  health care in, 80
  major influences on, 74
  time schedules in, 91
  traditional, 493-94
Primary school program
  curriculum
    art, 105-06
    development of, 99-100
    health education, 105, 300-01
    language arts, 102
    mathematics, 102-03
    music, 106
    natural science, 103-04
    physical education, 105
    reading, 100-02
    social studies, 104-05
  educational alternatives in small, 111-14
  evaluation of, 114-16
  in general, 95
  history of, 95-99
  teaching approaches in, 106-11
Principal-teacher relationship, 531-33
Professional groups, collective negotiations role of, 516-18
Programmed instruction, 107-08, 453-54
  reading and, 171-72
Progressive Education Association, xvii, xxvi, xxvii
Progressive education movement, xi, 5-6, 7-8, 240, 530
Project and activity approach, 108-09
Psychology, 270
Punishment, discipline and, 435-36
Pupils
  media center and, 155
  race relations behavior of, 474-78
  recording and reporting progress of, 412-18
  work samples of, 402
Purdy, C. Richard, 243

Quasi-controlled sectioning, 394

Race
  culture and, 19-20
  intelligence and, 491-92
  intergroup relations and, 471-72
  poverty and, 471

prejudice and, 470-71
Race relations (*see also* Integration, school)
  curriculum to promote, 469-74
  teacher and pupil behavior in, 474-78
Randomized sectioning, 394
Read, Katherine H., 81
Readiness
  and beginning reading, 181-83
  and learning, 27-29
Reading instruction
  appraisal of, 186-87
  beginning, approaches to, 167-75
    efficiency of, 177-81
    for special purposes, 175-77
  definition of, 162-63
  importance of, 161
  learning to teach, 185-86
  levels of
    aesthetic-appreciative, 163-64
    decoding, 162
    information, 162-63
  in the middle grades, 183-84
  in the preprimary curriculum, 81-82, 89
  in the primary curriculum, 100-02
  and study skills, 505-06
  testing achievement in, 184-85
Reading progress card, 413
Reading readiness, 181-83
Reading systems, 174-75
Ready? Set . . . Go (Logsdon and Barrett), 371, 373, 374, 375
Recording pupil growth, 412
  forms for
    cumulative health, 411
    permanent record, 408-09
Reform movement, education, 6
Reissman, Frank, 490
Remedial reading, 176-77
Report cards, 412, 414, 415
Reporting pupil growth
  appraisal of, 418, 420-21
  forms for, 414, 416-17
    teacher-parent conference, 419
  methods of, 412-18
    checklist, 415
    comparative marks, 412, 414, 415
    letter to parents, 418
    parent-teacher conferences, 415, 416, 419
    telephone reports, 418
Rice, Marion J., 210, 471
Riemer, George, 218
Roberts, Paul, 215
Rugg, Harold, 265

Safety (*see also* Health)
  accident prevention, 313
  fire prevention, 313-14
Safety education program (*see also* Health instruction)
  appraisal of, 314-15
  curriculum, 90-91, 314
Salaries, teacher, xxx-xxxi
Schem, Alexander, 384
School dropout programs, 499-500
School environment
  emotional problems, 296-97
  organization and routine, 289-90
  physical health problems, 291-96
  physical plant, 289
  teacher-pupil relations, 290-91
School Health Education Study (SHES), 310, 311
School health services, 297-99
Schooling, cultural values and, 482
School Mathematics Study Group (SMSG), 234-35, 449
School nurse, 299
Schools, social change and, 521-24
School systems, xxix-xxx
School years completed, xxviii-xxix
Schurr, Evelyn L., 370
Schwab, Joseph J., 310, 450
Science—A Process Approach, 252, 254, 256, 449, 526, 532
Science, teaching
  appraisal of, 261-62
  changed orientation in, 251-52
  objectives, 252-54
  organizing for, 254-57
  planning for, 357-61
  in the preprimary curriculum, 84-87
Scott Foresman New Basic Reader Series, 167
Sears, P. S., 34
Seating, race relations and, 475
Sectioning (*see also specific type*)
  in the integrated school, 476-77
Self-concept, disadvantaged and, 488
Self-contained classroom, 389-90
Self-realization objectives, 46
Sellery, C. Morely, 300
Separate subjects approach, 111
Severely mentally deficient children, 135
Sex education, 305-06
Sheldon, W. H., 30
Sherer, William J., 385
Sight-meaning approach (reading), 167, 169-71
Simons, Gene M., 83
Singing, 327-30
Skin, health problems related to, 293-94
Smith, Sarah L., 300
Social change, schools and, 521-24

index

Social class, language and, 488-90
Social control, classroom management and, 422-25
Socialization process, 20-23
　in the preprimary curriculum, 89-90
Socially handicapped children, 139-40. *See also* Disadvantaged children
Social mobility, as an educational objective, 48-49
Social studies
　appraisal of, 285-87
　concepts and concept clusters, 274, 275-76
　content of, 264
　curriculum development, 276-80
　curriculum projects 1960s, 280-83
　in general, 264
　goals and objectives in, 271-73, 275
　music in, 338
　in the preprimary curriculum, 84-87
　in the primary curriculum, 104-05
　projects appraisal, 284-85
　sequences in 1926-70, 280
　social science foundations of, 266-71
Society-oriented curriculum, 56-57
Sociograms, 403-05
Sociology, 270-71
Speaking, 196-97
　articulation, 197-200
　and listening, 206
　substandard speech, 200-04
　teaching English as a second language, 204-05
Spearman, Carl E., 25
Special classes, gifted children and, 133
Special health handicapped children, 138-39
Speech handicapped children, 137-38
Spelling, 207-12
Staffieri, J. R., 30
Staffing
　educating the disadvantaged and, 499
　media center and, 147, 150
　practices in, 529
Standardized tests, 405-06
Stanford-Binet intelligence tests, 490
Stanford project (mathematics), 235
Steffe, Leslie P., 88
Strodbeck, Fred L., 489
Student deployment, 393-95
　heterogeneous sectioning, 394-95
　homogeneous sectioning, 393-94
　interclass grouping, 395
Study skills, reading and, 505-06
Subject curriculum patterns, 64-66, 70
Substandard speech, 200-04
Summer schools, 501
Suppes, Patrick, 235
Supplemental phonics approach (reading), 171
Syllables, 194-95
Sylvester, Robert, 429

Syntatic Structure (Chomsky), 215
Systems approaches (reading), 174-75

Teacher deployment
　departmentalization, 390-91
　self-contained classroom, 389-90
　team teaching, 391-93
Teacher-made tests, 402
Teacher observation, 401
Teacher-parent conferences, 419
Teacher-principal relationship, 531-33
Teacher relations, Black-White, 477-78
Teachers
　as activists, 511-13
　characteristics of good, 441-44
　clarity and teaching, 506-07
　collective negotiations role, 516-17
　and exceptional children, 140-43
　and health education, 312-13
　general role of, 3-13
　and the media center, 154-55
　measuring effectiveness of, 444-47
　need for, xxxii-xxxiii
　numbers of, xxviii, xxx
　personality, physiques and, 32-33
　race relations behavior of, 474-78
　suitability of, 10-11
Teacher training, disadvantaged and, 500-01
Teaching English as a second language, 204-05
Teaching and learning
　methods for organizing, 60-63
　in the primary school, 106-14
　traits of good, 441-44
　unit organization, 439-41
Teaching schedules, 429-30
Team teaching, 391-93
Teeth, health problems related to, 292
Telephone reports, 418
Temperament, body build, ideal type and, 30-31
Templin-Darley Tests of Articulation, 198
Terman, Lewis M., 25, 26
Testing (*see also* Evaluation)
　articulation, 198-99
　culture and, 490-91
　listening comprehension, 206-07
　program for, 407
　reading achievement, 184-85
Tests
　achievement, 410
　essay, 402-03
　informal teacher-made, 402
　intelligence, 406, 410
　objective, 403, 406
　standardized, 405-06
Textbooks, history of use, xxi-xxiii
Thurstone, L. L., 25

Ticknor, Elisha, 96
Time schedule, 91
Torrence, E. Paul, 135
Trainable mentally retarded children, 134-35
Transportation, xxx
Triple-T program, 500
Turner, C. E., 300

United States Department of Health, Education, and Welfare, 367, 461, 463, 464, 466, 487
United States Office of Economic Opportunity, 484, 487, 497, 521
United States Office of Education, 479, 496, 500
United States v. Georgia, 463
United States v. Jefferson County Board of Education, 463, 522
Unit teaching method, 62-63, 109-10, 439-41, 457-61

Values, education and, xv-xvii, 45-46, 482
VISTA (Volunteers in Service to America), 500

Visually handicapped children, 136-37
Vocabulary development, 224-26
Vocational choice, 49
Vygotsky, L. S., 489

Wachowiak, Frank, 357
Walker, R. N., 30
Washburne, Carleton, 110, 111
Wechsler Intelligence Scale for Children (WISC), 26, 490
Wesley, Edgar Bruce, 265
Whorf, B. L., 189
Wilderspin, Samuel, 97, 98
Wilkerson, Doxey A., 492
Willson, Ella, 154
Wingo, Charles E., 209
Written composition, 219-21

Zeitler, W. R., 86
Zevin, Jack, 452
Zintz, Miles V., 204